WRITING TOGETHER: COLLABORATION IN THEORY AND PRACTICE

The Bedford/St. Martin's Series in Rhetoric and Composition

Assessing Writing: A Critical Sourcebook, edited by Brian Huot and Peggy O'Neill

Computers in the Composition Classroom: A Critical Sourcebook, edited by Michelle Sidler, Richard Morris, and Elizabeth Overman Smith

Disability and the Teaching of Writing: A Critical Sourcebook, edited by Cynthia Lewiecki-Wilson and Brenda Jo Brueggmann

Feminism and Composition: A Critical Sourcebook, edited by Gesa E. Kirsch, Faye Spencer Maor, Lance Massey, Lee Nickoson-Massey, and Mary P. Sheridan-Rabideau

Literacy: A Critical Sourcebook, edited by Ellen Cushman, Eugene R. Kintgen, Barry M. Kroll, and Mike Rose

An Open Language: Selected Writing in Literacy, Learning, and Opportunity, Mike Rose

Second-Language Writing in the Composition Classroom: A Critical Sourcebook, edited by Paul Kei Matsuda, Michelle Cox, Jay Jordan, and Christina Ortmeier-Hooper

Selected Essays of Robert J. Connors, edited by Lisa Ede and Andrea A. Lunsford

Style in Composition and Rhetoric: A Critical Sourcebook, edited by Paul Butler

Views from the Center: The CCCC Chairs' Addresses 1977–2005, edited by Duane Roen

Visual Rhetoric in a Digital World: A Critical Sourcebook, edited by Carolyn Handa

Writing and Community Engagement: A Critical Sourcebook, edited by Thomas Deans, Barbara Roswell, and Adrian J. Wurr

Writing Across the Curriculum: A Critical Sourcebook, edited by Terry Myers Zawacki and Paul M. Rogers

Writing on the Margins: Essays on Composition and Teaching, David Bartholomae

On Writing Research: The Braddock Essays 1975–1998, edited by Lisa Ede

WRITING TOGETHER: COLLABORATION IN THEORY AND PRACTICE

A Critical Sourcebook

Andrea A. Lunsford
Stanford University

Lisa Ede
Oregon State University

BEDFORD / ST. MARTIN'S   Boston   •   New York

For Bedford / St. Martin's

Executive Editor: Leasa Burton
Developmental Editor: Allie Goldstein
Production Supervisor: Nancy Myers
Marketing Manager: Molly Parke
Text Design: Anna Palchik
Project Management: DeMasi Design and Publishing Services
Cover Design: Marine Miller
Composition: Jeff Miller Book Design
Printing and Binding: Haddon Craftsmen, Inc., an RR Donnelley & Sons Company

President: Joan E. Feinberg
Editorial Director: Denise B. Wydra
Editor in Chief: Karen S. Henry
Director of Marketing: Karen R. Soeltz
Director of Production: Susan W. Brown
Associate Director, Editorial Production: Elise S. Kaiser
Manager, Publishing Services: Andrea Cava

Library of Congress Control Number: 2010943195

Manufactured in the United States of America.

6 5 4 3 2
f   e   d   c   b

For information, write: Bedford / St. Martin's, 75 Arlington Street, Boston, MA 02116   (617-399-4000)

ISBN: 978-0-312-60178-2

For our nieces, nephews, grandnieces, and grandnephews:
they continue to teach us the value of love, laughter,
and a life of writing.

CONTENTS

[1] Lisa Ede wrote this piece as a single author.
[2] Andrea A. Lunsford wrote this piece as a single author.

INTRODUCTION

Confluences

When we began writing together thirty years ago, we never expected to have an opportunity like the one afforded us here. Yet a set of serendipitous confluences came together and gave us this chance to gather pieces of our writing from across the decades and weave them, along with several new essays, into a collection. Sifting through our files brought many smiles and sometimes a shock of recognition: a box full of old computer punch-cards that once seemed so precious, handwritten notes to each other now beginning to crumble, draft after draft after draft of one essay or another, photos taken at the beginning of our careers and friendship, looking oh-so-young. Creating this collection has given us the gift of time to reflect, time to reread and to rethink, time to muse about the future of writing and of rhetoric and writing, time to be, once more, *writing together*.

Writing . . . is the idiom we live in, almost like the air we breathe. As far back as we can remember we have been writers, lovers of words and their power to conjure, to create. That love led us first to reading and the study of literature and then, increasingly and compellingly, to the field of rhetoric and writing. So writing, for many years, played the role of hero in our story: we resonated to the power of writing to make a difference, to give voice and empower, to work toward the principles we cherished (and still cherish): inclusivity, social justice, openness, and collaboration.

We still see writing as a potentially powerful force for good. But as we engaged with scholarly work in rhetoric and writing, particularly as we thought through issues involving audience, we increasingly recognized that writing can also disempower and even subjugate, can turn from hero to villain on a dime. In *Writing and Difference*, Jacques Derrida calls attention to the violence inscribed in the very word for writing: *scribere*, "to carve," and we could see the effects of that violence throughout history — and in the faces of many of our students. From Shirley Brice Heath's description of schooled writing in *Ways with Words: Language, Life, and Work in Communities and Classrooms* to J. Elspeth Stuckey's searing *The Violence of Literacy*, to Ebony Coletu's recent dissertation, "Forms of Submission," we tracked the way writing can not only liberate and empower but also ensnare, devalue, deprive. In teaching, we often begin undergraduate classes by drawing a long line on the chalkboard, labeling one end of it WRITING and the other end BEING WRITTEN. Over the years, our students have spoken passionately about where they feel they fall on that continuum and about those forces that keep them in check as well as those that help them gain agency.

Postmodernism taught us to question any master narrative, and this binary — writing as hero or as villain — is clearly overdrawn, though it still proves useful in engaging students in discussions about their own connections to and definitions of writing. Students often begin our classes holding fairly instrumentalist definitions of writing: you think something out, they say, and then you write it down; that's writing. Yet as the term wears on, they almost always begin to move beyond such easy definitions to grasp the epistemic potential of writing and its ubiquity in their lives. We take the journey with them, often rehearsing some of the changes in technologies of communication that we have lived through. Andrea tells of receiving her coveted "going to college" present: a small, portable manual typewriter she used to write every college assignment. Lisa tells of getting her first college teaching position and going out to buy — wonder of wonders — an electric, self-correcting typewriter. Such quaint stories help us generate further discussions. Noting that writing is one of the world's oldest technologies, we trace changes in its tools, looking at hieroglyphics; cuneiform and other early scripts; handwritten manuscripts on many different substances; carving instruments; the first movable type; quill pens; the pencil (several books have been written about its history); the typewriter; early computers (such as the IBM Andrea proudly bought in 1984, the one that was about as big as her desk but on which she could hardly do more than crank out a letter); and of course the contemporary tools that have brought such dramatic changes to writing.

"Writing," we have come to see, is increasingly hard to define. No longer just marks on paper or pixels on screen, writing has been electrified: today it is full of color, images, sound, and video. Walter Ong pointed out that we live in an age of secondary orality, where speech has been deeply influenced by written codes. But we also live in an age of secondary *literacy*, where writing is not only deeply influenced by spoken codes but can now encompass speech, as the sound of the spoken voice literally enters the text. In this scene, writing becomes reading becomes writing again, as the terms of the ancient rhetorical triangle fairly spin on their angles, dynamically interacting and interchanging. Students in this scene with access to technology are writing more than at any other time in history, texting, facebooking, tweeting, blogging, vlogging. We can only guess at what the future will hold. We live, it seems, in a world of writing, redefined broadly to include symbolic means of communication across a range of genres and media. Writers today can reach others across the world instantaneously, sending text messages and pictures for multiple purposes — whether to document the 2011 protests that brought down Egypt's Mubarak or to organize and participate in a mass entertainment event, such as the surprise flash mob performance by the Black Eyed Peas and an estimated crowd of twenty thousand Chicagoans that marked the twenty-fourth season of *The Oprah Show* and that stunned its unsuspecting host.

And yet new technologies of writing raise pressing questions. Who will control the hardware and software through which writing flows? Who will have access to these technologies and to information and conversations of all kinds necessary to keep writing going strong? Where will the bottom line of responsibility fall for writing that is seemingly unauthored or unattributed? Even closer to home for teachers, how can we most effectively teach writing — what some refer to as the "new literacies" — today? Should we incorporate new forms of writing such as audio and video essays, documentaries, and other mixed-media productions into required writing classes, and if we should, then how can we best evaluate these efforts? How can we teach students to be ethical as well as effective communicators, who can take on agency as well as understand the forces at work to control or curb that agency? And how can we do so within the constraints of contemporary academic structures, schedules, staffing models, and course limitations?

These and other questions swirl around in our consciousness and our conversation, leaving us sometimes dizzy: the subject we began to study nearly forty years ago has expanded, shifted and turned and twisted into new and amazing shapes. When we reflect on all these changes, our conversations often resemble gigantic word clouds in which writing envelops us, asking for all our attention, and then some.[1] We give that attention in the essays in this collection, and we continue to tackle the questions raised in these opening pages about writing. And, as always, we do so *through* writing together, sending our words back and forth, arguing and worrying them, patching them together, erasing them, and then starting over.

Together . . . is not what we have always been, however, either literally or figuratively. We met in graduate school, where being together meant hanging out, sharing our successes and failures as teachers, and commiserating over the stresses of comprehensive exams and dissertation writing. How to conjure up the togetherness of those early days: sitting in the library — or on a lush riverbank — trading stories of family and friends, experimenting with our first gardens, and spending lots of time cooking and eating together. These early experiences wove bonds between us, as did our interest in and growing commitment to rhetoric and writing. We became fast friends who shared a deep interest in teaching and learning and in the art, practice, and theory of rhetoric. So we were "together" in our friendship and in our interests before we were together as writers.

For us, friendship paved the way for the trust that underpins our relationship. And that friendship and trust have taken us through good times and bad, helped us "get over" this or that misunderstanding or problem and keep on going. Nevertheless, learning to write together was not always easy. We had to learn to give and take, to listen more carefully than we were wont to do, to negotiate differences in style and substance, to wait patiently for the other to speak or write, to be critical and supportive at the same time, to be responsible to one another, and to laugh rather than cry at frustrations and setbacks. And so much more.

The selections in Part One of this volume, "Why Write Together?," detail some of the challenges and satisfactions we experienced in moving from being friends, to friends who wrote together, to friends and coauthors devoted to changing understandings of writing and authorship in ways that would recognize and value the act of "writing double," to use Bette London's telling phrase. As we wrote together, we discovered a new voice, one that was part Lisa, part Andrea, part all our other interlocutors, sources, and friends, and part something else, something *together*. Once we began looking closely, we saw how much of the world's writing is done collaboratively, how much knowledge is cocreated and coproduced. We wrote passionately about the need to disavow the radical individualism of the Enlightenment and of late modernity and to conceive of writing as existing on a continuum — from the kind of subtle but real collaboration that the seemingly solitary writer practices with all those voices and words of others in her head, to the full-blown act of writing every single word with one or more coauthors. (While we couldn't have imagined Wikipedia in those days, we would have loved it at first sight.) We have spent decades working to bring collaborative writing practices into the academy, its policies and its practices.

Over the years colleagues have at times expressed bewilderment or skepticism in response to our collaboration. Lisa still remembers well, for instance, when a colleague looked at the cover of our 1990 book, *Singular Texts/Plural Authors*, and remarked rather acidly (to Lisa's ears), "My, it must be gratifying to see your and Andrea's names written over and over on the cover of your book." For readers unfamiliar with the book and its cover, the point of this repetition was to call attention to complex issues of authorship and attribution that we hoped in this way to challenge. On the spine of the book, the authors are listed as Ede and Lunsford. On the cover, which superimposes the title over our names repeated continuously without spacing breaks, Andrea's name is highlighted first above the title and then Lisa's is highlighted below. In this case, what seemed to Lisa's colleague like a narcissistic display of authorship has actually served to achieve the goal we set: we see that book cited both as Ede and Lunsford and Lunsford and Ede.[2] Such intentional ambiguity is, of course, not acceptable to institutions such as the Library of Congress. For the purpose of that catalogue, Lisa was identified as the first author of *Singular Texts/Plural Authors*. Hence our decision to have Andrea's name appear first in bibliographic entries for this collection. We hope, however, that readers will read this entry and title page as Lunsford and Ede/Ede and Lunsford. It is in this spirit that the "About the Authors" section of this collection lists our credentials as a coauthor team rather than as separate authors.[3]

Does our emphasis on the primacy and equality of our collaboration mean that we feel no sense of autonomy or "individual" voice? Not by a long shot. Rather, our writing together has given us a stronger sense of our own stylistic proclivities, our own ways of thinking, knowing, writing, organizing, and revising. Kenneth Burke describes two fundamental modes for humans, which he labels "identification" and "division." To oversimplify Burke's complex concepts, just as people yearn for identification, for true joining with another or others, they also need division, a sense of separation and separateness. In our experience, the act of writing together and of seeking "identification" allows us to better see ourselves as distinct. As a result, we've felt free to experiment in writing together, aiming for a seamless voice in one piece, such as this introduction, and for clearly demarcated but communicating voices in another, as is the case with "Dear Lisa/Dear Andrea: On Friendship and Collaboration," a new essay we wrote for this collection.

As we kept writing together, we noticed that our interest in collaboration seemed in some ways to color everything we did. James Kinneavy once said, joking about his devotion to rhetorical taxonomies in general and to the concept of the rhetorical triangle in particular, "I fully expect to be buried in a triangular coffin." Similarly, we began to joke that we saw collaboration and collaborative writing blooming in every nook and corner of the biosphere. We certainly knew that most scholars in the humanities still failed to share our views, but we also saw what we considered progress: collaborative work being published in rhetoric and writing journals, collaborative work being accepted (though usually hesitantly) for promotion and tenure, even a collaborative dissertation or two making their way through to acceptance (see Valek and Knott). So we kept writing, pursuing our commitment to collaboration and collaborative writing as well as our interests in feminist theory and practice, in theories of audience, and in the work we did as administrators of writing programs and writing centers. The years sped by, publications mounted, and we found ourselves increasingly looking for time to think about where our scholarly journeys have taken us, to trace out the threads of our work, to look for big pictures where we might find them, and to do so *together*.

Confluences . . . When did we begin to recognize the extent to which all of our scholarly work ultimately mixes and swirls together, as happens when the Ohio River flows into the Mississippi in Cairo, Illinois? This recognition had been nibbling at the edges of our thinking for a while, brought on no doubt by our work on this collection. But it was as we were working on " 'Among the Audience': On Audience in an Age of New Literacies" (2011) that we saw most clearly that our scholarly work on audience and on collaboration — projects that we had up to that point viewed as discrete — had, thanks to both new literacies and new technologies, in important ways come into confluence with one another.

This recognition stimulated further thought, particularly when we developed the table of contents for this collection. About a year ago, when we were together in Corvallis, Oregon, as we are now writing this introduction, we sat in Lisa's study with copies of some two dozen previously published essays scattered around us, rereading, talking about which pieces we might include in this collection, and wishing that we had completed all the new essays we planned to write for it. Then we began to winnow and shape, discarding some and wondering how best to arrange the others. The major categories were obvious: we would include sections on our own collaborative writing, on our research on collaboration, on audience, on feminism and rhetoric, and on writing centers, and we would print the contributions to each part in chronological order. Arranging the parts was a little more difficult, and we indulged ourselves in moving parts around and examining the effects of different clusterings. The sequence we eventually decided on moves from Parts One and Two, which deal explicitly with collaboration in practice and in theory, to Parts Three, Four, and Five, which address other areas of inquiry that intersect — both obviously and subtly — with collaboration. We decided when we undertook this project not only to collect, organize, and comment upon previously published work, but also to reimmerse ourselves in the questions that have proven so generative over the years. Thus each part of this collection contains a new essay written specifically for *Writing Together*.[4]

We see strong connections among all sections of this collection. For instance, our personal commitment to feminism certainly informed (and continues to inform) both our friendship and our determination to write together, even when others warned us of the risks involved or of difficulties such as geographic distance that posed a hindrance. Feminist thought also informed our thinking about audience — particularly our recognition of the need to critique our original formulation of audience in "Audience Addressed/Audience Invoked: The Role of Audience in Composition Theory and Pedagogy" (1984), and to do so through the lens of difference (see "Representing Audience: 'Successful' Discourse and Disciplinary Critique" [1996]). And like many committed to writing centers, for some time now we have consciously viewed our centers as sites for feminist inquiry, social action, and collaboration. As we have said, these strands of our research seem now to us to cohere, to mark our most unwavering interests and deepest commitments. It has been more than a great pleasure to weave these essays, old and new, into what we hope will encourage and support the interests and commitments of our readers.

In Part One, "Why Write Together?," we reprint two previously published essays and an interview followed by a new essay that attempts to convey the reasons we have chosen to write together, how we have negotiated this process over time, and the role that our friendship has played in our collaboration. The first two essays, "Why Write . . . Together?" (1983) and "Collaboration and Compromise: The Fine Art of Writing with a Friend" (1988) represent our earliest efforts to inquire into our own collaborative writing practices. The interview (1991) that follows these essays represents the efforts of others to understand our commitment to coauthorship. We close this section with a new essay, "Dear Lisa/Dear Andrea: On Friendship and Collaboration," where we write more personally than we ever have about the role that our friendship has played in our collaboration and the challenges, costs, and difficulties — as well as the benefit and joys — of writing together.

Part One of this collection focuses primarily on our practices as coauthors — friends who have chosen to write together and to inquire into the complexities of our personal and professional relationships. Part Two,

"On Collaboration," moves from issues of personal preference and practice to focus more generally on theory and research on authorship, intellectual property, and collaborative writing. It reprints three chapters of *Singular Texts/ Plural Authors* (1990), our Fund for the Improvement of Postsecondary Education (FIPSE)-funded study of collaborative writing, a selection of "Intertexts" from that book, and three other essays that report on various aspects of our research. The new essay in this part, "Collaboration and Collaborative Writing: The View from Here," attempts to summarize our work on collaboration and to see where, in effect, we stand now.

As we noted earlier in this introduction, for many years we viewed our research on collaborative writing and on audience as streams that ran alongside each other — reflecting our grounding in rhetorical and feminist history and theory, for instance — but that did not converge. We now recognize that these two "streams" have become interwoven in important ways. The essays in Part Three, "On Audience," chart this development. In Part Three we reprint two *College Composition and Communication* (CCC) essays, the first of which attempts a theory of audience and identifies and maps both "addressed" and "invoked" audiences. "Audience Addressed/Audience Invoked: The Role of Audience in Composition Theory and Pedagogy" (1984) firmly established our interest in understanding the rhetorical concept of audience, and we were pleased, over the years, to see it reprinted and referred to by other scholars working on audience. As we reread the essay roughly ten years after it was published, however, we saw a need to return to our earlier work and to look at it with critical eyes. Hence our "Representing Audience: 'Successful' Discourse and Disciplinary Critique" (1996) turns back to our earlier essay, providing a critique and commentary on our own work. The final essay in Part Three, "'Among the Audience': On Audience in an Age of New Literacies" (2011), updates our thinking on audience, reflecting what we have learned by considering both audience and collaboration in a digital age.

Part Four, "On Rhetorics and Feminisms," also makes visible developments in our thinking over time. When we wrote "On Distinctions between Classical and Modern Rhetoric" (1984), we did not see clearly how we might intertwine our commitments to rhetorical and feminist theory and practice. The next three essays in this part show us exploring differing ways in which we could draw upon both rhetorics and feminisms in our teaching, research, and writing. Thus our 1984 essay is followed by three essays that explore connections between women and writing/rhetoric, including "Border Crossings: Intersections of Rhetoric and Feminism" (1995), coauthored with Cheryl Glenn, and one in which we attempt to reread the classical canons of rhetoric in feminist terms. We conclude Part Four with a new essay, "The First Rhetoric(s) and Feminism(s) Conference and Its Legacy," which recounts the history of the Feminisms and Rhetorics Conference, a conference that has proven a powerful and productive site for our work, and for many feminist scholars in our field. We hope that this look back at the history of this conference will prove helpful as feminist scholars in our field chart pathways for the future.

Part Five of *Writing Together*, "On Writing Centers," also looks back in order to look forward. The subtitle of this collection is "Collaboration in Theory and Practice," and we believe that writing centers are particularly important in this regard. By their very nature, writing centers are sites of multiple collaborations — between writing centers and faculty across the curriculum, other units that support student success and retention, writing across the curriculum (WAC) programs, the schools, and the community, for instance. Perhaps most important, writing centers serve as rich sites of collaboration between student writers and peer tutors. Our years of working with writing center tutors (or writing consultants/assistants) as well as the students they serve have taught us that this collaboration yields mutual benefits: tutors regularly report that their own writing improves, sometimes dramatically, as they work to help other students improve and to meet the demands of both academic and self-sponsored writing. We have each devoted substantial portions of our careers to writing center work, and we are especially grateful for the opportunity this collection provides to connect this work with our other scholarly efforts. In Part Five, we reprint individually authored essays from the *Writing Center Journal* that inquire into theoretical models that might most effectively guide writing center practice. Also included is a collaboratively written reflection published in that same journal about the future of writing centers from the standpoint of the new millennium. The final essay in Part Five, "Collaboration, Community, and Compromise: Writing Centers in Theory and Practice," written for this collection, looks back to that essay and reconsiders those reflections from our contemporary moment. Given our long-standing engagement with and commitment to writing centers, it is particularly satisfying to us to have this essay close this collection.

In addition to the five parts of this book outlined earlier, we have included a brief section of archival materials, "Artifacts of Collaboration," which directly follows this introduction. The purpose of this section is to document in a material way the decades during which we have written together. Thus we include a few photos of ourselves working together as well as a treasured shot taken at a surprise panel presentation in honor of our mutual mentor, the late Edward P. J. Corbett (p. 15). Such images illustrate how our lives and our research have been interanimated and remind us, as feminists especially have emphasized, of the importance of embodiment. Following the photographs, we have included the first page of four different drafts (pp. 17–20) of the essay that eventually was published as "Representing Audience: 'Successful' Discourse and Disciplinary Critique." When we consider these drafts, which vary significantly in their approach and methodology, and the two-plus years that we spent working on this essay, we are positive that we could not have carried on if we had not shared a commitment to completing this project — and also shared a collaborative writing process that enabled us to persevere in the face of major difficulties. Next, artifacts of our collaborative writing from different periods (pp. 21–23) serve as a reminder of how important technologies of communication are to all writing. We both have very clear memories of the ferry ride from Vancouver to Vancouver Island when we wrote the first and very rough draft of the FIPSE grant proposal that led to our research on collaborative writing and, ultimately, to *Singular Texts/Plural Authors*. When we look at the page of that 1983 draft that survived in Lisa's files, we are startled to see our handwriting and to recall the ways that, even then, we wrote through and beyond each other's writing. A page of a 2008 draft of "'Among the Audience': On Audience in an Age of New Literacies," full of track changes and comments and replies, represents the way we typically compose when we are writing at a distance. However, even now, with all of the digital and online aids to collaborative writing that exist, our preferred mode of composing is to be physically together, often sitting next to each other at the computer. A page of a 2009 draft of "Collaboration and Collaborative Writing: The View from Here," which is typed but covered in a handwritten conversation, shows how we compose when we are in the same room and able to physically pass pages back and forth. Given the complexities of our lives and schedules, that luxury is not always possible. The "Artifacts of Collaboration" section concludes with the "Writer's Block" column and drawings (p. 24) that represent the efforts of others to wrap their heads around — and sometimes poke fun at — our commitments to coauthorship.

However, just as we don't want to overemphasize our "togetherness," we don't mean for this collection to suggest a seamless or totalizing quality to all of our research. We have not, as Casauban does in *Middlemarch*, spent our careers searching for anything resembling his key to all mythologies. Still, when we look at the table of contents for this collection, we now see that our commitment to collaboration merges and finds embodiment in important ways in much of our research and writing. It is both gratifying and humbling to come to such a recognition at this point in our careers, to recognize and celebrate the confluences in our research. We feel grateful and lucky to have found work that is so meaningful to us and that has rewarded our efforts.

Those familiar with our research will know that we at times pause to consider or describe the material conditions in which we write, marking time and space and the rhythms of our work. In the process of writing this introduction, we have exchanged texts, written over each other, argued, taken breaks to read poetry or take walks, trying to wring as much as possible out of every precious moment of our working time together. We completed this introduction in September 2010, working sometimes together at one computer and at other times on dueling computers in Lisa's light and airy study in Corvallis, and we paused to savor completing these last pages. We relished, one last time, looking at the artifacts that would be included in this book and joking about how often during these days we have interrupted or finished each other's sentences. We made a brand-new computer file labeled "Writing Together Collection Final Drafts" and prepared to email it to our editor in Boston. Sometime in late 2011, we will hold *Writing Together* in our hands, a material object that embodies thirty years of writing together. We will celebrate and be grateful for the confluences that brought this volume to fruition, but we will know that the meaning of this book, as with all books, escapes its material boundaries, taking real root only in those who pick it up and engage its ideas.

Along with Susan Leonardi and Rebecca Pope, we know that "One thing that collaboration teaches you is that there is no last word on anything. Someone looking over your shoulder or over your draft is going to find a better word or cross out your word entirely" (631). Leonardi and Pope's statement is a reminder that reading, as well as writing, is a collaborative act.

ACKNOWLEDGMENTS

As we put it in "Dear Lisa/Dear Andrea: On Friendship and Collaboration," we find ourselves at a moment in our lives and careers when we are leaning toward retirement, yet still very much treasuring our work with students and colleagues. This seems an apt time to acknowledge colleagues who paved the way for and, in many cases, mentored us. In this regard, we acknowledge, with thanks, Ann Berthoff, Lynn Bloom, Edward P. J. Corbett, Jim Corder, Peter Elbow, Janet Emig, James Golden, Maxine Hairston, Win Horner, William Irmscher, James Kinneavy, Richard Larson, Janice Lauer, Erica Lindemann, Richard Lloyd-Jones, Susan Miller, Jerry Murphy, Donald Murray, Mina Shaughnessy, Geneva Smitherman, Gary Tate, Ross Winterowd, and Richard Young. We are grateful for the energy and commitment that these and many other scholars demonstrated in conducting important scholarly projects while also working to professionalize the field of rhetoric and writing.

Over the years, Southern Illinois University Press (SIUP) has played a particularly important role in providing a venue for scholarly work in rhetoric and writing. Kenney Withers had a vision for the field and supported much work in the 1980s and 1990s — including our own *Singular Texts/Plural Authors* — that might not have otherwise seen the light of day. Karl Kageff, current editor-in-chief at SIUP, has carried on Withers's vision and tradition. While we are grateful that scholars in rhetoric and writing now have a number of well-regarded outlets for their work, we want to acknowledge the role that SIUP played, and continues to play, in the field's development.

This collection of essays makes it possible for us to, among other things, reaffirm our commitment to feminist theory and practice. The Coalition of Women Scholars in the History of Rhetoric and Composition has played a particularly important role in this regard. We thank the scholars who founded the organization: Win Horner, Nan Johnson, Jan Swearingen, Kathleen Welch, and Marjorie Curry Woods. We are grateful that this book afforded us an opportunity to document the history of the first Rhetoric(s) and Feminism(s) Conference, a conference that came to be sponsored by the Coalition.

Just as feminist scholars in rhetoric and writing have worked over the last twenty years to create a visible and viable presence in the field, so too have those committed to writing center theory and practice. We thank Kenneth Bruffee, Paula Gillespie, Nancy Grimm, Muriel (Mickey) Harris, Brad Hughes, Christina Murphy, Harvey Kail, Lou Kelly, Joyce Kinkead, Stephen North, Michael Pemberton, Jeanne Simpson, Byron Stay, and many others who helped establish and nurture this field. Thanks to their efforts, writing center theory and practice is now a thriving endeavor. We cannot acknowledge all who have contributed and are contributing to the ongoing work of writing centers, but we want to thank those with whom we have worked most closely: Lex Runciman, Jon Olson, Wayne Robertson, Dennis Bennett, John Tinker, Wendy Goldberg, and Clyde Moneyhun.

Another strong commitment that we have made is, of course, to collaboration and collaborative writing. We want to acknowledge the work of those such as Linda Hutcheon, Bette London, Sidonie Smith, Marjorie Stone and Judith Thompson, Susanna Ashton, Vera John-Steiner, and Holly Laird, who have worked within the field of English studies to make a clearer and safer space for collaboration. Many in our field of rhetoric and writing have stood with us as we argued for the value of writing together. In this regard we would particularly like to acknowledge the contributions of two pairs of co-authors: Kathleen Blake Yancey and Michael Spooner, and Michele Eodice and Kami Day.

So many scholars of our generation and subsequent generations have played a key role in encouraging and supporting our work — and enlarging our vision and understanding — that it is difficult to determine whom to acknowledge. Elizabeth Flynn and Suellynn Duffey were among our closest graduate school friends, and we are grateful to have moved through our lives and careers with them. Cheryl Glenn was Andrea's first graduate student at Ohio State, then Lisa's colleague, and now our treasured friend. Though Andrea has had the great good fortune of being colleagues with, and thus particularly indebted to, Beverly Moss and Jacqueline Jones Royster, we are both grateful for the role they have played in our lives and for how very much they have taught us. Others whose friendship and research have been particularly important to us include Bob Connors as well as David Bartholomae, Patricia Bizzell, James Berlin, Deborah Brandt, Suzanne Clark, Lester Faigley, Erika Lindemann, Anne Gere, Shirley Brice Heath, Susan Jarratt, Joyce Irene Middleton, Susan Miller, Shirley Wilson Logan, Krista Ratcliffe, Mike Rose, John Ruszkiewicz, Jim Slevin, John Trimbur, and Keith Walters.

Other important institutional and professional communities have made our work possible. Lisa has taught at Oregon State University (OSU) for thirty years. Though the Center for Writing and Learning (CWL), which Lisa directed during that time, no longer exists, Lisa would nevertheless like to thank her CWL colleagues Dennis Bennett, Robin Pappas, and Jeanna Towns for their support and to wish them all the best in their new academic homes: the Academic Success Center and the Center for Teaching and Learning. During the decades Lisa has been at OSU, colleagues in the English department have been unfailingly supportive and generous. She particularly thanks Robert Frank, Robert Schwartz, Tracy Daugherty, and Kerry Ahearn, who over the years have chaired the department and led it through perilously difficult times. She would also like to acknowledge the support and friendship of her colleagues in rhetoric and writing: Chris Anderson, Anita Helle, Sara Jameson, Susan Meyers, and Vicki Tolar Burton. One final community that has encouraged and supported her research is OSU's Center for the Humanities. A resident research fellowship at the Center during 2004–2005 played a key role in

Lisa's engagement with new technologies and literacies. Thanks to Director David Robinson and Assistant Director Wendy Madar for helping to make the year so rich and productive.

Andrea spent the first decade of her career at the University of British Columbia, where her association with Judy Segal, Will Garrett-Petts, Amanda Goldrick-Jones, Douglas Brent, Henry Huber, and many other students enriched her life and her understanding of rhetoric and writing. Her twelve years at Ohio State brought her into contact with one of the most imaginative and productive rhetoric and writing groups in the country; her ties to that group, including Beverly Moss, Nan Johnson, Brenda Brueggemann, Kay Halasek, Louie Ulman, Scott DeWitt, Jackie Royster, and Jim Fredal, remain strong and deep. The last eleven years at Stanford have afforded Andrea the opportunity to build an extraordinarily fine undergraduate writing program and writing center. To her partner in crime and pursuit of worldwide domination, Marvin Diogenes, she owes the deepest debt of gratitude. Working with Marvin, with the original coordinators of the writing center, John Tinker and Wendy Goldberg, and its first full-time director, Clyde Moneyhun, and with the magnificent writing teachers/researchers who form the heart of the Program in Writing and Rhetoric has been the gift of a lifetime.

During many summers between 1990 and the present, Andrea headed off from Columbus, Ohio or Palo Alto, California to join the Bread Loaf School of English. Her experiences there, with faculty and teachers from all over the country, have been jewels in the crown of her professional career. Director Jim Maddox and the truly wise and intrepid Dixie Goswami have created a professional development program like no other in the world, one that year after year brings teachers to one of four campuses to pursue an MA while engaging some of the most pressing questions facing education in America today. Andrea is grateful to the faculty and students of Bread Loaf for some of the deepest and most meaningful professional and personal friendships of her life.

Family and friends make both work and life meaningful. We will never be able to adequately thank those closest to us. Andrea thinks of and thanks her family — sister Ellen Ashdown; nephew Lance Ashdown, his wife Jennifer, and grandnieces Audrey and Lila, the best and most beloved playmates of all time; Liz, John, Brendan, Connor, and Logan Middleton, her sine qua non; niece (and colleague) Karen Lunsford; her longtime friends and traveling companions Helen and Don Gilbart; and her other sisters-for-life, Shirley Heath and Betty Bailey. Lisa thanks her husband Gregory Pfarr for collaborating with her in marriage, life, and work. She also thanks and acknowledges her nine siblings as a source of strength, perspective, and balance: Leni Ede Smith, Andrew Ede, Sara Ede Rowekamp, Jeff Ede, Robin Ede Bravard, Michelle Ede Smith, Laurie Ede Drake, Julie Ede Campbell, and Rob Ede.

We are grateful to Bedford/St. Martin's for encouraging us to collect previously published work, to embark on new explorations of topics of deep significance to us, and to reflect upon forty years of friendship and thirty years of writing together. We thank Joan Feinberg, president of Bedford/St. Martin's, for her support and vision. Joan's many years of experience as an editor, then editorial director, and now president have prepared her well to lead Bedford/ St. Martin's into the twenty-first century. We would also like to thank executive editor Leasa Burton for her engagement with and continued support for our project, and we feel particularly blessed in having had Allie Goldstein as our editor. Allie not only helped us clarify our thoughts and smooth out infelicities but also engaged our ideas in the new essays we wrote for this collection in deep and powerful ways. These essays particularly benefited from Allie's intelligence and her ability to ask thought-provoking, challenging questions. We would also like to acknowledge Nancy Perry for her guiding comments on early drafts and our production manager, Andrea Cava, for transforming our manuscript into the book you now hold.

Finally, we offer our deepest gratitude to the many, many students whom we have worked with and learned from over the years — whether in undergraduate or graduate classes, in our writing centers, or via community outreach. You are, after all, what has made the journey worthwhile.

— Corvallis, Oregon, September 2010

NOTES

1. The Wordle on the inside cover of this collection, composed of the words of our newest essays, represents such a word cloud.

2. On the first page of their introduction to *Literary Couplings: Writing Couples, Collaborators, and the Construction of Authorship* (Madison: U of Wisconsin P, 2006) editors Marjorie Stone and Judith Thompson list their names as follows: Marjorie Stone & Judith Thompson/Judith Thompson & Marjorie Stone. In a note at the end of their introduction they comment that "We have reversed the 'normal' alphabetical order of our names to draw attention to the way in which conventions of indexing introduce inequalities and hierarchies even in collaborative authorship" (35). We were attempting to make a similar point with the cover of our book.

3. When compiling the table of contents for this collection, we found that our attempt to share equally in first authorship over our careers was largely successful. As the source notes for the selections show, we are each the first author on almost exactly half of the previously published coauthored pieces included here.

4. "'Among the Audience': On Audience in an Age of New Literacies" appeared in an earlier form in *Engaging Audience: Writing in an Age of New Literacies* (Urbana: NCTE, 2009). The experience of looking again at "Audience Addressed/Audience Invoked: The Role of Audience in Composition Theory and Pedagogy" and "Representing Audience: 'Successful' Discourse and Disciplinary Critique," also included in *Engaging Audience*, was a powerful stimulus to our current project. We want to thank editors M. Elizabeth Weiser, Brian M. Fehler, and Angela M. González for their encouragement and support. Their collection makes it clear why audience remains a critical issue in an age of new literacies.

WORKS CITED

Burke, Kenneth. *A Rhetoric of Motives*. Berkeley: U of California P, 1950. Print.
Coletu, Ebony. "Forms of Submission: Acts of Writing in Moments of Need." Unpublished diss.: Stanford U, 2009. Print.
Derrida, Jacques. *Writing and Difference*. New York: Routledge Classics, 2001. Print.
Ede, Lisa, and Andrea Lunsford. *Singular Texts/Plural Authors: Perspectives on Collaborative Writing*. Carbondale: Southern Illinois UP, 1990. Print.
Heath, Shirley Brice. *Ways with Words: Language, Life, and Work in Communities and Classrooms*. Cambridge: Cambridge UP, 1983. Print.
Kinneavy, James L. *A Theory of Discourse: The Aims of Discourse*. New York: W. W. Norton, 1971. Print.
Leonardi, Susan J., and Rebecca A. Pope. "(Co)Labored Li(v)es; or, Love's Labors Queered." *PMLA* 116 (May 2001): 631–37. Print.

London, Bette. *Writing Double: Women's Literary Partnerships.* Ithaca: Cornell UP, 1999. Print.

Ong, Walter J. *Orality and Literacy: The Technologizing of the Word.* London: Methuen, 1982. Print.

Stone, Marjorie, and Judith Thompson, eds. *Literary Couplings: Writing Couples, Collaborators, and the Construction of Authorship.* Madison: U of Wisconsin P, 2006. Print.

Stuckey, J. Elspeth. *The Violence of Literacy.* Portsmouth, NH: Boynton/Cook, 1990. Print.

Valek, Lynne, and Toni Knott. "Working as One: A Narrative Study of the Collaboration of Male-Female Dyads in the Workplace." Unpublished diss.: The Fielding Institute, 1999. Print.

Weiser, M. Elizabeth, Brian M. Fehler, and Angela M. González, eds. *Engaging Audience: Writing in an Age of New Literacies.* Urbana: NCTE, 2009. Print.

ARTIFACTS OF COLLABORATION

In Corvallis, Oregon, in 1982, making pesto and working on our first coauthored essay. Left: Andrea A. Lunsford; right: Lisa Ede.

At the College Composition and Communication Conference in 1983 presenting a Festschrift to our mutual mentor Edward P. J. Corbett. From top left: Nan Johnson, Lisa Ede, Edward P. J. Corbett, and Michael Halloran. From bottom left: Andrea A. Lunsford and Bob Connors.

In Corvallis, Oregon, in 1992, working on "Collaborative Authorship and the Teaching of Writing."

In Lisa's study, 2009, working on this collection.

Four Drafts of a First Page

These are the first pages of four different drafts of the essay that was eventually pub-
lished as "Representing Audience: 'Successful' Discourse and Disciplinary Critique"
(included in this collection). We wrote the first draft as a dialogue with bell hooks. We
decided that we were uncomfortable using hooks's words in this way, so we abandoned
this idea and wrote two completely different frames before settling on one that worked.
In terms of collaboration, this was a demanding process. However, we feel confident
that our collaboration gave us the resolve we needed as we worked on this essay, which
we submitted to College Composition and Communication *in June 1995, two*
years after we began working on it.

10/11/93

REPRESENTING AUDIENCE

"To make the liberated voice, we must confront
the issue of audience--we must know to whom we
speak." (bell hooks, Talking Back: Thinking Feminist, Thinking Black, p. 3)

When we first began working on this essay, we did not imagine
that it would turn into an extended dialogue with bell hooks. Finding ourselves together for several days of collaboration at the start
of long-dreamed-of sabbaticals, we imagined that the essay we
hoped to draft would reconsider the notion of audience articulated
in an earlier study, "Audience Addressed/Audience Invoked: The
Role of Audience in Composition Theory and Pedagogy" (hereafter
referred to as AA/AI), and would do so in fairly standard ways. We
assumed, for instance, that we would review research on audience
that has appeared in the ten years since AA/AI was published, and
that we would articulate our current understanding of audience in
relation to these studies. Along the way, we would respond to various readings of our essay and would indicate the extent to which
our thinking about audience has changed in the last decade.

Our motive in wishing to do so was simple: through citations,
analyses, and reprintings, AA/AI has been both appropriated
and critiqued by later theorists who, like us, have been fascinated by the richness and difficulty of the concept of audience.
Just as our 1984 essay situated itself in relation to earlier studies of audience, so too does it now stand in an intellectual field of
prior and subsequent work. Moreover, our own relation to this

4/20/94

REPRESENTING AUDIENCE

"To make the liberated voice, we must confront the issue of audience--we must know to whom we speak." (bell hooks, Talking Back: thinking feminist, thinking black, p. 3)

The days are sunny here in Ohio, blue October skies punctuated by goldred effusions of maple leaves and the occasional wisp of a cloud. At dusk, we walk toward the river, watching for the moon and evening star, moving through falling leaves, talking, talking. As always, our talk leaps across times and places, touching old aches and new longings, workday woes and family stories, still more best-ever recipes and our most current reading. Beginning long-dreamed-of sabbaticals, we have come together to savor just such moments and to reflect on questions about audience, about authorship, about collaboration that have occupied us for over a decade now. Among these issues, we have been fretting over the concept of audience longer than any other, an interest that grew most directly out of our reading in traditional rhetorical theory and our experience of listening to and talking with (being audiences for and with) one another and that resulted in, among other things, a collaboratively written article on the concept of audience, "Audience Addressed/Audience Invoked: The Role of Audience in Composition Theory and Pedagogy" (hereafter referred to AA/AI).

Writing now, in the cool autumn days and nights a decade later, we propose to revisit our earlier article and to reexamine issues of audience raised there, for these issues seem as crucial

10/94

REPRESENTING AUDIENCE

RHETORIC, DIFFERENCE AND THE SUBJECT(S) OF DISCOURSE

> "[Recently there]...has been unprecedented sup-
> port among scholars and intellectuals for the inclu-
> sion of the Other--in theory. Yes! Everyone seems to
> be clamoring for 'difference.'"
>
> bell hooks
> Yearning, p. 54

Difference has become an important and even fashionable term in postmodern and feminist discourses. But speaking only for ourselves, we find that it has been easier to reflect theoretically about difference than it has been to recognize the extent to which our own material and discursive positions have caused us to see and understand the experiences of some writers, and to ignore and devalue the experiences of others. In this essay, we hope to demonstrate some of the ways in which inattention or resistance to difference can influence what those of us in composition studies see, or do not see, when we attempt to understand how writers, and writing, work--and in particular how they "work" with audiences.

Why engage in such a project? Contemporary theoretical, pedagogical, and professional debates both within and beyond the field of composition studies call, we believe, for a turn to self-reflection, to self-conscious examination of personal, cultural, disciplinary and institutional assumptions, frameworks, and methods. In the spirit of such self-critique, we wish to engage in the kind of analysis that leads not to new theories or taxonomies but rather to new insights about our own unexamined desires and positionings. And what better way to engage in self-a:/audmar, revised by Lisa 4-16-95

REPRESENTING AUDIENCE:
"SUCCESSFUL" DISCOURSE AND DISCIPLINARY CRITIQUE

We are wedded in language, have our being in words.
Language is also a place of struggle.

bell hooks (146)

In his February, 1994 College Composition and Communication editor's column, Joseph Harris provides a brief overview of the kinds of work he hopes to publish in the journal, noting, among other things, that he is "especially interested in pieces that take a critical or revisionary look at work in composition studies" (7). Given the contemporary turn to self-conscious disciplinary critique, Harris's call is hardly surprising. In its relatively brief disciplinary history, in fact, composition studies has engaged in a great deal of revisionary looking back: witness the several paradigm shifts or theoretical revolutions the field has experienced during the span of the last three decades. This disciplinary critique has for the most part, however, been carried out in the agonistic manner characteristic of traditional academic discussion, with each wave of criticism, each revisionary look establishing its own efficacy by demonstrating the flaws of prior conceptions.[1]

The notion of disciplinary progress--or success--enacted by these discourses has in many ways served our field well (15).[2] For though composition studies could hardly be described as an established or mainstream academic discipline, it has succeeded to a considerable extent in legitimizing and professionalizing its position in the academy. And the critical discourses of such

WRITING TOGETHER ACROSS TECHNOLOGIES

This is a page from the first handwritten draft of our Fund for the Improvement of Postsecondary Education (FIPSE) grant proposal, which we wrote en route to a vacation together, on a ferry from Vancouver, British Columbia, to Vancouver Island in the late summer of 1983. The page is a material artifact of our dynamic collaborative writing process: you can see our different handwriting, our cross-outs and notes to each other. On the ferry, we passed pages of this draft back and forth to each other and paused often to talk through ideas. The FIPSE grant, which we eventually received in 1984, supported the research that led to our first coauthored book, Singular Texts/ Plural Authors.

Technological advances — most notably the Internet — have in some ways made it easier for us to write together. Now we can send drafts back and forth instantly, crossing out passages, posing questions, and writing over and beyond each other just as we do when we're in the same room (or on the same ferry) — even when there are hundreds or even thousands of miles between us. This page, taken from a June 2008 draft of "'Among the Audience': On Audience in an Age of New Literacies" (included in this collection), was sent as an e-mail attachment from Lisa to Andrea, who responded to Lisa's lowercase comments and questions in all caps, deleting some passages and inserting others. We often use track changes when writing together at a distance.

20

various kinds of audiences: the participatory audience of peer review, for instance, can be theorized and interrogated by students in their composition classes, that is, rather than simply responding to one another, they can take time to get to know these real-life audiences, along with the assumptions and values they bring to their fellow students' texts, literally examining where these members of the audience are coming from. Or students can create a genealogy of audiences for a particular social networking site, exploring the many diverse individuals and groups that have access to the site and asking which audiences the site invokes and which it seems to address.

Comment: This has always struck me as an odd example as we know that (thanks to Anna Gere) peer review has in various forms been happening for a long, long time. Or maybe that's not the issue. I'm wondering how theorizing and interrogating in-class peer review will help students better understand online audiences.

Am I missing something? SEE MY EDITS.

Students could examine the many issues raised, for instance, by by various Pro Ana (pro anorexia) sites on the Web. Who are the sponsors of these sites? Just what kind of collaborative relationships are being invoked and addressed by those who post to and read this site?

Comment: I deleted the rest of this paragraph because I'm going to move it to the concluding discussion of ethical issues at the end of the essay. GO FOR IT.

As we have noted in this essay, what began for us as two different strands of research—one on audience, another on collaboration—have all but merged during the last couple of years as we have seen how frequently writers become audiences and vice versa. Yet more often than not, students resist collaboration in their schoolwork even as they collaborate constantly in their out-of-class online writing. There are reasons for this seeming contradiction or tension: school writing is part of a deeply individualistic system that rewards individual students through a system of grades and points and values the individual GPA: working collaboratively runs counter to that system. But while we work to change the hyper-individualistic base of higher education in the United States, we need also to engage students in intense discussions of this issue. As we have been arguing for some time, we know that most of the innovative work that gets done in the world today gets done in collaborative groups (see Sawyer, Tapscott and Williams, Sunstein, Ede and Lunsford)—including, increasingly, teams that work primarily

Deleted: In addition, teachers and students need to consider the reciprocal responsibilities entailed in writer-audience relationships. What does a student writer posting to Facebook owe to all the potential audiences of that post, from a former partner to a potential employer? And what responsibilities do audiences have toward those whose messages they receive, seek, reject, or encounter? One goal of future research on audience must surely be to explore the ethical dimensions of such relationships.

Deleted: almost twenty years

Deleted: , in collaborative teams

Though collaborating from a distance is certainly more efficient than it used to be, we still prefer — and covet — the time we are able to spend physically together when working on a project. This is a page from an August 2009 draft of "Collaboration and Collaborative Writing: The View from Here" (included in this collection), written when we were together in Corvallis. Though we now often write on the computer, we also like to print out drafts so we can pass them between us, making handwritten notes. In addition to the conversation that's apparent on the page, we also do lots of talking out loud.

agonistic. We think of this as running from the mutually composed wedding vow to the war-like engagement of negotiators).

In addition to a continuum from the most fully collaborative (our most enjoyable practice) to the most distantly distributed or from the most to least cooperative, we early on identified two distinct forms of collaboration, which we called "hierarchical"—the mode typical of much business and organizational writing, with a leader who assigns tasks—and "dialogic," which we described as mutually enabling and non-hierarchical though often not as efficient or product-oriented as hierarchical collaboration. In working on this essay, we have asked just how well these forms still hold up today. Lisa, if this seems OK so far, here we need to add two or three examples from today's writing world and show how they exemplify either dialogic or hierarchical collaboration.

So if hierarchical and dialogic forms of collaboration still seem viable, are there other forms we might identify today? Most notably would surely be kind of "wiki writing" discounted as collaborative by Yancey and Sooner, in which "countless authors anonymously revise a text composed by unknown persons" (actually, that anonymity turns out not to be so complete after all). Such collective forms of writing still seem collaborative to us, though we would label such writing "distributed" and note that it may sometimes also be dialogic (think of writers on Wikipedia working together toward one "perfect" entry) or hierarchical (think of the developing status differentiations at Wikipedia, where some editors are "more equal" than others). Each of these forms (hierarchical, dialogic, and distributed) realizes authority in different ways, and each offers a variety of possibilities for organizing structures to enable collaboration. Perhaps

WRITER'S BLOCK

The inaugural issue of Writing on the Edge *(WOE) included the first of a series of drawings by Tim Flower that featured a little square object he titled "Writer's Block." These cartoons appeared in the journal until 1995, then made a reappearance from 1999 to 2001, and most recently in 2010. The "Writer's Block" column that often accompanied the cartoons ran from WOE's first issue in 1989 until 1998. Editor John Boe recalls that these "guest columns" were sometimes written by the author(s) and sometimes concocted by Boe and his colleague Eric Schroeder. The one that appears here was written by Boe — with hearty approval from Andrea and Lisa, thus yielding another collaborative act. Facing this "column" were two of Flower's "writer's block" cartoons.*

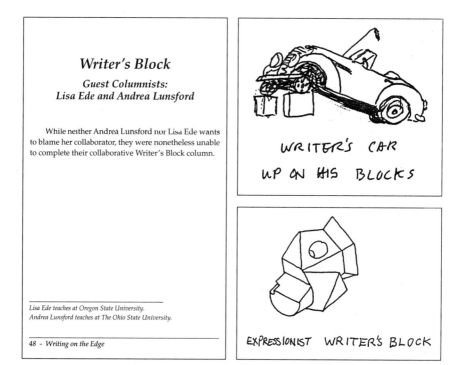

Writer's Block

Guest Columnists:
Lisa Ede and Andrea Lunsford

While neither Andrea Lunsford nor Lisa Ede wants to blame her collaborator, they were nonetheless unable to complete their collaborative Writer's Block column.

Lisa Ede teaches at Oregon State University.
Andrea Lunsford teaches at The Ohio State University.

48 - *Writing on the Edge*

WRITER'S CAR UP ON HIS BLOCKS

EXPRESSIONIST WRITER'S BLOCK

PART ONE

Why Write Together?

1   *Why Write . . . Together?*

I t was 10:00 P.M. We had just spent another twelve-hour day working on our paper. Lisa was settling into a chair with a hot toddy. Andrea was shoving off for a shower. We were grumpy, tired, full of self-pity; this was the third day we had worked at such a pace. Only one day remained before Lisa had to begin the eight-hour trek from Andrea's home in Vancouver to her own in Corvallis. We had to finish a draft of the paper, our first joint writing project, the next day.

All at once — we both remember it this way — Lisa sat upright and announced: "Andrea takes a shower every night; Lisa takes one every morning." Since the meaning of this toddy-stimulated statement was hardly self-evident, Lisa went on to explain that suddenly the significance of all our differences, of which this was just one example, seemed clear. How could two such opposite people ever hope to write a paper — together?

Warming to the silliness of the topic, we began to list all the ways we differ. Andrea showers every night; Lisa, every morning. Andrea drinks only iced tea, even at breakfast; Lisa drinks only the hottest of hot tea. Andrea hates milk and most dairy products; they form a staple of Lisa's diet. Andrea always wears her hair pulled back; Lisa gets a headache from even the thought of a single barrette. Andrea is a meticulous housekeeper; Lisa, so-so at best.

As the list of opposites grew, we felt a giddy sense of relief. No wonder the past few days had been so trying. Two such contrary, often downright cantankerous, people should have *expected* trouble. The struggle began to make sense: not just our personalities but our composing processes and, to a lesser degree, our styles, differed radically. After all, didn't Lisa love dashes, sprinkling them liberally through her prose, while Andrea seldom used them? Andrea preferred long paragraphs; Lisa's were usually shorter. Lisa wrote at a desk or (in a pinch) at a table; Andrea worked sitting cross-legged on the floor or on the bed. Andrea was a sprinter; she liked to write a draft straight through, as quickly as possible, revising and typing later. Lisa worked more slowly, dividing a paper into small sections, revising and typing as she went.

From Lisa Ede and Andrea Lunsford, in *Rhetoric Review* 1 (1983): 150–57.

We decided that night that if we ever did complete our joint essay, we would someday explore the mystery — or the madness — of co-authorship. Since that time, we have co-authored two other articles and have several joint projects in mind. Thus, while we continue individual research efforts, our status as sometime co-authors seems assured. Somehow, despite the difficulties, we not only manage to write essays together, but actually like doing so. And, as we have worked together, the question that arose that night — how can two people with different interests, personalities, habits, and composing processes together write one essay? — has expanded into many questions. This article is a brief anecdotal response to some of those questions. In it, we wish to sketch the outlines of the process of co-authorship as we have come to understand it, to set forth the advantages and disadvantages we encountered, and to pose a series of questions which we hope will be explored in future research.

In our experience, co-authorship has meant the two of us creating one text — together. We discovered and thought through ideas together, talked through almost every section and draft of the papers together, and often wrote drafts by talking and then recording directly. Such is not always the case. Indeed, our use of the term is probably atypical. More typically, no doubt, two authors contribute separate sections, which are then put together. Only at that point do the co-authors revise the whole text, and even in revising authors may work separately. In this way, people can co-author articles without ever being together or doing any writing together. This second form of co-authorship may best describe the kind of academic writing done by, say, a professor and a student, or the kind done by many researchers in science. It may also describe co-authorship in much professional and business writing. Yet a third concept covered by the blanket term "co-authorship" is that of group writing. It is not unusual, especially in business, for a number of people to contribute to a single text. The head of the writing division for an international mining corporation recently told us that as many as fifteen people contribute sections to their annual report. Subsequently, four or five of those people come together to revise the entire report, which generally goes through a dozen drafts.

We believe that important distinctions exist among these types of co-authorship and, indeed, that other types of co-authorship can be identified. Since our experience has been primarily of the first type, however — that of conceiving, drafting, and revising a text together — we will concentrate on that concept and will use the term "co-authorship" in this essay to refer to this type of writing together.

We are also here referring only to academic writing. The essays we have co-authored have all been addressed to those in our field, readers of *College Composition and Communication, College English*, and rhetoric journals. In that sense, we have gone into each project with a clear sense of audience, medium of publication, and purpose (although we could, of course, easily misjudge our audience or medium or alter our purposes). As with much academic writing, we began by working within only our own time constraints. But as so often is the case, this internal control soon gave way to external pressures. An invitation to speak at a conference was accepted; an article was solicited for a journal or committed to a book — and suddenly the external pressure to write on demand appeared. In this important regard, that of writing on demand, much academic writing may be closer to professional writing than we usually consider it to be. But in other ways, the genres vary markedly. As writers of an article for *Rhetoric Review*, for instance, we have a different kind of control over shape and substance than we would if we were writing an annual report for a mining company. As with the various types of co-authorship, we think these generic distinctions are important ones that need to be explored. While we hope to pursue these questions in the future, we are speaking here not of business or professional writing, but only of the academic genre with which we are all so familiar.

So what is this process of co-authoring an academic paper? We've drawn boxes and arrows, spirals and loops, but will offer no schematized representation of the process we have experienced. If you can imagine the words *talk . . . write . . . talk . . . read . . . talk . . . write . . . talk . . . read . . .* written in a large looping spiral — that comes closest a description of the process as we know it. We wish especially to emphasize the frequency and proportion of *talking* in this process.

As we noted earlier, each of our projects grew out of a particular rhetorical situation: we were constrained by a broad topic and by a medium of publication and an audience. Within those guidelines, our first and longest talks occurred. These early talks were characterized by a lot of foolishness (Why not claim that the concept of audience simply doesn't exist? or, How about writing a dialogue between Aristotle and Wittgenstein?), fantasy (What if we could visit Kenneth Burke for a month?), and unfocused rambling (Where do you suppose we've put our notes on those ten articles? What do you think is the best reading for *krisis*?) In our first project, these talks helped us sound the depths of our topic and, most importantly, discover the enormity of what we did not know. Intensive periods of reading and research followed, as did more and more talking, trading of notes, and posing of yet more unanswered questions. All told, this first co-authored essay took us six months, during which we met four times for two- to four-day writing sessions. These sessions were pressure-filled, frustrating — and very exciting. For one of them, we met halfway between our homes, in Seattle, and worked for two-and-a-half days in a hotel room, distracted only by the person trying unsuccessfully to "tidy up" around the stacks of books, articles, and drafts, and by our husbands, who insisted on reporting on all the fun they were having while we worked. We estimate writing and talking time in these sessions to be almost equal, with more time given to writing in the last session and more to talk in the earlier ones. At the end of each session the process of talk . . . write . . . talk . . . read . . . talk . . . write . . . talk . . . read . . . left us tired but exhilarated. And in each case the process produced a draft, one we could take back home, work on, and talk about in our frequent phone calls. We have kept every draft, all our notes, and some protocols from each of our projects, but we do not wish to turn this into a full-blown case study of our admitted idiosyncrasies. Rather, we wish to turn to a brief discussion of how co-authoring altered our individual writing processes.

Most noticeable, as we have mentioned, was the much larger proportion of talking together about our research and writing. Papers written singly have never been completely silent affairs; we talk to others about our work or ask colleagues to read and discuss essays or drafts with us. But never had either of us (both prodigious talkers to begin with) ever talked so much or for so long while writing a paper. This talking, in fact, seemed to be a necessary part of co-authoring, one that made our writing more productive and efficient. Nor is this result surprising. Our "talks," after all, gave us the constant benefits of dialectic, the traditional counterpart of rhetoric.

Co-authorship effected a second, less pleasurable change in our ordinary writing processes. All academic writers are accustomed to the pressure of deadlines, but in single authorship these deadlines are more or less manageable. Co-authorship presented us with completely rigid time-schedules and hence with more pressure than either of us was used to working under: if we had only two-and-a-half days to work together, then we had to come up with a text at that very time. Or else.

We also noted shifts in our usual revision strategies. In the first place, neither of us was accustomed to having *talk* serve as the basis for a majority of the revisions we made. When writing alone, writers usually revise while or after reading. We found also that our individual revising strategies differed substantially: Lisa generally revises and types each section as it is drafted; Andrea favors long periods of staring into space during which she composes various alternative drafts in her head before beginning a long burst of writing. Editing strategies were equally affected. In the co-authored articles, we found ourselves attending much more closely to quotation format and footnote citations in our early drafts than we would ordinarily have done. We were concerned to get the citations exactly right, since our resources were split up between us and our two libraries. Going back to find a missing source would be much more difficult than usual.

These changes in revision strategies reflect, we believe, a change in the rhetorical situations co-authors work within: they must cooperate and collaborate at every turn. Co-authorship, then, demands flexibility and compromise, traits single writers can often eschew. For us, this changed situation meant giving up some of our cherished stylistic tics — like Lisa's dashes — or a favored revision strategy.

The spirit of cooperation and compromise necessary to co-authorship helped us identify two additional ways in which our customary experience with writing was changed. As of this writing, we feel less ego involvement with the pieces we have co-authored than those we have written alone. Hence, we have a greater distance from the work. At this point, we cannot report whether co-authorship gives us more — or less — confidence in the written product. But the questions of confidence and of ego involvement raise a number of issues, some of which we will address in the concluding section of this essay. Most importantly, we found that co-authoring led us to alter our normal problem-solving styles. In spite of the tendency to work on writing and revising a paper one small section at a time, Lisa's basic approach to problems is broad and synthetic; she ordinarily begins by casting a very wide net. Andrea, on the other hand, approaches problems analytically, narrowing and drawing out implications, searching for closure almost at once. Working as co-authors identified this difference in approach for us and led us to balance the two styles continually against one another. As a result, one often felt we were circling endlessly, spinning our wheels, while the other alternatively felt we were roaring hell-bent toward our conclusion.

Such changes obviously require significant accommodation and compromise, which can be seen as either advantages or disadvantages of co-authorship. Had we not finally decided on the former, we would not be writing this now. Many others, in similar situations and with similar interests, might choose differently. Indeed, some time in the future our own circumstances or any of a number of other internal or external changes could prompt us to decide that the advantages of co-authorship no longer outweigh the disadvantages. Co-authorship, as we have pointed out, makes the whole process of writing more difficult in some ways. (Perhaps our worst moment occurred one afternoon in Seattle when Lisa revised the midsection of our first project three times — requiring Andrea to change the following pages, which she was working on at the time, substantially every time.) Those problems were offset for us, however, by the stimulation of working with someone who shares the same interests. Even more important to us was the strong sense that in some writing situations we were more likely to achieve a better understanding, generate potentially richer and fresher ideas, and develop a stronger overall argument than we might have done working alone. (We specify "some writing situations" to emphasize that we chose the projects on which we collaborated carefully and for a number of particular reasons; as we have noted, we continued to work on independent research efforts during this period.)

We felt, in short, a kind of synergism when we worked together. This synergism, the sense that by combining our efforts we could in some instances achieve more together than alone, carried us through some difficult times. But other factors also played a role. Although we knew before we began writing together that we differed in our composing habits and stylistic preferences, we each shared a respect for the other's abilities. Also, each of us knew the other was a person on whom we could count, once committed, to complete a project no matter how much or how violently we differed. Finally, we *wanted* to work together, both because we are friends (who now can deduct the expenses for all the trips we would have taken anyway) and because we feel that collaboration and collegiality are ideals much discussed but little practiced in academic life.

Although we have gone into some detail about our relationship as co-authors, we have by no means given a full accounting of the ups and downs, ins and outs, arguments and counter-arguments involved in working together. (For a while we planned to include process footnotes such as [1]"Believe it or not, Andrea put this dash in here"; or [2]"At this point, Lisa *begged* to be able to type what we had written.") We hope in future research to investigate further the concepts and kinds of co-authorship and the implications co-authoring may hold for our field. In the meantime, we would very much like to hear from other co-authors about their experiences writing with others. We hope shortly to begin a more formal gathering of data about co-authoring in various disciplines and professions. Even this brief exploration, however, has raised a number of questions we believe need to be addressed.

(1) What specific features distinguish the processes of co- or group-authoring from those of single authorship? Are these features the same for the three types of co-authorship described above? Can these features of process be linked to any features of the resulting products? In short, how can we best *define* co-authorship?

(2) Is there a limit to how many people can write together? Are projects such as the *Oxford English Dictionary*, *Bible*, *Short Title Catalogue*, elaborate computer programs, encyclopedias — all often involving more than 100 authors — examples of co-authorship? That is to say, what are the parameters of co-authorship?

(3) In what ways, if any, does co- or group-authorship affect the way we view the traditional rhetor-audience relationship?

(4) How does technology affect the processes of co-authoring? In our experience, writing together would have been much more difficult and much slower without the telephone, xerox, and self-correcting typewriter. Had we each had word processors at home and a computer link, what other differences might we have noted?

(5) What epistemological implications does co-authorship hold for traditional notions of creativity and originality? Our own strong sense that two may create ideas that neither would have reached alone argues for the value of dialectic as invention.

(6) How might the ethics of co-authorship be examined and defined? We spoke earlier of noting less ego involvement in our co-authored pieces. Perhaps this factor is related to our sense of shared responsibility: if we are wrong, at least we are wrong together. But in cases of group authorship, where does the responsibility lie? Who stands behind the words of a report written by fifteen people? As group authorship becomes more and more the norm in some genres, such questions gather urgency.

(7) Is the emphasis on or weight of various cognitive and rhetorical strategies different when co-authoring than when writing alone? As we noted, many of our customary revision strategies were altered by the process of co-authorship, and the rhetorical situation, which demanded collaboration and compromise, strongly affected our usual processes.

(8) Finally, we were led to think most seriously of the pedagogical implications of co-authorship. What do we know as a discipline about the advantages or disadvantages of having students participate in co- or group-writing? If advantages do exist, don't they in some ways contradict our profession's traditional insistence on students working alone? And perhaps most importantly, do we have ways to teach students to adjust readily to co- or group-writing tasks?

Although this whimsical report of our experiences as co-authors is severely limited, perhaps serving best to raise questions, the issue of co- and group-authorship in general is not of limited or peripheral significance. As a rule, writers in the humanities have tended to ignore co-authorship, both in writing and in teaching, while colleagues in the sciences and the professions have long used it as a major mode. In view of this anomaly, the images of the lonely writer in a garret, or students hunched against the solitary ordeal of writing proficiency examinations, seem particularly inappropriate. We are, after all, most often responsible for teaching those who go into science and the professions how to write. And when we consider that these students are going into jobs already making use of rapidly developing computer technology, which holds such potential significance for co-authoring, the question for both writers and teachers may be not "Why write together?" but "Why *not* write together?"

2 Collaboration and Compromise: The Fine Art of Writing with a Friend

> Talk is central to our collaboration in a way that it seldom has been for us as individual writers. We find ourselves talking through to a common thesis and plan, talking through the links in an argument, talking through various points of significance or alternative conclusions. Talk is also central to our planning, which must be both more explicit and more detailed when we write together than either of us is accustomed to when working alone.

In this essay we hope to describe what happens when two people, each of whom has a fairly extensive history of writing alone, decide to collaborate on professional writing projects. We are those two people — friends who first co-authored an essay almost by accident, liked both the process and the product, and have continued often to write together. As the following discussion will illustrate, melding our two styles was less difficult than melding our originally quite diverse composing processes. Though our writing together will always involve a delicate balancing of tensions, the process of collaborative writing has changed both the way we write and the way we think about writing. To help illustrate the nature of that change, we will first each briefly describe our individual composing processes. We will then discuss how we write together, a process that involves both collaboration and compromise.

WRITING ALONE: ANDREA

Most of the professional writing that I do results from an "assignment" of some kind: I have agreed to give a conference paper, contribute a chapter to a book, or write a journal article. But in one respect, such "assignments" or invitations are themselves the result of questions I have asked myself, questions which eventually led me into certain areas of study and research: What consti-

---

From Andrea A. Lunsford and Lisa Ede, in *Writers on Writing*, vol. 2, ed. Tom Waldrep (New York: Random House, 1988) 121–27.

tutes development in writing during the college years? What happened to the rhetorical tradition in the nineteenth century? Why do we think of writing almost exclusively as a solitary process? For me, then, the writing process begins almost always with curiosity. What follows is generally a period of intense concentration and brainstorming, followed by a lot of reading, some of which is apparently desultory. I rarely take notes as I read, but my internal eye is watching for what I call the "shape" of whatever I want to write. This process of conceptualization is extremely important to me; during it I envision the direction of any essay, article, or book — where it will go and how it will get there. I can write without going through this internal and largely silent process, but I am uncomfortable doing so and will avoid it if possible.

Once I see — internally — the shape and direction of an essay, I commit them to paper, usually in a series of schematized jottings. From this point on, I write quickly, anxious to see each sentence appear, to see if my conceptualization will pan out. At this stage, I prefer to write for as long a stretch as possible and will finish an entire draft if I can. If not, I aim to complete a draft of a section and to begin the next section before I stop, since it makes it easier to pick up the thread of my argument the next day. I seldom take breaks and am very irritated by interruptions during this stage. I still prefer to write first drafts in longhand, and I always write sitting cross-legged on the floor or on the sofa in my study, *never* at a desk. Generally, I cast each sentence or series of sentences roughly in my head and then write them, revising as I go and writing "metadiscourse" notes to myself in the margins ("Expand this point"; "Give an example"; "Fix syntax," etc.). And I include bibliographical citations in the first draft — I can't face the boredom of doing a list of sources after the essay is finished.

As I've already suggested, revision is a constant in my writing process, beginning as soon as I start to think about my subject and continuing throughout the drafting stage. I often read aloud to myself, revising for rhythm and sound, particularly if I am writing a conference paper or address. My completed draft, which I often know by heart, most often looks like a road map with arrows and cross-outs and such indicators as "See over" or "Go to next page, paragraph three." As I type this draft, I may make further revisions, and I may revise the typescript one or more times. But often I can type a finished copy from my much-revised and often-recited handwritten draft. I hate typing and am just in the process of learning to use a word processor, which I will probably also hate in spite of its flexibility and powers. Only if I can manage to use it while sitting cross-legged on the floor will the computer become an integral part of my writing process.

WRITING ALONE: LISA

When I write professional articles, my strongest inclination is to proceed slowly, carefully — even cautiously. (Letters, journal entries, and routine memos are another matter: I zip through these fairly speedily.) As an undergraduate, I allowed myself the pleasure of polishing each sentence before I moved on to the next, even though I might finally toss half of them. During, but especially since, graduate school I learned to push myself, forcing ideas down, leaving words and sentences alone until later. I can now, if I have to, write professional articles and essays with some speed. But my inclination, my desire, with any important scholarly project is always to write slowly, stopping often to monitor and reassess what I've written.

The impetus for my writing comes from a variety of sources. Sometimes, like Andrea, I accept "assignments" and thus willy-nilly find myself with a task I must complete. But the questions that catalyze my research also come from my teaching — my interest in audience began that way — and from my personal experience. I am aware of two broad stages in my composing: information gathering and writing. But they're not discrete. I generally make a number of notes as I read, for instance, but I also do so as I write; and as I write, I often realize that I need to return to a source to find or clarify information. I find it difficult to separate planning and revising, except in the broadest, most obvious ways; for as I write I'm constantly both making changes in my writing and recasting my plans for the rest of an essay, often in notes at the top of the page or on scrap paper. If I have time, I like to type sections of an essay as I go; I seem to need to see a relatively clean typed copy to be able to distance myself from my writing.

When I write I am most aware of my struggle to shape meaning: to say what I want to say about a specific topic. But I am also aware of being engaged in a dialogue with others who have written compellingly on my subject. These people become a particularly important audience for me, whose expectations and standards I want to try to meet. But since the world of composition studies is relatively small, I sometimes also find myself envisioning a very specific person as I write. ("What would X think of this?" "This may answer what Y said in that recent article.") And I am aware of the constraints posed by the means of publication. I don't sit down simply to write my thoughts on Chaim Perelman or audience; from the start I am aware of writing an article on Perelman for a scholarly journal in speech communication or on audience for *College Composition and Communication*.

Like many writers, I have my rituals. I have always preferred to write at my own desk, which I have, ideally, both physically and emotionally cleared — paid all the bills, written the most overdue letters to friends, made neat lists of what I need to do in the next few weeks or over the quarter break. (I used to have to clean the house and bake bread before I could begin writing, but I've broken myself of those habits.) I am easily distracted when I write, especially by noise. I write almost everything but letters or routine memos longhand; the latter I compose at the typewriter or, more recently, at the word processor. (I love the way word processing simplifies editing, but I can't imagine ever composing anything important at the computer.) I feel happiest when I have a chunk of time — two days at least — in which to work on a project of any magnitude. And I write best in the morning. If I'm at my desk and writing by 9 A.M. that's a powerful signal to me that this will be a good day.

WRITING TOGETHER: COLLABORATION AND COMPROMISE

As the preceding brief summaries suggest, our composing processes when we write alone differ considerably. Lisa writes slowly and synthetically; thinking through writing is essential to her. Andrea writes more quickly. And even more important, she is more analytic; she does in her head — by simply sitting and thinking things through — what Lisa often needs pen and paper to work out. Andrea most prefers to write in one long spurt; stopping for any reason is an irritant and a serious interruption of her writing process. Lisa likes to stop often to reread, rethink, and if there's time, type up what she's written. Lisa, in other words, thinks and writes in stages or segments; Andrea, in one single extended burst of energy. Andrea can write almost anywhere — except at a desk! — and has, in general, fewer writing rituals than Lisa. Lisa tends to fret over her writing; Andrea is more businesslike.

We are, in other words, from this perspective as different as the proverbial tortoise and hare. How have we managed to write together, and why? One powerful impetus, and subsequent reinforcement, for our collaboration is our friendship. We enjoy being together, and even though we spend much of the brief periods we're together — a weekend during the term, four to six days over Christmas, a luxurious two weeks in the summer — working, we always find time for jokes, shopping sprees for exotic foods, and laughter-filled late-night dinners. Before we coauthored our first essay, we had coordinated several workshops, so we weren't strangers to collaboration. We knew that we shared a similar attitude toward professional commitments: if we agreed to finish a project by a certain deadline, we generally would. We also knew we could count on each other. In addition, we shared a number of intellectual interests: what, for example, constitutes the "new" rhetoric? and how might research on audience affect the teaching of writing? And finally, of course, we came to share an interest in the phenomenon we were experiencing — collaboration.

Looking back on our four years' experience as coauthors, we are surprised to note the relative ease with which we have modified or given up some of our writing habits or rituals in order to collaborate. Andrea now willingly, if not enthusiastically, takes more frequent breaks when writing and will even type up parts of a draft to please Lisa, if necessary. Lisa, on the other hand, now writes faster and for longer, more sustained periods than she was accustomed to doing alone. Important as such changes in habits are, however, they do not reflect what we believe to be the single most significant change in our writing processes demanded by collaboration. What for Andrea is largely a lengthy internal process of conceptualization must now be made external and explicit. And what for Lisa is largely a silent conversation with colleagues must now become a concrete verbal conversation with an all too unideal Andrea. (Yes, Andrea wrote this sentence, against Lisa's protestations.) *Talk*, then, plays a vital role in our collaborative writing. In fact, . . . talk is central to our collaboration in a way that it seldom has been for us as individual writers. We find ourselves talking through to a common thesis and plan, talking through the links in an argument, talking through various points of significance or alternative conclusions. Talk is also central to our planning, which must be both more explicit and more detailed when we write together than either of us is accustomed to when working alone.

Although we generally organize our projects so that we can divide up tasks and do part of the work — gathering information or writing a section of an essay or chapter — alone, most of our writing, especially final drafts, has been done together. This presents a number of practical problems, which we'll discuss shortly. But the advantages, especially given the role face-to-face talk (which can only partly be simulated over the phone) plays in our writing, make the effort to be together not only worthwhile but essential. When we are working, whether in Vancouver, Corvallis, or Seattle's University Inn, our halfway meeting place, we usually stake out different rooms to write in. But we move constantly back and forth, talking, trading texts (one of our favorite collaborative strategies is to revise one another's writing), asking questions. Often, when one or both of us is stuck, we'll work together on the same text, passing a single pad of paper back and forth, one of us completing the sentence or paragraph that the other began. By the time that most essays are finished, we simply couldn't say that "Lisa wrote this section, while Andrea wrote that." Our joint essays are truly collaborative efforts.

This collaboration is a crucial factor in our coauthored projects, from the earliest point in our composing through the final editing process. The simple physical act of meeting to work, for instance, has come to serve as a powerful writing ritual for both of us. However we feel individually — tired, cranky, concerned with other projects or issues — once we're together (after the 8-hour drive or the quick airplane flight) we know it's time to work. We have already commented on the importance of talk in our joint composing process, especially in the earlier or prewriting stage. Throughout our writing, however, we are much more aware of the way in which our joint ideas and understandings enable us, via the crucible of our conversations and collaboration, to discover new meanings — meanings simply not available to us working alone. Finally, we believe that we feel somewhat less ego involvement with our coauthored essays, that we are more willing to loosen our proprietary connection or hold on our "own" words. This latter point may be reflected both in the care with which we alternate our names as first authors — we thought that listing our names alphabetically would indicate that we were equal collaborators, but were quickly disabused of that notion — and our ability to negotiate differences in our individual styles, such as Lisa's love of dashes or Andrea's fondness for periodic sentences.

As we mentioned earlier, our collaboration has presented a number of practical challenges and problems. Since we live 400 miles apart, our need to be physically together at certain crucial times in our composing process requires careful planning. (As we write this in December 1985, we are also deciding when and how we can meet the following summer — and discovering a number of difficulties, even though we're planning six months in advance.) Money is also a constraint. Without the support of our departments, which have generously paid for our numerous long-distance telephone calls, and, more recently, our FIPSE-funded Shaughnessy Scholars grant, we simply could not have afforded to meet as often as we have, and hence would have been forced to limit our collaboration. Pragmatic constraints have also affected our research and writing. We try to have duplicate copies of important reference materials, for instance, but must often pass books and articles back and forth, with the attendant inevitable confusion. ("Do you have the Grimaldi?" "Where did we put that article by David Bartholomae?" "Did you remember to make me a Xerox of Lynn Troyka's essay?") We must also take much greater care keeping reference notes and bibliographic references straight, especially in articles with numerous citations. Finally, we simply could not collaborate without photocopying. We are constantly mailing copies of notes, references, and drafts back and forth. One of our standard jokes involves our usually desperate efforts in Seattle to find a quick-copy center open early Sunday morning so we can Xerox what we've written over the weekend and begin our separate journeys home and arrive in time to unpack and prepare for Monday's classes.

We will soon be faced with a new practical challenge: Andrea will begin in fall 1986 teaching at a large Midwestern university — 5–7 driving days, not 8 hours, from Lisa's university in Oregon. We have of course discussed the problems this move will create for us as coauthors. We will almost certainly, for instance, have to commit ourselves to fewer joint projects, especially those with immediate deadlines, since we'll no longer be able to meet in Seattle in an emergency. We have both recently acquired personal computers, however, and we hope that these, and modems, may alleviate some of our anticipated difficulties. We expect, then, that our joint composing process will have to change. But we expect also to keep writing together. Collaborative writing has taught us too much for us entirely to abandon the practice of writing together; it has taught us how to read each other's illegible scrawls; how to be patient and flexible; how to listen to and criticize a draft over the phone; how to laugh, not cry, when one of us announces that something the other has just written is not quite right. Most important, perhaps, it has taught us what we know as writers but often forget: that there is no simple, single, static writing process. Rather, there are writing processes — repertoires of strategies and habits that writers can learn, and change, if they have a strong enough motive for communicating. We view our writing processes, then, whether single or collaborative, as flexible and multifaceted, as rooted in various rhetorical and social situations, as growing and changing — even as we grow and change.

3

An Interview with Andrea Lunsford and Lisa Ede: Collaboration as a Subversive Activity

ALICE HEIM CALDERONELLO, DONNA BETH NELSON, AND SUE CARTER SIMMONS

The three of us sit at Andrea Lunsford's kitchen table, sipping tea and talking with Andrea and her long-time friend and co-author, Lisa Ede. They have spent an exhausting day, side by side before a computer screen, collaborating on their recent book, *Singular Texts/Plural Authors: Perspectives on Collaborative Writing* (Southern Illinois University Press, 1990), but they greet us warmly and appear eager to talk. Undoubtedly the most ardent proponents of collaboration in our discipline, the two women speak easily, candidly, and address a variety of issues germane to their new book, including their research findings, their own history of writing together, and collaboration as a subversive activity.

In the course of describing the book, Andrea provides us with the titles of the book's five chapters, "Old Beginnings," "Collaborative Writers at Work," "The Concept of Authorship: Explorations and (Dis)Closures," "The Pedagogy of Collaboration," and "New Beginnings." Intrigued, one of us asks, "Who is your intended audience for the book?" Andrea replies, "You. So you'd better buy it." We laugh and she continues, "Certainly our primary audience is our colleagues in the English profession, although we would hope that the book might be read by people in other disciplines as well."

Andrea and Lisa talk for a couple of hours, one often finishing a statement — or paragraph — that the other has begun. During the course of the interview we come to understand that authorship is a function which cannot be easily attributed to a single person; therefore we decided to present our voice as a collective voice, Donnalisue Simderonelson — a tenured, Full Professor, Assistant Professor, Acting Director of Freshman Composition at a mid-sized state university. The editors of WOE, however, have recast us into their own image.

WOE: When did the two of you first begin to collaborate?

EDE: We first decided to collaborate when we both lived in the Northwest. We were driving along the coast in Oregon, just having fun, and we began talking

---

From Alice Heim Calderonello, Donna Beth Nelson, and Sue Carter Simmons, in *Writing on the Edge* 2.2 (1991): 6–18.

about the book we wanted to do with Bob Connors in honor of Ed Corbett (*Essays on Classical Rhetoric and Modern Discourse*). So it must have been about 1983. Anyway, we were riding along and one of us said that Ed was such a wonderful person that surely he'd be very pleased to see his students were friends and that they were working with one another. Then we got to talking about what we might do for the book; each of us had thought of writing an essay as well as editing the collection. Suddenly one of us said, "Why don't we collaborate on something together?"

LUNSFORD: I don't think we even said "collaborate," though. I don't think that verb was in our vocabulary. We just said "do it together."

EDE: After we made the decision to write together, we told Ed and got an astonished response. He said that he couldn't figure out how we'd do it, that our writing together was the most extraordinary thing! We got a lot of remarkable reactions. People would take us aside and give us advice, or treat us like we were Martians or as if we had some kind of weird game going. Colleagues seemed astounded or worried.

LUNSFORD: Or suspicious.

WOE: What were they suspicious of?

LUNSFORD: How we could write together. Who was doing *what* writing? Who was the author? Where did the authority lie?

EDE: People also asked very specific questions. They would say, "All right, you are co-authoring this, but *really* Andrea wrote the first part and you wrote the second, right?" Or they'd ask, "One of you had final control over the style, didn't you?" And when we would say "no," they treated us like we were people who had just been to the New World. Or like we were incapable of doing something by ourselves — so feebleminded alone that we had banded together. Two women with ONE BRAIN!

WOE: Were some of the people who were "warning you off" colleagues in your respective departments?

LUNSFORD: Yes. They just couldn't understand.

EDE: One colleague even called me up and said, "Lisa, you've got to *stop* doing this. You're not going to get tenure."

WOE: Did anyone say what a wonderful idea your collaboration was, that it was so exciting?

LUNSFORD AND EDE: Nope.

WOE: Not one?

EDE: Not to me.

LUNSFORD: Never.

WOE: But you'd known each other for a long time; you were good friends and that helped you with all of this. Right?

LUNSFORD: Yes, we got to know each other in graduate school. Lisa graduated ahead of me in '75, and I graduated in '77. After we finished we went on to other places, but we kept in touch. We have always been friends.

EDE: During the years when I was in Brockport and you were in Columbus and then in Vancouver, though, we were not as close as when I moved to the West Coast. Our physical proximity was an absolute precondition for working together in those early years, don't you think?

LUNSFORD: Yes. It would have been impossible otherwise.

EDE: But also, we already knew that since we had similar work habits and styles we would not have radical problems, although our writing styles have changed somewhat.

WOE: Have your styles changed in the same direction?

LUNSFORD: A little; my style has gotten more complex and Lisa's has gotten a bit more simple syntactically.

EDE: I like dashes.

LUNSFORD: And I like things sort of stark. Lisa left-branches and embeds and I tend to move relentlessly from subject to verb.

WOE: Sounds like an effective collaboration.

LUNSFORD: Well, it took us a while to realize that. I'd go through and remove dashes; Lisa would put them back.

WOE: What about your collaborative styles; have they changed?

LUNSFORD: We have done a number of different kinds of collaboration. In fact, today, for the very first time, we sat and composed together at the computer, with me moaning every moment because I *hate* composing at the computer. In the past, we have divided things up, drafted separate parts and then traded them, or we've worked on the same text longhand. We've even written things over the phone.

WOE: How do you do that?

EDE: It's not hard, actually, except you have to be very explicit about what you're referring to.

LUNSFORD: The very last part of our most recent book was written that way. We talked for probably an hour and a half and then I wrote it down. I was the one who put the words down on paper; Lisa was in Rhode Island, or somewhere.

EDE: Massachusetts.

LUNSFORD: Massachusetts, and she didn't have any equipment or anything. In essence, we wrote it on the long distance telephone call, and then I just marked it down.

WOE: You sound like remarkable friends and collaborators. Have you ever had tugs-of-war or disagreements over your writing?

LUNSFORD: Sure. We've had some squabbles.

EDE: But we usually negotiate things. Although I remember a very difficult time in Seattle when Andrea and I were meeting at a motel to write.

LUNSFORD: We would arrive with our typewriters.

EDE: And they would extend check-out time for us. We were doing an article for *Written Communication*; it was Andrea's 40th birthday. We worked until midnight that night. We really had trouble with that article and had already gotten an extension on the deadline. We got up the next morning and worked on it, but it still wasn't finished, and we had to leave. Since Andrea can write anywhere, she said, "Let's just go finish this in our car," which was in an incredibly horrible parking lot. I said, "Andrea, I can't. I just cannot." And Andrea was saying, "Yes you can; you can do it." Finally, I just had to put my foot down and we ended up going to a noisy restaurant.

WOE: Did you take your typewriters in with you?

EDE: No. We were exhausted.

LUNSFORD: I think if we hadn't been friends, really committed friends, we would have had a big fight, because that was also the time when Lisa kept changing the opening sentence. Everything depended on the opening, and Lisa would say, "No, I think I have to take Rosenfeld and move him up here." And I would say, "Okay," and rewrite that part and then she would change her mind and tell me to put it back the other way. This went on and on and on.

EDE: It was a complicated article.

LUNSFORD: It was; it was very hard for us. But I was peeved — although there was nothing Lisa could do about it in trying to make it right. I was irritated, and here I was staying up all night on my 40th birthday — supposedly a "big" one.

WOE: Wait a minute. Andrea, you wanted to write in a grungy parking lot on your birthday?

EDE: No. No. Her birthday was actually the night before, and *then* we'd written until late in a grungy motel room with plaster of paris flamingos hanging on the wall. We were dead. Right before midnight, Andrea took a shower and said, "What's for dinner? Let's have a party."

But seriously, I don't think we have ever had really big disagreements, certainly not about content. We just work our way through, and if one of us says something doesn't feel right, then we talk about it.

LUNSFORD: I think, too, that because we have been friends a long time, we have been through some periods of real adversity together, the kind of experience that you most often have with family members. Those struggles tie you to someone and make you want to stretch yourself around difficulties. Lisa and I have that history, which makes it pretty unlikely that we'd fall out over something like a pair of dashes.

WOE: Given your own experiences and problems with collaboration and the skepticism of your colleagues, is collaboration something you'd recommend to other faculty — especially to those just starting out?

EDE: My immediate response is that you need a supportive relationship. And whether you are working with someone who is more established than you are or whether you are working with a peer and are both first-year people, collaboration can be very efficient. There are things that you can do together that you might not be able to do alone, and often that allows you to have a kind of scope and significance that you're simply unable to have by yourself. When Andrea and I started writing together, she knew more about classical rhetoric, and I was more immersed in contemporary rhetoric. Working together, we could teach each other.

LUNSFORD: I enjoy my collaboration with Lisa so much that I prefer doing projects together over writing alone. However, I would never suggest that a young faculty member do all scholarship collaboratively and simply hope that everything will be all right. I think that new faculty members should discuss collaborative writing with their chairs or with those who will be evaluating their scholarship. If possible, a beginning faculty member should choose a department with a senior person in Rhetoric and Composition who could make a strong case for the value of the junior member's collaboratively produced work. Fortunately, our professional organization is starting to support faculty members as they begin to challenge traditional modes of scholarship. In today's mail I got a copy of the CCCC's statement for chairs, deans, and provosts on how to evaluate work in rhetoric and composition; included is a strong statement about collaboration.

EDE: Andrea's cautionary statements are really important; people at the start of their careers have to be careful. And if they choose to collaborate, they have to be careful about whom they collaborate with.

WOE: What advice about selecting a good partner would you offer to people who have never collaborated?

LUNSFORD: A Collaborative Writing Dating Service. You get matched up.

EDE: But assuming you couldn't rely on *that*, there are a few suggestions I could make. First of all, I think the selection of one or more collaborators should depend in part on your needs. I could imagine, for example, a situation where I would choose to work with someone primarily because of what she knew or because that person and I have been investigating the same subject. Under these circumstances we might or might not be friends, but for pragmatic reasons a collaboration makes sense. On the other hand, I don't think anyone would embark on the kind of sustained collaboration that Andrea and I have had over the years without there being other reasons to work together.

LUNSFORD: For instance, if a job is too big for one person. I think that is one of the reasons that graduate students or faculty with heavy teaching loads can collaborate successfully and productively: they want to do big projects and there's not enough time to do them alone.

EDE: I think there are some other requirements also. Successful collaborators probably share certain work habits and ways of thinking. A couple of years ago, Andrea and I began to realize that we approached work somewhat similarly. For instance, if we make commitments, we tend to keep them, we can meet deadlines within reason, and we are both fairly linear thinkers. Then too, we tend to behave similarly as writers: one of us doesn't prewrite pages and pages to discover one nugget while the other outlines everything. As a result of our collaboration with one another and with others, we have also discovered that interpersonal skills are very important. The ability to articulate how you're feeling, to stop and comment, or to be aware that someone is demonstrating discomfort and to respond to that before she goes crazy is absolutely essential.

LUNSFORD: One of the most interesting things about collaborative writing is that you become less invested in your writing. Lisa and I have talked for many years about our perception that we have less ego involvement in the things that we write together than we used to have in things that we wrote alone. The quality of a collaborative experience is strongly related to each collaborator's ability to be receptive, to let everything show — the stupidities, the backsliding and illogicalities, and everything else that goes into writing a text — as well as to be open to those things in the other person, and to the other person's strengths. Something necessary within our own collaboration is our willingness to lead or to follow or to do both in a particular project. That is largely unstated between us, but important, I think.

WOE: Collaboration certainly creates special challenges for all of us in our roles as scholars. Does it also present problems for us in our roles as teachers?

LUNSFORD: Yes. In my opinion it does, especially with respect to assigning grades. In a recent graduate class that I taught, I saw that I was going to have trouble grading the students' performance, since much of the work was to have been done collaboratively. I brought my dilemma to the class, explaining that grading could discourage people from taking risks and might undercut the trust we were trying to establish. The students' reactions were extraordinarily varied: some felt a need for a grade; others didn't want any grades. We finally agreed they would write analyses of their contributions to and performance in class and that grades would be individually negotiated in conference with me. The evaluation process required a great deal of time, although the class had only 13 people in it. I could not undertake this kind of process with an undergraduate class of 45 students.

WOE: Was it difficult to discuss pedagogical problems associated with collaboration in your book?

EDE: We struggled with our fourth chapter, "The Pedagogy of Collaboration," all the way to the very end.

LUNSFORD: I had a goal, something driving me, to make that chapter as pragmatic as possible. I wanted to instruct teachers how to use collaboration in their classes, to provide them with a little blueprint of what to do on Monday, and so on. When Lisa started to resist that idea, we changed the pedagogy section of the book significantly. Through a series of discussions with Lisa, I came to see the potential problem of teachers reading our chapter and going into their traditional, institutionally-constrained, patriarchal classrooms, attempting to introduce collaboration without any introspection or any changes in the way that power is distributed in the class or the academy.

WOE: What did you finally decide to do with that chapter as a result of your discussions?

EDE: We made our difficulties part of the chapter itself. At the start of Chapter 4, we discussed our initial vision of the chapter and explained why we couldn't write it that way, *why* it wasn't right to do that. The crunch comes when you try to take theoretical ideas and apply them. I still have a kind of uneasiness about the chapter.

LUNSFORD: And I'm just not completely satisfied with what we came up with. It is going to be very interesting to me to see the reaction to that chapter.

WOE: I certainly can see that writing Chapter 4 presented you with many difficulties to work out. Were there any other parts of the book that presented particular challenges?

LUNSFORD: Oh, yes — how to list our names. For instance, when we started writing together, we decided we would list our names alphabetically, but someone said to us —

EDE: Ed Corbett. He asked us how we were going to list our names. We told him we were going to list them alphabetically, a decision that we thought would be perfectly clear to people. But he said, "No way!" Then we started alternating our names.

WOE: When you publish together, you alternate whose name is listed first?

EDE: Yes. We have tried to do so, though we have not always been able to keep in sequence.

LUNSFORD: I have completely lost track of whose turn it is to go first.

EDE: Me too. Still, we definitely have made the effort to alternate.

LUNSFORD: In this book, we wanted very much to subvert the tradition of first and second author. We played around with a lot of different things. In the preface of the book, we say we thought about taking a new name, like Analisa Lunsede, or Edesford.

WOE: Oh, I like that!

LUNSFORD: But we decided that taking a new name would put people to so much trouble that it didn't seem like a good idea in the long run. Next we tried my favorite idea, having our names in a Mobius-strip design. We tried to do that on the computer, but we just couldn't get the three dimensional perspective right. Then the editor thought of what we finally used. The verso and recto of the title page have a border at the top, starting in the middle of one of our names and running them together. The border reads, "drealunsford-lisaedeandrealunsfordlisaedean . . ." and trails off. The border begins again on the bottom of the pages. Lisa's name will actually be listed first in the card catalog because the names will be cataloged alphabetically. But still, we wanted some typographical representation of our attempt to subvert the tradition of first author, something that would say to our readers, "We know you will look for the first author, and we have tried to keep you from being able to find her."

WOE: Aside from Ed Corbett's initial concern with how your names would be listed when you first began to write together, were there other people or experiences that made you become so concerned with how the authorship of this book would be attributed?

EDE: I think it came out, in part, from my tenure experience. My department has been very supportive of our co-authoring, but even so they have treated it as a difficult problem that they had to solve. First, my Chair asked Andrea to write a letter talking about our collaboration. Later, the college committee also wrote and asked Andrea for comments. We took these requests very seriously because we knew of individuals who were denied promotion because their co-authored and co-edited works were not considered.

WOE: At all?

EDE: At all. As though they didn't exist. In addition, I had been party to many discussions at my university about how co-authored or co-edited books are evaluated. There is a very strong belief throughout our field and others that there is a first or "primary" author who must be identified. My Chair and I argued about this with other university administrators, who were fairly unrelenting. Andrea's and my desire to subvert the tradition of who is the first author in our book grew out of our personal experience, but also out of all the anomalies we were finding in our research. While we were doing our research and talking about our own problems with the tradition of first author, we would get these bits of material from people who had found out about our research.

LUNSFORD: We had big files, slips of this, little notes of that, pieces cut from newspapers. We didn't know what to do with all these materials, so we just kept stuffing them into our files. One day while Lisa was here in my house — we were sitting out in the sun room — we decided to put them in the book. We decided that preceding each chapter, there would be some pages set in different type where we would put all of these little bits of things. We decided to call them intertexts. Our practical goal was to get as many of these intertexts into the book as possible, but our theoretical goal was to demonstrate the ways in which our book was written by many people besides ourselves. Many voices, many names appear in between the chapters.

EDE: With the intertexts, we tried to make a pastiche that would have these voices talk with each other; they are just presented with no comment. We have, for example, a piece about a computer program that writes poetry; a statement by John Gardner about how much his wife helped him write his book and how had the world been different, he might have called her co-author; and a clipping from the Hershorn Museum catalog about collaboration in the arts a friend of mine from Brockport had sent me. Next to that, we have a wonderful statement by the one surviving member of the two Irish co-authors, Sommerville and Ross. After one of them had died, the survivor said that just as an established legal firm does not change its name when one of the partners dies, she will not either.

WOE: From these examples, it seems you found that when people write together, the concept of authorship, of "who the author is," becomes very complicated.

LUNSFORD: Yes, especially in fields like the sciences where credit and power are toted up based on who is listed as the first author.

WOE: Do you mean that even if the authors are listed alphabetically, the assumption is that the first author listed gets all or most of the credit as the "primary" author?

LUNSFORD: Yes, the first author is *the* author. In some fields, there are huge fights over who gets credit for authorship. You might have heard in the news recently about the AIDS research that was delayed in publication for 10 years because some of the people were fighting over who would be listed as first author.

EDE: Occasionally, we found that one journal within a discipline might encourage authors to be listed alphabetically, but that is very rare. The prevailing practice is still that the first author is the primary author. Not only that: the practice of cataloging and indexing compounds the already-complicated ethical questions about how authorship is attributed when there are multiple authors. For example, some indexes that routinely deal with material by scientists who are working as professors require that a first author and any other authors be listed. But other indexes that deal with research done on a contract basis will not mention authors, even if they are listed on the title page. As a result of these arbitrary practices, some indexing services are taking authorship away from people who want it and giving authorship to people who don't.

WOE: In the humanities, or at least in literary studies, the concept of authorship has been problematic for theorists for some time now. Did you come across similar concerns in other fields?

EDE: Yes, we came across research in several fields about the practical, procedural, and logistical questions of co-authorship as it is being practiced today. If you read articles about how computers are making authorship obsolete, you can see that we are actually in a state where the material conditions of authorship have changed. All of a sudden Foucault in "What Is an Author?" doesn't seem to be looking ahead —

LUNSFORD: — but seems, instead, almost old fashioned.

EDE: Yes, Foucault was discussing, on a theoretical level, practices those of us in the humanities have been completely oblivious to, even though they are happening all around us.

LUNSFORD: And meanwhile, those people in other fields are completely unaware of the attacks on the construct of the author and the subject in literary theory. One of the most surprising items on this topic was a book by a librarian, a cataloger, called *Corporate Authorship: Its Role in Library Cataloging*.

EDE: Addressed to other catalogers, his book is a practical guide, completely isolated from the theoretical concerns of our field. Yet the author does a deconstruction — although he would not call it that — of authorship, describing writing as writing in, writing out, writing down, writing up, and writing over. All these *functions* for writing. The consequence of his deconstruction is that library catalogers have to abandon any concept of authorship as originary, as "intellectual property."

WOE: What does he propose to replace it with?

LUNSFORD: Author function, as Foucault would say.

WOE: You have said on other occasions that you think collaboration is potentially a subversive activity. Why is that?

LUNSFORD: We obviously think it is subversive; in fact, Lisa and I were writing about that today. But potentially only.

EDE: Collaboration, as it is predominately practiced in the United States today, seems to us not to be subversive but just a very efficient means towards achieving a goal. As such, the subversive potential can easily be co-opted, and all kinds of complicated issues having to do with ownership can be raised. One of the people we interviewed, for example, was an engineer. After five hours of interviewing him and his team members we found out, at the very end, that his secretary played a substantial role in the production of their texts, not just coordinating various aspects of the process, but in actually doing a lot of the writing, gathering together boilerplate materials, and so forth.

LUNSFORD: But the engineer was so dominant — his voice and stance were so powerful — that he erased everybody else. Another potential problem with collaboration is that it can create a set of circumstances where responsibility is totally absent; authority isn't situated *anywhere,* and so it exists nowhere. You think of the *Challenger* disaster as sort of the perfect example of collaboration gone berserk, where nobody is willing to take responsibility and things fall apart. Or collaboration can be a masquerade for the same old patriarchal, hierarchical structures — the patriarchal wolf in collaborative sheep's clothing.

EDE: Still, collaboration can be subversive even if it is hierarchical. A group of people can get together in many different ways that could be characterized as subversive. Collaborative writing is a culturally-situated activity; we could do an ethnographic study of two teams that seem to be hierarchically organized and find that one is functioning radically differently from the other. So we need to resist any kind of categorical statements about the relationship between how a group is structured and its potential for subversive activity.

WOE: Do you think that collaborative writing is subversive within the Academy?

LUNSFORD: Yes, within the institution, to some extent, and within the classroom collaboration is subversive because it challenges notions of individual authorship and responsibility for an autonomous text. We know also that it challenges our whole system of testing, measurement, and evaluation and that it questions the way we, as teachers, respond to and assess our students. Collaborative practices are often at odds with traditional classroom structure, which locates the authority for assigning a grade solely with the teacher. Our whole system of evaluation is shot through with the notion that a "creator" resides somewhere in the head of each person, and that this creator can be isolated, defined, tested, measured, and compared; everything that Lisa and I discovered in the course of our project challenges that notion and makes us uncomfortable as teachers and evaluators.

WOE: What future studies in collaboration would you suggest?

LUNSFORD: Certainly there is a lot of room for pedagogical research. No one knows enough about how collaborative groups really work.

EDE: We need to do ethnographic and longitudinal studies.

LUNSFORD: We also need to think more about the concept of "The Author" — and how it may differ from "writer."

EDE: Yes. One of the wonderful things that we discovered in our research was a statement about authorship from an 18th century German dictionary, which basically said that the dictionary was a means of expressing God's truth and that many people worked on it. The writer was listed along with many others — the papermaker, the book binder, gilder, scholar — as contributing to this work.

LUNSFORD: One of our intertexts is from a woman who is writing interactive fiction for a computer program. She is writing the story — the plot, the dialogue, everything — but she is "just" the writer. The programmer is The Author.

WOE: But what do you call a person who buys the program and writes a story?

LUNSFORD: Good question.

4   *Dear Lisa/Dear Andrea:*
On Friendship and Collaboration

Dear Reader: The following essay has a history, one worth sharing. We conceived of the idea of writing this essay in the fall of 2008. We were working on the collection in which this essay now appears, and we wanted to include a new chapter on both the material conditions of our collaboration and the friendship that has been one of its primary motivations. Pressed for time, and intrigued by Michael Spooner and Kathleen Blake Yancey's collaborations over email, we decided to attempt such an effort ourselves. We originally hoped that drafting this chapter over email would expedite its completion; it would, we thought, be an easy and quick way to produce a draft. Circumstances proved us wrong. Lisa did not respond to Andrea's first email, sent to her in November 2008, until mid-July 2009 (for reasons discussed in her response). We drafted the first part of this essay as we had intended, emailing each other back and forth. After beginning the correspondence in 2008, we took a time-out, picking up the thread again in the summer of 2009 and then writing a substantial portion during time spent together in Corvallis in August 2009. After another time-out, we completed the exchange in the spring and summer of 2010, just prior to another writing-filled visit in September, when we completed the work necessary to put this collection of our old and new essays into production.

The resulting exchange can be read, we hope, as a continuous though frequently interrupted conversation that spans two years. As the correspondence makes clear, while we have been strongly drawn to collaboration and have found many intrinsic rewards in writing together, the journey has not always been easy. The process that led to this essay also demonstrates that while we have written apart when necessary, our favorite moments still occur when we are, as the title of this collection suggests, writing together. In what follows, we reminisce about our first meeting, our mutual admiration for mentor Edward P. J. Corbett, and our long friendship; about our differing roads to the field of rhetoric and writing studies; about the ups and downs of our collaborative writing and the personal losses we've experienced. The epistolary form of this essay aims to evoke the kind of steady dialogue that has been essential to our friendship and collaboration over four decades. This conversation forms a collage, reflecting in some ways this collection as a whole, which brings together many of our earlier works with a collection of archival materials, as well as five new essays written especially for *Writing Together*.

This essay, written by Andrea A. Lunsford and Lisa Ede, is new to this edition.

*D*ear Lisa: It's a Sunday afternoon in late November 2008: it's cool and sunny *in that late autumn California kind of way, tempting me outside rather than here in the office where I am preparing for the coming week. I'm teaching* Memoria: The Arts and Practices of Memory *this term, and the subject teases me, niggles away at me, leading me to abandon whatever I should be doing to simply remember. Ironically, my memory is terrible — I recall almost nothing, for instance, of my early childhood, nor can I remember the name of a single teacher before middle school. (This is one of our most notable opposites — you who remember so vividly and well.)*

So today I am remembering, or trying to remember, my first meeting with you. You drift up in brief glimpses from our shared history as graduate students at Ohio State University (OSU) in the 1970s: standing in the office of Denney Hall, near the cubbyhole mailboxes, I think, you with your open smile, long white/blonde hair, wearing perhaps a leotard with a skirt. You are (always have been) so much more generous and nonjudgmental than I, who am quick to accept first impressions, even when they turn out to be wrong. What first impression did I have of you? What I remember is thinking how interesting you looked, how much — how should I say this — how much yourself. I wonder if you remember our first meeting — and if so, how you remember it. How I wish this moment were documented in some way, for looking back now I see that it marked a turning point in my intellectual and emotional life: here, I see so clearly now, was a friend (not to mention a coauthor) for life.

I'm going to send this message to you, even though I know you may not have time to respond right away — I'm hoping that these musings will spark a conversation that summons up a host of memories, that limns our personal friendship and our professional collaboration, and that gives us a chance to reflect on how far we have come — together.

Dear Andrea: Well it is now mid-July 2009, so it has indeed taken a long time for me to respond. And here in Oregon we have finally settled into our pattern of summer weather: clear, hot but seldom too hot, dry — so different from the summer weather we experienced as grad students at Ohio State (overcast and often unbearably hot and humid). Where did the year go? I'm afraid that we both know. The tanked economy. The horrifying budget cuts at our universities — cuts that we were forced to implement in the writing programs that we direct and that made work on personal writing and research feel impossible. Of course not everything this past year was difficult or painful. We both, even after all these years, find teaching to be personally rewarding and intellectually stimulating. We both have developed new teaching and research interests: graphic narrative and new media, for instance. We both have family, friends, and colleagues who sustain us. And of course we have our long friendship and long relationship as coauthors and coresearchers.

You write about memory. I don't think of myself as having a stronger memory than you do. But I do find myself with a specific memory of our meeting. It was in 1972 — possibly in the fall, shortly after you arrived at Ohio State. In my memory, I was in line in the cafeteria in Pomerene Hall, next to the library, preparing to have lunch with Miriam Nathanson. You were also in line, and Miriam, also in our grad program, introduced me to you. We talked briefly, and I remember being astonished when you said that you had come to Ohio State, after several years teaching at a community college in Florida, because you wanted to study rhetoric and the teaching of writing. "How could anyone do that?" I remember thinking to myself. I was preparing to write a dissertation on the Victorian nonsense of Edward Lear and Lewis Carroll. I didn't even know it was possible to study rhetoric and writing.

What I don't remember very clearly is the trajectory that took us from being colleagues in a very large PhD program to such close friends that we wept buckets when I took my first job at State University of New York (SUNY) Brockport and left Columbus. I do remember how our growing friendship, which quickly included Suellynn Duffey and Beth Flynn, was impossible to separate from the development of the (to me) strange new field of composition studies. You were the first PhD student at Ohio State to profess this as your area of disciplinary expertise, even as you worked with Edward P. J. Corbett to create a new area of study in the English department at OSU from scratch.[1] Only later would a clearly defined field of study in composition studies be developed at Ohio State.

Dear Lisa: I certainly did want to "profess" this new area, but I almost didn't get to. Remember, there were no real courses in rhetoric or writing in the English department at Ohio State in those early days. We had to declare four areas to be examined on before we could advance to the dissertation, and I chose American literature to 1900, old English and medieval literature, eighteenth-century literature, and Renaissance literature. Some six months before my examination, I was allowed to substitute "rhetoric and composition" for one of these areas, so I dropped the Renaissance and took on all of rhet/comp. I got a pretty decent education in composition studies because I had the incredible good fortune of serving as Ed Corbett's assistant during his editorship of College Composition and Communication (CCC); *on the rhetoric side, I had been conducting a reading program, in chronological order, starting with Plato and going up to Kenneth Burke. I would read several texts and then bother Ed with a list of questions. In addition, I was in graduate school when OSU's speech department had a strong rhetoric group. I audited courses from Jim Golden, "Goody" Berquist, and others: when I was cleaning out my Stanford office in anticipation of a move a year ago, I came across a folder full of notes I had taken in some of those classes, now practically crumbling with age! In retrospect, I realize that my tendency toward interdisciplinarity (rhetoric, we have long agreed, is the Ur interdiscipline) grew up naturally during those years as I took courses in speech and communication, in English, and also in education, where I audited several courses on quantitative research methods. So while I never had any formal coursework, I patched together a pretty fair education, and one that led me to feel increasingly committed to our field of study.*

In some ways, the mid-to-late '70s were heady days: after the horror of the '60s' assassinations (JFK, Martin Luther King Jr., Malcolm X, Bobby Kennedy) we watched, mesmerized and cautiously hopeful, the hearings that led up to Nixon's resignation in 1974; we hailed the end of the Vietnam War (at long last!) in 1975. We counted the gains made by people of color and women. These were also the days of open admissions at City University of New York (CUNY), of the push to burst open the academy's doors, and of the work of Mina Shaughnessy and her colleagues in what came to be called "basic writing." We felt we had a chance to change institutions and to attend more fully and respectfully to students who had previously been denied access to college. And these days saw the 1977 publication of two books that I still teach in tandem: Shaughnessy's Errors and Expectations *and Geneva Smitherman's* Talkin' and Testifyin'. *These texts, and the message they carried about the literate lives of young people, marked me in lasting ways. I still remember my first publication in a major journal: it was about the work I had done with basic writers — and it elicited a response, in the* Chronicle of Higher Education, *from a fellow who called me "a handmaiden of the Lord." In hindsight, I have to admit to at least a little missionary zeal, for our young field, for all our students.*

Dear Andrea: I had already completed my coursework when you started at Ohio State. I had *avoided* taking courses with Ed Corbett, partly because I wasn't particularly interested in eighteenth-century studies (which was how I then identified his area of expertise) and partly because of his reputation for strictness: he was famous for giving a quiz in grad seminars the moment the bell rang and anyone not there was counted absent for the day! I will always be grateful that in later years I got to know Ed so well and to appreciate his marvelous eccentricities and equally wonderful strengths: his love of reciting *Gunga Din* and of telling long and complex jokes and stories — remember the one about swimmers and Luftanza? — as well as his complete commitment to our field and generosity to students and colleagues.

Dear Lisa: I on the other hand was dying to take classes with Ed, if only he would teach something besides The Bible as Literature *and eighteenth-century lit. Before I left Ohio State, however, Ed had begun teaching his graduate seminar on style, and he went on to offer other courses on rhetoric to the growing number of grad students interested in the field. Beyond his teaching, however, we both knew Ed as a mentor for many, many scholars in our field: his National Endowment for the Humanities (NEH) summer seminars included Sharon Crowley, Jim Porter, and others who are now senior scholars — Jan Swearingen, Kathleen Welch, Gail Hawisher, and David Schwalm — along with Ed's students Bob Connors, Cheryl Glenn, Pat Sullivan, Roxanne Mountford, and a host of others who knew him as an unfailingly supportive friend and colleague.*

Dear Andrea: Ed was certainly an important mentor for me as I made the transition from being a Victorianist who was very interested in the teaching of writing to a rhet/comp scholar. I will always be grateful as well for my involvement in OSU's first-year writing program, which played such an important role in my "conversion." (Another equally important experience was my year-long NEH seminar at Carnegie Mellon University in 1979–80.) At that time, thanks to both Ed and Susan Miller, change was in the air in the writing program at Ohio State. Susan brought in exciting young scholars like Rick Coe and David Bartholomae. I remember having the sense that the teaching of writing was an area where I could make a difference. To be quite truthful, it was also an area where I might have a chance of finding a tenure-line position. The job market of the mid-1970s was the worst job market for PhDs in English since the Depression. Colleges and universities in the United States were in the midst of a self-proclaimed literacy crisis. (Later, many would realize that the crisis simply reflected the fact that students who would previously not have attended college were doing so.) Colleges and universities had financial resources, and many were putting them into new basic writing programs, like the one that you helped develop at Ohio State and that was the subject of your dissertation. They were hiring faculty with expertise in the teaching of writing to head these programs. You arrived at Ohio State committed to rhetoric and writing. By the time I left Ohio State, I shared that commitment and identification.

Dear Lisa: As we write these messages back and forth in the summer of 2009 that awful job market is with us again, and threatens to get worse before getting better (if it ever does). Looking back, I again see how fortunate I was when I went "on the market" in 1977: I was thunderstruck to be offered more interviews than I could accept — my memory is that I did about twenty. My dissertation on basic writing and my work with writing and rhetoric somehow struck a chord with a number of schools. But in both my Modern Language Association (MLA) and on-campus interviews, I was met with puzzlement and curiosity by many faculty members. Clearly, while the schools I interviewed with were increasingly interested in having faculty who could work with burgeoning enrollments of "unprepared" students, they found it hard to share my excitement at the prospect of actually doing so. At the time, I used my extensive study of literature to help cover the many gaps in conversation, especially during on-campus interviews with their required "social" dinners and receptions. Later, I thought of what Linda Flower has often said, echoing Mina Shaughnessy: that your own excitement about the work of rhetoric and literacy can usually attract one or two others, and from there it's up to that small group to slowly create a community. I think of the growth of rhet/comp as being like that: slow, steady, and persistent.

Dear Andrea: I'm reminded of the panel on collaborative writing that we participated in at the 2008 Conference on College Composition. There, in conjunction with Kathleen Blake Yancey, Michael Spooner, Michele Eodice, and Kami Day, we explored the question "Why Still Write Together?: Collaborative Writing in the Twenty-First Century." I've never forgotten one moment in the Q&A that followed our presentations. Someone asked the panelists to talk about how important it was to be able to be together physically when writing together. Kathleen and Michael responded that they *couldn't* write together if they had to be together physically — and we responded that if we *weren't* together a good deal of the time when working on a project we couldn't imagine successfully writing together. What a contrast — and what a telling statement about the situatedness of all writing, including collaborative writing.

But back to your email and our respective job searches. In terms of looking for our first tenure-line positions, our experiences couldn't have been more different. You went on the job market as one of the first trained and professionalized scholars in composition studies. I originally went on the job market in 1974 (while you were just getting started on your dissertation) as a Victorianist, hardly a hot specialization in an extremely depressed job market. (I didn't know it then, but fellow Victorianists David Bartholomae and Linda Flower were facing the same difficulties.) I had interviews at the MLA the year I was finishing my dissertation — a few, not twenty! — with no luck. The following year, after I had finished my dissertation and graduated, I went again to the MLA for perhaps two interviews. After the conference, one of the colleges I'd interviewed with, SUNY Brockport, wrote me to say that they were interested in me but their budget was frozen. Given the economy and job market, I never expected to hear from them again.

I had decided not to go on the job market for a third grueling and in all likelihood fruitless year. I liked my job as an editor at a sociology research center on campus, and my husband had also been unsuccessful in his own job search. The year we both graduated — me with a PhD and Greg with an MFA in printmaking — there were four (yes four) tenure-line openings for printmakers in the entire United States. Many of our grad school friends were also unsuccessful in their job searches — several ended up in law school, while others undertook government work of various kinds — so we had plenty of company in our predicament. Ohioans by birth, it looked to Greg and me like we would continue living and working in Columbus. Then to my surprise in the summer of 1976, I received a letter from SUNY Brockport: their position, they said, was "unfrozen." One speedily arranged on-campus interview later and I suddenly found myself with a tenure-line position as Director of Composition. My story is fairly typical, I think, of many, such as Susan Miller, John Trimbur, Patricia Bizzell, and others, who "converted" to rhet/comp in the 1970s. Though we came to identify profoundly with the discipline of rhetoric and writing, the "push" that moved us in that direction was as much pragmatic as philosophical.

Dear Lisa: So with your move, our almost daily get-togethers ended, and I missed them in a visceral way. We visited a couple of times, but the distance made a difference: talking on the phone (no e-mail in those days) for us is NOT the same as talking face-to-face. We had not yet started to write collaboratively, but looking back now I can see that we were laying the groundwork for that work by staying as closely in touch as we could and building the friendship that became the bedrock of our collaboration.

Thinking back on our first postgraduate jobs — what a long time ago that was now — points up another contrast in our experience: while you found yourself thrust into a writing program administrator (WPA) job as a brand-new assistant professor, I wound up in a non-WPA position. If I'm remembering correctly, I had five job offers, three of which I considered very carefully. But as I weighed the options, I suddenly realized that I'd never even been west of the Mississippi River. That did it: in 1977 I moved to Vancouver, Canada. The ten years I spent at the University of British Columbia were professionally rewarding, and I made friends for life there. Best of all, though, you and Greg moved to Corvallis just three years later. No longer a continent apart, we got together as often as we could, and our friendship grew even stronger. Still, we never imagined that we would begin to write together.

Dear Andrea: We've written about our differing memories of the chance composition of our first coauthored essay in another chapter in this collection ("Collaboration and Collaborative Writing: The View from Here," p. 186 in this collection). But we've not written about the moment when we turned the corner from being friends and scholars who liked to collaborate on such topics as classical rhetoric and audience to scholars who actively studied collaboration and collaborative writing. Here's how I remember it. You were in Corvallis, and we were working on a project. (Given the technologies available to us at the time, I don't see how we could have successfully collaborated in the early 1980s if we hadn't been able to be together physically, lugging our electric typewriters four hundred miles up and down the I-5 corridor from Vancouver, BC to Corvallis — and sometimes, when the drive just seemed too long, the time available too short, and the deadline too pressing, meeting at the University Motel in Seattle.) We were driving to campus talking about the strong responses we consistently got to our collaboration — that it was risky (and it was), that it was wonderful that we could write together, but that (it was always somehow clear, though few said it explicitly) really no "normal" scholar could or would want to do so.

In my memory, one of us said something like, "What's wrong with them? Don't they know that people in business and industry write together all the time!" That observation catalyzed years of work. We gleefully sought out support for our position, such as Lester Faigley and Tom Miller's 1982 "What We Learn from Writing on the Job." Convinced that we were on to something important, we decided to apply for a FIPSE Shaughnessy Scholars grant to study the collaborative writing practices of two hundred members of seven professional associations. Do you remember writing that grant? We did the first draft on a ferry ride between Horseshoe Bay and Nanaimo, writing by hand, crossing out each other's text, and writing over one another (a page from this draft appears on p. 21 in this collection). Sometimes we would read aloud and make changes; other times we would work separately on sections, revising and editing. But for the first draft we literally wrote as we talked it out. (Our collaborative writing has continued in that way: we almost always begin with long, long talks followed by note taking and sketching, often done together.) We learned a lot during the course of that research. A particularly important realization was that the data we so carefully gathered could hardly displace the ideologies of individual authorship that over several centuries became deeply embedded in Western culture in general and in the humanities and literature in particular.

Dear Lisa: Oh that FIPSE grant! How elated we were to receive the grant, especially since it honored the work of Mina Shaughnessy, and then how overcome we were when the reality of the work confronting us sunk in. How many "pilots" did we do of our surveys? How many false starts on coding the data? Those were the days of punch cards: we carried around stacks of them as if they were little sheets of gold. The research we did, as you say, taught us a lot, and it deepened our belief in the social nature of all writing. It also deepened our friendship. The school years were punctuated by visits together, by bouts of drafting and revising, by frustrations as we faced our differing writing styles and differing sense of priorities, and most of all by the satisfaction we got from talking, listening, walking, hiking, cooking (and eating) together.

But the 1980s brought some tough personal times. My mother's death (at what now seems to me the impossibly young age of sixty-three) began an accumulation of loss. I know you well remember 1984: the year we received that FIPSE grant was also the year when colon cancer took my beloved "baby" brother, Gordon, just thirty-three. At the time I didn't think things could get much worse on the personal front. But I was wrong.

Dear Andrea: Yes, I do remember, and it seems like an appropriate time, after forty years of friendship and thirty years of coauthorship, to revisit some of the challenges we have faced. I'm thinking here especially of how we have had to negotiate the differences in our personal situations, beginning in the mid-1980s. Not long after we met in the early '70s, you and Steve were married. Greg and I married the following year — on the same month and day, though we only realized that later — and the four of us developed a deep and powerful friendship during grad school. When Greg and I moved to Corvallis and you and I began collaborating, it often felt like all four of us were writing together: you and I would write all day and then the four of us would talk about what you and I were working on while we cooked something sumptuous and celebrated being together. When you and Steve divorced, it was devastating to all of us. It is a sign of your generosity of spirit that we negotiated that change. It would have been easy for you to turn away from our collaboration as a painful reminder of the past. But you didn't.

Dear Lisa: Breakups of marriages are common as dirt — but never, I think, to those involved. You more than anyone know that this particular breakup shook me to the roots of my being. One reason I managed to live through it, and the spiraling series of losses I encountered between 1980 and 1996 (I lost my youngest sister, Kerry, my father, my brother-in-law, and my dear friend Christa in those years), was YOU and your friendship, so the last thing on my mind would have been turning away from our collaboration; rather, I clung to it, and to you and Greg like the lifelines that you were — and are. Indeed, hard times have taught me, like so many others, the incalculable value of friends, and in my case particularly women friends. How I am looking forward to visiting Corvallis next month so we can continue this conversation in person.

Dear Andrea: It is now late August 2009, and we are writing this section of our correspondence together, taking turns at the computer. Mainly we write only our own "emails," though every now and then one of us will ask the other a question or remember something and then insert a word or a sentence in the other's message. Even now, as we take turns writing to one another, it is hard to resist the urge to weave our voices together.

We almost did not get to have this time together — time we had especially coveted because it coincided beautifully with the ripening of Greg's corn and tomatoes. We've continued to endure a grueling period as WPAs, and we are also both deep into textbook revisions and facing frighteningly close deadlines. I'm so glad we got together anyway for four days of writing and being together. As you have said, friendship has certainly been of the utmost importance in our collaboration. I wonder if we would or could have continued to write together, given the logistical difficulties, had we not been such fast friends. Working through draft after draft together often seemed like great fun because the work was punctuated with lots of laughter. But I don't want to idealize or romanticize our process. We've written plenty of articles and book chapters working primarily at a distance and using various technologies of communication, from phone to email, to keep in touch. Even when we're physically together as we are now, if we've got a really clear conception of how an essay or a chapter should be organized (or a really pressing deadline), we'll divide the work up: it's only efficient to do so. But as soon as we can, you'll start revising my writing and I'll start revising yours. In the early years, we *had* to be together physically — writing and revising over the phone was just too difficult. But even though the technologies of communication have changed dramatically since we first started writing together, I don't think our basic process has changed that much. Do you?

Dear Lisa: I agree that our writing process hasn't changed in fundamental ways. We do a huge amount of talking before and during writing, we often literally write together at the computer, and we revise each other's work constantly. For longer pieces especially, we often write sections individually and then revise together. Or we send drafts back and forth using track changes. I have written two essays with other collaborators using Google.docs, but for some reason you and I have not used that tool. Maybe we should give it a try for our next essay.

Dear Andrea: I find myself with a mixed response at the thought of using Google.docs. This may be simply because I've not used it, but I think it also says something about me generationally. As much as I try to keep up with new technologies, especially since this is a teaching interest of mine, I resist technological change at the level of daily practice. Word and track changes feel so familiar and comfortable to me. Having said that, I might be willing to give Google.docs a try.

It is interesting to reflect on all the transitions we've made during our thirty-plus years of writing together. And like all writers, we've at times had our difficulties. Some of these have been relatively trivial, like differences in our prose styles, me with my love of dashes and you with your desire to delete all of them. We also have somewhat different composing preferences. You are what I call in my textbook *The Academic Writer* a "heavy planner." You can and have "composed" entire essays and book chapters in your head and more or less transcribed them. (Remember how your grad students at Ohio State liked to refer to you as Andrea "Product Not Process" Lunsford?) As a "sequential composer," I can't do as much of the work of writing in my head as you can. I think we both agree, though, that the way in which collaboration requires us to externalize our thought processes and muck about in each other's words, sentences, paragraphs — and most importantly in each other's ideas and arguments — has enriched our scholarly and pedagogical work.

We both have strong work ethics and tend to meet deadlines — something essential in any effective collaboration — but especially in our early years of writing together you were more disciplined than I was. I remember writing the draft of our FIPSE grant application on that ferry as we were heading to the north coast of Vancouver Island for a vacation. I wanted to just go out on the deck and look at the water, sky, city, and distant mountains. I remember being just a wee bit resentful when you wanted to take advantage of the ferry crossing (something you'd done many times, but I hadn't) to at least make a start at drafting that proposal. In retrospect, we might well not have gotten that grant if we'd not gotten that early start.

Dear Lisa: I don't remember that Ohio State grad students sometimes called me Andrea "Product Not Process" Lunsford. But I do remember that the students sometimes referred to me as "The Encyclopedia," given my memory for citations. And while I am certainly focused on getting that product out, I really cannot write whole essays in my head! I am, however, stubbornly self-disciplined. I remember being invited to write a review of Mina Shaughnessy's Errors and Expectations *when I was still in grad school and being terribly intimidated. So I told myself that I could not get up from my desk until I had written five pages. It took me a ridiculous nine and a half hours, but I stuck to my self-imposed rule. That may be self-discipline, but it is also just silly! So in many ways we complement each other: My dogged stick-to-it-or-else is leavened by your sense that writers need breaks. My desire to blast through to a first draft is mediated by your tendency to carefully rewrite sentences and paragraphs as we go. But of course we don't always agree. I often chafe at what seems to me to be over-qualification of every single statement (and the dashes!), and I know that you often warn me about overgeneralizing or about sketching in too-broad strokes. Somehow we have managed to balance our disagreements, in large part because we trust each other.*

Dear Andrea: It's so interesting that you don't remember your students' nickname for you! Perhaps it was an in-joke — Andrea who advocates for revision but hates to revise herself! — that one of the grad students shared with me on one of my many visits to Columbus. And, yes, I remember "The Encyclopedia." I love recalling these moments from the past, and I also love taking time to reflect on our friendship and collaboration, something that this exchange has allowed us to do. In that regard, trust couldn't be more crucial to our collaboration. It is something that I at least experience in a deeply embodied way. I know in my bones that if we just continue to talk/write our way through conceptual, process, or stylistic difficulties, we will ultimately get there. In that regard, I find my mind going back to one of our 1983 work sessions at the University Motel in Seattle. We had chosen it because it was cheap and also because it had so-called suites. There was a mini-kitchen and a living/work area, as well as two bedrooms. On one memorable occasion we were working on our "On Distinctions between Classical and Modern Rhetoric" (included on p. 261 in this collection). (Doesn't the "Modern" in that title seem dated now?) We had agreed to bring only one of our typewriters since only one of us could type our evolving draft anyway — we were still several years away from our first behemoth computers. We kept taking turns writing and revising and typing, and what I remember (do you?) is that I kept announcing that I needed to reorganize the section I was working on, which also meant that you had to rewrite the transition into the section you were writing, not to mention that we had to keep retyping the essay. I remember working until 11 p.m. on our final day in Seattle — which was also your birthday. We called it quits, and you took a shower. I can still see you emerging from the bathroom saying brightly, "It's my birthday. Let's celebrate!" I could never have done that.

Dear Lisa: I remember that weekend like it was yesterday. We had been working really intensely for a couple of days but without making much progress, and I was ready to strangle you if you suggested one more reorganization. I remember complaining vociferously — and making vague threats. This was one occasion when your careful caution and my drive to closure really came head-to-head. In retrospect, we're probably lucky that it was my birthday and we decided to cook up a (really!) late dinner and drink a few glasses of wine rather than fight it out. I still think fondly of Seattle — we should take a little nostalgic trip there and see if that motel is still standing!

Dear Andrea: I'm for taking that trip — especially since it is now September 2009, and it's been weeks since you headed back to Palo Alto. We are once again drafting this essay via email. Fortunately, our history of writing together will help us pull through this. It has certainly helped me develop my own stamina and discipline as a writer, which came in handy when one summer I realized that if I kept trying to finish the book that became *Situating Composition: Composition Studies and the Politics of Location* while completing other projects (edited collections, textbook revisions) that I would never finish it. So that became my do-or-die summer, and I worked longer days that summer than I had imagined possible. I don't think I could have done that if we hadn't done the do-or-die summer that we spent together finishing *Singular Texts/Plural Authors*.[2]

Dear Lisa: Our work on that particular project was delayed by circumstances we've already talked about: the devastating breakup of my marriage, and my subsequent departure from the University of British Columbia (UBC) to take a position at Ohio State — that was in late 1986. I was pretty much flat broke at the time and had to scrape together money for a small down payment on a place to live and pray that my tiny ten-year-old Toyota would run well past 200,000 miles (it did!). And of course I had to try to settle into a new job and to come up with something resembling a life. So no more meeting halfway in Seattle for us, and this very material fact of life slowed us down considerably. But at long last, we were close to finishing — and even if we were no longer within driving distance of one another, we had a plan. During the summer of 1987 I would spend two weeks in Corvallis with you, and you would spend two weeks in Columbus with me. We'd be done!

Then I broke three bones in my ankle in a freak accident while hiking. Suddenly our plans had to change and you volunteered to come to Columbus for a month. During that time we either drafted or revised all the major chapters, checked and rechecked our statistical findings. We even had great fun choosing the "Intertexts" we put between chapters in the book. Remember how that happened? We'd been collecting quotations and passages about collaboration for years. We just about had a complete draft of our book, and we still had a big pile of texts we'd hoped to include, so we decided on the idea of intertexts. In retrospect, our book was one of the first in our field to experiment in this way, breaking up the chapters with voices other than our own and working to challenge the traditional linearity of texts. We were a little worried because we didn't have a model for what we were doing, but we egged each other on and did what we wanted!

On the other hand, we found the conclusion ("New Beginnings," included on p. 135 in this collection) especially difficult to write. With its focus on intellectual property and authorship as well as our qualitative and quantitative research results, and with our commitment to addressing pedagogical issues, Singular Texts/Plural Authors *had grown complex and multifaceted: we were deliberately mixing genres, from research report to personal narrative to historical overview to those little interchapter teasers. How best to bring this book — and this project — to a conclusion?*

Dear Andrea: Yes, those were hard years — made harder, as I'm sure you remember so well, by my bout with cancer in the mid-1980s. And, yes, that conclusion was difficult, to put it mildly. As I remember it, we also wanted our conclusion to challenge scholarly norms, which assume that even when authors write together they erase their differences and write with a singular, disembodied voice. We wanted this conclusion to be rooted materially in time and space. So it's no accident that the third to the last paragraph of the conclusion begins: "It is 6:00 p.m., 9 December 1988. We have been writing and talking and cooking and reading and listening and writing and talking and cooking and reading steadily for seven days now" (p. 147 in this collection). The second to last paragraph begins with another statement of material location and time: "And it is 8:30 p.m., 15 May 1989. Lisa is on a consulting trip in the East and Andrea is in her office, feet up, gathering notes for one more marathon telephone conversation" (p. 147). We wrote that conclusion — including the last paragraph with its reference to Edgar Allen Poe's purloined letter — during that conversation.

Dear Lisa: That we completed that book is a tribute to friendship, and to determination — which some might call stubbornness — and discipline, as well as some luck, especially in terms of your physical and my mental health: somehow we made it through, supported by colleagues and good friends who read and responded to our work. We realized at the time that we were trying to break some molds. We were writing collaboratively about collaboration; we were mixing formats (with the Intertexts) and methodologies: quantitative, qualitative, and interpretive methodologies all played a role in our study. We were writing personally as well as professionally.

Completing Singular Texts/Plural Authors *was certainly one of our most rewarding moments, which we celebrated in style on more than one occasion. But other projects have brought us great satisfaction as well, such as "Representing Audience: 'Successful' Discourse and Disciplinary Critique" (included on p. 225 in this collection). I know you remember that experience: we actually wrote four completely different frames for that essay.[3] With each version, lengthy conversations convinced us that another opening and frame would be better. Then when we had a draft we were fairly satisfied with, we got responses from others that led us back to the drawing board once more. And when we sent it to CCC, we had yet another set of responses to deal with, along with comments and challenges from editor Joe Harris. We began to think of "Representing Audience" as the essay that would never be completed, despite all our work. (Our first draft is dated October 11, 1993, and the essay finally appeared in the May 1996 issue of CCC.) But once again our friendship and our commitment to one another — and to our subject — kept us going, and the final draft we came up with managed to say just what we wanted to say in the way we wanted to say it. After a long struggle and some risk-taking in terms of how to write critically and reflectively about our own work, we had an essay we (and the editor of CCC) were happy with. It felt risky to attempt a self-critique of our most successful essay, "Audience Addressed/Audience Invoked: The Role of Audience in Composition Theory and Pedagogy" (included on p. 209 in this collection), especially when our goal was "neither to reject nor defend AA/AI but rather to embrace multiple understandings of it, and to acknowledge the extent to which any discursive moment contains diverse, heterodox, and even contradictory realities."*

Dear Andrea: Yes, we have taken plenty of risks over the years, including the risk involved in simply writing together — and in doing so before either of us was tenured. When I reflect back on our assumptions when we began writing together, I can see that we were quite naïve, especially about issues of authorship. Our original plan was to present our names in alphabetical order; that, we assumed, would tell readers that we were equal partners in our writing. But Ed Corbett quickly disabused us of that notion. So for most of our scholarly work, we have tried (and generally succeeded, when we could keep track) to simply alternate first authorship, as Ed suggested. (This choice didn't help when we came up for tenure and promotion, however, as we recount in other essays in this collection.) But there have been moments when it's been hard to negotiate authorship rights.

I still remember (and I'm sure you do too) when we were writing our essay "Collaboration and Concepts of Authorship" for *PMLA* (included on p. 167 in this collection). That essay ranks right up there with "Representing Audience" as one of the most difficult essays we've written together. I think we both felt a lot of pressure to write the best essay possible, given the importance of our topic and the rare opportunity to reach an audience of readers who profess literature and theory, not rhetoric and writing. You had recently run for president of the MLA and have always been much more prominent in that organization than I have (in part by my own choice admittedly). As we worked on that essay I found myself really wanting to be the first author. It was a hard topic to discuss, but we did — it's a sign of the strength of our friendship and collaboration that we were able to do so. And, yes, I ended up being the first author.

Dear Lisa: You are right that our sense of authorial ownership has, for all our critiques of ideologies of authorship, occasionally been a scene of discomfort, I think, for both of us. We have wanted to share equally, and alternating our names has been one way to do so. (Remember when we suggested combining our names and using that as our "author" name — to the horror of all our librarian friends? In retrospect, that might not have been such a bad idea after all.) But as you say, we'd done pretty well keeping to our alternating scheme, and we went so far as to list our names as "Ede and Lunsford" on the spine of Singular Texts/Plural Authors *but to confound that order by putting my name above yours on the cover: to this day, I see that book cited as both "Ede and Lunsford" and "Lunsford and Ede." When* PMLA *wrote and asked me to contribute an essay on collaboration to one of their issues, I accepted right away. But then it occurred to me that it would be very odd for me to write about collaboration as a single author. So I wrote* PMLA *and said I would accept the invitation as long as the essay could be written collaboratively, and they agreed. Better still, YOU agreed. And you're right that that was a hard, hard essay for us, partly I think because we were writing out of long experience about a topic we knew very, very well but one we thought our audience would not have thought about, at least in the ways we wanted them to.*

I can't remember how the listing of names came up: were we trying to figure out whose turn it was to be first? My (foggy) memory is that it was my turn and that I was surprised when you told me you felt it was important for your name to be listed first and, moreover, why you felt that way. I agreed to the change instantly. But that doesn't mean it didn't unsettle me. It seemed at least a little unfair and it also seemed to undercut in some fundamental way our stance of absolute equality in authorship. Moreover, it made me realize that had the roles been reversed, I would never have asked to switch the order because I would have lacked the courage to admit that I wanted it to happen. And indeed, I also lacked the courage to object, even though a part of me wanted to do so. So there we were — two people utterly committed to collaborative authorship still both holding on to the power of the single author as evidenced in the continuing power of the privileged first author.

Dear Andrea: Looking back at this incident I feel more than a little embarrassed and am fighting the impulse to explain myself further. (Until I read your section above I'd forgotten, for instance, that *PMLA* originally asked you, not us, to write that essay!) But what seems really important to me is that our long friendship and collaboration enabled me to request something that was then important to me and for you to agree to it and move beyond your own unsettlement. I also think it's testimony to our friendship that we have managed to write about some of the difficulties we have experienced here.

Dear Lisa: We have weathered more than a few storms together, and I hope we will have the opportunity to weather a few more. Our friendship and the time we spend together (whether we are working on a writing project or not) have certainly made a difference. In fact, the idea for this collection occurred to us when we were reminiscing while on vacation about our earliest collaboratively written essays (more than twenty-five years ago!) and decided to reread them with an eye for putting together a collection that we could then add some new essays to. As we sketched out the collection and the new essays we wanted to write, we were led irrevocably to look back not just at our essays but also at our careers and our friendship.

Dear Andrea: It's interesting to reflect on the process that led to this collection and to this essay. The first table of contents for *Writing Together* that I have in my file is dated March 2008. That was roughly the time when we began talking with Bedford/St. Martin's about this project. You sent me the email that begins this essay in November 2008, both of us hoping for a quick exchange of emails and an early draft. Now here we are trying to wrap this essay up so we can write the introduction and complete this project in late August 2010. The composition of this essay spans almost that entire time period. Sometimes we've written apart, sometimes together, but my sense is that our decision to compose this essay as an epistolary-like exchange over email between the two of us has been a powerful stimulus to memory and to reflection, even when we've been physically together.

Dear Lisa: Yes, this exchange is now about two years old — it feels like we've been writing these reflections forever. But as they say, stuff happens, and this last year or so has been intense and at times difficult for both of us. Under different circumstances and for different reasons, we have both wound up our administrative positions, for instance, and that has taken a lot of time and effort. At Stanford, I completed ten years as director of the Program in Writing and Rhetoric — and you left the Center for Writing and Learning after directing it for thirty years. These changes lead me to reflect on our long commitment to writing program administration and to the role that collaboration and friendship have played in that commitment. We both have valued this work partly because we see writing programs in fact as large collaboratories, as spaces for experiments in collaboration. We've both found this work intensely satisfying, yet we are moving on to a new phase in our careers, leaning forward toward retirement yet savoring our ongoing association with colleagues and with young people. But for us, retirement will not mean stepping away from our work together. Forty years of friendship and countless words written together have woven a tight bond: I can no more think of giving up our writerly ways than I could of giving up breathing . . . or eating. So this long exchange of memories and reflections ends with a renewed commitment to writing together, to sustaining our friendship, and to taking up those challenges that will inevitably confront us. Like the old song says, we'll "travel the road, sharing the load, side by side." See you and Greg soon, and please have the corn and tomatoes ready for me.

Dear Andrea: Can't wait! It's been a cooler than usual summer, but the tomatoes and corn are coming on strong and should be at their peak when you're here. Here's to time celebrating our friendship and enjoying the bounty of the garden, as well as more time at the computer. This year we are going to complete not only this email exchange but *Writing Together*!

— Lisa and Andrea, September 2, 2010

NOTES

    1. A photograph of Ed appears on p. 15 of this collection.

    2. Three chapters from *Singular Texts/Plural Authors* are included in this collection: "Old Beginnings" (p. 78), "Collaborative Writers at Work" (p. 91), and "New Beginnings" (p. 135).

    3. These false-start drafts are included on pp. 17–20 in this collection.

PART TWO

On Collaboration

5 *Why Write . . . Together?: A Research Update**

W hy write . . . together? We first raised this question in an article published in the January 1983 issue of *Rhetoric Review* (pp. 27–33 in this collection). This essentially anecdotal discussion attempted to describe our own experiences as coauthors, chronicled our growing interest in the nature and concept of collaboration, and formulated a series of questions for possible future study. Since that time, we have been engaged in a more formal research project, a three-stage study of coauthorship and group authorship in six major professional associations. In the following brief update, we would like to share the preliminary results of this research.

The original questions we posed as a result of our own experiences as coauthors and our own early research efforts were relatively obvious. How often and in what situations do coauthorship and group authorship occur? What specific features distinguish the processes of coauthors and group authors from those of an individual writing alone? What is the potential impact of technologies such as the computer on coauthorship and group authorship? As we thought about collaborative writing and talked with people who wrote as part of teams or groups, however, we came to see that answers to these and other questions, though useful and informative, represented only a first step. An analysis of the feasibility and efficiency of coauthorship and group authorship will be of little consequence, for instance, unless it addresses the powerful assumption, one particularly dominant in the humanities, of the link between individual genius, "originality," authorship, and authority for a text. Similarly, analyses of the role of coauthorship and group authorship which fail carefully to consider the social context in which such writing occurs — the influence of established institutional review procedures, for instance — may distort or oversimplify. Finally, we realized that we could not separate an interest in the nature, incidence, and significance of coauthorship and group authorship from a concern for the ethical issues involved.

From Andrea Lunsford and Lisa Ede, in *Rhetoric Review* 5.1 (1986): 71–81.
*This research was supported by a grant from FIPSE's Shaughnessy Scholars Program.

Underlying all these questions was our growing recognition of the dichotomy between current models of the composing process and methods of teaching writing, almost all of which assume single authorship, and the actual situations students will face upon graduation, many of which may well require coauthorship or group authorship. This recognition gave a sense of urgency to our investigations. Consequently, in 1983 we applied for, and subsequently received, a FIPSE-sponsored Shaughnessy Scholars grant to study the theory and practice of co- and group writing.

Our research project, which is still in progress, comprises three interrelated stages, only one of which is at present complete. Hence, this report should be regarded as tentative at best. The first stage of our research involved designing a questionnaire to survey 1,200 randomly selected members of six major professional associations (the American Psychological Association, the American Consulting Engineers Council, the American Institute of Chemists, the International City Management Association, the Professional Services Management Association, and the Society for Technical Communication) to determine the frequency, types, and occasions of collaborative writing in these six associations. Our final rate of response for this survey was just under fifty percent, and we have recently compiled and analyzed its results.

On a separate sheet accompanying this first questionnaire we asked respondents to indicate whether they would consider participating in the next stage of our research, a more open-ended and detailed questionnaire designed to identify more fully a spectrum of collaborative writing forms and strategies. We have sent this survey to twelve members of each of our six professional associations. We chose these seventy-two individuals because they are representative of a range of collaborative writing situations, and we are currently analyzing their responses. The last stage of our research involves on-site interviews with between six and twelve respondents who regularly write as part of a team or group. We completed these interviews in the summer of 1985 and will report the overall results of our research in a monograph.

As is perhaps already clear, this is a fairly ambitious research design, especially for two people at institutions far apart, each of whom has had only fifty percent released time to devote to our project, which is itself supported by a relatively small budget. But though we have sometimes been daunted by the task we have set ourselves, the suggestiveness of our preliminary analyses (and even when completed, our results will be preliminary at best) has encouraged us. Rather than simply reporting these preliminary results, however, in this brief research update we wish to highlight those areas or questions which the first survey indicated were most problematic and in need of further clarification.

Our own research and experience had led us early on to identify the concept of writing, and especially of authorship, as one particularly problematic area. We can report, at this relatively early stage in our investigation, that the responses to our initial survey confirmed the problematic nature of this concept and, in fact, confounded the problem. To our surprise, respondents clung to the notion of writing as a solitary activity in spite of overwhelming evidence to the contrary. More specifically, respondents in every field most often answered the question "Please indicate the percentage of the time you spend in writing activities that is spent writing alone or as part of a team or group" by saying that they wrote alone between 75% and 85% of the time. A full 60% of these respondents, however, contradicted themselves by answering a series of later questions in ways which revealed that they often wrote as part of a team or group. One respondent from the American Institute of Chemists, for instance, reported that he wrote 100% of the time by himself and then, in response to a later open-ended question, confided that every one of his publications had been coauthored. This seeming anomaly is, of course, easily accounted for in one way: Respondents think of writing almost exclusively as writing "alone" when, in fact, they are most often collaborating on the mental and procedural activities which precede and co-occur with the act of writing, as well as on the construction of the text.

But in another way, the responses to these questions suggested to us that the concept of authorship is even more problematic than we had anticipated. Preliminary results for members of each organization, for instance, suggest that many professionals regularly make use of in-house or "boiler-plate" materials, and that they may use such materials verbatim in something they are writing without acknowledging or documenting their use of this "silent" coauthor's work. Indeed, in a number of instances, the authorship of such in-house materials is unknown. When we add to this use of unacknowledged materials the assistance provided by what one respondent referred to as "idea men" and changes made — again silently — by various technical and legal reviewers, the concept of "authorship" as most English teachers think of it, becomes increasingly fuzzy. We believe that the concept will in fact be made even more problematic by the proliferation of information data bases which may, in fact, finally force us to reexamine our definition of copyright laws. We hope that our research will clarify the questions we need to ask in such a reexamination, even though it may not provide us with readymade answers. More immediately, we hope that we may be able to design curricular models which would broaden the conception of writing so that the term need no longer be primarily associated with an isolated, solitary act, and which would build in a more flexible and realistic definition of authorship.

A second problematic area revealed by this first stage of our research is the lack of a vocabulary to describe what people do when they write collaboratively. We first encountered this problem in writing the title of our grant proposal: What should we call the phenomenon we hoped to study? The term *collaborative writing*, which in many ways was most appealing to us, is most often associated with the kind of peer-group response techniques developed by Ken Bruffee. Hence, we ultimately found it necessary to qualify the term *collaborative writing* with the extremely clumsy *coauthorship and group authorship* and even then we ended up having to define and illustrate the phrase carefully in order to avoid confusion. (In spite of our difficulty with the term *collaborative writing*, we are very much indebted to the research on collaborative learning and to studies of professional writing such as those of Odell and

Goswami and Faigley and Miller.) Once the problem of a title term was solved, however, we faced a much more difficult problem in designing our first survey questionnaire, as we tried to elicit information about what we finally agreed to call "organizational patterns," plans used by groups to assign duties for completing a project. After extensive piloting and revising, we managed to describe seven such patterns, of which the following are examples:

A. Team or group plans and outlines. Each member drafts a part. Team or group compiles the parts and revises the whole.

B. One person plans and writes the draft. This draft is submitted to one or more persons who revise the draft without consulting the writer of the first draft.

C. One member assigns writing tasks. Each member carries out individual tasks. One member compiles the parts and revises the whole.

Responses to the first questionnaire indicate that such "patterns" are used widely and frequently, though very few respondents have a name for them. Some respondents, in fact, told us that they realized they were following such pre-established "organizational patterns" only after completing our survey, demonstrating in the most vivid way that what we do not have a name for we simply do not recognize. Other respondents, particularly in the technical writers' group, indicated that having such a pattern was indispensable to success and that following an "ineffective" pattern would produce "disastrous results." Our preliminary findings, then, suggest that procedural strategies or patterns are very important in collaborative writing, and that naming and defining these practices will enable us to think about them in ways that have heretofore been unavailable to us. In addition, we hope to identify those patterns which are most likely to be effective in a given situation and hence to draw conclusions that will have significant pedagogical implications. While it would be premature to draw such conclusions now, it seems likely to us that teachers of writing may well want to introduce students to various ways of organizing a group-authored project and let them experiment with this process.

A third extremely problematic area emerging from the initial stage of our research has to do with affective responses to group writing. To put it most briefly, we are realizing that a complex set of largely unidentified, or perhaps even unrecognized, variables creates general satisfaction or dissatisfaction with both the processes and products of group writing. On our initial survey, responses to our questions about organizational patterns elicited, almost incidentally, information about the frustrations some group writers felt. As a result, our second questionnaire attempted to define these frustrations more clearly and to gather additional information about affective concerns by asking questions such as "which of the writing activities do you find most [or least] productive to work on as part of a group." Our comments in this area must necessarily be very cautious. Nevertheless, we have tentatively identified a number of variables which seem related to the degree of satisfaction experienced by those who typically write with one or more people. These include:

1. the degree of control the writer has over his or her text;

2. the way credit (either direct, as in a name on a title page, or indirect, as in a means of advancement within an organization) is assigned;

3. the ability to respond to others who may modify a writer's text;

4. an agreed-upon procedure for resolving disputes among coauthors;

5. the amount of flexibility tolerated in using pre-established organizational patterns or standardized formats;

6. the number and kind of bureaucratic constraints (such as deadlines, length requirements, etc.) imposed on the writer;

7. the status of the project within the organization.

Again, we hope our eventual findings will help us establish what we might not too facetiously refer to as a "satisfaction index" and a "frustration index" and elaborate on these in ways that should be helpful to those already writing on the job in groups as well as to teachers of writing who want to prepare their students for co- and group writing experiences.

These problematic areas represent the issues related to group writing that were most clearly illuminated by the responses to our initial survey and that we hope to clarify further in the second and third stages of our research. We should not, however, close with the idea that this initial questionnaire identified only problematic areas or areas of contention. On several major points, our results are both conclusive and highly gratifying to teachers of writing. First, our hypothesis that co- and group writing is a widespread and well-established phenomenon among major professions has been clearly confirmed. Of 530 respondents to our initial questionnaire, 87% reported that they sometimes wrote as part of a team or group. The extent of this collaboration is perhaps best indicated by participants' responses to a question which asked them to "indicate how frequently, in general, you work on the following types of writing," from letters and lecture notes to reports, proposals, and books. Although the frequency of response varied from type to type, some participants indicated that they very often, often, or occasionally worked on every type of writing with one or more persons.

Forty-two percent of those we surveyed occasionally wrote short reports with one or more persons, for instance, while 17% often and 4% very often wrote professional articles and essays as part of a team or group. Twenty-nine percent of our respondents occasionally wrote professional articles or essays as part of a team or group, with 9% often and 2% very often writing these forms with one or more persons. We were not surprised by these results since we had anticipated that on-the-job writers would collaborate on such documents as reports and proposals. We were surprised, however, to discover that our survey participants were almost as likely occasionally or often to write books or monographs collaboratively as they were to do so alone. The same held true for proposals for contracts and grants, case studies, user manuals, and long reports. (The percentage of difference between the frequency of writing alone and with one or more persons for these types varied from 0 to 5%.)

Finally, we can report that 59% of those who participated in co- or group writing projects indicated that they found such collaboration to be either "productive" (45%) or "very productive" (14%).

Our results did speak eloquently to the significant role writing plays in all of the organizations we studied. On the average, respondents in all six fields reported that almost 50% of their professional time is spent in some kind of writing activity. Moreover, 98% of all respondents indicated that effective writing is either "very important" or "important" to the successful execution of their job. Many went on to elaborate on this importance in notes to us, some of which contained passionate pleas for help and for more and better training in writing and general communication skills. Such results are gratifying to us as researchers because they suggest that our interest in coauthorship and group authorship is justified. Much more importantly, however, the results should be gratifying to every teacher of writing because they graphically demonstrate what we have been "professing" for so long: that writing allows us to know, understand, and act on our worlds in unique ways; that through writing, in fact, we most often create these worlds. And finally, the preliminary results strongly suggest that such creation is least often an isolated, solitary act created *ex nihilo*, and most often a communal, consensual act, one that is essentially and naturally collaborative.

As we write this update, we have just completed three long interviews with a clinical psychologist, a consulting engineer, and a technical writer. Our visits to their workplaces, the transcripts of the interviews, our notes, and our on-going conversations and reflections will help us enter the world these writers inhabit. In the process of such collaboration, we hope to reshape, to recreate, our own worlds as writers and teachers of writing and to present that reformulation in our final report on this project.* In the meantime, we would very much like to hear from others who have experienced the difficulties and satisfactions of coauthorship or who are engaged in research on collaborative writing and learning.

*This final report appears as "Collaborative Writers at Work," p. 91 in this collection. — Eds.

6   *Intertexts**

Ιn collaborating on writing this book we searched for a single voice — a way of submerging our individual perspectives for the sake of the collective "we." Not that we denied our individual convictions or squelched our objections to one another's points of view — we argued, tried to persuade, even cried at times when we reached an impasse of understanding — but we learned to listen to each other, build on each other's insights, and eventually to arrive at a way of communicating as a collective what we believe. Hence, this book is not separated into parts that we wish to attribute to one or the other of us, even though each of us took the primary responsibility for different parts. There may be stylistic differences from one section to the next, but the book as a whole is the product of our joint efforts and interchange of ideas. — Mary Field Belenky, Blythe McVicker Clinchy, Nancy Rule Goldberger, Jill Mattuck Tarule, *Women's Ways of Knowing*

*   *   *   *   *

A Kinsey Institute sex survey that could help researchers understand how AIDS spreads was delayed for almost a decade because two of its authors fought over whose name should appear first on the title page. . . . Publication was scheduled in 1980, when an intense dispute broke out about whose name should appear on the title page. . . . The survey languished for years, unavailable to most researchers, until [an Institute Director] persuaded the authors to settle their differences. — "What Revolution?"

*   *   *   *   *

The authorship or compilership of a dictionary . . . is, indeed, a question like that of the identity of the darned and redarned stockings with the original pair. — *Spectator* 14 December 1867, quoted in *Oxford English Dictionary*

From Lisa Ede and Andrea Lunsford, in *Singular Texts/Plural Authors* (Carbondale and Edwardsville: Southern Illinois UP, 1990) 1–4.

*Before every chapter in our 1990 book *Singular Texts/Plural Authors*, we included *intertexts*, or thought-provoking excerpts on collaboration from a wide range of sources. The following intertexts appeared before "Old Beginnings" in the original collection.

*   *   *   *   *

In film, theater, and dance, collaboration among creative individuals is taken for granted. Even when dominated by one person — writer, director, or choreographer, for example — the ensemble is integral to the realization of the work. Similarly, joint authorship of books and articles occurs frequently, and teamwork in scientific research is standard.

In the visual arts, too, there is a rich collaborative tradition, which, however, has been overlooked until recently. From medieval workshops and Renaissance ateliers through the nineteenth-century Beaux-Arts studios, projects were created by pairs or teams of painters, sculptors, and printmakers. In our own time, collaborators also include photographers, filmmakers, and video and performance artists. Since the period of artistic as well as political ferment preceding the outbreak of World War I, most avant-garde movements have had significant collaborative components. — Artistic Collaboration in the Twentieth Century, Hirshhorn Museum Exhibit, Smithsonian Institution

*   *   *   *   *

As most young scientists learn in the early stages of their careers, the key to success is to master a nettlesome paradox. To thrive in science, you must be both a consummate collaborator and a relentless competitor. You must balance, with an almost gymnastic precision, the need to cooperate against the call to battle. Modern science has become too broad and complex a venture for any one researcher to go it alone; scientists need other scientists. At the same time, those scientists who avoid the often vitriolic squabbles and races that are such prominent features of doing science risk professional failure. By a generally accepted rule of thumb, if you don't publish your results before your opponent does, you may as well not publish at all. And in science, if you don't publish, you don't survive.

Casual and sentimental observers may wish that society could somehow encourage scientists to cooperate more. There's an old stereotype of the selfless scientist who seeks to solve the puzzles of nature for the joy of helping humanity, and that stereotype dies hard. Besides, doesn't extreme competition lead to all sorts of problems — name-calling, data stealing, even scientific fraud? Wouldn't science be more efficient and productive if scientists could devote themselves entirely to research and leave political warfare behind? — Natalie Angier, "Nice Guys Don't Win Nobel Prizes"

*   *   *   *   *

"People said [The Talisman, a novel written collaboratively with Peter Straub] would be like a teenage marriage," says Stephen King, who first proposed a collaboration . . . six years ago. "They said we'd ruin a good thing and wind up hating each other for life." The writing, however, went almost completely according to plan. — Charles Leerhsen, Review in Newsweek

*   *   *   *   *

Nancy Mitford's best-seller, *The High Cost of Death*, was co-authored with her lawyer husband; however, her publisher said that two authors would mean fewer sales, and only her name appears on the title page. — Alleen Pace Nilsen, "Men and Women: Working Together in Changing Times"

*   *   *   *   *

"Increasingly in recent years we do write together very much more than we used to. In working on the sequel to *Madwoman*, there are something like five enormous chapters in the opening sections, and we've been writing every word together." — Sandra M. Gilbert, quoted in Laura Shapiro, "Gilbert and Gubar"

*   *   *   *   *

If the old boys' network in psychiatry has a code of discretion, Jesse O. Cavenar Jr. has offended it. He says he had cause. Cavenar, a 47-year-old professor of psychiatry at Duke, sued in December for recognition as top editor of a major textbook whose cover gives first credit to someone else.

The other person is Robert Michels, 51, chairman of Cornell University's Department of Psychiatry and director of the prestigious Payne-Whitney Clinic in New York City. Cavenar says the publisher considered Michels' name more marketable and gave it first rank, even though Michels did not edit the book.

The court decided that Cavenar had been wronged . . . [and] Cavenar is satisfied. He also claims to have struck a blow for scientific integrity, and his case sets out in grimy detail the way in which publishers, editors, and academics carve up the rewards in multi-authored texts. The credit goes mostly to those who are already prominent, and the labor is done by those who are not. — Eliot Marshall, "Textbook Credits Bruise Psychiatrists' Egos"

*   *   *   *   *

Can it be that the notion of individualism, so sacred to the United States, also is its fatal flaw — the basic strength that works against itself to reduce strength? — Andrew Polack, "Scholars Reconsider Role of Trendy High-Tech Entrepreneurs"

7 *Old Beginnings*

What we want is not terms that avoid ambiguity, but terms that clearly reveal the strategic spots at which the ambiguities necessarily arise.

— KENNETH BURKE (*GRAMMAR* xviii)

QUESTIONING ASSUMPTIONS

In his essay "Common Sense as a Cultural System," Clifford Geertz argues that one of the most effective ways an anthropologist can begin to understand another culture is to study what that culture takes to be commonsense wisdom — the knowledge in our advanced Western society, for instance, that "rain wets and that one ought to come in out of it, or that fire burns and one ought not play with it" (75). Such analysis can, Geertz notes, reveal how a "culture is jointed and put together" much better than traditional functionalist accounts (93). Not that such analysis is easy. "There is something," Geertz comments, "of the purloined-letter effect in common sense; it lies so artlessly before our eyes it is almost impossible to see" (92).

The research that led to this book began when we caught a glimpse of a purloined letter in our own field: the pervasive commonsense assumption that writing is inherently and necessarily a solitary, individual act. What caused us, six years ago, to look not through this assumption but at it, to see the purloined letter? (In Edgar Allan Poe's mystery of that name, detective C. Auguste Dupin locates a very important missing letter that has been "hidden" in plain view "upon a trumpery fillagree card-rack of pasteboard" and thus prevents a major political crisis [49].) The answer to our mystery is simple and even perhaps predictable: our own experience as coauthors. Most succinctly, our interest in collaborative writing grew out of the dissonance generated by the difference between our personal experience as coauthors and the responses of many of our friends and colleagues.

From Andrea Lunsford and Lisa Ede, in *Singular Texts/Plural Authors* (Carbondale and Edwardsville: Southern Illinois UP, 1990) 5–16. This is the first chapter in this monograph.

Though we began writing together almost by accident — deciding on the spur of the moment to write an article together for a volume of essays to be published in honor of our mutual friend and mentor Edward P. J. Corbett — we found the experience so natural and so productive that we continued to write together. What seemed natural to us, however, seemed anything but natural to our English department colleagues. Some in our field cautioned us, for instance, that we would never receive favorable tenure decisions or promotions if we insisted on publishing coauthored articles. Even those who did not caution us about the dangerous consequences of our habit professed amazement at our ability to write together, questioning us in detail as though we had just returned from a strange new country. Our own experience as co-authors, then, provided the lens through which we initially took a new and intensely curious look at work in our own field of composition studies. What view of writing was inscribed there? On the occasions when writing teachers have attempted to describe writing in the most straightforward or common-sensical terms, the solitary nature of writing has emerged.

In his essay "Writing/Speaking: A Descriptive Phenomenological View," Loren Barritt attempts to define this relationship through phenomenologi-cal analysis, a method that has as its goal "'naive' looking, which is achieved by 'bracketing' popular beliefs, be they doubts or theories" (125). Conse-quently, a phenomenological study of speaking-writing relationships, Barritt adds, "involves a direct exploration and description of these language phe-nomena *as they are experienced*." Barritt then presents five statements that, he argues, "seem to me to be at the heart of the experience of written compo-sition" (127):

When I write, I sit down, pick up my pen,
and begin to write words on paper. (127)

When I write, I have some idea what I
intend to say. (128)

I write for someone, with a purpose in
mind. (129)

When I write, my thoughts tumble over one
another. I have trouble moving my pen to keep
up with my thoughts. (129)

You are alone when you write. (130, our emphasis)

Interestingly, Barritt goes on to connect this inevitable solitariness with the difficulties many writers experience: "Because writing is a solitary . . . activity, I find it easy to avoid getting started on a writing task. Writing means going off somewhere to be alone with my thoughts and plans" (130).

We found this generally unspoken and commonsensical assumption that "writers work in solitude, where they address absent persons virtually all of whom are and always will be totally unknown to them" silently informing both the theory and the practice of the teaching of writing (Ong 1982: 184).

James Moffett's theory and method in his influential *Teaching the Universe of Discourse* rest largely on the assumption that "the most critical adjustment one makes [in learning to write] is to relinquish collaborative discourse, with its reciprocal prompting and cognitive cooperation, and go it alone" (87). Much research on the composing process, such as the early work of Flower and Hayes (1981, 1984) or Bereiter and Scardamalia (1982), examines writers in the act of writing alone, using the data thus collected as the basis of proposed models of the composing process. Even most of the early work on collaborative learning in composition classes, such as the pioneering efforts of Kenneth Bruffee (1978, 1981, 1983a, 1983b, 1984a, 1984b), limited collaboration in practice to peer responses to a text already drafted by an individual student. As Donald Murray notes in "Writing as Process: How Writing Finds Its Own Meaning," "*Once the writing* is *produced*, it is shared" (27, our emphasis). For Murray and many others, we discovered, the writing process itself inevitably occurs in isolation.

SETTING A RESEARCH AGENDA

Yet our own experience as coauthors and our growing awareness that at least some work-related writing is highly collaborative belied the commonsensical view of writing as an individual act. So in 1984, with the help of a grant from the Fund for the Improvement of Post-Secondary Education (FIPSE) Shaughnessy Scholars program, we set out to investigate this anomaly. The following research questions, first articulated in our grant proposal, guided our early explorations:

1. What specific features distinguish the processes of co- or group authorship? Is it possible to locate from the range of potential co- and group authorship situations (which can vary from intensive collaboration between two individuals to large and often loosely organized group-writing efforts) a corpus of shared models and strategies?

2. How frequently and in what situations are members of representative professions called upon to write collaboratively?

3. Is the emphasis on or weight of various cognitive and rhetorical strategies different when writing collaboratively than when writing alone?

4. How do computers and other technologies, such as dictating, affect the process of co- or group authorship?

5. What epistemological implications do co- and group authorship hold for traditional notions of creativity and originality?

6. How might the ethics of co- or group authorship be defined?

7. What are the pedagogical implications of co- and group authorship? Can we develop ways to teach students to adjust readily to co- or group writing tasks?

Readers of this volume will note that our interest in co- and group authorship grew directly out of pragmatic, practical concerns. Did the view of writing implicit in composition theory and practice conflict with the view of writing emerging from work experience? How supportable and accurate was the view of writing we were presenting to our own students? Why were our coauthored articles received with alarm by many of our colleagues? Should writing teachers be encouraged to prepare their students for on-the-job collaborative writing? With such pragmatic questions in mind and with a set of research questions articulated, we devised a multilevel research project designed to provide some baseline data and preliminary answers, particularly to questions regarding the incidence and kinds of collaborative writing utilized on the job.

For the first stage of this research, we developed a questionnaire to survey 1,400* randomly selected members (200 from each group) of the American Institute of Chemists, the American Consulting Engineers Council, the International City Management Association, the Modern Language Association, the American Psychological Association, the Professional Services Management Association, and the Society for Technical Communication. Our goal in this initial survey: to determine the frequency, types, and occasions of collaborative writing among members of these associations.

After analyzing the results of this first survey — especially the problematic or anomalous results — we developed a second questionnaire, a longer, more open-ended instrument to be completed by twelve members of each of these seven professional associations who had responded to our first survey. This second questionnaire explored such issues as the kinds of documents respondents most typically write as part of a group; the way in which respondents and fellow group members divide such writing activities as brainstorming, information gathering, and editing; their use of organizational patterns or set plans to assign duties for completing a project; the assignment of authorship or credit; and the advantages and disadvantages of collaborative writing. In the third stage of this research, we held on-site interviews with at least one collaborative writer from each of these seven associations in locations as diverse as Lexington, Kentucky; Medford, Oregon; Columbus, Ohio; and Washington, D.C. These interviews — nonquantifiable as they are — have proven particularly valuable resources because they were informed by our analysis of the first and second surveys and because the open-ended format of the interviews allowed us to explore issues and problems at much greater length.

"Collaborative Writers at Work" (pp. 91–134 in this collection) reports the results of these surveys and follow-up interviews — results that play an important role in *Singular Texts/Plural Authors*'s argument, for they indicate that, in these seven professional associations at least, collaborative writing is a frequent activity. Perhaps even more importantly, these results provide insights into those social processes and contexts that can make collaborative writing a productive and satisfying — or an unproductive and frustrating — experience.

---

*On page 70, we say we planned to survey 1,200 members from six associations. Additional funding allowed us to add a seventh association.

SURVEYING LITERATURE ON COLLABORATION: EARLY ATTEMPTS

When we began to prepare for this research on collaborative writing in the professions, we found little research within the discipline of composition studies that directly addressed our concerns and questions. An early computer ERIC search and a review of all issues of the *Education Index* from 1975 to 1983 unearthed only a few scattered essays. Alleen Pace Nilsen's "Men and Women: Working Together in Changing Times" (1980), for instance, discusses the unusually high number of husband and wife teams currently writing books for children. Two other essays, L. Ray Carry's "Dissertation Publication: The Issue of Joint Authorship" (1980) and Cheryl M. Fields's "Professors' Demands for Credit as 'Co-Authors' of Students Research Projects May Be Rising" (1983), review the ethical issues potentially involved with joint publication by graduate students and their professors. While we could find very little information or research on collaborative writing, the late seventies and early eighties did produce calls for a collaborative pedagogy in writing classes. Bruffee's early essays and textbook (1972, 1973, 1978, 1980, 1983a, 1983b) called for such a pedagogy, as did studies by Hawkins (1976), Coe (1979), Gebhardt (1980), and Clifford (1981). Though these studies emphasize the importance of collaborative learning, all assume single authorship as a model. Peers can work collaboratively in every stage of the writing process except for drafting. In these and other early models of collaborative learning, students inevitably draft alone.

At the start of our project, then, we had little indication of interest or support in composition studies for research on collaborative writing. While Lester Faigley and Thomas P. Miller's 1982 article indicated that "the majority (73.5%) [of their respondents] sometimes collaborate with at least one other person in writing" (567), such observations provoked little response from those teaching and studying expository writing. The purloined letter — the assumption that writing is inevitably a solitary activity — had not yet come into view.

Because so little research in our field directly addressed our concerns and questions, of necessity we cast a wide net in our effort to locate studies that could help us better understand the phenomenon of collaborative writing. Our early inquiries produced surprisingly diverse leads. We discovered, for instance, a substantial (indeed overwhelming) body of research in sociology, psychology, speech communication, education, and business on group processes and decision making. As Bobby R. Patton and Kim Griffin note in *Decision-Making Group Interaction*, research in these areas on "the study of groups is largely a twentieth-century phenomenon" (3). From its start in the 1920s, this research has been largely empirically based; the emphasis, however, has shifted from a concern with productivity (the dominant concern from the 1920s to World War II) to the group process itself.

It is not possible here to survey the efforts of researchers involved in the study of group processes. This research is so diverse that it is difficult to develop a sufficiently broad perspective to enable integration, much less evaluation, of these multidisciplinary efforts. In the introduction to his 1982 study *Creativity in Small Groups*, A. Paul Hare notes the difficulties that inevitably arise when individuals in a variety of fields conduct research on a related problem or subject. In commenting on "the sources of research for . . . [his] analysis of social interaction and creativity in small groups," Hare observes that "psychologists dominate the field, followed by sociologists, and then by persons in the applied fields of psychotherapy, education, social work, and business." Inevitably, given these diverse disciplinary affiliations, not only methods but crucial definitions can vary considerably. "In some cases those who are part of the 'group dynamics school' are concerned with groups much larger than the typical 'small' group of five to twenty members. On the other hand, many of the social-psychologists who have made contributions to the understanding of social interaction in small groups were not studying groups as such but rather individual behavior in a social situation" (16). Finally Hare adds, "For all the research in this area, relatively few persons work in a general theoretical context that provides a way of integrating the various research results" (16).

If a researcher such as Hare, whose *Handbook of Small Group Research* is considered a basic resource for those studying small group processes, finds synthesis and application difficult, so inevitably will researchers in composition. In our unavoidably incomplete review of research on small group processes, we have nevertheless located researchers who have drawn a number of useful preliminary conclusions on the characteristics of effective and ineffective groups (Beebe and Masterson 1982, Hall and Williams 1970), the determinants of productivity (Steiner 1972, Jewell and Reitz 1981), and the role that pressures toward conformity, sometimes called groupthink, play in group interactions (Fisher 1980, Forsyth 1983, Janis 1983). These references might most fruitfully be viewed as starting points — places to begin exploring research in this area.

Investigations beyond our own disciplinary boundaries also revealed a related body of research in education on what is variously called cooperative learning (Johnson and Johnson 1974, 1985; Johnson and Johnson 1987; Sharan and Sharan 1976; Sharan 1980; Slavin 1980; Slavin et al. 1985; O'Donnell et al. 1985) or active learning (Bouton and Garth 1983). Although this research does not comment specifically on collaborative writing, it does contribute to our understanding of how teachers can more effectively encourage collaborative learning and writing in their classrooms. As was the case with studies of small group processes, the focus of this research is diverse. Bouton and Garth note in the introduction to *Learning in Groups* that those engaged in research on collaborative learning groups often have a variety of purposes, including: "overcoming student passivity in large classes . . . , developing liberal education skills and abilities . . . , teaching writing . . . , developing competent professionals . . . , improving scholarly ability among graduate students . . . , and encouraging learning beyond the classroom" (2). The studies cited by Bouton and Garth (1983), as well as the extensive research projects reviewed by Slavin (1980) and Sharan (1980), provide substantial evidence that, when effectively structured and guided, learning groups can help students improve their mastery not only of particular subject areas or academic skills, such as writing, but also increase their general cognitive skills and their engagement with and interest in learning.

Research in the sociology and history of science on the nature and impact of scientific collaboration also provided useful information about collaborative writing in the sciences. As Derek J. de Solla Price notes in *Little Science, Big Science*, such studies, whether statistical or interpretive, focus on "general problems of the shape and size of science and the ground rules governing growth and behavior of science-in-the-large" (viii). Price calls the growth of multiauthored over single-authored scientific papers "one of the most violent transitions that can be measured in recent trends of scientific manpower and literature" (89). And because of this trend, much attention is paid to the collaborative writing practices of scientists.

Typically in this research the focus is not on the process of collaborative writing but on its effect, particularly on the impact of collaborative practices on scientific productivity. As Mark Oromaner has noted, to this end "sociologists and historians of science have increasingly relied upon examinations of citations as a means of analysis. These analyses have been concerned with (1) the rate of growth and obsolescence of scientific literature; (2) the identification of the most important, eminent, influential, or visible scholars, publications, departments, invisible colleges and schools in particular disciplines or sub-disciplines; and (3) the sociometric networks among scholars, publications, departments, invisible colleges and schools among disciplines or within a particular discipline or sub-discipline" (98–99).

This research is of interest, obviously, for its detailed support of the collaborative practices – including collaborative writing — of modern scientists (Price 1963, Meadows 1974). But it also reveals that even in disciplines where collaboration is the norm, problems remain. Since the late seventies, a number of sociologists, such as Porter (1977), Long, McGinnis, and Allison (1980), and Lindsey (1980), have begun to argue against the established practice of noting only first authors in citation counts. Lindsey asserts that the practice of "count[ing] both publications and citations with procedures that take no account of multiple authorship" represents perhaps "one of the most serious errors in empirical judgment made in the sociology of science" (145).

A number of researchers in psychology and sociology explore what Meadows calls "one of the more arcane areas of scientific communication — the ordering of authors' names on research papers" from a somewhat different perspective, that of attempting to establish the fairest, most equitable means of attribution (197). These efforts include detailed analyses of the effects of name-ordering among authors of scientific papers (Zuckerman 1968, Nudelman and Landers 1972); proposals for the development of a coding system that would "provide more complete information on which author is responsible for what" (Simon 265); analyses of the causes and effects of collaborative research and publication in these disciplines (Over 1982, Over and Smallman 1973, Mitchell 1961); and discussions of the ethical standards governing the assignment of publication credit (Spiegel and Keith-Spiegel 1970).

As we analyzed responses to our surveys, we also continued to collect rich and varying sources on many issues surrounding collaborative writing. But despite their usefulness, our early reading and research, including our own surveys and interviews, could only answer some of the questions that continued to command our attention. They could not tell us why prohibitions against collaborative writing in the humanities have remained so strong or why the assumption that writing is a solitary activity has been so deeply and broadly accepted by English teachers. Nor could they help us probe larger issues, such as the nature of authorship or of knowledge, the essence of the latter brought into question most prominently by the growing influence of social-constructivist arguments in a variety of disciplines, including that of composition studies. As a result, at the time when we had planned to have our research project finished, we found ourselves shifting focus, no longer satisfied simply to report our results and have done with it. We were, in fact, at a new beginning.

REVISING OUR RESEARCH AGENDA

"The Concept of Authorship: Explorations and (Dis)Closures," the third chapter of our book *Singular Texts/Plural Authors*, charts the course of that new beginning, examining a number of theoretical questions raised by our research. This discussion, which is far from conclusive, ranges from the general (an analysis of those forces which together encouraged the identification of writing as inherently an individual activity in Western culture) to the specific (the consequences of electronic media for copyright and patent laws). Inevitably, we have drawn on research from a number of related disciplines — philosophy, history, anthropology, sociology, psychology, and literary theory. Such interdisciplinary explorations are always dangerous; one must be careful not merely to pick and choose that evidence which best supports one's own views, ignoring important disciplinary constraints. But the risk is, we feel, justified: only such a broad interdisciplinary approach can begin to suggest the implications of interrogating fully our traditional notions of what it means to be an author.

While our exploration of historical and theoretical dimensions of collaborative writing raised myriad questions, we hoped that our research would eventually yield answers to some important practical pedagogical questions. If men and women in the work force frequently write collaboratively, should not writing teachers help prepare them for an important part of their job? Our own experiences as coauthors have been both personally and professionally satisfying. Might students find writing more enjoyable and less alienating if they collaborated occasionally? How might such opportunities best be embedded in the curriculum? How are attacks on the subject in psychology and sociology and the destabilization of the author in literary studies reflected in our pedagogy? What would an effective collaborative assignment look like?

"The Pedagogy of Collaboration," chapter 4 in *Singular Texts/Plural Authors*, attempts to deal with such pedagogical issues and offers, where possible, tentative guidelines and suggestions for teachers who wish to include collaborative writing in their classes. But the more we worked with our materials in this chapter, the harder it became for us to devise a set of clear-cut, pragmatic recipes for collaboration. In fact, our subject proved as problematic pedagogically as it had theoretically and historically. Issues of power and authority, of consensus and conflict, of gender, race, and class raised questions about a pedagogy of collaboration that we could not ignore. And our growing awareness of and sensitivity to such issues made us particularly cautious in recommending any one kind of collaborative writing activity.

As this introduction suggests, the research odyssey on which we embarked six years ago has changed us, as we have changed it, as it has in turn changed us again. That first deceptively simple-sounding question we posed — is writing necessarily an individual activity? — did not plunge, straight and swift, toward safe answers but rather drifted in and out of currents and eddies, sending forth a rippled series of secondary and tertiary questions. Our attempt throughout *Singular Texts/Plural Authors* is to render our own sounding of these currents, our own processes of discovery and change. Though we originally strove to make it so, our book is not and could not finally be cast in the traditional patriarchal academic mode: a distanced, seamless, logical process, marching inexorably from proof to demonstration to conclusion. Our lived experience of this book's story has been filled with personal struggle and pain, false hopes and starts, rich rewards, even richer uncertainties. Thus we arrive, in "New Beginnings" (pp. 135–48 in this collection), not at a conventional set of proven conclusions but, as has most often been the case in our collaborative efforts, at a new beginning.

A NOTE ON DEFINITION

Before turning to "Collaborative Writers at Work" (pp. 91–134 in this collection), which reports the results of our FIPSE-funded study of collaborative writing practices in seven professional associations, we must address one particular site of uncertainty — term definition. The meaning of the term *collaborative writing* is far from self-evident. Like other aspects of this study, our understanding of this term and the role of definitions shifted as our research progressed.

Our first efforts to define the phenomenon we wished to study were motivated primarily by pragmatic considerations. We needed to identify, and then to describe, this phenomenon in such a way that the members of the associations we were studying could understand and respond to the questions in our survey. Rather than use the term *collaborative writing* in our first two surveys, we referred to *group writing* — a term that we believed respondents to our surveys would more easily identify and understand. Once we had decided upon a name for our object of inquiry, we needed to define it. After considerable reflection, we decided that we would do so in the broadest possible terms. Consequently, we posited the following series of definitions as an introduction to Survey 2:

> This survey explores the dynamics and demands of group writing in your profession. For the purposes of this survey, writing includes any of the activities that lead to a completed written document. These activities include written and spoken brainstorming, outlining, note-taking, organizational planning, drafting, revising, and editing. Written products include any piece of writing, from notes, directions, and forms to reports and published materials. Group writing includes any writing done in collaboration with one or more persons.

We chose such a broad-based strategy for several reasons. First, as those who study the history of invention are aware, modern students, writers, and teachers of writing have traditionally ignored or undervalued the numerous complex intellectual and social processes that constitute an important part of most writing activities. Despite the possible danger of collapsing distinctions between writing and all related intellectual activities, we wanted to explore the full range of processes our survey respondents might identify as related to their on-the-job writing. Finally, given the paucity of our knowledge of collaborative writing and the ways it might function in the seven professional associations we intended to study (or in society in general, for that matter), we did not want to restrict participants by defining either writing or group writing too rigidly. Our attempt at a broad definition rested, then, on the very pragmatic desire to get as much information as possible about our subject.

The analysis presented in "Collaborative Writers at Work" will demonstrate, we hope, the benefits derived from choosing such a broad lens through which to view our subject. Others interested in collaborative writing, however, have chosen more delimited definitions of the term. A group of researchers at Purdue University, for example, derived a definition from the descriptions provided by experienced collaborators, one that features three distinguishing features: (1) production of a shared document; (2) substantive interaction among members; and (3) shared decision-making power over and responsibility for the document (Allen, Atkinson, Morgan, Moore, Snow "Experienced").

The focus in this definition on the document directs their gaze in particular ways and leads to an efficient, pragmatic — though less broad — definition of both collaborative writing and writing. A similarly focused definition appears in the work of Deborah Bosley: "Collaborative writing is defined as two or more people working together to produce one written document in a situation in which a group takes responsibility for having produced the document" (6).

In practice, the term *collaborative writing* appears in many different settings and in fairly narrow — and often conflicting — definitions. In expository writing classes and in composition theory, the term has until recently most often described peer evaluation of individually written drafts. As Bosley's work demonstrates, researchers in professional and technical communication have also referred to any number of specific configurations as "collaborative writing" (4):

> supervisor's assignment of a document that is researched and drafted by a staff member, but carefully edited by the supervisor (Paradis, Dobrin, Miller)
>
> collaborative planning of a document that is drafted and revised by an individual (Odell)
>
> individual planning and drafting of a document that is revised collaboratively (Doheny-Farina)
>
> a peer's critiquing a co-worker's draft (Anderson) (4)

Countering these more specific implicit definitions are those of Jim Reither and other scholars, who tend to conflate writing and collaborative writing. For them, all writing is collaborative.

This unstructured and unsettled debate over definitions points up, most notably, just what is at stake in definitions in general and in definitions of collaborative writing in particular. We name in order to know, but that naming inevitably limits our knowing. Furthermore, these differing interpretations illustrate the problematic nature of defining terms. Each conception rests on a necessary but usually unstated definition of writing, a term that has of late proven highly resistant to simple or pat definitions. And definitions of writing, of course, reflect a set of ideological assumptions that we ignore only at our peril. Thus while we continue to use our broad definition — "any writing done in collaboration with one or more persons" — as a way of orienting our data and guiding readers through our study, we view this definition as largely unsatisfactory and just as problematic as any other. Indeed, the shifting and conflicting nature of the definitions revolving around the term *collaborative writing* seems to us to call not for simplification or standardization but for a Burkean complexifying — a series of perspectives by incongruity. By exploring such perspectives, we hope to contribute to an increasingly complex and enriched conversation about what it can mean to write collaboratively.

WORKS CITED

Allen, Nancy J., Dianne Atkinson, Meg Morgan, Teresa Moore, and Craig Snow. "What Experienced Collaborators Say about Collaborative Writing." *Iowa State Journal of Business and Technical Communication* 1 (Sept. 1987): 70–90.

Anderson, Paul V. "What Survey Research Tells Us about Writing at Work." *Writing in Nonacademic Settings.* Ed. Lee Odell and Dixie Goswami. New York: Guilford, 1985. 3–83.

Barritt, Loren. "Writing/Speaking: A Descriptive Phenomenological View." *Exploring Speaking-Writing Relationships: Connections and Contrasts.* Ed. Barry M. Kroll and Roberta J. Vann. Urbana, IL: NCTE, 1981. 124–33.

Beebe, Steven A., and John T. Masterson. *Communicating in Small Groups: Principles and Practices.* Glenview, IL: Scott, 1982.

Bereiter, Carl, and Marlene Scardamalia. "From Conversation to Composition: The Role of Instruction in a Developmental Process." *Advances in Instructional Psychology.* Ed. Robert Glaser. Vol 2. Hillsdale, NJ: Erlbaum, 1982. 1–64. 3 vols. 1978–87.

Bosley, Deborah. "A National Study of the Uses of Collaborative Writing in Business Communications Courses among Members of the ABC." Diss. Illinois State U, 1989.

Bouton, Clark, and Russell Y. Garth, eds. *Learning in Groups. New Directions for Teaching and Learning* 14. San Francisco: Jossey-Bass, 1983.

———. "Students in Learning Groups: Active Learning through Conversation." *Learning in Groups.* Ed. Clark Bouton and Russell Y. Garth. San Francisco: Jossey-Bass, 1983. 73–82.

Bruffee, Kenneth A. "The Brooklyn Plan: Attaining Intellectual Growth through Peer-Group Tutoring." *Liberal Education* 64 (1978): 447–68.

———. "Collaborative Learning and the 'Conversation of Mankind.'" *College English* 46 (1984a): 635–52.

———. "Collaborative Learning: Some Practical Models." *College English* 34 (1973): 634–43.

———. "Learning to Live in a World Out of Joint: Thomas Kuhn's Message to Humanists Revisited." *Liberal Education* 70 (1984b): 77–81.

———. *A Short Course in Writing.* 2nd ed. Cambridge, MA: Winthrop, 1980.

———. "The Structure of Knowledge and the Future of Liberal Education." *Liberal Education* 67 (1981): 177–86.

———. "Teaching Writing through Collaboration." *Learning in Groups.* Ed. Clark Bouton and Russell Y. Garth. *New Directions for Teaching and Learning* 14. San Francisco: Jossey-Bass, 1983a. 23–29.

———. "The Way Out: A Critical Survey of Innovations in College Teaching. . . ." *College English* 33 (1972): 457–70.

———. "Writing and Reading as Collaborative or Social Acts." *The Writer's Mind: Writing as a Mode of Thinking.* Ed. Janice N. Hays, et al. Urbana, IL: NCTE, 1983b. 159–69.

Burke, Kenneth. *A Grammar of Motives.* Berkeley: U of California P, 1969.

Carry, L. Ray. "Dissertation Publication: The Issue of Joint Authorship." *Journal for Research in Mathematics Education* 11 (1980): 391–93.

Clifford, John. "Composing in Stages: The Effects of a Collaborative Pedagogy." *Research in the Teaching of English* 15 (1981): 37–53.

Coe, Richard M. "Writing in Groups." *Working Together* 2 (1979): 29–31.

Doheny-Farina, Stephen. "Writing in an Emerging Organization: An Ethnographic Study." *Written Communication* 3 (1986): 158–85.

Faigley, Lester, and Thomas P. Miller. "What We Learn from Writing on the Job." *College English* 44 (1982): 557–69.

Fields, Cheryl M. "Professors' Demands for Credit as 'Co-Authors' of Students' Research Projects May Be Rising." *Chronicle of Higher Education* 14 (Sept. 1983): 7, 10.

Fisher, B. Aubrey. *Small Group Decision Making: Communication and the Group Process.* 2nd ed. New York: McGraw, 1980.

Flower, Linda, and John R. Hayes. "A Cognitive Process Theory of Writing." *College Composition and Communication* 32 (1981): 365–87.

———. "Images, Plans, and Prose: The Representation of Meaning in Writing." *Written Communication* 1 (1984): 120–60.

Forsyth, Donelson R. *An Introduction to Group Dynamics.* Monterey: Brooks, 1983.

Gebhardt, Richard. "Teamwork and Feedback: Broadening the Base of Collaborative Writing." *College English* 42 (1980): 69–74.

Geertz, Clifford. "Common Sense as a Cultural System." *Local Knowledge: Further Essays in Interpretive Anthropology.* New York: Basic, 1983. 73–93.

Hall, Jay, and Martha S. Williams. "Group Dynamics Training and Improved Decision Making." *Journal of Applied Behavioral Science* 6 (1970): 39–68.

Hare, A. Paul. *Creativity in Small Groups.* Beverly Hills: Sage, 1982.

———. *Handbook of Small Group Research.* 2nd ed. New York: Free, 1976.

Hawkins, Thom. *Group Inquiry Techniques for Teaching Writing.* Urbana, IL: ERIC Clearinghouse on Reading and Communication Skills, National Institute of Education, 1976.

Janis, Irving L. *Groupthink: Psychological Studies of Policy Decisions and Fiascoes.* 2nd ed. Boston: Houghton, 1983.

Jewell, Linda N., and H. Joseph Reitz. *Group Effectiveness in Organizations.* Glenview, IL: Scott, 1981.

Johnson, David W., and Frank P. Johnson. *Joining Together: Group Theory and Group Skills.* 3rd ed. Englewood Cliffs: Prentice, 1987.

Johnson, David W., and Roger T. Johnson. "Instructional Goal Structure: Cooperative, Competitive, or Individualistic." *Review of Educational Research* 44 (1974): 213–40.

———. "The Internal Dynamics of Cooperative Learning in Groups." *Learning to Cooperate, Cooperating to Learn.* Ed. Robert Slavin, et al. New York: Plenum, 1985. 103–24.

Lindsey, Duncan. "Production and Citation Measures in the Sociology of Science: The Problem of Multiple Authorship." *Social Studies of Science* 10 (1980): 145–62.

Long, J. Scott, Robert McGinnis, and Paul D. Allison. "The Problem of Junior-Authored Papers in Constructing Citation Counts." *Social Studies of Science* 10 (1980): 127–43.

Meadows, A. J. *Communication in Science.* London: Butterworths, 1974.

Mitchell, Mildred B. "Trends toward Multiple Authorship in Scientific Publications." *Journal of Psychology* 52 (1961): 125–31.

Moffett, James. *Teaching the Universe of Discourse.* 1968. Boston: Houghton, 1983.

Murray, Donald M. "Writing as Process: How Writing Finds Its Own Meaning." *Eight Approaches to Teaching Composition.* Ed. Timothy R. Donovan and Ben W. McClelland. Urbana, IL: NCTE, 1980. 3–20.

Nilsen, Alleen Pace. "Men and Women: Working Together in Changing Times." *School Library Journal* 27 (Sept. 1980): 29–32.

Nudelman, Arthur E., and Clifford E. Landers. "The Failure of 100 Divided by 3 to Equal 33 1/3." *American Sociologist* 7 (Nov. 1972): 9.

Odell, Lee. "Beyond the Text: Relations between Writing and Social Context." *Writing in Nonacademic Settings.* Ed. Lee Odell and Dixie Goswami. New York: Guilford, 1985. 249–80.

O'Donnell, Angela M., et al. "Cooperative Writing." *Written Communication* 2 (1985): 307–15.

Ong, Walter J. *Interfaces of the Word: Studies in the Evolution of Consciousness and Culture.* Ithaca: Cornell UP, 1977.

———. "Reading, Technology, and Human Consciousness." *Literacy as a Human Problem.* Ed. James Raymond. Tuscaloosa: U of Alabama P, 1982. 170–99.

Oromaner, Mark. "Career Contingencies and the Fate of Sociological Research." *Social Science Information* 12 (Apr. 1973): 97–111.

Over, Ray. "Collaborative Research and Publication in Psychology." *American Psychologist* 37 (1982): 996–1001.

Over, Ray, and Susan Smallman. "Maintenance of Individual Visibility in Publication of Collaborative Research by Psychologists." *American Psychologist* 28 (1973): 161–66.

Paradis, James, David Dobrin, and Richard Miller. "Writing at Exxon ITD: Notes on the Writing Environment of an R&D Organization." *Writing in Nonacademic Settings.* Ed. Lee Odell and Dixie Goswami. New York: Guilford, 1985. 281–307.

Patton, Bobby R., and Kim Griffin. *Decision-Making Group Interaction.* 2nd ed. New York: Harper, 1978.

Poe, Edgar Allan. "The Purloined Letter." *The Complete Works of Edgar Allan Poe.* Ed. J. A. Harrison. New York: Ames, 1965. 28–52.

Porter, Alan L. "Citation Analysis: Queries and Caveats." *Social Studies of Science* 7 (1977): 257–67.

Price, Derek J. de Solla. *Little Science, Big Science.* New York: Columbia UP, 1963.

Reither, James A. "Writing and Knowing: Toward Redefining the Writing Process." *College English* 47 (1985): 620–28.

Sharan, Shlomo. "Cooperative Learning in Small Groups: Recent Methods and Effects on Achievement, Attitudes, and Ethnic Relations." *Review of Educational Research* 50 (1980): 241–71.

Sharan, Shlomo, and Yael Sharan. *Small-Group Teaching.* Englewood Cliffs: Educ. Tech. Publ., 1976.

Simon, Julian L. "A Plan to Improve the Attribution of Scholarly Articles." *American Sociologist* 5 (1970): 265–67.

Slavin, Robert E. "Cooperative Learning." *Review of Educational Research* 50 (1980): 315–42.

Slavin, Robert, et al. *Learning to Cooperate, Cooperating to Learn.* New York: Plenum, 1985.

Spiegel, Don, and Patricia Keith-Spiegel. "Assignment of Publication Credits: Ethics and Practices of Psychologists." *American Psychologist* 25 (1970): 738–47.

Steiner, Ivan D. *Group Process and Productivity.* New York: Academic, 1972.

Zuckerman, Harriet A. "Patterns of Name Ordering among Authors of Scientific Papers: A Study of Social Symbolism and Its Ambiguity." *American Journal of Sociology* 74 (1968): 276–91.

8 *Collaborative Writers at Work*

> The ethical values of work are in its application of the competitive equipment to cooperative ends.
>
> — KENNETH BURKE (*PHILOSOPHY* 316)

SCENES OF COLLABORATION: FOREGROUNDINGS

In this chapter, we will contrast the conventional image of writers at work — an image that privileges the solitary writer working in isolation — with a different picture, that of writers planning, gathering information, drafting, and revising collaboratively. We know the first image well; the "reigning trope" for writing is, as Linda Brodkey observes, that of "the solitary scribbler" (55). In *Academic Writing as Social Practice*, Brodkey captures this image of the writer with rich specificity.

> Writing is a social act. People write to and for other people, yet when we picture writing we see a solitary writer. We may see the writer alone in a garret, working into the small hours of the morning by thin candlelight. The shutters are closed. Or perhaps we see the writer in a well-appointed study seated at a desk, fingers poised over the keys of a typewriter (or microcomputer). The drapes are drawn. Or we may even see the writer hunched over a manuscript in a magnificent public or university library, the walls and walls of books standing between the writer and the world. Whether the scene of writing is poetic or prosaic, the writer above the madding crowd in a garret, only temporarily free from family and friends in a study, or removed from the world in a library, it is the same picture — the writer writes alone.
>
> We do not easily picture writers in social settings. On those rare occasions when we do, we are likely to see a writer who is not writing. Maybe we see F. Scott Fitzgerald carousing, or Henry James dining out, or Tolstoy teaching peasants. Whether it is a picture of Virginia Woolf speaking

From Lisa Ede and Andrea Lunsford, in *Singular Texts/Plural Authors* (Carbondale and Edwardsville: Southern Illinois UP, 1990) 20–67. This is the second chapter in this monograph.

to undergraduate women at Oxford or Ernest Hemingway on the Left Bank, these are not images of writers at work. However caught up they may be by the details of their social lives, these are pictures of writers playing or working at something other than writing. The image we hold of the writer places social life on the other side of writing, that which occurs before or after writing, something or someone that must not be allowed to enter the scene of writing. (54–55)

Because images or pictures have such power, we wish to begin this report of our FIPSE-funded research project not with statistics but with descriptions of the writers we interviewed in order to discover more about collaborative writers at work. These descriptions are just that: descriptions. They should not be taken as generalizations or as representing ideal models for effective collaborative writing — though many of those we interviewed seemed to us to write quite effectively with others. Nor do our interviewees represent a comprehensive range or typology of collaborative writers. They are simply people who generously agreed to share their work and time with us. We have much to learn from them, both in terms of what these snapshots record about the everyday, commonsense collaboration that characterizes writing in the workplace and what these snapshots leave out or obscure. As this chapter progresses, then, we will attempt not only to report on collaborative writers at work but to problematize and to complicate that "report."

Collaborative Writing in a Large Consulting Engineering Firm

Bill Qualls describes himself as a city planner, but when we interviewed him for several days in the spring of 1985, he struck us as a modern Renaissance individual. His undergraduate degree is in architecture; his M.A., in city planning; and his Ph.D., in higher education with an emphasis on curriculum development. When we asked Qualls to explain his varied educational background, he indicated that he had moved from architecture to city planning because "I had more interest in complete city design as opposed to the design of individual buildings." His reasons for choosing a Ph.D. in higher education suggest a great deal about his interests and character:

After I had been out of school a number of years practicing as a city planner, I had become concerned about why we could develop a good plan for a community and try to explain it to people and they wouldn't seem to understand it. They wouldn't support it for one reason or another. And time and time again we would see a good plan go down the drain because people didn't agree with it or for some reason didn't actively support it. So I decided I needed more education. At first, I was going to get a Ph.D. in planning. But finally it occurred to me that, no, that was not what I wanted. I wanted to know more about the learning process — the educational process.

Bill Qualls works in a large consulting engineering firm in the South, and he is obviously successful in his work — he is a vice president of his firm. Qualls has the pragmatism characteristic of many engineers: "Once we get a

job we've got to do it and generally we find a way to do it." But in several respects Qualls struck us as different from many of his peers. When we asked
him how his varied education had influenced his approach toward his work,
Qualls responded that the "major difference is that we [Qualls and his team
members] feel hurt if we can't get the client to understand what we are doing.
Often, the professional doesn't really care about that as long as he gets paid
for what he's done." This concern for understanding, for true communication,
acts as a primary motivating force: "What motivates me is how I can help my
clients — how I can help them comprehend what I am talking about . . . in
order that they can better participate in the decision-making process. I will do
whatever I can to help them understand."

As his own words indicate, Bill Qualls is a self-reflective and systematic
collaborative writer. When we first arrived at his office, Qualls had a carefully
prepared presentation of the methods he and his co-workers use in their
work-related writing ready for us — complete with charts and examples. As
later discussion will indicate, Qualls possesses a particularly clear, detailed,
and highly articulated representation of his task, and he has developed innovative means of responding to its demands.

In these and other respects, Bill Qualls is not typical. He is not a typical
member of his firm, most of whom are engineers. He is not a typical member
of the American Consulting Engineers Council (ACEC), one of the seven professional associations whose members we surveyed. In fact, we learned when
we visited him, he is not a member of the ACEC at all. Our original survey
had been received by another member of the firm who had passed it on to
Qualls, who is unofficially considered his firm's writing expert. (Although in
planning our research we intended to interview at least one member from
each of the seven professional associations we surveyed — certainly a logical
and tidy pattern for our interviews — this expectation was confounded in this
and several other instances.)

Why highlight such an atypical individual? In the first place, we choose
to do so because we discovered in this and other interviews that the "typical"
individual is more than an apparent contradiction in terms. Each of the collaborative writers with whom we spoke was, in some sense, unique. There are
several other reasons why we chose to begin our description of scenes of collaborative writing with a discussion of Bill Qualls. One consideration was
practical. We were able to spend the longest amount of time (two and one half
days versus two to three hours) with Qualls and his colleagues. We thus have
the clearest, most complete view of collaborative writing as it is practiced by
these individuals. (Most of our interviews were with single individuals or, in
one case, with two persons who worked together regularly. We were able not
only to interview Bill Qualls several times but to conduct interviews of from
one to two hours with several of his co-workers.)

Finally, as noted earlier, Bill Qualls was one of the most self-consciously
reflective collaborative writers we interviewed. When we first chose those we
hoped to interview, we determined that we would attempt to talk with individuals who were satisfied, productive, and articulate collaborative writers

(as indicated by their responses to our first two surveys). Bill Qualls is such an individual. He is no more typical of all collaborative writers than the protagonist of a novel is typical of all humans. But just as we can learn a great deal about the human condition by describing and analyzing characters in a play or a novel, so too can we learn about collaborative writing by studying — and listening to — thoughtful and effective collaborative writers.

At the time of our interview, Qualls and his co-workers had most recently worked on several master plans for military installations. As Bill Qualls described it, such a project for a large army post may take three to five years to complete and involves planning for "a city of 60,000 or 70,000 people, a specialized city." As anyone who has dealt with the federal government can imagine, those preparing master plans for a new military base necessarily encounter numerous bureaucratic constraints. Bill and his team must, for instance, "come up with proposals for new buildings, new streets, other types of needs, based on what the army says a unit is due. . . . [We must always] estimate needs according to their regulations."

The most immediate difficulty posed by a project of this magnitude is simply comprehending precisely what their clients want. Though clients initiate the process by developing a scope of work, or statement of requirements for a project, Qualls generally finds these difficult to interpret. "I think to a great extent the people who put the scope of work together don't understand it. The people who respond to it [consulting firms such as Qualls'] don't know anything either, so they wander around in each other's ignorance and come up with something neither is satisfied with."

In response to these and other problems characteristic of the large projects which he typically manages, Qualls has developed a sophisticated method for analyzing and organizing all activities connected with a project. Over time, co-workers began affectionately to call Qualls' techniques the Critical Qualls Method — referred to in-house as the CQM — after the Critical Path Method sometimes used in their field to organize complicated activities.

We first learned of the CQM when we unfolded the large (30" × 32"), intricate chart that accompanied Bill Qualls' second survey. (We had asked respondents to send any information that they thought might help us understand collaborative writing better.) We studied this chart carefully, but even though its seven major sections were clearly labeled, as were subsections, we could not fully understand it. Only when we visited Bill Qualls and were able to question him and his colleagues about the chart and the method that it exemplifies were we able to understand the purpose and the function of the chart's seven major sections:

   I. Contract Data and Progress Bars

  II. Report Outline and Phases

 III. Base Map Index Sheet and Layout

 IV. Base Mapping Outline and Phases

  V. Information Mapping Outline and Phases

VI. End Products Submittal Record

VII. Submittal Time Sequence

This chart serves multiple functions. Qualls uses it initially as a means of clarifying the often vague or confusing language of the scope of work. The following excerpt is from a longer description of the ways in which the CQM "translates" the information in the scope of work into concrete objectives, responsibilities, and deadlines:

> We show [in the CQM] all the end products you the client want — in terms of the master plan report, mapping, etc. The number of times products are to be submitted is shown here. Some you want submitted just once, some twice, and some three times. . . . Here we indicate end products for maps and reports. These are the headings and chapters for your report, and we use this same organization for our cost proposal. Here I'll place the names of every person working on the report and how many days or hours they will be working on each chapter. We summarize these to develop many of our cost estimates.

Qualls and his team thus use this information, carefully organized according to the CQM format, "to explain to the client how we are translating their statement of work into something else that we think is a lot more understandable." If the client selects his firm, Qualls and his team develop a final CQM that reflects their negotiations and modifications. "When we sign a contract, the CQM becomes part of it, and it is used daily throughout the project."

Once Qualls' firm has signed a contract for a project, the CQM functions in different — and much more dynamic — ways. It is the means by which Qualls coordinates the efforts of team members. (The ten persons working on a recent project included the following: project manager [Qualls], project engineer, hydrology and sanitary engineer, mechanical engineer, architect, telecommunications engineer, electrical engineer, cartographer, planner, and secretary.) Although some of Qualls' staff, such as his planning technician and secretary, are permanently assigned to him, others vary depending upon the project.

One of Qualls' co-workers explained that as they work on a project the CQM "becomes a sort of homing point for everything that we are doing." Qualls and his co-workers use the CQM to monitor their progress: "Each month we select a color and we color in everything completed in that month. Visually, that tells you how much you have completed and what's left to be done. And if you have to check roughly when you did something, [you can] just go back to the CQM and look at the colors. . . . We also send copies of the CQM to each of our staff members . . . so they can redline what they are assigned to do as a reminder of what needs to be done."

The last two sections of the CQM, "End Products Submittal Record" and "Submittal Time Sequence," also enable team members to keep track of responsibilities and meet deadlines. Finally, because the CQM also includes all of the products the group must produce — the report in full outline form, and the numerous maps that will illustrate their plan — it also functions as a style guide, one that is particularly helpful in insuring that group members (most of whom are responsible for drafting the part of the report that involves their area of expertise) adhere to the same format. The CQM thus plays a role in every aspect of this group's efforts. The form itself maps every stage of the process — from their original analysis of the scope of work through the information-gathering and technical stages (including preparation of maps and other graphics) and through pencil, preliminary, and final drafts — relating each stage to the organizational format or outline of the final document.

At first glance — or even at second or third glance — the CQM looked formidably uninviting to us, more a maze in which to get lost than a map by which to find the way. We were surprised, therefore, when not only Qualls (its originator) but other team and firm members as well spoke of its wide-ranging usefulness. One of the team's cartographers said, "It helps as far as due dates and submittals and exactly what is needed — the title of each map and the tab number. We may have to refer back to the contract to get specifics, but this helps you see right away which maps you have done, which maps you have yet to do." An engineer who usually heads up another team in the firm has adopted the CQM for his projects. "It is," he says, "a very good concept." For his projects, the team "agree on the CQM, which essentially sets our outline and our process. . . . The bigger the job the more critical it is. We use it to the letter."

Not every team in this large firm uses the CQM; smaller projects especially seem to proceed efficiently without it. But this complex form, which is modified and tailored to each individual project, is more widely used — and praised — than we would ever have expected. The Qualls team member responsible for visiting the project site and gathering local background information said, "Oh, the big Qualls method: *everyone* respects it."

We have dwelt on the CQM at such length for several reasons. As is already obvious, this chart functions as a crucial part of the team's collaboration. It orchestrates the collaborative process — from the time it is conceived in response to a scope of work; through the team visit to the project site; through the contract negotiations; through the research and drafting of the plan (which team members carry out individually according to area of expertise); through the series of revisions, deadlines, and submittals. By the time the team leader — usually Qualls — checks off the blocks for the executive summary and the letter of transmittal (which he always writes), the CQM looks like a Klee painting — its bars ablaze with color. The CQM provides a visual representation of collaboration, a vivid picture of a job well done.

When one of the team members used the phrase "pride of authorship," we asked for elaboration. "We take great pride in doing these things, and we really help each other. Bill's knowledge expands our horizons and ours expands his. We all have a sense of pride in the [CQM and resulting report], because it makes us all shine more. An individual engineer — me included — would never put the time in to produce that quality. You look at a standard engineer's report, and you won't see anything like this." For members of this collaborative team, the final CQM serves as a symbol for this pride.

A second notable characteristic of the CQM also became apparent. Although its formality struck us as static and rigid, in practice it is a dynamic tool that intricately binds process and product. Although in one sense a product, the CQM drives the research, planning, writing, and illustrating processes forward; and they are in turn encoded in the complete report and charted on the CQM — an elegant enactment of the symbiotic relationship between product and process in any written discourse.

Finally, we have focused on the CQM because it demonstrates the way in which collaborative writing is highly goal oriented and context bound. An engineer in another firm reading about the CQM, for instance, might be tempted to import it and impose it on his or her own writing situation. Doing so might work but probably would not because the CQM was developed in response to a particular set of circumstances and needs. In addition, as a number of his colleagues' remarks indicated, the CQM is very much a product of Bill Qualls' personality and style. In that particular rhetorical situation, both CQM and his personal style are accepted and appreciated. "I have never met a professional more committed than Qualls," says one co-worker. Another elaborates, "Most engineers can't put their pragmatism into words, can't write it out so somebody can understand it or accomplish it. That is what makes Bill so rare and valuable."

Qualls' abilities include not only a gift for systematization but the tendency to see the project as a whole. Over and over again in our interviews with him, he came back to the importance of this way of perceiving reality — what he called "matrix thinking": "If you read a book or document, like a scope of work, what you may miss is the matrix that holds it all together. That to me is what is so important. Is there something that brings this all together so that when we finish we have something that holds water, that helps us understand the situation better?"

One of his colleagues describes this tendency to see the whole or the matrix as "thinking in terms of function *and* form." Bill puts it more graphically: "It is as though I am an overeater. I want to eat as quickly, enjoyably, and efficiently as I can, so I like to have the whole dinner laid out in front of me. I don't want people bringing me individual servings. Give me the whole buffet and let me go at it. I like to see everything at once when I am making certain decisions." And that is just what Qualls and his colleagues have developed in the CQM: a tool that brings them together (they often meet where it is posted to check on the phase of a project) and allows them to see "the whole thing at the same time."

A Clinical Psychologist Who Writes in a Variety of Collaborative Settings

Unlike most of the writers we interviewed, American Psychological Association member Albert Bernstein works independently, rather than for business or industry. Bernstein is a clinical psychologist in private practice, and he describes himself as very satisfied with his professional situation: "I would say that I am doing with my profession precisely what I want to do. I thought about what would be the ideal job for me and made it happen." In addition to his private clinical practice, Bernstein also presents workshops, acts as a consultant, develops videotapes, and writes a variety of documents. At the time that we interviewed him, for example, Bernstein had recently worked with a group of psychologists to draft a brochure describing the Oregon Psychological Association; met with administrators at a local college to draft guidelines for students who are disruptive because of mental health problems; consulted with businesses who wished to develop stress management programs and drafted brochures advertising these programs; and begun writing a popular psychology book in collaboration with a professional writer, who will help him transform his case studies into "stories that will interest people." All of these writing situations involve frequent collaboration with others.

These examples do not cover all of the collaborative writing that Bernstein has done and continues to do in his career. Bernstein has extensive grant-writing experience for example: "For years I worked for a mental health center. I was clinical director and had to write hundreds of grants, budget narratives, policies, and procedures." And he has worked with committees of the Oregon Psychological Association to draft laws dealing with such subjects as the rights of schizophrenics to treatment. More than any other individual we interviewed, Bernstein regularly wrote a wide variety of documents in an equally diverse range of situations. (According to Bernstein, the variety of writing he regularly works on is not typical of most clinical psychologists, many of whom primarily write clinical evaluations.)

Bernstein's answers to the open-ended questions in our second survey also indicated that he had thought a great deal about communication — and that he had a nice sense of wit. In response to the question "Please comment on how your high school or college English classes might have better prepared you for professional group writing tasks," Albert Bernstein had dryly responded: "My English teachers taught me how to scan poems and diagram sentences. Need I say more?"

Like Bill Qualls, Albert Bernstein is a particularly self-conscious and reflective writer. This interest in communication undoubtedly derives in part from his academic training: as a Ph.D. student he emphasized research in communication, and the popular psychology book he was working on at the time of our interview focused on the same subject. Bernstein also conveyed a strong sense of the importance of effective communication for his career. "If you want to achieve something you have to promote yourself. The good things go to people who promote themselves, whether we like it or not. And one of the ways you can promote yourself is to know how to write. If people ask me to write something or make a speech somewhere I never turn them down. That is my advertising." Bernstein was also conscious of the ways in which he varied language to suit different audiences. Early in our interview, for example, he informed us that "I write only English but I write six kinds of English: psychobabble, management jargon, formal psychology (journal article style), educationese, a little bit of hype (but not much), and everyday English." Finally, Bernstein cares about style. He told us that he prided himself "on never having used the word *utilize* in my life."

Unlike most of the individuals we interviewed, Bernstein had not consistently described collaborative writing as productive and satisfying in the answers to our first two surveys. He answered a question on the first survey that asked "How productive do you find writing as part of a team or group?" by indicating that he found such collaboration "not too productive." (The possible responses included: "very productive," "productive," "not too productive," and "not at all productive.") Thus we were not surprised when at the start of our interview Bernstein emphasized many of the problems he had encountered in collaborative writing situations.

One of the most difficult of all his group writing experiences occurred when he was charged with the task of writing a brochure for a statewide organization of which he was an active member. "This particular brochure took me four months to write, and it is not because I am a slow writer. It was because I had to go to board meetings and hear 'Well, I don't know about using this word, and this sentence might offend somebody.'"

Despite these problems — familiar to all who have engaged in similar group writing projects — Bernstein continued in his efforts. The negotiations involved in gaining approval for the final draft of the brochure were considerable. Members of the board argued about the order in which various items should be presented, as well as the wording. Because the brochure described the organization's various committees, it had to be approved by each committee. "Each committee had to approve the brochure, and they each wanted to add more information about their committee. I wanted the shortest, most direct brochure possible. It was a battle."

We were interested in the reasons why Bernstein, clearly a disciplined, task-oriented person ("I am very organized. So far as I know I have never missed a deadline for written work in my life."), originally accepted this task and then persevered in developing the brochure. Much of his resolve, apparently, grew out of frustration over the failure of past efforts." I knew that a group of people would be involved, and I was afraid they'd dither it to death. But I hoped I would be able to get the brochure through, because we had been trying to develop a brochure for four or five years, and nobody in the organization had been able to succeed in writing one people could agree on. . . . Not having a brochure seemed preposterous to me because there are a lot more controversial and difficult things to write than that." As Bernstein described it, the process of gaining acceptance of the brochure involved patience, persistence, and even what he called "manipulation": "I can stare people down . . . I usually don't operate like that, but it was necessary to get the brochure approved."

Given these difficulties, which Bernstein described at considerable length, we were surprised when he responded to the questions "What is your favorite way to write? What would be the ideal situation for you?" not by indicating that he most preferred to write alone, but that "the ideal setup would be working with one or two people and getting together and talking about what it is we want to say, what chapters we want to have, how we want to say it, how people will react to ideas. [Talking like this] helps you get fired up and also encourages you to ask each other hard questions."

We also asked Bernstein a question about the "pride of ownership" he felt when writing alone versus writing together. Again, his answer surprised us: "When I work with other people, one or two other people, I feel that I do a much better job than I would have done alone. I extend myself further and I think I have a clearer idea of what we are trying to do. *It brings more out of me so I think it is more mine.* I don't mind sharing the credit" (our emphasis). Bernstein elaborated on the advantages of writing with one or two coauthors (rather than with a large committee or group of people) in response to the question "Do you think that cognitive processes change when people work together in groups as opposed to writing by themselves?":

> Absolutely. When I am writing alone I always visualize an audience, but I hear my own experiences. . . . It's kind of a closed loop — there's no input from anyone else. When I'm working with other people there are several things that I must keep in mind: not just what the audience might say but what the person I'm working with is going to think of this line. And how to get the job done, how to get around some of the difficulties. . . . When I write with someone else I am engaging not just in a dialogue with the reader but with that other person. And I think it makes the result much better — unless I'm writing with too big a group, with a room full of picky people. . . . Working with someone else gives you another point of view. There is an extra voice inside your head; that can make a lot of difference. Others can see things about what I am doing or what I am saying that I can't see. And if they are good and we work well together, we can do that for each other.

Finally, we asked Bernstein to describe the characteristics of the people he has worked well with in the past. "First of all, a broad base of knowledge. I have a hard time dealing with people who only know their field and don't know anything else. . . . With any luck at all they will know some things that I don't know and so make [our writing] richer. I also work best with people who are task oriented, somebody who can enjoy an interesting conversation but realize that what we're here for is to get this article written. . . . And a sense of humor — that's a definite plus."

Clearly, though Bernstein has experienced his share of problems in writing collaboratively with others, in certain situations at least, for him the advantages outweigh the disadvantages: "In the real world you just can't operate alone unless you are a poet, and even then . . ." As we were preparing to leave, we asked Bernstein the question that closed most of our interviews: "What advice would you give teachers of writing who want to prepare their students for collaborative writing experiences?"

> What I wish is that somebody would have started out by teaching me what language is, why we are writing, what writing is, what writers are trying to do. I wish that somebody had told me that when I wrote I should think about my purpose and my reader. . . . I didn't really learn to write in school. I have a good friend — a poet and newspaper editor. He and I wrote things together; we worked together at the mental health center. He was trying to find out something about mental health, and I

was essentially teaching him about therapy. He was more a consultation and education person, back in the days when mental health clinics could afford to have people like that. I taught him about mental health, and he taught me about writing. And that's where I got my most important training in writing.

Technical Writers in a Construction Equipment Firm

"Correct," said Allan Warrior, a member of the Society for Technical Communication, when we asked if we had interpreted a printout accurately. "Not *right. Correct.* We do not use *right,*" explained Warrior, "unless it is the opposite of *left.* Everything else is *correct.*"

Defined exclusively as the opposite of *left, right* is part of a carefully constructed 2000-word controlled vocabulary developed especially for the international construction equipment manufacturing firm that employs Warrior as a technical writer. This prescriptively rigid style guide acts as a primary constraint on the technical writers who use it at the same time that it allows them to establish an intricate international collaboration.

Having a style guide is, as Warrior notes, far from unique: "Every technical writing group has to come up with a certain style guide. . . . Some of them are more formal than others but [even] if you go to a newspaper, they inevitably have a style guide." But the specificity and the formality of this guide is unusual. As is most often the case, this particular style guide grew out of very practical concerns. Faced with the need to produce operating and service manuals that could be used by diverse employees to assemble and maintain equipment in many non-English speaking countries, the firm turned to machine translation and to the loose translation produced by the people in the target country. The result was "pretty sterile." And, occasionally, pretty funny as well. One such translation problem featured a "feeler gauge": "There is a gauge we use in checking clearances, a machine gauge. It is a feeler gauge. Every mechanic in the U.S. knows what a feeler gauge is. But then it came back translated into French. The only word [the translator could find] for feelers were the little things on the end of a butterfly's antenna. This came back as 'Go catch a butterfly. . . .'"

The use of a strictly controlled vocabulary helped solve such problems. "The key element" in the language, notes Warrior, is that "one word can only have one meaning. Take, for instance, *switch*":

> We had a lot of trouble with *switch.* It is quite common for us to say "turn on the switch" or "turn off the switch." But switches don't turn. You see, we used to have oil lamps: you turned the light up, you turned the light down. Then the first electrical switches were rotary. But if you are in a country now where you have only had a wall switch that flips, try to tell them to turn the switch on. They wonder "What does that mean?" So we move the *switch* to the "on" position or . . . to the "off" position. . . . Another interesting point is that switch can be a noun or a verb in our language. We just throw it around and don't even pay attention to it. We are very careful about that. We just tell them it is a noun.

This vocabulary and "Max" (R Electronic Editor), the text editor program that checks the use of the vocabulary and several dozen other factors (such as no sentences longer than seventeen words; no more than two descriptors plus a noun; all negatives within four words of the verb; noun and verb close together; no inversion of word order; no use of *should, would,* or *could*; no passive verbs), are very much partners in the collaborative writing Warrior and his colleagues do. According to this team of writers, using the controlled vocabulary well "is kind of an art form. If we can write text so that the person reading it doesn't realize that it is in a controlled language, we think we have done our job."

The job cannot be done alone, however, as Warrior and his colleagues stressed again and again. Any piece of technical discourse they produce results from a complex and highly collaborative process, which typically begins when the company decides to come out with a new product. In such cases, Harold Scudder, head of the five-person writing division, assigns the project. "And then we go through and see what material has to be created. We make up a list. Then it is up to us to find out what engineering has done. A lot of times at that stage [the plans] are not complete yet, but we get involved as much as we can so we can learn about it. We start pulling out all the drawings and go through and interpret what there is, and we look for similarities to what else we have produced. . . ."

Eventually, the engineering division provides the writers with a "new product advance information guide," a set of preliminary drawings and a statement of aims, which the team studies for additional information. And as soon as a prototype and a rough draft of a manual to accompany it are developed, the writers "verify" or "try it out" by completely disassembling the product and checking to see if they can follow their own directions. In this stage of their work, they call not only on their own training (all have degrees in science and engineering as well as mechanical experience) but on the team engineers and team mechanics. "Afterwards," says Warrior, "we usually rewrite." The rewrite then travels back to the engineers: "We take what they give out and put it in our [language] and we feed it back through them. They mark it up again. And it is good because then we rewrite and it comes out better."

Throughout this process, the text editor program monitors the language and syntax of the manual, and the writers work with illustrators to create and label graphics. The draft copy is then "routed again to engineering, marketing, legal." The entire process, which takes "maybe six months," usually works smoothly: the team is small and comfortable with each other. Harold Scudder, the leader, "looks at the overall picture," "sets the priorities," and "does the choreography." In spite of the highly constrained nature of the writing that they do and the many levels of review to which their work is subjected, these writers find their collaborative experience "satisfying" and "challenging." Though each started out in some area of engineering, they moved into technical writing out of choice, not necessity. One team member said, "As an engineer, I always have to write . . . and all my life, words and language have been important. I enjoy words."

These writers also stressed the satisfaction that comes from the broadest form of collaboration their work calls for: establishing direct ties with one primary audience — those people around the world who operate and maintain their equipment. Ironically, they are able to establish this collaborative bond through the constraints imposed by their highly controlled language. Through it they create a text that readers in, say, Nepal, can use in constructing meaning. "We put things in our manuals that other people do not . . . but we do it because people need it, not only those people who will write the marketing information, but the people in the field who need to understand how it is supposed to work and how to fix it. We concentrate on writing for the end user." Thus in the work of this collaborative team, through reading and writing, readers and writers interanimate one another.

A Chemist Collaborating in Government-Funded Research

We asked George Irving, member of the American Institute of Chemists, retired research director of the United States Department of Agriculture, and a very active consultant/writer, if he could recall a particularly unsatisfying group-writing experience.

> I would say one group-writing project I put a great deal of work into was an evaluation of the research program of the Department of Agriculture before I became administrator. We called it a committee on research evaluation and came out with a core report. It took us the better part of a year. We [all the bureau heads] spent an awful lot of time together discussing what the research program of the department was and what it should be, and we wrote a strong report saying all these things. It was largely ignored. The Secretary's office, for whom it was done, chose to ignore it completely. That was a major disappointment to everybody.

Irving's comments highlight two typical problems. The first, disappointment or dissatisfaction when the document fails to achieve goals or make an impact, applies to single-authored texts as well as to documents written collaboratively. The second problem, time ("It took us the better part of a year.") is mentioned frequently as a drawback to collaborative writing. Certainly Irving, whose long career has called for many different kinds of collaboration, is very much aware of this problem. Collaborative writing, he says, is "a slow way, a ponderous way," to get things done. In spite of this drawback, he says: "I don't know of a better way to tap the expertise in your organization. If you presume you know enough to answer all questions, then you don't need an organization at all. But if you have an organization you'd better use it, work through all the stages and all the people involved. I don't know of any other way to tap all the information you have available in preparing a statement."

Irving should know. While administrator of the Agriculture Research Service from 1963 to 1971, he supervised 16,000 people in 400 locations. This position demanded at least three different types of collaboration. Letters and other kinds of correspondence would be drafted by a wide variety of individuals, often after conversations with Irving. These letters would "sediment their way up and go through various rewrites until eventually I would sign it if I liked it." Another kind of collaboration involved preparing speeches, which he frequently had to give, and statements for the press or for various organizations. For these occasions, Irving and his group of assistants would "talk extensively about what I wanted to say; then they would prepare a draft, and I would go over it with them, and that would go through a couple of cycles until we got what we wanted." Even with such a carefully crafted document, Irving said, he had to remain flexible and responsive to particular audiences. "On some occasions when I got to the site of action and took a look at the audience and got the smell of the grease paint and all the rest of it, I threw the thing away and did something else entirely." On such occasions, Irving often relied on earlier conversations with his assistants to "invent" appropriate new material. A third kind of collaborative writing — "perhaps even more important" — involved preparing testimony for appearances before Congress. For these appearances, Irving typically worked with "fiscal types" and "legal reviewers" in addition to his assistants.

For most of his career, Irving has acted as the leader in collaborative situations. And while he acknowledges the importance of leadership in effective group work, he likened the job to that of a "master of ceremonies," whose task "is like the person that stands beside the cement mixer; his job is to keep the stuff going down the chute. So . . . patience is probably the greatest virtue and then not necessarily wisdom but the ability to sit there long enough until the right answer comes up."

Patience is a virtue Irving had to call on in what he described to us as his longest collaborative effort. As consultant to the Federation of American Societies for Experimental Biology, Irving was asked to head up a team charged with evaluating the world's literature on all food additives — some 540 substances. The project took twelve years. In this effort, Irving assembled a group of fifteen — all experts "in practically all the fields needed for a thorough examination of additives — physiologists, biochemists, pharmacologists, allergists, nutritionists." When he identified "a few gaps," they added "a pediatrician and an oncologist and a food technologist." The large group seemed necessary to the task but went against the grain with Irving. As he said, "A group gets pretty big after you have more than three. After that you are working with a *gang*."

Nevertheless, Irving found this particular collaborative venture exciting and satisfying. Schedules presented a major problem since the group needed to meet "once a month for the first eight years" and "once every two months after that." Group members (usually two or three) carried out research and massive literature reviews and prepared drafts for the group. Initial drafts "were revised in the course of the sit-down meetings of the whole group." These were then "rewritten by our support staff [six professionals] and repolished and sent out for mail review. Quite a system, if you can imagine. We had 540 substances that were being reviewed and massive numbers of drafts in the air at all times, at all different stages."

When semifinal drafts were ready, the whole group went over them page by page, line by line. The work was very tedious and often controversial. If the group could not agree on precise wording, they talked the issue out until they all agreed "on the sense — what the group was willing to do." Then Irving "had the job of synthesizing it into language which again had to be approved by the whole group. It seems impossible, but we got there." After twelve years — twice as much time as Irving and the Federation had anticipated — all members became signatories to the report, which the FDA then used to make numerous decisions on additives, including such substances as MSG, sulphites, and caffeine. In retrospect, Irving says that he "and the whole group" enjoyed the effort. "I think we were surprised really that we could get that many people to stay together for twelve years on this rather rigorous business. We were all busy people — university professors and so forth — but once into this I think we were all just as immersed and enthusiastic as we could be."

In this brief glimpse of collaborative work among members of the chemistry profession, we were unable to speak with other team members whose perceptions — particularly of the enormous twelve-year project — might well have differed from Irving's. From his perspective as leader, however, Irving clearly felt the advantages of collaboration outweighed the disadvantages. He attributed his success at collaboration at least partially to "a natural extension of [my] writing efforts." Like most of the collaborative writers we interviewed, Irving reported a strong interest in language and communication, especially in writing. An assistant editor for an undergraduate publication, Irving went on to "write more newsletters for more different organizations than I can remember." The best way to become a writer — or a collaborative writer — is, in Irving's view, "to go at it and write. The more you write, the more you will find you are able to write and really communicate, work well, with people. If you don't write anything, then nobody can tell who you are. So — a lot of writing. No substitute for it."

A Manager of a Sanitary Authority

Several of Dick Miller's responses to our first two questionnaires intrigued us, so we were pleased when this member of the International City Management Association and manager of a sanitary authority (special district) in southern Oregon agreed to an interview. Miller's responses to our survey had been surprising in two respects. Unlike most respondents, even those who rated collaborative writing as productive and satisfying, Miller indicated that he could not list a single disadvantage to collaborative writing. Furthermore, again unlike most respondents, Miller noted that he had received substantial training that directly contributed to the effectiveness of his current on-the-job collaborative writing.

We began by asking Miller to describe the training he had received and to clarify how it had helped prepare him for collaborative writing tasks. As a preamble to his response, Miller detailed his long and successful career. This career began — and continued for twenty-seven years — in the air force. During this time Miller received extensive training in professional schools — "Squadron Officers' School of the air university, that sort of thing." He also continued his university studies, earning undergraduate degrees in chemistry from Boston University and in engineering from the University of Illinois and a master's degree in business administration from the University of Chicago. His formal education was sponsored by the United States Air Force.

Miller felt strongly that all of his educational experience had contributed to his current productivity and satisfaction with collaborative writing. He credited the air force with first enabling him to function well in groups: "In Squadron Officers' School you were organized as a group when you first arrived there . . . and you did everything as a group: group problem solving, group writing; everything was the group. . . . You wrote things — even reports — as a group." But Miller also cited his undergraduate report writing class at the University of Illinois and his engineering classes where, he said, "we had to work together and write up the experiments as a group, which was good." Finally, Miller commented on the helpfulness of his MBA classes at the University of Chicago, where (in the mid-sixties) he studied organization and group theory. By that time Miller "had been in several command positions and organizations, fairly large ones." Unlike many who return to the university after substantial practical experience, Miller found his studies both relevant and stimulating: "My professors had damn good ideas."

Dick Miller retired from the air force in 1970, and he spent the next five years as the city manager of a small town in Oregon. Finally, he signed on as manager of one of Oregon's special districts, a form of local government. His special district, a sanitary authority, is responsible for developing and overseeing such potentially controversial projects as the construction of new sewer systems. "Every one of our projects," Miller notes, "vexes somebody. Constructing new sewers and sewer systems costs money."

Miller's staff is small. The total number of employees is eighteen (this includes construction and maintenance staff). Miller works most closely with four people: the heads of the engineering, maintenance, and financial services departments plus his executive secretary. In the course of their work Miller and his staff write a variety of documents: reports for their governing board, letters, memos, speeches — whatever is necessary to get the job done and to maintain good relations with the public.

Miller's approach to his job as manager is pragmatic: "We have a goal of putting out a project that will do the job at the least cost." And so is his approach to on-the-job writing. Miller and his colleagues collaborate when they need to — which turns out to be about once a week. As Bill Corrin, director of financial services, noted in a brief interview: "We don't have any formal procedure [for group writing]. We just get together those people involved. We discuss the issues, try to get input from each individual as to how we should respond to the problem. Then one of us takes on or is assigned the responsibility of actively formulating a response. It is that simple." Corrin, an accountant who had previously worked in a savings and loan institution, noted that when he first began working at the sanitary authority he felt somewhat uneasy about Miller's group-oriented management style: "If it were up to me, I'd probably not do it [work collaboratively with others] as often." He credited the group's productivity and good relations to Miller's effective leadership and especially to his ability to motivate his co-workers. "He has a natural ability to motivate people to do things. That is probably the biggest factor . . . Dick's approachable and gets people together, and I guess he just encourages you to participate. . . . [He also] makes you feel that you have contributed something . . . that is probably the prime motivator."

When we questioned Miller about his strategies for managing collaborative writing, his comments suggested that Corrin's assessment of his goals and methods was accurate. In talking about the collaborative writing that he and his colleagues do, Miller took a pragmatic, task-oriented approach. When we asked him if he had a different sense of ownership or satisfaction when he wrote alone, rather than with others, Miller responded: "I don't think about that much. [For me] the satisfaction comes when the chairman of our governing board says 'You have done a great job.' That is the satisfaction. I don't think about private authorship or anything like that; I just want to know if I did a good job."

Similarly, when we asked Miller if he approached a writing task that he would complete on his own differently from one requiring collaboration, Miller felt there was no distinction; indeed, he seemed surprised by the question. "I do the same thing whether I am working with a group or by myself. You still have to pull stuff together that you need to write from. And whether you get it from people or several publications — whatever you are working from — you have to do the same thing."

Like many executives, Miller relies heavily on his secretary, who in fact plays a significant role in the collaborative writing that occurs in his office. Glenna Johnston, Miller's executive secretary, does — as many secretaries do — much more than type, file, and handle office administration. Miller commented on the importance of her role, indicating that he relies on Johnston heavily not just for correction and editing but also for substantive comments. "Glenna got here a few months before I did, and we have worked closely together since then. If she thinks that something should be changed — I don't mean a misspelling but an idea — she is not bashful at all about mentioning it. I never get excited about that. And I always look at her comments. Ninety percent of the time I agree with her, and 10 percent I don't. And she accepts that: there's no problem there."

At times, in fact, Johnston coordinates the team's efforts or writes documents, such as environmental statements, that draw heavily upon research or boilerplate materials. "She puts [many documents] together except the engineering and the financial data; she gets this from Bill or Gary. . . . She also does a lot of resolution writing and things like this." In describing the review process that he uses even for single-authored documents, Miller carefully noted Johnston's contribution: "I pick their [his staff's] brains and then I do the writing myself. After I get it written I will . . . route it to the proper people to get feedback. Glenna [then] has a go at it, and she will come back with suggestions. Then we put it in final form. The process works very well."

(Johnston's role in the collaborative writing that occurred in this office intrigued us. Consequently, we regret that we were able to have only a brief conversation with Johnston, who indicated that in general she was very satisfied with her job. In fact, she enjoyed its variety and collaborative atmosphere a great deal. She did indicate, however, that she believed her current title did not accurately reflect her numerous responsibilities.)

Unlike Bill Qualls and Albert Bernstein, who had obviously spent a great deal of time reflecting on the collaborative writing process and determining how better to manage that process, Dick Miller seemed to take collaborative writing for granted. Collaborating with others on reports, letters, memos: all this was simply an efficient way to get the job done. Miller was highly reflective about the larger questions of group dynamics and decision making, however. Two of his final comments to us reflect his approach to both collaborative writing and organizational management: "There is a time to speak and a time to listen. There is always time to do a job right."

A Research Associate at the Office of Educational Research and Information

Like Bill Qualls, the city planner with whom we began this series of snapshots of collaborative writers at work, Eleanor Chiogioji is not a typical member of her professional organization, the Modern Language Association. Chiogioji received a Ph.D. in English from the University of Maryland in 1981 — academic training that would most obviously prepare her for a career in teaching. And Chiogioji had, in fact, taught a variety of writing and literature classes at the University of Maryland while completing her degree and during the years immediately following. But rather than pursue a job in a college or university, Chiogioji accepted a position at the Office of Educational Research and Improvement (OERI).

The OERI is a large federally funded program designed to improve the quality of education in the United States. The OERI comprises five major program areas: Information Services, Library Programs, the National Center for Education Statistics, Programs for the Improvement of Practice, and the Office of Research. Chiogioji is employed as a senior research associate in the latter program area, which is itself subdivided into four units. Chiogioji works in the Learning and Instruction Division of the Office of Research. This division operates with the following mandate:

> The Learning and Instruction Division supports basic and applied research for which learning and its relationship to the instructional process are the central focus. It addresses such issues as how children acquire information, values, and character, and develop their knowledge of content areas; how human thought processes develop; how children develop intellectually and become mature citizens; and what the implications of these findings might be for instruction. It also addresses the efficacy and

efficiency of various instructional practices; examines interaction among teachers and students within classrooms; and studies the role of textbooks, workbooks, tests, and terminology in the instructional process. The work of the Division is currently focused on four major areas: content, learning, instruction, and assessment.

As this brief review of the organization of the OERI indicates, Chiogioji's research division is part of a very large, complex bureaucracy. In fiscal year 1984, the OERI had a budget of $154.9 million to operate its ten federally authorized programs.

Unlike many of those we interviewed, Chiogioji was at the start of her career. In the summer of 1986, she was completing her second year at the OERI. Many of the colleagues with whom she worked most closely were also relatively new to their positions. Chiogioji commented that she had felt particularly responsible for one collaborative project because "this was my third institutional grant competition, and my two colleagues had never been through one at all."

Chiogioji's position is clearly a demanding one. At the time of our interview she was acting as the monitor (or administrator) for one of her division's major programs, the Center for the Study of Writing, and she was also coordinating a major research grants competition in reading and literacy. When we asked her to describe a typical collaborative writing project, Chiogioji chose this grants competition, one still under way. She prefaced her remarks, however, by noting the important role that collaborative writing plays in all of her division's activities: "We could hardly get along here without any kind of collaborative writing. Everything we do here gets bounced back and forth — brainstorming, drafting, revisions. We're always working together." In fact, the process she described for us was collaborative from beginning to end, from the early conceptualization of the project, through the exploratory, drafting, and revision stages, and down to the final negotiations with superiors over the wording and the legality of the scope of work.

The research grants competition in reading and literacy, like many with which Chiogioji works, involved more than a year of effort. We spoke with Chiogioji during the summer of 1986, and she indicated that she and her colleagues had begun conceptualizing the project the previous January. After they had met a number of times independently, they invited a panel of national reading experts to meet in February in order to consider relevant research issues. Once this group had met, Chiogioji and three colleagues — her division director and two other research associates — met to "distill the panel's discussion." Together, this group of four individuals wrote an analysis of the panel's conclusions and drafted a memo with their own recommendations to the assistant secretary of education.

> We came in and we worked ten to twelve hours a day, including Saturdays and Sundays — just constantly. . . . We fed each other ideas. Anne, who is a reading person, would do some sort of writing draft, xerox it, and we'd all discuss it. We'd take what the panel of reading experts said

and our ideas and through that — just that constant going back and forth — we came out with a fairly good research agenda for the new reading center. We also came out with the research topics for the reading and literacy research grants competition.

In commenting on difficulties inherent in such a complex task, Chiogioji stressed the importance of the group developing a strong consensus, since they would bear joint responsibility for the recommendations they submitted to the assistant secretary of education.

After this task was completed and the memo accepted, the group faced another major task: drafting the scope of work. This part of the larger project took several months to complete. "We organized this project differently. We divided up tasks. We gave Conrad a lot of the boilerplate parts to put together because he was the only nonreading person, and he's got a wonderful legal mind. So he did that. Ann and I worked on the research areas, as well as the introduction and rationale. Our director came from his end, which was instruction and teacher education."

At the time of our interview, Chiogioji still had many months of work before this particular project would be completed. In describing the most recent work and what lay ahead, she again stressed the important role collaboration plays in this complex enterprise. After applications are received, for example, a review panel meets to evaluate them; the OERI team sits in on their discussions and later must synthesize them. "We have to be sure," Chiogioji says, that all team members "heard the same thing and that all of our notes meshed so that we could get a coherent evaluation for the secretary to read." In summing up, Chiogioji remarked that "the entire process of the competition is collaborative — the decisions and everything. But primarily the writing, because no one person can do this." Indeed, the pragmatic necessity of working collaboratively with members of her team was very clear to us, both from Chiogioji's comments and from the sample documents she shared with us. Chiogioji is herself a strong writer with an extensive knowledge of language and a highly refined sense of style. And yet she needs the full efforts of all team members. As she said, "It's impossible for any one person to complete this writing task alone."

Because of Chiogioji's advanced literary training, we were curious to know how she felt about the collaborative writing she did. Clearly, such a large and complex project could only be completed by a group of people working closely together. But did Chiogioji feel differently — experience less of a sense of ownership — about collaborative writing versus writing she completed alone? Her answer surprised us. "I hadn't even thought about it. No, I can't honestly say that I do feel differently about work I write alone or with others. I'm just as proud of what we produce together here. A lot of time that's a lot richer because we have multiple perspectives." In exploring this question further, Chiogioji speculated that her satisfaction and sense of ownership of collaboratively written documents may derive in part from the control that her group retains over the final form of the documents they produce. The writing that her group completes is reviewed by others, but because

Chiogioji and her colleagues are recognized as experts in their fields, the documents come back to them for negotiation and final approval. Thus far in her career, Chiogioji indicated, she had been satisfied with the result of negotiations over substantive and stylistic issues.

When we asked Chiogioji to cite the main advantages of collaborative writing, she emphasized the conceptual fruitfulness of working with others: "One advantage of working with others is that you get multiple perspectives and more feedback. You throw out something or somebody throws out something, but you agree or disagree — and this is where the value comes up. It opens up another line for you to pursue." Such interaction, though valuable, can exact its own price however — the reduction of time for individual reflection and analysis. "When I'm engaged in that kind of give-and-take in a group setting, I don't have the leisure to follow my own line of reasoning as far as I want to. And that can disturb me. I like to see where my thoughts would lead." Chiogioji also cited another problem that can occur with group writing: stylistic difficulties resulting from varying styles and levels of writing ability. Finally, Chiogioji noted that occasionally group members can lose the big picture and get bogged down worrying about minor points.

Chiogioji had clearly thought a great deal about the next question we raised: "What traits characterize an effective collaborative writer?" "One of the challenges of collaborative writing is being able to listen so you can synthesize different viewpoints. You don't always come to an agreement, but you have to be able to cooperate enough in that collaborative arrangement to be able to trust each other's opinions and to be able to compromise. It's not always easy to compromise, especially in front of other people. . . . You also must be fair but tactful, and you've got to be flexible." Compromising can be especially difficult, she noted, given our society's traditional emphasis on individualism: "We're such a competitive society. Even if we get together to play bridge, we're at each other's throats." Chiogioji suggested that training in listening and in group dynamics might enable individuals to collaborate more effectively. And what advice would she give to other writers? Her answer summarized themes touched on in almost all our interviews: "Learn to listen. If you don't listen, you can't succeed. Good collaboration rests on a very tenuous relationship. In any kind of group work, there's got to be a lot of give-and-take, and sometimes a lot of giving. And here's the rub: it should have nothing to do with egos."

As with our other interviewees, listening to Eleanor Chiogioji left us with much to ponder and with growing appreciation for the complex tasks in which these writers and their colleagues are engaged.

SCENES OF COLLABORATION: REFLECTIONS

In the opening paragraphs of this chapter, we noted that we wanted to contrast the conventional image of writers at work — an image that privileges the solitary writer working in isolation — with a different picture, that of writers planning, gathering information, drafting, and revising collaboratively. The scenes of writing that we have described thus far clearly and powerfully challenge that conventional image of the writer working alone in a garret, a well-appointed study, or a library. The writers we interviewed may have private offices (they may even, as Albert Bernstein does, work at home), but their scenes of writing are peopled, busy — full of the give-and-take of conversation and debate.

The scenes of writing depicted in this chapter can help us re-situate both the writer and the writing process, but these scenes have their own limitations. They are, first of all, little more than snapshots of writers at work. Because of both time and methodological limitations — we conducted interviews, not case studies — our descriptions provide neither the depth nor the critical perspective characteristic of case studies and ethnographies. Furthermore, photographs, even the most casual snapshots, are composed, not found. A photographer looks through the camera's viewfinder and in so doing creates the scene that will later emerge. Photographers know that what they exclude from an image is at least as important as what they include. The photograph's frame emphasizes, but it isolates as well.

As researchers, the lens through which we looked at collaborative writing in action was, of course, our research design. This design specified that we limit our observations to members of seven professional associations, representing the humanities, social sciences, sciences, business, government, and industry. Our research design enabled us to gain much useful information about the writing done by individuals in these professional associations — information we will highlight in the latter part of this chapter. And it also enabled us to identify individuals who found collaborative writing both productive and satisfying, and who were willing to share their experiences with us.

But our research design also excluded other realities. Readers will undoubtedly have noted, for instance, that there are very few women in the scenes we have presented, and there are also no minorities. With the exception of the Modern Language Association and the Society for Technical Communication, members of the seven professional associations we studied were, perhaps not surprisingly, predominantly male (75 percent male; 25 percent female). Furthermore, respondents typically were well advanced in their careers. Their perspective is that of leaders, those who set the tone and establish the explicit and implicit protocol for collaborative endeavors.

Almost completely absent from the scenes of writing depicted in this chapter, then, are those who play supportive, not leadership, roles in collaboration. These individuals — persons such as Glenna Johnston and the professional staff who worked with Irving and his colleagues — have their own stories to tell about collaborative writing — stories that do not appear in these pages. This absence disturbs us. Yet we are aware that it is our research lens itself that has enabled us to see so clearly that which is absent from the scenes of writing portrayed here. Future research on collaborative writing will, we hope, endeavor to bring these submerged elements more clearly into view.

We do not present these portraits of collaborative writers at work as models for imitation. Our own reading of the interviews presented here most strongly emphasizes the need to problematize descriptions that could, if read naively, seem "neutral" or "objective." We agree with Richard Ohmann, who notes in *Politics of Letters* that the process of interviewing emphasizes with particular clarity the fact that "the writer cannot dissolve into neutrality." As anyone who has worked with transcripts of interviews knows, transcripts may indeed present "the raw moment of the interview itself," but they inevitably "make the event appear inchoate . . . any attempt to rearrange and highlight the material, to delete what seems trivial or irrelevant, to paraphrase and organize . . . any such attempt at a deeper fidelity brings the writer into the act as interpreter and judge, as sure as if he or she comments explicitly on the interview and its subject." Any discussion of interviewing inevitably, Ohmann notes, "problematize[s] any naive standard of objectivity" (255).

The scenes of collaboration we present in this chapter are crafted visions, not slices of life, or raw moments of reality. These snapshots of collaborative writers at work have, we believe, great value. Articulate, experienced, productive writers like Chiogioji, Bernstein, Miller, and Qualls can help us better understand how collaborative writing works and how to make it work more effectively. But in considering these interviews, we hope that readers will listen not only to what these individuals say but to what they do not say.

Someone reading these interviews uncritically might, for example, pass over many of our interviewees' strong emphasis on efficiency — on collaborative writing as a means to an end — as a simple point of fact. Our interviewees' pragmatic approach to language in general and to collaborative writing in particular was so prevalent and so deep-seated that it came to represent for us another purloined letter: an assumption so deeply ingrained as to appear commonsensical and thus hidden from view. This goal-driven pragmatism tends to view language primarily as a tool, a means of getting a job done, one that in turn suggests that language itself is neutral, a conduit through which a kind of "pure" information can be transferred from writer to readers. Collaborative writers aiming pragmatically at efficiency do not have the occasion to consider the way language constructs varying economic or political agendas, which are in turn ideologically freighted. And yet this highly pragmatic view of language, to our surprise, coincided in almost every case with a marked appreciation, and at times even reverence, for language and its power. The potential contradiction between these two views of language represented for us an illuminating, though complex and largely hidden, site of struggle. In Bakhtinian terms, these interviews contain multiple and competing "voices" of language, the heteroglossic nature of which seemed not to concern our interviewees. (It perhaps goes without saying that the highly pragmatic view of language held by those we interviewed is also at odds with the view widely held in our profession — of writing as a means of discovery, of getting in touch with the self, of coming to know rather than to report.)

The pragmatism reflected in our interviewees' dominant view of language also no doubt accounts for their tendency to accept constraints, which raises for us a number of questions. Because they help to achieve the goal, a controlled language of only 2,000 words or a tightly controlled CQM chart received almost universal praise from their users. As the interviews reveal, such constraints are viewed as exceedingly efficient tools whose careful guidelines in a sense free their users to attend to other important matters. But they also constrain and regiment in ways that the users felt unnecessary to explore or interrogate. Nor did our interviewees criticize collaborative writing; as successful collaborators, they tended to accept the construct almost as a given. We are aware, however, that some collaborative writing situations are far from productive or satisfying and that, indeed, collaborative settings can reify traditional patterns of power and authority and can isolate rather than bring people together.

Finally, because of our own constraints of time and funding, we were unable to learn from these interviewees much about the institutional context in which they wrote. For the most part they seemed to take their contexts for granted. We and our readers, however, cannot afford to do the same. By presenting these snapshots, we are not implying that we can fruitfully study collaborative writers in isolation or that we can bracket questions of purpose and politics. I. A. Richards once defined "meaning" as that which is missing from any statement, picture, or context. We offer these vignettes, then, not simply for what they record but, more importantly, for what they suggest about that which is missing.

SCENES OF COLLABORATION: BACKGROUNDINGS

When we first began our FIPSE-funded study of the collaborative writing practices of members of seven professional associations, we had no idea what conclusions our data would reveal. We did not know what the pieces of our particular puzzle looked like; we did not, in fact, even have a picture on a box to go by. Since that time, research on collaborative writing has increased substantially. In 1984, for example, only one presentation at the Conference on College Composition and Communication — our own — focused on collaborative writing. In 1989 an entire strand of sessions investigated this topic.

As a consequence of this growing interest in collaborative writing, the context for this report on our two surveys has shifted considerably. When we developed these surveys, we were concerned primarily with providing evidence that collaborative writing is a fact of life for members of these seven professional associations. Most teachers and researchers in composition now recognize that individuals in a wide variety of professions regularly write collaboratively. But many other questions remain unanswered and in some cases unrecognized.

The results of our two surveys enable us to provide useful information about the collaborative writing practices of the members of the seven associations we studied. The results of these surveys, however, have been more generative than conclusive. Rather than providing definitive answers, the surveys have enabled us to articulate the probing questions that guided not only our interviews but our continuing theoretical and pedagogical explorations as well.

Research Methods

The three-tiered research project this chapter reports on began with our desire to survey a random sample of members of professional organizations representing the sciences, applied sciences, social sciences, information sciences, humanities, business, and government. We chose the seven organizations (six during the early stages of research; a seventh, the Modern Language Association, was added when we secured additional funds) on the basis of these criteria:

1. the organization was a major one for the field
2. membership was national and included both academic and nonacademic professionals
3. membership lists were public or could be made available to us
4. the president or other official representative of the organization agreed to cooperate with our plan of research

   Using these criteria as guides, we chose the following groups:

   The American Consulting Engineers Council

   The American Institute of Chemists

   The American Psychological Association

   The International City Management Association

   The Modern Language Association

   The Professional Services Management Association

   The Society for Technical Communication

Survey 1. We then developed a cover letter and a survey questionnaire to be sent to a random sample of 200 members of each organization. The questionnaire went through several pilot studies, one with members of the Oregon State University Survey Research Department, one with a group from the Environmental Protection Agency, and another with writers at CH2M Hill, an engineering consulting firm. After sending the initial survey, we followed up with a postcard reminder and later with a second copy of our letter and questionnaire. Our goals in this initial survey were relatively simple: to determine the frequency, types, and occasions of collaborative writing among members of these groups. The response rate for this first survey was just under 50 percent.

Survey 2. For the second, more in-depth survey, we chose a purposeful rather than random sample of twelve members of each organization that had responded to our first survey. In choosing the twelve individuals, we looked for the following characteristics:

1. experience and satisfaction with collaborative writing
2. variety of collaborative writing experience
3. willingness to participate in the research
4. diversity in age, years on the job, geographic location, and sex

This second, much longer and more open-ended survey also went through several pilot stages of development and benefited from the criticisms of many writers. The eventual response rate for this survey was 99 percent.

With the help of statisticians at Oregon State and the University of British Columbia, we subjected these data to a number of statistical analyses, including F- and T-tests, chi-square analysis, and multivariate analysis.

Results.   The mean responses of all seven groups combined, for both Survey 1 and Survey 2, appear on the following pages.

SURVEY 1
SURVEY OF WRITING IN THE PROFESSIONS

This survey is intended to identify and define the nature, types, and frequency of writing done in your profession. For the purposes of this survey, writing includes any of the activities that lead to a completed written product. These activities include written or spoken brainstorming, outlining or note-taking, organizational planning, drafting, revising, and editing. Written products include any piece of writing, from notes, directions, or forms to reports and published materials.

1. In general, what percentage of your professional time is spent in some kind of writing activity?

   44 percent

2. What percentage of the time you spend in writing activities is devoted to each of the following? (Your figures should total 100 percent.)

	Percent
a. Brainstorming and similar idea-generating activities	14 %
b. Note-taking	13 %
c. Organizational planning	13 %
d. Drafting (including dictating)	32 %
e. Revising	15 %
f. Editing (including proofreading)	13 %
Total	100 %

3. Technology is changing the way many people write. Please indicate the percentage of the time spent in writing activities that you use a word processor.

   28 percent

4. The situations in which people in the professions write may vary considerably. Please indicate the percentage of the time you spend in writing activities that is spent writing alone or as part of a team or group. (Your figures should total 100 percent.)

	Percent
a. Writing alone	82 %
b. Writing with one other person	9 %
c. Writing with a small group (2–5 persons)	7 %
d. Writing with a large group (6 or more persons)	2 %
Total	100 %

5. How important do you think effective writing is to the successful execution of your job? (Circle one number.)

(86%) 1 very important
(12%) 2 important
(2%) 3 not too important
(0%) 4 not at all important

6. Please indicate how frequently, in general, you work on the following types of writing, distinguishing between writing done alone and with one or more persons. (Circle one number for each.)

	Very Often	Often	Occasionally	Never
A. Letters				
a. Alone	1 (53%)	2 (23%)	3 (21%)	4 (3%)
b. With one or more persons	1 (1%)	2 (5%)	3 (43%)	4 (51%)
B. Memos				
a. Alone	1 (49%)	2 (24%)	3 (23%)	4 (4%)
b. With one or more persons	1 (1%)	2 (7%)	3 (40%)	4 (52%)
C. Short Reports				
a. Alone	1 (38%)	2 (29%)	3 (28%)	4 (5%)
b. With one or more persons	1 (2%)	2 (16%)	3 (43%)	4 (39%)
D. Long Reports				
a. Alone	1 (5%)	2 (21%)	3 (40%)	4 (14%)
b. With one or more persons	1 (4%)	2 (16%)	3 (43%)	4 (37%)
E. Professional Articles and Essays				
a. Alone	1 (21%)	2 (13%)	3 (37%)	4 (29%)
b. With one or more persons	1 (2%)	2 (8%)	3 (29%)	4 (61%)
F. Popular Articles and Essays				
a. Alone	1 (8%)	2 (4%)	3 (23%)	4 (65%)
b. With one or more persons	1 (1%)	2 (1%)	3 (12%)	4 (86%)
G. User Manuals or Other Detailed Instructions				
a. Alone	1 (14%)	2 (12%)	3 (35%)	4 (39%)
b. With one or more persons	1 (5%)	2 (11%)	3 (30%)	4 (54%)
H. Newsletters, Bulletins, or In-House Publications				
a. Alone	1 (10%)	2 (15%)	3 (36%)	4 (39%)
b. With one or more persons	1 (5%)	2 (9%)	3 (29%)	4 (57%)

I. **Case Studies**

		Very Often	Often	Occasionally	Never
a. Alone		1 (8%)	2 (9%)	3 (20%)	4 (63%)
b. With one or more persons		1 (1%)	2 (5%)	3 (18%)	4 (76%)

J. **Proposals for Contracts and Grants**

a. Alone		1 (14%)	2 (23%)	3 (32%)	4 (31%)
b. With one or more persons		1 (9%)	2 (21%)	3 (29%)	4 (41%)

K. **Lecture/Oral Presentation Notes**

a. Alone		1 (33%)	2 (20%)	3 (35%)	4 (12%)
b. With one or more persons		1 (1%)	2 (5%)	3 (33%)	4 (61%)

L. **Instructional or Course-Related Materials**

a. Alone		1 (23%)	2 (15%)	3 (31%)	4 (31%)
b. With one or more persons		1 (2%)	2 (7%)	3 (32%)	4 (59%)

M. **Books and Monographs**

a. Alone		1 (9%)	2 (8%)	3 (17%)	4 (66%)
b. With one or more persons		1 (1%)	2 (3%)	3 (16%)	4 (80%)

N. **Other**

a. Alone
(Please specify _____) 1 (31%) 2 (26%) 3 (14%) 4 (29%)

b. With one or more persons
(Please specify _____) 1 (9%) 2 (20%) 3 (30%) 4 (41%)

7. Collaboration in writing can, of course, take many forms. If you have written with a coauthor or as part of a group, please indicate how frequently you use each of the following organizational patterns for that writing. (Circle one number for each.) *If you never write with one or more persons, please skip to question 11.*

Organizational Patterns	Very Often	Often	Occasionally	Never
A. Team or group plans and outlines. Each member drafts a part. Team or group compiles the parts and revises the whole.	1 (7%)	2 (15%)	3 (45%)	4 (33%)
B. Team or group plans and outlines. One member writes the entire draft. Team or group revises.	1 (5%)	2 (21%)	3 (40%)	4 (34%)
C. One member plans and writes draft. Group or team revises.	1 (8%)	2 (23%)	3 (40%)	4 (29%)
D. One person plans and writes draft. This draft is submitted to one or more persons who revise the draft without consulting the writer of the first draft.	1 (3%)	2 (7%)	3 (20%)	4 (70%)

E. Team or group plans and writes draft. This draft is submitted to one or more persons who revise the draft without consulting the writers of the first draft. 1 (1%) 2 (2%) 3 (16%) 4 (81%)

F. One member assigns writing tasks. Each member carries out individual tasks. One member compiles the parts and revises the whole. 1 (6%) 2 (15%) 3 (40%) 4 (39%)

G. One person dictates. Another person transcribes and revises. 1 (2%) 2 (6%) 3 (17%) 4 (75%)

8. The list of organizational patterns described in question 7 is not exhaustive. If you use another organizational pattern, please describe it in the following space.

9. In general, how productive do you find writing as part of a team or group as compared to writing alone? (Circle one number.)

(13%) 1 very productive

(45%) 2 productive

(38%) 3 not too productive

(4%) 4 not at all productive

10. If you write with one or more persons, who most often assumes final responsibility for the written product? (Circle one number.)

(13%) 1 each member of the group or team shares equal responsibility.

(40%) 2 one member of the group or team takes responsibility.

(37%) 3 the head of the group takes responsibility.

(6%) 4 a superior or group of superiors outside the group takes responsibility.

(4%) 5 other (please specify _____)

11. Which one of the following best describes the type of employer for whom you work? (Circle one number.)

(38%) 1 business and industry

(24%) 2 college or university

(17%) 3 local, state, or federal government

(15%) 4 self-employed

(6%) 5 other (please specify _____)

12. About how many people are employed by your institution or company?

___4,373___ number

13. And how many are employed at your branch, division, or department of that institution or company?

___177___ number

14. How many years have you been doing the type of work characteristic of your present job?

___15___ years

15. Please state your title and briefly describe your major job responsibilities.

_____ title

_____ responsibilities

16. Please give the year of your birth.

___1937___ year

17. Are you: (Circle one.)

(75%)   1   male
(25%)   2   female

18. Is there anything else you can tell us about the writing you do in your profession that will help us better understand the nature, types, or frequency of that writing?

(Thank you very much for your cooperation.)

Survey 2
Survey of Writing in the Professions
Stage II: Group Writing

This survey explores the dynamics and demands of group writing in your profession. For the purposes of this survey, writing includes any of the activities that lead to a completed written product. These activities include written and spoken brainstorming, outlining, note-taking, organizational planning, drafting, revising, and editing. Written products include any piece of writing, from notes, directions, and forms to reports and published materials. Group writing includes any writing done in collaboration with one or more persons.

1. In general, do you work with the same person or persons in producing a written document? (Circle one number.)

1   Yes ⟶   (Please indicate the number of persons in this group.)

(35%)   ___6___ Number of persons in group

2   No ⟶   (Please indicate the number of persons in the three groups
            with which you most regularly work.)

   (65%)   3   Number of persons in first group

                        4   Number of persons in second group

                        5   Number of persons in third group

2. Please add any additional comments about the groups with which you work.

3. From the following list, please indicate the four kinds of documents that you
    most typically work on as part of a group, rank ordering them in terms of
    frequency written. (Place one letter in each of the appropriate boxes.)

   J   Most frequently   A. Memos
           written   B. Short reports
                               C. Long reports
   A   Second most   D. Professional articles and essays
           frequently written   E. Popular articles and essays
                               F. User manuals or other detailed
   B   Third most   instructions
           frequently written   G. Newsletters, bulletins, or other
                                in-house publications
   C   Fourth most   H. Letters
           frequently written   I. Case studies
                               J. Proposals for contracts or grants
                             K. Lecture/Oral presentation notes
                             L. Instructional or other course-related
                                materials
                           M. Books and monographs
                           N. Other (Please specify _____)

4. In general, which of the documents cited in question 3 do you find <u>most pro-</u>
    <u>ductive</u> to work on as part of a group, and why? Please refer to all of these
    documents, not just the four documents you most frequently write.

5. In general, which of the documents cited in question 3 do you find <u>least pro-</u>
    <u>ductive</u> to work on as part of a group, and why? Please refer to all of these
    documents, not just the four documents you most frequently write.

6. When you participate in a group writing project, do you generally carry out
    each of the following activities alone, with other group members, or partly alone
    and partly with the group? If you are generally not involved in one or more of
    these activities, please circle 4 for not applicable. (Circle one number for each.)

	Generally Alone	Generally as Part of Group	Partly Alone and Partly with Group	Not Applicable
a. Brainstorming and similar idea-generating activities	1 (5%)	2 (44%)	3 (50%)	4 (1%)
b. Information gathering	1 (33%)	2 (14%)	3 (53%)	4 (0%)
c. Organizational planning	1 (15%)	2 (35%)	3 (46%)	4 (4%)
d. Drafting (including dictating)	1 (63%)	2 (6%)	3 (29%)	4 (2%)
e. Revising	1 (32%)	2 (29%)	3 (39%)	4 (0%)
f. Editing (including proofreading)	1 (56%)	2 (4%)	3 (36%)	4 (4%)

7. Which of these activities (brainstorming, information-gathering, organizational planning, drafting, revising, editing) do you find most productive to perform as part of a group, and why?

8. Which of these activities (brainstorming, information-gathering, organizational planning, drafting, revising, editing) do you find least productive to perform as part of a group, and why?

9. Please indicate the frequency of use of prepared in-house or other "boilerplate" materials used in documents your group or groups produce. Such materials might include standard descriptions of equipment, facilities, staff, processes, or methods that are regularly included in various documents. (Circle one number.)

1	never (please skip to question #10)	(19%)
2	seldom used	(42%)
3	often used	(30%)
4	very often used	(9%)

9a. Approximately how many "boilerplate materials" do you use in a typical document? (Circle one number.)

(5%) 1   "boilerplate materials" comprise 75–100% of a typical document

(14%) 2   "boilerplate materials" comprise 50%–74% of a typical document

(18%) 3   "boilerplate materials" comprise 25%–49% of a typical document

(63%) 4   "boilerplate materials" comprise 0%–24% of a typical document

9b. How productive do you find the use of such in-house or "boilerplate" materials? (Circle one number.)

(26%)   1   very productive

(45%)   2   productive

(28%)   3   not too productive

(1%)   4   not at all productive

9c. Do you have any additional comments about the use or productivity of in-house or "boilerplate" materials in group writing?

10. How often do the group or groups with which you work assign duties for completing a project according to a set plan? (The set plan might specify, for instance, that the group will plan and outline a proposed document together, then divide writing tasks so that each member drafts a part, and then reconvene so that the group can compile and revise the entire document.) (Circle one number.)

1   never (please skip to question #11)   (10%)

2   seldom   (16%)

3   often   (51%)

4   very often   (19%)

5   always   (4%)

10a. When your group or groups follow a set plan to divide duties, who typically assigns the tasks each member of the group will accomplish? (Circle one number.)

(73%)   1   group leader

(1%)   2   superior outside the group

(1%)   3   group member other than leader

(22%)   4   the entire group

(3%)   5   other (please specify _____)

10b. When your group or groups follow a set plan, how productive do you find its use? (Circle one number.)

(31%)   1   very productive

(65%)   2   productive

(4%)   3   not too productive

(0%)   4   not at all productive

10c. Please briefly describe the set plan your group or groups most often use in assigning duties, or attach a copy of the plan with this questionnaire. (After describing this set plan, please skip to question #12.)

11. If the group or groups you write with do <u>not</u> follow a set plan to assign duties, how do you decide how those duties will be divided?

12. When you write as part of a group, how is authorship or credit most often assigned? (Circle one number.)

(40%)   1   to all those who participated in the project

(13%)   2   to the main writer(s)

(6%)   3   to the group leader

(3%)   4   to the writers of each section of the document

(1%)   5   to a superior outside the group

(30%)   6   to the company only (no person is cited as the author)

(7%)   7   other (please specify _____)

13. Are you satisfied or dissatisfied with the way authorship or credit is typically assigned in group writing projects in which you participate?

1   satisfied   (95%)

2   dissatisfied   (5%)

   13a. Please explain why you are satisfied or dissatisfied with the way authorship or credit is typically assigned in group writing projects in which you participate.

14. In your experience, to what extent are members of the group or groups with which you work likely to agree about each of the following areas? If you are generally not involved with one or more of these areas, please circle 5 for not applicable. (Circle one number for each.)

	Very Likely to Agree	Likely to Agree	Likely to Disagree	Very Likely to Disagree	Not Applicable
a. Division of duties	1 (34%)	2 (60%)	3 (1%)	4 (0%)	5 (5%)
b. Research methodology	1 (15%)	2 (64%)	3 (11%)	4 (0%)	5 (10%)
c. Content or substance	1 (11%)	2 (67%)	3 (14%)	4 (8%)	5 (0%)
d. Format or organization of document	1 (18%)	2 (65%)	3 (16%)	4 (0%)	5 (1%)
e. Style	1 (10%)	2 (56%)	3 (29%)	4 (3%)	5 (2%)
f. Grammar, punctuation, or usage	1 (26%)	2 (51%)	3 (14%)	4 (5%)	5 (4%)

g. Credit or
responsibility
for document   1 (40%)   2 (41%)   3 (7%)   4 (1%)   5 (11%)

h. Other   1 (0%)   2 (4%)   3 (4%)   4 (9%)   5 (83%)

Please specify _____

---

15. When the group or groups with which you work come to the revision stage of a project, who most often does the actual revision? (Circle one number.)

(33%) 1 group leader
(9%) 2 group member other than leader
(13%) 3 entire group
(23%) 4 several members of the group
(14%) 5 technical writer or editor within the group
(1%) 6 technical writer or editor outside the group
(7%) 7 other (please specify _____)

16. Please briefly describe the stages of review a group-written document typically goes through from the time the initial draft is complete to the time it is delivered to the intended receiver. (Please include all levels of review — legal, editorial, scientific, technical, etc.)

17. When you are working on a group writing project, how often do you use the following technologies? (Circle one number for each.)

	Very Often	**Often**	**Occasionally**	**Never**
a. Photocopying	1 (77%)	2 (22%)	3 (0%)	4 (1%)
b. Conference phone calls	1 (9%)	2 (14%)	3 (46%)	4 (31%)
c. Teleconferencing	1 (0%)	2 (3%)	3 (15%)	4 (82%)
d. Electronic mail	1 (3%)	2 (9%)	3 (20%)	4 (68%)
e. Computer links	1 (6%)	2 (14%)	3 (31%)	4 (49%)
f. Word processing	1 (80%)	2 (10%)	3 (5%)	4 (5%)
g. Dictaphones	1 (14%)	2 (17%)	3 (26%)	4 (43%)
h. Other	1 (17%)	2 (6%)	3 (12%)	4 (65%)
(Please specify _____)				

18. Have any of the technologies listed in the preceding question affected the writing you typically do as part of a group? (Circle one number.)

1   No   (25%)
2   Yes (75%)

18a. Please describe how any of these technologies have affected your writing.

19. In your experience, what are the three greatest <u>advantages</u> of group writing in your profession?

20. In your experience, what are the three greatest <u>disadvantages</u> of group writing in your profession?

21. Please comment on how your participation in group writing contributes or does not contribute to your overall job satisfaction.

22. What advice would you give to someone in your field about how to write effectively as part of a group?

23. Were you given any on-the-job training to prepare you for the group writing you do? (Circle one number.)

    1   No   (81%)
    2   Yes   (19%)

    23a. Please describe this training and comment on its effectiveness.

24. Do you feel that your high school and college English classes adequately prepared you for the group writing you do in your profession? (Circle one number.)

    1   Yes   (39%)
    2   No   (61%)

    24a. Please comment on how your high school or college English classes might have better prepared you for professional group writing tasks.

25. What degrees, if any, do you hold? Please list the degree (BA, MA, etc.), the major, the year awarded, and the awarding institution.

    Degree   Major   Year   Institution

    _____   _____   _____   _____
    _____   _____   _____   _____
    _____   _____   _____   _____

26. Please add any additional comments that will help us better understand group writing in your profession.

(Thank you for your cooperation.)

Discussion

To establish reliable baseline data, we began by asking some fairly simple questions. To those questions we received unequivocal and straightforward answers. We wanted to know, first of all, how much writing members of these professional organizations did and what importance they attached to writing. Even given the broad definition of writing we posited, their answers surprised us: professionals told us they spent about half their time (44 percent) in some writing-related activity, and 98 percent of them rated writing as important or very important to the successful execution of their jobs. In short, writing counts for these people, and they are doing a lot of it.

Beyond such general information lay our more specific goals. How much of this writing was conducted collaboratively, and how productive did respondents find such collaboration? Answering the first of these questions proved a problem, partly because of a weakness in our first questionnaire and partly because of deep-seated definitions of writing. An early question (4) asked what percentage of time these professionals spent writing alone and what percentage writing as a team or with a group: they reported writing alone 82 percent of the time. The wording of the question and the common-sense view of writing as the physical act of putting pen or typewriter key to paper probably contributed to this anomalous response, for later answers contradicted this one. Further analysis of following questions, particularly those asking how frequently respondents wrote particular types of documents with others, revealed that collaborative writing is a widespread and well established phenomenon among members of these professional organizations, with 87 percent reporting that they sometimes write as members of a team or a group. A member of the American Institute of Chemists epitomized this contradictory response for us: after saying that he wrote alone 100 percent of the time, he later answered an open-ended question by reporting that every one of his numerous publications was co- or group authored. And is such co- and group authorship a productive activity, compared to writing alone? Fifty-eight percent felt that it is productive or very productive; only 4 percent felt it is "not at all productive."

We attempted to explore responses to the question of productivity in open-ended questions in Survey 2 which called for a description of the advantages and disadvantages of collaborative writing. Of the disadvantages cited, perhaps that most often mentioned involved what one engineer called "the tough task of making a common single style from numerous styles." According to our respondents, disagreements about style occur frequently in collaborative writing projects. At times, these conflicts seem to represent major difficulties, particularly, according to another engineer, "when several members of the group have distinct and well-developed individual styles." In other instances, respondents described these disagreements as frustrating but not major problems. One member of the Professional Services Management Association noted that "differing writing styles make editing more tedious," while a psychologist commented that "disagreements on style . . . may slow down the [writing] process." Whatever the situation, negotiating a common style among individuals who often, in the words of one engineer, have "their own writing style which they are not willing to give up" seems to be a recurrent problem in collaborative writing.

Another difficulty, one cited almost as often as that of achieving stylistic consistency, is the additional time many respondents felt group writing requires. (One city manager's response to our request for three disadvantages of group writing was an emphatic "Time. Time. Time.") Since time was also cited as an advantage by a number of respondents, who felt group writing helped them "spread the workload" and thus meet crucial deadlines, this emphasis on time as a disadvantage first seemed anomalous to us. We are still exploring the reasons why so many respondents believe that collaborative writing takes significantly longer than individual writing, but we suspect that its emphasis by respondents may indicate a sense of a loss of control over their personal work time occasioned by the numerous meetings that many group-writing projects require. It may also reflect the fact that many group-writing projects are simply larger, more time-consuming endeavors than those undertaken by individuals in these professions.

Or it may express the frustration of individuals who have participated in inefficient, poorly run collaborative writing projects. As might be expected, interpersonal skills and group dynamics play an important role in influencing both the effectiveness of the product and the satisfaction with the process of those involved. A chemist spoke for a number of other respondents when he asserted that "responsibilities really do need to be defined in order to get maximum efficiency." Not all people feel comfortable participating in such tightly controlled efforts, even when they recognize their importance, as the following comment by a psychologist suggests: "In large groups, a careful management plan is absolutely necessary — which doesn't work with people like myself."

A related problem frequently cited involves the equitable division of tasks. All too often, according to one member of the Society for Technical Communication, "unless all the workers are extremely conscientious, one person may end up doing the greatest amount of the work." According to one member of the Professional Services Management Association, such a failure to share responsibilities may reflect the fact that "many group members shirk writing duties." (One city manager listed the tendency of group-writing projects to "reveal [the] writing deficiencies of participants" as one of its three major disadvantages.) Or it may result, in the words of another Professional Services Management Association member, from the team members' failure to make a "total commitment" to a project. In negotiating these tasks and responsibilities, often under the pressure of tight deadlines and a schedule that may require some persons to participate in several collaborative projects at the same time, personal disagreements can occur, especially when some participants are "prima donnas" (the first disadvantage of group writing cited by one engineer). One member of the Society for Technical Communication observed, "As in anything, a group is only as good as its weakest member."

Finally, a number of respondents noted that group writing can result in what one psychologist called the "diffusion of responsibility" and a loss of personal satisfaction and sense of creativity. "[It's] never exactly as *I* want it," observed another psychologist, while a member of the Society for Technical Communication commented that "sense of ownership of the project is lessened and therefore the taking of credit must be shared. If you happen to be the one who did most of the work, there may be a sense of feeling 'ripped off.'" Another technical writer simply wrote, "Loss of ownership to group (Ennui)."

These disadvantages, though perceived as serious, were balanced for the great majority of respondents by a number of important advantages. One of the most frequently cited advantages stressed the usefulness of having varying viewpoints, of "checks and balances," of "maximum input." Respondents also noted the following "advantages": joint knowledge, experience, and writing expertise; a variety of approaches and ideas; the strengths of all the members; different perspectives that generate better ideas for a better product. As this last comment indicates, a number of respondents believed that the increased participation of diverse group members resulted in a better, more accurate text. One person noted that group writing "enhances [the] completeness [of] the product [and] minimizes the inclusion of erroneous or potentially offensive material." Others cited the following related advantages: "reduces error"; "[the] brainpower of several professionals always results in better reports than that achieved alone"; "multiple input provides a richer document." Interestingly, a number of respondents also commented on the way in which the group-writing process can increase sensitivity to audience. Collaborative writing can encourage "clearer, more understandable documents," one chemist noted, "by involving group members of disciplines typical of the intended readers." A psychologist cited the way in which it helps participants develop a "better idea of [the] general impact [of a document] on [the] target audience." These comments suggest to us that collaborative writing is highly context based. What is productive in one situation may not be so in another. Nevertheless, our data support the conclusions that most professionals find collaborative writing a generally productive means of achieving their goals.

At this stage of our analysis, then, we had accomplished one early and largely unproblematized goal: to demonstrate the degree to which professionals engaged in collaborative writing and to get some sense of how useful they found such activities. But our two surveys provided at least rough answers to a number of other questions.

What Kinds of Documents Do Writers Collaborate On?   The answer to this question seems clear: Some writers work collaboratively on almost every document relevant to their jobs. We asked specifically about the following documents:

letters

memos

short reports

long reports

professional articles

user manuals/instructions

newsletters, bulletins, etc.

case studies

proposals

lecture/oral presentation notes

instructional or course-related materials

books and monographs

Although frequency of response varied from document to document, members of each professional group reported working collaboratively, at least occasionally, on each type of document. Forty-two percent said they occasionally write short reports collaboratively, while 29 percent occasionally write professional articles or essays as part of a team or a group. We had anticipated that on-the-job writers would collaborate on such documents as reports and proposals. We were surprised, however, to discover that these professionals were as likely "often or occasionally" to write books or monographs collaboratively as they were to do so alone. The same held true for contracts and grants, case studies, user manuals, and long reports. Results of the second survey gave us further information as respondents listed the four kinds of documents they most often write collaboratively: proposals, memos, short reports, and long reports. While these four documents are most often produced in collaboration, all the other types received some "votes." Our data suggest, then, that collaboration is not specific to a limited number of documents, but rather that it is a frequently used strategy in producing documents of all kinds.

How Are Collaborative Writing Groups Organized?   We had difficulty eliciting this information, primarily because we lack a vocabulary to discuss what people do when they write collaboratively. After extensive pilot testing and revising, we described the following seven organizational patterns and asked how often our respondents used them.

1. Team or group plans and outlines. Each member drafts a part. Team or group compiles the parts and revises the whole.

2. Team or group plans and outlines. One member writes the entire draft. Team or group revises.

3. One member plans and writes draft. Group or team revises.

4. One person plans and writes draft. This draft is submitted to one or more persons who revise the draft without consulting the writer of the first draft.

5. Team or group plans and writes draft. This draft is submitted to one or more persons who revise the draft without consulting the writers of the first draft.

6. One member assigns writing tasks. Each member carries out individual tasks. One member compiles the parts and revises the whole.

7. One person dictates. Another person transcribes and revises.

Our survey results suggest that writing groups use such patterns frequently, though hardly anyone had a name for them. In fact, some told us they realized that they were following set or preestablished organizational patterns only after completing our survey, vividly demonstrating the principle that what lacks a name, we often simply do not recognize. Others (particularly in the technical writers' group) said having such a pattern was indispensable to success and that following an "ineffective" organizational pattern could produce "disastrous results." Our second survey results confirmed these responses: 72 percent of these writers said their group writing followed a set organizational plan. More importantly, they perceived the plan as necessary and helpful: 95 percent found its use productive or very productive. We conclude, then, that collaborative efforts need to be carefully organized or orchestrated — a conclusion that our interviews bring dramatically to life.

Is Collaborative Writing Related to Overall Job Satisfaction?   Our answers to this question must be tentative, for we gathered most information from open-ended questions and can report no hard figures or percentages in support of our conclusions. We became interested in the question, in fact, only when responses to the first survey elicited, almost incidentally, information about the pleasures and frustrations some group writers felt. As a result, in the second survey we attempted to gather more information about affective concerns by asking questions like: "Which writing activities do you find most productive (or least productive) to work on as part of a group?"; or "Please comment on how your participation in group writing contributes or does not contribute to your job satisfaction." In response to such questions, our participants cited a number of social and organizational "pluses," including the positive impact of "team building" and "a sense of group accomplishment." Because in most collaborative writing projects those involved in some sense "share in the final product," such group efforts can contribute both to effective group dynamics — "promoting collegiality," in one psychologist's words — and to an overall sense of shared mission or purpose.

Several respondents also observed that collaborative writing offers an effective and satisfying way of initiating recent graduates into the demands of their profession and to the demands of a new position. One city manager noted that collaborative writing can "train participants in organizational policy and in the expectations and thought processes of the chief administrator," while an engineer cited the way in which it "provides leadership for younger workers." A number of respondents noted that collaborative writing has personal, as well as social or organizational benefits. "It helps me stay fresh by discussing writing and seeing how other writers work," one technical writer noted, while an engineer commented that group writing "contributes to my

job satisfaction in that it allows me to gain exposure and knowledge of different aspects of our profession in an actual work environment." Respondents
commented on "the intellectual stimulation provided by group writing," and
a number noted the importance of emotional support, which added to their
job satisfaction. One member of the International City Management Association, who reported that she had been "writing grants with the same people for
three years," observed that her "group is as much a support group as a professional team."

Put most briefly, these discursive responses suggest that a complex set of
largely unidentified (perhaps even unrecognized) variables creates general
satisfaction or dissatisfaction with both the processes and products of group
writing. From these responses, we can tentatively identify a number of factors
related to the degree of satisfaction experienced by those who typically write
collaboratively:

1. the degree to which goals are clearly articulated and shared

2. the degree of openness and mutual respect characteristic of group members

3. the degree of control the writers have over the text

4. the degree to which writers can respond to others who may modify the text

5. the way credit (either direct or indirect) is realized

6. an agreed upon procedure for resolving disputes among group members

7. the number and kind of bureaucratic constraints (deadlines, technical or legal
    requirements, etc.) imposed on the writers

8. the status of the project within the organization

These are the elements that appeared (in answers to these open-ended
questions) most closely related to job satisfaction. They are, of course, not
quantifiable or generalizable. Nevertheless, they provide a basis for further
study of the affective dimensions of collaborative writing.

What Characterizes Effective Collaborative Writers?   The last open-ended
question on our second survey (22) asked respondents to give advice to
"someone in your field about how to write effectively as part of a group." The
qualities most often recommended included listening well, flexibility, patience,
and not being overly sensitive about one's writing. As one engineer noted:
"Forget everything you learned in writing courses. Listen ultra intensely;
don't let your feelings get hurt by criticism; don't hesitate to ask questions or
change styles; and be verbose. It's always easier to erase than to go back and
reconstruct original thought processes." Similarly, a chemist exhorted colleagues to "resist being vain or sensitive; . . . be responsive but not submissive
to suggestions for change in what you have written; learn to recognize and
accept reasonable alternatives; avoid nit-picking beyond the point of dimin-
ishing returns; practice writing at every opportunity, even though in this era
of telephones and recorders there is a great temptation to avoid it." After recommending flexibility and adaptability, a city manager added a thoughtful

postscript regarding the importance of being able to vary perspectives on any given problem: "Think about your audience before writing and while writing, as if they were listening to your thoughts as you put them down."

A number of respondents also pointed to mentoring ability and leadership as characteristics of effective collaborative writers. Younger employees particularly stressed the cooperation, openness, and support a strong mentor can provide and noted the assurance gained by having a mentor as a collaborator. But those at the upper end of the hierarchy also stressed the importance of effective mentoring. A senior engineer, for example, spoke of helping the group's new members to "blossom as fast as they can" by "spending time after hours talking through problems and projects." One key to effective leadership in collaborative writing efforts seems to be flexibility. A number of professionals pointed out that leadership roles are rarely constant; group members must be able to lead on one project and follow on another. This flexibility, they also noted, is most often learned in what amounts to a kind of collaborative apprenticeship.

As with our question about job satisfaction, this question about the traits of effective collaborative writers yields no easy answers and certainly no quantifiable conclusions. Yet the many long answers we received to this open-ended question suggest an emerging profile of effective collaborative writers. They are flexible; respectful of others; attentive and analytical listeners; able to speak and write clearly and articulately; dependable and able to meet deadlines; able to designate and share responsibility, to lead and to follow; open to criticism but confident in their own abilities; ready to engage in creative conflict.

We were struck, as we tried to see the shape of this profile in our mass of data, by the number of people who listed "ability to work well with others" as the most important factor in success in their fields, often adding the "ability to write well" as a secondary — though not unimportant — criterion. As one technical writer vividly put it: "No one here loses a job because of incompetence; they lose jobs if they can't work with others." We do not take this comment as a justification for incompetence — far from it. Rather it suggests to us that competence is a necessary but not a sufficient condition for success. Today and in the twenty-first century, our data suggest, writers must be "able to work together." They must, in short, be able to collaborate.

Does Collaborative Writing Occur in Various Modes?   But what form(s) will the collaboration that future workers need to do take? As we studied responses to our survey, pushing hard to see profiles and patterns and guidelines, we noted a dominant language in descriptions of collaborative settings, organizational frameworks, and roles. This dominant language emerged as highly structured and hierarchical, with power and authority distributed vertically within the hierarchy. This hierarchical mode of collaboration was apparent in the responses to our surveys and to our interviews. But as we probed our data, sifting back through our transcripts of interviews and responses to our questionnaires, we found traces of descriptions that did not fit this hierarchical mode. These traces suggested a more loose, fluid mode of collaborative writing, one that focused more often on the processes of collaboration rather than on the end products, one that emphasized dialogue and exploration rather than efficiency and closure.

We will return to a discussion of these two modes, the hierarchical and the dialogic, in "New Beginnings" (pp. 135–48 in this collection). Our recognition of these varying modes, suggestive as they are of competing epistemologies and theories of language, had the effect of further problematizing our view of collaborative writing, forcing us once again to interrogate our original goals and assumptions and to ask what competing political and economic agendas may be inscribed in collaborative acts, how ideology may construct varying views of and purposes for collaboration. If writers have traditionally been written as solitary individual units, does collaboration necessarily write them in a different or differing way? Our seemingly simple, straightforward research project thus refused to be neatly packaged and reported but instead brought us into an ever-widening current of historical and theoretical issues, all focusing on what it means, in any particular time and place, to be "a writer."

WORKS CITED

Brodkey, Linda. *Academic Writing as Social Practice.* Philadelphia: Temple UP, 1987.
Burke, Kenneth. *The Philosophy of Literary Forms.* 3rd ed. Berkeley: U of California P, 1973.
Ohmann, Richard. *Politics of Letters.* Middletown, CT: Wesleyan UP, 1987.
Richards, I. A. *The Philosophy of Rhetoric.* Mary Flexner Lectures on Humanities 3. New York: Oxford UP, 1965.

9   *New Beginnings*

Let us try again. (A direct hit is not likely here. The best one can do is to try different approaches toward the same center, whenever the opportunity offers.)
— KENNETH BURKE (*RHETORIC* 137)

"And so," as Kenneth Burke is so fond of asking, "where are we now?" For us, and we hope for many readers who have joined the intertextual conversation represented in these pages, yet another new beginning beckons. When we began work on [*Singular Texts/Plural Authors*] six years ago, we thought of ourselves as embarking on a fairly straightforward data gathering project, one in which we would collect enough empirical information to demonstrate that collaborative writing is a typical mode of discourse and thus deserves greater attention by teachers of composition. (The original title for [*Singular Texts/Plural Authors*], *The Theory and Practice of Co- and Group Authorship*, reflects the "neatness" of our original research design.) The conclusion to the book we then envisioned writing would, we assumed, sum up our findings and offer a conceptual model for collaborative writing.

RESEARCH METHODS REVISITED

This rather naive aim broke down almost immediately, however. We quickly realized that we could not (and should not) depend on empirical research methods alone to bring our subject into focus. Rather, we needed to draw upon historical, theoretical, and pedagogical sources as well. Perhaps even more importantly, we recognized that any attempt neatly to resolve the paradoxes and ambiguities that multiplied as our research progressed would radically oversimplify the phenomenon we were studying. Rather than attempting to dissolve or minimize these paradoxes and ambiguities, we have endeavored

From Andrea Lunsford and Lisa Ede, in *Singular Texts/Plural Authors* (Carbondale and Edwardsville: Southern Illinois UP, 1990) 130–43. This is the fifth and final chapter in this monograph.

to heighten them in an effort to set into play a mutual interrogation of research methods and [. . .] of discourses [. . .]. Our "method," then, has been both exploratory and nontraditional. Far from proceeding in a linear, formally logical (or phallogocentric) manner, we have — in the Latin sense of *research, re + circare* — circled around and around the phenomenon of collaborative writing, seeing and re-seeing it from the vantage point of shifting terministic screens, striving to achieve a series of perspectives by incongruity.

In so doing, we have tried to join a number of different conversations — from group management theory to cognitive and social psychology, library science, medieval studies, history of science, literary and composition theory, and our own home disciplinary trope, rhetoric. Such an effort entails, we recognize, a number of potential dangers. The assumptions, methods, and concerns that characterize the discourse of library science differ substantially from those of group management theory or literary history. Researchers in these fields looking at the phenomenon called collaborative writing ask different questions, use different methods to attempt to answer their questions, and arrive at (often radically) different conclusions. Researchers engaged in interdisciplinary research must [. . .] take care not simply to pick and choose those methods and results which support their perspectives. We have tried to avoid such inappropriate use of sources. But we have attempted in this study not just to draw upon but to "push" or pressure these often incommensurable discourses. The risk entailed in such a method is, we believe, justified. For only by setting these discourses not so much in conversation as in debate and disputation have we been able to gain a rich, contextualized, multi-perspective on our subject.

In our reading, research, and discussions of collaborative writing, we have faced another very considerable risk — that of overstating our case, of using our sources to deny the subject and hence also deny the very possibility or value of individual authorship and authority and thus of doing what Jim W. Corder calls "fading into the tribe, relinquishing authority and autonomy to the tribe" (303). As teachers of writing and rhetoricians, however, we can never take such a stance, and so our project has led us not to assent to the "death of the author" but to try to conceive new and more expansive ways of experiencing and representing authorship. Like the editors of the recently published *Reconstructing Individualism*, we want neither the death "of the subject or a return to a lost state but rather an alternative conceptualization of the experience of subjectivity, enriched by the chastening experiences of the last century" (Heller 2).

Some scholars in psychology, resisting the long domination of the solitary and knowing self in that discipline, are calling for much the same kind of re-situating of the subject. In a series of articles dealing with the concept of individualism and its various permutations (see Perloff 1987, Spence 1985, Smith 1978), Edward Sampson argues that a form of Western individualism that he calls "self-contained individualism" has so dominated our experience that we have failed to recognize the potential of another form that he calls "ensembled" individualism. Sampson argues, in fact, that a great deal of "cross-cultural, historical, and intercultural evidence . . . suggests that the dominant meaning of individualism in U.S. society today is by no means universal" and further that this form may actually "thwart the very benefits" normally thought to stem from American individualism (15). Finally, he suggests that ensembled individualism is actually "more capable of achieving democratic ideals of freedom, responsibility, and achievement than is radical or self-contained individualism" (21).

Other researchers in psychology are challenging univocal psychological theories of the self. On the basis of empirical research, for instance, M. Brinton Lykes argues that her subjects evidenced at least "two different notions of the self" (which she calls "autonomous individualism" and "social individuality"), and further that "differences between women's and men's notions of the self are grounded in their different experiences of power" (356). And she calls for more work in psychology which would give us a better understanding of "women's psycho-social reality and fundamental revisions of currently biased psychological theories about the self" (357). Lykes' call is currently being answered in a number of important works in women's studies, including Gilligan's *In a Different Voice*, Chodorow's *The Reproduction of Mothering*, Noddings' *Caring*, and Belenky, Clinchy, Goldberger, and Tarule's *Women's Ways of Knowing*. Such investigations may help us to reconceive and redefine the ways in which selfhood and subjectivity are achieved and experienced.

The result of our circling and recircling around the questions raised by an investigation of collaborative writing has led us, then, to problematize rather than neatly to define and to classify or to anatomize collaborative writing and collaborative writers. In particular, our reading and discussions with students and colleagues about issues of gender, race, and class took us back more than once to our reams of data and led us to look once again at what Derrida calls "hinges" — those places where language deconstructs, undermines, or radically challenges itself. Our examination of such junctures (such as the contradiction between our personal experience of collaboration and our colleagues' skeptical and suspicious view of it or the tension between the views of language as a transparent tool and as a mysterious source of power held simultaneously by those we interviewed) confirmed our sense that collaborative writing, like the "self," is not a stable or coherent construct, but rather that it appears in complex and multiple modalities. Two of these modes, which we have only recently come to call the hierarchical and the dialogic, have been of particular interest to us because of the dialectical tension they embody.

HIERARCHICAL AND DIALOGIC MODES OF COLLABORATION

In our research, the hierarchical mode of collaboration emerged early on; it is, in fact, such a widespread means of producing texts in all the professions we studied that we failed at first to see that it was but one mode, not the whole reality, in spite of the fact that this mode belied in many instances our own experience of collaboration. This form of collaboration is carefully, and often rigidly, structured, driven by highly specific goals, and carried out by people playing clearly defined and delimited roles. These goals are most often designated by someone outside of and hierarchically superior to the immediate collaborative group or by a senior member or leader of the group. Because productivity and efficiency are of the essence in this mode of collaboration, the realities of multiple voices and shifting *authority* are seen as difficulties to be overcome or resolved. Knowledge in this mode is most often viewed as information to be found or a problem to be resolved. The activity of finding such information or solving such problems is closely tied to the efficient realization of a particular end product. This mode of collaborative writing is, we would argue, highly productive, typically conservative, and most often, in our experience, a masculine mode of discourse.

Along the highways and byways of our research and reading roads, however, we began to catch glimpses, perceive traces, of another mode of collaboration, one we came to call dialogic and one which, we ultimately realized, succeeded in naming our own mode of collaboration. This mode is not as widespread in the professions we studied as the hierarchical mode, and in fact, its practitioners had difficulty describing it, finding language within which to inscribe their felt realities. This dialogic mode is loosely structured and the roles enacted within it are fluid: one person may occupy multiple and shifting roles as a project progresses. In this mode, the process of articulating goals is often as important as the goals themselves and sometimes even more important. Furthermore, those participating in dialogic collaboration generally value the creative tension inherent in multivoiced and multivalent ventures. What those involved in hierarchical collaboration see as a problem to be solved, these individuals view as a strength to capitalize on and to emphasize. In dialogic collaboration, this group effort is seen as an essential part of the production — rather than the recovery — of knowledge and as a means of individual satisfaction within the group. This mode of collaboration can in some circumstances be deeply subversive. And because neither we nor our respondents had ready language with which to describe such an enterprise, because most who tried to describe it were women, and because it seemed so clearly "other," we think of this mode as predominantly feminine.

Both of these modes can be discerned in the interviews reported in ["Collaborative Writers at Work" (pp. 91–134 in this collection)]. In these interviews, the hierarchical mode of collaboration predominated: the twelve-year research project on food additives described by Dr. Irving is perhaps the clearest example of a strongly hierarchical collaborative effort. But dialogical modalities — if not pure examples of dialogic collaboration — were also evidenced, particularly by Dr. Bernstein and Dr. Chiogioji, who of all the persons we interviewed had most consciously and carefully considered the human and social potentialities of collaboration. These modes feature in the difference between the hierarchical concept of authorship operative in much scientific collaboration, where determining authorship is a pragmatic institutional and political problem, and that operative in the work of Bakhtin and some contemporary feminists. And they reappear [. . .] in the distinctions between cooperative learning (whose activities are highly structured and hierarchical) and the pedagogy of collaboration. . . .

It might be tempting, given these and other examples, to set these two modes, the hierarchical and the dialogic, in binary opposition and to argue for one (the dialogic) as liberatory and postmodern and for the other (hierarchical) as oppressive and phallogocentric. But such an opposition is both harmfully reductive in its oversimplification and false to our own experience as writers and teachers of writing.

The hierarchical mode can be, and indeed often is, realized in situations that locate power in structurally oppressive ways. Often the lowest-paid, least-recognized members of research teams perform most of the work on a project (including "writing up" the results). Yet these individuals often get no credit for their work or financial and professional rewards for their labor. But the hierarchical mode can also comprise scenes of shared power and authority and lead not only to efficiency but to great job satisfaction. During our two and one-half day visit with Bill Qualls and his team, for instance, we were struck by the sense of mutual respect, ease, and authority manifested by all the team members, not just by Qualls.

It is not possible or desirable, in other words, to develop a set of binary opposites that would neatly characterize collaborative writing situations as either hierarchical or dialogic, conservative or subversive, masculine or feminine. Perhaps only full-fledged ethnographic studies could provide the depth of detail and critical perspective necessary for such judgments. Like gender roles, discourse situations are, Burke reminds us, inherently mixed and paradoxical; they defy easy analysis and categorization. And surely it seems reasonable to find inscribed in any piece of collaboration or any particular collaborator the same kind of risks and tensions that are generally inscribed in our culture.

Similarly, we would resist efforts automatically to equate dialogic collaboration with "good" student-centered, process-oriented teaching and hierarchical collaboration with "bad" teacher-centered, product-oriented teaching. The dialogic mode of collaboration can be used with surprising ease in a traditional teacher-centered class, particularly when student groups are encouraged to view consensus as an end in itself (just as many of those whom we interviewed thought of efficiency as an end in itself). But a carefully structured and thus hierarchical mode of collaboration — one that defines tasks carefully and presents a series of steps students must follow in working together — can also be used in the ways George Hillocks calls "environmental" — ways which many have found conducive to student-centered learning.

Because the hierarchical mode of collaboration is dominant in our culture, however, dialogic collaboration can at least sometimes take the form of resistance and subversion. A number of acknowledgments and prefaces in recent books by women, for instance, have struck a markedly dialogic key.

Belenky, Clinchy, Goldberger, and Tarule preface *Women's Ways of Knowing* by noting:

> As we steeped ourselves in the women's recorded and transcribed words we found ourselves drawing even closer to their frames of mind. We emerged from this long process with an extraordinary sense of intimacy and collaboration with all the women. . . . So, too, during our work together, the four of us developed . . . an intimacy and collaboration which we have come to prize. We believe that the collaborative, egalitarian spirit so often shared by women should be more carefully nurtured in the work lives of all men and women. We hope to find it in all our future work. (ix)

This mode can serve a subversive purpose, then, by pointing not only to plural or multiple authors but to the degree to which even single-authored texts comprise a plurality of voices. In her acknowledgments to *Man Made Language*, for example, Dale Spender asserts that: "There is an assumption I wish to challenge: it is that people sit in garrets and write books on their own. I sat in the Women's Resources Center at the University of Utah in Salt Lake City, and I was not on my own. . . . While this book may represent a 'sum total,' its many parts have been shaped by many different people. . . . Not in isolation in a garret did this book come into existence, but in the co-operative and dynamic context of women's struggle. . . ." (xv, xvi).

Similar statements appear in the prefaces of works in composition studies, particularly, we find, among our colleagues interested in and sensitive to issues of class, race, and gender. Richard Coe's recent monograph *Toward a Grammar of Passages* provides a case in point.

> Although in traditional terms I am the author of this book, it is in fact very much a collaborative invention. With the exception of a very few paragraphs, I did all the "actual writing." . . . But if revision is really part of the "actual writing" process, the concepts you will read are not entirely "mine." They began as such, but were revised collaboratively whenever they proved inadequate for particular tasks. And the research presented to support and develop those revised concepts . . . was done by others, mostly graduate students. Although in traditional terms I wrote the book and in real terms I am the primary author, to count me as its only author would give the lie to our fine and important theories about writing as a social and collaborative process. (xii)

It is far from clear, however, that the mode of collaboration suggested in such prefatory remarks can succeed in resisting traditional Western phallogocentrism. It is important to note that statements about the importance of dialogic collaboration, like those cited above, have thus far been in effect marginalized by appearing in the prefaces or acknowledgments rather than in the body of the texts. Though many writers are convinced of the crucial importance and benefits of dialogic collaboration, they generally have not yet found ways to incorporate these concerns in the body of their texts, which as a rule do not yet challenge the conventions of single-authored documents.

Those in composition studies have also begun to recognize the difficulties inherent in any effort to resist or subvert the traditional culture of schooling. While a number of teachers and theorists in composition have recently argued for a social constructionist pedagogy — one that is often presented as inherently liberating — the claims for this pedagogy, and at times the methods, have been challenged as amelioristic and accommodating. In "Reality, Consensus, and Reform in the Rhetoric of Composition Teaching," for instance, Greg Myers criticizes advocates of collaborative learning for proffering a naive, idealistic vision of collaborative learning, one easily co-opted by the larger educational system. In his most recent work, John Trimbur says that "it would be fatuous . . . to presume that collaborative learning can constitute more than momentarily an alternative to the present asymmetrical relations of power and distribution of knowledge and its means of production" ("Consensus" 29). Trimbur asks us, as a result, to interrogate closely our notion of consensus and to "rehabilitate" it as a "way to orchestrate dissensus." In a like manner, Joseph Harris challenges us to examine more carefully the way in which we use the term "community" in "sweeping and vague" ways and notes that doing so often polarizes talk about writing: "One seems asked to defend *either* the power of the discourse community or the imagination of the individual writer" (12).

The dialectical tension between hierarchical and dialogic modes of collaboration mirrors the historical tension between the individual and society; the psychological tension between individual cognition, with its traditional focus on the inner, and the relational, the recognition of an "ensembled" self; the pragmatic tension between goal-directed work and process-oriented play. Because the phenomenon of collaborative writing calls up all of these dialectical tensions, we find it a particularly fruitful site of paradox and of promise. To define this phenomenon, to say that collaborative writing should be *x* or *y*, should proceed in ways *a* or *b*, would be, in Burke's words, not only to reflect and select but to *de*flect and ultimately to limit the usefulness of the concept. What seems much more powerful to us, as to Trimbur, is to allow the free play of the paradoxes animating collaborative writing to raise questions of power, politics, historiography, and ideology — questions of profound importance at the close of the twentieth century.

UNDERSTANDING AND OVERSTANDING

Borrowing "overstanding" from Wayne Booth's *Critical Understanding*, James Phelan defines the term as the "critical evaluation of what we have understood" (165). We wish to attempt here a bit of overstanding, for our study of collaborative writing has led us, finally, to embrace the full complexity of collaborative acts and, as a result, to dissolve the traditional boundaries between collaborative writing and writing. And contemplating the complex nature of this dissolution has led us to reexamine or overstand issues raised about the work-related, theoretical, and pedagogical implications of the construct we call collaborative writing.

In "Scenes of Collaboration: Reflections," chapter 2 [in *Singular Texts/Plural Authors*], we offered a beginning critique of the interviews we had conducted, noting that those with whom we spoke took an essentially pragmatic approach to language and to collaboration. These writers spoke eloquently to us about what makes collaborative writing work for them and about the personal and professional benefits of collaborative writing. But except for Dr. Chiogioji and Dr. Bernstein, they seemed generally unconcerned with questions of power and ideology. Collaborative writing for these individuals, then, is largely unproblematic and untheorized. Our surveys and interviews, our review of the history of the traditional concept of authorship and of contemporary theoretical and pragmatic challenges to this concept, and our investigation of pedagogical issues raised by collaborative learning and writing all confirm the necessity of a more critical perspective.

The relationship between power and *authority* is, for example, more complex than that described in much research on work-related writing. Limited as it has been, our research on collaborative writing in the workplace suggests that, contrary to what we might have thought, power and *authority* do not necessarily stand in isomorphic relationship to one another. An example may illustrate the unstable nature of this relationship. Early in our research, we had an opportunity to talk with a group of women involved in a FIPSE-funded program aimed at getting more women into government. These women, all lawyers or law students, were doing collaborative writing as part of an apprenticeship with various congressional committees and agencies. They reported that they were able to wield remarkable power in constructing the documents (often legislation) they worked on, but in no case did they have "authorship" or "authority." In fact, their power was effective, they felt, in proportion to their lack of authorship.

In our interviews, we saw the same principle at work, most notably in the case of Glenna Johnston. It was only during a second follow-up interview that Dick Miller, her supervisor, mentioned Johnston's contribution to the writing done by him and other team members. His comments emphasized the significant nature of her contribution — Johnston not only coordinates the team's efforts but also critiques his drafts and writes documents that draw heavily on boilerplate materials — yet as executive secretary, Johnston bears little authority, much less even minimal claims to authorship, for this work.

These findings support what many feminist critics of the workplace suspect — that in collaborative situations, women often play the "secretarial" role, one that by definition devalues their contributions. To the extent that rewards, both financial and professional, are associated with authorship, this conclusion seems to hold and may in fact constitute an ironic Catch-22 for many women working in collaborative teams. Power may be distributed and shared, may even be the province of these women. But such power is not necessarily tied to authority, on the basis of which traditional rewards most typically accrue.

Issues of gender raise other important questions about collaborative writing in the professional work world. We have commented earlier on the overwhelming male, Anglo-Saxonness of the large representative sample we studied. The fact that collaborative writing is so readily accepted in this world may be connected to this world's homogeneity. What, we wonder, will result when such a context changes, when the professional work scene is populated much more by women and people of color? In spite of its apparent embrace of collaborative writing and its ability, in the current context, to use it to fulfill its goals, America's professional work force may well not be prepared for the day-to-day implications such a demographic shift will have. But in a transformed context, collaborative writing and the pragmatic necessity to use it well will tend, we believe, necessarily to foreground issues of power, ideology, and difference — issues the collaborative writers we studied are now largely able to ignore.

If collaborative writers in the professional world tend not to reflect on or to recognize the theoretical implications and problems raised by their practice, many of the theorists in our study tend to lean in the opposite direction. Too often, that is, they seem not to recognize the practical implications of or the need to develop methods consonant with their theories. The latter tendency occurs most glaringly perhaps in the case of research in the sociology of science, where one method used in this research — counting the first author of studies and using this information to indicate the importance of a particular article or to derive maps of the structure of influence in disciplines — conflicts with one of this field's major theoretical assumptions: that modern science is inherently and necessarily a collaborative venture.

The failure to recognize the practical implications of theory also characterizes many literary theorists today. (There are, of course, exceptions to this trend: Richard Ohmann, Annette Kolodny, Gerald Graff, Wayne Booth, Robert Scholes, and others.) As we read and studied theoretical texts [. . .], and as we saw theoretical issues concerning the nature of the subject and of the author as privileged subject of the text, of power, ideology, and the situated nature of all discourse raised over and over again, we failed to find any sustained attention to a practical pedagogy that would enact such theoretical positions.

When we had an opportunity to speak personally with theorists about their research or their teaching, they seemed most often startled or irritated by questions about the pedagogical implications of their theories. One prominent feminist theorist answered our queries, for example, by saying that she could draw no pedagogical implications from her theory. A traditional classroom, in which the teacher/authority dispenses information to students/receivers seemed efficient, viable, and even necessary to her. In another instance, a noted reader-response critic refused to entertain a student's interpretation, even as a starting point of discussion, and was irritated when another student pointed out that such pedagogical practice seemed to confound — if not to deny — the critic's theoretical tenets. Theorists of various deconstructionist stripes have of course been roundly criticized for failing to face up to or to explore the political and pedagogical implications (and possible contradictions) of their theories, but these illustrative anecdotes suggest that it is not only deconstructionists who need to put their own pedagogical houses in order.

A study of the history of authorship also raises other questions about the relationship between theory and practice. Our investigations demonstrate that this history is heavily imbricated in material, technological change. Elizabeth Eisenstein's massive study of *The Printing Press as an Agent of Change* emphasizes the role that this technology played in establishing that "both the eponymous inventor and personal authorship appeared at the same time and as a consequence of the same process" (121). Similarly, later changes in the concept of revision are closely related to changes in the technology for text production (see Elizabeth Larsen's fascinating study of such changes in the eighteenth and the nineteenth centuries). So too, we believe, are shifts in and challenges to the traditional concept of authorship closely related to material changes in technology. Yet we — as well as many of the critical theorists we have studied — are too often ignorant of such material changes taking place all around us. Changes in copyright laws, in corporate authorship, in library cataloging systems, in artificial intelligence, in computer-generated discourse, in mixed-media texts, in networking systems, and in even more vast information storage, retrieval, and sharing systems seem necessarily related to theoretical challenges to the "author" construct and indeed to the whole notion of the codex book.

Just as many [. . .] theorists [. . .] fail to articulate and examine the pedagogical implications of their theory, so many teachers of writing fail to articulate and examine the theoretical implications of their practice. Too often we are content — as the collaborative writers whose interviews we presented in ["Collaborative Writers at Work" (pp. 91–134 in this collection)] were content — to focus simply on what works for us as teachers. Indeed, [. . .] theory and practice are often in radical disjunction, as they are in the classrooms of those who espouse collaborative learning and writing yet enact a theory of the author as originary, autonomous, and radically individual.

Toril Moi has recently charged Anglo-American feminists with a similar disjunction:

> If we are truly to reject the model of the author as God the Father of the text, it is surely not enough to reject the patriarchal ideology implied in the paternal metaphor. It is equally necessary to reject the *critical practice* it leads to, a critical practice that relies on the author as the transcendental signified of his or her text. For the patriarchal critic, the author is the source, origin, and meaning of the text. If we are to undo this patriarchal practice of *authority*, we must take one further step and proclaim with Roland Barthes the death of the author. (62–63)

Moi's criticism of Anglo-American feminists, and the implied criticism of many in composition studies who espouse collaborative learning or writing yet continue to view the individual author as the sole "source, origin, and meaning of the text," seems to us trenchant. Yet composition teachers face a difficulty that Moi and other theorists do not necessarily face: when we ask our students to free write, to plan an essay, or to revise, we observe these students striving to create and share their own felt meanings, and we participate in their acts of realizing intentions and purposes in their discourse. Theorists in composition may agree with Barthes or Moi about the need to replace or displace the traditional concept of the author, but the pedagogical implications of this "death" are hardly clear or simple. One possible response — replacing the concept of "author" with that of "writer" — is fraught with problems, as Barthes' discussion of "Authors and Writers" and the traditional academic distinction between literary "authors" and student "writers" suggest.

In fact, the challenge of responding to contemporary critiques of the author and of the subject comprises one of the most important tasks faced by those in composition in the coming years. In the meantime, we must focus even more insistently on critiquing our own practices, uncovering theoretical blind spots. As Tori Haring-Smith and others have shown, collaborative practices uncritically imposed on a classroom can yield merely a disguised version of the same old teacher-centered, authoritarian theory of learning, a version that confuses students with the mixed and contradictory messages it sends. Harris and Trimbur suggest, however, that such practices are not the only ones possible, and that examining the theoretical implications of collaboration — particularly in the dialogic mode — can be valuable precisely because it throws these practices into high relief, thereby allowing us and our students to question them, to open up the classroom to the free play of difference. Thus rigorously pursued, a theory of collaborative writing must lead us to question, in fact, not only the structure and management of our classrooms but our curricular and institutional structures as well.

Such a theory would, of course, radically re-situate authority or power in the classroom and our entire system of placing and testing students. But it would also challenge some of our most entrenched ways of rewarding academic progress through advancement and tenure. A theory of collaboration such as we envision would value community literacy work, for instance, or collaboratively conducted research as much as it would the single-authored codex book.

We have attempted in this last chapter [of *Singular Texts/Plural Authors*] to interrogate or overstand our own work [. . .] because we see such mutual interrogation and self-reflective overstanding as necessary for those working in composition studies today. In addition, our explorations suggest several other generalizations we think may be of particular importance to our colleagues in composition:

1. Conducting any mode of research always calls on the researcher to acknowledge and to attend to that which it is not, that which is absent or silent. Such recognition will inevitably be difficult and partial, but it will also allow for contextualization (and a fuller critique) of the research.

2. Interdisciplinary research brings challenges and dangers but carries its own rewards. Writing this book, for example, has graphically demonstrated for us the relevance of critical theory, which has been remarkably important to us in spite of the difficulties of negotiating the minefields of contemporary theoretical language. In a similar way, our excursions into library science and the sociology of science have allowed us to see our subject in new and clarifying ways.

3. Only through a mutual interrogation of theory and practice can we resist the powerful seduction of oversimplifying solutions. Such solutions are especially pressing in an age of accountability and almost blind faith in the power of tests as empirical means of measuring practice and achievement.

The work reviewed in this text strongly suggests that we have only begun to scratch the surface of what it means to describe writing as a social or collaborative process. Every aspect we have touched on — in the work world and in technological practices, in theory, in pedagogy — calls for further investigation, exploration, elaboration.

GROUNDINGS

Finally, it has been this capacity of collaborative writing to open out, to open up, to explore both the experiential present and the theoretically possible that has so intrigued us. In retrospect, we realize that our earliest discussion of collaboration ("Why Write . . . Together?") was unique in our publishing experience for just this grounding of our theoretical interest in collaborative writing in our deeply personal experience as coauthors. Throughout our research — and even in our surveys and interviews — we have never lost this connection between our "public" discourse and our "private" personal grounding, which is apparent both in our decision to focus on productive, satisfied collaborative writers in our interviews and in our eventual recognition and exploration of dialogic elements in those interviews.

As we worked on our project, what began almost whimsically in "Why Write" with personal anecdotes about collaborative pesto-making binges and our contrary but complementary natures grew into a conviction that we no longer wish to — indeed we no longer can — rigidly separate the public and the personal in our own discourse. In "Me and My Shadow," Jane Tompkins writes of the two voices inside her — one of a critic who wants to critique, the other of a person who wants to be personal in her responses — and notes that "I'm tired of the convention that keeps discussions of epistemology, or James Joyce, segregated from meditations on what is happening outside my window or inside my heart. The public-private dichotomy, which is to say the public-private *hierarchy*, is a founding condition of female oppression. I say to hell with it" (169).

In our own halting ways, we have said to hell with it too (when readers told us parts of [not "Old Beginnings"] were too personal and really belonged in a preface or when others noted that the "voice" in [*Singular Texts/Plural Authors*] changes from time to time), and we have been able to do so in and through our experience and our exploration of collaboration. For that experience has been for us finally not one of loss of self or subjectivity but instead a deeply enriching and multiplicitous sense of self, one that allows us to countenance and to speak our own voices — public and academic, personal and private — as well as to recognize, value, and credit the voices of others, many physically present, many others distantly echoed, which animate our text.

*　　*　　*　　*　　*

It is 6:00 P.M., 9 December 1988. We have been writing and talking and cooking and reading and listening and writing and talking and cooking and reading steadily for seven days now. We have before us a text, some 250 pages or so, one that looks physically solid, present, singular. The illusion still holds, but barely. For just these last few days, as has so often been the case during our work together, we have managed mutual negotiation of issues of power and control and paused to think upon them; we have rambled through discussions of a point only to turn a corner and suddenly see that point anew. We have read much, have imagined ourselves in deep conversation with Kenneth Burke, Luce Irigaray, Mikhail Bakhtin, Kenneth Bruffee, Carolyn Heilbrun. We have, in fact, been in conversation with our editor and with numerous friends and colleagues, and always with our students — and with each other and all the voices within. We will mail our draft next week, await reviewers' responses, and begin revising.

*　　*　　*　　*　　*

And it is 8:30 P.M., 15 May 1989. Lisa is on a consulting trip in the east and Andrea is in her office, feet up, gathering notes for one more marathon telephone conversation. The months of revising have been long ones, full of helpful and generous critiques, express mail and Fax exchanges, public presentations and private dreamings, and always the long-distance talking in which the "real" revisions have taken place, regardless of which of us "writes" the actual words. And once those words are written, of course, yet another collaboration begins, as we work with copy, line, and production editors to produce our *Singular Text* with *Plural* — indeed polyphonous — *Authors*.

*　　*　　*　　*　　*

We began this book, this project, with a glimpse of Poe's purloined letter embedded in our intellectual landscape, a sudden sighting of James' indistinct figure in the rug. Throughout our work, this figure — of a multivocal, multiplicitous, collaborative writer/text — has shifted in and out of view, in and out of focus. It is shifting still, in what for us is another beginning, a chance to continue the conversation pursued in and between these pages with you.

WORKS CITED

Bakhtin, Mikhail. *The Dialogic Imagination*. Ed. Michael Holquist. Trans. Caryl Emerson and Michael Holquist. Austin: U of Texas P, 1981.

Barthes, Roland. "Authors and Writers." *Critical Essays*. Evanston, IL: Northwestern UP, 1972. Rpt. in *A Barthes Reader*. Ed. Susan Sontag. New York: Hill, 1982. 185–93.

———. "The Death of the Author." *Image — Music — Text*. New York: Hill, 1977. 142–48.

Belenky, Mary Field, Blythe McVicker Clinchy, Nancy Rule Goldberger, and Jill Mattuck Tarule. *Women's Ways of Knowing: The Development of Self, Voice, and Mind*. New York: Basic, 1986.

Booth, Wayne C. *Critical Understanding: The Powers and Limits of Pluralism*. Chicago: U of Chicago P, 1979.

———. *Modern Dogma and the Rhetoric of Assent*. Ward-Phillips Lectures in English Language and Literature 5. Notre Dame: U of Notre Dame P; Chicago: U of Chicago P, 1974.

Burke, Kenneth. *A Rhetoric of Motives.* Berkeley: U of California P, 1969.

Chodorow, Nancy. *The Reproduction of Mothering: Psychoanalysis and the Sociology of Gender.* Berkeley: U of California P, 1978.

Coe, Richard M. *Toward a Grammar of Passages.* Conference on College Composition and Communication Studies in Writing and Rhetoric Series. Carbondale: Southern Illinois UP, 1988.

Corder, Jim W. "Hunting for Ethos Where They Say It Can't Be Found." *Rhetoric Review* 7 (Spring 1989): 299–316.

Eisenstein, Elizabeth. *The Printing Press as an Agent of Change: Communications and Cultural Transformations in Early Modern Europe.* Cambridge: Cambridge UP, 1979.

Gilligan, Carol. *In a Different Voice: Psychological Theory and Women's Development.* Cambridge, MA: Harvard UP, 1982.

Graff, Gerald. *Professing Literature.* Chicago: U of Chicago P, 1987.

Haring-Smith, Tori. "Is Peer Tutoring Collaborative?" Unpublished essay.

———. "When Collaborative Learning Backfires." Unpublished paper delivered at Conference on College Composition and Communication. St. Louis, Mar. 1988.

Harris, Joseph. "The Idea of Community in the Study of Writing." *College Composition and Communication* 40 (Feb. 1989): 11–22.

Heilbrun, Carolyn. *Toward a Recognition of Androgyny.* New York: Knopf, 1973.

Heller, Thomas C., Morton Sosna, and David E. Wellbery, eds. *Reconstructing Individualism: Autonomy, Individuality, and the Self in Western Thought.* Stanford: Stanford UP, 1986.

Hillocks, George, Jr. *Research on Written Composition: New Directions for Teaching.* Urbana, IL: ERIC Clearinghouse on Reading and Communication Skills, National Conference on Research in English, 1986.

Irigaray, Luce. *Speculum of the Other Woman.* Trans. Gilliam C. Gill. Ithaca: Cornell UP, 1985.

Kolodny, Annette. "Respectability Is Eroding the Revolutionary Potential of Feminist Criticism." *Chronicle of Higher Education* 4 (May 1988): A52.

Larsen, Elizabeth. "A History of the Composing Process." Diss. U of Wisconsin at Milwaukee, 1983.

Lykes, M. Brinton. "Gender and Individualistic vs. Collectivist Bases for Notions about the Self." *Journal of Personality* 53 (1985): 356–83.

Moi, Toril. *Sexual/Textual Politics: Feminist Literary Theory.* London: Methuen, 1985.

Myers, Greg. "Reality, Consensus, and Reform in the Rhetoric of Composition Teaching." *College English* 48 (1986): 154–74.

Noddings, N. *Caring: A Feminine Approach to Ethics and Moral Education.* Berkeley: U of California P, 1984.

Perloff, R. "Self-Interest and Personal Responsibility Redux." *American Psychologist* 42 (1987): 3–11.

Phelan, James. *Reading People, Reading Plots.* Chicago: U of Chicago P, 1989.

Sampson, Edward. "The Debate on Individualism." *American Psychologist* 43 (1988): 15–22.

Scholes, Robert. *Textual Power: Literary Theory and the Teaching of English.* New Haven: Yale UP, 1985.

Smith, M. B. "Perspectives on Selfhood." *American Psychologist* 33 (1978): 1053–63.

Spence, J. T. "Achievement American Style: The Rewards and Costs of Individualism." *American Psychologist* 40 (1985): 1285–95.

Spender, Dale. *Man Made Language.* 2nd ed. London: Routledge, 1985.

Tompkins, Jane. "Me and My Shadow." *New Literary History* 19 (Autumn 1987): 169–78.

Trimbur, John. "Collaborative Learning and Teaching Writing." *Perspectives on Research and Scholarship in Composition.* Ed. Ben W. McClelland and Timothy R. Donovan. New York: MLA, 1985. 87–109.

———. "Consensus and Difference in Collaborative Learning." Unpublished paper delivered at MLA Convention, San Francisco, Dec. 1987. Rpt. in *College English* 51 (1989): 602–16.

10   *Collaborative Authorship and the Teaching of Writing*

The concepts of author and authorship, so radically destabilized in contemporary literary theory — and in current discursive practice in fields as far removed as engineering and law — have also been problematized in the field of rhetoric and composition studies, where scholars have challenged the traditional exclusion of student writing from claims to "real writing" and "authorship," explored the ways in which *autho*rity is experienced by student writers, and increasingly sought to map various models of composing processes.

Beginning with a 1983 essay called "Why Write . . . Together?,"[1] we have attempted to add to this conversation by probing the concept of authorship that informs the teaching of writing in the United States. We began this research guided by the following questions:

1. What specific features distinguish the processes of collaborative authorship from those of single authorship? Can these features or processes be linked to any features of the resulting products? In short, how can we best *define* collaborative authorship?

2. Is there a limit to how many people can write together? Are projects such as the *Oxford English Dictionary*, the *Bible*, the *Short Title Catalogue*, elaborate computer programs, encyclopedias — all often involving more than 100 authors — examples of collaborative authorship?

3. In what ways, if any, does collaborative authorship affect the way we view the traditional writer-audience relationship?

4. What epistemological implications does collaborative authorship hold for traditional notions of creativity and originality?

5. How might the ethics of collaborative authorship be examined and defined? In cases of group authorship, where does the responsibility lie? Who stands behind the words of a report written by fifteen people?

6. Is the emphasis on or weight of various cognitive and rhetorical strategies different when co-authoring than when writing alone?

From Andrea A. Lunsford and Lisa Ede, in *Cardozo Arts & Entertainment Law Journal* 10.2 (1992): 681–702.

7. What are the pedagogical implications of collaborative authorship? What do we know about the advantages or disadvantages of having students participate in collaborative writing? If advantages do exist, don't they in some ways contradict our profession's traditional insistence on students working alone? And perhaps most importantly, do we have ways to teach students to adjust readily to collaborative writing tasks?

After a lengthy research project and eight years of study, we feel confident in saying that the traditional model of solitary authorship is more myth than reality, that much or most of the writing produced in professional settings in America is done collaboratively, and that, in fact, much of what we call "creative" writing is collaborative as well, though it almost always flies under the banner of single authorship.[2] But what of the college classroom and the teaching of writing that takes place there? That is to say, how may we best answer the last major research question, the one that challenges our pedagogy? While we will touch on those ways in which we have attempted to address all our original research questions, in the space provided here, we wish particularly to focus on writing pedagogy, relate its current forms to an epistemology that reifies radically individual forms and ways of knowing, and explore the potential for a reconstructed pedagogy that will allow for collaborative authorship.

I. HISTORICAL PERSPECTIVES ON COLLABORATION

In composition studies, interest in "discourse communities" has gone hand in hand with growing interest in social construction theories of knowledge, theories which attempt to situate the known in communal contexts. "Writing as a social process" has, in fact, become something of a buzzword or catchphrase, as articles on small-group collaborative efforts, peer-response techniques, and the social nature of writing and reading appear in growing numbers. We may best examine this movement, generally referred to as collaborative learning, by situating it in an historical context that represents one playing out of a persistent tension in American culture — that between the individual (the isolated Cartesian self) — and the community. This tension is vividly captured by Alexis de Tocqueville in his analysis of the American character. To describe this character, he uses a newly-coined word, *individualism* (which he differentiates from *egoism*): "Individualism is a calm and considered feeling which disposes each citizen to isolate himself from the main of his fellows and withdraw into the circle of family and friend; with this little society formed to his taste, he gladly leaves the greater society to look after itself."[3] As such an individualism increases, Tocqueville notes:

> More and more people who though neither rich nor powerful enough to have much hold over others, have gained or kept enough wealth and enough understanding to look after their own needs. Such folks owe no man anything and hardly expect anything from anybody. They form the habit of thinking of themselves in isolation and imagine that their whole

destiny is in their hands. . . . Each man is forever thrown back on himself alone, and there is danger that he may be shut up in the solitude of his own heart.[4]

Tocqueville feared the results of unmediated growth of "individualism" and argued that it could be best countered by a strong tradition of community and public discourse: "Citizens who are bound to take part in public affairs must turn from private interests and occasionally take a look at something other than themselves."[5] This strong civic involvement with public discourse was, in Tocqueville's view, the balancing factor that would keep America from developing into a society of naturally exclusive, autonomous individuals, a society which would not, he feared, easily be able to resist totalitarianism or despotism.

In part, the founding document of America, The Declaration of Independence, reflects both the profound drive toward individualism and the commitment to community and public discourse that Tocqueville found in the American character, dual ideals which are inscribed in our history and which are often seen as being in constant tension with one another.[6] We might expect to find evidence of this tension in American education and in the teaching of writing. And indeed we do. As Michael Halloran[7] has demonstrated, the earliest rhetorical instruction in America was influenced by Cicero and Quintilian, and the Roman concept of the "ideal orator" as the public-spirited person speaking well animated such instruction. But this essentially rhetorical emphasis on the Greek and Roman "commune," on communal values and shared meanings, diminished in the nineteenth century as oral discourse was displaced by writing, as new "objective" methods of testing arose, and as the academy emphasized competition over cooperation, autonomous electives over the classical "core" curriculum, and the autonomous individual over the social. By the end of the nineteenth century, traditional rhetorical instruction had been largely displaced by emerging English departments heavily imbued with romantic theories of "genius" and originality, with a concept of writing as an individual solitary act, and with philological and exegetical traditions that emphasized the autonomous writer and the text as individually held intellectual property.[8]

Nevertheless, some educators resisted the trend toward individualism and isolation in English instruction. Anne Gere's monograph on the history of writing groups in America reveals that peer response techniques and small group collaboration have been advocated and enjoyed by some citizens and teachers since the colonial period — in mutual improvement groups such as Benjamin Franklin's Junto, in the Lyceum- and Chatauqua-generated societies, and in the women's clubs and literary societies.[9] In nineteenth-century schools, Michigan's Fred Newton Scott and his student Gertrude Buck both advocated more natural social conditions for composition instruction *and* evaluation,[10] while Alexander Bain's *On Teaching English* praised the practice of writing with an eye toward reading draft versions to a society of peers and revising on the basis of discussion.[11] And in the colleges and universities, the great popularity of literary and other speaking societies offered an opportunity for cooperation and extensive collaboration.

As Mara Holt has demonstrated, collaborative pedagogy — while never dominant — has a rich history and tradition.[12] Basing her study on an examination of academic journals from 1911 to 1986, Holt traces this collaborative thread, arguing that "the rationales and practices of collaborative pedagogy consistently reflect social and intellectual and economic trends of the sociohistorical movement in which they are located."[13]

As the twentieth century proceeded, the dominant emphasis on individualism, on writing as an individually creative act, and on "objective" testing as a means of evaluating the intellectual property of solitary writers continued to be questioned by a marginal collaborative pedagogy. Most influential was the work of educational philosopher John Dewey, who argued tirelessly for seeing the education of each individual in a social and communal *context*. As he notes in *The Public and Its Problems*, "Individuals still do the thinking, desiring, purposing, but *what* they think of is the consequence of their behavior upon that of others and that of others upon themselves."[14] Dewey's calls for "new" or "progressive" education began early in this century. Throughout his career he insisted that learning occurs in *interaction*, that social context is of utmost importance in the classroom, and that we should reform our traditional model (which privileges the individual) by enhancing "the moving spirit of the whole group . . . held together by participation in common activities."[15]

Dewey influenced generations of teachers and scholars, among them Sterling Andrus Leonard, who argued as early as 1916, in *Two Types of Criticism for Composition Work*, that "oral and written composition are developed in a socially organized class to carry out real projects . . . in a spirit of hearty cooperation."[16] In his 1917 *English Composition As a Social Problem*, Leonard goes on to say:

> We must not make the mistake of assuming that training in composition is purely an individual matter. Most self expression is for the purpose of social communication. . . . Our whole use of language has a social setting. The futility of much of our past teaching has been due to our mental blinders to the social function of language. One has only to compare the situation of ordinary conversation with that of a class exercise in oral composition to realize how far we have forgotten the social genesis of speech. Worthy social conversation cannot be made at command of any person in authority. Ordinary human beings would not endure hearing the same item of discussion repeated by each person present. Nor would one care to say what everyone else had already said. Yet these are some of the striking characteristics of a composition exercise. If we are to make our training real, we must naturalize it, which is to say we must socialize our teaching of composition.[17]

Dewey's interactionist or constructivist approach to learning and knowledge gained increasing support in the 1930s from the work of George Herbert Mead, who argued that meaning is not individually wrought but is instead constructed through social interaction.[18] In *Invention as a Social Act*, Karen Burke LeFevre cites Mead's work as providing a theoretical foundation for a view of invention as collaborative, noting that "other social thinkers, such as Martin Buber and Ludwig Wittgenstein, [move from] what have traditionally been regarded as private psychological entities out into the realm of social interaction and contextualization of knowledge."[19] In addition, Piaget's work with children took a social constructivist approach to knowledge and learning as he demonstrated that children learn through *interaction* with others and with things in their environmental contexts.[20]

Dewey devotees[21] did much to rigidify and trivialize his original arguments; his influence faded during the exigencies of the war years. The critique of traditional education, with its teacher-centered classrooms and its emphasis on "working alone" and on "originality," continued, however, primarily in Britain. M.L.J. Abercrombie's *Anatomy of Judgment*[22] and her later *Aims and Techniques for Group Teaching*,[23] for instance, evolved from work with medical students. Abercrombie was convinced that small-group discussion provided the most effective way to help those students become more sophisticated and accurate at diagnosis and, hence, better physicians. Reacting to a Report of a Committee of the Royal College of Physicians, which argued that "the average medical graduate . . . tends to lack curiosity and initiative; his powers of observation are relatively undeveloped; his ability to arrange and interpret facts is poor; he lacks precision in the use of words,"[24] Abercrombie devised an experimental teaching course that would help students, through collaboration, learn to recognize diverse points of view, diverse interpretations of the results of an experiment, and thus to form more useful and accurate medical judgments:

> My hypothesis is that we may learn to make better judgements if we can become aware of some of the factors that influence their formation. We may then be in a position to consider alternative judgements and to choose from among many instead of blindly and automatically accepting the first that comes; in other words, we may become more receptive or mentally more flexible. The results of testing the effects of the course of [collaborative group] discussions support this hypothesis.[25]

Abercrombie's emphasis on contextualizing knowledge and her realization that communally derived diagnoses are generally more accurate and effective than those of a single medical student served as a direct challenge to the traditional individualism and isolated competitiveness endemic to most medical school curricula and higher education.

At roughly the same time, Edwin Mason, in his book, *Collaborative Learning*, presented a strikingly similar challenge to British secondary schools and, along the way, coined the phrase "collaborative learning." Charging that "to work in a school day after day and feel that we are doing more harm than good, and that with the best will in the world, is too much to bear,"[26] Mason set out to reform the school system, which he believed was "meeting neither the needs of the young nor the demands of the world."[27] As a result, Mason proposed a radical restructuring of this system, one which would replace the current competitive, authoritarian, overly specialized or departmentalized and hence "alienated" program with one emphasizing interdisciplinary study, small group work, collaboration, and dialogue — largely in the spirit of John Dewey. The remainder of his remarkable book describes such a curriculum and advises teachers on how best to implement it.[28]

As Abercrombie's and Mason's work began to have at least a small impact on pedagogical thinking, so too did that of the Brazilian teacher Paolo Freire, whose *Pedagogy of the Oppressed* appeared in 1968.[29] Arguing that literacy is best taught in the social contexts of people's own lives, Freire faulted traditional education with promoting not genuine public literacy but passivity, alienation, and conformity instead. In his work, Freire aims to empower his student-colleagues to reclaim, reinterpret, and hence reenact their own lives and to gain growing awareness of how social forces work in dialogic relationship with individual experience to enslave — or to liberate — and to create the realities they inhabit *communally*. Freire's work has most recently been presented as a challenge to the traditional teaching of writing in Ira Shor's *Freire for the Classroom*, which calls for a commitment to social and political contextualizing of all learning and on a renegotiation of power and authority in all classrooms.[30]

These examples demonstrate that the drive toward radically individual autonomy, competitiveness, and isolated selfhood has always been countered, often only in a whisper but at other times in a louder, clearer voice, by a call for community, for shared public discourse, for working together for some common good. And, as Anne Gere has shown, we could write part of the history of writing instruction in the twentieth century in just such terms.[31]

II. CONTEMPORARY WRITING PEDAGOGY AND COLLABORATIVE LEARNING

The last twenty years are generally regarded as having witnessed a large shift in writing pedagogy, sometimes as a growing awareness of process and context, sometimes (following the work of pioneers like Moffett, Emig, and Britton)[32] as a move from teacher-centered to student-centered learning models. Certainly we wish to acknowledge the effects of these largely positive shifts, most of which in our view run counter to the traditional valorization of autonomous individualism, privately held intellectual property, competition, and hierarchy. But in spite of these largely pedagogical efforts, most day-to-day writing instruction in American colleges and universities still reflects traditional assumptions about the nature of the self (autonomous), the concept of authorship (as ownership of singly-held property rights), and the classroom environment (hierarchical, teacher-centered).

We may look to contemporary composition studies as an illustration in point. Over the past few years, a number of scholars have attempted to understand this emerging field of study by, essentially, a naming of parts, by a taxonomizing. Thus Richard Young identifies as the two major "groups" the "new Romanticists" and the "new Classicists," the former stressing the interiority and essential mystery of writing, the latter stressing exteriority and structured procedures for composing.[33] Patricia Bizzell modifies and amplifies this distinction, grouping composition studies into two camps — those who view writing primarily as "inner-directed" and "prior to social influence" and those who view writing as "outer-directed" and based on "social processes whereby language-learning and thinking capacities are used and shaped in . . . communities."[34] In several essays and a monograph on twentieth-century writing instruction, James Berlin offers another taxonomy, contrasting what he calls "objective" and "subjective" rhetorics with a tripartite division of "transactional" rhetoric.[35] Similar arguments are advanced, though from differing perspectives, by several others, including Lester Faigley and Stephen M. North,[36] but are probably put most strongly by LeFevre. In *Invention as a Social Act*, LeFevre contrasts what she calls the Platonic view of inventing and composing ("the act of finding or creating that which is . . . written as individual introspection; ideas begin in the mind of the individual writer and then are expressed to the rest of the world") with a social view of inventing and composing.[37] This social view takes a constructivist approach to knowledge and posits that the "self," in some ways similar to Wayne Booth's "range of selves" or Foucault's "subject positions,"[38] is socially constituted and that, hence, writing is essentially a social and collaborative act. Interestingly, in his recent essay "On the Very Idea of a Discourse Community,"[39] Thomas Kent argues that social constructionists such as LeFevre are, from the perspective of Donald Davidson's coherence theory of truth and knowledge, internalists, not externalists.

These taxonomies of composition studies overlap and differ in a number of ways and, as all taxonomies inevitably do, they limit — indeed, they often distort — what we perceive about our own field of study. We mention them here, therefore, not to endorse any particular taxonomy of rhetoric and composition studies but to make one point that strikes us as particularly telling: the composition theorists and teachers most often identified with collaborative learning and peer response techniques — James Moffett, Donald Murray, Peter Elbow, Ken Macrorie — are also usually identified with Bizzell's "inner-directed" group,[40] Berlin's "expressionist" group,[41] LeFevre's Platonic group,[42] which posits the uniqueness of individual imagination and sees writing as a means of expressing an autonomous inner self. Ironically, then, the very scholars most often associated with collaborative learning hold implicitly to traditional concepts of autonomous individualism, authorship, and authority for texts. In addition, their versions of collaborative learning generally fail to problematize the role of the teacher/authority in the writing classrooms.

The work of Peter Elbow provides perhaps the best example of the tension and potential contradictions we have been describing. For years, Elbow has encouraged writers to work in groups, reading their work aloud for oral responses, out of which revisions grow. Many of his recommended classroom activities rely on freewheeling collaboration, and he continues to champion the use of collaborative learning. Yet in spite of this emphasis on the importance of audience response to revision and its advocacy of some form of collaboration, Elbow's work rests on assumptions about individualism and individual creativity that fail to sufficiently problematize traditional conceptions of "author" and that in fact come close to denying the social nature of writing. For Elbow, expressing personal authenticity requires not social interaction but mining the depths of the self, searching inside the self for a unique voice. As he says in *Writing without Teachers*, "The mind's magic. It can cook things instantaneously and perfectly when it gets going. You should expect yourself at times to write straight onto the paper words and thoughts far better than you knew were in you."[43] In his more recent books, Elbow continues to represent the individual self as the essentially mysterious source of creation, frequently calling on the "magical" ways writers discover their unified voices.[44] *Writing with Power*, in fact, ends with a chapter on "Writing and Magic."[45] As Greg Myers notes in a critique of Elbow, "Magic is the only possible source for such [individual] ineffable energies . . . [such] metaphors prevent any analysis of the social conditions of our writing."[46] Such a stance is reflected in Elbow's more recent essays, in which he argues that writers often must ignore audience (or any "others") in order to get to the heart and soul of what they want to say.[47]

The composition theorist most closely associated with social construction and collaborative learning theories in general and peer group response in particular is Kenneth Bruffee, who became interested in peer tutoring as a means of helping students "practice judgement collaboratively, through a progressive set of analytical and evaluative tasks applied to each other's academic writing in a context which fosters self-esteem."[48] Yet in his early work on peer tutoring and in his text *A Short Course in Writing*,[49] Bruffee also holds to the concept of single authorship and individual creativity (students write alone and then *revise* after getting peer response, much as in the Elbow method[50]) even while acknowledging the degree to which "knowledge is a social phenomenon, and the social context in which we learn permeates what we know and how we know it."[51] In addition, the mode of collaboration demonstrated in Bruffee's text is generally teacher-centered: the activities are set by a higher authority (the teacher), and the focus is on the revised end product — the intellectual property — of a text produced individually.

As Bruffee readily notes, only in the last few years has he come to contemplate the full theoretical significance of such an epistemology for the teaching of writing and reading.[52] Drawing on the work of scholars in a number of disciplines[53] — Bruffee argues that what and who we are and write and know is in large part a function of interaction and of community.[54] Thus writing and reading are, essentially and naturally, collaborative, social acts, ways in which we understand and in which "knowledge is established and maintained in the normal discourse of communities of knowledgeable peers."[55] As Berlin points out, Bruffee's later works have been "from the start based on a conception of knowledge as a social construction — a dialectical interplay of investigator, discourse community, and material world, with language as the agent of mediation. The rhetorical act is thus implicated in the very discovery of knowledge — a way not merely of recording knowledge for transmissions but of arriving at it mutually for mutual consideration."[56] But Bruffee's emphasis on collaboration and consensus continues to stand in contradiction to his implicit romanticist views of creativity and authorship. These views have been criticized most recently by Mas'ud Zavarzadeh and Donald Morton, who say that

> [t]here is in Bruffee no sense of the politics of cognition that organizes this socially constructed knowledge. Society and the social for him (as for Rorty) are cognitive domains — areas of such apparatuses as agreement and convention and so forth. As a result of such a conservative (cognitive) theory of knowledge . . . the subject is presented as an uncontested category. . . . Bruffee's collaborative learning/teaching is, in other words, the latest reproduction of the "management" of the subject and the latest effort to save it through "collaborative learning and the *Conversation of Mankind*." The teacher in this model is the manager of the classroom — an agent of social coalescence.[57]

Bruffee's particular brand of collaborative consensus has also been criticized by Greg Myers, who charges that

> while Bruffee shows that reality can be seen as a social construct, he does not give us any way to criticize this construct. Having discovered the role of consensus in the production of knowledge, he takes this consensus as something that just is, rather than as something that might be good or bad[58]

Myers is insisting that those interested in collaborative learning step back and ask *what* such practices will be used for, what aims and purposes and motives are served, where power and authority are located. Others in the composition community echo this concern. Richard Ohmann, for instance, has long criticized composition textbooks for treating student writers as though they were isolated, cut off from any cultural, political, or social contexts. Ohmann's *Politics of Letters* extends this critique to most contemporary teaching.[59] Similar critiques of the asocial and alienating nature of composition instruction appear in the works of Charles Yarnoff, David Bartholomae, Charles Bazerman, Patricia Bizzell, and particularly James Berlin.[60]

Other work has recently focused on context and on the communal aspects of learning. In particular, Shirley Brice Heath's ethnographic studies demonstrate how writing and reading must be seen as developing within a social context in which talk plays a major role.[61] David Bleich's *The Double Perspective: Language, Literacy, and Social Relativism* examines the ways in which learning is situated in and beyond our classrooms;[62] his chapter on "Collaboration among Students" offers particularly useful (and concrete) advice. At the Center for the Study of Writing, Linda Flower and her colleagues are working to relate the cognitive factors in composing to their social contexts.[63] Still others, focusing on professional and work-related writing, stress the importance of social and political contexts in such writing.[64]

The early work of Elbow and Bruffee has been augmented in this decade by a large and growing body of scholarship on collaborative learning, much of it linked to the National Writing Project and to writing across the curriculum movements.[65] In addition to the work of LeFevre[66] and Gere,[67] we now have major studies by Collette Daiute[68] and colleagues on collaboration among young school children,[69] by Anthony Pare and his colleagues on collaboration in high school settings,[70] and by the authors represented in Bouton and Garth's *Learning in Groups*,[71] to name only a few. This interest in, and growing commitment to, principles of collaborative learning grows out of, and is informed by, the philosophical tradition on which Bruffee's work builds. And, whether its advocates are aware of it or not, this tradition implicitly calls into question perceived notions of writing as inevitably and inherently *individual* and of intellectual property rights as belonging to radically individual selves. Whatever the strengths of the "collaborative learning" or "social constructionist" movement in composition studies may be, until scholars pursue the full implications of collaboration for these traditional notions of authorship and authority, they will fail to answer — or even to address — the questions with which we opened this essay.

III. The Challenge of Collaborative Writing

The work on collaborative learning surveyed here emphasizes the ways in which knowledge is constructed among members of communities. The recent attention given to collaborative *writing* might thus seem a natural extension or a subset of collaborative learning theory. Yet as the preceding pages have suggested, collaborative learning theory has from its inception failed to challenge traditional concepts of radical individualism and ownership of ideas and has operated primarily in a traditional and largely hierarchical way. Students in collaborative learning situations may work together on revising or on problem solving, but when they write, they typically continue to write alone, in settings structured and governed by a teacher/authority in whom final authority is vested. Studies of collaborative *writing*, on the other hand, make such silent accommodations less easy to maintain and as a result offer the potential to challenge and hence resituate collaborative learning theories.

Much of the work on collaborative writing has focused on the world of work. Studies by numerous authors examine collaborative writing in a number of job-related settings.[72] Others have attempted to build collaborative writing into classroom contexts.[73] In a 1986 survey, Hallie S. Lemon found that composition faculty at Western Illinois University use collaboration at every stage of the writing process, including drafting.[74] Extensive research on this kind of "shared document" collaboration is being carried out by members of a research team[75] in an effort to define kinds of collaborative writing and to describe the processes involved in such group writing tasks. Among their studies is an important case study of collaborative writing groups.[76] Also at the college level, O'Donnell and his colleagues have conducted experiments which support the claim that group-produced documents are perceived as "better" than those individually produced.[77] In a study of writers in seven contexts,[78] Stephen P. Witte identified four forms of collaborative writing and

concluded, among other things, that across these seven contexts "writing became increasingly more collaborative and collaborative in different ways."[79]
Thomas L. Hilgers[80] and Daiute[81] have explored the uses of collaborative writing with younger children.

Nevertheless, as Allen and her colleagues point out, because "very little
detail is known about collaborative writing processes in general . . . there is a
need for in-depth study of the features of collaborative writing [defined as] a
situation in which decisions are made by consensus."[82] We would add that
much more careful attention needs to be given to just what is meant by "consensus" and to the ways consensus is or is not achieved. John Trimbur begins
such an exploration in "Consensus and Difference in Collaborative Learning," in which he builds on the work of Habermas to argue that we must
"distinguish between consensus as an acculturative practice that reproduces
business as usual and consensus as an oppositional one that challenges the
prevailing conditions of production" by providing a "critical instrument to
open gaps in the conversation through which differences many emerge."[83]
Joseph Harris extends this critique of consensus and offers an argument for
"community without consensus" in his "Idea of Community in the Study of
Writing."[84]

Our own work has attempted to explore the varying and sometimes conflicting definitions of collaborative writing[85] and to identify the characteristics
of effective collaborative writing as well as its varying modes.[86] In our study
of collaborative writers in seven professional organizations, for instance, we
identified the following factors that serve to affect the degree of satisfaction
experienced by collaborative writers in their jobs:

1. the degree to which goals are clearly articulated and shared,
2. the degree of openness and mutual respect characteristic of group members,
3. the degree of control writers have over the text,
4. the degree to which writers can respond to others who may modify the text,
5. the way credit (direct or indirect) is realized,
6. an agreed upon procedure for resolving disputes among group members,
7. the number and kind of bureaucratic constraints (deadlines, technical or legal requirements, etc.) imposed on the writers, and
8. the status of the project within the organization.

Further questioning of our research subjects led to an emerging profile of effective collaborative writers. They are flexible and respectful of others; attentive, analytical listeners; able to speak and write clearly; dependable and able
to meet deadlines; able to dispute and share authority, to lead *and* to follow;
open to criticism but confident in their own abilities, and ready to engage in
creative conflict. As we sketched in this profile, however, we gradually became aware that collaborative writing on the job occurs in varying modes.
The dominant mode our research revealed emerged as highly structured and
hierarchical, with power and authority distributed vertically in the hierarchy,

and with productivity and efficiency as primary goals. A much less frequent mode of collaboration also emerged, however, one that we refer to as "dialogic." This alternate mode of collaboration is loosely structured, participants' roles are fluid, and the problem of articulating or reaching goals is of great importance.[87] Identifying these varying modes helped us to see how dramatically collaborative writing on the job offers theoretical challenges to traditional notions of originary authorship and radically individual intellectual property rights. Yet, in practice, such collaborative writing often gives the authority and intellectual ownership to "the boss" or the leader, without question, particularly in a rigidly hierarchical mode. In a number of cases, however, and particularly in those involving dialogic modes of collaboration, the writers involved were aware of at least a working sense of shared authorship, shared authority, and shared intellectual property, one far different from the traditional definition of a solitary, originary *author* holding individual intellectual property rights.

This review of research on collaborative writing suggests, first of all, that we need more and better studies of the processes and varieties of collaborative writing. It also points up, however, some directions that seem increasingly clear. First, collaborative writing offers a strong potential challenge to the hegemony of single, originary authorship and intellectual property and thus presents a series of challenges to higher education in general and to the teaching of writing in particular.

IV. IMPLICATIONS FOR THE COMPOSITION CLASSROOM

Closest to home is the challenge to traditional classroom format and to the teacher's role. Our classrooms most often continue to vest power and authority in the teacher. At best, students are in apprenticeship to authority; they do not help constitute it.[88] Richard Ohmann acknowledges this challenge when he probes the issue of student "powerlessness" in our classes: "The writer's situation is heavy with contradictions. She is . . . invited both to assume responsibility for her education and to trust the college's plan for it; to build her competence and to follow a myriad of rules and instructions; to see herself as an autonomous individual and to be incessantly judged."[89] As one concrete way of contesting such alienating tensions, Ohmann uses collaborative group interviews, including one of himself. Ohmann notes:

> This underlies their ownership of the writing task in two ways. First, it demystifies my role in the class, opening up my goals and values as a subject for inquiry on the students' terms, taking them off the secret agenda. Second, it changes the relationship of their writing to what I have said in class, turning the latter into material for analysis and criticism rather than the graven words of authority.[90]

But even in the most collaborative of our classrooms, the authority to organize and evaluate rests with the teacher. As John Trimbur notes,

> Even when I'm not in the room, my authority remains behind, embed-
> ded in the very tasks I've asked students to work on. . . . If anything, I
> have never felt more powerful than in the collaborative classroom pre-
> cisely because I know much more about what's going on, how students
> are thinking about the issues of the course, what language they are gen-
> erating to talk about these issues and so on.[91]

As Foucault's work suggests, collaborative writing itself constitutes a technology of power, one we are only beginning to explore.[92] As we carry out such
exploration, as we investigate the ethics of collaboration and the ways in
which collaborative writing challenges traditional power relationships, we
need to bring students into these discussions, asking them to work with us to
examine how authority is negotiated, shared, distributed. At least potentially,
we could argue, collaborative writing holds out the promise for a plurality of
power and authority among teacher and students, what Ohmann calls an
"opening up" of the classroom.[93]

The hierarchical bases of power in our classrooms, of course, reflect the
larger structure of our educational institutions: Most university calendars, divided neatly into semesters or quarters, reflect a positivistic approach to learning: knowledge is "packaged" into discrete segments and dispensed to passive
recipients, fast-food style, through four years. Such a system represents students as isolated units, all of whom learn in similar ways and at similar speeds.
The time necessary for group cohesion to occur, for the examination of group
dynamics involving consensus and dissensus to take place, much less for a
consideration of the issues at stake in seemingly simple questions such as
"Who is the author of this essay?" or "Who is responsible for these words?" is
not easily found in such a system. The research and scholarship reviewed here
strongly suggests that just as we must rethink our roles as teachers in a collaborative writing classroom, so also must we rethink our use of time in the
college curriculum. At the very least, we must become aware of how such
things as the use of time reflect assumptions and traditions that no longer fit
with our educational goals.

We could of course point out other institutional constraints that militate
against a pedagogy of collaboration. Most notable is no doubt traditional
classroom design. Large, cavernous lecture halls in which students see only
the backs of other students' heads and classrooms whose bolted down desks
face dutifully toward the slightly raised lectern in front present major stum-
bling blocks to collaborative learning and writing. Institutional practices,
bound as they are in ideology, may prove even more intractable to change
than will classroom settings. Among these, the examination system seems
particularly problematic. This system, barely a hundred years old, is rooted
solidly in positivistic assumptions: knowledge is objectifiably knowable and
can be measured and counted. Such a tradition, of course, goes hand in hand
with the conception of a solitary, sovereign — and usually male — writer
with individually "owned" property rights. This view of knowledge calls for
a "controlled" testing situation and valorizes the hard data such situations

yield as "proof" of success or failure. Testing as we know it is by definition a-contextual and anti-social, anti-communal, as far from a collaborative activity as could be imagined. In such a system, students must do "original" work, and they are individually judged on individual "quality of mind." Unfortunately, the dependence on and infatuation with mass testing at all levels of the educational system seems only to be growing, as evidenced most recently by a call from The National Council of Education Standards and Testing for yet another and more rigorous round of national exams for America's students.[94] Yet the movements discussed here all question the very foundations on which such testing and grading practices rest.

The institutional reliance on testing "norms" and the ideology it reflects can be found replicated, not surprisingly, in the writing classroom, where concerns over individual performance — and especially over plagiarism — can become near obsessions. Certainly collaborative writing calls such obsessive concerns into question and reveals the formalist, positivist, and individualist ideological assumptions on which common notions of plagiarism rest. But do such questions obviate the very notion of plagiarism? If not, how can we help students construct a more sophisticated and enabling understanding of this concept? Teachers of writing may best begin, it seems to us, by taking a rhetorically situated view of plagiarism, one that acknowledges that all writing is in an important sense collaborative and that "common knowledge" varies from community to community and is collaboratively shared. From this perspective, attribution of sources becomes not a means of avoiding the heinous sin of plagiarism, but of building credibility or writerly *ethos*, of indicating to readers that the writer is a full collaborative participant in the scholarly conversation surrounding whatever topic is at hand. Clearly, teachers wishing to implement a pedagogy of collaboration will need new ways of evaluating the process of collaborative writing and the products produced thereby.

Our current sense is that a thorough re-examination of the grounds of testing and grading practices in higher education in general and composition classes in particular will have to follow rather than precede curricular reform. And in this area, the research on collaborative writing reviewed here may have a more immediate impact. In spite of the reform efforts of Heath, Emig, and others, the current curriculum is still based on a model of content coverage: classes must clip along, "covering" a certain number of units in a certain number of days. But this model is under increasing attack on a number of fronts and for a number of reasons. Most obviously, it is simply no longer possible for any one person to "cover" all the material in any field, even a fairly narrow one. Less obvious but equally important is the growing realization that what we "teach" in this inexorable drive to cover a content area is not necessarily or even probably what is learned. Here the research in collaborative learning theory is clear and unequivocal: real learning occurs in *interaction* as students actively use concepts and ideas or strategies in order to assimilate them. The pedagogical implications are equally clear: less may well yield *more* in terms of learning. What follows from this line of reasoning is the need to reconsider course structure in terms of assignments that will engage students in interaction and in collaboration with their teachers and other students. What is much less clear is whether teachers are willing or able to make the next logical and necessary step — to move from such collaboration to collaborative *writing*. Doing so challenges, as we have shown, very deep-seated beliefs in radically individual ways of knowing and in the writing pedagogies accompanying such beliefs.

Yet the time seems particularly ripe for teachers of writing to accept this challenge and to explore further the questions raised in the opening section of this essay. The work summarized here, as well as the research we have conducted, barely scratches the surface in terms of understanding the full range of collaboration, of exploring its dangers as well as its potentialities, of establishing an ethics of collaboration. For teachers of writing, however, the most immediate need is for a pedagogy of collaboration, one that would view writing as always shared and social; writers as constantly building and negotiating meaning with and among others; and evaluation as based at least in part on a "range of selves" and on communal efforts. Articulating such a pedagogy of collaboration, we believe, would advance efforts on a number of fronts to reconceive intellectual property and selfhood and to value these reconceived notions in a way that is commensurate with the idea of a postmodern democracy.

NOTES

1. Lisa Ede & Andrea A. Lunsford, "Why Write . . . Together?," 1 *Rhetoric Rev.* 150 (1983).
2. See, e.g., Andrea A. Lunsford & Lisa S. Ede, *Singular Texts/Plural Authors: Perspectives on Collaboration* at ch. 3 (1990).
3. Alexis de Tocqueville, *Democracy in America* 506–08 (J. P. Mayer ed. & George Lawrence trans., 1969).
4. *Id.*
5. *Id.* at 510.
6. See Robert N. Bellah et al., *Habits of the Heart: Individualism and Commitment in American Life* (1985), and Robert N. Bellah et al., *The Good Society* (1991), for an examination of the ideals related to tensions in contemporary America.
7. See Michael Halloran, "Rhetoric in the American College Curriculum: The Decline of Public Discourse," 3 *Pre/Text* 245 (1982).
8. See Gerald Graff, *Professing Literature* (1987), for a recounting of this history, which treats English departments but not rhetorical instruction and/or theory.
9. Anne R. Gere, *Writing Groups: History, Theory, Implications* 32–54 (1987). See also David Potter, "The Literary Society," in *History of Speech Education in America: Background Studies* 238–58 (Karl R. Wallace ed., 1954).
10. Fred Newton Scott, *Composition-Rhetoric, Designed for Use in Secondary Schools* (1897); Gertrude Buck, "The Metaphor — A Study in the Psychology of Rhetoric," in 5 *Contributions to Rhetorical Theory* (Fred Newton Scott ed., 1899).
11. See Alexander Bain, *On Teaching English* (1901).
12. Mara Holt, Collaborative Learning From 1911–1986: A Sociohistorical Analysis 235 (1988) (unpublished Ph.D. dissertation, University of Texas (Austin)).
13. *Id.* at 235.
14. John Dewey, *The Public and Its Problems* 24 (1927).
15. *Id.* at 54–55.
16. Sterling A. Leonard, *Two Types of Criticism for Composition Work* 509 (1916).
17. Sterling A. Leonard, *English Composition As a Social Problem* at viii–ix (1917).
18. George H. Mead, Mind, *Self & Society from the Standpoint of a Social Behaviorist* (1970).
19. Karen B. LeFevre, *Invention as a Social Act* 63 (1987).
20. Jean Piaget, *The Construction of Reality in the Child* (1954).

21. Reductivist renderings of Dewey's work seem to have been uncritically accepted by E. D. Hirsch. See E. D. Hirsch, *Cultural Literacy: What Every American Needs to Know* (1987). Hirsch uses Dewey as a whipping boy in his cultural literacy argument.

22. M.L.J. Abercrombie, *The Anatomy of Judgment: An Investigation into the Process of Perception and Reasoning* (1969).

23. M.L.J. Abercrombie, *Aims and Techniques for Group Teaching* (1970).

24. Abercrombie, *supra* note 22, at 15–16.

25. *Id.* at 17.

26. Edwin Mason, *Collaborative Learning* 7 (1970).

27. *Id.* at 8.

28. See generally Mason, *supra* note 26.

29. Paolo Freire, *Pedagogy of the Oppressed* (Myra B. Ramos trans., 1970) (1968).

30. *Freire for the Classroom: A Sourcebook for Liberatory Teaching* (Ira Shor ed., 1987).

31. Gere, *supra* note 9.

32. See James Moffett, *Teaching the Universe of Discourse* (1968); Janet Emig, *The Web of Meaning* (1983); James N. Britton, *Language and Learning* (1970).

33. Richard Young, "Arts, Crafts, Gifts, and Knacks: Some Disharmonies in the New Rhetoric," in *Reinventing the Rhetorical Tradition* 53–60 (Aviva Freedman & Ian Pringle eds., 1980).

34. Patricia Bizzell, "Cognition, Convention, and Certainty: What We Need to Know About Writing," 3 *Pre/Text* 213, 215 (1982).

35. See James Berlin, "Contemporary Composition: The Major Pedagogical Theories," 44 *College English* 765–77 (1982). See also James Berlin, *Rhetoric and Reality: Writing Instruction in American Colleges, 1900–1985* (1987) [hereinafter Berlin, *Rhetoric and Reality*]; James Berlin, "Rhetoric and Ideology," 50 *College English* 477–94 (1988) [hereinafter Berlin, *Rhetoric and Ideology*].

36. See Lester Faigley & Thomas P. Miller, "What We Learn from Writing on the Job," 44 *College English* 557–69 (1982). See also Stephen M. North, *The Making of Knowledge in Composition: Portrait of an Emerging Field* (1987).

37. LeFevre, *supra* note 19, at 1.

38. See Wayne Booth, *Critical Understanding: The Powers and Limits of Pluralism* (1979); Michel Foucault, "What Is an Author?," in *Textual Strategies: Perspectives in Post-Structuralist Criticism* 141–60 (Josue V. Harari ed., 1979).

39. Thomas Kent, "On the Very Idea of a Discourse Community," 42 *CCC* 425 (1991).

40. See Bizzell, *supra* note 34.

41. See Berlin, *Rhetoric and Reality*, *supra* note 35, at 756.

42. See LeFevre, *supra* note 19.

43. Peter Elbow, *Writing without Teachers* 69 (1973).

44. See Peter Elbow, *Embracing Contraries: Explorations in Learning and Teaching* (1973); Peter Elbow, *Writing with Power: Techniques for Mastering the Writing Process* (1981) [hereinafter Elbow, *Writing with Power*].

45. See Elbow, *Writing with Power*, *supra* note 44.

46. Greg Myers, "Reality, Consensus and Reform in the Rhetoric of Composition Teaching," 48 *College English* 154, 165 (1986).

47. Peter Elbow, "Closing My Eyes as I Talk: An Argument Against Audience Awareness," 44 *College English* 50 (1987); Peter Elbow & Jennifer Clark, "Desert Island Discourse: The Benefits of Ignoring Audience," *The Journal Book* 19 (Toby Fulwiler ed., 1988).

48. Kenneth A. Bruffee, "The Brooklyn Plan," 64 *Liberal Education* 447, 450 (1978).

49. Kenneth Bruffee, *A Short Course in Writing* (2d ed., 1980).

50. See Elbow, *Writing with Power*, *supra* note 41, at 20–24, 139–45.

51. See Bruffee, *supra* note 48, at 116.

52. See Kenneth A. Bruffee, "Collaborative Learning and the 'Conversation of Mankind,'" 46 *College English* 635 (1984).

53. See, e.g., Stanley Fish, *Is There a Text in This Class?* (1980) (literary studies); Lev Vygotsky, *Thought and Language* (Eugenia Hanfmann & Gertrude Vakar, trans., 1962) (psychology); Thomas Kuhn, *The Structure of Scientific Revolution* (2d ed., 1979) (philosophy); Richard Rorty, *Philosophy and the Mirror of Nature* (1979) (philosophy); Clifford Geertz, *Local Knowledge: Further Essays in Interpretative Anthropology* (1983) (anthropology).

54. Bruffee, *supra* note 52, at 641–47. "[W]riting always has its roots deep in the acquired ability to carry on the social symbolic exchanges we call conversation." *Id.* at 641–42.

55. *Id.* at 640.

56. Berlin, *Rhetoric and Reality*, *supra* note 35, at 175–76.

57. Mas'ud Zavarzadeh & Donald Morton, "Theory Pedagogy Politics: The Crisis of "The Subject" in the Humanities," 15 *Boundary 2: A Journal of Postmodern Literature and Culture*, 1, 14–15 (Fall, Winter 1986–87).

58. See Myers, *supra* note 46, at 166.

59. See Richard Ohmann, *Politics of Letters* (1987).

60. See Charles Yarnoff, "Contemporary Theories of Intervention in the Rhetorical Tradition," 41 *College English* 552 (1980); David Bartholomae, "Inventing the University," in *When a Writer Can't Write: Studies in Writer's Block and Other Composing-Process Problems* 134 (Mike Rose ed., 1985); Charles Bazerman, "Scientific Writing as Social Act: A Review of the Literature of the Sociology of Science," in *New Essays in Technical and Scientific Communication: Research, Theory and Practice* 156 (Paul Van Anderson et al. eds., 1983); Bizzell, *supra* note 34, at 213–43 (1982); Patricia Bizzell, "Foundationalism and Anti-Foundationalism in Composition Studies," 7 *Pre/Text* 37–56 (1986); Berlin, *Rhetoric and Ideology*, *supra* note 35.

61. Shirley B. Heath, *Ways with Words: Language, Life, and Work on Communities and Classrooms* (1983).

62. David Bleich, *The Double Perspective: Language, Literacy, and Social Relativism* (1988).

63. *Reading-to-Write: Exploring a Cognitive and Social Process* (Linda Flower et al. eds., 1990).

64. See, e.g., *Writing in Non-Academic Settings* (Lee Odell & Dixie Goswami eds., 1985); Janis Forman & Patricia Katsky, "The Group Report: A Problem in Small Group or Writing Processes?," 23 *J. of Bus. Comm.* 23–35 (1986).

65. See John Trimbur, "Collaborative Learning and Teaching Writing," in *Perspectives on Research and Scholarship in Composition* 87 (Ben W. McClelland & Timothy R. Donovan eds., 1985) for a review of work on collaborative writing.

66. See LeFevre, *supra* note 19.

67. See Gere, *supra* note 9.

68. See Collette Daiute, "Do 1 and 1 Make 2? Patterns of Influence by Collaborative Authors," 3 *Written Comm.* 382–408 (1986).

69. *Id.*

70. See Anthony Pare, "How It Works: A Group-Authored Assignment," 7 *Inkshed* 5–7 (1988).

71. See *Learning in Groups, New Directions for Teaching and Learning* 14 (Clark Bouton & Russell Y. Garth eds., 1983).

72. See, e.g., Mary B. Debs, *Collaboration and Its Effects on the Writer's Process: A Look at Engineering* (1983); Janis Forman, "Computer-Mediated Group Writing in the Workplace," 5 *Computers and Composition* 19 (Nov. 1987); Stephen Doheny-Farina, "Writing in an Emerging Organization: An Ethnographic Study," 3 *Written Comm.* 158 (1986); Faigley & Miller, *supra* note 36, at 557; Geoffrey Cross, Editing in Context; An Ethnographic Exploration of Editor-Writer Revisions at a Midwestern Insurance Company (1988) (unpublished Ph.D. dissertation, Ohio State University). Two publications have recently devoted special issues to the subject of collaborative writing. See 38 *Technical Comm.* (Nov. 1991); 53 *The Bulletin* (Assoc. for Business Communication) (1990).

73. See, e.g., Deborah Bosley, A National Study of the Uses of Collaborative Writing in Business Communications Courses among Members of the ABC (1989) (unpublished Ph.D. dissertation, Illinois State University); Sharon Hamilton-Wieler, "How Does Writing Emerge from the Classroom Context? A Naturalistic Study of the Writing of Eighteen-Year-Olds in Biology, English, Geography, History, History of Art, and Sociology" (available in ERIC, Retrieval No. ED 284 209); Karen Spear, *Sharing Writing: Peer Response Groups in English Classes* (1988); Charles R. Cooper, *Responding to Student Writing, The Writing Process of Students* (Walter Petty & Patrick Finn eds., Report of the First Annual Language Arts Conference, State Univ. of N.Y. at Buffalo, 1975).

74. See Hallie S. Lemon, Collaborative Strategies for Teaching Composition: Theory and Practice, Unpublished Paper Delivered at the Conference on College Composition and Communication (St. Louis, Mar. 1988).

75. This research team began their work in a Purdue University Ph.D. program.

76. See Meg Morgan et al., "Collaborative Writing in the Classroom," 50 *The Bulletin* 20–26 (1987) (Assoc. for Business Communication).

77. Angela M. O'Donnell et al., "Cooperative Writing," 2 *Written Comm.* 307 (1985).

78. The seven contexts include: junior high school, high school, upper-division undergraduate, doctoral students, a chemist, a general manager, and a civil engineer.

79. Stephen P. Witte, Some Contexts for Understanding Written Literacy 2–3, Unpublished Paper Delivered at the Right to Literacy Conference (Columbus, Sept. 1988).

80. See Thomas L. Hilgers, On Learning the Skill of Collaborative Writing, Unpublished Paper Delivered at the Conference on College Composition and Communication (New Orleans, Mar. 1986).

81. See Daiute, *supra* note 68.

82. Morgan et al., *supra* note 76.

83. John Trimbur, "Consensus and Difference in Collaborative Learning," 51 *College English* 602 (1989).

84. See Joseph Harris, "The Idea of Community in the Study of Writing," 40 *College Composition and Communication* 11 (1989).

85. Lunsford & Ede, *supra* note 2, at 14–16.

86. *Id.*

87. For a more complete description of these modes, see Lunsford & Ede, *supra* note 2, at 133–36.

88. See Jane Tompkins, "Pedagogy of the Distressed," 52 *College English* 653 (1990).

89. See Ohmann, *supra* note 59, at 252.

90. *Id.* at 256.

91. See Trimbur, *supra* note 83, at 602.

92. See Foucault, *supra* note 38, at 141.

93. Ohmann, *supra* note 59.

94. Dennis Kelly, "National Standards," *USA Today*, Jan. 24, 1992, at D1.

11 Collaboration and Concepts of Authorship

[I]

Cogito, ergo sum.
— RENÉ DESCARTES

I yam what I am.
— RALPH ELLISON

Who am we?
— SHERRY TURKLE[1]

What does it mean to be an author? This question has been interrogated from just about every imaginable angle, as the status of the author has been problematized, deconstructed, and challenged to such an extent that discussions of the author problem now seem decidedly old-hat. Scholars now understand — in theory, at least — that the notion of author (like that of the founding or sovereign subject on which it depends) is a peculiarly modern construct, one that can be traced back through multiple and overdetermined pathways to the development of modern capitalism and of intellectual property, to Western rationalism, and to patriarchy. Foucault's assertion that "[t]he coming into being of the notion of 'author' constitutes the privileged moment of individualization in the history of ideas, knowledge, literature, philosophy, and the sciences" no longer surprises (141). The author, like the autonomous individual of Descartes's *cogito*, is, we understand with Raymond Williams, "a characteristic form of bourgeois thought" (192), one that Ralph Ellison parodies, for instance, when his protagonist, in a fleeting moment of self- and cultural integration, proclaims "I yam what I am" (260). The relentless intertextuality of Web culture, the rapid proliferation of multiple selves online, and the development of what Sherry Turkle has called "distributed selves" of postmodernity would seem to have moved us well beyond autonomous individualism (*Life* 14).

From Lisa Ede and Andrea A. Lunsford, in *PMLA* 116.2 (2001): 354–69.

Or have they? In spite of the works mentioned above, the question of what it means to acknowledge the death of the author and to proclaim the advent of distributed selves is hardly resolved. As Turkle recognizes, the opportunity to deploy virtual selves with distributed and potentially ever-changing identities can be a source of alienation and anxiety as well as of liberation — can make it hard indeed for us to determine "Who am we?" (1). Issues of agency also remain pressing. In 1988, for example, Barbara Christian began raising questions about the material consequences of critiques of the subject and of the author. Is it merely a coincidence, Christian asks in "The Race for Theory," that the death of the author was proclaimed just as women and scholars of color were beginning to publish? Other feminist scholars have been at pains to argue that the death of the author does not and cannot entail an abandonment of agency, as have some postcolonial and race theorists.[2] Such scholars have insisted as well on the urgent need to recover the voices of those whose otherness denied them *authority*. In the field of rhetoric and composition, researchers have expended considerable effort applying postmodern and poststructuralist critiques of subjectivity and the author construct to writing and the teaching of writing. The socially constructed nature of writing — its inherently collaborative foundation — functions as an enthymemic grounding for much contemporary research in the discipline.[3]

These efforts have spawned debates within debates over agency, subjectivity, and authorship. In feminism, for instance, conversations surrounding agency have catalyzed intense discussions about the place of the personal in academic criticism and theory (N. Miller; Tompkins; Scott; hooks). It is difficult indeed, feminist theorists have learned, to loosen the hold of the binaries that ground Western constructs of the subject and of the author. (See Cheryl Walker's "Feminist Literary Criticism and the Author" for an exploration of this issue and related ones.) Similarly, postcolonial and race theorists have debated the nature and status of hybridity, the splitting of the postcolonial subject posited by Homi Bhabha (207) and critiqued by, among others, Gloria Anzaldúa and Ania Loomba. In these fields, as in rhetoric and composition, the status of theory has been increasingly in question, as scholars recognize that, however we theorize the subject and author, problems of writing and of scholarly (and pedagogical) practice decidedly remain. Amid such intense questioning, a kind of paralysis seems possible, as Jane Flax notes when she asks, "How is it possible to write? What meanings can writing have when every proposition and theory seems questionable, one's own identity is uncertain, and the status of the intellectual is conceived alternatively as hopelessly enmeshed in oppressive knowledge/power relations or utterly irrelevant to the workings of the technical-rational bureaucratic state?" (5).[4]

Similar questions — about writing and the teaching of writing — find expression in rhetoric and composition, where the nature of voice and the role of the personal in academic writing are hotly contested issues.[5] Also open to debate are the nature and consequences of the social-constructionist turn that composition studies took in the 1980s. In their 1989 "Writing as Collaboration," for instance, James A. Reither and Douglas Vipond observe:

> Although the case for writing's social dimensions no longer requires arguing — it can be assumed — we would be hard put to point to a corresponding transformation in the ways writing is conceived and dealt with in our classrooms. In fact, even though radical changes in practice seem called for if we believe even some of what has been claimed about the social dimensions of writing, little substantive change in either course design or classroom practice has come about [. . .]. (855)

Our own experience as researchers and teachers supports Reither and Vipond: little has changed in the years since they wrote. Since the mid-1980s, when we began the research for *Singular Texts/Plural Authors*, we have been calling on scholars in rhetoric and composition, and in the humanities more generally, to *enact* contemporary critiques of the author and of the autonomous individual through a greater interest in and adoption of collaborative writing practices — and to do so not only in classrooms but in scholarly and professional work as well. Though we can certainly note some responses to this call at the level of scholarly and pedagogical practice, in general we would have to characterize these responses as limited.[6]

We are hardly alone in our concerns over disjunctures or contradictions between theory and practice in the academy. Literary scholars such as Jonathan Arac, James Sosnoski, Evan Watkins, Maria-Regina Kecht, and Paul Bové have pointed out the extent to which contemporary academic practices in English studies constitute, as Sosnoski puts it in the title of his 1995 study, "modern skeletons in postmodern closets." In his *In the Wake of Theory*, Bové explores the relation of theory and practice in English studies, noting that too often scholars have assumed "that 'theory-work' somehow would or could stand outside the given realities of our time and place" (5). Similarly, in *Work Time* Watkins calls attention to the importance of acknowledging that "actual practices of resistance depend on specific working conditions" and to the danger of "the dream of transubstantiation" — the dream that work done in one location (the writing of an article or a book, for instance) will effect political change in another location (28–29).

We scholars in English studies, it appears, are often more comfortable theorizing about subjectivity, agency, and authorship than we are attempting to enact alternatives to conventional assumptions and practices. In literary studies and in rhetoric and composition it has proved difficult, as Paul Smith observes in *Discerning the Subject*, to "produce a notion of subjectivity which will satisfy both the demands of theory and the exigencies of practice" (xxxii). What does or might it mean, after all, for scholars in the humanities to take the "exigencies of practice" seriously? Might one possible consequence of doing so require rethinking the "demands of theory"? In what follows we hope to trouble conventional understandings of authorship in contemporary theory — understandings that suggest that the problem of the author has been if not resolved then thoroughly critiqued — by looking at these understandings through the lens of actual collaborative (or noncollaborative) practices in and outside the academy. In our experience, looking at concepts of authorship through this materially grounded lens allows us to see, and then critique, assumptions and practices that otherwise appear natural or commonsensical. Doing so also reveals the powerful ideological, cultural, social, and political forces that work to resist, co-opt, or contain change — including those forces that work most intimately (and thus powerfully) in our personal and professional lives.

[II]

[A]lmost all the routine forms of marking an academic career — CVs, annual faculty activity reports, tenure and promotion reviews — militate against [collaboration] by singling out for merit only those moments of individual "productivity," the next article or grant or graduate course, creating a version of professional life that oddly yet almost seamlessly merges the roles of subaltern dissident and intellectual entrepreneur.

— JOSEPH HARRIS

The doctoral dissertation must be an original contribution to scholarship or scientific knowledge and must exemplify the highest standards of the discipline.

— STANFORD BULLETIN

Acknowledgments continue to present the indebtedness of a single individual, securely at the center of his or her authority, even at a time when, according to the poststructuralist or even postmodern critique, the author is either "dead" or so vitiated by various discourses as to be simply an "effect" of them.

— TERRY CAESAR

Every established order tends to produce (to very different degrees and with very different means) the naturalization of its own arbitrariness.

— PIERRE BOURDIEU[7]

As these epigraphs suggest, whatever scholars say about the nature of the subject and of the author, the ideologies of the academy take the autonomy of the individual — and of the author — for granted. And they do so in ways that encourage scholars not to notice potential contradictions between, say, poststructural and postmodern critiques of originality and the academy's traditional injunction that a PhD dissertation must represent an original contribution to a discipline.[8] In Pierre Bourdieu's terms, the result is a naturalization of contradictions that makes them appear not as contradictions but rather as cultural or disciplinary common sense. Clifford Geertz points out in "Common Sense as a Cultural System" that the more ideologically embedded the assumption, the less likely those who hold this assumption will recognize it: "There is something," Geertz comments, "of the purloined-letter effect in common sense; it lies so artlessly before our eyes it is almost impossible to see" (92). In this context it is not surprising that our examination of a number of university statements about PhD dissertations did not turn up a single explicit prohibition against collaborative dissertations. The most deeply held taboos are, after all, rarely specified in writing.

Whether one is an undergraduate hoping to do well in a class, an assistant professor working to meet explicit and implicit criteria for tenure and promotion, or a senior faculty member striving to gain national recognition for his or her scholarly work, everyday practices in the humanities continue to ignore, or even to punish, collaboration while authorizing work attributed to (autonomous) individuals. And as Terry Caesar notes in *Conspiring with Forms*, even potential acts of resistance to academic ideologies of individualism, such as acknowledgments, often reinscribe traditional assumptions about the individual ownership of intellectual property. In these and other ways, common-sense assumptions about individualism and authorship circulate in the humanities.

As an example of such common sense in action, Evan Watkins comments on the ideologies that inform academic understandings of *work*. After noting the potentially multiple significations of this term — from "work of literature" to "scholarly work" or "committee work" — Watkins points out that the commonsensical understandings of *work* in the academy might "easily be a source of confusion to outsiders, who might not understand that when [a colleague] asks you what you are working on now, s/he usually expects a brief summary of your latest article or book manuscript, not a report on your intro to Am Lit class or a blow-by-blow account of how you typed up the minutes for the last faculty meeting" (12). Watkins's anecdote exposes the commonsensical (and thus deeply ideological) valuing of certain kinds of practices as important work — work that in effect constitutes a person's primary academic identity — and other kinds as necessary but lacking personal or institutional significance once completed.

In his study, Watkins is concerned with (among other things) the ways in which "ideologies of 'the new'" circulate as "a privileged form of value" in English studies (14). He is concerned as well with the question of "[w]hether cultural work in English [. . .] can be politically effective" (8). These are concerns that we share — but we would point out (as Watkins does not) the extent to which ideologies of autonomous individualism and authorship inform the assumptions and practices that Watkins critiques. As we have already noted (and as the epigraph by Joseph Harris emphasizes), success in the academy depends largely on having one's work recognized as an individual accomplishment. Inherent in such individualism is the agonism central to patriarchy, an agonism requiring that the accomplishment of one scholar (or generation of scholars) can most easily win recognition by overturning the work of another scholar (or generation). In *The Academic Postmodern and the Rule of Literature*, David Simpson comments tellingly on this strategy, which he characterizes as "the rhetoric of self-definition." Simpson observes that this rhetoric "functions with a strongly presentist and individualist emphasis. We set up 'isms' and then go about the task of distinguishing them from other 'isms'" (105). While some scholars are beginning to recognize the problems inherent in this rhetoric — examples might include the conversation among Jane Gallop, Marianne Hirsch, and Nancy Miller published in "Criticizing Feminist Criticism" and Linda Hutcheon's Presidential Forum at the

2000 MLA convention, "Creative Collaboration: Alternatives to the Adversarial Academy" — the deep structure of the academy remains relatively untouched.

In calling attention to the sharp disjunction between scholarly critiques of the author and the material practices of the academy, we by no means advocate a reversal of business as usual in the form of an enforced ideology of collaboration, one that would circulate as rigidly and unitarily as the ideologies of individual agency and authorship now do. Nor do we wish to suggest that collaborative practices resolve ongoing questions of agency and of authors' rights. We are mindful of the concerns of many women and minority writers, who are only now claiming author-ity — and who for a variety of positive reasons may find it most productive to produce single-author texts (Lunsford 531). And we are mindful as well that, as John Trimbur argues in "Agency and the Death of the Author: A Partial Defense of Modernism," although critiques of the modernist figure of the author raise central issues for theory and practice, they risk "mistak[ing] the notoriously bad case of the belletristic author for the category itself" Trimbur goes on to argue that "(the point [. . .] is not just to rid ourselves of individualistic ideologies of the author and to take up a 'social view' of writing. The task, as Walter Benjamin poses it, is to *socialize* the author as producer" (296).

We agree. Our concern is not to propose a totalizing argument against single authorship and the practices conventionally associated with it. (In fact, given the current corporate appropriation of the author construct, to which we will shortly turn, we see increasing need to protect individual authors' rights.) Further, as we take pains to demonstrate in *Singular Texts/Plural Authors*, and as we will discuss more fully in the conclusion of this essay, collaborative practices, like individual practices, can only be evaluated through deeply situated analyses. The last thirty years of scholarly work in English studies have surely demonstrated that the power-knowledge nexus is a place of danger as well as opportunity and that the human ability to bracket one's own experiences and understandings from critique is substantial. This is as true of collaborative work as it is of work undertaken individually.

What we are arguing for is more attention to what Paul Smith terms "the exigencies of practice" and the ways in which practices do — or do not — intersect with contemporary theory. We hope to encourage scholarly work that interrogates these intersections and explores how demands of theory might be reconceived so that they allow for (or at least do not so deeply and strongly discourage) collaborative, as well as individual, projects. And we are particularly interested in provoking reconsiderations of disciplinary practices in English studies around issues of individualism and authorship. What might it mean, for instance, to acknowledge the inherently collaborative nature of dissertations and the impossibility of making a truly original contribution to knowledge? Would the sky fall if, on occasion, PhD students wrote dissertations collaboratively? And why has the ideological function of the single-author book — a virtual necessity for promotion and tenure in most research universities — not received the same attention from scholars that the author construct has received? Questions such as these remind us that, despite vigorous debates over theories and methods surrounding issues of subjectivity and authorship, ideologies of the individual and the author have remained largely unchallenged in scholarly practice.

Indeed, universities have increasingly co-opted the author construct, taking on more and more ownership of work produced in them as they are being restructured through a confluence of global capitalism and corporatization. If such a corporate scenario plays itself out in our universities, as a number of recent books argue it will (see, e.g., Readings; Lucas), then ownership and authorship will increasingly be held by the university, and knowledge produced by faculty members and students will belong exclusively to that entity. Such occurrences are perhaps most likely in distance and online learning programs, for which academics produce "content" that is owned by the corporate university. But in the current climate, the ownership of everything from course materials to dissertations and scholarly books, especially those produced with the aid of university hardware and software, can be disputed. In such a brave new world, understanding one's university's policies on intellectual property may be as important as understanding its policies on tenure and promotion; indeed, the two are intertwined. Far from being dead, the author is now working in the academy in ways that early framers of copyright and authorial autonomy could scarcely have imagined.[9]

Outside the academy, the ideology of the author also circulates powerfully through legal and corporate worlds. In the body of law governing copyright, for example, the solitary and sovereign "author" holds clear sway: copyright cannot exist in a work produced as a true collective enterprise; copyright does not hold in works that are not "original" (which, as Peter Jaszi has demonstrated, rules out protection for "nonindividualistic cultural productions, like folkloric works, which cannot be reimagined as products of solitary, originary, 'authorship'" [38]), and copyright does not extend to what the law sees as the basic components of cultural production (the rhythms of traditional music forms, for example). What copyright law does protect is "authors' rights," which have been repeatedly expanded during the last thirty years, effectively keeping a great deal of cultural material out of the public domain and further restricting the fair use of copyrighted works.

In a particularly ironic turn of events, corporate entities assuming the mantle of the author now lead the way in a kind of gold rush attempt to extend copyright in all directions. Bill Gates is trying to corner the world's market of images; Disney is working to extend the limits of copyright to well over a hundred years so that Mickey Mouse's move into the public commons is postponed; drug companies are patenting and copyrighting chemicals found in the plants of Third World countries to process and sell them as cures — and for a great profit; and scientists and the companies they work for are patenting genetic code. Most recent has been the move in legal and corporate worlds to apply the claim of proprietary authorship to computer hardware and software. In spite of their wide public use and the fact that they are the products of a highly collaborative process, computer programs (with a few notable exceptions) are increasingly defined in the law and in the economy as works of originality and creative genius — that is, as works that fall within the ever-expanding protection of copyright and authors' rights. In short, the old cloak of the originary author-genius has been spruced up and donned first by the law and then by corporate entrepreneurial interests — and the bigger and more global, the better. Today the same old cloak is being stretched to cover emerging Internet policies regarding authors' rights, though some of the suits associated with the Napster controversy are revealing holes in the fabric.[10] Nonetheless, as James Porter points out in examining the ethical frameworks available for use in Internet policy, the individualist frame of traditional authorship is almost universally accepted as the only valid choice ("Liberal Individualism"). These realities dramatically highlight the dangers inherent in continuing to extend the ideologies of the author and call attention to the extent to which scholarly critiques of authorship and individualism remain circumscribed within the academy. Academics who wish to resist late capitalist tendencies of commodification will need not only to critique conventional understandings of authorship but to enact alternatives as well.

[III]

I am not i can be you and me.

—Trinh T. Minh-ha

I didn't create language, writer thought. Later she would think about ownership and copyright.

—Kathy Acker

Today we stand at unmarked crossroads, knowing that our future depends on creatively rethinking who we are and what we do.

—Nellie McKay[11]

In our view, thinking of concepts of authorship and ownership as they are played out in realms far beyond the academy brings a new urgency to a number of recent calls for collaboration as well as for new forms, definitions, and understandings of authorship in the academy, calls that may help us understand, in other words, the potential power of Trinh T. Minh-ha's observation that "I am not i can be you and me" (90). In 1995, for example, David Damrosch's *We Scholars* made the case for replacing the academic culture of agonism and alienation with one of genuine collaborative community. Two years later, in "Shop Window or Laboratory: Collection, Collaboration, and the Humanities," Jonathan Arac asked why a model of exclusively individual ownership "is the fundamental way that we seem to value our intellectual activity" (123). In answering this question, Arac notes the degree to which humanities scholarship has focused "on the figure of the creator, treated as a distinctive, single, isolated individual" (118), and he goes on to explore knowledge produced by such isolated individuals (the shop window model) and to offer an alternative arena in which knowledge is produced collaboratively (the laboratory model). Arac's thoughtful essay sums up the increasingly obvious disjunction between the work that theory has done to critique "expressive totalities," such as the originary author, and the extent to which that work is carried out in "ways wholly compatible with a thoroughly discredited individualism" (120), a disjunction, as we noted above, that scholars in rhetoric and composition began exploring in the early 1980s.[12] In "What If Scholars in the Humanities Worked Together, in a Lab?" Cathy Davidson returns to Arac's question from a slightly different perspective. In productive labs, she says, "collaborative thinking" should be the outcome of work even if collaborative writing does not always, or even often, occur: "In a lab — or at least the platonic ideal of a lab — discovery of one sort or another is the shared, overt goal. [. . .] Labs are built around the process of discovery [and require] collaboration across fields and disciplinary subfields, as well as across generations" (B5).[13]

Paralleling and usefully augmenting calls for additional collaborative research models are the efforts of those who promote alternatives to the agonistic individualism characteristic of so much academic writing. For the last decade, scholars in the fields of rhetoric, composition, and communication have been describing and theorizing an invitational rhetoric, which grows out of collaborative rather than agonistic principles (Foss and Griffin; Frey; Barton). Considerable work as well has been done on alternatives to traditional forms of academic discourse — alternatives that, as Lillian Bridwell-Bowles notes in "Discourse and Diversity: Experimental Writing within the Academy," avoid traditional argumentative structures and provide "new processes and forms to express ways of thinking that have been outside the dominant culture" (349).[14]

In the 2000 MLA Presidential Address, Linda Hutcheon explores the human and intellectual costs the humanities have paid for what Deborah Tannen calls an "argument culture" (qtd. in Hutcheon).[15] In the address, which models an invitational argument, Hutcheon asks all scholars to practice thinking with as well as thinking against. Like Damrosch, Arac, and Davidson, Hutcheon points to the debilitating effects of continuing habits long associated with agonistic individualism and calls instead for new strategies of academic argument to replace those associated with combat, destructive critique, and aggression.

One compelling reason for taking up Hutcheon's challenge is resolutely practical: today many important and exciting research projects in the humanities — and particularly of the kind Arac suggests — simply cannot be carried out by a solitary (much less an alienated and aggressively destructive) scholar. What has become a commonplace for many in the natural and social sciences — scholars in physics and political science, for instance, carry out almost all their research as part of groups or teams — is now a feature of work across the humanities.[16] In "Doing Public History: Producing *The Great War* for PBS and BBC," Jay Winter describes the varying kinds of collaboration necessary to the success of this important documentary series and calls on senior scholars in the humanities to take the lead in creating and carrying out such large-scale projects. Indeed, Winter argues, the survival of public history depends on such a change in scholarly practices.

Projects like the one Winter describes almost always call for interdisciplinary collaboration, which can bring special challenges. The most recent work of Shirley Brice Heath provides a strong case in point. For the last dozen years, Heath and a group of researchers have been documenting the practices of youth art groups around the United States as part of an effort to demonstrate (to public policy makers, funding agencies, and the public) the essential value of the arts and humanities to young people. To make this case, Heath wanted to go beyond the traditional audiences that a book or research report might reach. The result, a documentary film entitled Art*Show* (screened during autumn 2000 on many local PBS stations), required two years of intensive collaboration among Heath, members of the research group, the young people involved in the four groups the film focuses on, film directors and editors, digital-sound and visual-effects experts, and other technical artists. Like Winter's *The Great War*, Heath's project aims at bringing humanities research to a broad public audience — and affecting public policy as well.

Other projects illustrate the degree to which humanities scholars are attempting collaborative research and writing. Based at the University of Alberta, the Orlando Project — whose participants come from schools in Canada, the United States, England, and Australia — is undertaking "the first full scholarly history of women's writing in the British Isles" while also "conducting an experiment in humanities computing" and providing "training and scholarly community for graduate students." Even a cursory look at the project's Web site (www.arts.ualberta.ca/~orlando/wordpress) indicates that this effort simply could not proceed without the kind of collaboration the site describes. The number of scholars involved, the breadth of the goal, and the multiple perspectives necessary to illuminate the writing of women across such a broad span of time — all suggest the crucial role collaboration plays in bringing this project to fruition.

Collaborative projects can extend beyond the humanities and indeed beyond the academy. At Carnegie Mellon University, a community-university collaborative — the Community Literacy Center — is at work on a range of issues related to community literacies. This project and the research carried out in it have identified, described, and enacted the "intercultural collaboration" that serves as the vision and mission of their center and have adumbrated a theory of "rivaling," a critical practice they argue constitutes effective youth involvement in the community (see http://english.cmu.edu/research/clc/default.html). On another front, efforts to establish a research agenda that could bring together the interests of scientists and humanists around issues of information technology are also under way. Launched at the 2000 meeting of the Rhetoric Society of America, the IText Working Group — whose participants come from eleven research universities — has collaborated to produce a white paper that "defines future directions for research on the relationship between information technology and writing." Like *The Great War*, Art*Show*, and the Orlando Project, the IText project demands precisely the kind of focused research and collaborative practices called for by Arac and others. In all

these projects, a group of humanities researchers has come together to identify an issue or a problem of shared interest or concern, drawn up plans for
addressing the issue from different perspectives and areas of expertise, and
begun the hard work of carrying out those plans. These projects reveal the
high stakes (the survival of public history, the record of women's writing, the
need for enriched community literacies, the crucial connections between new
technologies and humanities-informed theories of writing and reading) involved in achieving the collaborative goals they set. These projects also entail,
we hasten to add, considerable difficulties — in everything from gaining initial funding to negotiating the complex demands of collaboration, representing the significance of such work to others, and living with the realities of
current academic reward structures.

Institutional and professional change comes slowly — if it comes at all.
So we want to acknowledge the enormity of the challenges faced by those
who call for collaborative research and scholarship and for more cooperative,
less combative ways of exploring differences. Nevertheless, in optimistic moments we recognize that positive changes are in progress across a number of
fields. In addition to the collaborative work mentioned above, a particularly
productive constellation of projects is well under way at the intersection of
literary and legal scholarship. These projects aim not only to critique the author construct but also to historicize it in ways that call attention to its material
grounding in intellectual property and copyright. In "The Genius and the
Copyright," for instance, Martha Woodmansee provides a detailed portrait
of the struggles that took place in seventeenth- and early-eighteenth-century
Germany over the much-contested notion of authorship. Studies such as
Woodmansee's and later efforts such as Woodmansee and Jaszi's edited collection *The Construction of Authorship* and Mark Rose's *Authors and Owners*
estrange readers' familiar understanding of authorship and of intellectual
property, making possible (though not inevitable) new ways of conceiving
of — and enacting — the literate practices of writing and reading. Even more
recently, Rosemary Coombe's *The Cultural Life of Intellectual Properties* brings
together cultural studies, political and postcolonial theory, anthropology, and
legal studies to further complicate and enrich understandings of "the consti-
tutive role of intellectual properties in commercial and popular culture" (5).
For related efforts more squarely in the tradition of literary and historical
studies, see Carruthers; Meltzer; Stewart; Clanchy; H. Graff; Masten; and
Gere, *Intimate Practices*.

In legal studies, Lani Guinier is helping to think through the thicket surrounding agency, ownership, and political action. In an ingenious argument,
Guinier steers a course between the individual and the group, between liber-
tarian individualism and identity politics, situating authority in the connections a person makes among the discourses available. Out of these connections
can come what Guinier celebrates as a medley of component voices that is singular and plural at the same time. Guinier's valuing of connections echoes for
us the attempts of cybercitizen Esther Dyson, who claims that contemporary

cultural capital will "lie in the relationships surrounding and nurturing the movement of content through networks of users and producers" (184).

Contemporary writers have also done much to articulate and enact the medley of component voices that Guinier invokes. Of the many writers we might mention, the self-styled autoplagiarist Kathy Acker is particularly notable for the risks she takes. From such early pieces as *I Dreamt I Was a Nymphomaniac!: Imagining* (1974) through *Don Quixote, Which Was a Dream* (1986) to her final novel, *Pussy, King of the Pirates* (1996), Acker rewrites the so-called works of others, collapsing genres, time periods, genders, and selves in a series of dizzying texts. By these and other means, Acker acts out her theory that language cannot be owned — particularly not by a coherent, autonomous, individual author. Acker's willingness to challenge conventional forms of Western authorship is shared, though in very different ways, by Anna Deveare Smith, who constructs plays such as *Fires in the Mirror* or *Twilight: Los Angeles, 1992* from the words of others, thus flouting the prevailing assumption that as a playwright she must create character and plot from the smithy of her individual imagination.[17]

Feminist scholars have also attempted to enact alternatives to traditional authorship. Elizabeth G. Peck and JoAnna Stephens Mink's edited collection, *Common Ground: Feminist Collaboration in the Academy*, includes a number of examples of such alternatives. Particularly germane to the collaboration-authorship nexus are essays published in the fall 1994 and spring 1995 issues of the *Tulsa Studies in Women's Literature* devoted to explorations of collaboration. Inspired in part by the earlier work of Carey Kaplan and Ellen Cronan Rose, the essays in these issues "propose — indeed, in several cases enact — alternative modes of mutually acknowledged, reciprocally empowering intellectual collaboration" (Laird, "Preface" 231). In the introduction to the first of these issues, Holly Laird, the editor of the journal, acknowledges the difficulty of such enactments, wryly noting that "the first university to reward collaborative work by scholars in the humanities will not only be sponsoring interesting publications, but will also be promoting a different sort of society in literary studies. A collaborative literature department would look as different from today's hierarchical model as collaborative feminist scholarship looks when contrasted to traditional criticism."[18]

Indeed. These comments show once again that it is hard to overestimate the difficulty of effecting institutional change. So while we support these and other efforts to challenge conventional assumptions about authorship and to enact more collaborative models of writing and research, we see a need for caution. Anyone who has worked on a collaborative project is aware of the frustrations potentially accompanying such work, which have led more than one scholar to recall that during wartime, "collaboration" was a punishable offense. The dynamics of any collaborative research will be affected by a number of differences, primary among them those of gender, race, class, and discipline. In addition, personal preferences shaped by ideologies of the autonomous author will continue to make solitary scholarship and single-author publication seem the natural choice to many.

Beyond the difficulty of personal dynamics and preferences lie material and logistical problems that can also impede efforts at collaboration. In spite of the ease with which collaborators can now communicate, compose texts together, even work together in virtual archives, logistics are far from inconsequential: the seemingly simple paperwork requirements for a large collaborative project can daunt the most enthusiastic group member. Moreover, scholars in the humanities know little about how to organize such efforts effectively, about the modes of collaboration most appropriate to various projects.[19] And as we have pointed out repeatedly in this essay, the material conditions that enable most academic work exclude or discourage collaboration. Who, for example, has had a collaborative sabbatical? Insufficient attention to such logistical and material conditions may help to create naive or utopian expectations. Our own research on collaborative writers tells us, for example, that no single model — such as that of the laboratory — can effectively meet the diverse and situated needs of researchers in the humanities. (Moreover, the sciences have a poor record of including women and members of minorities — or their perspectives — in research.) Any serious move toward designing collaborative models in the humanities must expend time and effort on such material and logistical issues.

Of the many other challenges to collaboration and concepts of multiple authorship, questions of methodology and style stand out as particularly problematic as well as potentially productive. In collaborative research, participants almost always bring differing stylistic and methodological assumptions and practices — including not only the plethora of theoretical perspectives characteristic of literary studies but also the qualitative and quantitative methods used across varying fields.[20] Such plurality can lead to a waste of time, to conceptual incoherence, to the failures of shared innovative work noted by Arac (122). But it can also lead to a widening of scholarly possibilities (see, e.g., the discussion of such possibilities in the concluding chapter of Kathleen Welch's *Electric Rhetoric*). In the Orlando Project, for example, methods drawn from history and literary studies have been linked with those from computer sciences: in addition to undertaking feminist research on women's lives, texts, and material conditions, the participants have created a structure for storing and analyzing these materials through a new markup language. Such innovative methodological linkings also characterize a number of hypertext projects — such as the Victorian Web or the British Poetry 1780–1910 Hypertext Archive — now under way in the humanities.

If we in English studies are to meet the challenges just described, two conditions must obtain. First, we must make space for — and even encourage — collaborative projects in the humanities. But as we do so, we must address related professional standards and practices suggested by the following questions.[21] What do subtle but entrenched conventions (such as the use of *et al.*) do to erase the work of those who already engage in collaborative practices? What changes must occur for junior faculty members to participate in collaborative research projects without jeopardizing their careers? What work of redefinition will make way for the understanding that the contributions of doctoral dissertations come not from some abstract originality but rather from participation in complex layers of knowledge production? Are we willing to undertake the tedious and contentious work required to revise tenure and promotion guidelines so that collaborative research and publication count? And can we learn to take pleasure, as well as pride, in our scholarly work when the traditional egocentric rewards of proprietary ownership and authority must be shared? In short, are we prepared not only to critique conventional understandings of subjectivity and authorship but also to act on the implications of that critique? If scholars in the modern languages and humanities can answer this last question affirmatively, then perhaps we will be on our way toward taking up Nellie McKay's challenge to rethink creatively not only who we are but also what we do.

NOTES

Being an author means, it goes without saying, being in conversation and in debt to others. A number of generous friends and colleagues responded helpfully and creatively to queries and read drafts as we worked on this essay. They include Suzanne Clark, Elizabeth Flynn, Cheryl Glenn, Laura Gurak, Anita Helle, and Thaine Stearns. We note, however, that our citation practices relentlessly suppress such collaborative response and engagement while continuing to privilege traditional authorship. The assumption that the first author listed in a cowritten document must be the primary author is a case in point. In our twenty years of writing together, we have consistently alternated the order of our names as a small way of challenging the concept of first authors.

    1. Ellison 260; Turkle, "Who" 148.

    2. Representative feminist scholars include Flax; Code; Fuss; Butler; Hartman and Messer-Davidow; Butler and Scott; and Royster, *Traces*. Representative postcolonial and race theorists include Trinh; Mohanty; Lugones; hooks; Gates; Williams; and Bell.

    3. See LeFevre, *Invention*; Bartholomae, "Inventing"; S. Miller; Bizzell; Berlin; Flower; Crowley; Brodkey, *Writing*; Trimbur, "Collaborative Learning"; Bruffee; Royster, "When the First Voice"; Harkin and Schilb; and Sullivan and Qualley. *Collaboration* is a key term for composition studies, where it can refer both to collaborative learning activities, such as peer response and group problem solving, and to the actual practice of cowriting texts or negotiating power among members of workplace writing groups. This range of concerns is represented in three edited collections: Forman; Reagan, Fox, and Bleich; and Buranen and Roy.

    4. As readers may have already realized, Flax's comments apply as strongly to teaching as to writing.

    5. Bartholomae, "Writing"; Elbow; Bartholomae and Elbow; Kirsch and Ritchie; and R. Miller.

    6. Our comment about the limited impact that work on collaboration has had is not intended as a criticism of this research but rather as a reflection of the deeply held resistance to collaboration in the academy. The following include some particularly important works on collaboration in rhetoric and composition: Bleich; Brooke, Mirtz, and Evans; Cross; Dale; Forman; Howard; Lay and Karis; Reagan, Fox, and Bleich; Roen and Mittan; Spear; Spigelman; Trimbur, "Collaborative Learning"; and Yancey and Spooner.

    7. Harris 51–52; *Stanford* 359; Caesar 37; Bourdieu 77.

    8. In "Revising the Myth of the Independent Scholar," Patricia Sullivan provides a detailed discussion of the thoroughly collaborative nature of the dissertation and its process of production.

    9. While the traditional relation of scholarly work to authorship is called into question in the corporate university, access to research materials is potentially at risk in the wake of recent legislation. Those who have followed the progress of the Digital Millennium Copyright Act (which became law in 1998), the Copyright Term Extension Act (also passed in 1998), and the current efforts to pass the Uniform Computer Information Transactions Act (UCITA) in every state in the country will be aware of the degree to which hyperprotectionism is at work as well as the degree to which it affects the kind of information scholars can have access to and thus the work they can do. Karen Burke LeFevre has written extensively, for instance, on the dangers that recent limitations to fair use hold for writers and the ways in which these restrictions effectively place much unpublished

material outside the reach of humanities scholars ("Tell-Tale 'Heart'"). For discussion of these issues, see Porter (*Rhetorical Ethics*), Selfe, and Lunsford as well as Web sites for the Digital Future Coalition (www.dfc.org) and 4Cite (www.4Cite.org). The CCCC (Conference on College Composition and Communication) Caucus on Intellectual Property also maintains an online discussion group on these issues and related ones (www.ncte.org/ccc-ip/mailing.html).

10. See Boyle; Pareles; Mann; Heilemann; and Barlow. The Napster case has been widely reviewed and has already spawned legislation. HR 5274, for example, introduced on 27 September 2000 with the support of the Digital Future Coalition, would permit a person who lawfully owns a music compact disc to store music from it on the Internet and access the music for personal use at any time. See the DFC Web site for more information on this bill as well as other legislation.

11. Trinh 90; Acker, "Dead Doll" 21.

12. See, for instance, LeFevre, *Invention*; Gere, *Writing Groups*; Bruffee; and Brodkey, *Academic Writing*.

13. Both Davidson and Arac point to potential problems associated with adopting a laboratory model, even an ideal one, for humanities research. Others have also interrogated the laboratory model; see, e.g., Trimbur and Braun.

14. See also Zawacki; Annas; Schmidt; Bishop; Starkey; and Flynn.

15. Gerald Graff has recently taken issue with Tannen in "Two Cheers for the Argument Culture," noting that while rigorous and principled argument should be everywhere at work in the academy, it is actually in rather short supply.

16. Indeed, several relatively new humanities centers explicitly define their missions as collaborative (see, for example, Ohio State University's Institute for Collaborative Research and Public Humanities [www.huminst.osu.edu], as well as a newly funded lab for collaborative research in the humanities established at Stanford University [www.stanford.edu/group/shl]). According to a note in the *Chronicle of Higher Education*'s "Peer Review" column (8 Sept. 2000), the literary scholar Sander Gilman recently accepted a position at the University of Illinois, Chicago, because he was encouraged to develop a humanities lab that would serve "as an incubator of sorts for collaborative projects in the humanities involving professors, graduate students, and undergraduates" and would result in such products as "books, Web sites, and museum exhibitions." Earlier important collaborative efforts in the humanities are embodied in the mission of the Society for Critical Exchange (http://www.cwru.edu/affil/sce), in *Signs*, and in the publishing history of houses such as Aunt Lute Books, Arte Publico Press, and South End Books. It is also important to acknowledge the power of such collaborative efforts as the Combahee River Collective.

17. The reception of Acker's and Smith's work calls attention to tensions and paradoxes in contemporary culture. Most commentators, for instance, describe Acker and Smith as "unique" and "original" voices and highlight their individual accomplishments, in effect disregarding both writers' persistent challenges to these terms. At the same time, Acker and Smith have paid a price for their challenges to dominant ideologies of authorship. Harold Robbins, for instance, accused Acker of plagiarism and brought the wrath of publishers down on her. (See Acker's essay "Dead Doll Prophecy," which describes these events.) While Smith has not been accused of plagiarism, questions of her originality have surfaced repeatedly. An article on Smith in the 1994 volume of *Current Biography Yearbook*, for instance, recalls that "after having listed *Fires in the Mirror* as a finalist for the [Pulitzer], the committee disqualified *Twilight: Los Angeles, 1992* from consideration, reasoning that the text, because it had been taken from interviews, was not original" ("Smith" 547).

18. "Preface" 231. As this article went to press, we learned of Laird's recent study *Women Coauthors*. The headings of the three sections of this study indicate its focus. Part I is titled "Political Literary Alliances of Two"; part 2, "Coupled Women of Letters"; part 3, "Revisionary Collaborations." Another recently published study of women coauthors is Bette London's *Writing Double: Women's Literary Partnerships*. London's topics range from the Brontë juvenilia to the partnership of Edith Somerville and Martin Ross (Violet Martin) to the alternative writing practices of female mediums, spiritualists, and automatic writers.

19. Scholars of rhetoric and composition have begun the work of identifying and theorizing modes of collaboration, such as the dialogic and hierarchical modes described in *Singular Texts/ Plural Authors*. But many other modes surely can and should be studied. We think, for example, of these possibilities: additive, accretive, symbiotic, polyvocal, intertextual, and associational. Which of these might be most useful to humanities scholars — and in what situations?

20. For representative discussions of methodological issues, see Hirsch and Keller; Kirsch and Mortensen; and Addison.

21. Readers are invited to visit — and contribute to — a new Web site designed to encourage collaborative writing and research in higher education. The URL for the Web site, Collaborate!, is www.stanford.edu/group/collaborate/.

WORKS CITED

Acker, Kathy. "Dead Doll Prophecy." *The Subversive Imagination: Artists, Society, and Social Responsibility.* Ed. Carol Becker. New York: Routledge, 1994. 20–34.

———. *Don Quixote, Which Was a Dream.* New York: Grove, 1986.

———. *I Dreamt I Was a Nymphomaniac!: Imagining.* San Francisco: Empty Elevator Shaft Poetry, 1974.

———. *Pussy, King of the Pirates.* New York: Grove, 1996.

Addison, Joanne. "Data Analysis and Subject Representation in Empowering Composition Research." *Written Communication* 14 (1997): 106–28.

Annas, Pamela J. "Style as Politics: A Feminist Approach to the Teaching of Writing." *College English* 47 (1985): 360–71.

Anzaldúa, Gloria. *Borderlands/La Frontera: The New Mestiza.* San Francisco: Aunt Lute, 1987.

Arac, Jonathan. "Shop Window or Laboratory: Collection, Collaboration, and the Humanities." *The Politics of Research.* Ed. E. Ann Kaplan and George Levine. New Brunswick: Rutgers UP, 1997. 116–26.

Barlow, John Perry. "The Next Economy of Ideas: Will Copyright Survive the Napster Bomb?" *Wired* Oct. 2000: 240–52.

Bartholomae, David. "Inventing the University." *When a Writer Can't Write: Studies in Writer's Block and Other Composing Process Problems.* Ed. Mike Rose. New York: Guilford, 1985. 134–65.

———. "Writing with Teachers." Villanueva 479–88.

Bartholomae, David, and Peter Elbow. "Interchanges." Villanueva 501–10.

Barton, Ellen. "More Methodological Matters: Against Negative Argumentation." *College Composition and Communication* 51 (2000): 399–416.

Bell, Derrick. *Race, Racism, and American Law.* 4th ed. New York: Aspen, 2000.

Berlin, James. *Rhetoric and Reality: Writing Instruction in American Colleges, 1900–1985.* Carbondale: Southern Illinois UP, 1987.

Bhabha, Homi I. *The Location of Culture.* London: Routledge, 1994.

Bishop, Wendy, ed. *Elements of Alternate Style: Essays on Writing and Revision.* Portsmouth: Boynton, 1997.

Bizzell, Patricia. *Academic Discourse and Critical Consciousness.* Pittsburgh: U of Pittsburgh P, 1992.

Bleich, David, ed. *Collaboration and Change in the Academy.* Spec. issue of *JAC* 14.1 (1994): 1–316.

Bourdieu, Pierre. *Outline of a Theory of Practice.* Trans. Richard Nice. Ed. Jack Goody. Cambridge: Cambridge UP, 1979.

Bové, Paul. *In the Wake of Theory.* Hanover: UP of New England, 1992.

Boyle, James. *Shamans, Software, and Spleens: Law and the Construction of the Information Society.* Cambridge: Harvard UP, 1996.

Bridwell-Bowles, Lillian. "Discourse and Diversity: Experimental Writing within the Academy." *College Composition and Communication* 43 (1992): 349–68.

Brodkey, Linda. *Academic Writing as Social Practice.* Philadelphia: Temple UP, 1987.

———. *Writing Permitted in Designated Areas Only.* Minneapolis: U of Minnesota P, 1996.

Brooke, Robert, Ruth Mirtz, and Rick Evans. *Small Groups in Writing Workshops: Invitations to a Writer's Life.* Urbana: NCTE, 1997.

Bruffee, Kenneth. "Collaborative Learning and the 'Conversation of Mankind.'" *College English* 46 (1984): 635–52.

Buranen, Lise, and Alice M. Roy, eds. *Perspectives on Plagiarism and Intellectual Property in a Postmodern World.* Albany: State U of New York P, 1999.

Butler, Judith. *Gender Trouble: Feminism and the Subversion of Identity.* New York: Routledge, 1990.

Butler, Judith, and Joan W. Scott, eds. *Feminists Theorize the Political.* New York: Routledge, 1992.

Caesar, Terry. *Conspiring with Forms: Life in Academic Texts.* Athens: U of Georgia P, 1992.

Carruthers, Mary. *Book of Memory: A Study of Memory in Medieval Culture.* Cambridge: Cambridge UP, 1992.

Christian, Barbara. "The Race for Theory." *Feminist Studies* 14 (1988): 67–79.

Clanchy, Michael T. *From Memory to Written Record: England, 1066–1307.* Cambridge: Harvard UP, 1979.

Code, Lorraine. *Rhetorical Spaces: Essays on Gendered Locations.* New York: Routledge, 1995.

Combahee River Collective. "A Black Feminist Statement." *This Bridge Called My Back: Writings by Radical Women of Color.* Ed. Cherríe Moraga and Gloria Anzaldúa. New York: Kitchen Table, 1981. 210–18.

Community Literacy Center. English Dept., Carnegie Mellon U. 7 Sept. 2000 <http://english.cmu.edu/clc/>.

Coombe, Rosemary J. *The Cultural Life of Intellectual Properties: Authorship, Appropriation, and the Law.* Durham: Duke UP, 1998.

"Creative Collaboration: Alternatives to the Adversarial Academy." Presidential Forum. MLA Convention. Marriott Wardman Park Hotel, Washington D.C. 27 Dec., 2000.

Cross, Geoffrey. *Collaboration and Conflict: A Conceptual Exploration of Group Writing and Positive Emphasis.* Cresskill: Hampton, 1994.

Crowley, Sharon. *Composition in the University: Historical and Polemical Essays.* Pittsburgh: U of Pittsburgh P, 1998.

Dale, Helen. *Co-authoring in the Classroom: Creating an Environment for Effective Collaboration.* Urbana: NCTE, 1997.

Damrosch, David. *We Scholars: Changing the Culture of the University.* Cambridge: Harvard UP, 1995.

Davidson, Cathy. "What If Scholars in the Humanities Worked Together, in a Lab?" *Chronicle of Higher Education* 28 May, 1999: B4–5.

Descartes, René. *Discourse on the Method of Rightly Conducting Reason and Seeking Truth in the Sciences.* Online Literature Library. 9 Sept. 2000. <http://www.literature.org/authors/descartes-rene/reason-discourse/chapter-04.html>.

Dyson, Esther. "Intellectual Value." *Wired* July 1995: 136+.

Ede, Lisa, and Andrea A. Lunsford. *Singular Texts/Plural Authors: Perspectives on Collaborative Writing.* Carbondale: Southern Illinois UP, 1990.

Elbow, Peter. "Being a Writer vs. Being an Academic." Villanueva 489–500.

Ellison. Ralph. *The Invisible Man.* New York: Vintage, 1972.

Flax, Jane. *Thinking Fragments: Psychoanalysis. Feminism, and Postmodernism in the Contemporary West.* Berkeley: U of California P, 1990.

Flower, Linda. *The Construction of Negotiated Meaning: A Social Cognitive Theory of Writing.* Carbondale: Southern Illinois UP, 1994.

Flynn, Elizabeth. "Composing as a Woman." *College Composition and Communication* 39 (1988): 423–35.

Forman, Janis, ed. *New Visions of Collaborative Writing.* Portsmouth: Boynton, 1992.

Foss, Sonja, and Cindy Griffin. "Beyond Persuasion: A Proposal for an Invitational Rhetoric." *Communication Monographs* 62 (1995): 2–18.

Foucault, Michel. "What Is an Author?" *Textual Strategies: Perspectives* in *Poststructuralist Criticism.* Ed. Josué V. Harari. Ithaca: Cornell UP, 1979. 141–60.

Frey, Olivia. "Beyond Literary Darwinism: Women's Voices and Critical Discourse." *College English* 52 (1990): 507–26.

Fuss, Diana. *Essentially Speaking: Feminism, Nature, and Difference.* New York: Routledge, 1989.

Gallop, Jane, Marianne Hirsch, and Nancy K. Miller. "Criticizing Feminist Criticism." Hirsch and Keller 349–69.

Gates, Henry Louis. *The Signifying Monkey.* New York: Oxford UP, 1989.

Geertz, Clifford. "Common Sense as a Cultural System." *Local Knowledge: Further Essays in Interpretive Anthropology.* New York: Basic, 1983. 73–93.

Gere, Anne. *Intimate Practices: Literary and Cultural Work in U.S. Women's Clubs, 1880–1920.* Chicago: U of Illinois P, 1997.

———. *Writing Groups: History, Theory, and Implications.* Carbondale: Southern Illinois UP, 1987.

Graff, Gerald. "Two Cheers for the Argument Culture." *Hedgehog Review* 2 (2000): 53–71.

Graff, Harvey J. *The Labyrinths of Literacy: Reflections on Literacy Past and Present.* Pittsburgh: U of Pittsburgh P, 1995.

Guinier, Lani. *The Tyranny of the Majority: Fundamental Fairness in Representative Democracy.* New York: Free, 1994.

Harkin, Patricia, and John Schilb, eds. *Contending with Words: Composition and Rhetoric in a Postmodern Age.* New York: MLA, 1991.

Harris, Joseph. "Meet the New Boss, Same as the Old Boss: Class Consciousness in Composition." *College Composition and Communication* 52 (2000): 43–68.

Hartman, Joan E., and Ellen Messer-Davidow, eds. *(En)Gendering Knowledge: Feminists in Academe.* Knoxville: U of Tennessee P, 1991.

Heath, Shirley Brice, dir. Art*Show: Youth and Community Development.* Alweis Productions, 2000.

Heilemann, John. "David Boies: The Wired Interview." *Wired* Oct. 2000: 254–59.

Hirsch, Marianne, and Evelyn Fox Keller, eds. *Conflicts in Feminism.* New York: Routledge, 1990.

hooks, bell. *Talking Back: Thinking Feminist, Thinking Black.* Boston: South End, 1989.

Howard, Rebecca. *Standing in the Shadows of Giants: Plagiarists, Authors, Collaborators.* Norwood: Ablex. 1999.

Hutcheon, Linda. "Presidential Address 2000." *PMLA* 116.3 (2001): 518–30.

IText Working Group. "A Project to Define Future Directions for Research on the Relationship between Information Technology and Writing." Unpublished paper, 2000.

Jaszi, Peter. "On the Author Effect: Contemporary Copyright and Collective Creativity." Woodmansee and Jaszi 29–56.

Kaplan, Carey, and Ellen Cronan Rose. "Strange Bedfellows: Feminist Collaboration." *Signs* 18 (1993): 547–61.

Kecht, Maria-Regina, ed. *Pedagogy Is Politics: Literary Theory and Critical Teaching.* Urbana: U of Illinois P, 1992.

Kirsch, Gesa, and Peter Mortensen, eds. *Ethics and Representation in Qualitative Studies of Literacy.* Urbana: NCTE, 1996.

Kirsch, Gesa, and Joy Ritchie. "Beyond the Personal: Theorizing a Politics of Location in Composition Research." *College Composition and Communication* 46 (1995): 7–38.

Laird, Holly. "Preface to *On Collaborations I.*" *Tulsa Studies in Women's Literature* 13.2 (1994): 231–33.

———. *Women Coauthors.* Urbana: U of Illinois P, 2000.

Lay, Mary M., and William M. Karis, eds. *Collaborative Writing in Industry: Investigations in Theory and Practice.* Austin: Baywood, 1991.

LeFevre, Karen Burke. *Invention as a Social Act.* Carbondale: Southern Illinois UP, 1987.

———. "The Tell-Tale 'Heart': Determining 'Fair Use' of Unpublished Texts." *Law and Contemporary Problems* 55.2 (1992): 153–83.

London, Bette. *Writing Double: Women's Literary Partnerships.* Ithaca: Cornell UP, 1999.

Loomba, Ania. "Overworlding the 'Third World.'" *Colonial Discourse and Post-colonial Theory.* Ed. Patrick Williams and Laura Chrisman. New York: Columbia UP, 1994. 305–23.

Lucas, Christopher J. *Crisis in the Academy: Rethinking Higher Education in America.* New York: St. Martin's, 1996.

Lugones, María. "Playfulness, 'World' Traveling, and Loving Perception." *Hypatia* 22 (1987): 3–19.

Lunsford, Andrea Abernethy. "Rhetoric, Feminism, and the Politics of Ownership." *College English* 61 (1999): 529–44.

Mann, Charles. "The Heavenly Jukebox." *Atlantic* Sept. 2000: 39–59.

Masten, Jeffrey. *Textual Intercourse: Collaboration, Authorship, and Sexualities in Renaissance Drama.* Cambridge: Cambridge UP, 1997.

McKay, Nellie. Statement. *1997 MLA Elections Candidate Information Booklet.* New York: MLA, 1997. 5.

Meltzer, Françoise. *Hot Property: The Stakes and Claims of Literary Originality.* Chicago: U of Chicago P, 1994.

Miller, Nancy K. *Getting Personal: Feminist Occasions and Other Autobiographical Acts.* New York: Routledge, 1991.

Miller, Richard E. "The Nervous System." *College English* 58 (1996): 265–86.

Miller, Susan. *Textual Carnivals: The Politics of Composition.* Carbondale: Southern Illinois UP, 1991.

Mohanty, Chandra Talpade. "On Race and Voice: Challenges for Liberal Education in the 1990s." *Between Borders: Pedagogy and the Politics of Cultural Studies.* Ed. Henry A. Giroux and Peter McLaren. New York: Routledge, 1994. 145–66.

Orlando Project: An Integrated History of Women's Writing in the British Isles. English Dept., U of Alberta. 5 Sept. 2000 <http://www.ualberta.ca/ORLANDO/orlando.htm>.

Pareles, Jon. "Envisaging the Industry as the Loser on Napster." *New York Times on the Web.* 14 Feb. 2001: 2 pp. 3 Mar. 2001 <http://www.nytimes.com/2001/02/14/technology/14NOTE.html>.

Peck, Elizabeth G., and JoAnna Stephens Mink, eds. *Common Ground: Feminist Collaboration in the Academy.* Albany: State U of New York P, 1998.

"Peer Review." *Chronicle of Higher Education.* Sept. 8, 2000: A12.

Porter, James E. "Liberal Individualism and Internet Policy: A Communitarian Critique." *Passions, Pedagogies, and Twenty-First Century Technologies.* Ed. Gail Hawisher and Cynthia Selfe. Logan: Utah State UP, 1999. 231–48.

———. *Rhetorical Ethics and Internetworked Writing.* Greenwich: Ablex, 1998.

Readings, Bill. *The University in Ruins.* Cambridge: Harvard UP, 1997.

Reagan, Sally Barr, Thomas Fox, and David Bleich, eds. *Writing With: New Directions in Collaborative Teaching, Learning, and Research.* Albany: State U of New York P, 1994.

Reither, James A., and Douglas Vipond. "Writing as Collaboration." *College English* 51 (1989): 855–67.

Roen, Duane H., and Robert K. Mittan. "Collaborative Scholarship in Composition: Some Issues." *Methods and Methodology in Composition Research.* Ed. Gesa Kirsch and Patricia A. Sullivan. Carbondale: Southern Illinois UP, 1992. 287–313.

Rose, Mark. *Authors and Owners: The Invention of Copyright.* Cambridge: Cambridge UP, 1993.

Royster, Jacqueline Jones. *Traces of a Stream: Literary and Social Change among African American Women.* Pittsburgh: U of Pittsburgh P, 2000.

———. "When the First Voice You Hear Is Not Your Own." *College Composition and Communication* 47 (1996): 29–40.

Schmidt, Jan Zlotnick, ed. *Women/Writing/Teaching.* Albany: State U of New York P, 1998.

Scott, Joan. "'Experience.'" Butler and Scott 22–40.

Selfe, Cynthia L. *Technology and Literacy in the Twenty-First Century: the Importance of Paying Attention.* Carbondale: Southern Illinois UP, 1999.

Simpson, David. *The Academic Postmodern and the Rule of Literature: A Report on Half-Knowledge.* Chicago: U of Chicago P, 1995.

"Smith, Anna Deveare." *Current Biography Yearbook 1994.* Ed. Judith Graham. New York: Wilson, 1994.

Smith, Paul. *Discerning the Subject.* Minneapolis: U of Minnesota P, 1988.

Sosnoski, James J. *Modern Skeletons in Postmodern Closets: A Cultural Studies Alternative.* Charlottesville: UP of Virginia, 1995.

Spear, Karen. *Sharing Writing: Peer Response Groups in English Classes.* Portsmouth: Boynton, 1988.

Spigelman, Candace. *Across Property Lines: Textual Ownership in Writing Groups.* Carbondale: Southern Illinois UP: 2000.

Stanford Bulletin 2000–01. Stanford: Stanford U, 2000.

Starkey, David, ed. *Teaching Writing Creatively.* Portsmouth: Boynton, 1998.

Stewart, Susan. *Crimes of Writing: Problems in the Containment of Representation.* New York: Oxford UP, 1991.

Sullivan, Patricia. "Revising the Myth of the Independent Scholar." Reagan, Fox, and Bleich 11–30.

Sullivan, Patricia A., and Donna J. Qualley. *Pedagogy in the Age of Politics: Writing and Reading (in) the Academy.* Urbana: NCTE, 1994.

Tompkins, Jane. "Me and My Shadow." *New Literary History* 19 (1987): 169–78.

Trimbur, John. "Agency and the Death of the Author: A Partial Defense of Modernism." *JAC* 20 (2000): 283–98.

———. "Collaborative Learning and Teaching Writing." *Perspectives on Research and Scholarship in Composition.* Ed. Ben W. McClelland and Timothy R. Donovan. New York: MLA, 1985. 87–109.

Trimbur, John, and Lundy Braun. "Lab Life and the Determination of Authorship." Forman 19–36.

Trinh T. Minh-ha. *Woman, Native, Other: Writing Postcoloniality and Feminism.* Bloomington: Indiana UP, 1989.

Turkle, Sherry. *Life on the Screen: Identity in the Age of the Internet.* New York: Simon, 1995.

———. "Who Am We?" *Wired* Jan. 1996: 148+.

Villanueva, Victor, ed. *Cross-Talk in Comp Theory.* Urbana: NCTE, 1997.

Walker, Cheryl. "Feminist Literary Criticism and the Author." *Critical Inquiry* 16 (1990): 551–71.

Watkins, Evan. *Work Time: English Departments and the Circulation of Cultural Value.* Stanford: Stanford UP, 1989.

Welch, Kathleen. *Electric Rhetoric: Classical Rhetoric, Oralism, and a New Literacy.* Cambridge: MIT P, 1999.

Williams, Raymond. *Marxism and Literature.* Oxford: Oxford UP, 1977.

Winter, Jay. "Doing Public History: Producing *The Great War* for PBS and BBC." Presidential Forum. MLA Convention. San Francisco Hilton Hotel, San Francisco. 27 Dec. 1998.

Woodmansee, Martha. "The Genius and the Copyright: Economic and Legal Conditions of the Emergence of the 'Author.'" *Eighteenth Century Studies* 17 (1984): 425–48.

Woodmansee, Martha, and Peter Jaszi, eds. *The Construction of Authorship: Textual Appropriation in Law and Literature.* Durham: Duke UP, 1994.

Yancey, Kathleen Blake, and Michael Spooner. "A Single Good Mind: Collaboration, Cooperation, and the Writing Self." *College Composition and Communication* 49 (1998): 45–62.

Zawacki, Terry Myers. "Recomposing as a Woman — An Essay in Different Voices." *College Composition and Communication* 43 (1992): 32–38.

12 Collaboration and Collaborative Writing: The View from Here

On a Saturday evening in 1976, we were sitting together at Lisa's house in Brockport, New York, with several friends, chatting about words, and specifically about the distinctions to be drawn between "bogs," "fens," "mucklands," and other soggy bodies of land. Lisa was in her first tenure-track academic position, and several friends from Ohio State, including Andrea, had driven from Columbus, Ohio, to Brockport for a reunion. We'd spent Friday and Saturday exploring the area, and we'd noticed how much swampland surrounded Brockport (much of it planted in cabbages). The locals tended to refer to it as muckland. But what, we wondered, was the difference between a swamp, bog, fen, and muckland?

Semiamused and semiserious, we pulled out the trusty *Oxford English Dictionary* (*OED*), and Lisa began reading definitions of these and other terms to the group. Suddenly, we heard a knock on the back French doors, and there stood several students with drafts of essays they hoped Lisa would read over the weekend. How long had they been staring at their teacher reading earnestly from the dictionary before they knocked on the door? We weren't sure, but we could almost hear them thinking: "So *this* is what English professors do on Saturday nights."

We have laughed about this scene many times over the years, but it hasn't kept us from a fascination with words, and we've often pondered the fate of one particular set of words: *collaborate, collaborator,* and *collaboration.* The first instance of *collaborate* listed in the *OED* comes from an 1871 reference by J. H. Appleton to "those who collaborate for the *Academy.*" In 1801 H. C. Robinson speaks of a "body of poor students who help others" as *collaborators,* and during the 1860s the term *collaboration* denoted some form of working together. These terms experienced what critic Joseph Bentley has called "semantic gravitation" during the twentieth century, and by the time of the Second World War, *collaboration* was tantamount to treason and *collaborators* were dealt the death penalty. As a result, dictionaries today generally list two definitions of *collaboration* or *collaborate*: "to work together to achieve a common goal," and "treason or treasonous cooperation" — though the "working together" definition always appears first.

This essay, written by Lisa Ede and Andrea A. Lunsford, is new to this edition.

The rehabilitation of these terms seems to have come from the turn that took place after the war in disciplines from anthropology to education to sociology — that is, the turn toward social constructionism in general and toward the recognition that humans are by definition social animals. In any case, we see in the shifting fortunes of this set of terms a central, defining tension in Western culture between individualism and forms of collectivism, between the desire to be unique and singular and the need to connect to others, between what Kenneth Burke defines as "identification" and "division."[1] We see this same tension in the academy, where disciplines clearly "progress" through both collective and individual action, though individual action is what gets rewarded and valued, and far more so in the humanities than in the sciences. In the same vein, those in the academy in general and in English/humanities in particular have privileged intellectual over physical work at every turn: perhaps the "labor" buried in "collaboration" has also helped lead to the easy dismissal of collaborative work.

We are of course deeply interested in this terministic history and in the ways these words are used today. In the business and corporate worlds, "collaboration" has become the sine qua non, a practice that is expected if not outright demanded. The academy has been far less swift to embrace the concept or practice of collaboration, though the field of rhetoric and writing studies took a social turn of its own in the 1980s. During that time, we both strongly advocated for a theoretical "revolution," one that would recognize that the Western world's 300-plus-year devotion to the concept of radical individualism should give way to a view of writing and knowledge-making as social and material practices. We believed then, and still believe, that forms of collaboration describe writing as it actually occurs and enable scholars and teachers to think about writing and literacy in more productive ways than the old paradigm of the individual writer can do. This social turn also supported our arguments for the value of collaborative learning and, especially, collaborative writing. Now that it is late 2010, and not 1990, we want to look again at the nature and status of collaborative writing, both in the academy and in American culture in general and to do so in the context of composition's social turn. As we hope to suggest, the "view from here" for those who wish to practice and advocate for collaborative writing now seems both more complex and more mixed in terms of its implications than it did thirty years ago. It has proven easier, in other words, to theorize that writing is an inherently social process than it has been to significantly alter disciplinary and cultural assumptions and practices about writing, authorship, and intellectual property.

PERSONAL STORIES/SITUATED VISIONS

As we have just noted, we hope that our subtitle "The View from Here" reminds you of the deeply situated and motivated nature of our engagement with our topic. In this regard, at the remove of thirty years, it still surprises us to remember that our first coauthored essay happened by accident. As we have written in other accounts of our collaboration, Andrea's first academic position was at the University of British Columbia in Vancouver, British Columbia. Lisa's second academic position, following State University of New York (SUNY) Brockport, was at Oregon State University. Very close friends since graduate school, once we found ourselves living in the same part of the continent, we drove the four hundred or so miles between Corvallis, Oregon, and Vancouver often. At the time when we began coauthoring — a time before word processing and email — this physical proximity was essential to our collaboration.

Here's how Lisa remembers the moment when we decided to write our first coauthored article: We were at the coast having fun when our conversation turned to the essay collection that we and our friend Bob Connors were coediting to honor Edward P. J. Corbett, Andrea's and Bob's dissertation advisor and an important mentor to Lisa. We were talking about what a great person Ed was when one of us exclaimed, "I'll bet it would make Ed really happy to see former students collaborating. Why don't we work together on an essay for the collection?!"

Andrea's memory is somewhat different: she clearly remembers the conversation, but in place of Lisa's memory of collaborating to please their mutual mentor she recalls focusing on the practical, saying "Well, it would certainly save time if we wrote together rather than each contributing an essay." (These somewhat differing memories point up salient reasons we have worked together over the years, including friendship, personal preferences — and hardheaded practicality.) Indeed, we went on to write "On Distinctions between Classical and Modern Rhetoric" together, but Ed Corbett was anything but pleased that we had done so collaboratively. Don't get us wrong: Ed liked the essay itself. What he didn't like — or at least didn't understand — was why and how we had written it collaboratively. In his role as advisor and mentor, Ed warned us of the dangers ahead if we continued to write collaboratively: No one, he argued, would take us seriously if we continued to coauthor; indeed, coauthoring would surely create problems at promotion and tenure time.

So the story of our long collaboration begins with an irony. We coauthored our first essay to honor our friend and mentor Ed Corbett, but the collaborative process we undertook to write it shocked and worried him. So much so that when Ed saw that we were *not* going to take his advice to give up coauthoring, he made us promise to alternate our names as first authors rather than to present them in alphabetical order, as we'd been planning to do.

Ed Corbett was, it turned out, right to be concerned about responses by colleagues in the humanities to our collaboration. Andrea was awarded early tenure and promotion at the University of British Columbia, but her colleagues were careful to inform her that "of course" they had to discount all of our coauthored work when they reviewed her. Lisa's chair was more willing to credit our coauthored research but, anticipating that others might have reservations, he "informally" asked Andrea to write a "formal" letter describing our collaboration and assuring readers that we were equal partners in our

Edward P. J. Corbett, a mentor, colleague, and friend.

various publications. This letter became part of Lisa's dossier and made its way up the chain of review, where at one point the college promotion and tenure committee asked that we go through all of our publications and use magic markers to highlight just who had written which words, sentences, and paragraphs. Fortunately, when we explained that our writing process made this magic marker trick literally impossible, the committee accepted our claim to equal authorship. So we both were tenured and promoted, though in Lisa's case her dean felt compelled to warn her "You will never be promoted to full professor if you continue to insist on coauthoring" when he met with her to inform her of her promotion. (He turned out to be wrong, but his comment remains telling.)

THE MORE THINGS CHANGE

The stories we are telling here are now more than thirty years old, so it's important to note that in regard to the status of collaborative writing in the humanities, the more things change, the more (alas) they stay the same. Readers may be familiar with the MLA's 2006 "Report on Evaluating Scholarship for Tenure and Promotion." From one perspective, this report is positive in that it recommends that "The profession as a whole should develop a more capacious conception of scholarship by rethinking the dominance of the monograph, promoting the scholarly essay, establishing multiple pathways to tenure, and using scholarly portfolios" (12).

As the report makes clear, however, on the ground the reality is significantly bleaker. Research undertaken by the task force conclusively demonstrates that in recent decades, adherence to the single-authored monograph in English and foreign language departments has strengthened, not weakened — and that this has occurred "despite a worsening climate for book publication" (10). Indeed, "the status of the monograph as a gold standard is confirmed by the expectation in almost one-third of all departments surveyed (32.9%) of progress toward completion of a second book for tenure. This expectation is even higher in doctorate-granting institutions, where 49.8% of departments now demand progress toward a second book" (10).

In terms of our discipline of rhetoric and writing, and of the humanities in general, the "View from Here" vis-à-vis collaborative writing on the part of faculty members is no better than when we began writing together several decades ago. Certainly a few scholars in our field have, as we have, successfully resisted prohibitions against collaboration. However, we would be surprised if, like us, they have not paid a price for and/or experienced resistance to their collaborative efforts. When we think back to our own experience as coauthors, for instance, we are reminded that even those who did not caution us about the dangerous consequences of our decision to write together often professed astonishment at our ability to do so, questioning us in detail as though we had just returned from a strange new country.

Given these responses, perhaps there *was* a hint of defensiveness in our decision in the early 1980s to challenge the academy's (and our culture's) basic assumptions in regard to authorship, particularly the commonsense understanding that "real" writing must be single-authored. (We'll have more to say about that word "real" later.) In hindsight, our original goals for the research project that we initiated in 1984 were pretty naive. To put it most simply, we wanted to demonstrate that much of the writing that goes on in the workplace is collaborative — then we could say "told you so!" to our colleagues in English and the humanities. So with the help of a grant from the Fund for the Improvement of Post-Secondary Education's (FIPSE) Shaughnessy Scholars program, we set out to survey 1,400 randomly selected members of seven professional associations: The American Institute of Chemists, the American Consulting Engineers Council, the International City Management Association, the Modern Language Association, the American Psychological Association, the Professional Services Management Association, and the Society for Technical Communication. Our goal was to understand their collaborative writing processes as fully as possible and, especially, to learn what conditions and factors made for productive, satisfying, efficient, and effective collaboration.

Our research involved three stages: an initial questionnaire sent randomly to the members of the seven professional associations we have just named; a second questionnaire sent to twelve members of each association (members we chose because of the thoughtfulness of their responses to the first survey); and on-site interviews held across the country with survey respondents. The results of this study appeared in our 1990 *Singular Texts/Plural Authors: Perspectives on Collaborative Writing*, several chapters of which are included in this collection, so we don't want to belabor the discussion of those findings here. But we do want to point out what was perhaps the most important understanding we gained from this research on collaborative writing: it is impossible to separate any effort to study the material practices of collaborative writing from larger, and deeply ideologically embedded, assumptions about authorship and intellectual property, particularly as they inform conventional notions of what constitutes "real" (i.e., valued) forms of writing in the humanities.

From one perspective, this insight was wonderfully timed, as it coincided with a broad and deep interrogation of notions of authorship, writing, and intellectual property in literary and rhetorical theory, as evidenced in such widely discussed essays as Barthes's "The Death of the Author" and Foucault's "What Is an Author?" However, for us as scholars and coauthors, despite the intense interest in and challenge to the concept of the solitary genius, the "View from Here" remains mixed, at best. For despite widespread agreement in theory that the figure of the author requires critique and reconstitution, and despite changes in both hardware and software that make collaborative writing much easier than it was in the days when we lugged our electric typewriters back and forth from Oregon to British Columbia, collaborative writing in the humanities (whether on the part of faculty or students) remains difficult, challenging — and often ignored. In short, despite an extensive body of research on writing as social and collaborative, which we review briefly below, the figure of the single author still holds powerful sway.

MULTIDISCIPLINARY RESEARCH ON COLLABORATIVE WRITING

While a comprehensive review of research on collaborative writing is beyond the scope of this essay, we want to note some of the most important contributions to scholarly work on this topic. We kicked off our own efforts at such contributions in 1983 with "Why Write . . . Together?" which was followed in 1984 by Kenneth Bruffee's enormously influential "Collaborative Learning and the 'Conversation of Mankind.'" Bruffee, who went on to challenge epistemological, pedagogical, and professional business as usual in the academy, generated a great deal of interest in collaboration, and a spate of important new publications followed, including Anne Gere's 1987 *Writing Groups* and Karen LeFevre's *Invention as a Social Act*, also published in that year. These two studies played a key role in challenging the dominant Western view of invention as the act of an atomistic individual. While interest in and publication on collaboration fell off to some degree in the 1990s, important research on collaborative writing has been more recently undertaken by Kami Day and Michele Eodice, whose 2001 *(First Person)2: A Study of Co-Authoring in the Academy* provides a welcome addition to our understanding of collaborative writing.

While we think of research on and advocacy for collaborative writing as having been pioneered within rhetoric and writing studies, we are aware of important work in other fields, and particularly within feminist literary criticism. Not surprisingly, this work has often been carried out by women scholars on behalf of women coauthors: we think particularly of Holly Laird's *Women Coauthors*, Bette London's *Writing Double: Women's Literary Partnerships*, and Lorraine York's *Rethinking Women's Collaborative Writing: Power, Difference, Property*. The recovery work conducted by these and other feminist literary scholars has helped highlight collaborative creative work by women and challenge notions of singular authorship. The recent collection *Literary Couplings: Writing Couples, Collaborators, and the Construction of Authorship*, edited by Marjorie Stone and Judith Thompson, builds on this research, even as it extends it to consider collaborative relationships "formed not only by writers themselves but also by readers, critics, and literary historians" (5).

Within writing studies, on the other hand, the greatest attention to collaborative writing is found in scholarship on professional and technical writing. These studies — by scholars such as Mary Lay and William Karis, Nancy Blyler and Charlotte Thrall, and Rachel Spilka — document the range of collaborative practices and the "everydayness" of collaboration in the workplace, and thus stand in contrast to the literary feminist scholarship on collaboration, with its emphasis on gender and ideology.

In the broader field, much scholarly work blurs distinctions or addresses connections between collaborative learning and collaborative writing. Examples include Janis Forman's *New Visions of Collaborative Writing*, Sally Barr Reagan, Tom Fox, and David Bleich's *Writing With*, and Beverly Moss, Nels Highberg, and Melissa Nicholas's *Writing Groups Inside and Outside the Classroom*. From one perspective, such a blurring seems natural enough, given the distinct social turn that composition studies took in the 1980s. But this social "turn," as readers are aware, has generally not led to more collaborative assignments in most expository writing classes or to significant changes in the writing practices of scholars in the field.

We find it difficult to overemphasize the magnitude of the contradiction between composition's social "turn" — a movement that many scholars have heralded as a revolution in theory — and the continued emphasis on singular authorship in most beginning and advanced writing classes, not to mention in MA theses and PhD dissertations.[2] What does it say about American culture in general and our field and the academy in particular that the two scholarly areas that have demonstrated a marked interest in collaboration are feminist literary studies (where a central purpose has been to reclaim previously invisible or devalued authors) and professional and technical writing?

Answers to this question are elusive, but surely they begin with an acknowledgment of the marginal status of both these fields. Feminist criticism has been grudgingly accepted, but least often when its object has been the reclamation of women authors. Business and technical writing have often been viewed by English studies as more "other" than traditional writing and rhetoric, perhaps, again, because of their association with the workaday world. The empiricist leanings of technical writing led scholars to report on what they saw when they studied the world of work — and what they saw included a huge amount of collaboration. (In this regard, an important early catalyst for our research on collaborative writing was Lester Faigley and

Thomas Miller's 1982 article "What We Learn from Writing on the Job," which pointed to, among other things, the prevalence of collaboration in workplace writing.) And feminist critics bringing fresh eyes to the work of women authors were perhaps more able to recognize the extent of their collaborative practices than were colleagues whose ideological assumptions and training led them to valorize the singular male author.

On Questions of Terminology

As we consider the significant gap between our field's professed commitment to writing as a social process and its apparently entrenched (and often unacknowledged) prohibitions against coauthorship, we find ourselves wondering about the potential significance of the "slippage" that has occurred between collaborative learning and collaborative writing as these terms have circulated within the field. Consider, in this regard, Bruce W. Speck, Teresa R. Johnson, Catherine P. Dice, and Leon B. Heaton's 1999 *Collaborative Writing: An Annotated Bibliography*. In the introduction to their bibliography, the authors comment on the difficulty they had answering the apparently simple question "What exactly is collaborative writing?" (ix). Indeed, their bibliography covers an extraordinarily diverse range of topics, from collaborative planning to conferencing, researching, considering ethical issues, using computers/ technology, and literary collaborations (to cite only a few examples).

What is to be gained by blurring the distinctions between coauthorship (a specific, material practice where one or more persons collaboratively draft a document) and the inherently collaborative (or social) nature of writing and learning in general? We have claimed on many occasions and in numerous venues that writing is collaborative "all the way down." But to what extent have claims like this made it easy for both scholars and teachers to metaphorically pat themselves on the back for holding enlightened views even as they continue pedagogical and disciplinary business as usual? What about the potential danger, one cited by Kathleen Blake Yancey and Michael Spooner in "A Single Good Mind: Collaboration, Cooperation, and the Writing Self," that all-inclusive definitions of collaboration, definitions that insist that all writing is inherently social and collaborative, may have the unintended consequence of erasing distinctions that can illuminate and clarify materially grounded practices.

We will have more to say about these and related questions later, but for now we should point out that any efforts to address such questions need to explore the relationships among collaboration, collaborative writing, and intellectual property. Rebecca Moore Howard's *Standing in the Shadow of Giants* and Candace Spigelman's *Across Property Lines* are central to such efforts, for both probe the complex tensions existing between contemporary authorship and ownership, tensions that have become increasingly fraught as writers can and do make use of texts they "find" online, and as universities seek to control such use and to agonize over "plagiarism," an act that is increasingly difficult to define.

A collection of essays coedited by Rebecca Moore Howard and Amy E. Robillard, *Pluralizing Plagiarism: Identities, Contexts, Pedagogies*, emphasizes the limitations inherent in both the academy's and culture's tendency to essentialize, universalize, and moralize plagiarism and calls for greater attention to "the specificity of and variations among the many sites at which plagiarism occurs" (3). Sean Zwagerman's analysis of the hand-wringing over a supposed "rising tide" of cheating and plagiarism and his thoughtful discussion of ways to avoid such counterproductive discourse (one of those ways being through the use of more collaborative activities and assignments) demonstrate that we should come down "in favor of engaging the process rather than punishing the product" (702). If we needed any further evidence of the fraught nature of the very term *plagiarism* or of the difficulty today of parsing texts in order to determine what is "original" and what is not, then Jonathan Lethem's stunning "The Ecstasy of Influence: A Plagiarism," which presents a tissue of begged, borrowed, and stolen passages accompanied by details of their provenance, certainly provides it. (Those unfamiliar with Lethem's provocative essay can find it online in the February 2007 issue of *Harper's Magazine*.)

COLLABORATION AND CONTEMPORARY SCENES OF WRITING

Given the developments that we have thus far described — revolutionary changes in concepts of subjectivity, authorship, and writing in *theory* and the resistance to enacting these changes in our day-to-day disciplinary and pedagogical *practices* — the "view from here" a decade into the twenty-first century looks very different than it did in the early 1980s, when we first began thinking and writing about collaboration. As we have noted, resistance to collaborative writing has proven much more entrenched than we imagined. In addition, the contrast between the dizzyingly collaborative digital world that we and our students inhabit today and the world of the academy has grown even starker. Although this gap between the kinds of writing students are doing in and out of class is, as we have noted, not entirely new, little in our early experience as collaborators prepared us for what we see when we observe the scene of writing today.

That scene, which many of our students move through with ease, offers opportunities for inhabiting the roles of multiple authorship and for engaging exponentially expanding audiences. Indeed, in much web-based writing, traditional distinctions between author and audience now strike us as increasingly difficult to maintain — a situation that has caused us to recognize that research interests in audience and collaborative writing, which we once viewed as separate, have now more or less merged. (In Chapter 15 in this collection, we explore this merger in greater depth.) We have thus come to see the strands of our work on collaboration and on audience as intensely interwoven. We now understand that, in a digital age, audiences can and often do become collaborators who then, not to put too fine a point on it, face problems of authorial attribution, intellectual property, the possibility that their writing will be read by unintended and/or invisible audiences, and so on.

In the scene of writing we have just described, students are composing verbal and visual texts (such as short films and audio essays) more than ever before, and in sites unimaginable less than a decade ago. Email, for example, is now often described by students as "what you do when you need to get in touch with a teacher or supervisor" and has been outpaced by instant messaging systems of all kinds. Then there's the spectacular growth of social networking sites, which began in earnest with SixDegrees.com in 1997, hit the mainstream in 2003 with MySpace, and was followed by Facebook in 2004, YouTube in 2005, and Twitter in 2006. Add to these venues the staggering array of writing sites involved with fanzines, linked systems, blogs, and wikis — and the ready accessibility of *mountains* of information to be sampled, shared, and used in the design of "new" texts — and we see something of the huge digital canvas in and on which our students are crafting and responding to messages.

In such a setting, it is hardly surprising that students are more and more used to thinking of themselves as part of a network of people engaged in various discursive practices rather than as individual authors — at least when they are at work on self-sponsored activities. Nothing better exemplifies this new sense of textual interaction and shared ownership than Wikipedia, which — it's hard to remember — has been around only since 2001. With eleven million articles in two hundred-plus languages and growing, Wikipedia offers limitless opportunities for collaborative writing, or what our colleague Mark Otuteye describes as "authorless narrative" (that is, prose composed by many hands, largely without attribution). In the context of Wikipedia, contributors are simultaneously (co)authors *with* and the audience *for* the work of other (co)authors.

Our students consult Wikipedia almost obsessively; some also contribute to it. But students also engage in other kinds of online collaborative projects, often simultaneously as author and audience. In *Convergence Culture*, for instance, Henry Jenkins notes that more than 60 percent of the content for the video game *The Sims* has been generated by its fans (166). In his study, Jenkins points to many examples of fans playing central roles in what he refers to as transmedia storytelling. One example involves players who worked together as a group called the Cloudmakers to play "The Beast," a videogame created to promote Steven Spielberg's 2001 film *Artificial Intelligence: A.I.* (123). According to Jenkins, the number of players who participated in the Cloudmakers' collaborative effort ranged from 500 to more than 7,500. This collaboration engaged not only those working together to play the game but the game designers as well, since the designers often reacted to players in real time. As Tom, one of the players, said to Jenkins, as the Cloudmakers got "better and better at solving their puzzles, [the designers] had to come up with harder puzzles. They were responding to stuff we were saying or doing" (125).

To be sure, much of the collaborative online writing that students are so keen to do is self-sponsored writing, writing that can often be characterized as communicating for entertainment. But not always. We think, for instance, of Heather Lawver, a home-schooled teenager who, at age fourteen, launched *The Daily Prophet* (www.dprophet.com), a web-based school newspaper for

Harry Potter's fictional Hogwarts. By 2006 the newspaper had a staff of 102 children from around the world (Jenkins 171). More importantly, when Heather's site and other sites devoted to the Potter series were threatened by Warner Brothers, she formed the association Defense against the Dark Arts and worked with fans throughout the world to protect their freedom to publish fan fiction online. Pressing health issues (Lawver was diagnosed with Dercum's disease) led to closure of *The Daily Prophet*, though Lawver continues to collaborate extensively on sites devoted to education about Dercum's disease and to support for those living with this condition.

The examples of Tom the Cloudmaker and Heather Lawver emphasize the gap that currently exists between the highly collaborative, self-sponsored online writing that many students do and the writing that they are asked to do when they enter many of our classrooms. From one perspective, of course, this gap is hardly new. A gap has always existed between the values, expectations, interests, and experiences that students bring to the academy and the values, expectations, interests, and experiences of their teachers. Yet as our examples emphasize, the gap today seems especially wide and deep: students out of class are composing across a range of multimodal genres, most often in concert with other writers; yet in the great majority of their college writing classes they are still the "singular authors" that we described nearly twenty-five years ago. We are not alone in pointing out this discrepancy or in calling for change. In "The Movement of Air, the Breath of Meaning: Aurality and Multimodal Composing," Cynthia Selfe reviews the place of orality and au-rality in the academy, concluding that today we must move beyond the printed page and allow students to engage fully with "all the available means of persuasion." "Students," she says, "need to know that their role as rhetorical agents is open, not artificially foreclosed by the limits of their teachers' imaginations. They need a full quiver of semiotic modes from which to select, role models who can teach them to think critically about a range of communication tools, and multiple ways of reaching their audience" (645). Though Selfe doesn't mention it specifically, her essay suggests that using this "full quiver of semiotic modes" will call for collaboration.

WRITING — AND "REAL" WRITING

Ironically we see increasing evidence that in spite of all the extracurricular writing students are engaging in today, they may not think of much of it as "real" writing, nor would they necessarily characterize the highly participatory forms of such writing (in game playing, communicating on social networking sites, or texting, for example) as "collaboration." The Pew Internet and American Life Project's 2008 report "Writing, Technology, and Teens," by Lenhart and colleagues, for example, found that while as many as 93 percent of teens say "they write for their own pleasure" and "most teenagers spend a considerable amount of their life composing texts . . . , they do not think that a lot of the material they create electronically is real writing" (2). This report goes on to say that students today view "real" writing, which they associate with school writing and other high-stakes discourse, as very important, but they fail to include the vast amount of writing they do online in that category. In a similar vein, Stanford Study of Writing researchers asked student partici- pants every year of the five-year study to describe their collaborations. Most students reported that they did virtually no collaborative writing — and then went on to regale researchers with stories of the writing they did with others, in primarily extracurricular settings. They often seemed to resist the label "collaboration," even when they were deeply engaged in such practices. These findings raise additional questions about varying forms of collabora- tion: for instance, as Jeffrey Breitenfeldt asks, "Is collaborative writing differ- ent when you interact with 'funinthesun94' vs. a classmate whose name you know? Would they both seem to be equivalent coauthors?"

This tendency for contemporary students not to view the online writing they engage in every day as "real" writing is one demonstration of the power that deeply entrenched notions of authorship continue to hold. We gained an insight into the power of these assumptions early in our research on collab- orative writing. As we have already noted, that research involved several sur- veys. We knew that we needed to pilot our surveys, so at one point Lisa asked several of her colleagues to respond to an early version of the first survey.

One of these colleagues was at the time the coauthor of the second best- selling technical writing textbook in the country. He and Lisa had worked together for years and had coauthored more reports than they'd like to remem- ber. So imagine Lisa's surprise when this colleague returned his survey to her — a survey that indicated that he had never written collaboratively. When Lisa asked her colleague about this, his response stunned her. "Oh," he said, "I thought you meant *real* writing."

"Real writing." This comment forcefully demonstrated to us that while the data gathered in our surveys would be important, we needed to better understand and convey the ideologically grounded history of such constructs as authorship and intellectual property. Doing so added several years to our research project — but it also significantly enriched our analysis.

The need to fully understand the definition of "writing" as well as "real" writing has only gained in significance over the last thirty years. In fact, the definition and status of "writing" are clearly more in play today than at any time in our lives, and the differing responses of students to what is and what is not "writing" are clear indications of this fact of life in the age of Web 2.0. Indeed, much scholarship on new media raises important definitional ques- tions, at least indirectly. We think, for instance, of work by Cynthia Selfe, Anne Wysocki, Jeff Rice, the New London Group, and others who have done so much to illustrate the great potential that new media offer student writers and writing (no matter how students may label such work). In Wysocki, Johnson- Eilola, Selfe, and Sire's *Writing New Media: Theory and Applications for Expand- ing the Teaching of Composition*, the authors describe the current situation as akin to having a "thick, richly-printed rug" pulled out from under our feet (1) and say that their book, while it can never provide a complete new rug to replace the old one, is nevertheless "the equivalent of carpet scraps, some tentative weaves, bits and pieces of matting and colorful materials for you to consider" (2). In our view, these authors offer considerably more, exploring a series of questions about the relationship between new media and writing and demonstrating the ways that writing teachers can work more and more effectively with new media, arguing that a "writing teacher can . . . bring a humane and thoughtful attention to materiality, production and consumption" of new media texts (7). These authors go on to provide examples of teachers doing just that — and of students working with new media.

In one particularly compelling chapter, Selfe provides a case study of a young man — David — who doesn't do well in school or in traditional print-based academic writing but who gains both a fair amount of success and a great deal of satisfaction as a developer of websites and writer of popular articles (43–66). This and other chapters raise many issues, such as what will count as "real" writing in our classrooms and what the responsibilities of writing teachers will be in giving students opportunities to write across a wide range of genres and media. Selfe's student David doesn't find the "real" writing of school to be useful to him, and so he resists it.

There are, of course, many Davids out there. In *New Literacies: Changing Knowledge and Classroom Learning*, Colin Lankshear and Michele Knobel describe a whole group of Australian adolescent males who are identified as "trouble" and as having "problems with literacy" but who successfully worked with a team of researchers and teachers to develop a complex and successful website on motorcycles (182). As Selfe points out in her study of David, such stories present a huge challenge to teachers of writing: "how to design a meaningful course of study for composition classrooms that accommodates a full range of literacies, especially those literacies associated with new media texts" (56). That is, how can we design a course in which "real" writing includes what David wants and needs to do — and can we do so without abandoning the values long associated with traditional print text? These are very tough questions, especially considering the material conditions of most writing classes: we have between ten and fifteen weeks to teach students how to read, write, and think rhetorically; how to carry out research; and how to present that research in appropriate ways to a range of audiences. Can we say grace over these tasks — and work with new media as well?

In the face of such challenges, some teachers just give up. In " 'You Won't Be Needing Your Laptops Today': Wired Bodies in the Wireless Classroom," Kevin Leander describes what should be an ideal situation: a private high school where all students have laptops and all rooms are wired for Wi-Fi. And yet as Leander discovered, the mind-set of the teachers simply could not deal with the challenge to "traditional school space-time" that 24/7 access to the Internet and opportunities to work with new media represented. The teachers were so fearful of plagiarism, for example, that they agreed that all in-class essays had to be handwritten (Leander 35). In his study, Leander argues that the teachers at this elite private high school experienced a sense of "loss and nostalgia" for traditional school space-time when laptops and Internet access became universally available.

The "loss and nostalgia" for traditional school space-time writing and the tension regarding what counts as "real" writing seem to us to extend to discussions of collaboration as well (the teachers in that high school, for example, also feared letting the students work together). As we have pointed out, the default position in most writing classes today is still that of the single author, writing alone. Even when scholars attend to new writing spaces and forms, they most often attend to practices that are implicitly rather than explicitly collaborative. In short, some of this research continues to *assume* collaboration without attending carefully to it or its instruction. As a result, students who work in groups on projects, many of which engage new media, are too often left pretty much on their own to negotiate the material and practical — not to mention the ideological and theoretical — conditions of collaboration. (Selfe's recent collection *Multimodal Composition: Resources for Teachers* is a notable exception.)

At the present moment, research in composition studies and new media is beginning to discuss in detail just what it might mean for students to work collaboratively on a text. What Howard Rheingold says about new media writing — that students are "both self-guided and in need of guidance" — can be said even more emphatically for collaborative writing. Guidance is especially important in first-year writing, where students could be, but generally are not, receiving such detailed instruction on how to work effectively with others across a range of tasks. In regard to this point about first-year writing, it's telling to note that in a national study of first-year student writing that Andrea and coauthor Karen Lunsford recently conducted, not a single collaborative assignment emerged. Thus we continue to be struck by the need to confront the issue raised by Selfe — how to create classes that allow students to bring more of the kind of writing they are doing outside of class into the writing classroom while also preparing them for their most often more conservative academic assignments.

THE SPECTRUM OF COLLABORATION(S)

Behind these questions of definition (what is "real" writing?) and of practice (where and when do we teach collaboration?) lies what Knobel and Lankshear argue in *A New Literacies Sampler* is the development of a new cyberspatial, postindustrial mind-set in which "[t]he focus is increasingly on 'collectives' as the unit of production, competence, [and] intelligence" and "[e]xpertise and authority are distributed . . . collective . . . and hybrid" (11).[3] Such a mind-set will, by definition, depend on collaborative practices and could benefit from some work on our part to define and theorize such practices. Toward that end, we find ourselves musing (obsessing might be the better descriptive word here) about a question we have returned to again and again: How can we best define collaborative writing?

To begin, we should acknowledge Kathleen Blake Yancey and Michael Spooner's argument that not all writing is collaborative. In "A Single Good Mind: Collaboration, Cooperation, and the Writing Self," Yancey and Spooner argue that "the effect of an all-inclusive definition of collaboration has been to trivialize collaboration" (55). We take Yancey and Spooner's point, especially that viewing all writing as collaborative could potentially flatten out and empty the term of meaning. But such a degradation of meaning need not be the necessary outcome. Rather, seeing all writing as inevitably grounded in social exchange reminds us that collaboration can be hidden, repressed, and unacknowledged — yet still present. Moreover, recognizing such social grounding challenges us to explore, as Yancey and Spooner suggest, the careful differentiation among kinds or forms of collaborative writing (along with, we would add, kinds or forms of ownership).

Certainly one form of collaboration is that which we ourselves have most favored — two (or a very small group of) authors working closely together through all stages of the composing process. Through the years, we have drawn enormous satisfaction from such discursive acts, which have deeply strengthened, and been strengthened by, our friendship. Of course there are a number of other models for effective collaborative writing: a group of writers composes sections of a text separately and then stitches them together; or a group of writers composes sections and then hands them to a third party for editing, legal review, and so on. Using contemporary technologies, such groups can grow exponentially as collaborators shift in and out of the group and tasks divide and subdivide. In short, rather than labeling some texts "collaborative" and others "noncollaborative," we see a continuum of collaboration, from the single scholar who produces a monograph by silently "conversing" with other authors, readers, and editors to the huge and shifting coalitions that produce mass participatory texts such as Wikipedia. We should note that Yancey and Spooner do not see Wikipedia and other participatory or distributed writing as collaborative, arguing that multiple writers working to revise a text composed by anonymous others falls outside the bounds of collaboration. Such forms, however, still seem collaborative to us; indeed, we think of such wiki writing as "extreme collaboration" on the other end of the spectrum from the single scholar who "collaborates" only with his or her sources.

In addition to the degree of collaboration, we have also thought about a second continuum, from the most agreeable and cooperative forms of collaboration to those that border on or embrace the agonistic. We think of this continuum as one running from the mutually composed wedding vow to the agreement worked out by warlike negotiators. Many forms of writing, to be sure, fall squarely in mid-range. Think of the online news article, for instance, that is followed by a series of comments that create a cacophonous, overlapping, echoing conversation — or diatribe. In this example the article still holds pride of place, but it is complemented and/or challenged by commentary from other voices.

Yet a third continuum strikes us as increasingly germane to collaboration and collaborative writing, one that runs from texts over which writers exert most control to texts where that control is most limited. One of the reasons for holding doggedly to concepts of single authorship, it seems to us, may be the control that such authorship offers, such as the ability to make important choices about content, style, and publication venue. Such control is in many regards illusory: think of untenured assistant professors in the humanities whose professional lives depend upon their meeting expectations such as the increasingly high "gold standard" of the single-authored monograph, or who submit articles only to be told by editors that the length must be cut in half.

The tension between control and lack of control is even more visible in much digital communication. How many members of Facebook, for instance, are aware of the important role that privacy settings play in allowing them to control who can, and who cannot, access their profile, news feed and wall, and so on? How many such members are also aware of the control that Facebook itself requires as part of the price of enrollment? As readers are aware, any video posted on YouTube can be commented on, shared, altered, or parodied by others. Such issues of control also resonate in the increasing number of programs that allow for multiple writers working simultaneously.

The continua we have just described, and particularly the one focusing on degrees of control, bring us to a distinction that we identified early on in our research. In that study we identified collaboration that is "hierarchical" as a "form of collaboration [that] is carefully, and often rigidly, structured, driven by highly specific goals, and carried out by people playing clearly defined and delimited roles" (133). Dialogic collaboration, on the other hand, we described as "loosely structured and the roles enacted within it are fluid: one person may occupy multiple and shifting roles as a project progresses. In this mode, the process of articulating goals is as often as important as the goals themselves and sometimes even more important" (*Singular Texts* 133). In working on this essay, we have found that the concepts of hierarchy and dialogism still enable us to pose valuable if somewhat different questions about collaboration and collaborative writing. In most of the examples we have discussed here, hierarchy and dialogism exist in tension with one another. In the case of Heather Lawver's *Daily Prophet* online newspaper, for instance, as webmaster and editor Heather retained considerable control over this project, and in that sense the collaboration was hierarchical. Nevertheless, as a result of Heather's initiative and commitment, many young people engaged dialogically in the creation of content and were thus able to experience the satisfaction of published authorship.

So hierarchical and dialogic forms of collaboration still seem viable descriptors to us, though we often see them operating together, in a kind of give-and-take. We think of the dialogism at work as a small group of writers on Wikipedia collaboratively develops an entry on a topic of great importance to them, for example, alongside the hierarchy that views some editors as "more equal" than others. The experience of librarian Hope Leman, who developed the website ScanGrants to facilitate searches for funding health projects, allows us to explore further the complexity of the relationship between dialogic and hierarchical forms of collaboration. Here is Leman's account of her experience:

> Having read in a library blog that a link to one's site on Wikipedia raises the visibility of one's site . . . I added ScanGrants to the Research Funding page of Wikipedia as well as to the Wikipedia pages on basic science,

medicine, grants, etc. Within minutes, however, my links had been obliterated by two different editors on various grounds. Here is what one editor wrote: "Just possibly, if the NIH etc. do in fact discuss it as well as link to it, or if other references have been published in the 3rd party independent reliable published sources, print or online (but not blogs or press releases), then it just might be appropriate for an article. If you can furnish references here or on your talk page, someone else might be willing to write the article. But it has to be generally recognized as important first by other people as shown by published sources." In other words, to get into Wikipedia, you have to be published in journals so as to prove that you possess the credibility to get into Wikipedia. (22)

Leman's experience points up the strong hierarchical infrastructure that can and does exist on Wikipedia and calls attention to the diversity of writing practices and opportunities for authority, or for its lack, in that venue. But this single experience tends to obscure the multiple opportunities for dialogism that also exist on this site. Had she been initiating or contributing to an entry on some form of popular culture, such as mockumentaries, her actions probably would not have elicited the immediate vigilance of two eagle-eyed editors. Indeed, Leman could contribute to any number of entries in Wikipedia on a variety of topics. At this point, however, it's impossible to predict the ways others may use, engage with, or even obliterate her contributions. In any event, this discussion points up the limitations inherent in any effort to define collaborative writing in a singular or unitary way. Instead, we believe it is more important to engage collaboration and collaborative writing as richly complex, situated, and materially embedded practices.

The View from Here

When we began our research on collaboration, we were writing in one cultural and disciplinary moment. Today we write this essay in a very different moment, one often characterized as involving a tectonic shift in communication technologies similar to the transition from manuscript to print culture. At this moment, perhaps predictably, ordinary people, the media, and scholars alike seem drawn to either utopian or dystopian views of this transition. Consider, in this regard, George Landow, whose early analysis of the consequences of hypertext sometimes slipped into utopian visions; or Sven Birkerts, whose *The Gutenberg Elegies* mourned the fate of reading and saw only a dystopic wasteland in the new media.[4]

In our earlier work, we were constantly tempted to fall into such binary thinking and to valorize the kind of dialogic collaboration that we ourselves enacted and most enjoyed. Only our multiple on-site visits with collaborative writers helped us avoid such binary oversimplification.[5] We still vividly recall talking with the manager of a sanitary authority, who spoke at length of the pleasure he took in collaboration and in dialogical teamwork — music to our ears. His utopian representation of collaboration was challenged, however, when we recognized the largely unacknowledged role that his (female) secretary in this almost all-male office played in this process. Such recognitions have led us to reaffirm the continued importance of resisting Western culture's strong attraction to binaries, such as the one between dialogic and hierarchical collaboration, and to use the metaphor of continua to suggest the multilayered complexity of all writing practices. Thus the view from here confirms the position we originally took in *Singular Texts/Plural Authors*:

> It is not possible or desirable . . . to develop a set of binary opposites that would neatly characterize collaborative writing situations as either hierarchical or dialogic, conservative or subversive, masculine or feminine [or, we would add now, cooperative or agonistic, controlled or uncontrolled]. Perhaps only full-fledged ethnographic studies could provide the depth of detail and critical perspective necessary for such judgments. Like gender roles, discourse situations are, Burke reminds us, inherently mixed and paradoxical; they defy easy analysis and categorization. And surely it seems reasonable to find inscribed in any piece of collaboration or any particular collaborator the same kind of risks and tensions that are generally inscribed in our culture. (134)

It's encouraging to note that the work we envisioned so long ago is now being carried out. Selfe and Hawisher's case studies of students at work provide "the depth of detail and critical perspectives" we were hoping for, as does the work of danah boyd and her colleagues in the Digital Youth Project (see Ito et al.). While these researchers may not typically discuss the implications of their research for our understanding of collaboration, such collaboration is most often a given — a silent and potent partner — in their work. These studies are important to us, then, for they help us understand more concretely the material practices that make up the range of collaborative acts we have been studying for so long.

These recent studies are also important to us because of the way they position students as partners in, rather than the subjects of, research. In *Literate Lives in the Information Age: Narratives of Literacy from the United States*, Cynthia Selfe and Gail Hawisher explicitly discuss their decision to invite case study participants to coauthor chapters with them. In their introduction, they comment on the importance of giving "the participants more say in the politics of interpretation" (12) and argue that coauthorship represents "a viable, practical, and ethical resolution" for scholars undertaking qualitative research studies (13). In the same way, the Stanford Study of Writing research team includes student authors who are themselves part of the study, and readers will no doubt think of many other similar examples of such collaboration.

We see this move as a principle we should enact as fully as possible not only in our research but within our writing classrooms, where students work with us as partners, as coresearchers of their learning and growth as communicators. Students, after all, are the experts in their own experience of new media and new literacies: they have the potential to teach us a great deal. To achieve this goal, however, we need to confront at least two major obstacles. The first involves the structure of the university: as we lamented in *Singular*

Texts / Plural Authors, everything about the university — from individual grades, class rankings, and writing assignments and exams to large (and largely anonymous) lecture halls where "knowledge is packaged into discreet segments and dispensed to passive recipients, fast-food style" (120) — tells students that the kind of collaborative partnership described above is unavailable to them. While we cannot dismantle these structures, we can make our students increasingly aware of them and engage them in constructive critique as well as acts of resistance where possible.

The second obstacle grows out of assumptions that many students seem to hold about their engagement with new media and new literacies. At least according to the Pew study we cited earlier, students often fail to identify what they are doing online as "writing" at all. If we want them to become researchers of their own online communication, and to do so in partnership with other students and their teachers, we may well have our work cut out for us: We need, first of all, to engage students in some serious definitional work, helping them understand the nature of collaboration and the definition and scope of "writing" today. More importantly, we need to engage *with* them in exploring the deep ethical challenges and responsibilities (from questions of intellectual property, citation, plagiarism, and respect for others to a heightened sense of responsibility to self in terms of disclosure) inherent in their own practices. If successful, such engagement will help students uncover or make visible the rhetorical choices and strategies they enact in their everyday writing lives and thus help address the widening gap between what students are doing in their primarily online self-sponsored writing (whether they think of it as "writing" or not) and their school-based writing (whether that writing is print or multimodal). We see narrowing this gap as one of the most pressing challenges facing teachers of writing today.

Thirty years ago, we had a growing sense that the electronic revolution would lead to exciting changes in literacies (although at the time we would have used the word "literacy" in a sentence such as this one), but we had little sense at the time of the forms such changes would take or of the effects they would have on students. Now we are in the midst of these changes and are struggling to make sense of them for ourselves and for our students. The view from late 2010 reveals a devilishly complex and difficult terrain. As we consider our situation and the situation of our students — not to mention the troubled world beyond our classrooms — we see an urgent need for a clear-eyed and steady-handed understanding of collaboration and collaborative practices in all their fullness: the stakes are higher, the difficulties are greater, but the possibilities are more exciting for us as learners, educators, and as citizens than we could have imagined some thirty years ago.

NOTES

1. A recent example of this tension can be found in the debate over Jaron Lanier's book *You Are Not a Gadget,* in which he — the person who coined the term "virtual reality" and has been a guru of the digirati — argues that the openness and participatory collaboration on the Web have gone too far and are threatening individual creativity and responsibility.

2. We are heartened by MLA President Sidonie Smith's call for a revisioning of the dissertation in literature and languages. In the summer 2010 *MLA Newsletter*, she writes that if the profession moves in the direction she calls for "We will better prepare our graduate students to navigate a scholarly environment in which the modes of production are increasingly collaborative, the vehicles of scholarly dissemination increasingly interactive, the circulation of knowledge more openly accessible, and the audiences for which we compose purposefully varied. We will also better prepare them to develop supple and sophisticated pedagogies for teaching undergraduates whose habits of mind and attention, modes of learning, and repertoire of literacies are changing before us" (2). We couldn't agree more . . . though having made similar arguments for thirty years, we are not holding our breath.

3. While we appreciate the helpfulness of Knobel and Lankshear's distinction between different mind-sets, we note that this distinction represents a binary, and as such needs to be interrogated.

4. In *The Digital Sublime: Myth, Power, and Cyberspace*, Vincent Mosco explores the extent to which changes in technology encourage some to proclaim "an epochal transformation in human experience that would transcend time (the end of history), space (the end of geography), and power (the end of politics)" (2–3).

5. In fact, based on Yancey and Spooner's reading of our text, it seems that we were not successful in avoiding privileging one mode of collaboration over another, in spite of strenuous efforts on our parts to do so.

WORKS CITED

Barthes, Roland. "The Death of the Author." *Image Music Text*. Trans. Stephen Heath. New York: Hill and Wang, 1978. 142–48. Print.

Bentley, Joseph. "Semantic Gravitation: An Essay on Satiric Reduction." *Modern Language Quarterly* 30 (Mar. 1969): 3–19. Print.

Birkerts, Sven. *The Gutenberg Elegies: The Fate of Reading in an Electronic Age*. Boston: Faber and Faber, 2004. Print.

boyd, danah. "Taken Out of Context: American Teen Sociality in Networked Publics." Diss. UC Berkeley, 2008. Print.

Breitenfeldt, Jeffrey. Personal interview. 22 Aug. 2009.

Bruffee, Kenneth. "Collaborative Learning and the 'Conversation of Mankind.'" *College English* 46.7 (1984): 635–52. Print.

Burke, Kenneth. *A Rhetoric of Motives*. Berkeley: U of California P, 1950. Print.

Connors, Robert J., Lisa S. Ede, and Andrea A. Lunsford, eds. *Essays on Classical Rhetoric and Modern Discourse*. Carbondale: Southern Illinois UP, 1984. Print.

Day, Kami, and Michele Eodice, *(First Person)2: A Study of Co-Authoring in the Academy*. Logan: Utah State UP, 2001. Print.

Ede, Lisa, and Andrea A. Lunsford. *Singular Texts/Plural Authors: Perspectives on Collaborative Writing*. Carbondale: Southern Illinois UP, 1990. Print.

Ede, Lisa, and Andrea A. Lunsford. "Why Write . . . Together?" *Rhetoric Review* 1 (1983): 150–58. Print.

Faigley, Lester, and Thomas P. Miller. "What We Learn from Writing on the Job." *College English* 44 (1982): 557–69. Print.

Foucault, Michel. "What Is an Author?" *Textual Strategies*. Ed. Josue V. Harari. Ithaca: Cornell UP, 1979. 141–60. Print.

Gere, Anne. *Writing Groups: History, Theory, Implications*. Urbana, IL: NCTE, 1987. Print.

Howard, Rebecca Moore. *Standing in the Shadow of Giants: Plagiarists, Authors, Collaborators*. Stamford, CT: Ablex, 1999. Print.

Howard, Rebecca Moore, and Amy E. Robillard, eds. *Pluralizing Plagiarism: Identities, Contexts, Pedagogies*. Portsmouth, NH: Boynton/Cook, 2008. Print.

Ito, Mizuko, Heather A. Hurst, Matteo Bittanti, danah boyd, Beckyi Herr-Stephenson, Patricia G. Lange, C. J. Pascoe, and Laura Robinson. *Living and Learning with New Media: Summary of Findings from the Digital Youth Project*. Cambridge: MIT Press, 2009. Print.

Jenkins, Henry. *Convergence Culture: Where Old and New Media Collide*. New York: New York UP, 2006. Print.

Knobel, Michele, and Colin Lankshear. *A New Literacies Sampler*. New York: Peter Lang, 2007.

Laird, Holly. *Women Coauthors*. Champaign, IL: U of Illinois P, 2000. Print.

Landow, George. *Hypertext: The Convergence of Contemporary Critical Theory and Technology*. Baltimore: Johns Hopkins UP, 1992. Print.

Lanier, Jaron. *You Are Not a Gadget: A Manifesto.* New York: Knopf, 2010. Print.

Lankshear, Colin, and Michele Knobel. *New Literacies: Changing Knowledge and Classroom Learning.* New York: Open UP, 2004.

Leander, Kevin M. "'You Won't Be Needing Your Laptops Today': Wired Bodies in the Wireless Classroom." *A New Literacies Sampler,* eds. Michele Knobel and Colin Lankshear. New York: Peter Lang, 2007. Print.

LeFevre, Karen. *Invention as a Social Act.* Carbondale: Southern Illinois UP, 1986. Print.

Leman, Hope. "ScanGrants: A New Service for Libraries, a New Role for Librarians." *Computers in Libraries* 28.8 (Sept. 2008): 20–23. Print.

Lenhart, Amanda, Sousa Arafeh, Aaron Smith, and Alexandra Rankin Macgill. "Writing, Technology, and Teens." *Pew Internet.* Pew Research Center and American Life Project and the National Commission on Writing, 24 Apr. 2008. Web. 27 July 2010.

Lethem, Jonathan. "The Ecstasy of Influence: A Plagiarism." *Harper's* Feb. 2007: 59–71. Print.

London, Bette. *Writing Double: Women's Literary Partnerships.* Ithaca, NY: Cornell UP, 1999. Print.

Lunsford, Andrea A., and Lisa S. Ede. "On Distinctions between Classical and Modern Rhetoric." *Essays on Classical Rhetoric and Modern Discourse.* Ed. Robert J. Connors, Lisa S. Ede, and Andrea A. Lunsford. Carbondale: Southern Illinois UP, 1984. 37–59. Print.

Lunsford, Andrea, and Karen Lunsford. "'Mistakes Are a Fact of Life': A National Comparative Study." *College Composition and Communication,* 59.4 (2008): 781–807. Print.

Mosco, Vincent. *The Digital Sublime: Myth, Power, and Cyberspace.* Cambridge: MIT P, 2005. Print.

"Report of the MLA Task Force on Evaluating Scholarship for Tenure and Promotion." *Profession 2007.* New York: MLA, 2007. 9–71. Print.

Rheingold, Howard. "Vision of the Future." Education.au Seminar. Melbourne, Australia. 2 Oct. 2007. Web.

Selfe, Cynthia L. "The Movement of Air, the Breath of Meaning: Aurality and Multimodal Composing." *College Composition and Communication* 60 (2009): 616–63. Print.

Selfe, Cynthia L., ed. *Multimodal Composition: Resources for Teachers.* Cresskill, NY: Hampton P, 2007. Print.

Selfe, Cynthia L., and Gail E. Hawisher. *Literate Lives in the Information Age: Narratives of Literacy from the United States.* Mahwah, NJ: Erlbaum, 2004. Print.

Smith, Sidonie. "An Agenda for the New Dissertation." *MLA Newsletter.* Summer 2010: 2. Print.

Speck, Bruce W., Teresa R. Johnson, Catherine P. Dice, and Leon B. Heaton. *Collaborative Writing: An Annotated Bibliography.* Westport, CT: Greenwood P, 1999. Print.

Stanford Study of Writing. Stanford, 2008. Web. 9 Feb. 2011.

Stone, Marjorie, and Judith Thompson, eds. *Literary Couplings: Writing Couples, Collaborators, and the Construction of Authorship.* Madison: U of Wisconsin P, 2006. Print.

Wysocki, Anne Francis, Johndan Johnson-Eilola, Cynthia L. Selfe, and Geoffrey Sirc. *Writing New Media: Theory and Applications for Expanding the Teaching of Composition.* Logan: Utah State UP, 2004. Print.

Yancey, Kathleen Blake, and Michael Spooner. "A Single Good Mind: Collaboration, Cooperation, and the Writing Self." *College Composition and Communication* 49 (1998): 45–62. Print.

York, Lorraine. *Rethinking Women's Collaborative Writing: Power, Difference, Property.* Toronto: U of Toronto P, 2002. Print.

Zwagerman, Sean. "The Scarlet P: Plagiarism, Panopticism, and the Rhetoric of Academic Integrity." *College Composition and Communication* 59 (2008): 676–710. Print.

PART THREE

On Audience

13   *Audience Addressed/Audience Invoked: The Role of Audience in Composition Theory and Pedagogy*

One important controversy currently engaging scholars and teachers of writing involves the role of audience in composition theory and pedagogy. How can we best define the audience of a written discourse? What does it mean to address an audience? To what degree should teachers stress audience in their assignments and discussions? What *is* the best way to help students recognize the significance of this critical element in any rhetorical situation?

Teachers of writing may find recent efforts to answer these questions more confusing than illuminating. Should they agree with Ruth Mitchell and Mary Taylor, who so emphasize the significance of the audience that they argue for abandoning conventional composition courses and instituting a "cooperative effort by writing and subject instructors in adjunct courses. The cooperation and courses take two main forms. Either writing instructors can be attached to subject courses where writing is required, an organization which disperses the instructors throughout the departments participating; or the composition courses can teach students how to write the papers assigned in other concurrent courses, thus centralizing instruction but diversifying topics."[1] Or should teachers side with Russell Long, who asserts that those advocating greater attention to audience overemphasize the role of "observable physical or occupational characteristics" while ignoring the fact that most writers actually create their audiences. Long argues against the usefulness of such methods as developing hypothetical rhetorical situations as writing assignments, urging instead a more traditional emphasis on "the analysis of texts in the classroom with a very detailed examination given to the signals provided by the writer for his audience."[2]

To many teachers, the choice seems limited to a single option — to be for or against an emphasis on audience in composition courses. In the following essay, we wish to expand our understanding of the role audience plays in composition theory and pedagogy by demonstrating that the arguments advocated by each side of the current debate oversimplify the act of making

From Lisa Ede and Andrea Lunsford, in *College Composition and Communication* 35.2 (1984): 155–71.

meaning through written discourse. Each side, we will argue, has failed adequately to recognize (1) the fluid, dynamic character of rhetorical situations; and (2) the integrated, interdependent nature of reading and writing. After discussing the strengths and weaknesses of the two central perspectives on audience in composition — which we group under the rubrics of *audience addressed* and *audience invoked*[3] — we will propose an alternative formulation, one which we believe more accurately reflects the richness of "audience" as a concept.*

AUDIENCE ADDRESSED

Those who envision audience as addressed emphasize the concrete reality of the writer's audience; they also share the assumption that knowledge of this audience's attitudes, beliefs, and expectations is not only possible (via observation and analysis) but essential. Questions concerning the degree to which this audience is "real" or imagined, and the ways it differs from the speaker's audience, are generally either ignored or subordinated to a sense of the audience's powerfulness. In their discussion of "A Heuristic Model for Creating a Writer's Audience," for example, Fred Pfister and Joanne Petrik attempt to recognize the ontological complexity of the writer-audience relationship by noting that "students, like all writers, must fictionalize their audience."[4] Even so, by encouraging students to "construct in their imagination an audience that is as nearly a replica as is possible of *those many readers who actually exist in the world of reality*," Pfister and Petrik implicitly privilege the concept of audience as addressed.[5]

Many of those who envision audience as addressed have been influenced by the strong tradition of audience analysis in speech communication and by current research in cognitive psychology on the composing process.[6] They often see themselves as reacting against the current-traditional paradigm of composition, with its a-rhetorical, product-oriented emphasis.[7] And they also frequently encourage what is called "real-world" writing.[8]

Our purpose here is not to draw up a list of those who share this view of audience but to suggest the general outline of what most readers will recognize as a central tendency in the teaching of writing today. We would, however, like to focus on one particularly ambitious attempt to formulate a theory and pedagogy for composition based on the concept of audience as addressed: Ruth Mitchell and Mary Taylor's "The Integrating Perspective: An Audience-Response Model for Writing." We choose Mitchell and Taylor's work because

*A number of terms might be used to characterize the two approaches to audience which dominate current theory and practice. Such pairs as identified/envisaged, "real"/fictional, or analyzed/created all point to the same general distinction as do our terms. We chose "addressed/invoked" because these terms most precisely represent our intended meaning. Our discussion will, we hope, clarify their significance; for the present, the following definitions must serve. The "addressed" audience refers to those actual or real-life people who read a discourse, while the "invoked" audience refers to the audience called up or imagined by the writer.

of its theoretical richness and practical specificity. Despite these strengths, we wish to note several potentially significant limitations in their approach, limitations which obtain to varying degrees in much of the current work of those who envision audience as addressed.

In their article, Mitchell and Taylor analyze what they consider to be the two major existing composition models: one focusing on the writer and the other on the written product. Their evaluation of these two models seems essentially accurate. The "writer" model is limited because it defines writing as either self-expression or "fidelity to fact" (p. 255) — epistemologically naive assumptions which result in troubling pedagogical inconsistencies. And the "written product" model, which is characterized by an emphasis on "certain intrinsic features [such as a] lack of comma splices and fragments" (p. 258), is challenged by the continued inability of teachers of writing (not to mention those in other professions) to agree upon the precise intrinsic features which characterize "good" writing.

Most interesting, however, is what Mitchell and Taylor *omit* in their criticism of these models. "Neither the writer model nor the written product model pays serious attention to invention, the term used to describe those methods designed to aid in retrieving information, forming concepts, analyzing complex events, and solving certain kinds of problems."[9] Mitchell and Taylor's lapse in not noting this omission is understandable, however, for the same can be said of their own model. When these authors discuss the writing process, they stress that "our first priority for writing instruction at every level ought to be certain major tactics for structuring material because these structures are the most important in guiding the reader's comprehension and memory" (p. 271). They do not concern themselves with where "the material" comes from — its sophistication, complexity, accuracy, or rigor.

Mitchell and Taylor also fail to note another omission, one which might be best described in reference to their own model (Figure 13-1). This model has four components. Mitchell and Taylor use two of these, "writer" and "written product," as labels for the models they condemn. The third and fourth components, "audience" and "response," provide the title for their own "audience-response model for writing" (p. 249).

Mitchell and Taylor stress that the components in their model interact. Yet, despite their emphasis on interaction, it never seems to occur to them to note that the two other models may fail in large part because they overemphasize and isolate one of the four elements — wrenching it too greatly from its context and thus inevitably distorting the composing process. Mitchell and Taylor do not consider this possibility, we suggest, because their own model has the same weakness.

Mitchell and Taylor argue that a major limitation of the "writer" model is its emphasis on the self, the person writing, as the only potential judge of effective discourse. Ironically, however, their own emphasis on audience leads to a similar distortion. In their model, the audience has the sole power of evaluating writing, the success of which "will be judged by the audience's reaction: 'good' translates into 'effective,' 'bad' into 'ineffective.'" Mitchell and

FIGURE 13-1   Mitchell and Taylor's "General Model of Writing" (p. 250)

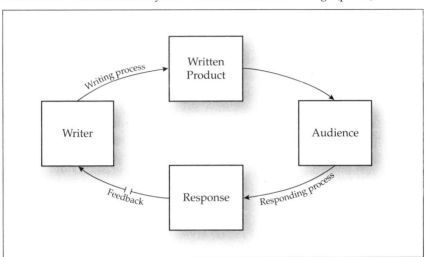

Taylor go on to note that "the audience not only judges writing; it also motivates it" (p. 250),[10] thus suggesting that the writer has less control than the audience over both evaluation and motivation.

Despite the fact that Mitchell and Taylor describe writing as "an interaction, a dynamic relationship" (p. 250), their model puts far more emphasis on the role of the audience than on that of the writer. One way to pinpoint the source of imbalance in Mitchell and Taylor's formulation is to note that they are right in emphasizing the creative role of readers who, they observe, "actively contribute to the meaning of what they read and will respond according to a complex set of expectations, preconceptions, and provocations" (p. 251), but wrong in failing to recognize the equally essential role writers play throughout the composing process not only as creators but also as *readers* of their own writing.

As Susan Wall observes in "In the Writer's Eye: Learning to Teach the Rereading/Revising Process," when writers read their own writing, as they do continuously while they compose, "there are really not one but two contexts for rereading: there is the writer-as-reader's sense of what the established text is actually saying, as of this reading; and there is the reader-as-writer's judgment of what the text might say or should say. . . ."[11] What is missing from Mitchell and Taylor's model, and from much work done from the perspective of audience as addressed, is a recognition of the crucial importance of this internal dialogue, through which writers analyze inventional problems and conceptualize patterns of discourse. Also missing is an adequate awareness that no matter how much feedback writers may receive after they have written something (or in breaks while they write), as they compose writers must rely in large part upon their own vision of the reader, which they create, as readers do their vision of writers, according to their own experiences and expectations.

Another major problem with Mitchell and Taylor's analysis is their apparent lack of concern for the ethics of language use. At one point, the authors ask the following important question: "Have we painted ourselves into a corner, so that the audience-response model must defend sociologese and its related styles?" (p. 265). Note first the ambiguity of their answer, which seems to us to say no and yes at the same time, and the way they try to deflect its impact:

> No. We defend only the right of audiences to set their own standards and we repudiate the ambitions of English departments to monopolize that standard-setting. If bureaucrats and scientists are happy with the way they write, then no one should interfere.
>
> But evidence is accumulating that they are not happy. (p. 265)

Here Mitchell and Taylor surely underestimate the relationship between style and substance. As those concerned with Doublespeak can attest, for example, the problem with sociologese is not simply its (to our ears) awkward, convoluted, highly nominalized style, but the way writers have in certain instances used this style to make statements otherwise unacceptable to lay persons, to "gloss over" potentially controversial facts about programs and their consequences, and thus violate the ethics of language use. Hence, although we support Mitchell and Taylor when they insist that we must better understand and respect the linguistic traditions of other disciplines and professions, we object to their assumption that style is somehow value free.

As we noted earlier, an analysis of Mitchell and Taylor's discussion clarifies weaknesses inherent in much of the theoretical and pedagogical research based on the concept of audience as addressed. One major weakness of this research lies in its narrow focus on helping students learn how to "continually modify their work with reference to their audience" (p. 251). Such a focus, which in its extreme form becomes pandering to the crowd, tends to undervalue the responsibility a writer has to a subject and to what Wayne Booth in *Modern Dogma and the Rhetoric of Assent* calls "the art of discovering good reasons."[12] The resulting imbalance has clear ethical consequences, for rhetoric has traditionally been concerned not only with the effectiveness of a discourse but with truthfulness as well. Much of our difficulty with the language of advertising, for example, arises out of the ad writer's powerful concept of audience as addressed divorced from a corollary ethical concept. The toothpaste ad that promises improved personality, for instance, knows too well how to address the audience. But such ads ignore ethical questions completely.

Another weakness in research done by those who envision audience as addressed suggests an oversimplified view of language. As Paul Kameen observes in "Rewording the Rhetoric of Composition," "discourse is not grounded in forms or experience or audience; it engages all of these elements simultaneously."[13] Ann Berthoff has persistently criticized our obsession with one or another of the elements of discourse, insisting that meaning arises out of their synthesis. Writing is more, then, than "a means of acting upon a receiver" (Mitchell and Taylor, p. 250); it is a means of making meaning for writer *and* reader.[14] Without such a unifying, balanced understanding of language use, it is easy to overemphasize one aspect of discourse, such as audience. It is also easy to forget, as Anthony Petrosky cautions us, that "reading, responding, and composing are aspects of understanding, and theories that attempt to account for them outside of their interaction with each other run the serious risk of building reductive models of human understanding."[15]

AUDIENCE INVOKED

Those who envision audience as invoked stress that the audience of a written discourse is a construction of the writer, a "created fiction" (Long, p. 225). They do not, of course, deny the physical reality of readers, but they argue that writers simply cannot know this reality in the way that speakers can. The central task of the writer, then, is not to analyze an audience and adapt discourse to meet its needs. Rather, the writer uses the semantic and syntactic resources of language to provide cues for the reader — cues which help to define the role or roles the writer wishes the reader to adopt in responding to the text. Little scholarship in composition takes this perspective; only Russell Long's article and Walter Ong's "The Writer's Audience Is Always a Fiction" focus centrally on this issue.[16] If recent conferences are any indication, however, a growing number of teachers and scholars are becoming concerned with what they see as the possible distortions and oversimplifications of the approach typified by Mitchell and Taylor's model.[17]

Russell Long's response to current efforts to teach students analysis of audience and adaptation of text to audience is typical: "I have become increasingly disturbed not only about the superficiality of the advice itself, but about the philosophy which seems to lie beneath it" (p. 221). Rather than detailing Long's argument, we wish to turn to Walter Ong's well-known study. Published in *PMLA* in 1975, "The Writer's Audience Is Always a Fiction" has had a significant impact on composition studies, despite the fact that its major emphasis is on fictional narrative rather than expository writing. An analysis of Ong's argument suggests that teachers of writing may err if they uncritically accept Ong's statement that "what has been said about fictional narrative applies ceteris paribus to all writing" (p. 17).

Ong's thesis includes two central assertions: "What do we mean by saying the audience is a fiction? Two things at least. First, that the writer must construct in his imagination, clearly or vaguely, an audience cast in some sort of role. . . . Second, we mean that the audience must correspondingly fictionalize itself" (p. 12). Ong emphasizes the creative power of the adept writer, who can both project and alter audiences, as well as the complexity of the reader's role. Readers, Ong observes, must learn or "know how to play the game of being a member of an audience that 'really' does not exist" (p. 12).

On the most abstract and general level, Ong is accurate. For a writer, the audience is not *there* in the sense that the speaker's audience, whether a single person or a large group, is present. But Ong's representative situations — the orator addressing a mass audience versus a writer alone in a room —

oversimplify the potential range and diversity of both oral and written communication situations.

Ong's model of the paradigmatic act of speech communication derives from traditional rhetoric. In distinguishing the terms audience and reader, he notes that "the orator has before him an audience which is a true audience, a collectivity. . . . Readers do not form a collectivity, acting here and now on one another and on the speaker as members of an audience do" (p. 11). As this quotation indicates, Ong also stresses the potential for interaction among members of an audience, and between an audience and a speaker.

But how many audiences are actually collectives, with ample opportunity for interaction? In *Persuasion: Understanding, Practice, and Analysis*, Herbert Simons establishes a continuum of audiences based on opportunities for interaction.[18] Simons contrasts commercial mass media publics, which "have little or no contact with each other and certainly have no reciprocal awareness of each other as members of the same audience" with "face-to-face workgroups that meet and interact continuously over an extended period of time." He goes on to note that: "Between these two extremes are such groups as the following: (1) the *pedestrian audience*, persons who happen to pass a soap box orator . . . ; (2) the *passive, occasional audience*, persons who come to hear a noted lecturer in a large auditorium . . . ; (3) the *active, occasional audience*, persons who meet only on specific occasions but actively interact when they do meet" (pp. 97–98).

Simons's discussion, in effect, questions the rigidity of Ong's distinctions between a speaker's and a writer's audience. Indeed, when one surveys a broad range of situations inviting oral communication, Ong's paradigmatic situation, in which the speaker's audience constitutes a "collectivity, acting here and now on one another and on the speaker" (p. 11), seems somewhat atypical. It is certainly possible, at any rate, to think of a number of instances where speakers confront a problem very similar to that of writers: lacking intimate knowledge of their audience, which comprises not a collectivity but a disparate, and possibly even divided, group of individuals, speakers, like writers, must construct in their imaginations "an audience cast in some sort of role."[19] When President Carter announced to Americans during a speech broadcast on television, for instance, that his program against inflation was "the moral equivalent of warfare," he was doing more than merely characterizing his economic policies. He was providing an important cue to his audience concerning the role he wished them to adopt as listeners — that of a people braced for a painful but necessary and justifiable battle. Were we to examine his speech in detail, we would find other more subtle, but equally important, semantic and syntactic signals to the audience.

We do not wish here to collapse all distinctions between oral and written communication, but rather to emphasize that speaking and writing are, after all, both rhetorical acts. There are important differences between speech and writing. And the broad distinction between speech and writing that Ong makes is both commonsensical and particularly relevant to his subject, fictional narrative. As our illustration demonstrates, however, when one turns to precise, concrete situations, the relationship between speech and writing can become far more complex than even Ong represents.

Just as Ong's distinction between speech and writing is accurate on a highly general level but breaks down (or at least becomes less clear-cut) when examined closely, so too does his dictum about writers and their audiences. Every writer must indeed create a role for the reader, but the constraints on the writer and the potential sources of and possibilities for the reader's role are both more complex and diverse than Ong suggests. Ong stresses the importance of literary tradition in the creation of audience: "If the writer succeeds in writing, it is generally because he can fictionalize in his imagination an audience he has learned to know not from daily life but from earlier writers who were fictionalizing in their imagination audiences they had learned to know in still earlier writers, and so on back to the dawn of written narrative" (p. 11). And he cites a particularly (for us) germane example, a student "asked to write on the subject to which schoolteachers, jaded by summer, return compulsively every autumn: 'How I Spent My Summer Vacation'" (p. 11). In order to negotiate such an assignment successfully, the student must turn his real audience, the teacher, into someone else. He or she must, for instance, "make like Samuel Clemens and write for whomever Samuel Clemens was writing for" (p. 11).

Ong's example is, for his purposes, well-chosen. For such an assignment does indeed require the successful student to "fictionalize" his or her audience. But why is the student's decision to turn to a literary model in this instance particularly appropriate? Could one reason be that the student knows (consciously or unconsciously) that his English teacher, who is still the literal audience of his essay, appreciates literature and hence would be entertained (and here the student may intuit the assignment's actual aim as well) by such a strategy? In Ong's example the audience — the "jaded" schoolteacher — is not only willing to accept another role but, perhaps, actually yearns for it. How else to escape the tedium of reading 25, 50, 75 student papers on the same topic? As Walter Minot notes, however, not all readers are so malleable:

> In reading a work of fiction or poetry, a reader is far more willing to suspend his beliefs and values than in a rhetorical work dealing with some current social, moral, or economic issue. The effectiveness of the created audience in a rhetorical situation is likely to depend on such constraints as the actual identity of the reader, the subject of the discourse, the identity and purpose of the writer, and many other factors in the real world.[20]

An example might help make Minot's point concrete.

Imagine another composition student faced, like Ong's, with an assignment. This student, who has been given considerably more latitude in her choice of a topic, has decided to write on an issue of concern to her at the moment, the possibility that a home for mentally-retarded adults will be built in her neighborhood. She is alarmed by the strongly negative, highly emotional reaction of most of her neighbors and wishes in her essay to persuade them that such a residence might not be the disaster they anticipate.

This student faces a different task from that described by Ong. If she is to succeed, she must think seriously about her actual readers, the neighbors to whom she wishes to send her letter. She knows the obvious demographic factors — age, race, class — so well that she probably hardly needs to consider them consciously. But other issues are more complex. How much do her neighbors know about mental retardation, intellectually or experientially? What is their image of a retarded adult? What fears does this project raise in them? What civic and religious values do they most respect? Based on this analysis — and the process may be much less sequential than we describe here — she must, of course, define a role for her audience, one congruent with her persona, arguments, the facts as she knows them, etc. She must, as Minot argues, *both* analyze and invent an audience.[21] In this instance, after detailed analysis of her audience and her arguments, the student decided to begin her essay by emphasizing what she felt to be the genuinely admirable qualities of her neighbors, particularly their kindness, understanding, and concern for others. In so doing, she invited her audience to see themselves as *she* saw them: as thoughtful, intelligent people who, if they were adequately informed, would certainly not act in a harsh manner to those less fortunate than they. In accepting this role, her readers did not have to "play the game of being a member of an audience that 'really' does not exist" (Ong, "The Writer's Audience," p. 12). But they did have to recognize in themselves the strengths the student described and to accept her implicit linking of these strengths to what she hoped would be their response to the proposed "home."

When this student enters her history class to write an examination she faces a different set of constraints. Unlike the historian who does indeed have a broad range of options in establishing the reader's role, our student has much less freedom. This is because her reader's role has already been established and formalized in a series of related academic conventions. If she is a successful student, she has so effectively internalized these conventions that she can subordinate a concern for her complex and multiple audiences to focus on the material on which she is being tested and on the single audience, the teacher, who will respond to her performance on the test.[22]

We could multiply examples. In each instance the student writing — to friend, employer, neighbor, teacher, fellow readers of her daily newspaper — would need, as one of the many conscious and unconscious decisions required in composing, to envision and define a role for the reader. But *how* she defines that role — whether she relies mainly upon academic or technical writing conventions, literary models, intimate knowledge of friends or neighbors, analysis of a particular group, or some combination thereof — will vary tremendously. At times the reader may establish a role for the reader which indeed does not "coincide[s] with his role in the rest of actual life" (Ong, p. 12). At other times, however, one of the writer's primary tasks may be that of analyzing the "real life" audience and adapting the discourse to it. One of the factors that makes writing so difficult, as we know, is that we have no recipes: each rhetorical situation is unique and thus requires the writer, catalyzed and guided by a strong sense of purpose, to reanalyze and reinvent solutions.

Despite their helpful corrective approach, then, theories which assert that the audience of a written discourse is a construction of the writer present their own dangers.[23] One of these is the tendency to overemphasize the distinction between speech and writing while undervaluing the insights of discourse theorists, such as James Moffett and James Britton, who remind us of the importance of such additional factors as distance between speaker or writer and audience and levels of abstraction in the subject. In *Teaching the Universe of Discourse*, Moffett establishes the following spectrum of discourse: recording ("the drama of what is happening"), reporting ("the narrative of what happened"), generalizing ("the exposition of what happens"), and theorizing ("the argumentation of what will, may happen").[24] In an extended example, Moffett demonstrates the important points of connection between communication acts at any one level of the spectrum, whether oral or written:

> Suppose next that I tell the cafeteria experience to a friend some time later in conversation. . . . Of course, instead of recounting the cafeteria scene to my friend in person I could write it in a letter to an audience more removed in time and space. Informal writing is usually still rather spontaneous, directed at an audience known to the writer, and reflects the transient mood and circumstances in which the writing occurs. Feedback and audience influence, however, are delayed and weakened. . . . *Compare in turn now the changes that must occur all down the line when I write about this cafeteria experience in a discourse destined for publication and distribution to a mass, anonymous audience of present and perhaps unborn people.* I cannot allude to things and ideas that only my friends know about. I must use a vocabulary, style, logic, and rhetoric that anybody in that mass audience can understand and respond to. I must name and organize what happened during those moments in the cafeteria that day in such a way that this mythical average reader can relate what I say to some primary moments of experience of his own. (pp. 37–38; our emphasis)

Though Moffett does not say so, many of these same constraints would obtain if he decided to describe his experience in a speech to a mass audience — the viewers of a television show, for example, or the members of a graduating class. As Moffett's example illustrates, the distinction between speech and writing is important; it is, however, only one of several constraints influencing any particular discourse.

Another weakness of research based on the concept of audience as invoked is that it distorts the processes of writing and reading by overemphasizing the power of the writer and undervaluing that of the reader. Unlike Mitchell and Taylor, Ong recognizes the creative role the writer plays as reader of his or her own writing, the way the writer uses language to provide cues for the reader and tests the effectiveness of these cues during his or her own rereading of the text. But Ong fails adequately to recognize the constraints placed on the writer, in certain situations, by the audience. He fails, in other words, to acknowledge that readers' own experiences, expectations, and beliefs do play a central role in their reading of a text, and that the writer who does not consider the needs and interests of his audience risks losing that audience. To argue that the audience is a "created fiction" (Long, p. 225), to stress that the reader's role "seldom coincides with his role in the rest of actual life" (Ong, p. 12), is just as much an oversimplification, then, as to insist, as Mitchell and Taylor do, that "the audience not only judges writing, it also motivates it" (p. 250). The former view overemphasizes the writer's independence and power; the latter, that of the reader.

RHETORIC AND ITS SITUATIONS[25]

If the perspectives we have described as audience addressed and audience invoked represent incomplete conceptions of the role of audience in written discourse, do we have an alternative? How can we most accurately conceive of this essential rhetorical element? In what follows we will sketch a tentative model and present several defining or constraining statements about this apparently slippery concept, "audience." The result will, we hope, move us closer to a full understanding of the role audience plays in written discourse.

Figure 13-2 represents our attempt to indicate the complex series of obligations, resources, needs, and constraints embodied in the writer's concept of audience. (We emphasize that our goal here is *not* to depict the writing process as a whole — a much more complex task — but to focus on the writer's relation to audience.) As our model indicates, we do not see the two perspectives on audience described earlier as necessarily dichotomous or contradictory. Except for past and anomalous audiences, special cases which we describe paragraphs hence, all of the audience roles we specify — self, friend, colleague, critic, mass audience, and future audience — may be invoked or addressed.[26] It is the writer who, as writer and reader of his or her own text, one guided by a sense of purpose and by the particularities of a specific rhetorical situation, establishes the range of potential roles an audience may play. (Readers may, of course, accept or reject the role or roles the writer wishes them to adopt in responding to a text.)

Writers who wish to be read must often adapt their discourse to meet the needs and expectations of an addressed audience. They may rely on past experience in addressing audiences to guide their writing, or they may engage a representative of that audience in the writing process. The latter occurs, for instance, when we ask a colleague to read an article intended for scholarly publication. Writers may also be required to respond to the intervention of others — a teacher's comments on an essay, a supervisor's suggestions for improving a report, or the insistent, catalyzing questions of an editor. Such intervention may in certain cases represent a powerful stimulus to the writer, but it is the writer who interprets the suggestions — or even commands — of others, choosing what to accept or reject. Even the conscious decision to accede to the expectations of a particular addressed audience may not always be carried out; unconscious psychological resistance, incomplete understanding,

Figure 13-2   The Concept of Audience

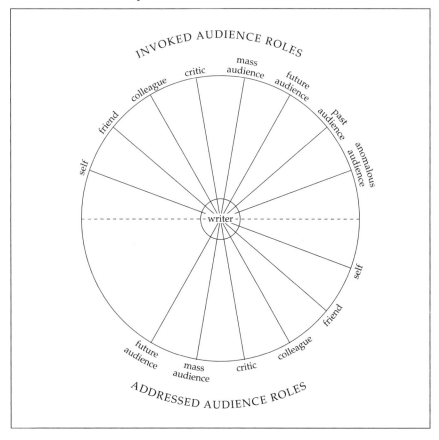

or inadequately developed ability may prevent the writer from following through with the decision — a reality confirmed by composition teachers with each new set of essays.

The addressed audience, the actual or intended readers of a discourse, exists outside of the text. Writers may analyze these readers' needs, anticipate their biases, even defer to their wishes. But it is only through the text, through language, that writers embody or give life to their conception of the reader. In so doing, they do not so much create a role for the reader — a phrase which implies that the writer somehow creates a mold to which the reader adapts — as invoke it. Rather than relying on incantations, however, writers conjure their vision — a vision which they hope readers will actively come to share as they read the text — by using all the resources of language available to them to establish a broad, and ideally coherent, range of cues for the reader. Technical writing conventions, for instance, quickly formalize any of several writer-reader relationships, such as colleague to colleague or expert to lay reader. But even comparatively local semantic decisions may play an equally essential role. In "The Writer's Audience Is Always a Fiction," Ong demonstrates how

Hemingway's use of definite articles in *A Farewell to Arms* subtly cues readers that their role is to be that of a "companion in arms . . . a confidant" (p. 13).

Any of the roles of the addressed audience cited in our model may be invoked via the text. Writers may also invoke a past audience, as did, for instance, Ong's student writing to those Mark Twain would have been writing for. And writers can also invoke anomalous audiences, such as a fictional character — Hercule Poirot perhaps. Our model, then, confirms Douglas Park's observation that the meanings of audience, though multiple and complex, "tend to diverge in two general directions: one toward actual people external to a text, the audience whom the writer must accommodate; the other toward the text itself and the audience implied there: a set of suggested or evoked attitudes, interests, reactions, conditions of knowledge which may or may not fit with the qualities of actual readers or listeners."[27] The most complete understanding of audience thus involves a synthesis of the perspectives we have termed audience addressed, with its focus on the reader, and audience invoked, with its focus on the writer.

One illustration of this constantly shifting complex of meanings for "audience" lies in our own experiences writing this essay. One of us became interested in the concept of audience during an NEH [National Endowment for the Humanities] seminar, and her first audience was a small, close-knit seminar group to whom she addressed her work. The other came to contemplate a multiplicity of audiences while working on a textbook; the first audience in this case was herself, as she debated the ideas she was struggling to present to a group of invoked students. Following a lengthy series of conversations, our interests began to merge: we shared notes and discussed articles written by others on audience, and eventually one of us began a draft. Our long distance telephone bills and the miles we travelled up and down I-5 from Oregon to British Columbia attest most concretely to the power of a co-author's expectations and criticisms and also illustrate that one person can take on the role of several different audiences: friend, colleague, and critic.

As we began to write and re-write the essay, now for a particular scholarly journal, the change in purpose and medium (no longer a seminar paper or a textbook) led us to new audiences. For us, the major "invoked audience" during this period was Richard Larson, editor of this journal, whose questions and criticisms we imagined and tried to anticipate. (Once this essay was accepted by *CCC*, Richard Larson became for us an addressed audience: he responded in writing with questions, criticisms, and suggestions, some of which we had, of course, failed to anticipate.) We also thought of the readers of *CCC* and those who attend the annual CCCC, most often picturing you as members of our own departments, a diverse group of individuals with widely varying degrees of interest in and knowledge of composition. Because of the generic constraints of academic writing, which limit the range of roles we may define for our readers, the audience represented by the readers of *CCC* seemed most vivid to us in two situations: (1) when we were concerned about the degree to which we needed to explain concepts or terms; and (2) when we considered central organizational decisions, such as the most effective way to introduce a discussion. Another, and for us extremely potent, audience was the authors — Mitchell and Taylor, Long, Ong, Park, and others — with whom we have seen ourselves in silent dialogue. As we read and reread their analyses and developed our responses to them, we felt a responsibility to try to understand their formulations as fully as possible, to play fair with their ideas, to make our own efforts continue to meet their high standards.

Our experience provides just one example, and even it is far from complete. (Once we finished a rough draft, one particular colleague became a potent but demanding addressed audience, listening to revision upon revision and challenging us with harder and harder questions. And after this essay is published, we may revise our understanding of audiences we thought we knew or recognize the existence of an entirely new audience. The latter would happen, for instance, if teachers of speech communication for some reason found our discussion useful.) But even this single case demonstrates that the term *audience* refers not just to the intended, actual, or eventual readers of a discourse, but to *all* those whose image, ideas, or actions influence a writer during the process of composition. One way to conceive of "audience," then, is as an overdetermined or unusually rich concept, one which may perhaps be best specified through the analysis of precise, concrete situations.

We hope that this partial example of our own experience will illustrate how the elements represented in Figure 13-2 will shift and merge, depending on the particular rhetorical situation, the writer's aim, and the genre chosen. Such an understanding is critical: because of the complex reality to which the term *audience* refers and because of its fluid, shifting role in the composing process, any discussion of audience which isolates it from the rest of the rhetorical situation or which radically overemphasizes or underemphasizes its function in relation to other rhetorical constraints is likely to oversimplify. Note the unilateral direction of Mitchell and Taylor's model (p. 5), which is unable to represent the diverse and complex role(s) audience(s) can play in the actual writing process — in the creation of meaning. In contrast, consider the model used by Edward P. J. Corbett in his *Little Rhetoric and Handbook*.[28]

Figure 13-3   Corbett's Model of "The Rhetorical Interrelationships" (p. 5)

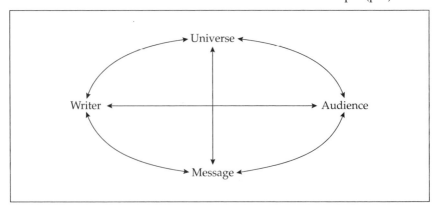

This representation, which allows for interaction among all the elements of rhetoric, may at first appear less elegant and predictive than Mitchell and Taylor's. But it is finally more useful since it accurately represents the diverse range of potential interrelationships in any written discourse.

We hope that our model also suggests the integrated, interdependent nature of reading and writing. Two assertions emerge from this relationship. One involves the writer as reader of his or her own work. As Donald Murray notes in "Teaching the Other Self: The Writer's First Reader," this role is critical, for "the reading writer — the map-maker and map-reader — reads the word, the line, the sentence, the paragraph, the page, the entire text. This constant back-and-forth reading monitors the multiple complex relationships between all the elements in writing."[29] To ignore or devalue such a central function is to risk distorting the writing process as a whole. But unless the writer is composing a diary or journal entry, intended only for the writer's own eyes, the writing process is not complete unless another person, someone other than the writer, reads the text also. The second assertion thus emphasizes the creative, dynamic duality of the process of reading and writing, whereby writers create readers and readers create writers. In the meeting of these two lies meaning, lies communication.

A fully elaborated view of audience, then, must balance the creativity of the writer with the different, but equally important, creativity of the reader. It must account for a wide and shifting range of roles for both addressed and invoked audiences. And, finally, it must relate the matrix created by the intricate relationship of writer and audience to all elements in the rhetorical situation. Such an enriched conception of audience can help us better understand the complex act we call composing.

NOTES

1. Ruth Mitchell and Mary Taylor, "The Integrating Perspective: An Audience-Response Model for Writing," *CE*, 41 (November, 1979), 267. Subsequent references to this article will be cited in the text.

2. Russell C. Long, "Writer-Audience Relationships: Analysis or Invention," *CCC*, 31 (May, 1980), 223 and 225. Subsequent references to this article will be cited in the text.

3. For these terms we are indebted to Henry W. Johnstone Jr., who refers to them in his analysis of Chaim Perelman's universal audience in *Validity and Rhetoric in Philosophical Argument: An Outlook in Transition* (University Park, PA: The Dialogue Press of Man & World, 1978), p. 105.

4. Fred R. Pfister and Joanne F. Petrik, "A Heuristic Model for Creating a Writer's Audience," *CCC*, 31 (May, 1980), 213.

5. Pfister and Petrik, 214; our emphasis.

6. See, for example, Lisa S. Ede, "On Audience and Composition," *CCC*, 30 (October, 1979), 291–295.

7. See, for example, David Tedlock, "The Case Approach to Composition," *CCC*, 32 (October, 1981), 253–261.

8. See, for example, Linda Flower's *Problem-Solving Strategies for Writers* (New York: Harcourt Brace Jovanovich, 1981), and John P. Field and Robert H. Weiss' *Cases for Composition* (Boston: Little Brown, 1979).

9. Richard E. Young, "Paradigms and Problems: Needed Research in Rhetorical Invention," in *Research on Composing: Points of Departure*, ed. Charles R. Cooper and Lee Odell (Urbana, IL: National Council of Teachers of English, 1978), p. 32 (footnote #3).

10. Mitchell and Taylor do recognize that internal psychological needs ("unconscious challenges") may play a role in the writing process, but they cite such instances as an "extreme case

(often that of the creative writer)" (p. 251). For a discussion of the importance of self-evaluation in the composing process, see Susan Miller, "How Writers Evaluate Their Own Writing," *CCC*, 33 (May, 1982), 176–183.

11. Susan Wall, "In the Writer's Eye: Learning to Teach the Rereading/Revising Process," *English Education*, 14 (February, 1982), 12.

12. Wayne Booth, *Modern Dogma and the Rhetoric of Assent* (Chicago: University of Chicago Press, 1974), p. xiv.

13. Paul Kameen, "Rewording the Rhetoric of Composition," *Pre/Text*, 1 (Spring-Fall, 1980), 82.

14. Mitchell and Taylor's arguments in favor of adjunct classes seem to indicate that they see writing instruction, wherever it occurs, as a skills course, one instructing students in the proper use of a tool.

15. Anthony R. Petrosky, "From Story to Essay: Reading and Writing," *CCC*, 33 (February, 1982), 20.

16. Walter J. Ong, S.J., 'The Writer's Audience Is Always a Fiction," *PMLA*, 90 (January, 1975), 9–21. Subsequent references to this article will be cited in the text.

17. See, for example, William Irmscher, "Sense of Audience: An Intuitive Concept," unpublished paper delivered at the CCCC in 1981; Douglas B. Park, "The Meanings of Audience: Pedagogical Implications," unpublished paper delivered at the CCCC in 1981; and Luke M. Reinsma, "Writing to an Audience: Scheme or Strategy?," unpublished paper delivered at the CCCC in 1982.

18. Herbert W. Simons, *Persuasion: Understanding, Practice, and Analysis* (Reading, MA: Addison-Wesley, 1976).

19. Ong, p. 12. Ong recognizes that oral communication also involves role-playing, but he stresses that it "has within it a momentum that works for the removal of masks" (p. 20). This may be true in certain instances, such as dialogue, but does not, we believe, obtain broadly.

20. Walter S. Minot, "Response to Russell C. Long," *CCC*, 32 (October, 1981), 337.

21. We are aware that the student actually has two audiences, her neighbors and her teacher, and that this situation poses an extra constraint for the writer. Not all students can manage such a complex series of audience constraints, but it is important to note that writers in a variety of situations often write for more than a single audience.

22. In their paper on "Student and Professional Syntax in Four Disciplines" (unpublished paper delivered at the CCCC in 1981), Ian Pringle and Aviva Freedman provide a good example of what can happen when a student creates an aberrant role for an academic reader. They cite an excerpt from a third year history assignment, the tone of which "is essentially the tone of the opening of a television travelogue commentary" and which thus asks the reader, a history professor, to assume the role of the viewer of such a show. The result is as might be expected: "Although the content of the paper does not seem significantly more abysmal than other papers in the same set, this one was awarded a disproportionately low grade" (p. 2).

23. One danger which should be noted is a tendency to foster a questionable image of classical rhetoric. The agonistic speaker-audience relationship which Long cites as an essential characteristic of classical rhetoric is actually a central point of debate among those involved in historical and theoretical research in rhetoric. For further discussion, see Lisa Ede and Andrea Lunsford, "On Distinctions Between Classical and Modern Rhetoric," in *Classical Rhetoric and Modern Discourse: Essays in Honor of Edward P. J. Corbett*, ed. Robert Connors, Lisa Ede, and Andrea Lunsford (Carbondale, IL: Southern Illinois University Press, 1984).

24. James Moffett, *Teaching the Universe of Discourse* (Boston: Houghton Mifflin, 1968), p. 47. Subsequent references will be mentioned in the text.

25. We have taken the title of this section from Scott Consigny's article of the same title, *Philosophy and Rhetoric*, 7 (Summer, 1974), 175–186. Consigny's effort to mediate between two opposing views of rhetoric provided a stimulating model for our own efforts.

26. Although we believe that the range of audience roles cited in our model covers the general spectrum of options, we do not claim to have specified all possibilities. This is particularly the case since, in certain instances, these roles may merge and blend — shifting subtly in character. We might also note that other terms for the same roles might be used. In a business setting, for instance, colleague might be better termed co-worker, critic, or supervisor.

27. Douglas B. Park, "The Meanings of 'Audience'" *CE*, 44 (March, 1982), 249.

28. Edward P. J. Corbett, *The Little Rhetoric and Handbook*, 2nd edition (Glenview, IL: Scott, Foresman, 1982), p. 5.

29. Donald M. Murray, "Teaching the Other Self: The Writer's First Reader," *CCC*, 33 (May, 1982), 142.

14 Representing Audience: "Successful" Discourse and Disciplinary Critique

> We are wedded in language, have our being in words. Language is also a place of struggle.
>
> — BELL HOOKS (*Yearning* 146)

In his February 1994 *CCC* editor's column, Joseph Harris provides a brief overview of the kinds of work he hopes to publish in the journal, noting, among other things, that he is "especially interested in pieces that take a critical or revisionary look at work in composition studies" (7). Given the contemporary turn to self-conscious disciplinary critique, Harris' call is hardly surprising. In its relatively brief disciplinary history, in fact, composition studies has engaged in a great deal of revisionary looking back, as can be seen in the several paradigm shifts or theoretical revolutions the field has experienced during the span of the last three decades. This disciplinary critique has for the most part, however, been carried out in the agonistic manner characteristic of traditional academic discussion, with each wave of criticism, each revisionary look establishing its own efficacy by demonstrating the flaws of prior conceptions.[1]

The notion of disciplinary progress — or success — enacted by these discourses has in many ways served our field well. For though composition studies could hardly be described as an established or mainstream academic discipline, it has succeeded to a considerable extent in legitimizing and professionalizing its position in the academy. And the critical discourses of such theorists as Janet Emig, James Berlin, and Susan Miller have, we believe, contributed substantially to our understanding of how very much is at stake when scholars in composition studies profess the teaching of writing.

We are grateful for this tradition of critical discourse. Indeed we wish to respond to Harris' call to participate in a "critical or revisionary" look at work

From Andrea A. Lunsford and Lisa Ede, in *College Composition and Communication* 47.2 (1996): 167–79.

in composition studies by building on this tradition — albeit with one significant exception. We attempt here to resist traditional oppositional critique, with its tendency to focus (usually in a negative way) on the work of others. Instead, we propose here to attempt a self-critique by revisiting an essay of our own, "Audience Addressed/Audience Invoked: The Role of Audience in Composition Theory and Pedagogy" (AA/AI, hereafter), the essay that (if citations, analyses, and reprintings are any indication) of all our coauthored work might be said to have been judged most "successful" by others in our field.

We've put "successful" in quotation marks for a reason. The conventional Western understanding of success emphasizes the role that individual agency plays in achievement. In this view, particularly as played out most often in American mythologies, success comes to those individuals who work hard for it, and who thus deserve it. Business persons who work hard, who fight the good fight, are successful. Writers who write well, who use the resources of language to persuade others, similarly merit whatever recognition and achievement come their way. As conventionally understood, success in the academy is measured by "objective" and largely individualist criteria, such as publications and reprintings, citations, and the degree of response the writing engenders.

That such a view of success — and of language — has been challenged on a number of fronts goes without saying. We may write language, but language also writes us. We may desire to express our ideas, but the ideas we express may reveal more than we have intended. Rather than emphasizing individual agency, this poststructuralist view of discourse calls attention to the role that shared assumptions and ideologies play in enabling or hindering communication. It reminds us as well of the locatedness and situatedness of all texts — and of the need to inquire into what Gesa E. Kirsch and Joy S. Ritchie in a recent *CCC* essay refer to as a "politics of location" (7). Such an effort challenges researchers, Kirsch and Ritchie argue, to "theorize their locations by examining their experiences as reflections of ideology and culture, by reinterpreting their own experiences through the eyes of others, and by recognizing their own split selves, their multiple and often unknowable identifies" (8). It is in the spirit of Kirsch and Ritchie's call that we turn to our earlier essay.

In attempting such a self-critique, we wish to be as clear about our goals as possible. In this essay, we intend to subject our earlier work to critical inquiry in an effort to foreground the rhetoricity of this work and to explore and learn from the cultural, disciplinary, and institutional forces at play in it. In so doing, we attempt to illuminate both the absences and presences in AA/AI, but to do so in a way that resists the lure of totalizing, oppositionalizing readings. We do not, in other words, wish to construct a bad-old-Ede-and-Lunsford, which we — in traditional agonistic fashion — will strike down in the service of representing an all-new-and-improved-Lunsford-and-Ede on audience. In revisiting our essay, then, we wish neither to reject nor defend AA/AI but rather to embrace multiple understandings of it, and to acknowledge the extent to which any discursive moment contains diverse, heterodox, and even contradictory realities — confirming (once again) the acuity of Kenneth

Burke's observation that "if any given terminology is a *reflection* of reality, by its very nature as a terminology it must also be a *selection* of reality; and to this extent it must function also as a *deflection* of reality" (45). As a result of such multiple understandings, we hope to raise heuristic questions not only about our own work but also about conventional narratives (and genres) of disciplinary progress and about the relationship between "success" and traditional academic critique.

AUDIENCE AND THE SUBJECT(S) OF DISCOURSE

At the time that it was written, AA/AI entered an ongoing debate on the nature and role of audience in discourse. Responding to a number of essays on the concept of audience that appeared in the late 1970s and early 1980s, AA/AI attempted to redirect current discussions of audience by arguing that previous commentators had generally taken a partial view of an unusually rich and complex concept. Some theorists, such as Ruth Mitchell and Mary Taylor, privileged what we called the *audience addressed*, "the concrete reality of the writer's audience . . . [and assumed] that knowledge of this audience's attitudes, beliefs, and expectations is not only possible (via observation and analysis) but essential" (AA/AI 156). Others, such as Walter Ong and Russell Long, emphasized the extent to which writers create or *invoke* audiences by using "the semantic and syntactic resources of language to create cues for the reader — cues which help to define the role or roles the writer wishes the reader to adopt" (160). Our own approach was to challenge the helpfulness of such dichotomous and polarizing views of audience as either wholly addressed or wholly invoked and to argue for a syntheses of these perspectives, one that acknowledges the creativity and interdependence of writers and readers, writing and reading, and that recognizes the "fluid, dynamic character of rhetorical situations" (165). Audience can perhaps best be conceptualized, we argued, as a "complex series of obligations, needs, resources, and constraints" that both enable and constrain writers and readers (165).

Ten years later, we still resist efforts to characterize audience as solely textual (invoked) or material (addressed), and we continue to affirm the importance of considering audience in the context of the rhetorical situation. Rereading our essay, we note its refusal to generate pedagogical formulas or rules for teachers and students and its attempt to argue that the most complex understanding of audience is — theoretically and pedagogically — the most useful. We also recognize, however, a number of absences in AA/AI — absences that reflect our personal and professional desire to turn away from the potential difficulties and costs entailed in successful communication.

By insisting that the concept of audience involves textual and material constraints as well as opportunities, and that it must always be considered in the context of the larger rhetorical situation, AA/AI sets the scene — but then fails to explore — the ways in which audiences can not only enable but also silence writers and readers. In addition, although AA/AI recognizes the possibility of readers rejecting "the role or roles the writer wishes them to adopt in responding to a text" (166), our essay consistently downplays the possibility of tension and contradiction, presenting the interplay of audience addressed and audience invoked as potential opportunities for the writer "catalyzed and guided by a strong sense of purpose, to reanalyze and reinvent solutions" (164). With good will and rhetorical sensitivity, AA/AI implicitly suggests, writers will be able to negotiate their ways into positions of discursive power, will achieve and maintain communicative success.

Such an understanding of writing assumes a negotiation of meaning among if not literal equals then among those with equal access to the resources of language. Such an understanding also necessitates, of course, a parallel series of assumptions about writers and readers, as well as about the genres they attempt to inhabit. We have already indicated that the subject of discourse invoked in AA/AI is a subject who feels both agency and authority — that subject is also implicitly stable, unified, and autonomous. Although we recognize in AA/AI that students have less power than teachers and thus less freedom in some rhetorical situations than in others, we do not pursue the multiple ways in which the student writer's agency and identity may be shaped and constrained not only by immediate audiences but also, and even more forcefully, by the ways in which both she and those audiences are positioned within larger institutional and discursive frameworks. Nor do we consider the powerful effects of ideology working through genres, such as those inscribed in academic essayist literacy, to call forth and thus to control and constrain writers and audiences.[2] That a student might find herself full of contradiction and conflict, might find the choices available to her as a writer confusing and even crippling — might in fact find it difficult, even undesirable, to claim the identity of "writer" — did not occur to us.[3]

That such ideas did not occur to us is a mark of the extent to which the students invoked in AA/AI were in important ways the students *we* had been — eager, compliant, willing to shape ourselves to rhetorical situations. Our desire to invoke such students and to (re)write experience in such a way as to highlight success not failure, consensus not conflict, progress not struggle, is, we have realized, deeply imbedded in our relationship to schooling as well as to discourse. In working on this essay, for instance, we have each recalled memories of struggle and failure, of negative educational experiences that reminded us of the degree to which, as students, we molded ourselves as willing subjects of education. Andrea found herself reflecting most often on her early grade school years, recalling, for instance, a moment when she perceived that a teacher simply did not like her — and noting the ways in which that perception led her not to challenge the teacher's views or goals but to attempt to remake herself in the image of a dutifully schooled subject less likely to invoke a hostile teacher audience. Lisa found herself drawn to memories of graduate school experiences and to the ways in which she repressed her confusion and anger as different courses required her to become not only a different audience for each professor but a different subject as well.

In reflecting on these memories, we have begun to explore the extent to which, very early in our educations, we identified with the goals and institutions of schooling. Our home communities were ones in which school was generally defined as a place for positive change and advancement. But our identification with schooling involved more than mere acceptance of these attitudes. Academic good girls, we studied, even excelled, and in so doing we came to associate both schooling and the writing we did in school with a positive sense of self, a means of validation and "success," and of hailing appreciative audiences. So powerful was this identification, in fact, that we recast those painful memories of struggle that we could not repress, reinterpreting experiences that might have led to resistance and critique as evidence of individual problems that we could remedy if only we would work harder, do (and be) better. Such an approach is congruent, of course, with the individualism inherent throughout our culture, educational institutions, and scholarly disciplines, an individualism that traditionally writes the kind of struggles we experienced as students as inevitable, even necessary and salutary, aspects of the Western narrative of individual success that AA/AI implicitly endorses.[4]

Does this critique suggest that we have now rejected our identification with schooling and its traditional individualist assumptions? It does not, or not monolithically at least, for it would be disingenuous indeed for us to ignore or devalue what we have gained both intellectually and materially as a result of our schooling. So while we recognize that schooling subjects and disciplines students, that writing is not necessarily and certainly not always a venue for power, we also recognize — and honor — the potential of both writing and schooling to enable students to enact subjectivities that they experience as positive and authorizing. Thus, like the audiences that it hails, schooling is both deeply situated and inherently paradoxical, full of contradictions and complexities — and opportunities. In this analysis of our earlier work, our goal is neither to embrace schooling unthinkingly (as we once did) nor to condemn schooling out of hand. Rather, we seek to recognize its multiple complexities and to understand as fully as possible our positioning among them as we strive not only to acknowledge but also to take responsibility for our own politics of location.

Part of this positioning, of course, involves our experiences and identities not only with schooling in general but with the field of composition in particular. When we reflect upon the disciplinary moment in which we wrote AA/AI, we find ourselves with multiple understandings and responses. From our current perspective, one informed by recent research in feminism, poststructuralism, rhetorical theory, and critical pedagogy, it is easy to look back at research in composition in the mid-1980s — with its emphasis on the writing process and cognitive models of that process — and note the field's generally uncritical identification with and appropriation of the goals of schooling. Paradoxes of institutional placement that now seem obvious — such as the tension inherent in our field's asserted desire to empower students and its curricular positioning as gatekeeper and certifier — were repressed in much of the work of the time, including our own. We want now to acknowledge and understand the implications of such repression, as well as to relinquish at least some of the dreams of disciplinary progress, of moving inexorably toward a time when we can "know" audiences, much less teach students to use such knowledge in straightforward ways to achieve "success" in writing. Yet we would not want to give up our field's commitment to teaching. Thus when we return to such efforts as Mina Shaughnessy's *Errors and Expectations*, or to early writing process studies, we find much to celebrate in their commitment to teaching, to opening up spaces in the academy for traditionally excluded students, and to the importance of striving for social and political change. We want now, at *this* disciplinary moment, to reaffirm these commitments, while acknowledging the importance of inquiring into the nature of both teacher and student subjectivities, and of recognizing the implications of our cultural, political, economic, and institutional embeddedness. Teachers and students are — we understand better now than in the past — not free individual agents writing their own destinies but rather constructed subjects embedded in multiple discourses, and the classroom is not a magic circle free of ideological and institutional influence. Such understandings have been and continue to be chastening to us; they encourage humility and modesty in teaching and research and an increased attentiveness to the motivated and situated — that is to say deeply rhetorical — nature of our assumptions and practices.

AUDIENCE, IDEOLOGY, AND THE RHETORICAL TRADITION

As we have tried to suggest, the writers and teachers speaking through AA/AI are, in many important ways, the writers and teachers we wanted and still want to be: negotiators of rhetorical situations who can gain a place for ourselves, our students, and our field at the academic and social conversational table. But we can also now see repressed in our essay — metaphorically smoothed or ironed out — traces of difficulties, of pain, failure, misunderstanding, and conflict. Such repressions were both encouraged and made possible not only by our personal identification with schooling and with the emergent field of composition studies, but also by our deep — and ongoing — commitment to the discipline of rhetoric.

In AA/AI, this commitment to traditional views of rhetoric, and particularly to the heuristic potential of the concept of the rhetorical situation, offered us a powerful framework for analyzing and enriching understandings of audience, a framework we still find useful. But this commitment also almost certainly insured that we would not notice the tradition's insistent impulse toward successful communication on the one hand and exclusion on the other. Indeed, the rhetorical tradition's focus on success in communicating with and persuading others is longstanding and enduring, discernible in the Western emphasis on efficiency, "getting the job done," and clarity, as well as in traditional theories and definitions of rhetoric. Think, for instance, of Aristotle's definition of rhetoric as "the faculty of discovering in the particular case what are the available means of persuasion" (7) or of Richards' view of it as "the study of misunderstanding and its remedies" (3).

This focus on successful communicative negotiation inevitably, albeit silently, casts misunderstanding, miscommunication, disagreement, resistance, and dissent as failure and, as such, as that which is to be avoided or "cured." Today it seems to us that this emphasis on "success" has exacted a high hidden price. For how better to avoid misunderstanding and failure (and to make "successful" communication more likely) than to exclude, to disenfranchise those who by their very presence in the arena of discourse raise increased possibilities for communicative failures. The student writers invoked in AA/AI, for instance, are always already within and compliant to academic discourse, and thus willing and able to "adapt their discourse to meet the needs and expectations of an addressed audience" (166). While we still hope to help students meet such needs and expectations, we would also hope to bring into relief the exclusions that will almost certainly be necessary to do so, as well as the choices students must consider in deciding to inhabit academic discourse in this way.

That the rhetorical tradition is one of persistent exclusion goes without saying. But seeing the desire for successful communication as deeply implicated in the tendency to exclude those (like women and slaves in the ancient world) who might tend to disrupt or stand in the way of that success seems to us particularly noteworthy. For the dual moves toward exclusion and successful persuasion tend to hide from view any value that misunderstanding, resistance, or similar "failures" might have in complementing and enriching our notion of "success" by opening up spaces for additional voices, ways of understanding, conversations, and avenues of communication. It's interesting to consider, in this regard, the ways in which the exclusionary tendencies of the rhetorical tradition are tied to a view of the human subject as coherent, autonomous, and unified. Such a view assumes that writers and readers have no options but to be either in — or out of — a particular rhetorical situation.

Suppressed by the double impulse toward exclusion and success are the ways in which lived experiences can cause people to create internalized audiences that can lead not only to successful communication but also to disabling silences or to attempts at manipulative control, or the ways in which the materiality of people's lives can have the same effects, can result in communicative failure, in audiences ignored, rejected, excluded, or denied. Most deeply suppressed in the persistent gesture toward success, with its accompanying silent embrace of sameness, is a concomitant inattention to issues of difference. Thus while traditional Western conceptions of rhetoric as a system do, we still wish to argue, leave a space for difference in the concepts of rhetorical situation and of audience, that space has been, in practice, more often apparent than real. But not always. For as bell hooks and many others traditionally excluded from the dominant discourse continue to demonstrate, the "place of struggle" that rhetoric encompasses *can* be broadened (albeit with difficulty) to enact differences. In terms of verbal communication, this rhetorical space is what we have to work with and in. And in order to do so in a way that makes that space as open and inclusive as possible, we must work hard to understand the complex choices, multiple responsibilities, and competing representations that communication always entails. Only thus can we open up more spaces for dialogue with others; only thus can we understand, with hooks, that:

> Spaces can be real and imagined. Spaces can tell stories and unfold histories. Spaces can be interrupted, appropriated, and transformed through artistic and literary practice. (*Yearning* 152)

RE-PRESENTING AUDIENCE

As we hope this discussion has suggested, situating AA/AI in a web of personal, professional, and disciplinary contexts draws attention to those multiple and sometimes conflicting desires that speak through our effort to communicate with others, to both address and invoke audiences. As we noted early on in this essay, however, this attempt at a rereading of our work has aimed not to dismiss or discredit the work we have discussed, and in this sense not to engage in the agonistic activities so characteristic of the academy and the rhetorical tradition. Rather, we have attempted to demonstrate here the value of reading one's own research with the same kind of rhetorical care often reserved for the work of others and to suggest that this kind of reading — which calls attention to absences as well as presences, to multiplicity, tension, and competing motives in discourse — can enrich our understanding in ways that oppositional or totalizing readings do not.

Reading AA/AI against the backdrop of our own commitment to and identification with schooling, for instance, helped us to understand that although we intended AA/AI both to invoke and address a broad range of audiences, it speaks most strongly to those whose identifications and experiences mirror our own, while turning away from the potential difficulties and costs often inherent in the effort to achieve the kind of academic "success" that our essay takes for granted as well as from those who would wish to subvert such "success." Similarly, reading AA/AI in the context of research in the field emphasizes the degree to which our text fails to examine common-sense understandings of the nature, purposes, and impacts of education. In addition, a single-minded focus on students' success, without an interrogation of the definitions and foundations of such success, effectively prevents us from fully recognizing the contradictions and conflicts inherent in our own (and students') positionings. Finally, seeing these desires for success and suppression of conflict as implicated in the larger project of the Western rhetorical tradition helps us to understand not only how implicated we are in that tradition but also the exclusions that that tradition necessarily entails.

Put another way, reading AA/AI in terms of its place in the field of composition studies as well as in the rhetorical tradition, as we have just done, requires us to acknowledge the extent to which our essay both inhabits and expresses what Lynn Worsham terms our field's modernist commitment "to the Enlightenment dreams of communication and consensus, emancipation and empowerment" (100). That we now question some aspects of these dreams is evident in our desire to interrogate AA/AI in order to reveal at least some of its exclusions and repressions. These exclusions and repressions need to be acknowledged, we believe, if (as both writers and teachers) we are to work effectively to further those goals that we remain unwilling to relinquish. For with Stanley Aronowitz and Henry Giroux we believe that "those ideals of the project of modernity that link memory, agency, and reason to the construction of a democratic public sphere need to be defended" (59).

Our understanding of what it means to work to further the goals of democratic education has changed, however, since we wrote AA/AI. We have learned to be suspicious, for instance, of claims to empower or do something "for" others, especially when that claim entails representations that may essentialize those on whose behalf these claims are made. (Current arguments about basic writing programs turn at least in part on this issue.) We have also learned to reassess what it means to be "successful" as both writers and teachers, and we have become aware of the ways in which "success" disciplines and shapes what we are allowed — generically, theoretically, pedagogically — to do. Perhaps most importantly, we now know in our bones that there is no pure or separate space from which we may write or teach. Representation, of ourselves as well as of those audiences that we both invoke and address, can never be innocent — whether that representation involves writing an essay (such as the one you are now reading) or teaching a class. Nevertheless, without representation we cannot engage in discourse, nor can we create spaces that, potentially at least, enable others — as well as ourselves — to speak. And without representation, we cannot teach writing or reading, for those acts depend absolutely on a willingness to represent and be represented.

CODA

In this rereading of AA/AI, we have attempted to engage in a series of reflections about what it means to represent audience, and, in doing so, to raise some questions about "successful" discourse, disciplinary critique, and progress. We have looked at AA/AI as an example of "successful" discourse and attempted to examine the nature of that success. In so doing, we have tried to indicate that "success" is — in every case — more charged with tensions, competing motives, and trade offs than we had imagined, tensions that, we have been at pains to suggest, can and should inform our teacherly and writerly practices.

In writing this essay we have also attempted to resist the impulse to engage in traditional academic critique by overturning our previous work. We have done so primarily because we have come to feel that such critical maneuvers, while necessary and helpful in many ways, make it particularly easy for us to forget how multiple, heterodox, and situated both teaching and writing are. They also contribute to a rhetoric of disciplinary progress that tends to exempt those effecting critique from inquiry into their own ethical responsibilities and choices. No critical reading can insure or guarantee that our field will effect positive pedagogical change, and we have no doubt that our analysis has failed to illuminate some of the ethical responsibilities and choices implicit in our earlier work. Nor do we doubt that the essay presented here could be effectively subjected to the same kind of positioning and exploration and critique. (Indeed, some of our reviewers have provided us with the beginnings of such a critique.)

What seems finally most important to us, however, is not the particular product of a particular critique of the intensely self-reflective kind attempted here, but the process, the intellectual habit of mind, necessary to doing so. In the long run, we have written (not to mention re-written and re-written) this essay over a period of some two years now because we are trying to enact a practice that can inform our teaching as well as our scholarship. What, after all, do we have to offer our students if we cannot pass out universal laws of correctness, absolute textual meanings, and guarantees of communicative success along with our syllabi? What we have to offer, we believe, is a way of being in language and a way of both inhabiting and shaping knowledge structures, ways that strive to be critically self-reflective, multi-perspectival, and complex.

In short, what we have been trying to do here is consonant with what Don Bialostosky argues we must teach our students to do: to interrogate not only the discourses of schooling but personal, communal, and professional discourses as well. For students, the cultivation of such habits of mind can lead, Bialostosky believes, to the development of "double-voiced" texts that are self-reflexive, aware of the situated nature of the words they write and speak (18). Such a pedagogy should, Bialostosky implies, not stop with students' awareness of their own situatedness but instead move toward a commitment to representing themselves as fully and ethically as possible — and toward an increased responsibility for their written and spoken words.

We should not, however, expect our students, as Bialostosky says, "to examine the words they arrive with" unless we ourselves are also engaged in just such an ongoing project (17). It is, we know from experience, much easier to call for scholarly and pedagogical changes than to enact such changes. In a footnote to "Beyond the Personal: Theorizing a Politics of Location in Composition Research," for instance, Kirsch and Ritchie acknowledge "the irony of the text . . . [they] have produced: a relatively univocal, coherent text that argues for experimental, multivocal writing" (27). And we can certainly find similar examples of such unintended discursive irony in texts we have authored or coauthored and in much other "successful" work in our field. Part of the burden of this essay has been to question the grounds of such discursive "success," but to do so in ways that suggest the possibility of non-agonistic disciplinary critique, a critique that we believe necessarily entails self-critique and self-reflection. We are not, however, arguing for the imposition of some "new" singular norm of scholarly practice. Rather, we hope that others will join us in articulating the multiple ways in which scholars may productively "examine the words they arrive with" whenever they engage in the representation of self and audience.

Acknowledgments: We are grateful to friends and colleagues who responded to sometimes wildly varying drafts of this essay: Sharon Crowley, Russell Durst, Tom Fox, Suzanne Clark, Vicki Collins, Cheryl Glenn, Anita Helle, and Gesa Kirsch.

NOTES

1. In "Wearing a Pith Helmet at a Sly Angle: or, Can Writing Researchers Do Ethnography in a Postmodern Era?," Ralph Cintron comments, for instance, on the extent to which "academic debates are to a significant degree performances. Differences — and they do exist — push themselves forward by creating caricatures of each other. Although it may seem paradoxical, differences are deeply relational: To denounce the other's position is to announce one's own" (376).

2. Many feminist scholars are working to challenge the generic constraints associated with the traditional academic essay and are claiming the essay, in fact, as a site of intense struggle and exploration. The student writer we invoke in AA/AI is involved in no such struggle, seeking instead to inhabit traditional genres "successfully."

3. We have been particularly aided in recognizing the potential conflicts and contradictions inherent in inhabiting various writerly identities by reading the many works of bell hooks — whose reflections on audience in particular (see, in this regard *Talking Back: Thinking Feminist, Thinking Black*) and literacy in general reflect her powerful understanding of how much is at stake in acts of reading and writing. We are aware of other projects that will help illuminate our understanding of these issues, such as Juanita Comfort's dissertation, "Negotiating Identity in Academic Writing: Experiences of African American Women Doctoral Students."

4. In "On Race and Voice: Challenges for Liberal Education in the 1990s," Chandra Talpade Mohanty makes a similar point when she observes that "if complex structural experiences of domination and resistance can be ideologically reformulated as individual behaviors and attitudes, they can be managed while carrying on business as usual" (157).

WORKS CITED

Aristotle. *The Rhetoric of Aristotle.* Trans. and ed. Lane Cooper. Englewood Cliffs: Prentice, 1932.

Aronowitz, Stanley, and Henry A. Giroux. *Postmodern Education: Politics, Culture, and Social Criticism.* Minneapolis: U of Minnesota P, 1991.

Bialostosky, Don H. "Liberal Education, Writing, and the Dialogic Self." *Contending with Words: Composition and Rhetoric in a Postmodern Age.* Ed. Patricia Harkin and John Schilb. New York: MLA, 1991. 11–22.

Burke, Kenneth. *Language as Symbolic Action: Essays on Life, Literature, and Method.* Berkeley: U of California P, 1966.

Cintron, Ralph. "Wearing a Pith Helmet at a Sly Angle: or, Can Writing Researchers Do Ethnography in a Postmodern Era?" *Written Communication* 10 (1993): 371–412.

Comfort, Juanita. "Negotiating Identity in Academic Writing: Experiences of African American Women Doctoral Students." Diss., Ohio State U, 1995.

Ede, Lisa, and Andrea Lunsford. "Audience Addressed/Audience Invoked: The Role of Audience in Composition Theory and Pedagogy." *CCC* 35 (1984): 155–71.

Harris, Joseph. "*CCC* in the 90s." *CCC* 45 (1994): 7–9.

hooks, bell. *Talking Back: Thinking Feminist, Thinking Black.* Boston: South End P, 1989.

———. *Yearning: Race, Gender, and Cultural Politics.* Boston: South End P, 1990.

Kirsch, Gesa E., and Joy S. Ritchie. "Beyond the Personal: Theorizing a Politics of Location in Composition Research." *CCC* 56 (1995): 7–29.

Long, Russell C. "Writer-Audience Relationships: Analysis or Invention?" *CCC* 31 (1980): 221–26.

Mitchell, Ruth, and Mary Taylor. "The Integrating Perspective: An Audience-Response Model for Writing." *College English* 41 (1979): 247–71.

Mohanty, Chandra Talpade. "On Race and Voice: Challenges for Liberal Education in the 1990s." *Between Borders.* Ed. Henry A. Giroux and Peter McLaren. New York: Routledge, 1994. 145–66.

Ong, Walter J. "The Writer's Audience Is Always A Fiction." *PMLA* 90 (1975): 9–21.

Richards, I. A. *The Philosophy of Rhetoric.* London: Oxford UP, 1936.

Shaughnessy, Mina P. *Errors and Expectations.* New York: Oxford UP, 1977.

Worsham, Lynn. "Writing against Writing: The Predicament of *Ecriture Feminine* in Composition Studies." *Contending with Words: Composition and Rhetoric in a Postmodern Age.* Ed. Patricia Harkin and John Schilb. New York: MLA, 1991. 82–104.

15 "Among the Audience":
On Audience in an Age
of New Literacies

With participatory media, the boundaries between audiences and creators become blurred and often invisible. In the words of David Sifry, the founder of Technorati, a search engine for blogs, one-to-many "lectures" (i.e., from media companies to their audiences) are transformed into "conversations" among "the people formerly known as the audience."

> — ANDREAS KLUTH, "Among the Audience:
> A Survey of New Media," *The Economist*, p. 4

Critics argue that privacy does not matter to children who were raised in a wired celebrity culture that promises a niche audience for everyone. Why hide when you can perform? But even if young people are performing, many are clueless about the size of their audience.

> — ARI MELBER, "About Facebook," *The Nation*, p. 23

When we wrote "Audience Addressed/Audience Invoked: The Role of Audience in Composition Theory and Pedagogy" (hereafter AA/AI), which was published in *College Composition and Communication* in 1984, we little realized the life that it would have. Much has changed in the teaching of writing — and in the technologies of communication — since we published AA/AI. Much has changed, as well, in our culture and cultural awareness. So much, in fact, that we saw the need in 1996 to critique our earlier essay, calling attention to several unexamined assumptions that we wished to expose and challenge. In "Representing Audience: 'Successful' Discourse and Disciplinary Critique," published in *College Composition and Communication* in 1996, we observed, for instance, that although we intended our essay "to invoke and address a broad range of audiences, it speaks most strongly to those whose identifications and experiences mirror our own, while turning away from the potential difficulties and costs often inherent in the effort to achieve the kind of academic 'success' that our essay takes for granted as well as from those who would wish to subvert such 'success'" (175).

This essay, written by Andrea A. Lunsford and Lisa Ede, is new to this edition.

More than a dozen years later, we still see the need to reflect yet again on the role of audience in composition theory and pedagogy. We are particularly interested in the role that new literacies are playing in expanding the possibilities of agency, while at the same time challenging older notions of both authorship and audience. In addition, observations of and talks with students — as well as changes in our own reading, writing, and researching practices — have alerted us to new understandings and enactments of textual production and ownership. As a result, our goal in this essay is both theoretical and pedagogical. We wish to subject the concept of audience to renewed inquiry, attempting to account for the way texts develop and work in the world in the twenty-first century. We hope, as well, that the resulting analysis will be useful in our classrooms. As we conduct this exploration, we will address the following questions.

- In a world of participatory media — of Facebook, YouTube, Wikipedia, Twitter, and Del.icio.us — what relevance does the term "audience" hold?

- How can we best understand the relationships among text, author, medium, context, and audience today? How can we usefully describe the dynamic of this relationship?

- To what extent do the invoked and addressed audiences that we describe in our 1984 essay need to be revised and expanded?

- What other terms, metaphors, or images might prove productive?

- What difference might answers to these questions make to twenty-first century teachers and students?

ON NEW MEDIA AND NEW LITERACIES[1]

Before turning to these questions, we would like to situate our discussion in the context of recent research on new media[2] and new literacies, for how we view their relationship matters a good deal to our understanding of both audience and authorship. Are new literacies "new" simply because they rely upon new media, or is the relationship more complex? This is a question that Michele Knobel and Colin Lankshear raise in the introduction to *A New Literacies Sampler*. Knobel and Lankshear argue that the latter is the case. While acknowledging that new media have certainly played an important role in the development of new literacies, they argue that what they term "paradigm cases" of new literacies have, as they put it, both "new 'technical' stuff and new 'ethos' stuff" (7). Central to the development of new literacies is the mobilization of "very different kinds of values and priorities and sensibilities than the literacies we are familiar with" (7). New literacies, they argue, are "more 'participatory,' 'collaborative,' and 'distributed' in nature than conventional literacies. That is, they are less 'published,' 'individuated,' and 'author-centric' than conventional literacies." They are also "less 'expert-dominated' than conventional literacies" (9).

Thus new literacies involve a different kind of mindset than literacies traditionally associated with print media. In their introduction to *A New*

Literacies Sampler, Knobel and Lankshear contrast what they refer to as a "physical-industrial" mindset — the mindset that the two of us certainly grew up with throughout our schooling and a good deal of our working lives — with a "cyberspatial-postindustrial mindset" (10). According to Knobel and Lankshear, those whose experience grounds them primarily in a physical-industrial mindset tend to see the individual person as "the unit of production, competence, intelligence." They also identify expertise and authority as "located in individuals and institutions" (11). Those who inhabit a "cyberspatial-postindustrial mindset," in contrast, increasingly focus on "collectives as the unit of production, competence, intelligence" and tend to view expertise, authority, and agency as "distributed and collective" (11). In a "cyberspatial-postindustrial mindset," the distinction between author and audience is much less clear than in that of the physical-industrial mindset of print literacy.

Those familiar with research in our field on new media and new literacies — research undertaken by scholars such as Cynthia Selfe, Gail Hawisher, James Porter, Anne Wysocki, Johndan Johnson-Eilola, James Gee, Heidi McKee, Cheryl Ball and James Kalmbach, Danielle DeVoss, Todd Taylor, the New London Group, and others — will recognize that the distinction that Knobel and Lankshear draw has been made before. (They will recognize, as well, the value of complicating this binary, useful as it is in a general sense.) The scholarly work of media historians is particularly helpful in this regard. (See, for instance, Lisa Gitelman and Geoffrey B. Pingree's *New Media: 1740–1915*.) The insights generated by these and other scholars in our field have been enriched by research in such related areas as literacy, cultural, and Internet studies. In works ranging from Gunther Kress's *Literacy in the New Media Age* to Howard Rheingold's *Smart Mobs: The Next Social Revolution*, Henry Jenkins' *Convergence Culture: Where Old and New Media Collide*, Lisa Nakamura's *Digitizing Race: Visual Cultures of the Internet*, Keith Sawyer's *Group Genius*, and Clay Shirky's *Here Comes Everybody*, those studying online and digital literacies — particularly Web 2.0 literacies — are challenging conventional understandings of both authorship and audience.[3]

As we have engaged this literature and have attempted to better understand what it means to be a reader and writer in the twenty-first century, we have come to see that what we thought of as two separate strands of our scholarly work — one on collaboration, the other on audience — have in fact become one. As writers and audiences merge and shift places in online environments, participating in both brief and extended collaborations, it is increasingly obvious that writers seldom, if ever, write alone. In short, when receivers or consumers of information become creators of content as well, it is increasingly difficult to tell when writers are collaborative writers or authors and when they are members of audiences.

THE END OF AUDIENCE?

In our contemporary world of digital and online literacies, it seems important to question the status and usefulness of the concept of "audience." Are the changes brought about by new media and new literacies so substantial that it is more accurate to refer to those who participate in new media writing, ranging from user-generated content and tagging to tweeting and digital remixing, as "the people formerly known as the audience," as David Sifry suggests in the first epigraph to this essay?

Even before the explosion of such social networking sites as blogs, Facebook, and Twitter, some scholars in the field of rhetoric and writing argued that the term "audience" may have outlived its usefulness. Some suggested, for instance, that the term "discourse community" better reflects social constructionist understandings of communication. This is the position that James Porter espouses in his 1992 *Audience and Rhetoric: An Archaeological Composition of the Discourse Community.* Others have wondered whether the term "public," as articulated and developed by Jürgen Habermas and explored and extended in Michael Warner's *Publics and Counterpublics*, might not be just as useful as — or more useful than — the term "audience." In *Citizen Critics: Literary Public Spheres*, for instance, Rosa Eberly argues that the term "public" is more helpful than the terms "reader" or "audience" for her study of letters to the editor about four controversial literary texts — two published early in the twentieth century, and two published later.

These and other efforts to re-examine and problematize the concept of audience reflect developments in the field over the last several decades. In the early 1980s, when we were talking, thinking, and writing about audience, the need for such problematization was anything but apparent to us. To put it mildly, our context was different. At that time, we were immersed in research on the contemporary relevance of the classical rhetorical tradition, as our 1984 essay "On Distinctions between Classical and Modern Rhetoric" attests. That same year saw the publication of our coedited *Essays on Classical Rhetoric and Modern Discourse.*

In the years since we published AA/AI, we have come to recognize the limitations, as well as the strengths, of the classical (and more broadly Western) rhetorical tradition. In our 1996 reflection on AA/AI, "Representing Audience," for example, we acknowledge the individualism inherent in this tradition. We also point out that the rhetorical tradition's commitment to *successful* communication has exacted a high hidden price, particularly in terms of efforts to address the ethics of diversity: "For how better to avoid misunderstanding and failure (and to make 'successful' communication more likely) than to exclude, to disenfranchise those who by their very presence in the arena of discourse raise increased possibilities for communicative failures" (174). The rhetorical tradition, as a consequence, risks indifference or hostility to issues of difference, to "audiences ignored, rejected, excluded, or denied" (174).

Does this mean that we wish to reject the term "audience"? No, it does not. We believe that "audience," like other terms such as "discourse community" or "public," is inevitably overdetermined but is still (as is the case with these other terms) in many contexts both helpful and productive. Finally, terms like "audience," "reader," "discourse community," and "public" gesture toward and evoke differing concerns, traditions, and interests. The emphasis on the reader in reader response criticism, for instance, was clearly a salutary response to the emphasis on the text in formalist New Criticism.[4] In the final analysis, one of the beauties of a fluid, multiplicitous term like "audience" is its heuristic value in exploring fine distinctions and teasing out important nuances in any communicative situation.

We continue to believe, then, that the concept of audience provides a helpful theoretical and practical grounding for efforts to understand how texts (and writers and readers) work in today's world. We also believe, as we stated in AA/AI, that a productive way to conceive of audience "is as an over-determined or unusually rich concept, one which may perhaps be best specified through the analysis of precise, concrete situations" (168). Indeed, in rereading AA/AI, we are struck by the powerful role that the analysis of such situations plays in our own essay. As readers may already realize, in remaining committed to the term "audience" we remain committed to rhetoric and to the rhetorical tradition. Our understanding of the rhetorical tradition has changed and expanded since we first wrote AA/AI, but we continue to find rhetoric's emphasis on the rhetorical situation to be theoretically and pedagogically enabling.

THE "RHETORICAL TRIANGLE" REVISITED

In AA/AI we described our own experiences with varying audiences, arguing that "the elements [of invoked and addressed audience roles] shift and merge, depending on the particular rhetorical situation, the writer's aim, and the genre chosen" (168). Thus we embedded our discussion of audience in the classical conception of the "rhetorical triangle," the set of relationships among text, author, and audience out of which meaning grows. Twenty-five years ago, while our work attempted to complicate these sets of relationships, this basic understanding served us simply and well. Today, however, we need a more flexible and robust way of understanding these traditional elements of discourse and the dynamic at work among them.

As a result, we now use the following figure to portray the basic elements of the rhetorical situation. Figure 15-1 includes speakers as well as writers, viewers, listeners, and readers. This figure captures more of the complexity of the rhetorical situation: it acknowledges the plurality of authorship/readership; it includes media as a key element of thinking about texts; and it includes context as the element that touches on, connects, and shapes all angles of the triangle. This element of the rhetorical situation calls attention to the diverse and multiple factors that writers must consider when they compose — from generic or situational constraints to ideologies that make some writerly choices seem obvious and "natural," while others are "unnatural" or entirely hidden from view. As suggested in the figure, the relationship among writer and message and medium (or media) is complex and full of reciprocity. In a digital world, and especially in the world of Web 2.0, speakers and audiences communicate in multiple ways and across multiple channels, often recipro-

FIGURE 15-1   The Rhetorical Triangle

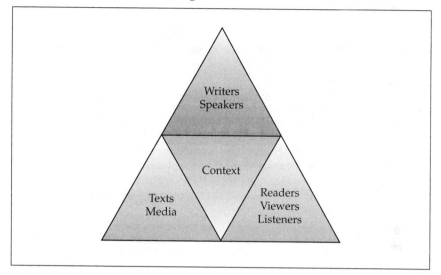

cally. This momentous shift has challenged not only traditional models of communication but also the relationship between "creators" of messages and those who receive them. Today, as we have pointed out, the roles of writers and audiences often conflate, merge, and shift.

The deeply participatory nature of much new media writing provides opportunities for writerly agency,[5] even as it challenges notions of intellectual property that have held sway now for over 300 years, leading — as we have been at pains to point out in our research on collaboration and collaborative writing — both to diverse forms of multiple authorship and to the kind of mass authorship that characterizes sites such as Wikipedia, Rotten Tomatoes, or collaborative blogs. To say that the music and film industries, along with some print-based companies, are resisting such shifts in authorship is an understatement. While these entities will continue to cling to traditional intellectual property regimes of the past, it seems clear that new ways of managing the relationship among texts, "authors," media, contexts, and audiences are emerging. In this regard, consider the alternative rock group Radiohead's decision to release its seventh album *In Rainbows* as a digital download on the Internet. Fans of this group could purchase the music collection on the web — for whatever price they wished to pay.[6]

In *The Economics of Attention*, Richard Lanham argues that we have moved from what he calls a "stuff economy" (one based on material goods) to a "fluff economy" (one based on immaterial information). With his typical humor and verve, Lanham shows that while in a "stuff" economy scarcity is the major economic principle at work, that principle utterly fails in a "fluff" economy, where information is anything but scarce. In fact, as Lanham points out, we are drowning in it. In such an economy, what is needed, according to Lanham, is *attention* — that is, a way of attending sensibly to the information pouring in:

> In an attention economy, the center of gravity for property shifts from real property to intellectual property. This shift has plunged us into confusions about the ownership of such property . . . that it will take some time to sort out. . . . Information, unlike stuff, can be both kept and given away at the same time. As long as the means of notation were fixed in physicality as books, reports, painted images, we could gloss over this major obstacle: that 'possession' means something different from a private property in stuff. Now, with information expressed on a digital screen, with its new means of dissemination, we can no longer continue this gloss. Hence the current agonies in the music and film business. They have been caught in a vise, squeezed between the macro and the micro economics of attention. (259)

We too are caught between the macro and micro economies of attention, since we cannot ignore the world of "stuff." But we are clearly in what Lanham calls a "revisionist" way of thinking. "Our locus of reality has shifted," he argues:

> We have not left the physical world behind and become creatures of pure attention. Neither has wealth become totally disembodied. Our view is now bi-stable. We must always be ready to move from one view of the world to another. They are always competing with each other. We are learning to live in two worlds at once. (258)

In a time of transition, some people are differentially advantaged or disadvantaged: individuals are — or are not — members of Lanham's "we," a fact that reminds us that inequalities and differing degrees of access persist in an attention economy.

As Lanham's discussion suggests, writers who want and need to shift among worlds must be able to hold flexible views of the real and potential relationships among text, context, author, medium, and audience. They must be able to negotiate distinctions between writing and reading, between author and audience that refuse to remain stable; they must also be able to sort out the competing claims of words, images, and sounds in choosing the best medium or media of communication. And they must become comfortable with new ways of thinking about property, about ownership of the messages that are created amidst the dynamic interaction of writers, audiences, and media.

In many ways, our students are already experienced inhabitors of Lanham's two worlds, and they are increasingly comfortable with new ways of thinking about textual ownership. Such new ways began to emerge in interviews with students conducted during the Stanford Study of Writing (SSW), when researchers asked the students in the study about their views on intellectual property. These interviews, which took place between 2001 and 2006, revealed what at first felt like a hard-to-describe, nebulous change: the best the researchers could say was that something seemed to be happening to the way students thought about intellectual property and ownership. But more recent analyses of the transcripts of some 150 interviews indicate the kind of flexible shifting back and forth described above.

Perhaps one vivid example will serve to limn this potential shift in understanding and attitude toward textual ownership. One participant in the study, Mark Otuteye, wrote a poem during the early weeks of his first year at Stanford. Titled "The Admit Letter," this poem was performed by Mark later that year during Parents' Weekend; it opens with a "so-called friend" saying to Mark, "Oh sure, you got into Stanford: you're Black." What follows in this spoken word poem is Mark's imagining of what his "so-called friend" thought his admit letter might have said. The two imaginary versions of the admit letter that Mark performed were biting — and very, very funny; together, they not only put the so-called friend in his place but managed to send up the university as well. On the Stanford campus, news of this poem spread like proverbial wildfire and Otuteye was called on to perform it in numerous venues. In one such venue, the poem changed significantly: now it was performed by Mark and a Chicana student, who powerfully wove together versions of their "admit letters."

"The Admit Letter" went through additional permutations during Otuteye's college career, and during one of the interviews with him SSW researchers asked, "So is this poem yours? Do you own it?" In a lengthy conversation, Mark said that he considered the poem to be his in significant and important ways — but not *exclusively* his; in fact, he said, his work is usually written and performed collaboratively, and he sees it as part of a large poetic commons. In short, this student was already beginning to move between the information and the attention worlds, and he was comfortable writing with as well as for others, and in a range of media. For Mark, and for many other students in this study, what has seemed at times to us the perplexing fluidity and even tension among writer, text, context, medium, and audience feels like home turf. This home turf, however, is not without its potential dangers and challenges (including challenges to notions of textual ownership). As we will discuss in a later section of this essay, other problems can arise if students fail to differentiate between the constraints and opportunities inherent in their self-sponsored writing and those of the academic rhetorical situation.

Taxonomizing Audiences

When we wrote AA/AI, we literally could not have imagined the textual and material worlds we inhabit today. At that time we were attempting to intervene in a then-contemporary debate over audience. In our effort to understand and give coherence to this debate, we grouped various scholars' work on audience under two constructs, that of audience invoked (the intended audience as well as those imagined and hailed by the writer) and of audience addressed (the actual people reading a writer's work). If reprintings and references to AA/AI are any indication, others have found the constructs of audience addressed/audience invoked useful. But we are also aware that the

impulse to taxonomize — to create binaries and various other sorts of categories — has disadvantages as well as advantages. Indeed, the felt need to go
beyond addressed and invoked audiences to acknowledge audiences that are
"ignored, rejected, excluded, or denied" motivated our effort to look again at
AA/AI when we wrote "Representing Audience" (174).

A quarter of a century after AA/AI was published, we want to look again
at these two constructs to determine what relevance they hold in an age of
new media and new literacies.[7] When we look at our earlier work, we continue to value the way that the constructs of audience addressed and audience invoked enable us to call attention to "(1) the fluid, dynamic character of
rhetorical situations; and (2) the integrated, interdependent nature of reading
and writing" (156). We value as well the extent to which they discourage
overly stark binaries — such as those that posit sharp dichotomies between
speaking and writing. In AA/AI we point out, for instance, that Walter Ong's
representative situations (in "The Writer's Audience Is Always a Fiction") of
"the orator addressing a mass audience versus a writer alone in a room" will
always "oversimplify the potential range and diversity of both oral and written communication situations" (161).

If this statement was true in 1984, it is even more compelling today with
the proliferation of electronic and online media and social networking sites.
Increasingly, for instance, students in our writing classes post messages to
course discussion boards and blogs and/or contribute to wikis. When they
compose academic texts, they may well insert images and sound or provide
tables or spreadsheets with supporting information. When students turn
from academic writing to self-sponsored communication, the possibilities
explode — including everything from instant messaging and texting to blogging, creating text and images on Facebook (and commenting on others'
pages), posting photos on Flickr, and sharing tags on Del.icio.us.

As we noted earlier in this essay, these kinds of participatory communications challenge conventional understandings of both authorship and audience, even as they provide an opportunity for anyone and everyone to become
author and audience, writer and reader.[8] But do they invalidate the general
constructs of audience addressed and audience invoked that we established
in AA/AI? In the most general sense, the kinds of participatory communication that we have just described can, we believe, be encompassed within
these two categories — which, we argue in AA/AI, are best understood as a
dialogic pair.

Consider, in this regard, our experience writing this chapter. Rather than
relying on the technologies of telephone, electric correcting typewriter, and
photocopy machines (technologies essential to the composition of AA/AI),
we relied on contemporary electronic technologies, particularly word processing, email, and the web. Yet our experience composing this text still required us to negotiate both addressed and invoked audiences — from the
readers we envisioned as we worked on drafts of this essay to colleagues and
students who actually read and responded to it. In short, we find that the
categories of invoked and addressed audiences still inform the much more

complex online communicating we do today. As we post to Listservs, look for videos on YouTube that we can use in our classes, or participate in a wiki devoted to developing an accreditation report for one of our institutions, we are conscious of both addressed and invoked audiences. In the case of the accreditation report, some thirty members of a task force are contributing to this document, which is addressed directly to the university's accreditation board. In a more indirect way, this document is also addressed to all members of the accreditation team and to our upper administrators as well. But to address these audiences, and especially the first one, we must invoke the accreditation board, which we have done very carefully and cautiously: a lot is at stake in our getting this particular invocation right.

Even so, we need to acknowledge that precisely because the constructs of audience addressed and audience invoked are so broad and encompassing, they can only take us so far in our understanding of audience, including contemporary online and electronic audiences.[9] A person who reads Barbara Kingsolver's *The Poisonwood Bible*, for instance, and then posts the 1,497th customer review on Amazon.com no doubt has an invoked audience in mind, while the addressed audience is potentially vast and largely unknowable.[10] We are likewise fascinated by the potential relationships among the photographers who (as of our last checking) posted 66,977 photos of black Labs on Flickr, tagging them so that other audiences with a similar passion for this breed of dogs can easily find them,[11] not to mention the relationship we might establish if we clicked on the profile of one of these photographers or if we commented on a photo we find particularly compelling. In these instances, we are invoking this photographer even as the photographer invokes other audiences, which may or may not include us. Further, our invocation of the photographer may lead us to address him or her directly — or not. In any case, the concepts "addressed" and "invoked" seem to ripple out, overlap, and echo one another in provocative ways.

And such examples proliferate. When Henry Jenkins in *Fans, Bloggers, and Gamers: Exploring Participatory Culture* refers to "the interactive audience" (136), it seems clear that those communicating with such an audience must necessarily both address and invoke each other. But having said that, what more might we add? How does the technology of gaming or blogging, for example, ignore or exclude certain audiences? What ideological positions may be unspoken in such activities? And how can we avoid the utopian/dystopian ways in which audiences and members of new online communities are often framed, both in the popular press and in more serious scholarly work? In attempting to answer this last question, Jenkins observes that "the interactive audience is more than a marketing concept and less than a 'semiotic democracy'" (136). Jenkins's comment suggests that interactive or participatory audiences fall somewhere along a continuum, from those who consume media and content on the web in fairly traditional ways to the full shared agency characteristic of many online communities.

We have additional issues and questions as well. In an online, participatory culture, the concerns that we articulated in "Representing Audience" about audiences "ignored, rejected, excluded, or denied" become even more salient (174).[12] As we will discuss more fully in the next section, many students easily forget that when they post something on the web they may encounter unwanted or future audiences — such as an employer checking their Facebook entries or a researcher checking on their use of his or her scholarly work.

Although these questions suggest potential limitations of the constructs of audience addressed and audience invoked, we believe that these constructs can still usefully remind us of the rich complexity of any form of communication, written or spoken, print or online. But as we have suggested, they are too general to directly address questions such as the ones we have just articulated. These questions require the kind of "analysis of precise, concrete situations" that we call for near the end of AA/AI (168).[13] Such work is currently being done, most often in qualitative studies that require the depth and breadth of ethnography. One powerful example of such work occurs in Angela Thomas's chapter "Blurring and Breaking through the Boundaries of Narrative, Literacy, and Identity in Adolescent Fan Fiction" in Knobel and Lankshear's *New Literacies Sampler*. In this four-year ethnographic study, Thomas explores the experiences of two adolescent females: "Tiana, aged 14 years, and Jandalf, aged 17 years, friends who met online and who have been collaboratively writing fan fiction for over a year" (139). These two young authors prove to be extraordinary in a number of ways, including the degree of self-reflexivity and flexibility that they exhibit. In characterizing their writing, both individual and collaborative, Thomas observes that Tiana and Jandalf move successfully "in and out of media type, text type, form, style and literary device with an ease and poetry of linguistic dexterity that is truly exceptional" (151). In doing so, they assume a range of audience roles for each other, taking turns, for example, at role-playing as they develop the outlines of plots and of characters for their fan fiction. Tiana explains: "[W]hen I transcribe over, I sort of become two people — Tiana and a narrator. I make myself see things from a third person POV [point of view] while still writing as my characters" (144). In describing the many kinds of writing the pair undertake, Thomas mentions "the role playing, the out-of-character discussions occurring synchronously within the role playing, the character journals, the art work, the careful plotting out of story lines, the forum discussions, the descriptions of worlds and cultures, the invention of language, the playful spoofing, the in-role poetry, the meta-textual allusions to sound effects, movie techniques" (145).[14]

Another instructive analysis of precise, concrete situations occurs in Kevin Brooks and his student Aaron Anfinson's study of Anfinson's own capstone project as well as Brooks's response to it. The study, "Exploring Postcritical Composition: MEmorials[15] for Afghanistan and the Lost Boys of Sudan," examined coauthor Anfinson's effort to meet the requirements of a senior English project while also, as Anfinson observed in an email to Brooks, writing "something different . . . I think I just wanted to do something I've never done and to truly learn something and have fun while doing it — quite a challenge caught up in the sometimes-captive atmosphere of the classroom" (78). As an active member of the National Guard who could be deployed at any time, Anfinson wanted to raise political issues and questions about the war in Afghanistan but was "reluctant to divulge much personal information" (85). In Anfinson's written reflections on his experience and in his discussions with Brooks, Anfinson did not focus extensively on audience. This choice was in part the result of his gradual decision to create what Gregory Ulmer terms "electronic monuments." Such monuments encourage writers to emphasize their own preferences over the interests and needs of readers and encourage such strategies as borrowing, collage, and intentional minimalism. In his only reflection on audience, Anfinson comments on how he drew upon his own inclinations in making decisions, even those related to his readers: "I think the idea for videos came actually from a bit of laziness. Rather than entertain, I wanted to be entertained . . . I enjoy finding videos . . . I too thought that a reader who is not so academically inclined would sit through a video or two, but would never read a huge block of text" (83). This example demonstrates how the role of audience can shift depending on the author's context, sense of agency, and personal inclinations.

In the case of Anfinson's capstone project, "A MEmorial for Afghanistan," genre played a more important role than audience. In Brooks' view, the MEmorial was an effective genre for Anfinson, who focused his self-evaluation on the role it played in increasing his own knowledge. In a reflective paper he submitted with his MEmorial, Anfinson observed that "Overall, in my MEmorial, I think I learned a lot. If nothing else, due to my 'public participation in monumentality . . . [and] deconsultancy,' [16] I learned what I truly think about an issue that I have been inactive in directly confronting" (86). In commenting on the power of Anfinson's project, Brooks observes that it inspired him to undertake a similar effort, "A MEmorial for the Lost Boys of Sudan." His own project is, he believes, "not as visually interesting as Aaron's and I have not been able to emulate his textual minimalism, but I have tried to learn from his various strategies of composing with others' videos (appropriation), and arranging video, text, and still images in various patterns on the screen (collage)" (86). Thus does the teacher learn from the student.

As the examples from Thomas and from Brooks and Anfinson demonstrate, understanding the complexity of writing processes, audience awareness, and collaboration calls for specific, grounded, and nuanced analysis that goes well beyond the analytic binary of addressed and invoked audiences. Issues of authority may play a particularly key role here. Tiana and Jandalf had a good deal of authority and autonomy in their self-sponsored writing. As Anfinson's teacher, Brooks also granted him considerable flexibility and authority.

TEACHING AUDIENCE IN THE TWENTY-FIRST CENTURY

Imagine this: A student in a required writing class composes a research-based argument and then presents an oral version of the argument as part of a panel at an in-class "conference" held at the end of the term. The teacher of the class creates a website and posts all of the student arguments on it, inviting response from the students as well as other audiences. Two years later, the teacher gets a response from a professor at another university, pointing out that the student's argument drew on the professor's work, citing that work but often failing to enclose directly quoted passages within quotation marks. The professor demands that the student's argument be taken off the website, accusing the student of sloppy habits at best, plagiarism at worst. Notified of this turn of events, the student — now a prospective graduating senior — is completely surprised — he had not meant to plagiarize, and he certainly had not imagined that one of his sources would go to the trouble of accessing his essay.

Like many others, this student experiences the Internet and many of its sites as fairly private, when the reality is that audiences are there all the time, browsing, searching, engaging, responding, sometimes accusing. Many scholars and commentators have noted the breakdown between private and public today and the somewhat contradictory attitudes students hold: students often say they are comfortable being in public — that a public stance comes with the territory of digital communication. But they also sometimes view sites — and especially social networking sites such as Facebook — as relatively private, away from the prying eyes of parents and other unwanted audiences. We had these students in mind when we quoted Ari Melber at the opening of this essay: "Critics argue that privacy does not matter to children who were raised in a wired celebrity culture that promises a niche audience for everyone. Why hide when you can perform? But even if young people are performing, many are clueless about the size of their audience" (23).[16]

Clearly, even though many of our students are completely at ease in the digital landscape, they nevertheless need to become more knowledgeable about the nature and complexity of the audiences for whom they perform, particularly as they shift back and forth from self-sponsored online writing to academic writing. The first lesson we draw from grappling with the questions we pose in this essay, then, is that we have a responsibility to join with our students in rich and detailed explorations of just what "audience" can mean in their writing and in their lives. Such explorations might well begin with exploring the problematics of viewing the teacher as the sole audience for student writing. As the real-life example above suggests, the teacher remains *an* audience for student texts but by no means the only audience, especially when student writing is posted on the web. Even if it is not posted, student writing often invokes and addresses audiences well beyond the teacher (who is also, often, both addressed and invoked).

Beyond unpacking the concept of teacher as audience, teachers can help students understand the contemporary complexities of audience by providing case studies that exemplify various kinds of audiences. The participatory audience of peer review, for instance, can be theorized and interrogated by students in their composition classes: that is, rather than simply responding to one another's texts, students can take time to get to know these real-life audiences, along with their assumptions and values, literally examining where these members of the audience are coming from. Or students can create a genealogy of audiences for a particular social networking site, exploring the many diverse individuals and groups that have access to the site and asking which audiences the site invokes and which it seems to address. Students could examine the many issues raised, for instance, by various Pro Ana (pro anorexia) sites on the web. Who are the sponsors of these sites? What kinds of collaborative relationships are being invoked and addressed by those who post to and read this site?

As we have noted in this essay, what began for us as two different strands of research — one on audience, another on collaboration — have all but merged during the last couple of years as we have seen how frequently writers become audiences, and vice versa. Yet more often than not, students resist collaboration in their schoolwork even as they collaborate constantly in their out-of-class online writing. There are reasons for this seeming contradiction or tension: school writing is part of a deeply individualistic system that rewards individual students through a system of grades and points that values the individual GPA, and working collaboratively runs counter to that system. Scholars and teachers need to challenge the hyper-individualistic base of higher education in the United States; we need also to engage students in substantial discussions of this issue. As we have been arguing for some time, we know that most of the innovative work that gets done in the world today gets done in collaborative groups (see Sawyer; Tapscott and Williams; Sunstein; Ede and Lunsford) — including, increasingly, teams that work primarily online. And we know that colleges and universities, for reasons mentioned above, are doing very little to prepare students to thrive in such an environment (see Bok; Light). We need to do more, then, than *assign* collaborative projects — we need to provide a theoretical rationale for such projects, along with data to support it. In addition, we need to craft collaborative projects that will work hard to engage every member of the group and guide the group in analyzing their work together from beginning to end. And we need to join with students in exploring the use of free collaborative writing tools such as Google Docs, Zoho, and Writeboard.

We also need to consider the impact that new literacies are having — and should have — in our teaching. Such literacies often call for producing new texts, often referred to as "new media" texts. The question of whether and how to teach such new media writing poses significant challenges to teachers of writing today. Thanks to the work of Anne Wysocki, Johndan Johnson-Eilola, Cynthia Selfe, and Geoffrey Sirc, their collaborative *Writing New Media* paints a rich picture of the kinds of writing students are increasingly doing today, both inside and outside of the classroom. In one chapter in this study, Cynthia Selfe points out the double-edged sword that comes along with new media texts, as she tells the story of David, a young man who teaches himself to produce effective new media texts only to fail his college classes because of his inability to create acceptable traditional print texts. The point Selfe makes is one all teachers of writing need to heed: We must help our students learn to conceive and produce a repertoire of texts, from the convincing academic argument to the compelling website or memorable radio essay. (Selfe has also recently published a helpful guide for teachers, *Multimodal Composition: Resources for Teachers*, as well as a passionate call for moving teacherly attention well beyond print literacy in "Aurality and Multimodal Composing.")

It is important to acknowledge the difficulties inherent in taking on such a task. At Stanford, when the Faculty Senate mandated that the Program in Writing and Rhetoric (PWR) develop a new second-level course that would go beyond academic writing to embrace oral presentations with multimedia support, the PWR teaching staff responded with great enthusiasm. By the time they began piloting courses to equally enthusiastic students, the sky seemed to be the limit: Students wanted to write and produce hour-long documentaries; to produce NPR-quality audio essays; to design, write, and produce online magazines; not to mention create other new media texts to be performed in a wide range of settings. By the end of the second quarter of the pilot, however, both teachers and students realized that their reach had clearly exceeded their grasp. Most notably, the writing that students were doing as they worked their way toward new media or multimodal texts was declining in quality. Both students and teachers recognized that time spent on perfecting visual design and enriching texts with multimedia was time — given the constraints of the ten-week academic term — that students could no longer spend on their written texts. As a result, before the new course was fully implemented, the teaching staff, working in conjunction with the Undergraduate Advisory Board, pulled back from some of their ambitions, focusing the course first on producing a research-based argument and then working the rest of the term to "translate" that argument into various genres and media. As the Stanford teachers continued to refine this new course and its assignment sequence, they were able to inch a bit back toward those earlier ambitions. But it is instructive to note the power of tradition in the face of challenging new ways of composing. It is even more instructive to note that the response of the upper administration to this new course, even though mandated by the Faculty Senate, was less than supportive: "Are you teaching 'real writing'?" they asked. The response to that question was, emphatically "yes," but even an extensive rationale for the answer failed to convince some colleagues and administrators.

As this discussion has suggested, universities and the culture at large seem not to have arrived at a consensus on what "writing" is and can be in this age of new literacies. In short, we don't yet know how best to balance our obligation to open opportunities for students to engage new media fully in their writing with our obligation to honor university mandates to strengthen and expand students' grasp of traditional print academic discourse. The way forward is neither easy nor obvious, but scholars, teachers, and students need to work together to explore and experiment with both theories and practices that can help guide us. In this section of our essay, we have explored several important implications for teaching the concept of audience in the twenty-first century, the most important of which is to engage our students in analyzing and theorizing the new literacies and new media themselves, especially as these practices call for collaboration, for new understandings of audience, and for a robust ethics of communication. Exploring new literacies and new media with students means crafting syllabi that leave time for such interrogations and for the experimentation they will demand. In addition to working closely with our students, we can revisit our assignments, looking in our required composition courses for ways to stretch the boundaries of academic discourse and to allow students collaborative opportunities for engaging with new media and new audiences. And we can offer advanced elective courses that move well beyond print literacy, calling on students to create innovative new media texts and to analyze them in the context of their audiences. Michigan State's program in professional writing offers a range of exciting courses on web authoring and multimedia writing, and other examples of such classes abound.[17] These sites offer, we believe, fertile ground for detailed ethnographic explorations of writerly agency and of audiences, including those invoked and addressed.

ETHICS AND PARTICIPATORY LITERACIES

As we have worked on this essay, we have found ourselves meditating on audiences across the millennia — from audiences who gathered before the ancient Greek rhapsodes, who "read" the scriptures along with literate scribes in the medieval period, who sat among the groundlings at the Globe and other Elizabethan theatres, who waited in rapt anticipation for the next issue of the latest Dickens novel, who gathered at whistle-stops throughout the United States to engage with political hopefuls, and who today log on to check in with Facebook friends or read and comment on their favorite blog. In some ways, there has always been a relational or participatory quality to audiences. Yet it seems clear that changes in technology and other material conditions that have brought us to the present moment have opened avenues for audiences to take on agency and to become participants and creators/shapers of discourse in more profound ways than ever before. While nineteenth-century audience members could meet in salons or coffeehouses to discuss the latest installment of *Great Expectations*, think of the possibilities for enhanced agency and participation that blogging or the ability to post comments online (to take just two examples) offers today.

In noting the opportunity for enhanced agency and participation in online writing, we do not intend to join those who characterize the web and social networking sites in utopian terms. If we have learned anything from our study of the rhetorical tradition, it is that the nature and consequence of any act of communication can never be determined in advance, and that inquiry into issues such as these requires a deeply situated, finely tuned analysis. When consumers post reviews to Amazon.com, for instance, are they expanding their possibilities for agency and for collaborations with others, or are they serving as unpaid volunteer workers for this ever-expanding company? There are no simple, decontextualized answers to questions such as these.

Our engagement with the rhetorical tradition, as well as our study of the history of communicative technologies, thus reminds us that both utopian and dystopian views of our current moment are likely to oversimply. They also remind us of how difficult it is to predict how various communication technologies will be employed. The earliest graphic symbols, it is good to remember, were used for accounting, not writing. We might consider in this regard Twitter, the social networking and microblogging service that allows users to publicly post 140-character "tweets" or send private 140-character "direct messages" to each other. "Tweets" are used by restaurants, clubs, bands, and stores — as well as by individuals — to promote and inform, and many users use Twitter as a source of personalized breaking news. Who would have expected, then, that some users of Twitter would decide that it provides the perfect online space to write haiku, much less that the haiku created on Twitter would invoke an avid audience? Just how much interest is there in the world today in Twitter haiku? We can't know for sure, but a quick check on Google instantly pulled up 1,750,000 hits. In searching the web, we have also found numerous references to Twitter contests. One frequent challenge invites writers to compose microessays and microstories limited to Twitter's 140 characters. In case you're interested, a search on Google using the term "Twitter contests" generated 136,000,000 hits.[18] Here's what one Twitter user, Calvin Jones, posted to his website Digital Marketing Success about his fascination with Twitter:

> I love the way twitter makes you condense your writing, squeezing the maximum out of every character. Here's my swiftly penned missive:
>
> She paused, shivering involuntarily; the wave of adrenalin surged through her, leaving her giddy and disoriented. It was quiet. He was gone!

Twitter was released to the public in October 2006, and we conducted these Google searches in late July 2010. Thus does a software program evolve in lightning speed on the web, making a space for readers to become writers who then become invoked and addressed audience members for still other writers/readers.

What if a friend or family member prefers not to know what someone close (or not so close) to them is doing throughout the day? Twitter.com addresses this issue by requiring users to sign up for Twitter to receive tweets and by allowing for privacy settings. But surely ethical issues remain. Twitter can be used to help groups gather quickly, whether for positive purposes (engaging in civic discussion or action) or negative. How can those interested in participating in this social networking and micro-blogging site best understand their responsibilities as writers and audiences for others? In this regard, we have been interested in the use of Twitter to call for and promote protests during the summer of the 2009 Iranian election. Of particular note during these demonstrations were the many signs protesting the validity of the elections written in English, both addressing and invoking audiences rejected by the official regime, which refused to allow Western reporters into the country.

In response to this prohibition, protesters used their cell phones and hand-held cameras to document and share these signs and images with the rest of the world.

At its strongest and most productive moments, the rhetorical tradition has acknowledged the potentially powerful ethical implications inherent in any act of communication. As we conclude this discussion of audience in an age of new literacies, then, we turn to several other ethical questions that seem compelling to us as teachers and scholars. Perhaps most importantly, in a world of participatory media, it seems essential for teachers and students to consider the multiple reciprocal responsibilities entailed in writer-audience relationships. What does a student writer posting to Facebook owe to all the potential audiences of that post, from a former partner to a potential employer? And what responsibilities do audiences have toward those whose messages they receive, seek, reject, or encounter? One goal of future research on audience must surely be to explore the ethical dimensions of such relationships.

It seems equally important for scholars, teachers, and students to explore collaboratively the increasingly complex issue of plagiarism/patchwriting in an online world.[19] As the example of the professor who found his work used without proper attribution in a student essay on a class website demonstrates, the ease of cutting and pasting and the wide availability of sources make holding to traditional norms of scholarly citation increasingly difficult. While students we know roundly condemn buying or downloading a paper whole-sale from a website as unacceptable cheating, they are much more ambivalent about using a form of sampling in their writing, and they are downright resistant to the need for what they often think of as excessive (or even obsessive) citation: If you go to the web with a question and get thousands of "hits" in answer to it, they say, shouldn't that answer be considered common knowledge that doesn't need to be cited? We're inclined to answer "yes" to this question, but if we answer "no," then which one of the thousands of sources should be *the* one to be cited? These questions, and the issues they raise, suggest that we must continue not only to explore students' understandings of intellectual property but also to engage them in a full discussion of where academic citation practices came from, why they have been so deeply valued, and what is at stake in developing alternative practices — such as a much broader definition of "common knowledge," as well as alternative forms of attribution.

If plagiarism and potential misuse of sources represent one ethical problem that contemporary audiences must address, then another problem has quite diverse origins and implications. What are the consequences for civic discourse in a world where those interested in a specific topic or audience can, if they have Internet access, easily find sites where they can communicate with like-minded individuals, where our culture seems to promise, as Ari Melber observes, "a niche audience for everyone" (23)? Is our culture likely to fragment into what legal scholar Cass R. Sunstein refers to as "information cocoons" (9)? And how can we best understand and enact an appropriate relationship between privacy and free speech on the web? One place to turn in exploring this set of ethical issues is the extensive work on public discourse being pursued by many scholars in rhetoric and communication studies.[20] Most generally, our goal as teachers should be to encourage (even inspire) students to build bridges between the seemingly private voices they inhabit online and the public ones they can establish as students, workers, and citizens.

In his 2007 "Vision of the Future," Howard Rheingold notes the need for students who use the web to take responsibility for determining the accuracy of what they find there and for parents and students alike to take responsibility for the ethical and moral choices they make in reading and writing online. (Rheingold cites, for example, the responsibility of parents in establishing rules for access that would protect their children from pornographic sites.) But in this talk, Rheingold is primarily interested in how young people can get beyond the small niches of the web to participate most effectively in online settings. Noting that while students today are "naturals" when it comes to point-and-click explorations, "there's nothing innate about knowing how to apply their skills to the processes of democracy" (4), Rheingold calls on teachers to help students make connections "between the literacies students pick up simply by being young in the 21st century and those best learned through reading and discussing texts" (5). We can help students make such connections, Rheingold argues, by allowing them to move "from a private to a public voice" that will help them "turn their self-expression into a form of public participation" (5). Public voice, Rheingold insists, is "learnable, a matter of consciously engaging with an active public rather than broadcasting to a passive audience" (5).

Thus while Rheingold recognizes the potential for fragmentation, for performing only for small niche audiences, and for existing "information cocoons," he also sees the potential for developing participatory public opinion that can "be an essential instrument of democratic self-governance" (5). We believe that Rheingold is right to argue that if we want such public voices to arise, we must teach to and for them. And along with Rheingold, we recognize that teaching to and for new publics and public voices calls for "a whole new way of looking at learning and teaching" that will, we believe, require close attention to the ethical issues raised by new literacies and new media (7). It will also call for resisting the dichotomy between those who dream utopian dreams of a vast collective and participatory democracy enabled by Web 2.0 and those who bemoan a collapse into fragmentation and solipsism that can come from talking only with those who already think just as you do. Limiting an audience to or collaborating only with like thinkers will almost surely fail to develop a "whole new way of looking at learning and teaching" or addressing the ethical issues we have raised.

At its best, the Western rhetorical tradition, however flawed, has encouraged both writers and teachers of writing to take a deeply situated perspective on communication — and thus to challenge the kind of binaries that we have just described. Whenever we write, read, speak, or (as Krista Ratcliffe has so eloquently reminded us) listen, there are no guarantees that either the process or outcome will be ethical. This is an understanding that we can — and should — bring with us when we enter our classrooms, especially our first-year writing classrooms. For there we have the opportunity to help our students experience the intellectual stimulation and excitement, as well as the responsibility, of engaging and collaborating with multiple audiences, from peers to professors to addressed and invoked audiences of all kinds.

NOTES

1. We are keenly aware of the irony inherent in this essay on new media and new literacies, composed as it is almost entirely of words and published in print. At least one reason for this irony is practical: we wrote this essay in response to an invitation to contribute to a print book, *Engaging Audience: Writing in an Age of New Literacies*, edited by M. Elizabeth Weiser, Brian M. Fehler, and Angela M. González. The essay has been revised since this publication.

2. In *Writing New Media*, Anne Wysocki argues that "we should call 'new media texts' those that have been made by composers who are aware of the range of materialities of texts and who then highlight the materiality; such composers design texts that help readers/consumers/viewers stay alert to how any text — like its composers and readers — doesn't function independently of how it is made and in what contexts. Such composers design texts that make as overtly visible as possible the values they embody" (15).

3. We use the term "Web 2.0" here and elsewhere recognizing that some have argued that this term is inaccurate and/or hyperbolic. In an interview posted on IBM's developerWorks site, for instance, Tim Berners-Lee argues that Web 2.0 is "a piece of jargon, nobody even knows what it means. If Web 2.0 for you is blogs and wikis, then that is people to people [as opposed to Web 1, which is sometimes described as computer to computer]. . . . But that was what the Web was supposed to be all along." Berner-Lee prefers to use the term "Semantic Web" rather than Web 2.0 (Laningham).

4. Two recent monographs helpfully remind us of the differing concerns, traditions, and interests that scholars have brought to the concept of audience. The first study, Mary Jo Reiff's 2004 *Approaches to Audience: An Overview of the Major Perspectives*, chronicles the development of research on audience within English studies in general and rhetoric and writing in particular. The second study, Denis McQuail's 1997 monograph *Audience Analysis*, is written from the perspective of communication studies, particularly mass communication and cultural studies.

5. Recent work on gaming and gamers sometimes explores agency in such venues. See the special issue of *Computers and Composition* devoted to Reading Games: Composition, Literacy, and Video Gaming and particularly the articles by John Alberti and Matthew S. S. Johnson.

6. After making their album available on the web, Radiohead also released their music as a conventional CD.

7. Other scholars have also examined these constructs in helpful ways. We would particularly like to call attention to Robert Johnson's "Audience Involved: Toward a Participatory Model of Writing," Jack Selzer's "More Meanings of Audience," Rosa Eberly's "From Writers, Audiences, and Communities to Publics: Writing Classrooms as Protopublic Spaces," Mary Jo Reiff's "Rereading 'Invoked' and 'Addressed' Readers Through a Social Lens: Toward a Recognition of Multiple Audiences," and the essays published in Gesa Kirsch and Duane H. Roen's edited collection *A Sense of Audience in Written Communication*. Though space limitations do not allow us to discuss these studies, we have benefited from these authors' analyses and critiques.

8. In "Agency and Authority in Role-Playing 'Texts'," Jessica Hammer identifies three kinds of authorship in video games: primary, secondary, and tertiary. As Hammer notes, "The primary author develops a world and a set of rules," while "the secondary author takes the work of the primary author and uses it to construct a specific situation or scenario. . . . The tertiary authors, then, 'write' the text of the game in play" (71).

9. In *Audience Analysis*, for instance, Denis McQuail helpfully identifies the following dimensions of audience: "degree of activity or passivity; degree of interactivity and interchangeability; size and duration; locatedness in space; group character (social/cultural identity); simultaneity of contact with source; heterogeneity of composition; social relations between sender and receiver; message versus social/behavioral definition of situation; degree of 'social presence'; sociability of context of use" (150).

10. As of July 25, 2010, this was the number of customer reviews of the Harper Perennial Modern Classic paperback edition of Kingsolver's novel on Amazon.com.

11. This search of Flickr was also conducted on July 25, 2010.

12. In *Rhetorical Refusals: Defying Audiences' Expectations*, John Schilb examines cases in which speakers and writers intentionally defy audience expectations.

13. Scholars in such areas as media and cultural studies, communication, sociology, and anthropology have undertaken research in media reception and audience ethnography. For an introduction to this interdisciplinary body of work, see Pertti Alasuutari's *Rethinking the Media Audience: The New Agenda*. Representative studies include Virginia Nightingale's *Studying Audiences: The Shock of the Real*, S. Elizabeth Bird's *The Audience in Everyday Life: Living in a Media World*, and Will Brooker and Deborah Jermyn's *The Audience Studies Reader*.

14. Thomas goes on to observe that "in addition to exploring the scope of the narrative worlds of the fan fiction, it is important to note that the girls also produce multimodal texts to enhance their fan fiction, making avatars (images to represent themselves) for role playing, making visual signatures as can be seen at the side and end of each post on the forum . . . , finding icons to reflect mood, creating music bytes, making fan fiction posters in the form of an advertisement and teaser, and creating mini movie trailers using their own spliced-together combination of existing movie clips, music, voiceovers, and text. They also draw maps and room plans of their world, draw and paint scenery, and sketch images of their many characters. As well as hand-drawn sketches, they create digital images, digital colorizations or enhancements of their sketches, or purely digitally-created images" (150–51).

15. See Gregory Ulmer's *Electronic Monuments* for a discussion of this concept.

16. Internet studies scholar danah boyd has done considerable research on this topic. See, for instance, her "Social Network Sites: Public, Private, or What?" Here boyd argues that "[n]ew social technologies have altered the underlying architecture of social interaction and information distribution," and that today's teenagers ". . . are embracing this change, albeit often with the clumsy candour of an elephant in a china shop."

17. Readers will know of many similar efforts, such as Advanced Studies in Digital Rhetoric and Writing in Digital Environments at the University of Texas, Austin; or the digital media writing courses in MIT's Department of Writing and Humanistic Studies; or Ohio State's Digital Media Studies Program. At the Bread Loaf School of English in the summer of 2008, Andrea's students used WordPress to build a class blog that allowed for tagging, searching, linking, and multiple forms of interaction, as well as opportunities for experimental writing that fell outside the bounds of what colleges usually call "academic discourse," including graphic memoirs and visual/audio narratives. Students in another class filmed documentary essays aimed at changing one or more policies at the schools where they teach during the regular academic year.

18. Both searches were conducted on July 25, 2010.

19. Rebecca Howard has written extensively and compellingly about the developmental nature of what she calls "patchwriting," as well as about the ways in which students and teachers understand (and often misunderstand) plagiarism.

20. Several essays in Section IV of *The Sage Handbook of Rhetorical Studies* explore such issues; see, especially, Gurak and Antonijevic and Beasley.

WORKS CITED

Alasuutari, Pertti, ed. *Rethinking the Media Audience: The New Agenda*. London: Sage, 1999. Print.
Alberti, John. "The Game of Reading and Writing: How Video Games Reframe Our Understanding of Literacy." *Computers and Composition* 25 (2008): 258–69. Print.
Ang, Ien. *Livingroom Wars: Rethinking Audiences for a Postmodern World*. New York: Routledge, 1995. Print.
Ball, Cheryl, and James Kalmbach. *RAW: Reading and Writing New Media*. Cresskill, NJ: Hampton Press, 2010. Print.
Beasley, Vanessa. "Between Touchstones and Touchscreens: What Counts as Contemporary Political Rhetoric." *The Sage Handbook of Rhetorical Studies*. Ed. Andrea A. Lunsford, Kirt Wilson, and Rosa Eberly. Thousand Oaks, CA: Sage P, 2009. 587–604. Print.
Bird, S. Elizabeth. *The Audience in Everyday Life: Living in a Media World*. New York: Routledge, 2003. Print.
Bok, Derek. *Our Underachieving Colleges*. Princeton: Princeton UP, 2006. Print.
boyd, danah. "Social Network Sites: Public, Private, or What?" *Knowledge Tree* 13. Australian Flexible Learning Network, May 2007. Web. 24 Aug. 2010.
———. "Viewing American Class Divisions through Facebook and MySpace." *Apophenia*. danah boyd Weblog, 24 June 2007. Web. 24 Aug. 2010.

Brooker, Will, and Deborah Jermyn, eds. *The Audience Studies Reader*. London: Routledge, 2003. Print.

Brooks, Kevin, and Aaron Anfinson. "Exploring Post-critical Composition MEmorials for Afghanistan and the Lost Boys of Sudan." *Computers and Composition* 26 (2009): 78–91. Print.

DeVoss, Danielle N., Gail E. Hawisher, Charles Jackson, Joseph Johansen, Brittney Moraski, and Cynthia L. Selfe. "The Future of Literacy." *Literate Lives in the Information Age: Narratives of Literacy from the United States*. Ed. Cynthia L. Selfe and Gail E. Hawisher. Mahwah, NJ: Lawrence Erlbaum, 2004. 183–210. Print.

Eberly, Rosa. *Citizen Critics: Literary Public Spheres*. Urbana: U of Illinois P, 2000. Print.

———. "From Writers, Audiences, and Communities to Publics: Writing Classrooms as Protopublic Spaces." *Rhetoric Review* 18 (1999): 165–78. Print.

Ede, Lisa, and Andrea Lunsford. "Audience Addressed/Audience Invoked: The Role of Audience in Composition Theory and Pedagogy." *College Composition and Communication* 35 (1984): 155–73. Print.

———. *Singular Texts/Plural Authors: Perspectives on Collaborative Writing*. Carbondale: Southern Illinois UP, 2000. Print.

Gee, James. *What Videogames Have to Teach Us about Learning and Literacy*. New York: Palgrave/Macmillan, 2004. Print.

Gitelman, Lisa, and Geoffrey B. Pingree, eds. *New Media: 1740–1915*. Cambridge: MIT P, 2003. Print.

Gurak, Laura, and Smiljana Antonijevic. "Digital Rhetoric and Public Discourse." *The Sage Handbook of Rhetorical Studies*. Ed. Andrea A. Lunsford, Kirt Wilson, and Rosa Eberly. Thousand Oaks, CA: Sage P, 2009. 497–508. Print.

Hammer, Jessica. "Agency and Authority in Role-Playing Texts." *A New Literacies Sampler*. Ed. Michele Knobel and Colin Lankshear. New York: Peter Lang, 2007. 67–94. Print.

Howard, Rebecca Moore. *Standing in the Shadow of Giants: Plagiarists, Authors, Collaborators*. Stamford, CT: Ablex, 1999. Print.

Jenkins, Henry. *Convergence Culture: Where Old and New Media Collide*. New York: New York UP, 2006. Print.

———. *Fans, Bloggers, and Gamers: Exploring Participatory Culture*. New York: New York UP, 2006. Print.

Johnson, Matthew S. S. "Public Writing in Gaming Spaces." *Computers and Composition* 25 (2008): 270–83. Print.

Johnson, Robert. "Audience Involved: Toward a Participatory Model of Writing." *Computers and Composition* 14 (1997): 361–76. Print.

Jones, Calvin. "Twitter Story Competition." *Digital Marketing Success*. 23 May 2008. Web. 5 June 2008.

Kirsch, Gesa, and Duane Roen, eds. *A Sense of Audience in Written Communication*. Newbury Park, CA: Sage, 1990. Print.

Kluth, Andreas. "Among the Audience: A Survey of New Media." *The Economist* 22 Apr. 2006: 4. Print.

Knobel, Michele, and Colin Lankshear, eds. *A New Literacies Sampler*. New York: Peter Lang, 2007. Print.

Kress, Gunther. *Literacy in the New Media Age*. New York: Routledge, 2003. Print.

Lanham, Richard A. *The Economics of Attention: Style and Substance in the Age of Information*. Chicago: U of Chicago P, 2006. Print.

Laningham, Scott. "Interview with Tim Berners-Lee." Host Scott Laningham. *developerWorks Interviews*. IBM, 22 Aug. 2006. Web. 5 June 2008.

Light, Richard J. *Making the Most of College*. Cambridge: Harvard UP, 2004. Print.

Lunsford, Andrea A., and Lisa Ede. "On Distinctions between Classical and Modern Rhetoric." *Essays on Classical Rhetoric and Modern Discourse*. Ed. Robert J. Connors, Lisa S. Ede, and Andrea A. Lunsford. Carbondale: Southern Illinois UP, 1984. 37–49. Print.

———. "Representing Audience: 'Successful' Discourse and Disciplinary Critique." *College Composition and Communication* 47 (1996): 167–79. Print.

McKee, Heidi, and James E. Porter. "The Ethics of Digital Writing Research: A Rhetorical Approach." *College Composition and Communication* 59 (June 2008): 711–49. Print.

McLuhan, Marshall. *The Medium Is the Massage*. New York: Bantam, 1967. Print.

McQuail, Denis. *Audience Analysis*. Thousand Oaks, CA: Sage P, 1997. Print.

Melber, Ari. "About Facebook." *The Nation* 7/14 Jan. 2008: 23. Print.

Nakamura, Lisa. *Digitizing Race: Visual Cultures of the Internet*. Minneapolis: U of Minnesota P, 2007. Print.

New London Group, The. "A Pedagogy of Multiliteracies: Designing Social Futures," in *Multiliteracies, Literacy Learning, and the Design of Social Futures.* Ed. Bill Cope and Mary Kalantzis. London: Routledge, 2000. 9–38. Print.

Nightingale, Virginia. *Studying Audiences: The Shock of the Real.* London: Routledge, 1996. Print.

Ong, Walter J. "The Writer's Audience Is Always a Fiction." *PMLA* 90 (1975): 9–21. Print.

Porter, James. *Audience and Rhetoric: An Archaeological Composition of the Discourse Community.* Upper Saddle River, NJ: Prentice Hall, 1992.

Radiohead. *In Rainbows.* Ato Records, 2008. Web and CD-ROM.

Ratcliffe, Krista. *Rhetorical Listening: Identification, Gender, Whiteness.* Carbondale: Southern Illinois UP, 2005. Print.

Reiff, Mary Jo. *Approaches to Audience: An Overview of the Major Perspectives.* Superior, WI: Parlay P, 2004. Print.

———. "Rereading 'Invoked' and 'Addressed' Readers through a Social Lens: Toward a Recognition of Multiple Audiences." *JAC* 16 (1996): 407–24. Print.

Rheingold, Howard. *Smart Mobs: The Next Social Revolution.* Cambridge: Basic Books, 2002.

———. "Vision of the Future." *Education.au Seminar.* Melbourne, Australia. 2 Oct. 2007. Web. 24 Aug. 2010.

Sawyer, Keith. *Group Genius: The Creative Power of Collaboration.* New York: Basic Books, 2007. Print.

Schilb, John. *Rhetorical Refusals: Defying Audiences' Expectations.* Carbondale: Southern Illinois UP, 2007. Print.

Selfe, Cynthia. "Aurality and Multimodal Composing." *College Composition and Communication* 60 (June 2009): 616–63. Print.

———. *Multimodal Composition: Resources for Teachers.* Cresskill, NJ: Hampton P, 2007. Print.

Selfe, Cynthia L., and Gail E. Hawisher, eds. *Literate Lives in the Information Age: Narratives of Literacy from the United States.* Mahwah: Lawrence Erlbaum, 2004. Print.

Selzer, Jack. "More Meanings of Audience." *A Rhetoric of Doing.* Ed. Stephen P. Witte and Neil Nakadate. Carbondale: Southern Illinois UP, 1992. 161–77. Print.

Shirky, Clay. *Here Comes Everybody: The Power of Organizing without Organizations.* New York: Penguin, 2008. Print.

Stanford Study of Writing. Andrea Lunsford. Stanford U, Sept. 2001–Sept. 2006. Web. 24 Aug. 2010.

Sunstein, Cass R. *Infotopia: How Many Minds Produce Knowledge.* Oxford: Oxford UP, 2006. Print.

Tapscott, Don, and Anthony D. Williams. *Wikinomics: How Mass Collaboration Changes Everything.* New York: Penguin, 2006. Print.

Taylor, Todd. "Design, Delivery, and Narcolepsy." *Delivering College Composition: The Fifth Canon.* Ed. Kathleen Blake Yancey. Portsmouth, NH: Boynton/Cook, 2006. 127–40. Print.

Thomas, Angela. "Blurring and Breaking through the Boundaries of Narrative, Literacy, and Identity in Adolescent Fan Fiction." *A New Literacies Sampler.* Ed. Michele Knobel and Colin Lankshear. New York: Peter Lang, 2007. 137–66. Print.

Ulmer, Gregory. *Electronic Monuments.* Minneapolis: U of Minnesota P, 2005. Print.

Warner, Michael. *Publics and Counterpublics.* New York: Zone Books, 2005. Print.

Weiser, Elizabeth M., Brian M. Fehler, and Angela M. González, eds. *Engaging Audience: Writing in an Age of New Literacies.* Urbana: NCTE, 2009. Print.

Wysocki, Anne, Johndan Johnson-Eilola, Cynthia Selfe, and Geoffrey Sirc. *Writing New Media: Theory and Applications for Expanding the Teaching of Composition.* Logan: Utah State UP, 2004. Print.

PART FOUR

*On Rhetorics
and Feminisms*

16 *On Distinctions between Classical and Modern Rhetoric*

The tentative emergence of a modern or a "new" rhetoric has been characterized by the attempt both to recover and reexamine the concepts of classical rhetoric and to define itself *against* that classical tradition. The works of Richard Weaver, Richard McKeon, Kenneth Burke, Donald Bryant and, later, Albert Duhamel, Chaim Perelman, and Edward Corbett helped draw attention to major tenets and values of the classical system. Daniel Fogarty's important *Roots for a New Rhetoric* (1959) stands at a metaphorical crossroads, affirming the continuing need for a viable rhetoric and sketching in the broad outlines of a "new" rhetoric that would meet that need:

> [The new rhetoric] will need to broaden its aim until it no longer confines itself to teaching the art of formal persuasion but includes formation in every kind of symbol-using . . . ; it will need to adjust itself to the recent studies in the psychology and sociology of communication; and, finally, it will need to make considerable provision for a new kind of speaker-listener situation.[1]

The years since 1959 have witnessed numerous attempts to define modern rhetoric more fully — attempts that consistently have rested on distinctions drawn between classical rhetoric and an emerging "new" system.[2] We believe that focusing primarily on distinctions between the "old" and the "new" rhetoric has led to unfortunate oversimplifications and distortions. Consequently, our purpose in this essay is to survey the distinctions typically drawn between classical and modern rhetoric, to suggest why these distinctions are inaccurate and, most importantly, to note the compelling similarities between classical and modern rhetoric. These similarities, we believe, can help clarify the features essential to any dynamic theory of rhetoric.

Although stated in widely varying terms, the distinctions persistently drawn between classical and modern or "new" rhetoric fall under four related

From Andrea A. Lunsford and Lisa Ede, in *Essays on Classical Rhetoric and Modern Discourse*, ed. Robert J. Connors, Lisa S. Ede, and Andrea A. Lunsford (Carbondale: Southern Illinois UP, 1984) 37–49.

heads. Images of man and of society provide one area frequently cited as distinguishing the two rhetorical periods. According to many definers of new rhetoric, the classical tradition, and especially Aristotle, defined man as a "rational animal" who dealt with problems of the world primarily through logic or reason and who lived during a time characterized by stable values, social cohesion, and a unified cultural ideal.[3] In contrast, modern rhetoric defines man as essentially a "rhetorical" or "symbol-using" or "communal" animal who constitutes the world through shared and private symbols.[4] And this modern man is said to live not in a simple, cohesive society but in an aleatoric universe in which generally agreed upon values and unifying norms are scarce or nonexistent.[5] In such a universe, it is argued, the bases of classical rhetoric are simply inadequate.

The second distinction often drawn between classical and contemporary rhetoric — that classical rhetoric emphasizes logical proofs while modern rhetoric stresses emotional (or psychological) proofs — is closely related to the first. Richard Young, Alton Becker, and Kenneth Pike argue, for example, that Aristotle's image of man as a rational animal had a direct influence on his rhetoric: "Underlying the classical tradition is the notion that although men are often swayed by passions, their basic and distinguishing characteristic is their ability to reason. . . . [Thus for classical rhetoricians] logical argument . . . was the heart of persuasive discourse."[6] According to Douglas Ehninger, this preference for logical proof is also evident in classical invention, which focuses on the analysis of subject matter at the expense of a concern for "the basic laws of human understanding." As a result, Ehninger notes, a successful classical orator has to be "an expert logician," while the modern speaker or writer needs, in contrast, to be "a keen student of practical psychology."[7]

A third often-cited distinction between the two periods concerns the rhetor-audience relationship, a relationship said to be characterized in the classical period by manipulative, antagonistic, one-way or unidirectional communication.[8] The new rhetoric is conversely said to posit not an antagonistic but a cooperative relationship between rhetor and audience, one based upon empathy, understanding, mutual trust, and two-way or "dialogic" communication.[9] In *Rhetoric: Discovery and Change*, for instance, Young, Becker, and Pike reject what they see as the classical model of "skillful verbal coercion" and introduce instead a "Rogerian rhetoric" of "enlightened cooperation."[10] In his 1967 and 1968 essays describing systems of rhetoric, Ehninger labels the new rhetoric "social" or "sociological" and argues that it is an "instrument for understanding."[11]

The final distinction often drawn between the two periods is inextricably related to the rhetor-audience relationship just described. This distinction results from identifying the goal of classical rhetoric as persuasion, while the goal of the new rhetoric is identified as communication. In his widely influential 1936 study, *The Philosophy of Rhetoric*, I. A. Richards articulates this view:

> Among the general themes of the old Rhetoric [which he associates with
> Aristotle] is one which is especially pertinent to our inquiry. The old

Rhetoric was an offspring of dispute; it developed as the rationale of pleadings and persuadings; it was the theory of the battle of words and has always been itself dominated by the combative impulse.[12]

Wilbur Samuel Howell, whose works on sixteenth-, seventeenth-, and eighteenth-century rhetoric have become standard texts, also identifies persuasion as the goal of classical rhetoric and specifically argues that the "new" eighteenth-century rhetoric explicitly embraced exposition and communication as goals.[13] Recent articles by Otis Walter, Richard Ohmann, Herbert Simons, Douglas Ehninger, Richard Young, and Paul Bator describe classical (and often specifically Aristotelian) rhetoric as emphasizing success or winning above all else, often depicting rhetors as attempting to coerce or impose their will on others.[14] In Ohmann's words, classical rhetoric is "concerned, fundamentally, with *persuasion*. The practical rhetorician — the orator — seeks to impel his audience from apathy to action or from old opinion to new, by appealing to will, emotion, and reason. And the novice . . . learns the tricks."[15] Most of these writers claim that the new rhetoric, on the other hand, stresses not coercive persuasion but communication, understanding, and reduction of threat through dialogue.

Table 16-1 summarizes the four distinctions which are persistently drawn between classical and modern rhetoric. Of the many points which could be made about these distinctions, one seems particularly crucial: they resolve to two contradictory claims about the nature of classical rhetoric. The first two distinctions, which view the classical image of man as a rational being and the logical proofs as supreme, discount classical rhetoric as too rationalistic.[16] The latter two, which present the rhetor-audience relationship in classical rhetoric as antagonistic and unidirectional and its goal as persuasion (in the narrowest, most limited sense), discount classical rhetoric as too dependent upon emotional manipulation and coercion.

TABLE 16-1   Major Distinctions Typically Drawn between Classical and Modern Rhetoric

Classical Rhetoric	*Modern Rhetoric*
1. Man is a rational animal living in a society marked by social cohesion and agreed-upon values.	1. Man is a symbol-using animal living in a fragmented society.
2. Emphasis is on logical (or rational) proofs.	2. Emphasis is on emotional (or psychological) proofs.
3. Rhetor-audience relationship is antagonistic, characterized by manipulative one-way communication.	3. Rhetor-audience relationship is cooperative, characterized by emphatic, two-way communication.
4. Goal is *persuasion*.	4. Goal is *communication*.

This disconcerting contradiction is perhaps the strongest evidence that the conventional understanding of classical rhetoric, as embodied in the above distinctions, is seriously flawed. The resulting confusion has led not only to major distortions and misrepresentations of classical rhetoric but to critical misunderstandings of our own potential system as well. Although we believe a strong argument can be made that these distinctions distort classical rhetoric in general, space restrictions do not permit us to make such a case here.[17] Instead, we have chosen to use Aristotle as the locus of our discussion because the Aristotelian theory is the most complete of all classical rhetorics and, more importantly, because many current misconceptions grow out of a limited reading of Aristotle's *Rhetoric*. In particular, we wish to argue that the distinctions we have outlined reflect two major problems: 1) a failure to relate Aristotle's *Rhetoric* to the rest of his philosophy; and 2) serious, persistent misunderstandings about the nature and function of the *pisteis* and of the *enthymeme* in Aristotelian rhetoric.

One of the most essential characteristics of Aristotle's philosophical system is its integration. It is no accident, for example, that Aristotle begins his work on rhetoric by carefully noting its relationship with dialectic. As William M. A. Grimaldi observes in his *Studies in the Philosophy of Aristotle's Rhetoric,* Aristotle in this work "insists from the outset upon showing the relation of his comments to his work on dialectic, epistemology, ethics, and even metaphysics. . . . Throughout the analysis his constant explicit and implicit reference to his own philosophical work clearly reveals that he was working with his own philosophical system in mind."[18]

A recent article by Christopher Lyle Johnstone on "An Aristotelian Trilogy: Ethics, Rhetoric, Politics, and the Search for Moral Truth," demonstrates how the failure to relate Aristotle's analysis of rhetoric to his discussion of ethics and politics has resulted in critical misinterpretations of Aristotle's intent.[19] As an example, Johnstone cites the often-quoted passage in the *Rhetoric* in which Aristotle emphasizes the necessity of "putting the judge in 'a certain' or 'the right' frame of mind," a statement often used as evidence that Aristotle advocates crass emotional manipulation (p. 9). What commentators have failed to recognize is that in the *Nichomachean Ethics* Aristotle consistently uses the same phrase to mean "the *morally* right condition, the state in which emotion is amenable to rational guidance" (p. 9). This emphasis on rational guidance should not, however, be interpreted as support for the view that Aristotle advocates an exclusively rational rhetoric since the end of rhetoric, as Aristotle clearly indicates, is *krisis* (judgment), "an activity of the practical intellect, and thus one directed by *logos* and *pathos* functioning in a complementary relationship. As a result 'the right frame of mind' can only be taken to refer to that emotional state that, when joined by reason in the process of judging or deciding, makes intelligent and responsible choice possible" (pp. 9–10).[20]

This example is symptomatic of the misunderstandings that can occur when commentators ignore the fundamental connections among Aristotle's writings. Lawrence Rosenfield makes a similar point in "Rhetorical Criticism and an Aristotelian Notion of Process," which explores the relationship between Aristotle's concept of process, or "the way in which an object acquires characteristics or properties," and his concept of animism.[21] Basic to Rosenfield's argument is his assertion that "the essential contribution of the concept of animism to Aristotle's notion of process is that of dynamic interaction between an agent and an object undergoing change" (p. 4). As a result, Rosenfield questions whether in Aristotelian rhetoric "the figure which best captures the communicator's role . . . is not that of a puppeteer, who manipulates his audience according to his skill at persuasion, but that of a mid-wife who focuses and directs energies inherent in the listener himself" (p. 8). In fact, Aristotle's metaphysics intrinsically rejects exploitive or "monologic" communication from speaker to listener (p. 15).

As even this brief discussion should suggest, investigations of the relationship between Aristotle's rhetorical and philosophical writings can help us locate alternatives to previous interpretations of the *Rhetoric* which have, simplistically, tended to characterize that work as exclusively committed either to rational or emotional appeals. In order fully to resolve the reductive dilemma posed by these contradictory interpretations, however, we must finally turn to the *Rhetoric* itself, particularly to the *pisteis* and the *enthymeme*. For much of the confusion surrounding the *Rhetoric* can be traced, finally, to an inadequate understanding of the nature of and interrelationships among Aristotle's methods of proof.

As Grimaldi observes, the traditional conception of the nature and role of the *pisteis* is that they are "three independent modes of rhetorical demonstration: non-logical (or quasi-logical) demonstration by the use of *ethos* and *pathos*, and logical demonstration by means of the *enthymeme*, the syllogism of rhetoric" (*Studies*, p. 65).[22] Such a view encourages the conflict between the role of reason and emotion in the *Rhetoric*, which has complicated interpretations of that work and led to the contradiction noted above. For if the *pisteis* are viewed as discrete, separable elements of discourse, then *logos* and its tool the *enthymeme* may be isolated and crowned supreme (as some commentators have done). Or *pathos* may hold sway instead, resulting in a view of rhetoric as overly emotional and manipulative. The solution to this dilemma must be to replace an oversimplified notion of the *pisteis* as elements that can be added to discourse — rather like ingredients in a recipe — with a more complex understanding of the inseparable strands that link people engaged in discourse.

In his *Studies in the Philosophy of Aristotle's Rhetoric* and *Aristotle, Rhetoric I: A Commentary*, Grimaldi articulates such an enriched, corrective perspective.[23] His complex argument cannot be fully described here, but particularly central to his discussion are: 1) his analyses of the multiple uses of the words *pistis* and *pisteis* in the original text[24] and of the pre-Aristotelian history of the word *enthymeme*; and 2) his discussion of the relationship of the *eide* and *koinoi topoi* to the *pisteis* (*logos*, *ethos*, and *pathos*) and of these *pisteis* to *enthymeme* and *paradeigma* (example). The resulting analysis represents a powerful alternative explication of the basic method of rhetorical discourse as outlined in the *Rhetoric*. In this method, the *enthymeme* is not a mere tool of *logos*, nor do the three *pisteis* of *logos*, *ethos*, and *pathos* function independently of one another. Rather, they interact in the *enthymeme* and *paradeigma*, the two central methods of rhetorical demonstration — the former deductive, the latter inductive. Thus Grimaldi clarifies our understanding of the *enthymeme*, broadening its generally accepted definition as the limited tool of *logos* to one of the two modes of inference through which rhetor and audience together move toward *krisis*.

Grimaldi's analysis thus dissolves the apparent contradiction between reason and emotion in the *Rhetoric* and demonstrates that the contradictory interpretations of classical rhetoric we described earlier represent a false dichotomy. Aristotle's *Rhetoric* is neither an abstract theoretical treatise in praise of *logos* nor a handbook of manipulative emotional tricks. Rather, through the *enthymeme*, which (along with *paradeigma*) integrates and organizes the *pisteis* of *logos*, *ethos*, and *pathos*, Aristotle develops a system of language use whereby individuals unite all their resources — intellect, will, and emotion — in communicating with one another. The *Rhetoric*, then, acknowledges that we are moved to *krisis* not just by knowledge but by emotion as well: "In rhetorical discourse the audience must be brought not only to knowledge of the subject but knowledge as relevant and significant for they are either indifferent, opposed, or in partial agreement. . . . If the whole person acts then it is the whole person to whom discourse in rhetoric must be directed" (*Studies* pp. 146–47).

An understanding of how Aristotle's *Rhetoric* relates to his entire philosophical system and of how the *enthymeme* and the *pisteis* function in the *Rhetoric* suggests that the characterization of classical rhetoric summarized in Table 16-1 is inadequate and misleading. The first distinction, which posits classical man as solely a rational being living in a stable society, seems particularly oversimplistic. As our discussion of the *enthymeme* indicates, the rational man of Aristotle's rhetoric is not a logic-chopping automaton but a language-using animal who unites reason and emotion in discourse with others. Aristotle (and indeed, Plato and Isocrates as well) studied the power of the mind to gain meaning from the world and to share that meaning with others.[25] And far from being a highly stable society marked by agreement on all values, Aristotle's Greece was one of upheaval: old beliefs in the gods were increasingly challenged, the political structure of the Greek city state system was under attack, and the educational system was embroiled in deep controversy.[26]

Equally inadequate is the second distinction, held by those who argue that classical rhetoric privileges logical proofs. As we have seen, such a view oversimplifies Aristotle's own complex analysis of the nature of reason, ignoring his careful discrimination of the speculative and practical intellect. In addition, this distinction misrepresents the nature and function of the *enthymeme* and the *pisteis*.

If *logos*, *ethos*, and *pathos* are dynamically related in the *enthymeme*, the third traditional distinction, which characterizes the rhetor-audience relationship in classical rhetoric as antagonistic and unidirectional, is equally unacceptable. Further support to this position is given by Lawrence Rosenfield's discussion of Aristotle's concept of process and by Lloyd Bitzer's analysis of the *enthymeme* in "Aristotle's Enthymeme Revisited," which argues that since "enthymemes occur only when speaker and audience jointly produce them . . . [they] intimately unite speaker and audience and provide the strongest possible proofs."[27] Far from being "one-way," "manipulative," or "monological," Aristotle's rhetoric provides a complete description of the dynamic interaction between rhetor and audience, an interaction mediated by language. Seen in the light of Aristotle's entire system of thought, the rhetorical elements of rhetor, audience, and subject matter are dynamic, interlocking forces.

Finally, if the relationship between the rhetor and the audience in Aristotle's system is indeed dynamic and interdependent, then the goal of Aristotelian rhetoric can hardly be persuasion in the narrow or pejorative sense in which it is used by those who equate persuasion with manipulation and coercion. We suggest that a much more accurate way to describe Aristotle's concept of the goal of rhetoric is as an interactive means of discovering meaning through language.[28] It is, as Richard Hughes notes in "The Contemporaneity of Classical Rhetoric," "a generative process," one in which the rhetor "is both investigator and communicator."[29] As Grimaldi observes, rhetoric was for Aristotle "the heart of the process by which man tried to interpret and make meaningful for himself and others the world of the real" (*Studies* p. 54). This process may be termed "persuasion," only in the broad sense that all language is inherently persuasive. In his discussion of the function of rhetoric, Kenneth Burke says that "there is no chance of our keeping apart the meanings of persuasion, identification ('consubstantiality') and communication." We have thus, Burke notes, "come to the point at which Aristotle begins his treatise on rhetoric."[30]

In spite of the large body of scholarship which should have kept us from drawing misleading distinctions, the view of classical rhetoric as manipulative, monologic, and rationalistic persists. We believe that we, therefore, must also come back to Aristotle, to a richer understanding of how his theory can enrich and illuminate our own. Indeed, major distinctions between Aristotelian and contemporary rhetoric do exist, but these distinctions are more fundamental than those traditionally cited. While we shall note these distinctions, we wish to stress what we believe are compelling similarities between the two rhetorics, similarities which draw contemporary rhetoric closer to the classical system rather than further away from it. Our understanding of these similarities and of the profound distinctions which must accompany them, as outlined in Table 16-2, will help us identify those qualities which must characterize any vital theory of rhetoric.

One similarity between classical and modern rhetoric is their shared *concept of man as a language-using animal who unites reason and emotion in discourse with another*. Central to this concept is the role of language in the creation of knowledge or belief and its relationship to the knowing mind. We have already demonstrated the ways in which Aristotle's *Rhetoric* unites reason and emotion. In addition, Aristotle's works on logic, ethics, and epistemology as well as the *Rhetoric* demonstrate that Aristotle recognized the powerful

TABLE 16-2   Similarities and Qualifying Distinctions between Classical and
Modern Rhetoric

---

1. Both classical and modern rhetoric view man as a language-using animal
who unites reason and emotion in discourse with another.

Qualifying distinction:

Aristotle addresses himself primarily to the oral use of language; ours is
primarily an age of print.

---

2. In both periods rhetoric provides a dynamic methodology whereby rhetor
and audience may jointly have access to knowledge.

Qualifying distinction:

According to Aristotle, rhetor and audience come into a state of knowing
which places them in a clearly defined relationship with the world and with
each other, mediated by their language. The prevailing modernist world
view compels rhetoric to operate without any such clearly articulated theory
of the knower and the known.

---

3. In both periods rhetoric has the potential to clarify and inform activities in
numerous related fields.

Qualifying distinction:

Aristotle's theory establishes rhetoric as an art and relates it clearly to all
fields of knowledge. Despite the efforts of modern rhetoricians, we lack
any systematic, generally accepted theory to inform current practice.

---

dynamism of the creating human mind. These works further indicate that
Aristotle was aware of man's ability to use symbols and that he viewed language as the medium through which judgments about the world are commu-
nicated.

Modern theories, of course, also posit language as the ground of rhetoric.
This view is articulated in Burke's famous statement that rhetoric "is rooted in
an essential function of language itself, a function that is wholly realistic, and
is continually born anew; the use of language as a symbolic means of inducing cooperation in beings that by nature respond to symbols."[31] Theorists as
dissimilar as I. A. Richards, Chaim Perelman, and Wayne Booth hold parallel
views on the relation between language and rhetoric.

As expected in rhetorics removed by twenty-three hundred years, however, Aristotle's system of language use differs from ours. The resultant distinction between the two periods is potentially profound: Aristotle addressed
himself primarily to oral discourse; modern rhetorics have addressed themselves primarily to written discourse. Our understanding of the historical and
methodological ramifications of the speaking/writing distinction has been
hampered by the twentieth-century split among speech, linguistics, philosophy, and English departments. Despite the work of scholars such as Walter
Ong, Kenneth Burke, and Jacques Derrida, many questions about the relationship of speech and writing remain unanswered and, in some cases,
unexplored.[32]

The second major similarity we find between Aristotelian and modern rhetoric is the view of rhetoric as a *techne or dynamic methodology through which rhetor and audience, a self and an other, may jointly have access to knowledge.*[33] We have already examined Aristotle's concept of the *enthymeme* and the ways in which it united speaker and audience, *logos, ethos,* and *pathos,* in the pursuit of knowledge leading to action. In modern theory, particularly the work of Kenneth Burke, rhetoric provides the means through which we may both achieve identification with another and understand that identification through the attribution of motives. Similarly, Chaim Perelman's rhetorical system posits rhetoric as the process through which rhetor and audience gain access to knowledge.

We believe that such a view of rhetoric as creative or epistemic must characterize any viable, dynamic rhetoric and, indeed, any other view reduces the role of rhetoric to a "naming of parts" or to stylistic embellishment, reductions characteristic of many rhetorical theories. But this basic similarity should not mask an equally important distinction between classical and modern rhetoric. As we have seen, this distinction concerns not the notion of man, the nature of proof, the speaker-audience relationship, nor the goal of rhetoric. Instead, this distinction concerns the nature and status of knowledge.[34]

In Aristotle's system, knowledge may be either of the necessary or the contingent. Knowledge of the necessary or universal, *episteme,* operates in the realm of the theoretical or scientific. Breaking with Plato, Aristotle admits of another kind of knowledge, that of the contingent. Such knowledge, *doxa,* is the way of knowing contingent reality (that is, the world around us that is both characterized and limited by change). Rhetoric's realm is limited to the contingent, and the connections among language, thought, and that reality are grounded in an epistemology which posits reality independent of the knower. In short, rhetoric uses thought and language to lead to judgment (*krisis*) as the basis of action in matters of this world. And for Aristotle, that world of contingent reality, though itself in a state of flux, could be understood by systematic application of the intellect because that reality was itself thought to be informed by stable first principles.

Modern rhetorical theory rests on no such fully confident epistemology, nor does knowledge enjoy such a clearly defined status. In fact, we are in radical disagreement over what "knowledge" may be, though we generally agree on man's ability to communicate that disagreement. Hence, for the modern period, connections among thought, language, and reality are thought to be grounded not in an independent, chartable reality but in the nature of the knower instead, and reality is not so much discovered or discoverable as it is constituted by the interplay of thought and language. Though we lack a fully articulated theory, Kenneth Burke, Richard Weaver, and Wayne Booth offer intensive investigations into the rhetoric of this interplay; and works in disciplines as diverse as anthropology, language philosophy, literary criticism, philosophy, psychology, and the physical sciences suggest that, as Michael Polanyi says in the opening of *Personal Knowledge,* "We must inevitably see the universe from a centre lying within ourselves and speak about it in terms of a human language shaped by the exigencies of human intercourse. Any attempt rigorously to eliminate our human perspective from our pictures of the world must lead to absurdity."[35]

Rhetoric's grounding in language and its potential ability to join rhetor and audience in the discovery of shared (communicable) knowledge suggests a third compelling similarity between classical and modern rhetoric: *in both periods rhetoric has the potential to clarify and inform activities in numerous related fields*. By establishing rhetoric as the *antistrophos* or corollary of dialectic,[36] Aristotle immediately places rhetoric in relation to other fields of knowledge, and these relationships are painstakingly worked out in the *Organon*. Rhetoric, poetics, and ethics all involve *doxa*, knowledge of contingent, shifting reality. Hence, rhetoric is necessarily useful in addressing complex human problems in any field where certainty is unachievable.

In addition, Aristotle's *Rhetoric* provided a theory that was intimately related to practice. For the Greeks, and indeed for the Romans who followed them, rhetoric was a practical art of discourse which played a central role in education and in the daily affairs of citizens. Aristotle's work established a theoretical relationship among belief, language, and action; Cicero and Quintilian adapted and acted out that theory, Quintilian using it as a basis for a rhetoric which would serve as a way of knowing and a guide to action throughout a person's life.

From the time of Quintilian, the history of rhetoric has been haunted by a whittling away of domain, a compartmentalization of its offices, and a frequent dramatic separation of theory and practice. The most obvious instance of rhetoric's diminution is Ramus' assignment of *inventio* and *dispositio* to logic, thus leaving rhetoric with a concern only for style. Even George Campbell and Alexander Bain, both of whom attempted to ground rhetoric in a full psychology, did not fully admit invention into the province of rhetoric. Not until philosophers began to recapture the crucial conception of language as a meaning-making activity, an essential element in the social construction of reality, has rhetoric had the opportunity to regain some of its lost status and scope, to inform both education and ordinary behavior and thus clarify a number of related fields.

Why, thus far at least, has this opportunity not been realized? A partial answer to this question must lie in what we see as a final qualifying distinction between classical and modern rhetorics. Aristotle's theory is revolutionary in that it establishes rhetoric as an art and relates it clearly to all fields of knowledge. Despite the efforts of modern rhetoricians, we lack any such systematic theory to inform current practice. In fact, our age has witnessed a curious divorce between rhetorical theory and practice and an extreme fragmentation of our discipline. Earlier in this essay, we alluded to the large body of rhetorical "theory" which argues that modern rhetoric is characterized by understanding, mutual sharing, and two-way communication. Yet how well does such theory account for or describe twentieth-century rhetorical practice, which has surely reached new heights (or depths) of manipulative use of language?

The position of rhetorical theory and practice in education is equally fragmented. While theorists in speech departments consider the theoretical concept of "dialogic communication," their counterparts in English departments struggle over abstruse questions of intentionality in literary texts, and scholars in linguistics departments strive to describe the abstract grammar of a sentence. Meanwhile, instruction in rhetorical practice — speaking, writing, and reading — is usually relegated to graduate students and part-time instructors and looked upon as menial "service." As a result, most of our textbooks offer compendia of "how-to" tips but fail to ground that advice in a theoretical framework that would relate language, action, and belief.[37]

Such a situation is a far cry from Aristotle's elegant theory, from Cicero's powerful statesmanship, or from Quintilian's masterful pedagogy. But if our failure to articulate a systematic theory which informs current practice is great, our need is even greater. We believe that the work of such theorists as Kenneth Burke, Chaim Perelman, Wolfgang Iser, Richard Weaver, and Wayne Booth offers a modern ground for the reunion of rhetorical theory and practice. But such a reunion demands that we attempt to reinstate rhetoric at or near the center of our curriculum, as the art of using language in the creation — and sharing — of knowledge and belief.

One way to begin this task is by eschewing the false distinctions that have been drawn persistently between classical and modern rhetoric and by building instead on their powerful similarities. If we see Aristotle's *Rhetoric* as a work which unites rhetor and audience, language and action, theory and practice, then we have a model for our own *antistrophos*. If rhetoric is to reach its full potential in the twentieth century as an informing framework for long-divorced disciplines and for instruction and conduct in reading, writing, and speaking, then we must define ourselves not in opposition to but in consonance with the classical model.

NOTES

1. Daniel Fogarty, S.J., *Roots for a New Rhetoric* (New York: Russell and Russell, 1959), p. 130.
2. We are thinking particularly of Otis M. Walter, "On Views of Rhetoric, Whether Conservative or Progressive," *Quarterly Journal of Speech*, 49 (Dec. 1963), 367–82; rpt. in *Contemporary Theories of Rhetoric*, ed. Richard Johannesen (New York: Harper and Row, 1971), pp. 18–38; Richard Ohmann, "In Lieu of a New Rhetoric," *College English*, 26 (Oct. 1964), 17–22; rpt. in Johannesen, pp. 63–71; Wayne E. Brockriede, "Toward a Contemporary Aristotelian Theory of Rhetoric," *Quarterly Journal of Speech*, 52 (Feb. 1966), 33–40; rpt. in Johannesen, pp. 39–49; Herbert W. Simons, "Toward a New Rhetoric," *Pennsylvania Speech Annual*, 24 (Sept. 1967), 7–20; rpt: in Johannesen, pp. 50–62; Douglas Ehninger, "On Rhetoric and Rhetorics," *Western Speech*, 31 (1967), 242–49, and "On Systems of Rhetoric," *Philosophy and Rhetoric*, 1 (Summer 1968), 131–44; rpt. in *Contemporary Rhetoric*, ed. Douglas Ehninger (Glenview, Ill.: Scott, Foresman and Co., 1972), pp. 49–58; Howard Martin and Kenneth Andersen, *Speech Communication: Analyses and Readings* (Boston: Allyn and Bacon, 1968); Richard Young, Alton Becker, and Kenneth Pike, *Rhetoric: Discovery and Change* (New York: Harcourt, Brace, and World, 1970); S. Michael Halloran, "On the End of Rhetoric, Classical and Modern," *College English*, 36 (Feb. 1975), 621–31, and "Tradition and Theory in Rhetoric," *Quarterly Journal of Speech*, 62 (Oct. 1976), 234–41; Robert L. Scott, "A Synoptic View of Systems of Western Rhetoric," *Quarterly Journal of Speech*, 61 (Dec. 1975), 439–47, and its companion piece of the same title by Douglas Ehninger, 448–53; Richard Young, "Paradigms and Problems: Needed Research in Rhetorical Invention," in *Research on Composing*, ed. Charles Cooper and Lee Odell (Urbana, Ill.: NCTE, 1978), pp. 28–48; Frank Zappen, "Carl R. Rogers and Political Rhetoric," *Pre-Text*, 1 (Spring–

Fall 1980), 95–113; and Paul Bator, "Aristotelian and Rogerian Rhetoric," *College Composition and Communication*, 31 (Dec. 1980), 427–32.

3. See, for example, Ehninger, "A Synoptic View of Systems of Western Rhetoric," p. 452; Young, Becker, and Pike, *Rhetoric: Discovery and Change*, p. 6; Halloran, "Tradition and Theory in Rhetoric," 236; and Zappen, "Carl R. Rogers and Political Rhetoric," 98.

4. These definitions stem primarily from Kenneth Burke's profound efforts to articulate a contemporary rhetoric, though Burke in no way upholds or sets forth the problematic distinctions we have previously detailed. For a discussion of man as communal, see Young, Becker, and Pike's *Rhetoric: Discovery and Change*, pp. 7–9, and the articles on dialogic communication listed in note 9.

5. Halloran, "On the End of Rhetoric, Classical and Modern," 624.

6. *Rhetoric: Discovery and Change*, p. 6. This notion is reiterated by Paul Bator in "Aristotelian and Rogerian Rhetoric."

7. Douglas Ehninger, "George Campbell and the Revolution in Inventional Theory," *Southern Speech Journal*, 15 (May 1950), 274.

8. See, for example, Robert L. Scott, "Dialogue and Rhetoric," in Rhetoric and Communication, ed. J. Blankenship and H. G. Stelzner (Urbana: Univ. of Illinois Press, 1976), p. 101; David B. Strother, "Communication and Human Response: A Heuristic View," also in the Blankenship and Stelzner volume; and Paul Bator, "Aristotelian and Rogerian Rhetoric," previously cited in note 2. *Rhetoric: Discovery and Change* also perpetuates this view.

9. Richard L. Johannesen, "The Emerging Concept of Communication as Dialogue," *Quarterly Journal of Speech*, 57 (1971), 373–82; John Stewart, "Foundations of Dialogic Communication," *Quarterly Journal of Speech*, 64 (1978), 183–201; John Poulakos, "The Components of Dialogue," *Western Speech*, 38 (1974), 199–212; Floyd Matson and Ashley Montagu, eds., *The Human Dialogue* (New York: Macmillan, Free Press, 1967); Frank Keller and Charles Brown, "An Interpersonal Ethic for Communication," *Journal of Communication*, 16 (1968), 73–81.

10. *Rhetoric: Discovery and Change*, pp. 8–9.

11. Ehninger, "On Systems of Rhetoric," in *Contemporary Rhetoric*, p. 53.

12. I. A. Richards, *The Philosophy of Rhetoric* (New York: Oxford Univ. Press, 1936), p. 24.

13. Wilbur Samuel Howell, *Eighteenth-Century British Logic and Rhetoric* (Princeton, N.J.: Princeton Univ. Press, 1971), pp. 441–42.

14. See note 2 for full citations.

15. Ohmann, "In Lieu of a New Rhetoric," rpt. in *Contemporary Theories of Rhetoric*, p. 64.

16. They do so often in reference to Aristotle's condemnation, early in Book I, of *pathos* in the hands of the technographers. Yet Aristotle by no means denies that *pathos* is part of the rhetorical art. He is rather questioning the misuse of *pathos* by these technographers. See William Grimaldi, *Aristotle, Rhetoric I: A Commentary* (Bronx, N.Y: Fordham Univ. Press, 1980), p. 7.

17. As we were completing this essay, we were fortunate to receive a copy of an article by Floyd D. Anderson, "The Classical Conception of Communication as Dialogue." Professor Anderson makes a very persuasive argument in his essay for all of classical rhetoric as sharing what we argue is an Aristotelian view of communication. We are indebted to Professor Anderson for sharing his insights with us.

18. William M. A. Grimaldi, *Studies in the Philosophy of Aristotle's Rhetoric* (Wiesbaden: Frans Steiner Verlag, 1972), p. 18. Subsequent references will be cited in the text as *Studies*.

19. Christopher Lyle Johnstone, "An Aristotelian Trilogy: Ethics, Rhetoric, Politics, and the Search for Moral Truth," *Philosophy and Rhetoric*, 13 (Winter 1980), 1–24. Subsequent references will be cited in the text.

20. The failure to read the *Rhetoric* in light of Aristotle's other works is further exacerbated by difficulties in translation. In "The Greekless Reader and Aristotle's *Rhetoric*," Thomas M. Conley demonstrates that Lane Cooper's popular translation is seriously flawed in a number of places. In particular, Conley argues that where Aristotle discusses the importance of getting the "judge into the right frame of mind," the Greek does not "express the one-way view of persuasion" usually inferred. *Quarterly Journal of Speech*, 65 (1979), 75.

21. Lawrence W. Rosenfield, "Rhetorical Criticism and an Aristotelian Notion of Process," *Quarterly Journal of Speech*, 33 (Mar. 1966), 1–16. Subsequent references will be cited in the text.

22. Douglas Ehninger notes, for example, in his discussion of "Campbell, Blair, and Whately Revisited," *Southern Speech Journal*, 28 (Spring 1963), 169–82, that in classical rhetorical theory the *pisteis* "were viewed as autonomous. Each was considered as complete in itself, and as entirely capable of effecting conviction without the aid of the others" (172).

23. Grimaldi, *Aristotle, Rhetoric I: A Commentary*. Subsequent references will be cited in the text and notes as *Commentary*.

24. The heart of Grimaldi's analysis reveals that the Greek word for *pisteis* is used by Aristotle to indicate both *logos, pathos,* and *ethos* (the *entechnic pisteis*) and *enthymeme* and *paradeigma* (the *apodeictic pisteis*). See especially the Appendix, "The Role of the *Pisteis* in Aristotle's Methodology," *Commentary,* pp. 349–56.

25. See Aristotle, *The "Art" of Rhetoric,* trans. John Henry Freese (Cambridge: Harvard Univ. Press, Loeb Classical Library, 1926), 1355a 27–28, 1395b 31–1396a 4, 1402a 33–34.

26. We are indebted to Michael Halloran for pointing out that the oratory of fourth-century B.C., Athens reveals much about contemporary cultural turmoil.

27. Lloyd Bitzer, "Aristotle's Enthymeme Revisited," *Quarterly Journal of Speech,* 45 (Dec. 1959), 408.

28. Grimaldi makes essentially the same point: "As soon as it is understood that rhetoric for Aristotle is an activity which engages the whole person in an effort to communicate meaning by way of language a major obstacle toward understanding the *Rhetoric* is removed" (*Studies,* p. 53).

29. Richard Hughes, "The Contemporaneity of Classical Rhetoric," *College Composition and Communication,* 16 (1965), 158–59.

30. Kenneth Burke, *A Rhetoric of Motives* (1950; rpt. Berkeley: Univ. of California Press, 1969), p. 46.

31. Ibid., p. 43.

32. In "Rhetoric in the American College Curriculum: The Decline of Public Discourse" *Pre/Text,* 3 (1982), 245–69, Michael Halloran traces the move from oral discourse to written discourse in American colleges and draws a number of provocative and insightful conclusions about the results of that move.

33. Grimaldi provides an illuminating discussion of the relationship of *techne* to *dynamis* in *Commentary,* pp. 5–6.

34. Among the articles we have read which draw distinctions between classical and modern rhetoric, Michael Halloran's works cited in note 2 deal substantively with this epistemological difference.

35. Michael Polanyi, *Personal Knowledge: Towards a Post-Critical Philosophy* (Chicago: Univ. of Chicago Press, 1962), p. 3.

36. Otis Walter has recently argued that the opening sentence of the *Rhetoric* be interpreted as "Rhetoric must follow the lead of an informed, searching and brilliant intellect," and that this sentence is the most significant in the *Rhetoric* because it "carries Aristotle's revolutionary intent, because it suggests his concern for knowing, [and] because it contains the ethical case for knowledge." Such an interpretation fits well with, and indeed supports, our view of Aristotle's concept of rhetoric and its relationship to knowledge and human action. See "The Most Important Sentence in Aristotle's *Rhetoric,*" *Rhetoric Society Quarterly,* 12 (1982), 18–20.

37. In "An Adequate Epistemology for Composition: Classical and Modern Perspectives," [. . .], John Gage presents a persuasive discussion of how the concept of the enthymeme has been reduced to sterile formulae in modern texts, and he goes on to show how a fuller understanding of Aristotle's enthymeme can provide the kind of theoretical framework we are calling for here.

17 Rhetoric in a New Key: Women and Collaboration

Stories, Carolyn Heilbrun has recently reminded us in *Writing a Woman's Life*, are powerful. They enable us to explore, try out, and sometimes to embody new ways of seeing, doing, and being. Far from recounting mere anecdotal evidence, stories tell us what is imaginable, possible, or — in Clifford Geertz's terms commonsensical — in our culture. In this brief essay, we wish to tell a number of stories about a phenomenon that we have come to call collaborative writing. These stories point, we think, to the possibility of a new rhetoric, a rhetoric in a new key that rejects what Toril Moi has called "the model of the author as God the Father of the Text" (62) for a dialogic or polyphonal model of communication. These stories only *point* to this new rhetoric, however. Rather than telling a single narrative, these stories as a group function in a Burkean perspective-by-incongruity fashion to point to a site of struggle, a site we see also as one of opportunity.

Any story we tell, of course, is necessarily a version of our own story, and that story, as it relates to our work on collaborative writing, is a long and in some ways unsettling one to us. Our interest in collaboration grew directly out of our personal experience as long-time friends and coauthors, piqued by our surprised realization that coauthorship was not valued in our own departments of English. At the time, we did not associate this devaluation of a mode which seemed important and productive to us with the phallogocentric nature of the academy; we were merely irritated. And so we set out, rather naively, to "prove" how unreasonable this devaluation was. We would simply collect enough empirical "information" to demonstrate that collaborative writing is a feature of much contemporary discourse — and, voilà, the importance and efficacy of collaborative writing would be "obvious." In fact, we went on to gather such data, the story of which we have published in two earlier *Rhetoric Review* essays.

In the six years since we began what we originally thought of as a fairly straightforward data gathering project, we have come to situate the issue of

From Andrea A. Lunsford and Lisa Ede, in *Rhetoric Review* 8.2 (1990): 234–41.

collaborative writing in a much broader historical, political, and ideological context and to contemplate the ways in which our society locates power, authority, authenticity, and property in an autonomous, masculine self. It was not hard to find provocative discussions of this phenomenon all around us — in literary and feminist theory, of course, but also in fields as diverse as anthropology, psychology, and library science. But while the "author" as construct was revealed, challenged, declared dead, and so on, people continued authoring — most often as solitary writers who signed single names to their texts.

Our interest in collaboration at this point took on the typical characteristics of a binary opposition: Against the solitary, sovereign author-ity of the single writer, we would investigate the multivoiced power of collaborative writers. And so as we began our study of collaborative writers in seven major professions, we expected (or, more accurately, hoped) to find that collaboration offered a mode that would serve a postmodern conception of writing.

What we found, however, was not A mode of collaborative writing but a number of modes, each deeply embedded in specific political, social, and ideological contexts. From this variety of modes, we eventually identified two that are particularly interesting to us as women and as collaborative writers. These modes we have come to call the hierarchical mode and the dialogic mode. In our research the hierarchical mode of collaborative writing emerged early on; it is a widespread means of producing texts in all the professions we studied. This form of collaboration is linearally structured, driven by highly specific goals, and carried out by people who play clearly assigned roles.

These goals are most often designated by someone outside of and hierarchically superior to the immediate collaborative group or by a senior member or "leader" of the group. Because productivity and efficiency are of the essence in this mode of collaboration, the realities of multiple voices and shifting authority are seen as problems to be overcome or resolved. Knowledge in this mode is most often viewed as information to be found or a problem to be solved. The activity of finding this information or solving this problem is closely tied to the realization of a particular end product. This mode of collaborative writing is, we would argue, typically conservative. It is also, need we say, a predominantly masculine mode of discourse.

Along the highways and byways of our research and reading roads, however, we began to catch glimpses, perceive traces, of another mode of collaboration, one we came to call dialogic. This mode is not as widespread in the professions we studied as the hierarchical mode and, in fact, its practitioners had difficulty describing it, finding language within which to inscribe their felt realities. This dialogic mode is loosely structured, and the roles enacted within it are fluid; one "person" may occupy multiple and shifting roles as the project progresses. In this mode the process of articulating and working together to achieve goals is as important as the goals themselves. Those who participate in dialogic collaboration generally value the creative tension inherent in multivoiced and multivalent ventures. What those involved in hierarchical collaboration see as a problem to be solved, these individuals view as a strength to be capitalized on and emphasized. In dialogic collaboration this group effort is seen as essential to the production — rather than merely the recovery — of knowledge and as a means of individual satisfaction within the group. This mode of collaboration, we argue, is, potentially at least, deeply subversive. And because our respondents had no ready language with which to describe such an enterprise, because many of those who tried to describe it to us were women, and because this mode of collaboration seemed so much the "other" — we think of this mode as predominantly feminine.

At present, our thinking about the nature and implications of hierarchical and dialogic collaboration is tentative and preliminary. We have found this way of viewing collaborative writing provocative and clarifying, yet we are aware that there are not only questions we have not answered but questions we have not even thought to ask. And we know that we need to "converse" or collaborate with many others — French and Anglo-American feminists, educational and political analysts, critical theorists, as well as (we would want to emphasize) those who collaborate regularly on the job or in their research or creative writing — before we can present a full, complex picture of these modes of collaboration.

For now, however, we want to tell our story but, as Emily Dickinson does, "tell it slant," by pointing up a persistent but not very surprising irony revealed in our research: The two professional fields in our study most populated by women — the Society for Technical Communication, of which 62 percent are women, and the Modern Language Association, of which 46 percent are women — are generally not enacting the dialogic mode of collaboration. Let us look briefly at what our study revealed about collaborative writing among members of these two professional groups.

The Society for Technical Communication members who responded to our call for information described a collaborative process that is very often hierarchical. Typically, a document begins with the technical writer, who produces it after consultation with various information sources within the organization. The document then travels in a rigidly linear way, through level upon level of bureaucratic authority. We have many stories we could tell to illustrate what is a fairly standard mode of collaboration experienced by technical writers. One such story emerged as we were testing one of our survey instruments with technical writers at the Environmental Protection Agency. The writers, who work in a strongly bureaucratized and thus deeply hierarchical context, indicated in their responses that they experienced dissatisfaction with collaborative writing in proportion to their sense of loss of control over the documents they were charged with initiating and "authoring."

A similar story emerged in an ethnographic study of a collaboratively produced document in a very large insurance firm undertaken by one of our graduate students (Cross, 1988). This document, a report to stockholders originally written by a technical writer, went through the same kind of upward series of steps, being altered and criticized at every step. At the end of this process, the report was so unsatisfactory to the chief officer who was to sign it that the whole project was scrapped — at great cost of time and money. In this instance the hierarchical mode turned out to be not only unsatisfactory to the technical writer and to the senior officer but inefficient and unproductive as well. Most often, though, our data indicate that collaborative writing in the hierarchical mode is perceived as efficient and productive if sometimes unsatisfying — and that it is embraced by technical writers as essentially unproblematic and as "the way things are."

The Modern Language Association, 46 percent of whom are women, did not in their responses to us embrace ANY concept or mode of collaboration but rather seemed suspicious of work that was produced in concert with others, saying that almost all their writing was done alone, the sole exception being writing they did to secure grants. Of course, we hardly need demonstrate that the humanities in general and English in particular valorize and reward single authorship and disregard collaboratively produced texts. Even those few scholars in our field who do write collaboratively fail to connect their own collaborative practices with larger theoretical, political, or pedagogical issues. But if we need to remind ourselves of the power of this particular authorial construct and its power in our own sphere, we can offer numerous exempla:

> A prestigious English department decided to withdraw its undergraduate poetry prize when the anonymous "author" of the winning poem turned out to be three undergraduate collaborators.

> Two women who petitioned and were granted permission to conduct collaborative research on a dissertation project were later told they would have to produce two separate and "different" dissertations.

> At a large research institution, a woman who often writes collaboratively was tenured and promoted to associate professor — but warned that her promotion to full professor would be contingent on producing single-authored books and articles.

> A well-known feminist scholar, whose work is collaboratively written, stated that she can draw no compelling pedagogical implications from her practice. The classroom structure of teacher-lecturer giving information to student-listeners seems perfectly efficient and reasonable to her.

> Those who work on collaborative projects "cannot apply for grants from the NEH under the fellowship program available for single authors," but must instead apply only under "Research Programs" and hence compete with universities and other large institutions. (See, for example, Smith, 1987.)

We could go on with such stories of our own profession's antipathy toward collaboration in spite of the challenges posed by poststructuralist and feminist critiques. But you know these stories — and many other ones as well — yourselves.

Given that the dialogic mode of collaborative writing can be discerned or glimpsed at work in certain places, the major issue for us then becomes to what extent such a mode represents the possibility of subverting traditional phallogocentric, subject-centered discourse — for a rhetoric, if you will, in a new key. As we have studied this question, we have found responses in some likely — and other unlikely — places. Particularly important to realizing what we call a dialogic model of collaborative writing is work in women's studies. We are thinking here particularly of books such as Carol Gilligan's *In A Different Voice* and Belenky, Clinchy, Goldberger, and Tarule's *Women's Ways of Knowing* — works that challenge and subvert conventional Western conceptions of the self. We could also point to work women are doing in sociology, especially that of Laurel Richardson, on the nature of teaching styles and the relations of those styles to traditionally masculine and univocal concepts of self. Psychologists such as M. Brinton Lykes are also helping to articulate a view of the self as ensembled or social, rather than autonomous and independent.

In practice we see the dialogic mode of collaboration enacted in interesting and subtle ways. We hear echoes of this mode, for instance, in a series of prefaces and acknowledgements to recent books. Read together, these strongly personal statements stand as a powerful challenge to and indictment of the concept of a single-authored, authoritative, univocal text. Let us cite here only a few of the many we have collected, almost all of which, by the way, are by women:

> From Dale Spender's *Man Made Language* (xv–xvi) — "there is an assumption I wish to challenge: it is that people sit in garrets and write books on their own. I sat in the Women's Resources Center at the University of Utah in Salt Lake City, and I was *not* on my own. . . . While this book may represent a 'sum total,' its many parts have been shaped . . . by many different people. . . . Not in isolation in a garret did this book come into existence, but in the co-operative and dynamic context of women's struggle. . . .''

> From Belenky, Clinchy, Goldberger, and Tarule's *Women's Ways of Knowing* (ix) — "As we steeped ourselves in the women's recorded and transcribed words we found ourselves drawing ever closer to their frames of mind. We emerged from this long process with an extraordinary sense of intimacy and collaboration with all the women. . . . So, too, during our work together, the four of us developed . . . an intimacy and collaboration which we have come to prize. We believe that the collaborative, egalitarian spirit so often shared by women should be more carefully nurtured in the work lives of *all* men and women. *We* hope to find it in all our future work."

> From Shirley Brice Heath's *Ways with Words* (ix) — "Those to whom the greatest acknowledgement of gratitude is due for help writing this book are the community members of Roadville and Trackton, and the school, mill, and business personnel of the Piedmont Carolinas with whom I lived and worked for nearly a decade."

> From Bellah, Madsen, Sullivan, Swidler, and Tipton's *Habits of the Heart* (xi) — "The people who let us into their homes and talked to us so freely during the course of our study are very much part of the authorship of this book."

And from Karen Burke LeFevre's *Invention as a Social Act* (xiii) — "In the chapters . . . that follow . . . I attempt to identify those points at which the voices of others — those necessary others whose words I have read, and those with whom I have spoken and thought and worked — are particularly evident."

These and other statements are provocative — and, to us at least, moving. But it's important to note that these assertions about the importance of collaboration are marginalized by appearing in prefaces or acknowledgements, rather than in the bodies of texts. Though many writers are convinced of the crucial importance and benefits of collaboration, then, they generally have not yet found ways to incorporate these concerns in the body of their texts, which as a rule do not challenge the conventions of single-authored documents.

Other scholars are helping us reenvision authorship along the lines of what we are calling a dialogic collaborative mode, one that radically subverts the status quo. We think particularly here of LeFevre's studies (1988) of Frances Steloff, of the famed New York Gotham Book Mart, studies which have done much to illuminate a scene of writing and publishing in which Steloff's voice is a crucial and integral part not of a series of monologic individual productions but of a creative polylogue. LeFevre's work helps us to see "authorship" in this case as grounded not in individual writers (such as Hart Crane and e e cummings, to name two who were members of this circle) but in dialogic and relational acts. Still others show us that the dialogic mode of collaboration we are trying to bring into focus has a history or, more appropriately, a herstory. We see traces of it in the women's writing groups described in Anne Gere's study (1987), and we see it powerfully revealed in Jacqueline Jones Royster's chronicling of the tradition of black women writers.

Primarily through the work of women, then, we have found evidence of a dialogic mode of collaboration, one that allows a contextualized, multivocal text to appear. This mode, this "new key," as Suzanne Langer says in her preface to *Philosophy in a New Key*, is not one which we alone have struck. "Others," she says, "have struck it, quite clearly and repeatedly" (viii). It is a key, we would argue, that has been and is being struck clearly and repeatedly by many of the women and a few men we have mentioned, but which has not often been heard — by our professional organizations, by our institutions, by the culture within which we are all so deeply inscribed. Our challenge, then, is not to *strike* a new key but to hear within that key the full texture of layered, polyphonic chords — and to create institutional and professional spaces within which those chords may be played and echoed.

WORKS CITED

Belenky, Mary Field, Blythe McVicker Clinchy, Nancy Rule Goldberger, and Jill Mattuck Tarule. *Women's Ways of Knowing.* New York: Basic Books, 1986.
Bellah, Robert, et al. *Habits of the Heart.* Berkeley: U of California P, 1985.
Cross, Geoff. "An Ethnographic Exploration of Editor-Writer Revision at a Midwestern Insurance Company." Diss. The Ohio State University, 1988.
Ede, Lisa, and Andrea Lunsford. "Why Write . . . Together?" *Rhetoric Review* 1 (January 1983): 57–68.

———. "Why Write Together: A Research Update." *Rhetoric Review* 5 (Fall 1986): 71–84.

Geertz, Clifford. "Common Sense as a Cultural System." *Local Knowledge: Further Essays in Interpreting Anthropology.* New York: Basic Books, 1983. 73–93.

Gere, Anne Ruggles. *Writing Groups: History, Theory, and Implications.* Carbondale: Southern Illinois UP, 1987.

Gilligan, Carol. *In a Different Voice: Psychological Theory and Women's Development.* Cambridge, MA: Harvard UP, 1982.

Heath, Shirley Brice. *Ways with Words: Language, Life, and Work in Communities and Classrooms.* Cambridge: Cambridge UP, 1983.

Heilbrun, Carolyn. *Writing a Woman's Life.* New York: Norton, 1988.

Langer, Suzanne. Preface to *Philosophy in a New Key.* New York: The New American Library, 1942.

LeFevre, Karen Burke. *Invention as a Social Act.* Carbondale: Southern Illinois UP, 1987.

———. "Studying Writers in Literacy Communities: A Social Perspective." CCCC Convention, St. Louis, March 17–19, 1988.

Lykes, M. Brinton. "Collective Action and the Development of Social Individuality in Women." The Annual Convention of the American Psychological Association, Toronto, August 24–28, 1984.

Moi, Toril. *Sexual/Textual Politics: Feminist Literary Theory.* London: Methuen, 1985.

Richardson, Laurel, et al. "Down the Up Staircase: Male and Female University Professors' Classroom Management Strategies." *Feminist Frontiers.* Ed. Laurel Richardson and Verta Taylor. New York: Random. 280–86. 1983.

Royster, Jacqueline Jones. "Contending Forces: The Struggle of Black Women for Intellectual Affirmation." Columbus, Ohio, March 1, 1989.

Smith, Nicolas D. "Collaborating Philosophically." *Rhetoric Society Quarterly* 17 (Summer 1987): 247–62.

Spender, Dale. *Man Made Language.* London: Routledge and Kegan Paul, 1980.

———. "Studying Writers in Literacy Communities: A Social Perspective." CCCC Convention, St. Louis, March 17–19, 1988.

18 *Border Crossings: Intersections of Rhetoric and Feminism*

WITH CHERYL GLENN*

One quality or action is nobler than another if it is that of a naturally finer being; thus a man's will be nobler than a woman's.

— ARISTOTLE, *Rhetoric* 1.9

The work of *mestiza* consciousness is to break down the subject-object duality that keeps her a prisoner and to show in the flesh and through the images in her work how duality is transcended.

— GLORIA ANZALDÚA, *Borderlands/La Frontera* 82

STANDING AT THE BORDER

Western rhetoric began, or so one predominant disciplinary narrative tells us, as a response to disputes regarding property, regarding borders.[1] As language awareness became closely linked with the expedient workings of the newly democratic Syracuse, rhetoric flourished as a practical art, a vital part of civic life in this democracy fraught with a mass of litigation on property claims. Corax and Tisias, the heroes of this narrative, crossed borders to establish boundaries, pioneers armed only with an *enchiridion* of successful rhetorical practices.

After dedicating its early years to settling boundary disputes, rhetoric soon found itself submitting to the same kinds of boundarying. Unsettled by Plato's sound drubbing in the *Gorgias* and increasingly disarmed by philosophy's

From Lisa Ede, Cheryl Glenn, and Andrea Lunsford, in *Rhetorica* 8.4 (1995): 401–41.

*In addition to the many voices of rhetoricians and feminists that animate our text, we are particularly grateful to Danielle Mitchell, who graciously, expertly — and valiantly — helped us prepare this manuscript for publication. We also thank Jean Williams, Melissa Goldthwaithe, and Jennifer Cognard-Black for their heroic long-distance research. Finally, we thank Jon Olson for his careful and astute readings as this essay took shape.

Please note that the alphabetical listing of our names represents one attempt to resist the privileging of a "first" author and indicates the degree to which the thinking about and writing of this essay have been equally shared and thoroughly collaborative throughout.

disvaluing, rhetoric has, for much of its history, been viewed as either the codification of and instruction in discursive, persuasive practices or as a sophisticated system of tropes. But even within these bounds, rhetoric contained and remembered its power. In his *In Defence of Rhetoric*, Brian Vickers joins other twentieth-century scholars as he works to release that power and reemphasize rhetoric's central role in public discourse. As Vickers argues, the "conception of rhetoric as public debate in a society guaranteeing free speech, a debate in which both sides of the case are heard and those qualified to vote come to a decision binding on all parties, has much more to offer us . . . than Plato's equation of it with cosmetics, cookery, and other more disreputable arts designed, according to him, to satisfy base pleasures rather than promote knowledge.[2] Other scholars, such as Kenneth Burke, Samuel IJsseling, and -Ernesto Grassi,[3] have interrogated philosophy's traditional disvaluing of rhetoric, exposing the willed misreadings that support such a view, and thus they have rehabilitated rhetoric's epistemic status and heuristic value across the disciplines. Rhetoric may well border other studies, but it is not necessarily circumscribed by them.

Thanks to both broad and deep shifts in our contemporary epistemological assumptions and practices — shifts that call into question what Jane Flax terms western culture's "Enlightenment story" — rhetoric's boundaries are no longer so clearly delimited or contested.[4] Indeed, as John Bender and David E. Wellbery note in *The Ends of Rhetoric: History, Theory, Practice*, "rhetorical inquiry, as it is thought and practiced today, occurs in an interdisciplinary matrix that touches on such fields as philosophy, linguistics, communication studies, psychoanalysis, cognitive science, sociology, anthropology, and political theory."[5] Each of us doubtless has his or her own response to Bender and Wellbery's list — and to the larger issue of appropriation that disciplinary border-crossing inevitably raises.[6] As teachers of writing and scholars of rhetoric, we note, for instance, the absence from this catalogue of both classics and composition studies, two fields of disciplinary inquiry whose borders often intersect with those of rhetoric. In this essay, however, we wish to focus on another disciplinary field whose borders have upon occasion intersected with those of rhetoric, but which still remain largely at the margins of rhetorical inquiry: feminism. More specifically, we explore the intersections of rhetoric and feminism — intersections that Gloria Anzaldúa might refer to as "the Borderlands/*La Frontera*."[7]

As a political movement — as resistance to patriarchal assumptions and practices — feminism is as old as, well, at least as old as Aphrodite. But as a self-conscious academic field of inquiry, feminism is more recent, its history having developed over the last thirty years. Although much feminist work is grounded in the humanities, considerable work in the social sciences and sciences has taken place.[8] Like rhetoric, feminism is both multidisciplinary — situated in multiple academic disciplines — and, in many instances at least, also interdisciplinary.[9] In spite of its multidisciplinarity and the inevitable accompanying methodological differences, the feminist project was, until the 1970s, marked by a strong degree of consensus. As Michele Barrett and Anne

Phillips tell us in *Destabilizing Theory: Contemporary Feminist Debates*, "1970s feminism assumed that one could specify a *cause* of women's oppression. Feminists differed substantially (and fiercely) as to what this cause might be . . . but did not really question the notion of a cause itself. Nor was there any difficulty with the idea of *oppression*, which seemed to have self-evident application."[10]

Since that time, a number of factors have radically destabilized this consensus. African American and third-world/postcolonial women writers have pointed out the extent to which feminism's claims for authority and representation rested upon racist and ethnocentric assumptions about women's nature and oppression; they have also charged feminism with ignoring the intersections of gender with race and class. Marianne Hirsch and Evelyn Fox Keller explored and documented such *Conflicts in Feminism* in their 1990 collection: Mary Childers and bell hooks held a "Conversation about Race and Class"; Elizabeth Abel asked (and answered) some cogent questions about "Race, Class, and Psychoanalysis"; and Jane Gallop, Marianne Hirsch, and Nancy K. Miller "Criticiz[ed] Feminist Criticism."[11] In addition, poststructuralist and postmodern theorists have also raised questions about many of feminism's traditional assumptions and practices. Theorists such as Carla Freccero, Amy Ling, Joan W. Scott, Elaine Showalter, and Gayatri Chakravorty Spivak have characterized feminism (or certain strains of feminism) as relying upon individualist, rationalist, and universalist assumptions.[12] From such a perspective, feminism's traditional dream of freedom from oppression and equality for women appears complicitous with both Enlightenment and modernist narratives of individualism and progress.

As a result of such contemporary debates, those writing within feminism have increasingly been drawn to the term "feminisms," rather than "feminism," as a marker for their projects.[13] For purely stylistic reasons, we have chosen to use the singular form throughout this essay, yet we wish to acknowledge the extent to which feminism — like rhetoric, for that matter — is not only a construction but a place of contest and difference. Although both feminism and rhetoric have at times been represented as having continuous traditions and innocent encounters with others (peoples, disciplines, cultures), their situations are, of course, much more complex.

In "Towards a Transactional View of Rhetorical and Feminist Theory," Barbara A. Biesecker calls for "putting into contact the genius of Rhetoric and the (very different) genius of feminism."[14] In this essay, we attempt to respond to Biesecker's call as we inhabit and unsettle the conventionally understood borders between rhetoric and feminism. We hope that further engagement between these two disciplinary projects will be beneficial, but we cannot anticipate, much less predict, the consequences of ongoing dialogue — though we tend to agree with Biesecker, who suggests that the contact may "both uncramp the orthodoxy of rhetorical theory and advance the theory and practice of feminism."[15] We, too, see our project as encouraging the kind of border crossings that might allow both feminists and rhetoricians to reflect upon, and possibly even to reconsider, their disciplinary projects.

CANONICAL MAPPINGS

Aristotle may well have been the first cartographer of western rhetoric; in the fourth century BCE, he charted the canons of invention, arrangement, and style for the edification and ease of his students. Together, his *Rhetoric* and Anaximenes' *Rhetorica ad Alexandrum* serve as baseline maps for the author of *Rhetorica ad Herennium* as well as for Cicero and Quintilian, all of whom added the dimensions of memory and delivery. Throughout the ages, then, this map of rhetoric has evolved. All maps are cultural artifacts that reveal value, and the value of the canons of invention, memory, arrangement, style, and delivery has remained uncontested — regardless of deviations in their forms and influence in varying historical eras. Whether studied separately or in truncated form, the canons today retain their "tendency toward completeness, interaction, and interdependence."[16]

As a result of their long history, the traditional rhetorical canons provide familiar guides for us as we attempt to explore the borderlands of rhetoric and feminism. We have chosen to use the canons to mark the sections of our essay not only because of their enthymematic familiarity, but also in order to emphasize the mutually heuristic nature of the border crossing that we envision for rhetoric and feminism. Feminist theories and practices pose interesting questions and challenges for traditional understandings of the canons. But the canons also help illuminate how much is at stake in feminism's scholarly and performative enterprise, providing a fertile context for exploring the radical nature and significance of contemporary feminist efforts.

As Burkean terministic screens, then, the canons provide a framework that enables us to gain new perspectives on both rhetoric and feminism by inhabiting their borders. But as is the case with all terministic screens, our framework entails certain limitations. Although the linearity of print demands that we treat the canons consecutively, we wish to call attention at the outset to their tendency to overlap and interact. As Kathleen Welch writes, in this regard the canons represent "the aspects of composing which work together in a recursive, synergistic, mutually dependent relationship,"[17] one we find particularly apt for the collaborative process we have enjoyed in composing this essay.

ON INVENTION AND MEMORY

> [Invention] is the most important of all the divisions, and above all is used in every kind of pleading.
>
> — CICERO, *De inventione* I.7.9

> Now let us turn . . . to the custodian of all parts of rhetoric, memory.
>
> — *Rhetorica ad Herennium* I.2.3

We begin our exploration by linking invention, the heart and soul of inquiry, with memory, the very substance of knowledge. Although these canons have, of course, traditionally been treated separately, with invention often relegated to the province of philosophy, and memory often ignored or deleted without comment, there seem to us to be compelling reasons for considering them together, not the least of which is the rich overlap between inquiring (*inventio*) and knowing (*memoria*), one that demonstrates interconnections and blurrings characteristic of all canonical boundaries. Sharon Crowley tells us that

> until the modern period, memory held a central place within rhetorical theory. . . . In ancient times even people who could write easily . . . relied on their memories, not merely as storage facilities for particulars, but as structured heuristic systems. In other words, memory was not only a system of recollection . . . ; it was a means of invention.[18]

Even in the most traditional terms, then, the canon of invention leads the rhetor to search "in any given place [for] the available means of persuasion" and to use the topics and the *pisteis* to do so.[19] But additionally, the rhetor must surely rely heavily, in all searches, on *memoria*, for where else would the ancients have stored their commonplaces, their topics? Cicero tells us that the "structure of memory, like a wax tablet, employs places [*loci*] and in these gathers together images."[20] Thus memory ignites the process of invention. With the dominance of print over oral culture, however, memory became misremembered, and, eventually, associated not with the full powers of invention but with mere rote memorization.

Much important work of the last thirty-five years has sought to reclaim the canons of invention and memory for contemporary rhetoric. For invention, the work of James Kinneavy, Janice Lauer, Edward P. J. Corbett, Richard Young, Chaim Perelman and L. Olbrechts-Tyteca, and Burke has been particularly significant.[21] For memory, similar reclamation has been carried out by Mary Carruthers, Brian Stock, Fred Reynolds, Sharon Crowley, and Kathleen Welch.[22] But even this contemporary work on invention and memory, though valuable, all too often focused on method, such as new ways of recovering information, locating topics, using heuristics, and building proofs, without acknowledging the degree to which these tools are themselves always situated within larger discursive and ideological systems that tend to valorize some methods while silently rejecting others.

From a postmodern perspective, invention and memory are hardly neutral methods but rather represent socially and historically constructed — and constructing — language games.[23] Like other games, more is at stake in acts of invention and memory than might first seem apparent, for invention and memory constrain and shape both who can know and what can be known. Consider, for instance, the frequent references (including our own) to such ancient Greek city-states as Syracuse as democracies. In order to identify Syracuse as a democracy — to remember this "fact" and to select it as an example and an "available means of persuasion" — the rhetor must accept as natural and commonsensical these city-states' exclusion of slaves and women from civic participation. Feminist efforts not only to remember these exclusions, but also to employ them in contemporary arguments about the nature and significance of western democracies, aim to expose the political and ideological assumptions that inevitably inform any act of invention or memory.

Before they could engage in this act of memory, invention, and argumentation — or at least before they could claim a public space for this engagement — feminists had to recognize, remember, and challenge traditional understandings of the rhetor, for until recently, the figure of the rhetor has been assumed to be masculine, unified, stable, autonomous, and capable of acting rationally on the world through language. Those who did not fit this pattern — women, people of color, poorly educated workers, those judged to be overly emotional or unstable — those people stood outside of the rhetorical situation, for they were considered neither capable of nor in need of remembering and inventing arguments. From a feminist vantage point, however, it is impossible to take the subjectivity of the rhetor for granted, impossible not to locate that subjectivity within the larger context of personal, social, economic, cultural, and ideological forces, impossible not to notice not only the context itself, but also who is absent from this context as well as what exclusionary forces (regarding knowledge and argument, for example) are at work there.

Equally challenged by this perspective is what counts as knowledge. In this regard, feminist theory has consistently challenged any public/private distinction, arguing that knowledge based in the personal, in lived experience, be valued and accepted as important and significant. In describing her own way of speaking and writing, of inventing, hooks says she must "incorporate . . . a sense of place, of not just who I am in the present but where I am coming from, the multiple voices within me. . . . When I say then that these words emerge from suffering, I refer to that personal struggle to name the location from which I came to voice."[24] Women have also sought to include the intuitive and paralogical, the thinking of the body, as valuable sources of knowing, as sites of invention. Audre Lorde writes, "As women, we have come to distrust that power which rises from our deepest and nonrational knowledge. We have been warned against it all our lives by the male world, which values this depth of feeling enough to keep women around in order to exercise it in the service of men, but which fears this same depth too much to examine the possibilities of it within themselves."[25]

If in making these claims, contemporary feminists have implicitly sought to expand the canon of invention, they have often done so by linking it with memory, which Toni Morrison tells us is "a form of willed creation. It is not an effort to find out the way it really was. . . . The point is to dwell on the way it appeared and why it appeared in that particular way," which, she insists, is the province of *memoria*.[26] A brilliant example of Morrison's point about the relationship between invention and memory is readily available in the work of Isabel Allende, especially her *House of Spirits*. In this text, Allende weaves together past, present, and future events, resulting not in "individualistic autobiographical searchings [but in] revelations of traditions, re-collections of disseminated identities . . . [that] are a modern version of the Pythagorean arts of memory: retrospection to gain a vision for the future."[27] Hooks also comments on this intricate connection in a discussion of works such as the film *Freedom Charter* (which portrays the anti-apartheid movement in Africa) and Gloria Naylor's novel *Mama Day*. She notes that in these and other works, "fragments of memory are not simply represented as flat documentary but constructed . . . to move us into a different mode of articulation . . . [, a] re-membering that serves to illuminate and transform the present."[28]

As this discussion indicates, as human beings we are both limited and empowered by our individual and collective memory and invention. This recognition spurred our interest in working collaboratively on this article, for we realized that any effort to inhabit the borderlands of feminism and rhetoric could only be enriched by such dialogue. We also quickly realized the centrality of invention and memory to conceptions of subjectivity and knowledge as well as to understandings of the other canons. We wish to emphasize, then, that the following discussions of arrangement, style, and delivery both assume and depend upon a rethinking of invention and memory — one that recognizes the role that both these canons play in current efforts to reconceptualize and reenact what it means to know, speak, and write.

On Arrangement

> A speech has two parts. You must state your case, and you must prove it.
>
> — ARISTOTLE, *Rhetoric* III.13

Aristotle's cryptic injunction to arrange discourse into "two parts" was elaborated into a powerful, seven-part architectonic for the creation of ideas (*inventio*). Indeed, Cicero's adumbration and exploration of *exordium, narratio, partitio, confirmatio, reprehensio, digressio*, and *conclusio* established a highly flexible pattern for what Richard Enos calls "structuring compositions to the limits of the situation."[29] This structure has, in many respects, stood the test of 2,500 years. Certainly it has worked well to realize the traditional ends of rhetoric: to deploy, in Aristotle's terms, "all the available means of persuasion,"[30] or in Burke's, to use "language as a symbolic means of inducing cooperation in beings that by nature respond to symbols."[31] In short, if speakers/writers wanted to "state a case and prove it," they would be hard pressed to find more effective ways of disposing their cases and proof than in this logical, linear chain aimed at persuasion.

Or so western writers have generally assumed. But what if what constitutes "your case" and "your proof" are not clear-cut, are instead themselves highly contested sites? And what if the traditional aim of persuasion, of winning over an audience, is also highly contested? What might such disruptions suggest for the venerable canon of arrangement? While few theorists of rhetoric or of feminism have addressed these questions directly and in quite these terms, many feminist scholars have approached them obliquely. In a widely-cited early article, for instance, Sally Miller Gearhart charges that rhetoric is based on a "conquest model" and that "any intent to persuade is an act of violence."[32] Over fifteen years later, Sonja Foss and Cindy Griffin elaborated

Gearhart's claim, tracing the ways in which rhetoric's focus on winning has led to the dominance of several master narratives — of progress and exclusion, of subjection, of conversion.[33] All of these narratives, Foss and Griffin insist, invoke patterns of arrangement aimed at winning, at control.

Other scholars have noted the ways in which patterns of control are inscribed in seemingly innocuous conventions related to the arrangement of discourse, such as those governing endnote/footnote and works cited lists, all of which are relegated to the margins, to the periphery or very end of discourse. The text exerts its own univocal control, taking center stage and pushing beyond its borders the voices of others. Many women writers, such as Tillie Olsen, have sought to open up this textual space, to allow for the sharing of space and authority.[34] Perhaps no one on the contemporary scene has done so as consistently and consciously, however, as hooks. Early in her career, hooks chose to eschew the use of footnotes and to open up her text and her style to multiple voices. She has done so out of her belief that such discursive conventions are exclusionary, that they mark discourse "for highly educated, academic audiences only." Hooks aims instead to reach out, *sans* footnotes, to a very broad audience, "to speak simply with language that is accessible to as many folks as possible" — even if such practices lead critics to label her "anti-intellectual" and "unprofessional."[35]

But these narratives of control and exclusion, of subjection/winning, of conversion, no longer seem to encompass or to respond to many writers' goals. Consider the well-known case of literary critic Jane Tompkins, invited to contribute a critical response to the work of another scholar for the journal *New Literary History*. In traditional rhetorical terms, Tompkins' goal is clear: she should make her case, that the other scholar's essay is mistaken in its view of epistemology; and she should do so (as she puts it) by "using evidence, reasons, chains of inference, citations of authority, analogies, illustrations, and so on."[36] Tompkins does not want to do so, however, or to dispose her arguments in traditional form, for such a response ignores what she calls her "other voice," the one that is deeply in sympathy with the other scholar's goals, the one that wants to write about her feelings that the kind of academic discourse she is expected to write is a "straitjacket" she longs to throw off, the one that wants not to fight, not to "beat the other person down," not, in short, to *win*.[37] In rejecting the master narrative of triumphing over an opponent, Tompkins also eschews traditional patterns of arrangement, suggesting, at least indirectly, that the aim and the means of realizing the aim are inextricably linked. Instead, Tompkins opts for an alternation, and a dissonant juxtaposition, of her "two voices," concluding not on a note of victory or of traditional closure but of rage: "I can't strap myself psychically into an apparatus that will produce the right gestures when I begin to move. . . . This one time I've taken off the straitjacket, and it feels so good."[38]

Tompkins has not been alone in wishing to loosen the "straitjacket" of agonistic aims and patterns of discourse. Of the many feminists who have attempted to slip its holds (from Sappho to Mary Wollstonecraft and from Emily

Dickinson to Audre Lorde), we would like to call special attention to Margaret Fuller, the only woman admitted as an intellectual equal to the rarefied Transcendental Club of Ralph Waldo Emerson, Bronson Alcott, and other highly educated and influential mid-nineteenth-century Bostonians. In a detailed reading of Fuller's *Woman in the Nineteenth Century*, Annette Kolodny demonstrates the revolutionary nature of Fuller's rhetorical patterning.[39] In particular, Kolodny responds to Fuller's contemporary critic Orestes Brownson, who archly assessed Fuller's book to be "no book, but a long talk. . . . It has neither beginning, middle, nor end, and may be read backwards as well as forwards, and from the center outwards each way, without affecting the continuity of the thought or the succession of ideas. We see no reason why it should stop where it does, or why the lady might not keep on talking in the same strain till doomsday, unless prevented by want of breath."[40] Kolodny's essay demonstrates the epistemological and ideological grounds on which this judgment of incompetence rests. Fuller, herself thoroughly versed in classical and contemporary rhetoric and having developed a rhetoric class for women derived in part from a detailed and highly insightful reading of Richard Whately,[41] was perfectly capable of producing the rhetorical forms Brownson values. Rather, Kolodny shows, Fuller rejected the "authoritarianism of coercion and the manipulative strategies [of traditional forms] . . . , endeavoring instead to create a collaborative process of assertion and response in which multiple voices could — and did — find a place." As Kolodny concludes, Fuller's use of a conversational and collaborative structural pattern, rather than one based on traditional ways of disposing an argument, led to her devaluation, one that still prevents our hearing the brilliant rhetorical lessons she had to teach. If we view Fuller from the perspective gained by standing on the borderlands of rhetoric and feminism, however, we may read her refusal to order her discourse in conventional ways not as a failure at winning a traditional argument but instead as a striking success at conducting "the inclusive, collaborative, and open-ended conversations"[42] she and many other women before and since have valued.

Learning to look anew at discourse that does not follow conventional patterns, that does not pursue a master narrative of subjection, can yield major insights for rhetoricians and theorists of rhetoric, as Kolodny has clearly shown. In the same way, we have much to gain by reexamining the traditional rhetorical drive toward closure, with its reliance on those structures that lead readers inevitably to an ending, that follow Aristotle's advice that discourse must have a beginning, a middle, and an end. In this regard, we also have much to gain by crisscrossing the borders of rhetoric and feminism, particularly in terms of long-standing feminist attempts to disrupt the linear orderliness of prose, to contain contradictions and anomalies, to resist closure. These goals have been pursued vigorously by Hélène Cixous, whose attempts at "writing the body" introduce disruptive forms that push against traditional patterns of discourse and closure.[43] Drawing on Cixous' work, Lynn Worsham argues that conventional standards of unity and coherence, standards that rely on linearity and closure, rest on a logic that is thoroughly masculine — but that alternative logics, those that value indeterminacy, nonclosure, and multiplicity of meanings, are also possible.[44]

Julia Kristeva is another theorist who has written extensively of alternative discursive possibilities. In "Women's Time," for example, Kristeva invokes a discursive attitude that could allow for, indeed invite, "parallel existence[s] . . . in the same historical time or even . . . interwoven one with the other."[45] This possibility of simultaneity and multiplicity offers, Suzanne Clark suggests, a "dialogic rhetoric,"[46] one based not on oppositions or conquest but on collaboration, relationality, and mutuality, one that "can interrupt the rigidities of language and open it to a subject in process, to the unsettling and nonlogical life of the body."[47] Kristeva's project, which resists the domination of sameness and order by offering a way to transform language from within, aims to provide a pathway through the crisis of modernity and away from the "colonizing discourse of mastery."[48] Ironically — especially in light of rhetoric's long association with democratic ideals — this discourse of mastery, so familiar to traditional rhetorical forms of arrangement and aim, is itself a great threat; in Kristeva's view, the future of political democracies will depend on their ability to include in material and practical as well as rhetorical ways all those within their borders. As Clark points out in a studied understatement, "There are high stakes involved in finding more inclusive forms of argument."[49]

If Cixous' and Kristeva's attempts to enact and to theorize alternative discursive possibilities are perhaps best known in academic circles, particularly in North America and Europe, many other writers are currently working to embody and arrange language in nontraditional and more inclusive ways. Within our own limited frame of reference, for example, we think in this regard of Lorde's open letter to Mary Daly, in which she explicitly rejects traditional hierarchical, linear patterns of argument in attempting a critique that is open, dialogic, accepting and, indeed, loving.[50] We also think of Patricia Williams' personalized and nonlinear analysis of the law in *The Alchemy of Race and Rights*.[51] And we think of Nobel prize winner Toni Morrison's remarkable use of nonlinear and multiplicitous orderings, and her refusal of closure, in *Beloved*[52] — and, more remarkably still, in her acceptance address for the Nobel award. Further examples abound, increasingly and importantly from third-world/postcolonial women writers such as Rigoberta Menchú, Mariá Lugones, and Tey Diana Rebolledo.

As we hope these examples suggest, the borderlands of feminism and rhetoric offer provocative signposts toward a reexamination of the canon of arrangement. Drawing on rhetoric's (potential) plasticity, its attention to context, and its goal of finding discursive forms to meet the needs of particular audiences; and drawing on feminism's insights regarding the ideological freight and exclusionary result of many influential contemporary forms — as well as on women's long-standing attempts to create alternative discursive patternings — we may find our way toward a reimagined *dispositio*, one we may both theorize and enact.

ON STYLE

> The right thing in speaking really is that we should be satisfied not to annoy our
> hearers, without trying to delight them. . . . [N]evertheless the arts of language
> cannot help having a small but real importance, whatever it is we have to ex-
> pound to others: the way in which a thing is said does affect its intelligibility. Not,
> however, so much as people think. All such arts are fanciful and meant to charm
> the hearer. Nobody uses fine language when teaching geometry.
>
> — ARISTOTLE, *Rhetoric* III.1

One has only to think of Aristotle's comments on style in the *Rhetoric* to be
reminded of the extent to which style functions as a site of tension and contest
within rhetoric. As readers will recall, in Book III Aristotle provides copious
advice about style and delivery, but he does so with some ambivalence. For
bordering Aristotle's emphasis on style — "it is not enough to know *what* we
ought to say; we must also say it *as* we ought"[53] — is an anxiety about the
extent to which language can be used to obscure and mislead, to play upon
the emotions of the audience. As Aristotle notes, the speaker "must disguise
his art and give the *impression* of speaking naturally and not artificially" (our
emphasis).[54]

Inscribed in Aristotle's comments on style are a series of oppositions —
between *res* and *verba*, reason and emotion, demonstration and persuasion,
and fact and interpretation — that for centuries have troubled those working
within the rhetorical tradition. An example from Corbett's *Classical Rhetoric
for the Modern Student* provides a useful instance of one such difficulty. In this
work, Corbett introduces his discussion of style by noting that "once arguments had been discovered, selected, and arranged, they had to be put into
words. Words . . . serve as the medium of communication between speakers
or writers and their audience."[55] Corbett's definition of style is certainly conventional, but it nevertheless represents a potential dilemma for rhetoric. If
ideas and arguments are separate from and prior to language, as Corbett's
definition seems to suggest, then they are epistemologically foundational, and
rhetoric, however necessary and helpful, is open to the charge of being "mere
outward show for pleasing the hearer."[56] Aware of this potential difficulty,
Corbett quickly modifies his opening statement, commenting that "one notion about style that needs to be erased at the outset is that style is simply 'the
dress of thought.' "[57]

It is no accident, of course, that Corbett uses the derogatory — and
gendered — phrase "dress of thought" to characterize undesirable views of
rhetoric. As Susan Jarratt observes in *Rereading the Sophists: Classical Rhetoric
Refigured*, "Both rhetoric and women . . . [have been] trivialized by identification with sensuality, costume, and color — all of which are supposed to be
manipulated in attempts to persuade through deception."[58] The history of
rhetoric as a scholarly and pedagogical discipline, as well as a performative
tradition, is marked by recurring tensions and oscillations as both theorists
and rhetors have negotiated the relation of rhetoric, poetics, and logic — and
in so doing have often challenged the centrality, and at times even the validity,

of attention to style. Think of Plato's dismissal of rhetoric in the *Gorgias* as mere "pandering," akin to "cookery" and "beauty-culture"[59]; of Ramus' bifurcation of invention and arrangement from style and delivery; and of the Royal Society's effort, reported by Thomas Spratt, to "reject all the amplifications, digressions, and swellings of style; to return back to the primitive purity, and shortness, when men deliver'd so many *things*, almost in an equal number of *words*."[60]

As feminists have noted, the "primitive purity" that the rejection of style entails has generally necessitated the exclusion of women from the rhetorical scene, for how could women, with their inferior reason and their involvement in the stylish, the embodied, and the material, hope to attain such rigorous rationality? But not only women have been excluded: inherent in rhetoric's internalized ambivalence about style is an anxiety about rhetoric's relationship with audience in general, particularly popular audiences. (For instance, Plato handily forces Gorgias to agree that "a popular audience means an ignorant audience."[61]) In her study of modernism and its unsettled relationship with "sentimental" literature — literature that transgresses modernist values both in its gendering and in its identification with popular audiences — Clark exposes the extent to which "modernism is both caught in and stabilized by a system of gendered binaries."[62] In such a situation, Clark asks, "What kind of subject or ethos may function [in discourse] with authority? What kind of relationship to the audience — what pathos — may be seen as legitimate?"[63]

Given rhetoric's own construction of (and construction within) similar binaries, these questions resonate with equal fullness for the rhetorical tradition, emphasizing that although rhetoric may desire to decenter style, style — as the material embodiment of the relationships among self, text, and world — resists such displacement. For though some writers (including a number of feminists) experience style primarily as technique, many others find that style raises powerful and difficult personal, political, and ethical issues. Acutely aware of the patriarchal nature of the western phallogocentric tradition, many feminist writers feel themselves to be in a double bind. In order to claim authority and agency, to function as subjects in the discursive arena and thus further feminism's emancipatory goals, some feminists choose (as we choose in this essay) to adhere to the stylistic conventions of traditional western discourse — conventions that sharply dichotomize the public and the private, that devalue personal experience in favor of "objective" facts, "rational" logic, and established authorities.

For many, however, Lorde's well-known dictum that "the master's tools will never dismantle the master's house" powerfully evokes the potential limitations of such an approach. For even when women employ the style of traditional argumentation, gender-related concerns and questions can and often do influence both the immediate and subsequent reception of their work. Consider, for instance, the case of Emma Goldman, the Russian-born American anarchist, lecturer, writer, and editor who achieved great notoriety in the United States from the 1890s to 1917. Although Goldman's politics were radical (she was a passionate anarchist and argued [among other things] in favor of free love and birth control), her argumentative style in many ways resembled "standard American rhetoric."[64] Nevertheless, Goldman often scandalized contemporary popular audiences, while intellectuals and critics — both then and now — have tended to dismiss her as sentimental and romantic.

Such a double bind was almost inevitable, Clark argues. As a speaker, Goldman's *ethos* and style of delivery violated the expectations of mass audiences, for Goldman "broke their most sacred codes of womanly behavior. She did not smile; she did not defer" as she uttered her passionately held and expressed ideas.[65] Goldman's more intellectual listeners and readers had different reservations; they found her lacking because her "language was not like the symbolist or modernist practice, not experimental."[66] In the "twentieth century . . . struggle over how emotion is to be regulated and distributed," modernism came down on the side of a refined aestheticism that favored irony and restraint, not passion.[67] Goldman resisted these (gendered) conventions, preferring to emulate such earlier American writers as Ralph Waldo Emerson — an unacceptable practice given modernism's critique of American romanticism. As a consequence, from a modernist perspective, Goldman occupied "the impossible position of the passionate woman."[68]

Goldman did succeed in creating a space for her words and ideas in her own time; and if she stirred controversy and strong response (a response that eventually led to her deportation to Russia), she "generated not only antagonists but also adherents."[69] Goldman's writing could not survive the critique of modernism, however, for her passion and her adherence to a once-revered Emersonian style was an embarrassment. Consequently, "under the regime of the new criticism, Goldman's connections to literary history became unspeakable, and forgotten."[70]

Mindful of the fate of Goldman and of the previously discussed Fuller, "the most forgotten major literary figure of her own times,"[71] a number of women have attempted to forge not only alternative styles but also alternative discourses. Perhaps one of the most radical of such efforts is that of Daly, whose "co-conjured" *Websters' [sic] First New Intergalactic Wickedary of the English Language*[72] represents an attempt to "conceive of language itself as a fabric that was originally woven by women in conversation with one another."[73] In so doing, Daly often reclaims earlier meanings of words, giving back to the term "spinster," for instance, its significance as "a woman whose occupation is to spin."[74] Such projects are not without their own risks, however. After reading Daly's earlier *Gyn/Ecology: The Metaethics of Radical Feminism*,[75] Lorde wrote "An Open Letter to Mary Daly," which questioned the sources of Daly's alternative vision for feminism, asking, among other things, why Daly's "goddess-images [are] only white, western-european, judeo-christian."[76] Lorde's letter is of interest not only for its suggestive treatment of arrangement, noted above, and its commentary on Daly's work, but also for its direct, dialogic, and invitational style. Rather than relying upon confrontational, agonistic strategies, Lorde employs personal disclosures, frequent addresses to readers, and questioning rather than critique or dismissal to convey her reservations about Daly's work. Lorde concludes her letter with these words:

> We first met at the MLA [Modern Language Association] panel, "The Transformation of Silence Into Language and Action." Shortly before that date, I had decided never again to speak to white women about their racism. I felt it was wasted energy, because of their destructive guilt and defensiveness, and because whatever I had to say might better be said by white women to one another, at far less emotional cost to the speaker, and probably with a better hearing. This letter attempts to break this silence.
>
> I would like not to have to destroy you in my consciousness. So as a sister Hag, I ask you to speak to my perceptions.
>
> Whether or not you do, Mary, again I thank you for what I have learned from you.
>
> This letter is in repayment.[77]

In this closing passage, Lorde fuses the public and the private, the personal and the political, using direct address, many first- and second-person pronouns, and personal reminiscence to demonstrate her gratitude and make connections that unsettle the traditional borders between speaker and listener.

We have already discussed the work of Cixous and Kristeva, continental writers who resist traditional western stylistic conventions of unity, coherence, linearity, and closure and whose texts challenge traditional distinctions between poetry and prose. In "If I Could Write This in Fire, I Would Write This in Fire," Jamaican Michelle Cliff similarly composes a text that offers stylistic explorations while occupying the borderlands between poetry and prose.[78] Her essay moves with poetic intensity from personal reflections to snatches of texts and remembered sayings, interweaving a sustained, though hardly traditional, critique of race relations in her country and abroad. In the closing paragraph, Cliff comments upon her writing and its relationship to her experience:

> There is no ending to this piece of writing. There is no way to end it. As I read back over it, I see that we/they/I may become confused in the mind of the reader: but these pronouns have always co-existed in my mind. . . . I am Jamaica is who I am. No matter how far I travel — how deep the ambivalence I feel about ever returning. And Jamaica is a place in which we/they/I connect and disconnect — change place.[79]

Other writers, such as Anzaldúa and Sandra Cisneros,[80] portray the various stylistic borderings they inhabit by blending English, Spanish, and "Spanglish" throughout their fiction and essays; in so doing, they not only portray the multiple realities through which they live and write, but also provide opportunities for others to experience such multiplicities.

A number of feminists in the United States have enacted yet another form of stylistic resistance to conventional expectations. These (largely academic — and tenured) writers compose what literary critic Nancy K. Miller terms "personal criticism," criticism that engages, rather than distances, the writer's experiences.[81] Such criticism, Miller argues, represents an intervention into contemporary cultural and theoretical practices, and it does so at the level of style: "[B]y turning its authorial voice into spectacle, personal writing theorizes the stakes of its own performance. . . . Personal writing opens an inquiry on the cost of writing — critical writing or Theory — and its effects."[82]

Not all feminists agree with Miller's assessment of the value of the personal style or with Daly's effort to create a language free of patriarchal influence. In "Surviving to Speak New Language: Mary Daly and Adrienne Rich," Jane Hedley argues that Daly's efforts to construct a feminist discourse are ultimately totalizing, "*self*-contextualizing and autotelic to a quite remarkable degree."[83] Many postmodern feminists are also suspicious of efforts to develop more personally grounded forms of criticism, believing that such efforts reinscribe the western tradition's emphasis on individualism and authenticity, while feminists of color such as hooks and Trinh T. Minh-ha challenge the ease with which many white feminists have felt comfortable representing (or, from hooks's and Trinh's perspectives, ignoring or misrepresenting) the experiences of others. Even recent attempts on the part of feminists to acknowledge the extent to which feminism has ignored race and class and to affirm what Rich terms a "politics of location" often have the effect, critics such as hooks argue, of "recentering the white authorial presence."[84]

For these and other reasons, in contemporary feminism few issues are as contentious as issues of style. While some feminists engage in agonistic arguments about the disadvantages and advantages of experimental efforts such as those of Kristeva and Cixous and of personal criticism as practiced by Tompkins and Miller, others focus their inquiry on the difficulty of writing itself. In *Woman, Native, Other*, for instance, Trinh calls for feminists to embrace "a practice of language which remains, through its signifying operations, a process constantly unsettling the identity of meaning and speaking/writing subject, a process never allowing I to fare without non-I."[85] In the context of such a practice, style marks the borderland where conflicting ideological, cultural, political, and other forces important to both rhetoric and feminism contend.

ON DELIVERY

> [Delivery] is, essentially, a matter of the right management of the voice to express the various emotions. . . . Those who . . . bear [delivery] in mind . . . usually win prizes in the dramatic contests; and just as in drama . . . , so it is in the contests of public life, owing to the defects of our political institutions.
>
> — ARISTOTLE, *Rhetoric* III.1

Aristotle's barest outline of the canon of delivery emphasized "the three things — volume of sound, modulation of pitch, and rhythm — that a speaker bears in mind." Fully aware of rhetoric as public display, as performance art, as the one-time demonstration before a judge and jury, Aristotle lamented rhetoric's "unworthy" yet necessary concern with the delivery of "appearances." After all, we should "fight our case with no help beyond the bare facts: nothing . . . should matter except the proof of these facts." But "owing to the defects of our hearers" (that is, to the defects of our humanness), "we must pay attention to the subject of delivery . . . because we cannot do without it."[86]

Theophrastus, Aristotle's successor as head of the Peripatetic School, later elaborated and codified this canon, dividing delivery into matters of voice and gesture — or action — and providing rules for each. His now-lost but influential *On Delivery* informed rhetoric throughout antiquity, as numerous texts attest. The author of *Rhetorica ad Herennium* details delivery's "exceptionally great usefulness,"[87] for example, and Cicero addresses delivery in *De oratore* as "the dominant factor in oratory; without delivery the best speaker cannot be of any account at all, and a moderate speaker with a trained delivery can often outdo the best of them."[88] Delivery is presented in *Brutus* as that element of rhetoric that "penetrates the mind, shapes, moulds, turns it,"[89] and in the *Orator* a "sort of language of the body."[90] Quintilian notes that "the nature of the speech we have composed within our minds is not so important as the manner in which we produce it, since the emotion of each member of our audience will depend on the impression made upon his hearing."[91] And both Cicero and Quintilian took apparent pleasure in recounting Demosthenes' memorable response when asked to list the three most important components of rhetoric: "Delivery, delivery, delivery."[92]

Delivery remains vital to rhetoric, given that it is, indeed, the culmination of the composing process, the combination and culmination of all five canons. Whether written, oral, or visual/aural (electronic), each rhetorical act culminates in delivery. Just as the ancient teachers went to great lengths to teach their students rhetorical effectiveness, so, too, have all students, from antiquity to this postmodern era, hoped to inhabit rhetorical power. In writing this essay, for example, we aimed throughout at effective delivery. Just a glance at the lengthy annotated endnotes, the copious examples (our artistic and nonartistic proofs), and our use of time-honored sources indicates how thoroughly we three academic women have attempted to embody the traditional delivery medium of the professional academic essay. Our introduction with its aims of establishing good will, common ground, and good sense; our presentation of topic and explanation of methodology; the very linearity of our argument, in which we use the canons of rhetoric as organizing principles — all these strategies comprise the public performance, the appearance before and attention to a university-trained, international audience, all of whom have easy familiarity with the delivery system represented by an academic journal.[93]

But our ability to enter this arena of public academic discourse and to deliver our message is utterly dependent on one crucial item: access not only to the conventions regarding delivery but also to the system of delivery itself. Cicero conflates delivery with the "language of the body,"[94] making us particularly conscious of the privilege we enjoy since, as Biesecker (among others) notes, "Rhetoric is a discipline whose distinctive characteristic is its focus on *public* address, a realm to which women as a class have historically been denied access."[95] Indeed, for most of the history of rhetoric in the western world, women generally could not have entered the public arena as we have here. Most women have been closed out of a rhetorical tradition of vocal, public, and, therefore, privileged men, silenced by force and by means of their educations. Nevertheless, women have not been excluded entirely from effective communication.

Those whose work we will note here represent only a fraction of the largely as-yet unexplored number of women who have turned to alternative, often private, forms of delivery (in secondary sources, mystical visions, autobiographies, translations, letters, lists, prose-poems, teachings, humor, and recordings by educated males).[96] First of all, these women had to gain access to a medium of delivery; then they most often found themselves altering that medium in whatever ways would allow them to speak (through the writings of others, for example), even if those voices reached no attentive audience for centuries. Other women reached a highly educated audience only by translating, filtering their erudition through the words of men. Still others, those who took hold of a system designed for men, shaped the traditionally masculine medium of oral delivery to their own advantage and pushed the boundaries of platform rhetoric to include a broader listening audience. Although largely ignored until very recently, the rhetorical deliveries of these women have ultimately proved as powerful and long-lasting as traditionally masculine displays.[97]

By means of secondary sources, fifth-century BCE Aspasia of Miletus, for example, provides one of the earliest examples of women's use of alternative delivery methods: her work has been delivered to us by the way of men's writing, for none of Aspasia's work exists in primary sources.[98] Aspasia's reputation as both a rhetorician and philosopher, as well as the text of her various speeches, have been preserved by men.[99] Given the cultural constraints that limited her, Aspasia used the only media of delivery available — that is, media employed by men. The most important of her compositions may well be Pericles' Funeral Oration, a moving, patriotic epideictic that the Platonic Socrates recites from memory in the *Menexenus*.[100] Although we have no access to her original text, the Platonic version (an exaggerated encomium abounding with historical misstatements and anachronisms) aligns well with the Platonic Aspasia's opinions on the efficacy of rhetoric: "It is by means of speech finely spoken that deeds nobly done gain for their doers from the hearers the meed of memory and renown."[101] This version of Pericles' Funeral Oration also aligns with Aspasia's reputation as rhetorician, philosopher, and influential colleague in the Sophistic movement, a movement devoted to the analysis and creation of rhetoric — and of truth. Aspasia's oral text, delivered to us in the print medium of secondary sources, not only provides a compelling demonstration of rhetoric's potential to create belief, but perhaps just as important, her dispersed but still powerful text has at last reached an appreciative audience.[102]

In old age, illiterate medieval mystic Margery Burnham Kempe (1373–c.1439) used the oral system of delivery to dictate the story of her life to scribes. *The Book of Margery Kempe,* left unidentified until five hundred years after it was written, recounts the trials and triumphs of her worldly and spiritual pilgrimages, gives voice to the silent, middle-class, uneducated woman, and appears to be the earliest extant autobiography in the English language.[103] Despite her lack of formal literacy and training, Kempe located herself within the particular discourse of Franciscan affective piety, where she could self-consciously author and own the story of her life, create her self, record her spiritual development, and, most importantly, validate her life and her mystical visions.[104] Kempe knew well the power of the written word, so she attached herself to the oral component of that written word, studying (listening to and memorizing) with a priest until she became literate — without being able to read and write (without being text-dependent). And her employment of an amanuensis enabled her to leave a written record of her oral deliveries, a written record intended, no doubt, for oral performance or delivery. Thus, her *Book* is Kempe's unique inscription of rhetorical practice and delivery. It demonstrates the way in which one woman, denied ready access to the print medium, refracted her oral discourse through a scribe and sent her message down to us.

Renaissance intellect Margaret More Roper (1504–44), daughter of Thomas More, delivers her rhetorical skill in her translation of Erasmus' *Devout treatise upon the Pater noster* (1524). Considered derivative, defective, and muted, the feminine art of translation posed no threat to the masculine art of composition — not even when the translation itself became a major intellectual influence. Roper's translation remains one of the earliest examples of the Englishing of Erasmian piety; in addition, it broke new ground as part of a broad campaign directed at the English-reading public in that it domesticated and disseminated Erasmus' view of the devotional life. Translations provided Roper an outlet for her rhetorical skills and a measure of intellectual and religious influence — but only because she chose decorously to conceal her voice and identity as a writer in the work of a known and accepted author, only because she delivered her thoughts through the words of men, within the constraints of womanly modesty, piety, and humility.

Like Kempe, Sojourner Truth (1797–1883) remained illiterate all her life, though she drew deep from the wellsprings of oral tradition, delivering her own words through her own body. This former slave commanded large audiences whenever she spoke to the two most crucial political and social issues of her day: slavery and suffrage. At a time when the science of voice, gesture, and elocution was all the rage in rhetorical circles, at a time when (white) women's presence at a pulpit, a podium, a platform, or the bar was often illegal (the presence of a black woman would have been unimaginable), Truth's rhetoric of practicality shot through the fog of belletristic display. Like Kempe, she, too, appropriated the medium of oral delivery to her own end. Indeed, in contrast to most contemporary oral delivery, Truth made use of simple, straightforward language in an attempt to reach the broadest possible audience, fusing her simple style with her simple delivery. As Suzanne Pullon Fitch notes, Truth's "use of the simple language of the uneducated, which she could weave into striking narrative and metaphors, her nearly six-foot frame that revealed the strength developed working as a farmhand and house maid, and her powerful low voice telling of her denied rights as a woman and an African-American made her one of the most forceful instruments of reform."[105] Truth's physical bearing, enhanced by her use of simple language and memorable stories, helped her reach her goal, that of a more inclusive audience engagement and participation.

How different the "plain style" delivery of this woman was from the formal rhetorical delivery so common among nineteenth-century American public speakers, nearly all of whom were males. So memorable (and perhaps threatening) was this alternative rhetorical display — in terms of her style, her delivery, her arrangement, and her subject — that one pro-slavery newspaper wrote: "She is a crazy, ignorant, repelling negress, and her guardians would do a Christian act to restrict her entirely to private life."[106] Yet this "ignorant" woman continued in the public sphere, exhorting note-taking college students to "put their notes in their heads"[107] and parlaying her illiteracy into stylized delivery: "You know, children, I don't read such small stuff as letters, I read men and nations. I can see through a millstone, though I can't see through a spelling-book. What a narrow idea a reading qualification is for a voter! I know and do what is right better than many big men who read."[108] On these and many other occasions, Truth clearly practiced Cicero's dictum for delivery as the "language of the body." Still, hers was an alternative delivery, the only practice available for an illiterate, slave-class, black woman, particularly a woman who wanted to transform hostile and separatist audiences with a rhetoric of inclusion.

Truth is only one in a long tradition of women who have attempted to appropriate conventional oral delivery to their own ends. If we turn to contemporary America for another example, we might well point to the former governor of Texas, Ann Willis Richards, who, like Truth, uses oral delivery — valorized speech and language — to seek out, speak, and listen to new voices. In the United States, Richards, perhaps best known for her 1988 keynote address to the Democratic National Convention, participates fully in public, political, argumentative, powerful rhetoric — rhetoric in our most traditional(ly masculine) sense.

But her participation is on her own terms, that of a woman, a feminist, who easily conflates the public with the private, inviting more and more people into her audience. If a commonplace in feminist theory is the link between where one stands — and delivers — in society and what one perceives, then feminist Richards self-consciously enters the political arena, perceiving with great clarity not only her own position but that of male privilege. Ever-mindful of her audience, Richards carefully avoids elitism, agonism, and paternalism, enacting, instead — in her platform delivery — a fierce "maternalism" that embraces her constituents. From the platform, she reads letters from the disempowered and downtrodden. From the platform, she testifies

to the benefits of inclusion, cooperation, and connection, qualities often associated with the feminine. From the platform, she reaches out to all women
who worry about their families and children, to all grandmothers who want
life to promise steady improvements for their generations, to all feminists
who join Richards in hoping that her granddaughter Lily may never believe
"that there was a time when blacks could not drink from public water foun-
tains, when Hispanic children were punished for speaking Spanish in the
public schools and women couldn't vote."[109] She delivers all these messages
with homely examples (a staple of platform rhetoric) and common sense (one
of her favorite lines is, "Tell it so my Mama in Waco can understand it"). As
she fuses her style with her delivery, she transforms her politics through her
female body, and she speaks from the borderlands of women in politics — all
to the advantage of her rhetorical power.

In addition to providing us an example of (traditionally masculine) delivery informed by feminine/feminist ethics, Richards also exemplifies an oral
delivery inscribed in and by different media. With (seemingly) full access to
all systems of delivery, Richards speaks aloud from her written text to a "live"
audience as well as to the audiences who hear her on the radio, watch and
listen to her on television, and read excerpts from her speech in the newspaper — a merger of electronic, written, and oral media.

With this electronic delivery comes electronic writing, a new means of
delivering text and graphics that offers another productive space within
which rhetoric and feminism may work. At least some electronic media, such
as hypertext, seem to allow for feminist concerns of inclusion, participation,
and dialogue, and here we find the potential, at least, to allow full audience
engagement in the establishment of the text itself. For example, in hypertext software designed for MacIntosh platforms, Deena Larsen offers *Marble
Springs*,[110] a hypothetical space in nineteenth-century Colorado populated
by many women. Primarily a collection of poetry written by and about the
women of Marble Springs and detailing their many contributions to the
town's history and development, the texts of *Marble Springs* can be rewritten,
revised, and added to by the hypertext user. Thus like all hypertext, and electronic media in general, *Marble Springs* holds out the promise of an inclusion-
ary rhetoric. But like all systems of delivery, electronic rhetoric also harbors
the threat of exclusion, as George Landow's dystopic vision of the fate of writers in such a world makes alarmingly clear.[111] If the electronic medium establishes itself as the major delivery system of the next century, then rhetoricians
and feminists together must continue to examine the power relations of its
rhetorical situation: Who gets to speak/write? Who gets to listen? Who gets to
rewrite? How many of us will have material access to the electronic media
and to all their concomitant delivery systems?

Just as the history of rhetoric cannot be written from rhetoric books alone,
neither can the canon of delivery be theorized beyond the point of successful
practice. As we hope this discussion has revealed, border-crossings between
rhetoric and feminism can help us better to appreciate the power of past practices. In looking to present and future practices, we have suggested that when

rhetoric and feminism come together, as in this interrogation of the canon of delivery, both are transformed. Rhetoric, a vibrant process of inquiring, organizing, and thinking, offers a theorized space to talk about delivery. And feminism offers a reason to "bridge differences (rather than to create them), to include (rather than to exclude), and to empower (rather than to seek power or weakness)."[112] So when our discussion of delivery includes theories and artifacts that represent both the traditions of agonism, confidence, and competitiveness as well as more recently embodied examples of inclusion, cooperation, and identification, and when we put these influential feminine voices in dialogue with traditionally masculine deliveries, we move beyond a rhetoric of masculine privilege to a transformed rhetorical practice. Standing on the borderlands of rhetoric and feminism allows us to imagine a much wider, much more inclusive range of successful deliveries and fruitful border-crossings.

CONCLUSION

> The duty of rhetoric is to deal with such matters as we deliberate upon without arts or systems to guide us.
>
> — ARISTOTLE, *Rhetoric* I.2

> Culture forms our beliefs. We perceive the version of reality that it communicates. Dominant paradigms, predefined concepts that exist as unquestionable, unchallengeable, are transmitted to us through the culture.
>
> — GLORIA ANZALDÚA, *Borderlands/La Frontera* 16

In taking this *excursus* among the rhetorical canons, we have been especially conscious of our central metaphor — the borderlands (*la frontera*) of rhetoric and feminism. For us, this metaphor has been most powerful in its nuanced indeterminacy, its quiet reminder that borderlands shift and overlap, that they are, as Anzaldúa notes, in "a constant state of transition."[113] Indeed, as our discussion of the rhetorical canons has demonstrated, their borders also inevitably blur. At one point in working on this essay, we found ourselves disagreeing, to cite just one instance, as to whether we should discuss as style or delivery the dissonance between Goldman's presentation of public self (her refusal to smile, to defer) and the gendered expectations of her popular lecture audiences. How can it be possible to separate style from delivery, we wondered; when both are so intimately connected with the rhetor's subjectivity and *ethos* and with the specifics of the particular rhetorical situation? We thus found relevant to our experience in composing this essay Trinh's insight that "despite our desperate, eternal attempts to separate, contain, and mend, categories always leak."[114] Such leakage is, we believe, not only inevitable but helpful, for it reminds us that categories — and their boundaries and borderlands — are "sites of historicized struggles."[115]

In some of these historical moments, rhetoric and feminism have had few if any intersections. As the headnote from Aristotle's *Rhetoric* that begins this essay indicates, rhetoric was constituted as a patriarchal, exclusionary discipline, and it remained so for centuries. When Aristotle, Cicero, Quintilian, and Augustine considered the nature and province of rhetoric, they did not imagine that women — or those gendered feminine by their race, class, psychology, or other characteristics — might wish or be able to employ what Aristotle terms "the available means of persuasion" to communicate their ideas. As our discussion indicates, however, those whom rhetoric has gendered as "Other" have, nevertheless, employed strategies that those working within the rhetorical tradition have recognized as "rhetoric" to form, shape, and express their ideas.

In our contemporary historical moment, feminism and rhetoric stand, along with a number of other disciplines, amid a rich and intricate landscape — a landscape that postmodern and poststructural critique has complicated with its skeptical probings. In such a landscape, congruences as well as dissimilarities between rhetoric and feminism appear. Both fields, for example, place high value on *process*, as the longevity and influence of the canons and feminism's persistent commitment to working through to an understanding rather than to (premature) closure both demonstrate. In both fields, this focus on process signals a larger commitment to linking theory with practice, to recognizing and valuing local and applied knowledges. And both fields share a long-standing concern for public values and the public good, for creating spaces within which human subjectivities, at least potentially, can be realized, celebrated, and expanded.

Both fields have also demonstrated, it goes without saying, that they are capable of both conscious and unconscious hierarchies and exclusions, that they are, as Burke so eloquently indicates, "rotten with perfection."[116] We have already discussed feminism's belated recognition of the extent to which its scholarly and political project excludes women of color. As feminist theory has gained academic respectability — as scholars who viewed themselves as radical in the 1970s and 1980s have become tenured professors in the 1990s — a number of feminists, such as Kolodny, have become concerned that "Respectability Is Eroding the Revolutionary Potential of Feminist Criticism."[117] And feminists have been forced to recognize that they can be as agonistic, as competitive, as the most traditionally masculinist academic. In Gallop, Hirsch, and Miller's "Criticizing Feminist Criticism," for instance, Miller describes a particular vehement public attack on her work and her resulting recognition that she had "learned to fear other women in a way [she] hadn't done until that point."[118]

At the level of practice, then, feminists have become increasingly aware of the need to develop an ethics of communication. Such an ethics would also address an urgent theoretical question of concern to many contemporary feminists: how to justify and forward feminism's scholarly and political project given postmodern and poststructural skepticism about traditional humanistic argumentation. Once aware, as Judith Butler notes, that "the subject who theorizes is constituted as a 'theorizing subject' by a set of exclusionary and selective procedures,"[119] feminists must acknowledge the interestedness and situatedness of their own discourse. As a consequence, they must address, rather than evade, the question of rhetoric.

In *Thinking Fragments*, for instance, Flax begins her last chapter with this statement:

> A fundamental and unresolved question pervading this book is how to justify — or even frame — theoretical and narrative choices (including my own) without recourse to 'truth' or domination. I am convinced we can and should justify our choices to ourselves and others, but what forms these justifications can meaningfully assume is not clear to me.[120]

As a tradition that has for centuries concerned itself with the question of how rhetors can and should justify their choices, rhetoric has, we believe, much to offer contemporary feminist theory and practice. For as our discussion of the canons has, we hope, indicated, rhetoric offers a rich conceptual framework and terminology that could prove heuristic as feminists attempt to probe and articulate these and other concerns. As Susan Brown Carlton notes, rhetoric could enable feminists to reconstruct what many have experienced as a contentious "philosophical impasse as a map of rhetorical options available for voicing the feminist stance."[121]

Rhetoric would also benefit, we believe, if the borderlands between rhetoric and feminism were more fully explored. Mining the borders of feminism and rhetoric would seem to offer intriguing interconnections and new ratios among *logos, pathos,* and *ethos,* ones that would expand the province of rhetorical proof and hence speak to and with wider and more diverse audiences. In insisting on the value of the local, the personal, the private, the mythic, for example, Anzaldúa's discourse embodies a set of proofs that transcends dualisms by embracing multiple understandings. The complex processes of knowing that Anzaldúa's work enacts (and invites) resituate proofs so that, as Lata Mani observes, "The relation between experience and knowledge is now seen to be not one of correspondence but one fraught with history, contingency, and struggle."[122]

In addition, sustaining a position on the borderlands of rhetoric and feminism holds promise of more complex and multiplicitous understandings of human communication, of how meanings arise and are inscribed. From this vantage point, the angles of the rhetorical triangle — speaker, hearer, text — become shape-shifters, three-dimensional and elastic points of contact, of location. Discussing this elasticity in another context, Michele Wallace describes the movement involved in this way of apprehending the world not as one of fixed stances (as writer *or* reader, for example), but as self-consciously "travelling from one position to another, thinking one's way from one position to another" and back again.[123]

Perhaps most importantly, Anzaldúa's *mestiza* borderland consciousness may create a space for public discourse that is inclusive, that accepts difference and Others, as Kristeva, Spivak, and hooks insist it must, without colonizing and also without shutting down exchange. Such an effort calls for considerable self-reflectiveness, a self-reflectiveness that requires rhetors to "become accountable for . . . [their] own investments in cultural metaphors and values," as well as a willingness to experiment, to take risks.[124] It also calls, as hooks wisely observes, for the continuing recognition that "it is not just important what we speak about, but how and why we speak."[125] As this essay has argued, from a perspective that borders rhetoric and feminism, attention to "what we speak about" and "how and why we speak" urges all of us not only to continued exploration and interrogation but also to a renewed responsibility for our professional and personal discursive acts.

NOTES

1. We are aware that many historians of rhetoric challenge the foundational stories of western rhetoric (Richard Enos, *Greek Rhetoric before Aristotle* [Prospect Heights, IL: Waveland, 1993]; Cheryl Glenn, *Rhetoric Retold: Regendering the Tradition from Antiquity through the Renaissance* [Carbondale: Southern Illinois University Press, 1997]; Susan Jarratt, *Rereading the Sophists: Classical Rhetoric Refigured* [Carbondale: Southern Illinois University Press, 1991]; Jasper Neel, *Plato, Derrida, and Writing* [Carbondale: Southern Illinois University Press, 1988]; Takis Poulakos, *Rethinking the History of Rhetoric* [Boulder: Westview, 1993]; C. Jan Swearingen, *Rhetoric and Irony* [New York: Oxford University Press, 1991]; Victor Vitanza, *Writing Histories of Rhetoric* [Carbondale: Southern Illinois University Press, 1994]; Kathleen Welch, *The Contemporary Reception of Classical Rhetoric* [Hillsdale, NJ: Erlbaum, 1990]; and many others).

Jane Sutton, for example, counters this story with "a scene in history when the earth was young and the Amazon ruled, [allowing] no Tyrant to direct the affairs of society" ("The Taming of the *Polos/Polis*: Rhetoric as an Achievement without Woman," *Southern Communication Journal* 57 [Winter 1992]: 99–100). Sutton goes on to relate the Amazon story to Aphrodite and to link rhetoric's beginning to Aphrodite's female entourage, thus offering an intriguing parallel between the Amazonian myth and the story of Corax and Tisias, in both of which the hero(ine)s slay the Tyrant.

2. (Oxford: Clarendon-Oxford, 1988), p. viii.

3. See Burke, *A Rhetoric of Motives* (Berkeley: University of California Press, 1950); IJsseling, *Rhetoric and Philosophy in Conflict: An Historical Survey*, trans. Paul Dumphy (The Hague: Martinus Nijhoff, 1976); and Grassi, *Rhetoric and Philosophy: The Humanist Tradition* (University Park and London: The Pennsylvania State University Press, 1980).

4. In *Thinking Fragments: Psychoanalysis, Feminism, and Postmodernism in the Contemporary West* (Berkeley: University of California Press, 1990), pp. 30–31, Flax populates the "Enlightenment" story with "major themes and characters": (1) a coherent, stable self (the author); (2) a distinctive and privileged mode of storytelling — philosophy (the critic and judge) — and a particular notion of "truth" (the hero); (3) a distinctive political philosophy (the moral) that posits complex and necessary interconnections among reason, autonomy, and freedom; (4) a transparent medium of expression (language); (5) an optimistic and rationalist philosophy of human nature (character development); and (6) a philosophy of knowledge (an ideal form).

5. (Stanford: Stanford University Press, 1990), p. vii.

6. Dwight Conquergood ("Rethinking Ethnography: Toward a Critical Cultural Politics," *Communication Monographs* 58 [June 1991]: 179–98) observes that boundaries and borderlands pose multiple possibilities, not all of which are positive. Using the situation of refugees as a trope for the multiple possibilities inherent in borders, he notes that "with displacement, upheaval, unmooring, come the terror and potentiality of flux, improvisation, and creative recombinations" (p. 185). We cite Conquergood's observations to acknowledge that the rhetorical "turn" in the humanities and social sciences brings potential dangers and losses, as well as opportunities.

7. As we crossed disciplinary borders in this essay, we appreciated the work (and implications thereof) of Gloria Anzaldúa. Her compelling *Borderlands/La Frontera: The New Mestiza* (San Francisco: Aunt Lute, 1987) brilliantly articulates the promises — and dangers — inherent in crossing borders: cultural, political, racial, ethnic, and sexual borders. Anzaldúa tells us that to survive the Borderlands, we must "live *sin fronteras* [without borders]" (p. 195). To be conscious of Borderlands is, according to Anzaldúa, to develop a new consciousness, a *mestiza* consciousness and tolerance of blurring, instability, struggle, contradictions, and ambiguity (pp. 77ff.) — the very fabric of full human consciousness itself.

We are not the first, of course, to explore the intersections of rhetoric and feminism. Although we cannot hope to survey all such efforts, we will whenever possible acknowledge current feminist work in the history of rhetoric. Helpful introductions to this work include: Barbara Biesecker, "Coming to Terms with Recent Attempts to Write Women into the History of Rhetoric," *Philosophy and Rhetoric* 25 (1992): 140–61; Karlyn Kohrs Campbell, *Man Cannot Speak for Her: A Critical Study of*

Early Feminist Rhetoric, 2 vols. (New York: Greenwood, 1989); Cheryl Glenn, "Remapping Rhetorical Territory," *Rhetoric Review* 13 (Spring 1995): 287–303; and Andrea Lunsford, *Reclaiming Rhetorica* (Pittsburgh: University of Pittsburgh Press, 1995). Cf. note 1.

8. Of course, it is beyond the scope of our essay and abilities to list all the feminist scholarship (cf. notes 1 and 4) that recuperates and analyzes women's contributions in the broad history of culture-making, but we want to provide at least a bare sketch. Feminist cultural analyses continue to sweep through philosophy (Linda Lopez McAlister, "Some Remarks on Exploring the History of Women in Philosophy," *Hypatia* 4 [Spring 1989]: 1–5; Nancy Tuana, *The Less Noble Sex: Scientific, Religious, and Philosophical Conceptions of Woman's Nature* [Bloomington: Indiana University Press, 1993]; Mary Ellen Waithe, *A History of Women Philosophers*, 2 vols. to date [Dordrecht: Martinus Nijhoff, 1987–]); literature (Sandra M. Gilbert and Susan Gubar, *The Madwoman in the Attic* [New Haven: Yale University Press, 1979]; Peggy Kamuf, *Fictions of Feminine Desire* [Lincoln: University of Nebraska Press, 1982]; Nancy K. Miller, *The Poetics of Gender* [New York: Columbia University Press, 1986]); language (Dennis Baron, *Grammar and Gender* [New Haven: Yale University Press, 1986]; Cheris Kramerae, *Women and Men Speaking: Frameworks for Analysis* [Rowley, MA: Newberry, 1981]; Dale Spender, *Man Made Language* [London: Routledge, 1980]); writing (Elizabeth Abel, "Race, Class, and Psychoanalysis? Opening Questions," in *Conflicts in Feminism*, eds. Marianne Hirsch and Evelyn Fox Keller [New York: Routledge, 1990], pp. 184–204; Cynthia L. Caywood and Gillian R. Overing, *Teaching Writing: Pedagogy, Gender, and Equality* [Albany: State University of New York Press, 1987]; Lisa Ede and Andrea Lunsford, *Singular Texts/Plural Authors* [Carbondale: Southern Illinois University Press, 1990]); societal structure (Edwin Ardener, "The Problem Revisited," in *Perceiving Women*, ed. Shirley Ardener [London: Malaby, 1975], pp. 19–28; Jean Bethke Elshtain, *Public Man, Private Woman* [Princeton: Princeton University Press, 1987]; Jane Gardner, *Women in Roman Law and Society* [New York: St. Martin's Press, 1987]; bell hooks, *Yearning: Race, Gender, and Cultural Politics* [Boston: South End Press, 1990]; Joan Kelly, *Women, History, and Theory: The Essays of Joan Kelly* [Chicago: University of Chicago Press, 1984]); Christianity (Mary Daly, *The Church and the Second Sex* [New York: Harper-Colophon, 1968]; Rosemary Radford Ruether, *Religion and Sexism: Images of Woman in Jewish and Christian Traditions* [New York: Simon and Schuster, 1974]); history (Simone de Beauvoir, *The Second Sex* [1952; rpt. New York: Vintage-Random, 1976]; Gerda Lerner, *The Majority Finds Its Past* [New York: Oxford University Press, 1981]; Joan Wallach Scott, *Gender and the Politics of History* [New York: Columbia University Press, 1988]); education (Sara Munson Deats, *Gender and Academe: Feminist Pedagogy and Politics* [Latham, MD: Rowman, 1994]; Madeleine R. Grumet, *Bittermilk: Women and Teaching* [Amherst: University of Massachusetts Press, 1988]; Kathleen Weiler, *Women Teaching for Change* [New York: Bergin, 1988]); reading (David Bleich, *The Double Perspective: Language, Literature, and Social Relations* [New York: Oxford University Press, 1988]; Elizabeth Flynn and Patrocinio Schweikart, eds., *Gender and Reading* [Baltimore: Johns Hopkins University Press, 1986]); psychology (Nancy Chodorow, *The Reproduction of Mothering* [Berkeley: University of California Press, 1978]; Carol Gilligan, *In a Different Voice: Psychological Theory and Women's Development* [Cambridge: Harvard University Press, 1982]; Juliet Mitchell, *Psychoanalysis and Feminism* [New York: Pantheon, 1974]); gender (Judith Butler, *Gender Trouble: Feminism and the Subversion of Identity* [New York: Routledge, 1990]; Peter Brown, *Body and Society* [New York: Columbia University Press, 1988]; Thomas Laqueur, *Making Sex* [Cambridge: Harvard University Press, 1990]); and science (Donna Haraway, *Primate Visions: Gender, Race, and Nature in the World of Modern Science* [New York: Routledge, 1989]; Evelyn Fox Keller, *Reflections on Gender and Science* [New Haven: Yale University Press, 1985]; Sara Ruddick and Pamela Daniels, eds., *Working It Out: 23 Women Writers, Artists, Scientists, and Scholars Talk About Their Lives and Work* [New York: Pantheon, 1977]) — all of which, including the many others unnamed here, help create a space for reconceiving the rhetorical tradition in terms of feminism.

9. For example, biologist Donna Haraway demonstrates the pandisciplinarity of feminist work in her *Primate Visions*.

10. (Stanford: Stanford University Press, 1992), p. 2.

11. The essays cited here are in Hirsch and Keller, *Conflicts in Feminism*, pp. 60–81, 184–204, and 349–69, respectively.

12. Freccero, "Notes of a Post-Sex Wars Theorizer," in ibid., pp. 305–25; Ling, "I'm Here: An Asian American Woman's Response," in *Feminisms*, eds. Robyn R. Warhol and Diane Price Herndl (New Brunswick, NJ: Rutgers University Press, 1991), pp. 738–45; Scott, "Deconstructing Equality-Versus-Difference: Or, the Uses of Poststructuralist Theory for Feminism," in Hirsch and Keller, *Conflicts in Feminism*, pp. 134–48; Showalter, "A Criticism of Our Own: Autonomy and Assimilation in Afro-American and Feminist Literary Theory," in Warhol and Herndl, *Feminisms*, pp. 168–92; and Spivak, "Three Women's Texts and a Critique of Imperialism," in ibid., pp. 798–814.

13. Warhol and Herndl's 1991 *Feminisms* argues for the regular use of the term, which acknowledges the diversity of motivation, method, and experience among feminist academics. In their introduction, the editors tell us that from the outside, "feminism may appear monolithic, unified, or singularly definable. . . . [But, actually, there is a] multiplicity of approaches and assumptions inside the movement. While this variety can lead to conflict and competition, it can also be the source of movement, vitality, and genuine learning. Such diversity — if fostered, as it has been in some feminist thought — can be a model for cultural heterogeneity."

14. *Southern Communication Journal* 57 (Winter 1992): 88.

15. Ibid.

16. Kathleen Welch, "Reconfiguring Writing and Delivery in Secondary Orality," in *Rhetorical Memory and Delivery*, ed. John Frederick Reynolds (Hillsdale, NJ: Erlbaum, 1993), p. 17.

17. "The Platonic Paradox: Plato's Rhetoric in Contemporary Rhetoric and Composition Studies," *Written Communication* 5 (1988): 5–6.

18. "Modern Rhetoric and Memory," in Reynolds, *Rhetorical Memory and Delivery*, p. 35.

19. Aristotle, *The Rhetoric and the Poetics of Aristotle* (1954; rpt. New York: Modern Library, 1984), I.2.

20. *Partitiones Oratoriae*, trans. E. W. Sutton (Cambridge: Harvard University Press, 1979), p. 26.

21. Kinneavy, *A Theory of Discourse* (1971; rpt. New York: Norton, 1980); Lauer, "Heuristics and Composition," in *Contemporary Rhetoric: A Conceptual Background with Readings*, ed. W. Ross Winterowd (New York: Harcourt, 1975), pp. 79–90; Corbett, *Classical Rhetoric for the Modern Student* (1965; rpt. New York: Oxford University Press, 1990); Young, "Invention: A Topographical Survey," in *Teaching Composition: Ten Bibliographic Essays*, ed. Gary Tate (Fort Worth: Texas Christian University Press, 1976), pp. 1–44; Perelman and Olbrechts-Tyteca, *The New Rhetoric: A Treatise on Argumentation*, trans. John Wilkinson and Purcell Weaver (Notre Dame: University of Notre Dame Press, 1969); Burke, *A Rhetoric of Motives*.

22. Carruthers, *The Book of Memory: A Study of Memory in Medieval Culture* (Cambridge: Cambridge University Press, 1990); Stock, *Listening for the Text* (Baltimore: Johns Hopkins University Press, 1990); Reynolds, *Rhetorical Memory and Delivery*; Crowley, "Modern Rhetoric and Memory," in ibid., pp. 31–44; Welch, "Reconfiguring Writing and Delivery in Secondary Orality," in ibid., pp. 17–30.

23. The term "postmodern" is itself a contested construction, both broadly and within feminism. We have found Flax's analysis of the central characteristics of postmodernism persuasive. Flax represents postmodern theorists as "masters of suspicion" (*Thinking Fragments*, p. 31) who argue that mind, reason, and truth are all effects of discourse; that discourses are "local, heterogeneous, and incommensurable" (p. 36), and thus caught up in issues of power, struggle, and hierarchy; and that such once-privileged narratives as philosophy and history can best be viewed as stories that are as rhetorically grounded and interested as any other story.

24. "Choosing the Margins as Space of Radical Openness," *Framework* 36 (1989): 16.

25. "Uses of the Erotic: The Erotic as Power," in *Sister Outsider* (Freedom, CA: Crossing, 1984), pp. 53–54.

26. "Memory, Creation, and Writing," *Thought* 59 (1984): 385.

27. Michael M. J. Fischer, "Ethnicity and the Post-Modern Arts of Memory," in *Writing Culture: The Poetics and Politics of Ethnography; A School of American Research Advanced Seminar*, eds. James Clifford and George E. Marcus (Berkeley: University of California Press, 1986), p. 198.

28. *Yearning: Race, Gender, and Cultural Politics*, p. 147.

29. "Ciceronian *Dispositio* as an Architecture for Creativity in Composition; A Note for the Affirmative," *Rhetoric Review* 4 (Sept. 1985); 108.

30. *Rhetoric* I.2.

31. *A Rhetoric of Motives*, p. 43.

32. "The Womanization of Rhetoric," *Women's Studies International Quarterly* 2 (1979): 195. Gearhart's claims are echoed in the work of those who have lately focused our attention on what Elspeth Stuckey calls "the violence of literacy." Writing itself is, as Derrida long ago observed, an act of dis-placement. Even the word itself is related etymologically to cutting/carving, to acts of violence.

33. "Beyond Persuasion: A Proposal for an Invitational Rhetoric," *Communication Monographs* 62 (Mar. 1995): 2–18.

34. Olsen's prose, with its frequent ellipses, fragments, and erasures, its insistent inclusion of other women's words, calls attention not only to alternative forms of arrangement, of course, but to her methods of invention and even more to her style, demonstrating once again how the canons inevitably blur when put into practice. For a view of Olsen's method and rationale for opening up

textual space, see "One Out of Twelve: Writers Who Are Women in Our Century" (in *Silences* [New York: Delacorte, 1978], pp. 41–66), a revealing overview of twentieth-century women writers.

35. *Talking Back: Thinking Feminist, Thinking Black* (Boston: South End, 1989), p. 77.

36. "Me and My Shadow," *New Literary History* 19 (Autumn 1987): 172.

37. Ibid.

38. Ibid., p. 178.

39. "Margaret Fuller: Inventing a Feminist Discourse," in Lunsford, *Reclaiming Rhetorica*, pp. 137–66.

40. Ibid., pp. 139–40.

41. See *Elements of Rhetoric* (1828; rpt. in *The Rhetoric of Blair, Campbell, and Whately*, eds. James L. Golden and Edward P. J. Corbett [Carbondale: Southern Illinois University Press, 1990]).

42. "Margaret Fuller," p. 159.

43. "Laugh of the Medusa," in *The Signs Reader*, eds. Elizabeth Abel and Emily K. Abel (Chicago: University of Chicago Press, 1983), pp. 279–97.

44. "Writing Against Writing: The Predicament of *Ecriture Féminine* in Composition Studies," in *Contending With Words*, eds. Patricia Harkin and John Schilb (New York: Modern Language Assoc., 1991), pp. 82–104.

45. In Warhol and Herndl, *Feminisms*, p. 458.

46. "Julia Kristeva and the Woman as Stranger," in Lunsford, *Reclaiming Rhetorica*, p. 309.

47. Ibid., p. 308.

48. Ibid., p. 314.

49. Ibid., p. 305.

50. "An Open Letter to Mary Daly," in *Sister Outsider*, pp. 66–71.

51. (Cambridge: Harvard University Press, 1991).

52. (New York: Plume-New American, 1987).

53. *Rhetoric* III.1.

54. Ibid.

55. P. 380.

56. Aristotle, *Rhetoric* III.1.

57. *Classical Rhetoric for the Modern Student*, p. 381.

58. P. 65. Such "sensuality, costume, and color" have often found embodiment in a theory of figures and tropes as discursive excesses and linguistic means of manipulation, although another view holds tropes to be central to all language and meaning. (J. Hillis Miller is one prominent contemporary proponent of this view.) In any case, feminist theorists have begun to carry out further forays into tropology. Jane Sutton, for example, attempts a tropological argument that moves "metaphorically, metonymically, synecdochically, and ironically" to unseat traditional tropes that inscribe woman ("The Taming of the *Polos/Polis*," p. 97). In another intriguing and nontraditional analysis, Foss and Griffin compare the rhetorics of Burke and feminist writer-activist Starhawk, noting the differing ways in which the two theorists use (and do not use) certain tropes (see "A Feminist Perspective on Rhetorical Theory: Toward a Clarification of Boundaries," *Western Journal of Communication* 56 [Fall 1992]: 330–49).

59. Trans. Walter Hamilton (London: Penguin, 1960), p. 44.

60. Qtd. in Michael Mooney, *Vico in the Tradition of Rhetoric* (Princeton: Princeton University Press, 1985), pp. 58–59.

61. *Gorgias*, p. 37.

62. *Sentimental Modernism: Women Writers and the Revolution of the Word* (Bloomington: Indiana University Press, 1991), p. 8.

63. Ibid., p. 3.

64. Ibid., p. 52.

65. Ibid., p. 55.

66. Ibid., p. 53.

67. Ibid., p. 31.

68. Ibid., p. 47.

69. Ibid., p. 54.

70. Ibid., p. 65.

71. Ibid., p. 45.

72. (Boston: Beacon, 1987).

73. Jane Hedley, "Surviving to Speak New Language: Mary Daly and Adrienne Rich," *Hypatia* 7 (Spring 1992): 43. Similar efforts include Monique Wittig and Sande Zeig's *Lesbian Peoples: Material for a Dictionary* (New York: Avon, 1979); and Cheris Kramerae and Paula A. Treichler's *Amazons, Bluestockings, and Crones* (London: Pandora, 1992).

74. *Websters'*, p. 167.

75. (Boston; Beacon, 1978).

76. P. 67.

77. Ibid., p. 71.

78. In *Multi-Cultural Literacy: Opening the American Mind*, eds. Rick Simonson and Scott Walker (Saint Paul, MN: Graywolf Press, 1988), pp. 63–81.

79. Ibid., p. 8l.

80. See Cisneros, *House on Mango Street* (New York: Random House, 1994).

81. Recent examples include Alice Kaplan's *French Lessons: A Memoir* (Chicago: University of Chicago Press, 1993); hooks's *Talking Back*; Tompkins' "Me and My Shadow," pp. 169–78; and Marianna Torgovnick's edited collection *Eloquent Obsessions: Writing Cultural Criticism* (Durham: Duke University Press, 1994).

82. *The Poetics of Gender* (New York: Columbia University Press, 1986), p. 24.

83. P. 47.

84. *Yearning*, p. 21.

85. (Bloomington: Indiana University Press, 1989), p. 76.

86. Aristotle, *Rhetoric* III.1.

87. Trans. Harry Caplan (Cambridge: Harvard University Press, 1954), 3.11.19.

88. Trans. E. W. Sutton (Cambridge: Harvard University Press, 1979), 3.56.213.

89. Cicero, *Brutus, On the Nature of the Gods, On Divination, On Duties*, trans. Hubert M. Poteat (Chicago: University of Chicago Press, 1950), 28.142.

90. Cicero, *Brutus, Orator*, trans. G. L. Hendrickson and H. M. Hubbell, respectively (Cambridge: Harvard University Press, 1949), 17.55.

91. *Institutio Oratoria*, trans. H. E. Butler, 4 vols. (1920; rpt. London: Heinemann, 1969), 11.3.2.

92. Ibid., 11.3–6.

93. We have not, however, used only traditional strategies. For example, we have chosen to collaborate, a nontraditional academic way to write and publish, in order to share equally the work and the credit of this essay, following the feminist tradition of "connected knowing" recorded in Mary Field Belenky, Blythe McVicker Clinchy, Nancy Rule Goldberger, and Jill Mattuck Tarule's *Women's Ways of Knowing* (New York: Basic, 1986) and expanded in Inderpal Grewal and Caren Kaplan's *Scattered Hegemonies* (Minneapolis: University of Minnesota Press, 1994). As Grewal and Kaplan note, "We must work collaboratively in order to formulate transnational feminist alliances" (p. 1). Nontraditionally, then, we deliver the third collaboratively written essay in *Rhetorica* (two earlier pieces, both on the rhetoric of science, were contributed by J. E. McGuire and Trevor Melia). In another nontraditional move, we use postmodern feminist examples and methodology, and we depend on a number of women writers and speakers who may not be familiar to our non-American readers.

94. *Orator* 17.55.

95. "Toward a Transactional View of Rhetorical and Feminist Theory: Rereading Hélène Cixous's *The Laugh of the Medusa*," *Southern Communication Journal* 57 (Winter 1992): 87.

96. Nor can we here explore the delivery of silence, a traditionally undervalued feminine mode, given the western tendency to valorize speech and language. Elaine Hedges and Shelley Fisher Fishkin (*Listening to Silences* [New York; Oxford University Press, 1944]) have recently helped us understand the expressive, positive powers of silence when it denotes alertness and sensitivity, when it signifies attentiveness or stoicism, and particularly when it seeks out and listens to new voices. Such explorations remind us of how much more we may yet learn here.

97. Throughout this essay, our examples have come from women using literate (print) delivery systems. In this section, we concentrate mostly on women's use of the oral medium of delivery. We do not speak to issues of facial and bodily gestures, nor will we comment on voice-timbre; except for our example of Ann Richards, we have no access to the actual physical delivery of these women.

98. Nor, of course, does any of Socrates' work, but the historical tradition has readily accepted secondary accounts of his influence, teaching, and beliefs. The same cannot be said for any female counterpart.

99. Discussions of Aspasia's intellectual activity can be found in the works of Plato (437–328 BCE), Xenophon (fl. 450 BCE), Cicero (100–43 BCE), Athenaeus (fl. AD 200), and Plutarch (AD 46–c.120).

100. Plato, *Timaeus, Critias, Cleitophon, Menexenus, Epistles*, trans. R. G. Bury (1929; rpt. London: Heinemann-Loeb, 1981), 240e ff.

101. Ibid., 236e.

102. For a thorough account of Aspasia's contributions to rhetoric, see Cheryl Glenn's "sex, lies, and manuscript: Refiguring Aspasia in the History of Rhetoric," *College Composition and Communication* 45 (1994): 180–99.

103. In 1934, Hope Emily Allen identified and helped Sanford Brown Meech edit the unique manuscript, long the possession of the W. Butler-Bowden estate. (Margery Kempe, *The Book of Margery Kempe*, eds. Hope Emily Allen and Sanford Brown Meech [London: Oxford University Press, 1940].)

104. See Cheryl Glenn's "Reexamining *The Book of Margery Kempe*: A Rhetoric of Autobiography" (in Lunsford, *Reclaiming Rhetorica*, pp. 53–71) for a fuller argument regarding Kempe's significance as a rhetorician.

105. "Sojourner Truth," in *Women Speakers in the United States: 1800–1925; 1925–1993*, ed. Karlyn Kohrs Campbell, 2 vols. (Westport, CT: Greenwood, 1993), 1:421.

106. Qtd. in ibid., 1:428.

107. Harriet Carter, "Sojourner Truth," *Chautauquan* 7 (May 1887): 479.

108. Elizabeth Cady Stanton, Susan B. Anthony, and Matilda Joslyn Gage, eds., *History of Woman Suffrage* (Salem, NH: Ayer, 1985), 2:926.

109. Richards, Ann. Keynote Address to Democratic National Convention. July 18, 1988. <http://gos.sbc.edu/~/richards.html>

110. Illus. Kathleen Turner Suarez (Cambridge: Eastgate System, 1993).

111. *Hypertext: The Convergence of Contemporary Theory and Technology* (Baltimore: Johns Hopkins University Press, 1992).

112. Jamie R. Barlowe, conversation among the contributors in the "Afterword," Lunsford, *Reclaiming Rhetorica*, p. 327.

113. *Borderlands/La Frontera*, p. 3.

114. *Woman, Native, Other*, p. 94.

115. Kaplan, *French Lessons*, p. 149.

116. Kenneth Burke, *Language as Symbolic Action: Essays on Life, Literature, and Method* (Berkeley: University of California Press, 1966), p. 16.

117. *The Chronicle of Higher Education*, May 4, 1988, p. A52.

118. See *Conflicts in Feminism*, p. 352.

119. "Contingent Foundations: Feminism and the Question of 'Postmodernism,'" in *Feminists Theorize the Political* (New York: Routledge, 1992), p. 8.

120. P. 222.

121. "Voice and the Naming of Woman," in *Voices on Voice: Perspectives, Definitions, Inquiry*, ed. Kathleen Blake Yancey (Urbana, IL: NCTE, 1994), p. 240.

122. "Multiple Mediations: Feminist Scholarship in the Age of Multinational Reception," *Inscriptions* 5 (1989): 4.

123. "The Politics of Location: Cinema/Theory/Literature/Ethnicity/Sexuality/Me," *Framework* 36 (1989): 53.

124. Kaplan, *French Lessons*, p. 139.

125. *Yearning*, p. 151.

19 *Crimes of Writing and Reading*

Since the publication in 1989 of Karlyn Kohrs Campbell's two-volume *Man Can Not Speak for Her*, scholars of rhetoric and writing have done much to reclaim and describe women's contributions to rhetorical history and practice. Such work has necessarily entailed a challenge to the scope and definition of the rhetorical tradition, and to traditional understandings of historiography. The following chronology indicates the significance and breadth of this work:

1990

Kathleen Welch. *The Contemporary Reception of Classical Rhetoric*

Lisa Ede and Andrea Lunsford. *Singular Texts/Plural Authors: Perspectives on Collaborative Writing*

1991

Karen Foss and Sonja Foss, eds. *Women Speak: The Eloquence of Women's Lives*

Susan Jarratt. *Rereading the Sophists: Classical Rhetoric Refigured*

C. Jan Swearingen. *Rhetoric and Irony: Western Literacy and Western Lies*

1995

Shirley Wilson Logan, ed. *With Pen and Voice: A Critical Anthology of Nineteenth-Century African-American Women*

Catherine Hobbs, ed. *Nineteenth-Century Women Learn to Write*

Andrea Lunsford, ed. *Reclaiming Rhetorica: Women in the History of Rhetoric*

Krista Ratcliffe. *Anglo-American Feminist Challenges to the Rhetorical Traditions: Virginia Woolf, Mary Daly, Adrienne Rich*

1996

JoAnn Campbell, ed. *Toward a Feminist Rhetoric: The Writing of Gertrude Buck*

From Andrea Lunsford and Lisa Ede, in *Teaching Rhetorica: Theory, Pedagogy, Practice*, ed. Kate Ronald and Joy Ritchie (Portsmouth, NH: Boynton/Cook, 2006) 13–30.

1997

Gere, Anne. *Intimate Practices: Literacy and Cultural Work in U.S. Women's Clubs, 1880–1920*

Cheryl Glenn. *Rhetoric Retold: Regendering the Tradition from Antiquity through the Renaissance*

Jacqueline Jones Royster, ed. *Southern Horrors and Other Writings: The Anti-Lynching Campaign of Ida B. Wells, 1892–1900*

1998

Carol Mattingly. *Well-Tempered Women: Nineteenth-Century Temperance Rhetoric*

1999

Shirley Wilson Logan. *"We Are Coming": The Persuasive Discourse of Nineteenth-Century Black Women*

Molly Meijer Wertheimer, ed. *Listening to Their Voices: The Rhetorical Activities of Historical Women*

Christine Mason Sutherland and Rebecca Sutcliffe, eds. *The Changing Tradition: Women in the History of Rhetoric*

Karen Foss, Sonja Foss, and Cyndi Griffin, eds. *Feminist Rhetorical Theories*

Susan Kates. *Activist Rhetorics and American Higher Education: 1885–1937*

Christine Nguyen Fredrick. *Feminist Rhetoric in Cyberspace*

2000

Jacqueline Jones Royster. *Traces of a Stream: Literacy and Social Change Among African American Women*

2001

Michelle Bailiff. *Seduction, Sophistry, and the Woman with the Rhetorical Figure*

Joy Ritchie and Kate Ronald, eds. *Available Means: An Anthology of Women's Rhetoric*

Kami Day and Michele Eodice. *(First Person)²: A Study of Co-Authoring in the Academy*

2002

Jane Donawerth, ed. *Rhetorical Theory by Women Before 1900*

Nan Johnson. *Gender and Rhetorical Space in American Life: 1866–1910*

Elizabeth A. Flynn. *Feminism Beyond Modernism*

Carol Mattingly. *Appropriate[ing] Dress: Women's Rhetorical Style in Nineteenth-Century America*

2003

M. Jacqui Alexander, Lisa Albrecht, Sharon Day, and Mab Segrest, eds. *Sing, Whisper, Shout, Pray!: Feminist Visions for a Just World*

Beth Daniell. *A Communion of Friendship: Literacy, Spiritual Practice, and Women in Recovery*

Gesa E. Kirsch, Faye Spencer Maor, Lance Massey, Lee Mickoson-Massey, and Mary P. Sheridan-Rabideau, eds. *Feminism and Composition: A Critical Sourcebook*

Roxanne Mountford. *The Gendered Pulpit: Preaching in American Protestant Spaces*

Susan Zaeske. *Signatures of Citizenship: Petitioning, Antislavery, and Women's Political Identity*

2004

Joyce Blackwell. *No Peace Without Freedom: Race and the Women's International League for Peace and Freedom, 1915–75*

Katherine Chandler and Melissa Goldthwaite. *Surveying the Literary Landscapes of Terry Tempest Williams*

Lisa Ede. *Situating Composition: Composition Studies and the Politics of Location*

Cheryl Glenn. *Unspoken: A Rhetoric of Silence.*

Karyn Hollis. *Liberating Voices: Writing at Bryn Mawr Summer School for Women Workers*

Gwendolyn Pough. *Check It While I Wreck It: Black Womanhood, Hip-Hop Culture, and the Public Sphere*

Sarah Robbins. *Managing Literacy, Mothering America: Women's Narratives on Reading and Writing in the Nineteenth Century*

Wendy Sharer. *Vote and Voice: Women's Organizations and Political Literacy 1915–30*

2005

Lindal Buchanan. *Regendering Delivery: The Fifth Canon and Antebellum Women Rhetors*

Krista Ratcliffe. *Rhetorical Listening: Identification, Gender, Whiteness*

Jacqueline Rhodes. *Radical Feminism, Writing, and Critical Agency: From Manifesto to Modem*

In the introduction [to *Teaching Rhetorica: Theory, Pedagogy, Practice*, editors] Kate Ronald and Joy Ritchie acknowledge this impressive body of work and go on to raise a number of thought-provoking questions about our field's ongoing efforts to document and inquire into women's rhetorical practices. We need to continue to build on this work, Ronald and Ritchie argue — and we need to do so on multiple levels. What challenges to conventional understandings of history and theory, they ask, do women's rhetorical practices represent? What are the potential consequences of recent efforts to reclaim and redefine women's rhetorical practices for the actual *teaching* of writing?

As we worked on this chapter, we found that these questions reverberated for us in powerful ways. Most generally, they reminded us that as important as it has been to reclaim women's contributions to rhetorical history and practice, these contributions will not automatically have consequences for the day-to-day teaching of writing. Hence the need for [*Teaching Rhetorica*]. The questions that Ronald and Ritchie pose also encouraged us to bring together two lines of inquiry with which we have for some time been engaged. As teachers of writing and writing program administrators, we have long recognized the need to subject our pedagogical practices to ongoing critique — to never assume that we have (at last) determined the best way to understand and teach writing. We have not necessarily linked this effort, however, to our historical and textual inquiry into women's discursive theories and practices. The opportunity to place these two strands of our work in dialogue has stimulated much productive thought.

As teachers of writing, for instance, we have been aware that the institutional, cultural, political, and economic contexts in which we work hold the potential to co-opt, subvert, or in other ways discipline our teaching. We recognize as well that the ideologies that most strongly inform our assumptions and practices are not necessarily shared by our students — and thus conflict is an important element of the rhetorical situation of our classrooms.

Reading and thinking about the discursive practices of Marguerite Porete, Anne Hutchinson, Geneva Smitherman, Kathy Acker, and Anna Deavere Smith — some of the women we will consider in this chapter — reminds us that we cannot know how students will experience various rhetorics. We regularly invite students, for example, to experiment with discursive practices that in one way or another transgress conventional academic norms: we do so when we invite students to write collaboratively or to compose texts that experiment or "play" with language. Placing this pedagogical invitation in the context of crimes of writing and reading reminds us that whereas some students will experience our invitation as a stimulating opportunity to experiment with new and interesting ways of enacting writing, others will consider this same invitation a threatening and an unwanted solicitation to crime.

Later in this chapter, we will have more to say about the insights we have gained as teachers as a result of considering both our and our students' discursive practices from the perspective of crimes of writing and reading. We turn now, however, to a discussion of these crimes — one that is wide-ranging not only in its historical breadth but also in the diversity of examples we discuss. We are not the first, of course, to observe that women's practices of reading and writing have all too often been represented as "crimes" that posed such serious threats to the rhetorical status quo that, for many women throughout history, the mere desire to learn to write and read becomes a suspicious and even criminal act. In sketching in this history, we will point to specific women who insist on pursuing "improper" discursive behaviors and reflect on the ways in which our engagement with their texts and practices has influenced both our theoretical understandings and pedagogical enactments. As we do so, we will attend to the specific historical conditions in which people write and read. Such a focus can, we believe, cast additional light on the tensions among readers' and writers' desires and those cultural, political, social, economic, and rhetorical assumptions and practices that can work to limit or even criminalize them.

Our interest in crimes of reading and writing grew most immediately out of our own experiences as coauthors who, especially when we began collaborating, felt "othered" by our desire to write together. (In reviews for tenure and promotion, for instance, both our chairs and departmental and college committees made it clear that they did not know how to "count," or in other ways assess our collaborative scholarly work, and hence they did not value it.) Our earliest explorations of the extent to which coauthoring is not only devalued but proscribed — especially by those in the humanities — focused on the discursive practices of the many writers in the workplace who are called on to work collaboratively on both the production of knowledge and of texts. Early on in our research, we realized that simply documenting the practices of these writers would do little to dislodge deeply held assumptions about the nature of authorship and of intellectual property — or of transgressions against these assumptions — so our efforts expanded to encompass historical and theoretical efforts to rethink what it means to be an "author" or to have an "original" idea.

This work eventually led to the publication in 1990 of *Singular Texts/Plural Authors: Perspectives on Collaborative Writing* and to a series of essays and conference presentations on collaboration and intellectual property, especially as they relate to women's discursive practices. Along the way, we became increasingly interested in identifying and studying the work of women who — sometimes consciously, sometimes unconsciously — have written texts that others view as either deviant or criminal. (This range stretches from the eccentric, as in the case of Sojourner Truth, to the actionable, as our discussion of Kathy Acker will demonstrate.) As we did so, we often had to remind ourselves that the very definition of a "crime" of writing is historically situated. In the Middle Ages, for instance, perhaps the worst crime of writing for either a man or a woman was blasphemy, since at that time it was God who could be said to "own" language and its power. In more secular periods, such as the Elizabethan period in Great Britain, sovereign states held that power — and sedition was the prime crime of writing. For the last three hundred years, anything that threatened the hegemony of the originary author (whether an individual person or a corporate entity) or author construct was likely to be viewed as a violation of copyright law, and thus as a crime.

Once we took the focus even momentarily off singular authorship, a whole range of practices came into view, practices that challenge the authorial tradition or are in other ways transgressive — from medieval women mystics' collaborative writing with scribes (or with God, for that matter, who "authored" their visions); to Renaissance women translators who smuggled their own subversive ideas into prefaces to the translated or "proper" material; to the conversational rhetoric women such as Margaret Fuller practiced as a mode of resistance to the linearity so favored at the time; to the many contemporary women who have insisted on pursuing practices of writing that challenge the norm.

CRIMES OF WRITING

Among such contemporary writers whose acts have been criminalized, few are more visibly transgressive than Kathy Acker. Susan Stewart concludes her study *Crimes of Writing* with a brief discussion of Acker's *Don Quixote: Which Was a Dream*. "Here," says Stewart, "it is important not to consider this [book] a matter of rewriting or revision, for there is no attempt to translate, update, or improve upon the fabric of history other than to parody such a gesture of renovation" (1991, 286). Here, in short, is a book that will "plagiarize" to forge whatever "identity" it might arrive at. In Acker's work, Stewart notes in a concluding understatement: "all the relations between attribution, authority, theory and practice, primary and secondary texts, intention . . . become exaggerated" (288).

And that's putting it mildly. Acker, born — according to various "official" sources, in 1943, 1945, 1947, or 1948 — and raised in New York City, attended a private girls' school before her parents disowned her. In subsequent years, she continued her education both on the streets and at other schools, eventually studying for (but not completing) a PhD in English literature at New York University. From her first novel, *Politics* (1972), to her final novel, *Pussy, King of the Pirates* (1996), Acker produced a significant body of work that went, as she herself might have said, well beyond experimentalism. Combining high theory and low street talk, dreams of friendship and scenes of sadomasochistic cruelty, Acker rewrites the so-called works of others, collapsing genres, time periods, genders, and selves in a series of dizzying texts that have been called everything from "literary trash compactors" (LeClair 1986, 10) to "prose assemblages" (McCaffery 1996, 14) to texts of great "outlaw intelligence" (Olsen 1994, np).

What accounts for these descriptions? We can fairly easily chart the characteristics of Acker's work that seem most threatening, that may account for her being labeled an outlaw, a criminal, or the term she herself preferred, a "pirate." Identity in Acker's works, for example, and especially *sexual* identity, is completely fluid. As a result, any traditional sense of "intentionality" or "voice," and hence of authorial power or agency, is absent. One way that Acker consistently challenged notions of agency was through her rejection of or play with personal pronouns. She seldom uses first person, for instance, as this opening to the second part of *Don Quixote: Which Was a Dream* demonstrates: "Being dead, Don Quixote could no longer speak. Being born into and part of a male world, she had no speech of her own. All she could do was read male texts which weren't hers" (1984, 39). Likewise, in her essay "Humility," a description of the ordeal she went through when Harold Robbins and his attorneys charged her with plagiarism and her "feminist" publisher did little to help (even though Acker carefully refuted each of the charges brought against her), she consistently drops out the pronouns: "In Paris decided that it's stupid to live in fear. . . . Still trying to explain . . . the deconstructionist needs to use the actual other texts" (1990, 128). Such striking omission of personal pronouns is part of Acker's insistent rejection of traditional authority, an insistence that resulted in many charges against her, including that of plagiarism.

Indeed, in her terms, Acker could not keep from plagiarizing, *Don Quixote: Which Was a Dream*, for example, mixes such real-life events as an abortion with passages from and references to not only Cervantes and the Cid, but to Borges (whose "Pierre Menard, Author of the Quixote" pairs well with Acker's text), de Sade, Machiavelli, Milton, Shakespeare, *Wuthering Heights*, *Waiting for Godot*, and the work of many literary and feminist theorists. Her *Great Expectations*, another "piratical" text, operates on a similar trajectory. In these and other novels, Acker acts out her theory that language cannot be owned — particularly not by coherent, organic "individuals."

The use of extreme violence, pornography, and explicit sexual material — another hallmark of Acker's work that led to censure — is related to her effort to resist what she sees as the degradation brought on the world by global capitalism and commodification, including the commodification represented by the author construct. Though many (including us) find aspects of her work shocking, she insisted that "I'm really not interested in shocking people in the usual sense but the idea of shock as a form of teaching . . . I want to show them that their perceptual habits are distorted, too rigidified" (McCaffery 1996, 16). Thus in her life and in her work, Acker attempted to define a space outside the patriarchal laws of discourse and society she believed trapped most artists and, she acknowledged over and over, *all* women — including those who identify themselves as radical feminist theorists. (In his dissertation study, John Logie devotes a chapter to a reading of Acker and Cixous that does much, we think, to contribute to an understanding of Acker's own brand of feminism.) To do so, Acker used the "criminal" techniques described earlier to wrench genres and languages completely out of context, to remake them through and with one another, to both deconstruct and construct. In interviews, she talked in detail about her exploration of deconstruction and her use of deconstructive methods as well as her eventual rejection of these techniques as finally too limited and limiting. Throughout her life, Acker searched for a way to reject and escape the confines of genre, which she saw as related to, indeed created by, hegemonic and patriarchal practices.

Acker's willingness to challenge the conventional assumptions and forms of Western authorship — to deny the myth of individual genius and originality and to engage in the crimes we have just described — is shared by another contemporary writer we find fascinating. Anna Deavere Smith, playwright, actress, and author and sole performer of such plays as *Fires in the Mirror: Crown Heights, Brooklyn, and Other Identities* and *Twilight Los Angeles, 1992*, is in a number of ways less scandalous than Acker, both in terms of her intentions and in terms of the nature and consequences of the texts she writes and performs. But Smith's work, like Acker's, though valued by many, has nevertheless at times been viewed as a crime of writing.

Some background about Smith's project may be helpful in exploring this reaction. For almost twenty years, Smith has been engaged in an extended project titled *On the Road: A Search for an American Character* ("Theater in Search of the American Character" n.d.). Whether she is writing and performing a play about the Crown Heights riots or the civil unrest and destruction that engulfed Los Angeles in the wake of the initial Rodney King verdict, Smith deliberately and self-consciously constructs dramas solely from the words of others, thus flouting the prevailing assumption that as a playwright she must create character and plot from the "smithy" of her own individual imagination. As author, Smith (depending on your perspective) thus collaborates with — or appropriates and thus "steals" — the words of those she interviews. There are additional ways in which Smith's plays depend on collaboration with others. In *Twilight Los Angeles,* for instance, Smith worked with four individuals of various races who functioned as dramaturges and thus assisted her in the preparation of the play. In the introduction to the print version of *Twilight Los Angeles,* Smith calls attention to the importance of their role, noting that "these dramaturges brought their own real-world experiences with race to bear on the work. They reacted to *Twilight* at every stage of its development" (A. Smith 1994, xxii).

The scope and ambition of Smith's project are substantial. As part of her work for *Twilight Los Angeles,* for instance, Smith interviewed more than two hundred individuals, from relatively anonymous persons, such as the wife of a Korean store owner injured in the riots, to such well-known figures as Maxine Waters, Cornell West, and Daryl Gates. In this project, as in others, once the interviews were completed Smith listened to the tapes over and over — and over and over. Her goal, as she has explained, is to listen carefully not only to her interviewees' words but to the rhythms, the tics and tremors of their language, and thus to arrive at the essence of their characters.

In performance, and using minimal props and costume changes, Smith attempts as fully as possible to embody the individuals whose words she speaks. In so doing, Smith operates out of a sophisticated Bakhtinian understanding of the relationship between language and subjectivity. In speaking about her work, for instance, Smith says:

> My sense is that the American character lives not in one place or the other but in the gaps between the places, and in our struggle to be together in our differences. It lives not in what has been fully articulated but in what is in the process of being articulated, not in the smooth-sounding words but in the very moment that the smooth-sounding words fail us. It is alive right now. We might not like what we see, but in order to change it, we have to see it clearly. (Stepanek n.d.)

In describing her work, Smith acknowledges the ethical complexity of her effort, " 'Acting isn't nice,' she has said. . . . 'It's giving but it's also stealing' " (Lloyd 1998). Although Smith has not been accused of stealing the words of others, as Acker was in her dustup with Harold Robbins, questions of originality have nevertheless played a role in the reception of her writing. For though in recent years Smith has encountered a good deal of success — in 1996 she was awarded a "genius award" of $280,000 from the MacArthur Foundation, an Obie Award, and the Ford Foundation's first artist in residency, and she also served as the founding director of the Institute on the Arts and Civic Dialogue, a Harvard University institute devoted to socially conscious art — she has nevertheless paid a price for her reliance on the words of others (Lloyd 1998). An article on Smith in the 1994 volume of the *Current Biography Yearbook* details, for instance, the decision of the Pulitzer Prize committee, which "after having listed *Fires in the Mirror* as a finalist for the award, disqualified *Twilight: Los Angeles, 1992* from consideration, reasoning that the text, because it had been taken from interviews, was not original and that other actors could not perform the play, since its authenticity lay in Smith's having conducted the interviews" ("Anna Deavere Smith" 1994, 547).

Yet Acker and Smith — in different ways and for different reasons — have succeeded in challenging powerful and deep-seated understandings about the nature of authorship and creativity, even if they have been punished or disciplined for doing so. We believe that scholars and teachers of writing need to pay very close attention to such challenges, exploring their causes as well as the uses to which they are put. As we do so, we need to take care to avoid oversimplifications and easy oppositions. As the examples of Acker and Smith illustrate, despite the ongoing critique of the sovereign subject and *his* ownership of text, the gap between theoretical critique and change at the level of praxis is broader and deeper than many have wished to acknowledge. Thus, although we are eager to recognize the power of Acker and Smith's transgressions, it would be a mistake to think of them as unidimensional exemplars of resistance or as easily comparable.

In looking at Acker's and Smith's lives and works, for example, one might be tempted to contrast them in various ways — according to race, for instance, or to the differing receptions of their work. These certainly are not insignificant issues, but they are almost certainly more complex than they at first appear. In comparison with Smith's work, for example, Acker's oeuvre has been more thoroughly and consistently marginalized in significant and ongoing ways. (As readers may be aware, Smith also appeared as a regular character in the popular TV series *West Wing*.) For though Kathy Acker certainly succeeded in publishing a significant body of work — a selected bibliography included in Larry McCaffrey's interview with Acker lists fourteen books of fiction, as well as other publications — many were published in nonmainstream presses, such as the Empty Elevator Shaft Press and Diana's BiMonthly Press. Even Grove Press's publication of her later works did not bring her into the mainstream — or into favor with many feminist critics. Acker's marginality interests us a great deal, since some of it at least is the direct result of Acker's own choices. She was, after all, a white woman who had the benefit of private and advanced higher education; her privileged position in terms of class and race needs to be factored into any understanding of how marginalization works in her case, since this privilege allowed her some freedom to take the risks, to commit writerly crimes, and to choose to deeply distrust the mainstream.

Anna Deavere Smith's case is, we find, equally complex. Acclaimed in 1993 when she was named *Glamour Magazine*'s Woman of the Year for "put-

ting race center stage" (qtd. in N. Martin 1994), Smith responded by emphasizing that her goal was not to shift anything to the center. Rather, she said,
her goal was to be "present," to be "available," to be "a witness to the changes
taking place in American culture" (N. Martin 1994). In calling attention to this
fact, we are by no means disvaluing the potentially radical nature and consequences of Smith's work but rather noting differences between Smith's stated
intentions and the way in which her work is most often characterized.

In broadest terms, if Acker's work continues to be represented as that of
the bad girl of postpunk sensibility and often dismissed on those grounds,
then Smith's work is often figured in heroic terms, as "theatre's antidote to
social irrelevance" (Lloyd 1998). Clearly, both Smith's production and the
public text of her dramas have been broadly accepted and disseminated. (*Fires
in the Mirror*, for instance, was broadcast on PBS's Great Performances, and
Twilight Los Angeles was much in the news during the tenth anniversary of the
Los Angeles riots.) Whether she is being profiled in *The New Yorker* (Lahr 1993)
or hailed by *Newsweek* as "the most exciting individual in American theatre"
(Kroll 1993), the *newness* and *uniqueness* of the effort — and the transformation she brings about via her individual acting skills — are consistently
emphasized.

As writers such as Jacqueline Jones Royster, bell hooks, Victor Villanueva,
Gloria Anzaldúa, and others have taught us, those whom our society constitutes as *other* may in our contemporary world find themselves allowed (as
they might not have been in the past) to speak and to write. But it is a rare day
when they are genuinely *heard*.[1] Our inquiry into the work and lives of Kathy
Acker and Anna Deavere Smith confirms this understanding. For whether
they are being reviled or adored, Acker and Smith both exemplify and demonstrate very strong challenges to traditional concepts of voice and singular
authorship. Yet, in many ways, their work has not been *heard* in these terms, a
fact we find to be strikingly ironic. In fact, most commentators continue to
describe both Acker and Smith as "unique" and "original" voices and to comment on their individual accomplishments, in effect disregarding (refusing to
hear) the persistent challenges both writers make to these very terms. Whether
this irony reflects the unerring ability of late-capitalist individualism to co-opt
acts of resistance or whether it reflects a kind of profound ambiguity and tension within Smith's and Acker's work (or perhaps some of both?) is not at all
clear to us at this point.

CRIMES OF READING

What *is* clear is that we can learn important lessons by examining such complex cases and by setting them in a broader communicative context that considers not only writing but reading. When we first began work on crimes of
writing, it seemed to us that reading has been a much safer activity for women
than writing has been. On reflection, however, we recognized that unsanc-
tioned ways of reading have also been marked as misinterpretations, thefts,
even felonies or immoral behaviors. This understanding reminded us that

although reading often does not result in a material product, it — like writing — is an act of meaning-construction. It reminded us, in other words, that just as inquiry into acts of writing crimes can provide unique insights into some of the most commonsensical, and thus ideologically invisible, assumptions about what it means to write "properly," so too with reading crimes.

As we began exploring crimes of reading, we noted that these acts seemed more pervasive, but also less recognizably dangerous, than crimes of writing. In the midst of our research on this topic, however, we read Azar Nafisi's *Reading Lolita in Tehran*, a gripping memoir that describes, among other things, an underground (and highly dangerous) class on English and American literature that Nafisi taught in her home for two years after resigning from Tehran University in protest of its fundamentalist practices. In a society where the legal age for marriage at that time was nine, the punishment for female adultery was stoning, and a woman could be punished if a few strands of her hair fell out of her veil, gathering a group of young women together to read banned literature — and to spend a few hours free of their veils and chadors — was dangerous indeed. Yet Nafisi took this risk to maintain her intellectual and emotional life and to help other women resist some of the most severe restrictions of Muslim fundamentalism.

Reading Lolita in Tehran is for us a powerful reminder of just how dangerous — how criminal — acts of reading can be. Obviously, the nature of this danger can vary depending on culture and time period. In some cases, all that is at risk is a reader's social and cultural standing: there are reasons, after all, why a contemporary academic with a secret passion for popular romance novels might slip her current reading away in a drawer before welcoming her distinguished colleagues to a party. (Janice Radway's *Reading the Romance: Women, Patriarchy, and Popular Literature* is a fascinating ethnographic study of a group of women readers of such novels.) As Laura Smyth's work on Marguerite Porete demonstrates, however, reading can be not only dangerous but also a crime: Porete, a French beguine, was burned at the stake for heresy in 1310 on the evidence of her only book, *A Mirror for Simple Souls*. As Smyth notes, contemporary accounts and the *process-verbal* of Marguerite's trial strongly suggest that her greatest crime was not the writing of her text but her persistence in making copies of it available for reading, and that her condemnation and murder could well have been precipitated by her accusers' deliberate misreading of her text.

Other examples of dangerous reading acts are not hard to summon up. Think of Abelard and Heloise, for example, whose textual partnership and collaboration led to pleasure and eventually to sexual union, not to mention to disastrous consequences for both. In a recently completed dissertation, Kimberley Benedict explores the relationships between medieval women mystics and their scribes, relationships that sometimes highlight the sensuality of reading and recording, the ways in which sexuality and textuality could, and sometimes did, interact. Such acts of reading God's messages could be particularly dangerous, for the mystic receiver of those messages as well as for the transcriber of them.

Similar crimes of reading abound in early European America. Janice Knight, for example, explores the antinomian controversy, looking closely at how women's claims to interpretive or readerly authority were debated, and deplored. Of such claims, Anne Hutchinson's was surely strongest, eliciting charges of conspiracy, heresy, and spiritual harlotry. When Hutchinson continued to claim that her readings of the Bible came from God and were thus indisputable, John Winthrop called her heretical opinions "brats hatched from her leprous mind," and she was brought to civil trial and eventually banished — all for her insistently prophetic acts of reading.

In her keynote address at the conference "The Emergence of the Female Reader, 1500–1800," held at Oregon State University in May 2001, Janice Radway contrasted conventional schooled reading practices, which call for reading as transfer, delivery, and assessment, with what she characterized as "promiscuous practices of reading," practices that make it difficult to tell where the author begins and ends and where the reader takes up, where interpretation can morph into poaching or stealing, as happens, for instance, when *Star Trek* fans claim the right to read new meanings into episodes by casting Mr. Spock and Captain Kirk as lovers or when online groups of *X-Files* fans rewrite episodes and, indeed, write new episodes in which Scully and Mulder's relationship is far from platonic. Radway has coined the term "interpersonation" to designate such transgressive practices of reading and writing. As an earlier example of such interpersonation, we might recall the Brontë children, whose reading of their own private language, world, and writings has been labeled pathological by many critics, even as the power of this reading for Charlotte and Emily, especially, has been acknowledged.

We might also consider the fears created when, in nineteenth-century America, new reading materials became available to the general public. As Cathy Davidson has shown in her analysis of novels written early in the Republic, these materials challenged elite authority, because new forms of popular literature (the newspaper, the romantic novel, and so on), unlike traditional poetry, could be read by anyone who possessed even modest literacy skills.[2] Whereas some saw an enlarged reading public as a positive sign of political and social change, others feared that these new readers, especially readers marked as marginal by gender, race, or class, would corrupt conventional standards of reading taste. Without a new group of women readers who relished the transgression of traditional taste by preferring sentimental to "serious" literature, the "mobs of scribbling women" derided by Hawthorne could not have been successful.

Who was right? Those like Hawthorne who upheld conventional "high" standards of reading and literature, or the new and transgressive readers of popular novels? We raise this question not to attempt an answer (and black-and-white questions like this one don't usually lend themselves to answers anyway, but only to heated debate) but rather to emphasize the importance of how reading practices, whether transgressive or conventional, are evaluated or valued. Certainly, it is tempting to identify marginalized readers and then to praise their implicit resistance to conventional elite cultural texts, to cheer on those who challenge the disciplinary tendencies of traditional reading in clearly transgressive ways. As Trysh Travis points out in "Divine Secrets of the Cultural Studies Sisterhood: Women Reading Rebecca Wells" (2003), it has become commonplace in cultural studies to identify and privilege narratives that resist hegemonic practices. Such practices, in Travis's view, too often obscure real material connections between readers and the texts they choose to read.

In one of her own attempts to look hard at specific historical conditions, Travis considers the phenomenon of the *Divine Secrets of the Ya-Ya Sisterhood*, which achieved national prominence in the United States and spawned many Ya-Ya Sisterhood clubs, not as a result of public relations efforts by major presses but rather through word of mouth from readers and independent bookstores. Initially drawn to the Ya-Ya Sisterhood phenomenon, which seemed to represent a potentially effective naming and claiming of women's experiences, Travis ultimately developed reservations. Her study of the publishing history of the Ya-Ya Sisterhood, as well as personal interviews with relevant individuals in the publishing industry and online discussions with members of Ya-Ya clubs, suggest that the *Divine Secrets of the Ya-Ya Sisterhood* is more about commercial shaping of readerly desires than the enabling of women's actual desires. Although Travis applauds the benefits that grow out of a book that encourages women to meet for regular conversation, she also argues that critics should not interpret the Ya-Ya Sisterhood phenomenon as a challenge to existing discursive authority. In short, the more Travis studied the purportedly transgressive acts of the Ya-Ya Sisterhood readers, the more she saw that these acts are already scripted in the text and in claims for it. Rather than contesting existing authority, then, these readers seem at least potentially caught up in the workings of an ever more efficient, subtle, and complex cultural industry, one that continues to discipline readers.

Other studies that focus on "specific historical conditions in which people make and read books," such as Jacqueline Jones Royster's *Traces of a Stream: Literacy and Social Change Among African American Women* (2000) and Anne Ruggles Gere's *Intimate Practices: Literacy and Cultural Work in U.S. Women's Clubs 1880–1920* (1997), cast additional light on the tensions between readers' desires and those of institutions intent on creating — or restricting — markets for particular texts and ways of reading them. Gere's *Intimate Practices*, for instance, considers (among other topics) the ways in which male professors of English (there were no other professors of English in American colleges at that time) from 1880 to 1920 figured women's acts of critical reading — acts that often took place in women's clubs throughout the United States — as inconsequential and amateur, reserving "real" reading for themselves. The women who met together on a regular basis to discuss their responses to various texts were hardly criminals, but their responses were nevertheless trivialized and disvalued by the male academic establishment.

In *Traces of a Stream*, Royster tells an equally compelling story that links transgressive reading and writing practices. In this study, which brings together "what we know now about literacy with what we know now about

African American women," Royster focuses on "the material conditions and the activities of African American women" (2000, ix, x). In the introduction to her study, Royster characterizes her effort as "A Call for Other Ways of Reading" (3), and reading figures prominently in her analysis. Like Gere, Royster focuses particularly on the club woman movement — in her case the rise of the Black Club women's movement. As she does so, Royster consistently emphasizes the ways that African American women's insistent efforts to read texts that would otherwise be denied to them have led to the writing of their own texts — and to social change as well.

As Gere's and Royster's studies evidence, the forces of control and discipline are ever at work in our culture. Particularly in the lived experience of the historical moment, it can be difficult to ascertain whether a particular literate act constitutes a (resistant) crime or a (co-opted) accommodation. In any literate act — whether of reading or writing — there will always be a tension between control and discipline, between self-expression and (variously bounded) acts of communication with others. This tension is especially apparent today in the debates within feminism and in rhetoric/composition over the nature and consequences of the growing use of such alternative discourses as personal criticism and multivoiced texts. Some feminists, for instance, find the use of the personal to be a liberating and productive practice; for others, it represents a self-indulgent solipsism. Likewise, some in rhetoric and composition advocate the teaching of alternative discourses, whereas others project dire warnings about the consequences of doing so. In these debates we see the forces of control and discipline predictably hard at work.

In fact, it's possible to trace the forces surrounding this particular debate all the way back to the many struggles over use of vernacular languages in the West, and certainly to the beginnings of the American experience. In this regard, the African American struggle for language rights has been particularly intense and long lasting. In her contribution to the double fiftieth anniversary issue of *CCC*, "CCCC's Role in the Struggle for Language Rights" (1999), Geneva Smitherman chronicles this struggle and argues that scholars in rhetoric and composition need to know this history and to continue to learn its lessons. We have learned a great deal from Smitherman, beginning with our reading of *Talkin' and Testifyin'* in 1977, and we have been very much aware of the transgressive nature of her writing practices. In fact, the reception of her work — especially early on — suggests that the very forces of control and discipline we have examined in this essay have worked to marginalize her writing and reading practices.

In this regard, it's telling that *Talkin' and Testifyin'* (1977) was published at virtually the same time Mina Shaughnessy's *Errors and Expectations* (1977) appeared — yet at the time it was Shaughnessy's text that attracted the lion's share of attention and accolades. In our view, both Smitherman's forceful and (for some) controversial argument and her transgressive writing practices (especially her masterful code switching) contributed to the easiness with which audiences turned away from her text and toward Shaughnessy's. In recent years, Smitherman's work has received more attention: she was honored, for instance, in 2001 with the CCCC Exemplar Award. But we believe the significance of her ongoing project continues to be deflected by the forces that regulate academic and public discourses.

DISCURSIVE CRIMES AND THE TEACHING OF WRITING

How does this discussion of struggles over vernacular Englishes and the ways in which they influence the reception of writers' texts relate to the issues that teachers of writing — and the students in our classes — face when we decide whether particular discursive acts constitute "proper" (lawful) or "improper" (criminal) discourse? Our answer to this question is perhaps predictable, given our engagement with rhetoric and its traditions, for we believe that questions such as the one we pose here can be answered only by a rhetorically sensitive and situated analysis. Feminists, for example, can justifiably disagree about Acker's work. Does her writing, in its dependence on sexual violence, strike a blow for liberation or further enslave and degrade women? Does her work represent an "alternative" discourse that we should value and teach, or does it represent a crime, a violation of literary, social, and cultural norms that we should abjure? Do her practices hold potential theoretical implications for or constitute an implicit alternative to the traditional rhetoric of authorship and intellectual property, or are they simply examples of the crime of plagiarism? Teaching Acker's work demands attention to such questions as well as a full exploration of their implications for students and their lives.

What is true of Acker's texts is, of course, potentially true for any student text as well. A student writing a personal narrative or experimenting with alternative discourse strategies in a first-year writing class may indeed experience the writing of such texts as an act of productive resistance to the hegemonic assumptions and practices of the academy. But there is no guarantee that such will be the case. The student may just as likely feel that writing such essays means nothing more or less than meeting yet another academic requirement and may associate truly resistant writing with hip-hop, email, blogs, instant messaging, fanzines, and other self-sponsored writing and reading. (A Christian student attending a secular university might, for instance, find participating in a weekly Bible study group more transgressive in that particular context than reading a secular text.) Other students may feel that personally grounded writing assignments represent an unwarranted invasion of their privacy; they might prefer to respond to assignments that emphasize the conventions of academic discourse.

The divergent experiences and understandings we have just described are a reminder that although teachers can and must plan our writing classes — and can and must intervene in our students' writing processes via such activities as creating syllabi, making assignments, and evaluating essays — we cannot control the results of these activities for students' learning. We cannot, in other words, guarantee that an assignment that we hope will function as an invitation to a productive "crime" of writing and reading will be experienced in this way. Think, for instance, of the resistance that many students express when teachers ask them to engage published texts in highly critical ways. To the extent that students' previous education and culture have encouraged them to view texts as authoritative and/or as the neutral transmitters of established knowledge, this invitation to critical inquiry may strike students as a textual "crime." Our observations here may strike readers as unnecessarily pessimistic, and in one sense they are. We do believe that teachers cannot predict or control what students learn in our classes; but we also believe that teachers can think and act in creative ways about both the decisions we need to make as teachers and the decisions students need to make as writers. When we recognize that assignments we present to students as invitations to innovative, critical, and perhaps even experimental writing and reading may strike students as crimes to be avoided if at all possible, for instance, we can better understand why students can be so reluctant to take risks in both their writing and reading and why they can be so critical of others (whether published or student writers) who do so.

When we think of discursive risk-taking as potentially criminal, we can understand why even experienced writers and readers can find it difficult to challenge the conventions of the academy. In this regard, one of us recalls a particularly difficult conversation with a graduate student whose thesis she was directing. This graduate student, a feminist, wanted to write a thesis that was grounded not only in scholarly work but also in her own experience. Doing so, she argued, was itself a feminist act, and yet this graduate student found it extraordinarily difficult to write her thesis. When asked about this difficulty, she spoke at length about the power that the single word *thesis* exerted on her. "Every time I start to write something related to my own experience," she said, "I think of the word 'thesis' — and of the theses I've read in the library — and I think that what I'm trying to do is wrong, impossible, inappropriate. A thesis is supposed to have a thesis, which means it needs to be objective, neutral, and traditionally scholarly. How can I do that and also relate my ideas to my personal experience?"

If a graduate student who has both studied and enacted feminist theory and practice can find that her desire to write a resistant text is disciplined by the fear that she is undertaking a criminal act, imagine how powerful such understandings can be for less experienced, less confident, less self-conscious students. When teachers recognize the power that the academy holds to discipline students and to convince them that some kinds of acts represent crimes of writing and reading, we can use this understanding as we make decisions about syllabi and assignments. Teachers who want to encourage students to take risks that may strike students as crimes of writing or reading, for instance, may make these assignments low-risk activities in terms of the role they play in students' final course grades. Or they may build in strategic elements of choice in major assignments so that students can find an appropriate comfort level as they experiment with new discursive practices.

Teachers may also find it helpful to talk with students about issues related to crimes of reading and writing. Like many colleagues, for instance, we regularly raise issues of power and authority as they are related to acts of reading and writing. "Why does Annie Dillard get to have comma splices in her writing, but you don't?" we might ask. In discussions of such resistant texts as Anzaldúa's *Borderlands* (1987), we try to create opportunities for students to reflect on the risks — and benefits — inherent in such writing practices. More generally, we attempt explicitly to theorize our pedagogical practices and to share this theorizing with students. If we assign an activity that students may experience as criminal, dangerous, or offensive (such as asking students to articulate and then interrogate their racialized and gendered reading practices), we explicitly discuss those aspects of the assignment that students may consciously or unconsciously view as unlawful or miscreant.

Although we believe that the perspective on crimes of writing and reading that we have articulated here can help teachers make important day-to-day decisions in their classrooms, we conclude this essay by commenting on several important challenges that remain — challenges that are grounded in potential gaps and differences among the assumptions, values, and practices of teachers and students. As feminist teachers, for instance, we want to encourage our students to take risks and to challenge conventional understandings of gender and patriarchy. In our experience, our goals often differ from those of our students. How hard do we push students in encouraging them to take risks in their thinking, reading, and writing? Recognizing the key role that affect plays in student learning, how can we distinguish between an assignment that will provide an opportunity for students' growth and one that will seem so criminal that students will, in effect, shut down — meeting the letter of the assignment perhaps, but not its spirit.

Another difficult question involves the extent to which teachers should bring alternative discourses, which by their very nature represent potential crimes of reading and writing, into the classroom. From one perspective, doing so seems reasonable. If we as teachers find alternative discourses powerful, why not teach students to write such discourses? Yet if we do so, are we implicitly "disciplining" the challenge that these texts represent to hegemonic academic practices by turning them into schooled assignments? And what about students' own desires? As we noted earlier, many students already enact resistant writing practices. What are we telling students if we ignore these practices and focus on those we favor?

Questions such as these remind us that there is much that remains unclear and contested about both crimes of writing and reading and feminist practices in rhetoric and composition. As readers are aware, feminists often disagree about basic issues in feminist theory and practice. Similarly, there is much room for disagreement about crimes of writing and reading. Though we believe that certain discursive practices (such as Azar Nafisi's 2003 heretical and dangerous reading of Vladimir Nabokov and F. Scott Fitzgerald in Tehran) clearly constitute crimes of writing and reading, the answer to the question, what represents a (resistant) crime versus an accommodation to or variation of conventional practices, is hardly obvious. Consider in this regard Oprah Winfrey's book club, which she reintroduced in 2003. From one perspective, this book club can be seen as a potential act of resistance to the corporatized and masculinized world of publishing. It can also be viewed, however, as an accommodation to, or even a capitalization of, this same world.

In closing, we return to a question that we posed at the start of our essay: What are the potential consequences of recent efforts to reclaim and redefine women's rhetorical practices for the actual *teaching* of writing? As our analysis suggests, these consequences have less to do with advocating for particular pedagogical practices and more to do with general understandings of what is at stake when we teach writing. They remind us, as we pointed out earlier, that as teachers we cannot control the results of our pedagogical practices for students' learning. Thus, although we continue to invite students to write collaboratively or to compose texts that experiment or play with language, we do so knowing that depending on their own interests and situations students may experience these invitations in quite diverse ways. Given this diversity, it becomes all the more important for teachers to inquire into both our and our students' rhetorically and materially grounded situations. The results of this inquiry will always be tentative and uncertain: rhetoric is, after all, the search for the best available means of persuasion in a particular situation — whether that situation involves writing an argument or teaching a class.

NOTES

1. We have learned a great deal from Krista Ratcliffe's important work on how to listen rhetorically, an act that makes it possible for others to be heard.

2. See the discussion of this topic in Charles Paine's *The Resistant Writer: Rhetoric as Immunity, 1850 to the Present* (1999, 66). The Davidson reference is to *Revolution and the Word: The Rise of the Novel in America* (1986).

WORKS CITED

Acker, Kathy. *Bodies of Work: Essays.* London: Serpent's Tail, 1997.
———. *Don Quixote: which was a dream.* New York: Grove, 1984.
———. *Great Expectations.* New York: Grove, 1989.
———. "Humility." *The Seven Cardinal Virtues,* ed. Alison Fell. London: Serpent's Tail, 1990.
———. *Politics.* New York: Papyrus, 1972.
———. *Pussy, King of the Pirates.* New York: Grove, 1996.
Alexander, M. Jacqui, Lisa Albrecht, Sharon Day, and Mab Segrets, eds. *Sing, Whisper, Shout, Pray!: Feminist Visions for a Just World.* Fort Bragg: EdgeWork Books, 2003.
"Anna Deavere Smith." American Repertory Theatre Online. <http://www.fas.harvard.edu/~art/anna.html>
Anzaldúa, Gloria. *Borderlands/La Frontera: The New Mestiza.* San Francisco: Aunt Lute Books, 1987.
Bailiff, Michelle. *Seduction, Sophistry, and the Woman with the Rhetorical Figure.* Pittsburgh: U of Pittsburgh P, 2001.
Benedict, Kimberley Michelle. "Authorial Alliances: Collaboration between Religious Women and Scribes in the Middle Ages." Diss. Stanford University: 2002.
Blackwell, Joyce. *No Peace Without Freedom: Race and the Women's International League for Peace and Freedom, 1915–75.* Southern Illinois UP, 2004.
Buchanan, Lindal. *Regendering Delivery: The Fifth Canon and Antebellum Women Rhetors.* Southern Illinois UP, 2005.
Campbell, JoAnn. *Toward a Feminist Rhetoric: The Writing of Gertrude Buck.* Pittsburgh: U of Pittsburgh P, 1996.
Campbell, Karlyn Kohrs. *Man Cannot Speak for Her: A Critical Study of Early Feminist Rhetoric.* 2 vols. New York: Greenwood, 1989.
Chandler, Katherine, and Melissa Goldthwaite. *Surveying the Literary Landscapes of Terry Tempest Williams.* U Utah P, 2004.

Current Biography Yearbook 1994. "Anna Deavere Smith." New York: H. W. Wilson: 544–47.

Daniell, Beth. *A Communion of Friendship: Literacy, Spiritual Practice, and Women in Recovery.* Carbondale: Southern Illinois UP, 2003.

Davidson, Cathy N. *Revolution and the Word: The Rise of the Novel in America.* Oxford: Oxford UP, 1986.

Day, Kami, and Michele Eodice. *(First Person)²: A Study of Co-Authoring in the Academy.* Logan: Utah State UP, 2001.

Donawerth, Jane, ed. *Rhetorical Theory by Women before 1900.* Lanham: Rowman & Littlefield, 2002.

Ede, Lisa. *Situating Composition: Composition Studies and the Politics of Location.* Carbondale: Southern Illinois UP, 2004.

Ede, Lisa, and Andrea A. Lunsford. *Singular Texts/Plural Authors: Perspectives on Collaborative Writing.* Carbondale: Southern Illinois UP, 1991.

Flynn, Elizabeth A. *Feminism Beyond Modernism.* Carbondale: Southern Illinois UP, 2002.

Foss, Karen, and Sonja Foss, eds. *Women Speak: The Eloquence of Women's Lives.* Prospect Heights: Waveland, 1991.

Foss, Karen, Sonja Foss, and Cyndy L. Griffin, eds. *Feminist Rhetorical Theories.* Thousand Oaks: Sage, 1999.

Fredrick, Christine Ann Nguyen. *Feminist Rhetoric in Cyberspace.* Routledge, 2004.

Gere, Anne Ruggles. *Intimate Practices: Literacy and Cultural Work in U.S. Women's Clubs: 1880–1920.* Urbana: U of Illinois P, 1997.

Glenn, Cheryl. *Rhetoric Retold: Regendering the Tradition from Antiquity through the Renaissance.* Carbondale: Southern Illinois UP, 1997.

———. *Unspoken: A Rhetoric of Silence.* Carbondale: Southern Illinois UP, 2004.

Hobbs, Catherine, ed. *Nineteenth-Century Women Learn to Write.* Charlottesville: UP of Virginia, 1995.

Hollis, Karyn L. *Liberating Voices: Writing at Bryn Mawr Summer School for Women Workers.* Carbondale: Southern Illinois UP, 2004.

Jarratt, Susan. *Rereading the Sophists: Classical Rhetoric Refigured.* Carbondale: Southern Illinois UP, 1991.

Johnson, Nan. *Gender and Rhetorical Space in American Life: 1866–1910.* Carbondale: Southern Illinois UP, 2002.

Kates, Susan. *Activist Rhetorics and American Higher Education: 1885–1937.* Carbondale: Southern Illinois UP, 1999.

Kirsch, Gesa E., Faye Spencer Maor, Lance Massey, Lee Mickoson-Massey, and Mary P. Sheridan-Rabideau, eds. *Feminism and Composition: A Critical Sourcebook.* Boston: Bedford/St. Martin's, 2003.

Knight, Janice. "The Word Made Flesh: Reading the Body in Puritan America." The Emergence of the Female Reader, 1500–1800. Oregon State University. Corvallis, Oregon. 19 May 2001.

Kroll, Jack. "Fire in the City of Angels." *Newsweek,* 28 June 1993: 62–63.

Lahr, John. "Under the Skin." *The New Yorker,* 28 June 1993: 90–94.

LeClair, Tom. "The Lord of LaMancha and Her Abortion." Review of *Don Quixote. New York Times Book Review,* 30 November 1986, sec. 7:10.

Lloyd, Carol. "Voice of America." *Salon Magazine Online.* <http://www.salon.com/bc/1998/12/cov_08bc.html>

Logie, John. "The Author('s) Proper(ty): Rhetoric, Literature, and Constructions of Authorship." Unpublished dissertation, Pennsylvania State U, 1999.

Logan, Shirley Wilson, *"We Are Coming": The Persuasive Discourse of Nineteenth-Century Black Women.* Carbondale: Southern Illinois UP, 1999.

———, ed. *With Pen and Voice: A Critical Anthology of Nineteenth-Century African American Women.* Carbondale: Southern Illinois UP, 1995.

Lunsford, Andrea, ed. *Reclaiming Rhetorica: Women in the History of Rhetoric.* Pittsburgh: U of Pittsburgh P, 1995.

Martin, Neil. *On race, riots and national recognition.* "Stanford's Anna Deavere Smith Looks Back at Two Frantic, Fabulous Years." <http://www.service.com/PAW/morgue/cover/1994_Mar_18.QAAR18.html>

Mattingly, Carol. *Appropriate[ing] Dress: Women's Rhetorical Style in Nineteenth-Century America.* Carbondale: Southern Illinois UP, 2002.

———. *Well-Tempered Women: Nineteenth-Century Temperance Rhetoric.* Carbondale: Southern Illinois UP, 1999.

McCaffery, Larry. "The Path of Abjection: An Interview with Kathy Acker." *Some Other Frequency: Interviews with Innovative American Authors.* U Pennsylvania P, 1996. 14–35.

Mountford, Roxanne. *The Gendered Pulpit: Preaching in American Protestant Spaces.* Carbondale: Southern Illinois UP, 2003.

Nafisi, Azar. *Reading* Lolita *in Tehran.* New York: Random House, 2003.

Olsen, Lance. "Introduction to Kathy Acker." Artist in Society Conference. Chicago, October 1994. <http://www.uidaho.edu/LS/Eng/Fugue/fugue10.html>

Paine, Charles. *The Resistant Writer: Rhetoric as Immunity, 1580 to the Present.* Albany: State U of New York P, 1999.

Pough, Gwendolyn D. *Check It While I Wreck It: Black Womanhood, Hip-Hop Culture, and The Public Sphere.* Northeastern UP, 2004.

Radway, Janice. "On the Sociability of Reading: Books, Self-fashioning and the Creation of Communities." Keynote Address. The Emergence of the Female Reader, 1500–1800. Oregon State University. Corvallis, Oregon. 18 May 2001.

——. *Reading the Romance: Women, Patriarchy, and Popular Literature.* Chapel Hill: U of North Carolina P, 1984.

Ratcliffe, Krista. *Anglo-American Challenges to the Rhetorical Traditions: Virginia Woolf, Mary Daley, Adrienne Rich.* Carbondale: Southern Illinois UP, 1996.

——. *Rhetorical Listening: Identification, Gender, Whiteness.* Southern Illinois UP, 2006.

Reynolds, Nedra. *Geographies of Writing: Inhabiting Places and Encountering Difference.* Carbondale: Southern Illinois UP, 2004.

Ritchie, Joy, and Kate Ronald, eds. *Available Means: An Anthology of Women's Rhetoric(s).* Pittsburgh: U of Pittsburgh P, 2001.

Robbins, Sarah. *Managing Literacy, Mothering America: Women's Narratives on Reading and Writing in the Nineteenth Century.* Pittsburgh: U of Pittsburgh P, 2004.

Royster, Jacqueline Jones, ed. *Southern Horrors and Other Writings: The Anti-Lynching Campaign of Ida B. Wells, 1892–1900.* Boston: Bedford/St. Martin's, 1997.

——. *Traces of a Stream: Literacy and Social Change Among African American Women.* Pittsburgh: U of Pittsburgh P, 2002.

Sharer, Wendy B. *Vote and Voice: Women's Organizations and Political Literacy, 1915–1930.* Carbondale: Southern Illinois UP, 2004.

Shaughnessy, Mina P. *Errors and Expectations: A Guide for the Teacher of Basic Writing.* New York: Oxford UP, 1977.

Smith, Anna Deavere. *Fires in the Mirror: Crown Heights, Brooklyn, and Other Identities.* New York: Doubleday, 1992.

——. *Twilight Los Angeles, 1992.* New York: Doubleday, 1994.

Smitherman, Geneva. "CCCC's Role in the Struggle for Language Rights." *College Composition and Communication* 50 (1999): 349–76.

——. *Talkin' and Testifyin': The Language of Black America.* Boston: Houghton Mifflin, 1977.

Smyth, Laura. Preaching with Their Hands: The Role of the Carthusians in the Transmission of Women's Texts in Late Medieval England. Unpublished diss. Stanford U, 2001.

Stepanek, Marcia. "Creative Reality: Anna Deavere Smith." *Women in Communications.* <www.awic-dc.org/text/womennews_Deavere-Smith.html>

Stewart, Susan. *Crimes of Writing: Problems in the Containment of Representation.* New York: Oxford UP, 1991.

Sutherland, Christine Mason, and Rebecca Sutcliffe, eds. *The Changing Tradition: Women in the History of Rhetoric.* Calgary: U of Calgary P, 1999.

Swearingen, Jan. *Rhetoric and Irony: Western Literacy and Western Lies.* New York: Oxford UP, 1991.

"Theater In Search of the American Character." Ford Foundation. <http://www.forfound.org/publications//ff_report/view_ff_report_detail.cfm?report_index=111>

Travis, Trysh. "Divine Secrets of the Cultural Studies Sisterhood: Women Reading Rebecca Wells." *American Literary History* 15.1 (Spring 2003): 134–61.

Welch, Kathleen. *The Contemporary Reception of Classical Rhetoric.* Hillsdale: Erlbaum, 1990.

Wertheimer, Molly Meijer, ed. *Listening to Their Voices: The Rhetorical Activities of Historical Women.* Columbia: U of South Carolina P, 1999.

Zaeske, Susan. *Signatures of Citizenship: Petitioning, Antislavery, and Women's Political Identity.* Chapel Hill: U North Carolina P, 2003.

20 *The First Rhetoric(s) and Feminism(s) Conference and Its Legacy*

> A word is dead
> When it is said,
> Some say.
> I say it just
> Begins to live
> That day.
> — EMILY DICKINSON

This essay came about when Lisa happened to glance at the table of contents for this volume and saw the title of this section, "On Rhetoric(s) and Feminism(s)," with fresh eyes. "Do you remember," she emailed Andrea, "when we couldn't have imagined putting those two words together?" "We only have to look at the first essay in this section to remind ourselves of that," Andrea replied.

There was a time, and not so long ago, when conjoining the disciplinary projects of rhetoric and feminism was a radical idea. Cheryl Glenn, who co-authored the third essay in this section of *Writing Together*, played a key role in this effort with her 1997 *Rhetoric Retold: Regendering the Tradition from Antiquity Through the Renaissance.*[1] Thanks to the work of Glenn and many other scholars, in the early 1990s the terms "rhetoric" and "feminism" ceased to be strange bedfellows and instead pointed to an exciting area of research, teaching, and practice. As the decade progressed, these terms themselves came to be interrogated — most often by scholars of color. In recognition of the multiple groundings and experiences of both rhetoric and feminism, the terms "rhetoric(s)" and "feminism(s)," rather than the singular "rhetoric" and "feminism," increasingly came into play.

A primary purpose of this essay is to narrate the history of a conference held at Oregon State University from August 28–30, 1997, one that marks an important moment when the terms "rhetoric(s)" and "feminism(s)" were spoken with particular force and clarity and thus began, in Dickinson's terms, "to

---

This essay, written by Lisa Ede and Andrea A. Lunsford, is new to this edition.

live" and to increase in disciplinary vigor and influence. The conference was titled "Feminism(s) and Rhetoric(s): From Boundaries to Borderlands" and was co-coordinated by Cheryl Glenn and Lisa Ede. Andrea Lunsford was one of four keynote speakers at this conference. As readers may be aware, this conference — which the co-coordinators had imagined as a one-time-only event — took on a force of its own and ultimately became a biennial conference sponsored by the Conference on College Composition and Communication's Coalition of Women Scholars in the History of Rhetoric and Composition. Here are subsequent conferences, the years in which they were held, and the conference themes:

- 1999, The University of Minnesota, Minneapolis, "Challenging Rhetorics: Cross-Disciplinary Sites of Feminist Discourse"
- 2001, Millikin University, "Feminist Literacies: Resisting Disciplines"
- 2003, Ohio State University, "Intersections: Critical Locations of Rhetorical Practice"
- 2005, Michigan Technological University, "Affirming Diversity"
- 2007, The University of Arkansas, Little Rock, "Civic Discourse"
- 2009, Michigan State University, "Enabling Complexities: Communities/ Writing/Rhetoric"

As we write this essay, faculty at the University of Minnesota, Mankato are planning the 2011 Feminisms and Rhetorics Conference, whose theme is "Feminist Challenges or Feminist Rhetorics?: Locations, Scholarship, and Discourse." The coordinators of the 2009 conference removed the parentheses around the "s" in each term as in their view they were no longer necessary.[2]

In this essay, we want both to document the history of the first Feminism(s) and Rhetoric(s) Conference and to comment upon its primary goal — which was to encourage dialogue among feminists in a variety of academic disciplines — and the extent to which this goal has and has not been achieved. We also want to describe the process that led to the eventual affiliation of the conference with the Coalition of Women Scholars in the History of Rhetoric and Composition. Such documentation is important, we believe, in contributing to institutional and disciplinary history. How many of those attending the annual Conference on College Composition and Communication (CCCC), with its thousands of attendees and hundreds of sessions, for instance, realize that the organization that sponsors this event grew out of what Richard Lloyd-Jones describes as just "another session . . . at the annual NCTE conference" (487)? The description of that session from Lloyd-Jones's 1992 *College Composition and Communication* essay "Who We Were, Who We Should Become" follows:

> The Conference on College Composition and Communication began in Chicago in the Fall of 1948 simply as another session for the college people at the annual NCTE convention. The folks who came to that meeting were pressed by what seemed to be a crisis and wanted to have practical talk about how to deal with a flood of new students — many of

whom were first-generation college students, most somewhat older vet-
erans. . . . In a single year — 1946 — college enrollments had doubled. . . .
Survival under the mob of students required that colleges develop "programs" with administrative conveniences, like placement and exemption
tests. That is, new quasi-administrators had to solve unfamiliar problems. They came to their NCTE session in desperate need of help and
wanted to keep raising problems and solutions indefinitely. They were
persuaded to quit only when the program chair . . . agreed to organize a
Spring meeting in Chicago to continue the discussion. These were not
people trying to get ahead in academic hierarchies; they wanted help in
dealing with what was often described as a short-term enrollment problem. Not high theory, but practical need brought them together. (487)[3]

From a contemporary perspective, those participating in ongoing Feminisms
and Rhetorics conferences might well imagine that the existence of this conference was somehow foreordained or inevitable, just as the CCCC itself may
appear to be to many unfamiliar with its history. As the following narrative
will explain, this was anything but the case.

THE 1997 CONFERENCE: A BRIEF NARRATIVE

That the 1997 Feminism(s) and Rhetoric(s) Conference responded to a strong
disciplinary exigency seems clear in hindsight, as the continuing legacy of the
conference suggests. But the incident — and there was a single incident —
that most immediately led to the conference was connected not to scholarly
work at the intersections of these two areas of inquiry but rather to more local
concerns, in this case the desire of the chair of the English department at
Oregon State to call attention to the department's strengths in rhetoric and
writing.

In the fall of 1995, then English department chair Robert Schwartz asked
Lisa, who joined the faculty in 1980 as the first faculty member to profess
rhetoric and writing as her scholarly and professional interest, to meet with
him. Since that time, the department had hired a number of faculty members
in the area, including Chris Anderson, Cheryl Glenn, Anita Helle, and Vicki
Tolar Burton. When Schwartz and Lisa met, he said that he wanted the department's strengths in the field to be broadly recognized, and that one way
to achieve this goal was to sponsor a national conference. He was willing to
contribute $8,000 toward that conference — though, he added, ideally the
conference would be self-supporting.

Schwartz left the topic of the conference entirely open. As far as he was
concerned, it could have focused on writing and assessment, the rhetoric of
argument, style, service learning, or any of an almost infinite number of topics. Lisa and Cheryl were intrigued by the possibility of hosting a national
conference and immediately knew the topic they wanted the conference to
address. In 1995 they and Andrea Lunsford had published "Border Crossings:
Intersections of Rhetoric and Feminism" in the journal *Rhetorica* (the article is
included on pp. 281–309 in this collection). They were acutely aware of the

ways in which their collaboration had emboldened them to take on a challenging subject and to publish the resulting essay in a then fairly traditional journal.

Cheryl and Lisa knew many other scholars across North America who shared their interest. The conference could play a key role, they believed, in providing a forum where scholars in rhetoric and writing working on feminist projects could gather, exchange ideas, and network — and perhaps even gain the confidence, support, and synergy that encourage productive risk-taking. But they also very much hoped to expand that conversation by encouraging feminist scholars in other disciplines to participate in the conference, for while feminist scholars in rhetoric and writing read and cited work by scholars such as Evelyn Fox Keller, Linda Alcoff, Judith Butler, Trinh T. Minh-ha, bell hooks, and Joan K. Scott, this was primarily a one-way conversation. There was little indication that feminist scholars working in history, literary criticism, philosophy, and other areas were familiar with feminist work taking place in the field of rhetoric and writing. Cheryl and Lisa hoped nothing less than to take a step toward challenging disciplinary barriers. Hence the subtitle of the conference: "From Boundaries to Borderlands."

One of their earliest and in their view most important decisions was to have an equal number of keynote speakers from within rhetoric and writing and from without. Thus while two of the keynote speakers, Andrea Lunsford and Jacqueline Jones Royster, represented the field of rhetoric and writing, two additional keynote speakers, Nancy Tuana and Barbara Warnick, represented philosophy and speech communication, respectively. The titles of the four keynote addresses reflect an attempt at interdisciplinarity:

- Jacqueline Jones Royster, "Borderlands and Common Spaces: Care and Maintenance in Our Neutral Zones"
- Barbara Warnick, "Masculinizing the Feminine: Inviting Women Online ca. 1997"
- Andrea Lunsford, "Feminism, Composition, and the Politics of Ownership"
- Nancy Tuana, "Fleshing Rhetoric: Speaking Bodies, Refiguring Sex/Gender"

In addition to the four keynote speakers, the co-coordinators invited sixteen scholars working on feminist history, theory, and practice to participate as featured speakers. Eight of the scholars responded to keynote speakers (two for each speaker); eight served in two featured panels, where each participant had seven to ten minutes to present one or more issues or questions for panelists and conference attendees to discuss. The featured speakers included Jamie Barlowe, Susan Carlton, Suzanne Clark, Elizabeth Flynn, Maria Gonzalez, Angelletta Gourdine, Susan Jarratt, Shirley Logan, Arabella Lyon, Joyce Irene Middleton, Krista Ratcliffe, Joy Ritchie, Patricia Sullivan, C. Jan Swearingen, Kathleen Welch, and Molly Meijer Wertheimer.[4]

Lisa remembers the anxiety that she and Cheryl experienced when they distributed the call for proposals in the spring of 1996. (They had spent the year on the countless details that all conference organizers know well:

everything from lining up keynote and featured speakers to finding a venue, negotiating the university's bureaucracy, dealing with housing and dining issues, etc.) Would the list of keynote and featured speakers prove attractive enough that scholars would want to attend the conference? Would the call for proposals generate a sizable body of strong and substantial work? They set the submission deadline for October 30, 1996 and were jubilant when they received almost 250 proposals for the conference, roughly 150 of which they accepted. They were particularly pleased that scholars from areas other than rhetoric and writing found the conference appealing. Speech communication scholars Sonja and Karen Foss submitted proposals, as did philosopher Lorraine Code and educator and anthropologist Patty Lather — all very established in their disciplines and in feminist theory and practice. The fact that well-known feminist scholars outside the primary field represented at the conference chose to use precious travel funds or their own income to attend the conference boded well for the conference's success. Also exciting was the fact that in addition to scholars from North America, presenters from Hong Kong and Russia planned to attend.

"Feminism(s) and Rhetoric(s): From Boundaries to Borderlands" was held at Oregon State University from August 28–30, 1997. In addition to the four keynote addresses with responses and the two plenary panels with featured speakers, the conference included 40 concurrent sessions and roughly 150 presenters. There were moments of crisis and last-minute snags, but in general the conference went smoothly and generated considerable energy and enthusiasm. Conference mealtimes found participants clustered around tables enjoying the bounty of the Northwest harvest and talking animatedly about what they were hearing and learning — clearly the conference had struck a very strong chord. In fact, both Cheryl and Lisa remember hearing conference participants express how much they were enjoying the conference and how they hoped it might go beyond a one-time occurrence.

Given the budget realities at Oregon State University, however, the English department was in no situation to host the conference in future years.[5] Lisa and Cheryl had run the conference on a shoestring, constantly worried about balancing expenses and income.[6] As the final day of the conference began, it appeared that the Feminism(s) and Rhetoric(s) Conference had generated great enthusiasm and catalyzed many conversations and future research projects — but that it would not have a life beyond that day. Then during the final dinner of the conference, Lillian Bridwell-Bowles and Lisa Albrecht came forward to make a surprise announcement: This conference did indeed have to continue, they said, and the University of Minnesota would host it in 1999.

The Second and Third Feminism(s) and Rhetoric(s) Conferences: Assuring a Future for the Conference

If the first conference at Oregon State jump-started the Feminisms and Rhetorics Conference, the second conference at the University of Minnesota increased its scope and size and helped create the sense that the conference was, to put it simply, both necessary and inevitable as a biennial event. The conference coordinators included Lillian Bridwell-Bowles, Hildy Miller, Lisa Albrecht, Laura Gurak, and Ann Browning, and the conference was sponsored by the Center for Interdisciplinary Studies of Writing, which Bridwell-Bowles directed. Whereas the first Feminism(s) and Rhetoric(s) program was sixteen pages long, the second conference program totaled 127 pages, including abstracts of all talks at the conference. The second conference continued the first conference's tradition of including featured speakers from within and without the field of rhetoric and writing. Joining feminists within rhetoric and writing, such as Susan Jarratt, Elizabeth Flynn, Nan Johnson, Gesa Kirsch, and others, were nationally known feminist scholars and creative writers, including Dorothy Allison, Judith Butler, Deborah Cameron, Lorraine Code, Suzette Haden Elgin, Jane Gallop, Janice Gould, Judith Halberstam, Joy Harjo, Florence Howe, Evelyn Fox Keller, Robin Lakoff, Julia Penelope, and Dale Spender. In addition to the thirty-nine featured speakers, the program included nine University of Minnesota writers and scholars, including eminent scholars and writers Karlyn Kohrs Campbell, Patricia Hampl, Mary Lay, and Valerie Miner. All told, the program listed 420 participants. The Feminism(s) and Rhetoric(s) Conference had arrived.[7]

This does not mean, however, that the future of the conference was assured. Although the coordinators of the second conference confidently titled it the "Second *Biennial* Feminism(s) and Rhetoric(s) Conference," the conference still had no ongoing institutional home or sponsorship. The coordinators were acutely aware of this situation. In an effort to encourage scholars in other universities to take on the conference, they developed the extremely helpful and detailed "Feminism(s) and Rhetoric(s) Planning Guide." As one of its recommendations, the planning guide suggests that the Coalition of Women Scholars in the History of Rhetoric and Composition might want to support the conference. The authors of the planning guide note that "If the coalition continues to evolve, it may well want to ask for dues and offer a discount to members for this conference. Having a budget up front from dues would help considerably" (10).

As this comment suggests, the Coalition was itself still a work in progress. Here is a brief history of the Coalition, as narrated on its "About Us" web page:

> The Coalition of Women Scholars in the History of Rhetoric and Composition began in a series of discussion and brainstorming sessions attended by Winifred Horner, Jan Swearingen, Nan Johnson, Marjorie Curry Woods, and Kathleen Welch in 1988 and 1989. These five women rhetoricians met during assemblies of the Conference on College Composition and Communication (CCCC), The Speech and Communication Association, and the Rhetoric Society of America. At these meetings, participants talked about how isolated work on women in rhetoric was, and how very difficult such work was to carry out. These early conversations produced a draft of a constitution, and led to a larger meeting of interested women

scholars during the 1990 CCCC. The constitution articulates the goals for the Coalition:

- to foster and encourage scholarship, research, and interest in the history of rhetoric and composition;
- to encourage exploration of women's roles in the stories we tell about rhetoric and composition;
- to build and sustain a network of scholars who share these interests.

The group met formally for the first time during the 1993 Conference on College Composition and Communication meeting in San Diego and has met every subsequent year, on Wednesday evening before the formal opening of the Conference.

The Coalition had been involved with the Feminism(s) and Rhetoric(s) Conference from the start. One of the concurrent sessions held at Oregon State in 1997 was "Working at the Intersections of Feminism(s) and Rhetoric(s): Professional Concerns." This session was sponsored by the Coalition, chaired by Kathleen Welch, and included statements by and conversation among Lillian Bridwell-Bowles, Cheryl Glenn, Shirley Logan, Danielle Mitchell, C. Jan Swearingen, and Kathleen Welch. Although the Coalition for Women Scholars did not formally sponsor the third Feminism(s) and Rhetoric(s) Conference at Millikin University, the program for that conference included two pages devoted to the history of the Coalition and a listing of its current officers, so the connection between the conference and the Coalition was already visible if still implicit. However, the Coalition did not officially affiliate with the Feminism(s) and Rhetoric(s) Conference until the fourth conference at Ohio State University in 2003.

The fact that the third conference even occurred in 2001 was a result of a moment of serendipity.[8] This moment occurred when Nancy DeJoy, then director of the writing program at Millikin University in Decatur, Illinois, agreed to step in when a previously chosen location fell through. In a presentation at the 2003 Feminism(s) and Rhetoric(s) Conference, DeJoy described the circumstances that enabled her to take on the conference:

> The fact that I was at a small private university meant that I could move quickly, get the Provost's approval, reserve rooms, plan for meals and refreshments, etc. The fact that I was in Decatur, Illinois — a depressed town that no one really wanted to reserve rooms in — meant that I could get a block of rooms at the local Holiday Inn on short notice. The fact that I was at an undergraduate institution that required two semesters of first-year writing for first-year students and multiple writing seminars for English writing majors meant that I had a pool of students who had developed an interest in writing studies to draw from for inspiration, assistance, and motivation while pulling off that conference.

The third Feminism(s) and Rhetoric(s) Conference was a significantly smaller event than the second conference — closer in size to the first conference held at Oregon State. The program for this conference was 23 pages long, rather than the 127 pages that comprised the program for the second conference. Nevertheless, one need only study the program for the conference, available at the Coalition's website (http://cwshrc.org), to see how ambitious an undertaking it was and to recognize that the talks presented at this conference were as stimulating and wide-ranging as at previous conferences. The third conference shared with the first two conferences a strong emphasis on fostering dialogue among feminist scholars working in a range of disciplines. The call for papers for the conference, for instance, pointedly observed that "Currently the list of featured speakers includes scholars from the fields of adult literacy, anthropology, history, literary studies, performance, photography and the visual arts, political science and rhetoric." The call for proposals identifies the third conference as the "Third Biennial *International* Feminism(s) and Rhetoric(s) Conference." The presence of such featured speakers as Samantha Manchester Earley, Hannington Ochwada, and Beatrice Quarshie Smith certainly justified the designation "international." Another notable feature of the third conference was the significant involvement of undergraduate students, who played a key role in planning and running the conference and also presented several talks. In addition, DeJoy observed, "It was the undergraduate students who pushed me to invite visual artists to present at featured sessions, and to do everything I could to get people from lots of different disciplines to submit papers."

By the time Nan Johnson and Susan Delagrange were beginning to prepare for the fourth conference, held at Ohio State University in 2003, the Coalition was ready and able to take on the conference. According to Delagrange and Johnson, the Coalition gave the co-coordinators $1,500 in start-up funds, which was returned to the Coalition once it was clear that the conference would break even financially. Currently the major role that the Coalition plays in the ongoing development of the conference is to provide start-up funds and to determine future hosts for the conference.[9] As suggested in the now decade-old planning guide, Coalition membership funds indirectly help fund the conference. Due to the partnership with the Coalition, the Feminisms and Rhetorics Conference now enjoys some degree of stability.

Diversity of Participants, Diversity of Thought

In the years since the first three conferences, attendance has varied somewhat depending on location. The Coalition "Conference Site CFP" web page indicates, however, that conference sites "must accommodate approximately 400+ people." This rough attendance figure suggests that the conference has a record of attracting a significant group of feminist scholars in rhetoric and writing. And despite the fact that the conference is sponsored by the "Coalition of Women Scholars in the *History* of Rhetoric and Composition," presentations at the conference cover a wide range of topics while continuing to celebrate a range of diversities.

The Ohio State conference (the fourth biennial conference, held in 2003) focused on inclusivity in the work of feminists, in papers on Tongan-American feminism, Bolshevik women's rhetoric, women's literacy programs in India, and mestiza feminist consciousness. With its theme of "Critical Locations of Feminist Rhetorical Practice," this meeting explored embodied rhetorics extensively. Particularly memorable was a strand of sessions focusing on disabilities and exclusionary discourses and a gripping evening of performances that explored disability, gender, sexuality, and identity.

The 2005 conference, held at Michigan Tech, took "Affirming Diversity" as its theme, thus maintaining this central value of both the Coalition and the earlier conferences. Keynote speakers at this 5th biennial conference included Min-Zhan Lu, Helena Maria Viramontes, Donna Haraway, and Jacqueline Jones Royster, and presenters came from Cyprus and the Middle East, Canada, Europe, and Mexico. In an email to the authors, Beth Flynn reflected on choosing diversity as the overriding theme, the first Feminisms and Rhetorics Conference to do so explicitly. She also wryly noted that the upper peninsula of Michigan is not the easiest place to visit: "some presenters went to heroic efforts to get here," she wrote, noting that they flew into Minneapolis or Green Bay or Marquette and then drove rental cars the rest of the way. The year 2005 also was the year of Hurricane Katrina, and as Beth noted, "Patty Sotirin and Ann Brady coordinated a special session" on this massive tragedy. The conference was dedicated to the victims and survivors of Katrina.

Even a glance at the titles of concurrent panels offered during the opening session of the 2007 Feminism(s) and Rhetoric(s) Conference shows careful attention to a broad diversity of topics as well as to diversity in general, indicating that the work of feminist scholars at this conference extended well beyond the academy:

- "Framed! Feminist Interventions in Civic Discourse"
- "Rhetorics of Science and Healthcare"
- "Conduct Manuals through the Ages"
- "Women in Literature and Television"
- "Margins, Grassroots, and Bully Pulpits: Women Occupying Space in Politics"
- "Talking and Teaching Post-9/11 and Katrina"
- "Creating Changes with Administration"
- "Chinese Civic Discourse"
- "Women's Activism and Advocacy: A Century of Continuity and Change"
- "Issues in Community Literacy"
- "New Possibilities for the Composition Classroom"
- "Defining Sexuality and Gender: Theoretically and Legally"

This 6th conference, held in 2007 at the University of Arkansas, took "Civic Discourse" as its theme and was timed to coincide with the anniversary of the integration of Little Rock's high school. With its memorable visit to Little Rock Central High School and its riveting keynote address by U.S. Surgeon General Jocelyn Elders, this conference reconnected many attendees to Little Rock's powerful local history and celebrated the remarkable work of civic discourse carried out by women in Arkansas — and around the world.

As we have noted, these conferences not only encourage and celebrate pluralism and diversity but also have been particularly proactive in encouraging nontraditional, engaged, performative presentations. Here, for instance, is the call for proposals for the 2009 Feminisms and Rhetorics Conference, held at Michigan State University in East Lansing, Michigan from October 7–10, 2009:

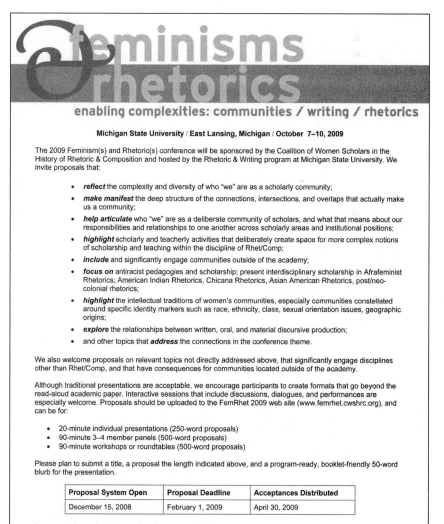

feminisms rhetorics

enabling complexities: communities / writing / rhetorics

Michigan State University / East Lansing, Michigan / October 7–10, 2009

The 2009 Feminism(s) and Rhetoric(s) conference will be sponsored by the Coalition of Women Scholars in the History of Rhetoric & Composition and hosted by the Rhetoric & Writing program at Michigan State University. We invite proposals that:

- *reflect* the complexity and diversity of who "we" are as a scholarly community;
- *make manifest* the deep structure of the connections, intersections, and overlaps that actually make us a community;
- *help articulate* who "we" are as a deliberate community of scholars, and what that means about our responsibilities and relationships to one another across scholarly areas and institutional positions;
- *highlight* scholarly and teacherly activities that deliberately create space for more complex notions of scholarship and teaching within the discipline of Rhet/Comp;
- *include* and significantly engage communities outside of the academy;
- *focus on* antiracist pedagogies and scholarship; present interdisciplinary scholarship in Afrafeminist Rhetorics; American Indian Rhetorics, Chicana Rhetorics, Asian American Rhetorics, post/neo-colonial rhetorics;
- *highlight* the intellectual traditions of women's communities, especially communities constellated around specific identity markers such as race, ethnicity, class, sexual orientation issues, geographic origins;
- *explore* the relationships between written, oral, and material discursive production;
- and other topics that *address* the connections in the conference theme.

We also welcome proposals on relevant topics not directly addressed above, that significantly engage disciplines other than Rhet/Comp, and that have consequences for communities located outside of the academy.

Although traditional presentations are acceptable, we encourage participants to create formats that go beyond the read-aloud academic paper. Interactive sessions that include discussions, dialogues, and performances are especially welcome. Proposals should be uploaded to the FemRhet 2009 web site (www.femrhet.cwshrc.org), and can be for:

- 20-minute individual presentations (250-word proposals)
- 90-minute 3–4 member panels (500-word proposals)
- 90-minute workshops or roundtables (500-word proposals)

Please plan to submit a title, a proposal the length indicated above, and a program-ready, booklet-friendly 50-word blurb for the presentation.

Proposal System Open	Proposal Deadline	Acceptances Distributed
December 15, 2008	February 1, 2009	April 30, 2009

For more information: Contact Bets Caldwell, caldwell@msu.edu.

This call for proposals from the most recent Feminisms and Rhetorics Conference resulted in a notable group of featured speakers at Michigan State. While most of them represented rhetoric and writing or other areas within English studies, such as creative writing or ethnic studies, they were a particularly diverse group in terms of racial and cultural identity and research interests. The featured speakers and the titles of their talks follow:

- Gwendolyn D. Pough, "On Prince Charming and the Strong Black Woman: Race, Representations, Rhetoric and Romance"
- Cecilia Rodríguez Milanés, "'My English Is Not Very Good Looking' — Accents and Identities"
- Rochelle L. Harris, "From Zombies to Writing Groups and Motorcycle Rallies to Memoir: My Search for the Fifth Trope of Rhetoric"
- Resa Crane Bizzaro, "Diagnosing Intergenerational Post Traumatic Stress Disorder: Or, A Fat Old Indian Woman Fistfights the American Psychiatric Association in East Lansing"
- Terese Guinsatao Monberg, "Pinay Peminists: Listening for New Locations and Re/visions of Rhetorical Theory"
- Dora Ramirez-Dhoore, "Racial and Scientific Rhetoric in Eco-Political Matters: Third World Women Workers in Helena Maria Viramonte's *Under the Feet of Jesus* and Alicia Gaspar de Alba's *Desert Blood*"

The 2009 call for proposals — and the diverse group of presenters who responded to that call — powerfully demonstrates, we believe, the spirit that motivates this innovative and collaborative biennial gathering of feminist scholars.

THE CHALLENGE OF INTERDISCIPLINARITY

But what about the original goal of the first conference: to move beyond disciplinary boundaries to borderlands, where feminist scholars working in the context of different disciplines could engage in dialogue? Certainly, as we've noted, the conferences have continued to pursue that goal, and the utopian hope for cross-disciplinary exchange that Lisa and Cheryl brought to the first conference remains. The call for proposals for the 2011 conference, hosted by the University of Minnesota, Mankato, reiterates this desire for interdisciplinarity: Here is that call, as represented on the Coalition's website (see facing page).

In spite of conference organizers' best efforts, however, this goal — of achieving a fully interdisciplinary conference — has proven much harder to achieve. While most conferences have included well-known feminist scholars from disciplines outside of rhetoric and writing as keynote or featured speakers, and while some scholars from other disciplines also choose to attend the conference, the participants at the biennial Feminisms and Rhetorics Conference most typically identify with the field of rhetoric and writing. This is a powerful reminder that even at a time when interdisciplinarity is being touted as the next best thing for the academy, the silent but powerful tug of tradi-

Feminist Challenges or Feminist Rhetorics?: Locations, Scholarship, and Discourse

Feminisms and Rhetorics 2011

Call for Proposals

The theme of the 2011 Feminisms and Rhetorics conference is "Feminist Challenges or Feminist Rhetorics?: Locations, Scholarship and Discourse." The Feminisms and Rhetorics conference is sponsored by the Coalition of Women Scholars in the History of Rhetoric and Composition, and will be hosted by Minnesota State University, Mankato October 12-15, 2011.

The conference committee is strongly interdisciplinary and therefore our theme seeks to recognize the spaces between disciplines and communities. The conference theme is meant to acknowledge the academic and socio-discursive spaces that feminisms, and rhetorics on or about feminisms, inhabit. Major political, religious and social leaders have recently discussed feminism, including the Dalai Lama, but the discussion seems to revolve around cultural or essentialized discourses of feminism. This spotlight on feminism is, of course, not new, and the way feminism is engaged in public discourse is much different than that of academic discourse. However, in Rhetoric and Composition, we have seen many significant publications lately focusing on what it means to be a woman in the field, how to be a successful woman in the field, and the connections between feminist theory and feminist pedagogy.

We seek proposals that speak to the challenges and diversities of feminist rhetoric and discourse, in public and private life, in the academy, and in the media. We welcome proposals on topics that significantly engage disciplines other than Rhetoric and Composition, and that have consequences for communities located outside of the academy.

Questions to consider include:

- What are the discourses of feminism? Where are they located?
- What does feminist scholarship look like in the 21st century?
- What is the politic of feminist scholarship?
- How does feminist inquiry impact our understanding of scholarship?
- What are the challenges faced by feminists inside and outside of the academy?
- Where do we find feminist rhetorics? How do we understand the function of feminist rhetoric?
- How has interdisciplinarity impacted the feminist agenda?
- How do we understand the politics of inclusion in 21st century feminism?
- How might we add to Joanna Russ' invective: "She wrote it, BUT...?"

In the past few years, women have made, yet again, publicly recognized strides in breaking through a variety of glass ceilings, however, current events in places like Arizona, illustrate the necessity of a renewed feminist politic. The recursive nature of feminism is not new, and is, in fact, embodied in the rhetorical struggle for place in dominant discourse.

On the submission and registration page, you will find options for panel, roundtable, or individual submissions. If you have any questions, please email Kirsti Cole at kirsti [dot] cole [at] mnsu [dot] edu.

Abstracts due: April 15th, 2011.

Acceptance to the conference will be sent out no later than May 15, 2011.

tional disciplines keeps scholars in place. How many of those in rhetoric and writing, for instance, attend the National Communication Association, or even the Modern Language Association (MLA), meetings? In addition, as a field, rhetoric and writing is still often equated with first-year writing programs in the minds of many in the academy and thus continues to struggle for cultural capital and legitimacy. Finally, it may be that Stanley Fish had a point when he argued that "Being Interdisciplinary Is So Very Hard to Do."

A LOOK AT THE CONFERENCE'S LEGACY AND FUTURE

Clearly, the Feminisms and Rhetorics Conference has created a space where scholars' commitment to feminist theory and practice is both visible and valued as the heart of the conference's endeavors — something that is not always the case at larger and more diversified conferences, such as the Conference on College Composition and Communication, the Rhetoric Society Conference, and the Modern Language Association Conference. In addition, through its various calls for proposals, the conference encourages scholars to experiment, to collaborate with each other and with nonacademic communities, to work toward social justice, and to weave multiple voices together. And not to put too fine a point on it, despite the fact that the conference lacks the kind of financial, bureaucratic, and material support that a group like the National Council of Teachers of English or CCCC can provide their annual meetings, the conference keeps on keeping on; feminist scholars of rhetoric and writing just don't give up. Some years a highly visible and fairly elite (in terms of its research profile) university hosts the conference; other years less well-known colleges and universities play this role. The Feminisms and Rhetorics Conference strongly benefits, we believe, from this diversity in sponsorship, institutional situation, and geographical location. In an email to the authors, Krista Ratcliffe, President of the Coalition from 2000 to 2002, pointed out that this diversity "enables larger schools with more money to bring in more outside speakers. The smaller conferences offer an intimate setting that facilitates developing relationships among people in the field, which affects, to some extent, who gets recommended to do promotion and tenure reviews and to read manuscript submissions for journals and presses."

Both the Feminisms and Rhetorics Conference and the Coalition have also had a very strong commitment to supporting and mentoring graduate students.[10] The Coalition devotes a substantial part of its traditional Wednesday evening workshop at the CCCC, for instance, to mentoring graduate students and early-career faculty members. From the first conference to the present, graduate student participation has also been strongly encouraged and has made a difference in many students' lives and careers, as the following comments from Barbara L'Eplattenier, past president of the Coalition, suggest. In reflecting on her presentation at the first Feminism(s) and Rhetoric(s) Conference at Oregon State University, L'Eplattenier noted that while this was not her first conference presentation, "it was definitely the first presentation I did where I felt like a scholar, and not someone tagging along after someone else's work. This was the conference where I presented the seed of the idea that became my dissertation, which led to my first book, *Historical Studies of Writing Program Administration*." L'Eplattenier goes on to add that she met her coeditor of this collection, Lisa Mastrangelo, "at one of the Coalition Wednesday night gatherings in Nan Johnson's historiography group. We were both looking at Progressive Era women and knew of no one else who was doing similar work. It was a match made in heaven! We've been friends and collaborators ever since!" L'Eplattenier and Mastrangelo's collection won the 2004–2005 WPA best book award.

For all the reasons we have discussed, the Feminisms and Rhetorics Conference has proven to be a powerful stimulus to both scholarly work and pedagogical and community-based actions. In the acknowledgments to their edited collection *Teaching Rhetorica: Theory, Pedagogy, Practice*, Kate Ronald and Joy Ritchie affirm that "The Coalition of Scholars in the History of Rhetoric and the Biennial Conference on Feminism(s) and Rhetoric(s) have . . . provided us with stimulating and supportive forums in which to extend our thinking" (vii). Cheryl Glenn similarly acknowledges the Coalition for providing "a safe venue for trying out my latest ideas within the good company of intellectual sisters" (xvii). That venue is, of course, the Feminisms and Rhetorics Conference. We are sure that there are many, many more scholars in rhetoric and writing who remain profoundly aware of the important role that the Feminisms and Rhetorics Conference has played in both their scholarly, pedagogical, and personal lives — for, ideally, the personal and the professional (as well as the political) inspire one another.

Another indication of the power of both the Coalition and the Feminisms and Rhetorics conference is the Studies in Rhetorics and Feminisms Series co-edited by Cheryl Glenn and Shirley Logan and published by Southern Illinois University Press. In her September 1998 proposal to Southern Illinois University Press to establish the series, Glenn commented on the extent to which the 1997 conference was a "whopping success" (3). She noted that the conference, and the series that she was proposing, performed an important function in bringing together scholars who up to this point were often limited to conferences and book series that *either* focused on rhetoric *or* on feminist theory and practice. "Scholars working at the crossing of rhetoric and feminism," Glenn observed, are thus "offered two, often markedly different lines of opportunity" (9). The new Studies in Rhetorics and Feminisms series could address this difficulty by offering authors working in both areas "the perfect home for their work, a place where rhetoric and feminism constantly interanimate each other" (9).

Southern Illinois University Press instituted the series and has, thus far, published nine titles:

- Carol Mattingly, *Appropriate[ing] Dress: Women's Rhetorical Style in Nineteenth-Century America* (2002)

- Nan Johnson, *Gender and Rhetorical Space in American Life, 1866–1910* (2002)

- Elizabeth Flynn, *Feminism Beyond Modernism* (2002)

- Roxanne Mountford, *The Gendered Pulpit: Preaching in American Protestant Spaces* (2003)

- Karyn Hollis, *Liberating Voices: Writing at the Bryn Mawr Summer School for Women Workers* (2004)

- Wendy B. Sharer, *Vote and Voice: Women's Organizations and Political Literacy, 1915–1930* (2004)

- Lindal Buchanan, *Regendering Delivery: The Fifth Canon and Antebellum Women Rhetors* (2005)

- Krista Ratcliffe, *Rhetorical Listening: Identification, Gender, Whiteness* (2005)

- Suzanne Bordelon, *A Feminist Legacy: The Rhetoric and Pedagogy of Gertrude Buck* (2007)

Readers will agree, we are sure, that this is an impressive list of publications that has been well reviewed and, in at least one case, recognized with major scholarly awards.[11] Many of these monographs might well have been published if the Feminisms and Rhetorics Conference (and the SIUP series on Rhetorics and Feminisms that grew out of the conference) had not come to be. But it seems clear that the conference has indeed proven itself to be generative. Indeed, we can testify to the impact of the Coalition and conference in our own work, as presented in this section of this collection.

So the future of the Feminisms and Rhetorics Conference seems fairly secure. But we shouldn't delude ourselves: the values of inclusivity, diversity, collaboration, and coalition building that form the foundation of this conference don't often fit well with the hegemonic ideologies of the academy, and these ideologies are still very strong. For example, even as the Modern Language Association has called for a loosening of the stranglehold of the single-authored monograph, it has acknowledged that the requirement has increased at elite universities, which often specify that assistant professors must have *two* single-authored monographs — one in print and one at least in contract — for promotion to associate professor with tenure. And even though 2010 MLA President Sidonie Smith argues that scholars in the humanities must recognize that our students will enter

> a scholarly environment in which the modes of production are increasingly collaborative, the vehicles of scholarly dissemination increasingly interactive, the circulation of knowledge more openly accessible, and the audiences for which we compose purposefully varied

— and that the dissertation should be rethought in ways that might encourage collaboratively-written works — we are not holding our breath. As we have noted in other essays, however, since we and other feminist scholars of rhetoric and writing have been making a similar argument for some thirty years now, we don't want to give up either. Thus we still hope that Smith's call for change may make a difference and that the academy in general and the humanities in particular will be more open to the values espoused and embodied in the Feminisms and Rhetorics Conferences. If and when that time comes, we firmly believe that there will be a Feminisms and Rhetorics Conference ready to reaffirm those values, to embody change, and to remind us that words such as "feminism" and "rhetoric" not only can and should but *must* be linked together, and in so doing "live that day." And linked together they are in the Biennial Feminisms and Rhetorics Conferences that embody collaborative partnership and coalition building; create spaces for nontraditional, experimental modes of research and presentation; and celebrate and affirm the work of feminist scholars in rhetoric and writing studies.

Acknowledgments: We would like to thank a number of colleagues who read and responded to this essay as it neared completion. They helped us fill in details that our archives (and our memories) missed or were unclear about. They also reminded us of the power and passion that is so characteristic of the

Feminisms and Rhetorics Conference and of the Coalition for Women Scholars in the History of Rhetoric and Composition, which has sponsored the conference since 2003. Thanks to Nancy DeJoy, Susan Delagrange, Elizabeth Flynn, Cheryl Glenn, Nan Johnson, Barbara L'Eplattenier, Hildy Miller, and Krista Ratliff.

NOTES

1. For a chronological listing of work that has played an integral role in challenging the scope and definition of the rhetorical tradition and in bringing feminist theory and practice in conversation with that tradition, see our "Crimes of Writing and Reading," pp. 310–329 in this collection.

2. In this essay, we tend to use the original name up to the 2009 conference and drop the (s)'s after that. We use the most current spelling — "feminisms and rhetorics" — when referring to the conference in general as it has been enacted over time.

3. For further discussion of the founding of the CCCC, see *On Writing Research: The Braddock Essays 1975–1998*, ed. Lisa Ede. Boston and Urbana: Bedford/St. Martin's P and NCTE, 1999.

4. The programs for many of the Feminisms and Rhetorics conferences are available at http://cwshrc.org.

5. Throughout the 1980s and 1990s several other universities already hosted regular annual or biennial conferences for scholars in rhetoric and writing. The hosting institutions include the University of Wyoming, Pennsylvania State University, and the University of New Hampshire. As far as the authors know, the histories of these conferences have not been documented, which seems regrettable. Conferences such as these played an important role during the years that rhetoric and writing was professionalizing itself as a discipline.

6. Neither Cheryl nor Lisa now has access to the final budget for the conference, but a tentative budget that Lisa submitted on August 10, 1997, a few weeks before the conference occurred, showed conference expenses at $23,794 and conference income at $21,205.

7. In an email to the authors, Hildy Miller recalled how hard the coordinators of the conference worked to achieve diversity in multiple arenas. Miller noted their excitement about setting up a keynote panel featuring the work of African American scholars Jacqueline Jones Royster, Beverly Moss, Shirley Logan, and Joyce Irene Middleton and their determination to continue the tradition of inviting speakers from outside rhetoric and writing. Miller added that they "showcased figures like Judith Butler, Judith Halberstam, and Dorothy Allison in key spots, not only because they were outside rhet/writing, but because they reflected intersections of gender with sexuality — it seems like fem/rhet generally is still struggling to articulate this intersection, even ten years later. Besides inviting feminist scholars from many disciplines, we tried to be inclusive of rhetoric proper by including scholars from the oral dimension of it from linguistics (Deborah Cameron, Julia Penelope, Robin Lakoff) and speech (Karlyn Kohrs Campbell). . . . And we tried to reach out to literary studies (Jane Gallop) and creative writing (Dorothy Allison) — again, mindful of the splits within English studies. We looked back and tried to honor feminist foremothers via Robin Lakoff (often scapegoated) and Florence Howe and to look to the future, especially with technology (Dene Grigar, Mary Lay) and through encouraging alternative discourses (Harjo's performance)."

8. Serendipity often plays a role in the creation and institutionalization of professional entities and projects. *The Writing Lab Newsletter*, for instance, grew out of what Michael Pemberton and Joyce Kinkead describe as a "volatile session" on writing centers at the 1977 Conference on College Composition and Communication. In their introduction to *The Center Will Hold: Critical Perspectives on Writing Center Scholarship*, Pemberton and Kinkead describe the well-known story of how at the end of the session Muriel Harris of Purdue University "took out pen and pad, invited participants to write their names and addresses, and, using that list, mailed out the first issue of the *Writing Lab Newsletter (WLN)*, produced on a Sears typewriter at her kitchen table" (3).

9. For details see the "Conference Site CFP" (http://cwshrc.org/conference-site-cfp) page on the Coalition's website.

10. In reflecting on the 2004 conference at Ohio State University, for instance, Nan Johnson observed that she and co-coordinator Susan Delagrange "held the conference at the Holiday Inn rather than the fancy conference center down the block because the Holiday Inn gave us room rates we felt graduate students and younger scholars could afford."

11. Krista Ratcliffe's *Rhetorical Listening*, for instance, was recognized with the 2006 Gary A. Olson Rhetoric and Cultural Studies Award and with the 2007 Rhetoric Society of America Book Award and the CCCC Outstanding Book Award.

WORKS CITED

Buchanan, Lindal. *Regendering Delivery: The Fifth Canon and Antebellum Women Rhetors.* Carbondale: Southern Illinois UP, 2005. Print.

Call for Proposals 2001: Feminist Literacies: Resisting Disciplines. Decatur, IL: Milliken University. Print.

Call for Proposals 2009: Enabling Complexities: Communities/Writing/Rhetorics. Lansing, MI: Michigan State University. Web. 3 Sept. 2010.

Call for Proposals 2011: Feminist Challenges or Feminist Rhetorics: Locations, Scholarship, and Discourse. Mankato: Minnesota State University. Web. 3 Sept. 2010.

Dejoy, Nancy. "Reflecting on Feminism(s) & Rhetoric(s): Looking Forward, Looking Back." The Sixth Biennial Feminism(s) & Rhetoric(s) Conference. Little Rock, Arkansas. 4–6 Oct. 2007. Lecture, sent to the authors by e-mail.

Dickinson, Emily. "A Word Is Dead." *The Complete Poems of Emily Dickinson.* Ed. Thomas H. Johnson. Boston: Little Brown, 1961. 534. Poem 1212. Print.

Fish, Stanley. "Being Interdisciplinary Is So Very Hard to Do." *Profession* 89. New York: Modern Language Association, 1989. 15–22. Print.

Flynn, Elizabeth. *Feminism Beyond Modernism.* Carbondale: Southern Illinois UP, 2002. Print.

———. "Fems/Rhets Conference." Message to Lisa Ede. 31 Aug. 2010. E-mail.

Glenn, Cheryl. "Studies in Rhetorics and Feminisms: A Series of Southern Illinois University Press." Proposal submitted Sept. 1998. Print.

———. *Unspoken: A Rhetoric of Silence.* Carbondale: Southern Illinois UP, 2004. Print.

Hollis, Karyn. *Liberating Voices: Writing at the Bryn Mawr Summer School for Women Workers.* Carbondale: Southern Illinois UP, 2004. Print.

Johnson, Nan. "Fems/Rhets Conference." Message to Lisa Ede. 30 Aug. 2010. E-mail.

———. *Gender and Rhetorical Space in American Life, 1866–1910.* Carbondale: Southern Illinois UP, 2002. Print.

L'Eplattenier, Barbara. "Feminism(s) and Rhetoric(s) Essay." Message to Lisa Ede. 30 Aug. 2010. E-mail.

L'Eplattenier, Barbara, and Lisa Mastrangelo. *Historical Studies of Writing Program Administration: Individuals, Communities, and the Formation of a Discipline.* Anderson, SC: Parlor Press, 2004. Print.

L'Eplattenier, Barbara, and Marcia Smith, co-chairs. *The Sixth Biennial Feminism(s) and Rhetoric(s) Conference: Civic Discourse.* Program of Feminism(s) and Rhetoric(s) Conference, 4–6 Oct. 2007, University of Arkansas, Little Rock. The Coalition of Women Scholars in the History of Rhetoric and Composition, n.d. Web. 3 Sept. 2010.

Lloyd-Jones, Richard. "Who We Are, Who We Should Become." *College Composition and Communication* 43.4 (1992): 486–96. Print.

Mattingly, Carol. *Appropriate[ing] Dress: Women's Rhetorical Style in Nineteenth-Century America.* Carbondale: Southern Illinois UP, 2002. Print.

Miller, Hildy. "Some Comments." Message to Lisa Ede. 29 Aug. 2010. E-mail.

Mountford, Roxanne. *The Gendered Pulpit: Preaching in American Protestant Spaces.* Carbondale: Southern Illinois UP, 2003. Print.

Pemberton, Michael A., and Joyce Kinkead, eds. *The Center Will Hold: Critical Perspectives on Writing Center Scholarship.* Logan: Utah State UP, 2003. Print.

Ratcliffe, Krista. "The First Feminisms and Rhetorics." Message to Lisa Ede. 31 Aug. 2010. E-mail.

———. *Rhetorical Listening: Identification, Gender, Whiteness.* Carbondale: Southern Illinois UP, 2005. Print.

Ronald, Kate, and Joy Ritchie, eds. *Teaching Rhetorica: Theory, Pedagogy, Practice.* Portsmouth, NH: Boynton/Cook, 2006. Print.

Sharer, Wendy. *Vote and Voice: Women's Organizations and Political Literacy, 1915–1930.* Carbondale: Southern Illinois UP, 2004. Print.

Smith, Sidonie. "An Agenda for the New Dissertation." *MLA Newsletter* Summer 2010: 2. Print.

University of Minnesota, Center for Interdisciplinary Studies of Writing. *Feminism(s) and Rhetoric(s) Conference Planning Guide.* Twin Cities: University of Minnesota, 1999. Print.

PART FIVE

On Writing Centers

21   *Writing as a Social Process: A Theoretical Foundation for Writing Centers?* *

We all have stories that help us define who we are in our personal and professional lives. For those of us who work in writing centers, these stories are generally convoluted and circuitous. Few of us planned as graduate students to direct or work in writing centers, at least few graduate students of my generation (the early 70s) did. Yet most of us are now fully committed to our centers. The work that we do is demanding and undervalued — and we'd never consider changing jobs.

I would like to begin this essay by telling you the story of my own involvement with writing centers. Like many of you, I suspect, I began my graduate studies blissfully unaware of composition as a professional field. Sometime during my dissertation years my attitude toward composition changed. And sometime during my first job teaching at a SUNY college in upstate New York, my sense of my own professional identity changed: I defined myself as a teacher and researcher of composition studies.

I read research in composition studies; I began to write articles myself. And in 1980 I accepted a job at Oregon State University where, in addition to teaching composition, I became both the coordinator of the English department's writing program and the director of the Communication Skills Center, an independent support service with a Writing Lab and non-credit classes in reading and study skills. I will spare you the saga of my early years at the Communication Skills Center — my shocked recognition that I knew nothing about running a Writing Lab, the budget deficits, the frustration of hours spent making appointments, ordering supplies, and paying bills.

I survived these and other administrative traumas, thanks to an extraordinarily supportive staff and to English department colleagues. And thanks to my tutors (now called writing assistants, to avoid the remedial connotations of "tutor") I became educated about collaborative learning and peer tutoring as well. My writing assistants educated me by showing me what writing assistants can — and can't — do. With good humor and wisdom, they helped

From Lisa Ede, in *The Writing Center Journal* 9.2 (1989): 3–14.
*Lisa Ede wrote this piece as a single author.

me understand collaborative learning as it occurs in actual peer conferences, not in the pages of a book.

On my campus, I became an advocate of collaborative learning and of writing centers. I spoke with conviction of the unique nature and benefits of peer tutoring to colleagues, students, administrators — anyone who would give me ten minutes of their time. At first I fought for the Center's survival. Once we managed to get a still inadequate but permanent budget, I and my staff had the luxury of focusing on other issues.

These were satisfying years, but I was aware of a lingering sense of unease. For as I grew into my job as director — as my staff and the writing assistants continued to educate me — I recognized a troubling contradiction. Despite my convictions about the importance of our Writing Lab and the benefits of peer tutoring, I couldn't connect my pragmatic experience and understanding of the importance of this work with my more theoretical research in composition and rhetoric. Furthermore, the research that most interested me — research on classical and contemporary rhetorical theories — seemed to intersect little with my work in the Writing Lab.

I want to be as clear as possible about the nature of this contradiction and the reasons why it troubled me. In a sense, my awareness of this contradiction simply exacerbated a schizophrenic-like bifurcation already implicit in my situation. (I have two offices in two separate buildings, for instance, and until recently I reported to two different deans.) But my unease went deeper than that. I believe strongly in the interdependence of theory and practice, as do most in our profession. Theory without practice is likely to result in ungrounded, inapplicable speculation. Practice without theory, as we know, often leads to inconsistent, and sometimes even contradictory and wrongheaded, pedagogical methods.

Yet here I was, theorizing at nights and on weekends in ways that didn't seem to connect with my week-day work. I wondered if I was continuing the ghettoization of composition, only in a new form. The old version had literary critics theorizing, while underpaid teaching assistants and instructors toiled in composition classes. Had I managed to internalize that opposition, so that the Writing Lab part of me couldn't find anything interesting or relevant to say to the weekend theorizer? If so, I gradually realized, I was implicitly contributing to the general perception that writing centers are "extras," helpful additions to composition or writing across the curriculum programs that fall into the nice-to-have-if-you-can-get-it-but-not-essential category.

I have come to believe that my situation is not uncommon. For a variety of reasons, those of us who direct or work in writing centers have seldom been able to articulate theoretical support for our work that goes beyond the basic principles of collaborative learning. The most common reason for this failure, of course, is that we have been too busy working ourselves to death — running centers on inadequate or even nonexistent budgets, functioning as director, secretary, tutor, and public relations expert all at once — to take the time to theorize. Because we have in a sense been inventing ourselves as we started, developed, and defended our centers, we have naturally focused on the pragmatic.

Anyone who has found a solution to a pressing problem by consulting a treasured collection of *Writing Lab Newsletters* knows how crucial the exchange of ideas and experiences is. We need to draw upon our shared experiences, to find out how others have solved problems that we face. But one consequence of our enforced pragmatism is that we have tended to talk mainly with one another. We have succeeded in creating a niche for ourselves in the larger world of composition studies, but we have not, I fear, convinced others in our field of our centrality. We are part of but not fully integrated into our own discipline.

In *Writing Centers: Theory and Administration*, Gary Olson observed that writing centers ". . . have always been diverse in their pedagogies, philosophies, and physical make-ups. But the writing center's period of chaotic adolescence is nearly over. Center directors are slowly articulating common goals, objectives, and methodologies; and writing centers are beginning to take on a common form to evolve into a recognizable species" (vii). Olson is right: our period of adolescence is nearly over. Part of our passage into professional adulthood, however, involves grounding this "common form" in a fully articulated theory. For by so doing, we will not only clarify and justify the work we do, we will also connect in important ways with others in our field.

I believe that the time is right for those of us who direct or work in writing centers to place our work in a rich theoretical context. And we don't need to start from scratch. We can build not only on theories of collaborative learning, as articulated by Bruffee, Hawkins, and others, but on the work of those who have recently challenged us to view writing as a social, rather than a solitary and individual, process.

In this essay, I would like to comment on several lines of research that either explicitly or implicitly place writing centers at the heart, rather than the periphery, of current theory in composition studies. I also hope to suggest some of the ways that those of us who work in writing centers can contribute to this intellectual dialogue. For we have an important contribution to make. Because of our experiences in writing centers, we know things that composition specialists who work only with graduate students — or even those who teach undergraduate writing classes — can't know. And our centers can provide unique opportunities for research.

Most of us are familiar with the research that stimulated current interest in collaborative learning — Thom Hawkins' *Group Inquiry Techniques for Teaching Writing* and Kenneth Bruffee's articles and textbook. Enough time has passed since this research was published — Bruffee's first article on collaborative learning appeared in 1972, while Hawkins' book was published in 1976 — for us to gain distance from it. As . . . [many readers are aware] recent interest in collaborative learning grew out of a crisis, a rapid increase in student enrollment in the 70s, which drew many underprepared students who previously would not have attended college to our campuses. One response to this crisis was the establishment of writing centers, places where these and other students could get the help they needed. Those who directed these centers were pragmatists. To the degree that they grounded their work in theory — and few had time to do this — they looked primarily to such educational reformers as John Dewey, M. L. J. Abercrombie, Edwin Mason, and Paolo Freire. They emphasized the important role that social interaction played in learning, and they argued that students who participate in collaborative learning experiences learn more effectively — do better on exams, write more effective prose — than their peers.

Although this early research emphasized the importance of the social and cultural contexts of teaching and learning, it still tended to view both writing and thinking — the creation of knowledge — as inherently individual activities. In his early essays, for instance, Bruffee at times praises collaborative learning as a means of helping student writers escape the inevitable solitariness of writing, whose self-imposed isolation is often seen as particularly troubling for beginning writers. Cognitive-developmental research does suggest that basic writers find it difficult to move from the collaboration of conversation to the more independent creation of meaning that writing entails.

Bruffee's and others' claims for collaborative learning have potentially negative implications, however. For if writing is naturally and inevitably solitary, then collaborative learning is in a sense an unnatural and, for most writers, unnecessary interruption. Implicitly, then, such a view of writing suggests that only beginning or second-best writers would need the support and collaboration that in-class peer groups and writing centers provide. *Real writers*, experienced and professional writers, wouldn't need or seek out such concrete dialogue. Recognizing that writers naturally write alone and that, as Walter Ong states in a well-known article in *PMLA*, "The Writer's Audience Is Always a Fiction," they would happily seclude themselves in their study or carrel.

I want to emphasize this point: as long as thinking and writing are regarded as inherently individual, solitary activities, writing centers can never be viewed as anything more than pedagogical fix-it shops to help those who, for whatever reason, are unable to think and write on their own. This understanding of thinking and writing not only places writing centers on the periphery of most colleges, where our second-class status is symbolized by our basement offices and inadequate staffs and budgets, it also places us on the periphery of our own field of composition studies. Think for a moment, for instance, of Flower and Hayes' cognitive-based research — research that has been particularly influential during the past decade. Where in the flow charts depicting task representation, audience analysis, and short-term and long-term memory is the box representing collaboration and conversation? As Marilyn Cooper says in "The Ecology of Writing":

> The ideal writer the cognitive process model projects is isolated from the social world. . . . The solitary author works alone, within the privacy of his own mind. He uses free writing exercises and heuristics to find out what he knows about a subject and to find something he wants to say to others; he uses his analytic skills to discover a purpose, to imagine an audience, to decide on strategies, to organize content; and he simulates how his text will be read by reading it over himself, making the final revisions necessary to assure its success when he abandons it to the world

of which he is not a part. The isolation of the solitary author from the social world leads him to see ideas and goals as originating primarily within himself and directed at an unknown and largely hostile other. *Writing becomes a form of parthenogenesis, the author producing propositional and pragmatic structures, Athena-like, full grown and complete, out of his brow.* (365–66, my emphasis)

The assumption that writing is inherently a solitary cognitive activity is so deeply ingrained in western culture that it has, until recently, largely gone unexamined. Indeed, many people find it difficult to recognize that the term *authorship* refers not to the physical act of inscription, the process of writing texts, but to a concept. One of the best ways I've found to understand the concept of authorship is to take an historical perspective. I think you may be surprised, as I was when I first began this research, by what history tells us.

In the Middle Ages, for instance, authors simply didn't exist: no distinction was made between the person who wrote a text and the person who copied it. In *The Friar as Critic: Literary Attitudes in the Middle Ages*, Judson Boyce Allen attempts to help scholars understand what it meant to be an author or reader in this period. Aware of the difficulty of his task, Allen comments that:

> when we are faced with medieval authors . . . we are faced with a foreign, nonempirical sensibility. We are confronted by authors who are for the most part content to repeat inherited materials, making their own primary contribution . . . in the area of decoration, and often content to remain anonymous: if they name themselves, it is only in the later Middle Ages that they are not primarily doing so in order to solicit prayer. (59)

Or consider the Elizabethan period in England. When we think of this period, of course, we think of Shakespeare — now enthroned as one of the greatest authors in English literature. Surely Shakespeare typifies our contemporary notion of what it means to be an author? The fact is, however, that the conditions of the period precluded any such conception. During the Elizabethan period, for instance, only those playwrights who were also actors, and thus members of the company performing their work, could expect to receive any financial benefit other than a one-time payment. For, with a few exceptions, the actors, members of companies that functioned much like present-day cooperatives, owned the plays the company produced. Most plays, including Shakespeare's early plays, appeared without an author's name on the title page. Furthermore, once a company purchased a play, it felt free to make whatever alterations the actors wished. As Albert Feuillerat notes in *The Composition of Shakespeare's Plays*, "A certain amount of reworking came naturally enough during the rehearsals, but far more important revisions of an author's text were frequent and often went so far as to change the very nature of the play" (7).

I wish that I could discuss the history of the concept of authorship more fully. Even a cursory historical examination indicates, however, that our modern concept of authorship, which might best be characterized as intellectual property rights (property rights that can, by their very nature, only be owned by a single person), is clearly an overdetermined concept. You can trace its development in literary history, from the tentative assertions of the claims of originality in the Renaissance to the Romantic's fully conceived argument for the primacy of the individual imagination. (In *Literary Theory: An Introduction*, Terry Eagleton notes that since the Romantics, literary theory has "assumed that, in the main, at the centre of the world is the contemplative individual self, bowed over its books, striving to gain touch with experience, truth, reality, history, or tradition" [196].) The impact of Cartesianism, which established epistemology as the central branch of philosophy, further supports the assumption that the individual thinking and writing in isolation is the source of all truth worth knowing.

It is also possible to trace the impact of technology on the concept of authorship, as Elizabeth Eisenstein does in *The Printing Press as an Agent of Change*. According to Eisenstein, "both the eponymous [or named] inventor and personal authorship appeared at the same time and as a consequence of the same process," the development of the printing press. "Scribal culture," she argues, "worked against the concept of intellectual property rights. It did not lend itself to preserving traces of personal idiosyncrasies, to the public airing of private thoughts, or to any of the forms of silent publicity that have shaped consciousness of self during the past four centuries" (229–30).

Still others have analyzed the way that copyright laws, which we take for granted but which were a bitter source of controversy in the eighteenth and nineteenth centuries, codified and extended authorship. It is startling indeed to read German intellectuals in the 1840s argue that writers can no more claim their texts as permanent property, theirs for a lifetime, than a cabinetmaker can expect to profit each time a chest that he has made is purchased. Once sold, both are gone forever; they are the property of the purchaser (Woodmansee). The inextricable link between writers and their ideas, one that undergirds our notions of both authorship and plagiarism, simply didn't exist.

I hope that this brief historical excursion doesn't strike you as a digression, a curiosity. Recognizing that authorship is a concept, not a physical activity, and then tracing how that concept developed can help us understand why collaborative learning, and our writing centers, have always been resisted, marginalized. For although we may be unaware of it, our effort to encourage collaboration and dialogue is inherently subversive — not just of our traditional educational institutions (we have always known that), but of one of the most important, because most hidden and commonsensical, assumptions of our culture: that writing and thinking are inherently individual, solitary activities.

This historical excursion also clarifies what has always, for me at least, been a puzzling and frustrating mystery: the fact that those who most resist or misunderstand the kind of collaborative learning that occurs in writing centers are often our own colleagues in departments of English. Their immersion in our Romantic and Post-Romantic literary tradition, as well as their experience as students and teachers, has reinforced their often unconscious allegiance to the image of the solitary writer working silently in a garret. Though they often want — and try — to support us, their acceptance of writing as a solitary act prevents them from fully doing so.

I indicated previously that the time is right for those of us who are committed to collaborative learning and writing centers to locate our work in a rich theoretical context — one that places us at the center of current theory. A number of researchers are endeavoring to articulate a theory of writing that recognizes, as Marilyn Cooper notes, that "language and texts are not simply the means by which individuals discover and communicate information, but are essentially social activities, dependent on social structures and processes not only in their interpretive but also in their constructive phases" (367). These researchers — Marilyn Cooper, Anne Ruggles Gere, Patricia Bizzell, Kenneth Bruffee, Karen LeFevre, James Reither, Linda Brodkey, and others — are attempting to enrich the cognitive approach to writing with what Cooper calls "an ecological model of writing, whose fundamental tenet is that writing is an activity through which a person is continually engaged with a variety of socially constructed systems" (36).

If you aren't familiar with this research, you may be surprised to discover the diverse range of disciplines upon which these writers draw. Kenneth Bruffee's later essays, which attempt to lay the framework for a social constructivist epistemology, cite studies in philosophy, education, sociology, anthropology, psychology, and literary criticism. Such a display of learning may seem pretentious — the unnecessary piling up of sources — but I don't think that's the case. What we're witnessing is a fundamental epistemological shift, one that both draws on and will influence a broad range of disciplines, including our own.

I don't want to mislead you, however. Not all these discussions of writing as a social process are as scholarly as Bruffee's. Some, such as Min-Zhan Lu's recent essay "From Silence to Words: Writing as Struggle," are surprisingly personal. We're not used to reading essays whose authors ground their theoretical observations in personal experience, as Min-Zhan Lu does when she discusses the conflicts she experienced growing up in China during the Cultural Revolution. For despite our adherence to an individualist and subjectivist ideology, as scholars, at least, we have insisted, in Eagleton's words, on "abstracting personal values and qualities from the whole concrete context . . . in which they are embedded" ("The Subject of Literature" 103). We have granted AUTHORity — and I hope that by now you see the "author" in authority — only to those who establish their claims by referring to other texts. A number of those who advocate a social view of writing resist such restrictions, choosing instead to place themselves in a particular, contextualized scene of writing and reading (as I have tried to do in this essay).

We've got a lot at stake, I've been arguing, in the research on writing as a social process that I've been describing here, for such research implicitly argues for the centrality of what we do in our writing centers. We've also, I believe just as strongly, got a lot to contribute. A recent critique of Bruffee's work

by Greg Myers, for instance, charges Bruffee and other advocates of collaborative learning with naively refusing to recognize the role that ideology (which
Myers defines as "the thoughts that structure our thinking so deeply that we
take them for granted" [156]) plays in collaborative learning. Bruffee and others talk, Myers charges, as though the social construction of reality is inevitably positive and beneficial to our students, presenting an idealized view of
writing that has little resemblance to actual group dynamics.

I think that Greg Myers is at least partly right, and that those of us who
work in writing centers are just the right folks to help keep theoreticians like
Bruffee honest. We can do case studies, or even more detailed ethnographic
analyses, for instance, of what actually happens when two or more peers collaborate. And we can learn something about the role that power and ideology
play in our writing classrooms by comparing our experiences as teachers and
as participants in the culture of writing centers. Last year, for instance, I kept
a reading journal during a quarter when I taught a section of my university's
freshman composition class and read the journals and essays written by students working as writing assistants in our lab. I was shocked to discover that
my experience of reading my freshmen's essays and writing assistants' journals differed so fundamentally that I could hardly call both experiences reading. I am still considering the implications of this recognition for my teaching
and for my work with students in the Writing Lab.

These examples suggest, I hope, that it is hardly necessary to master the
philosophical tradition before one can contribute to the ongoing conversation
about writing as a social process — though an understanding of the degree to
which this movement constitutes a genuine epistemological revolution is certainly helpful. *Those of us who work in writing centers need* to *be part of this conversation.* This means that many of us will first have to fight for the time we
need to do such thinking and writing. We will have to convince our deans or
vice-presidents that our job requires us to do more than hire and train tutors,
balance budgets, and promote our centers. We will, in other words, have to
argue for a revised definition of our positions. But then, precisely because of
our work in writing centers, we have known for quite some time that, as Min-
Zhan Lu notes, writing is struggle.

I'd like to close this essay with a quotation from Mikhail Bakhtin that I
think applies both to us and to our students. Language, Bakhtin says, "lies on
the borderline between oneself and the other. The word in language is half
someone else's. It becomes 'one's own' only when the speaker populates it
with his own intentions, his own accent, when he appropriates the word,
adapting it to his own semantic and expressive intention. Prior to this moment of appropriation, the word does not exist in a neutral and personal language . . . but rather it exists in other people's mouths, in other people's
contexts, serving other people's intentions: it is from there that one must take
the word, and make it one's own" (293–94). It is time for us to take the word
and make a real place for ourselves in the world of composition studies, and
of the academy.

WORKS CITED

Abercrombie, M. L. J. *Aims and Techniques for Group Teaching.* Guildford: U of Guildford P, 1970.

Allen, Judson Boyce. *The Friar as Critic: Literary Attitudes in the Middle Ages.* Nashville: Vanderbilt UP, 1971.

Bakhtin, Mikhail. "Discourse in the Novel." Ed. Michael Holquist. Trans. Caryl Emerson and Michael Holquist. Austin: U Texas P, 1981.

Bizzell, Patricia. "Foundationalism and Anti-Foundationalism in Composition Studies." *Pre/Text* 7 (1986): 37–56.

Brodkey, Linda. *Academic Writing as Social Practice.* Philadelphia: Temple UP, 1987.

———. "Modernism and the Scene(s) of Writing." *College English* 49 (1987): 396–418.

Bruffee, Kenneth. "The Brooklyn Plan: Attaining Intellectual Growth through Peer-Group Tutoring." *Liberal Education* 64 (1978): 447–68.

———. "Collaborative Learning and the 'Conversation of Mankind.'" *College English* 46 (1984): 635–52.

———. "Collaborative Learning: Some Practical Models." *College English* 34 (1973): 579–86.

———. *A Short Course in Writing.* 2d ed. Cambridge, MA: Winthrop, 1980.

———. "Social Construction, Language, and the Authority of Knowledge: A Bibliographic Essay." *College English* 48 (1986): 773–90.

———. "The Structure of Knowledge and the Future of Liberal Education." *Liberal Education* 67 (1981): 177–86.

———. "The Way Out." *College English* 33 (1972): 457–70.

Cooper, Marilyn. "The Ecology of Writing." *College English* 48 (1986): 364–75.

Dewey, John. *Experience and Education.* 1938. New York: Collier, 1963.

———. *The Public and Its Problems.* Denver: Alan Swallow, 1927.

Eagleton, Terry. *Literary Theory: An Introduction.* Minneapolis: U of Minnesota P, 1983.

———. "The Subject of Literature." *Cultural Critique* 2 (1985–86): 95–104.

Eisenstein, Elizabeth. *The Printing Press as an Agent of Change.* Cambridge: Cambridge UP, 1979.

Feuillerat, Albert. *The Composition of Shakespeare's Plays.* New Haven: Yale UP, 1953.

Flower, Linda, and John R. Hayes. "A Cognitive Process Theory of Writing." *College Composition and Communication* 32.4 (1981): 365–87.

Freire, Paolo. *Pedagogy of the Oppressed.* New York: Leabury, 1968.

Gere, Anne Ruggles. *Writing Groups: History, Theory, and Implications.* Carbondale, IL: SIUP, 1987.

Hawkins, Thom. *Group Inquiry Techniques for Teaching Writing.* Urbana, IL: NCTE, 1976.

LeFevre, Karen. *Invention as a Social Act.* Carbondale: Southern Illinois UP, 1986.

Lu, Min-Zhan. "From Silence to Words: Writing as Struggle." *College English* 49 (1987): 1–8.

Mason, Edwin. *Collaborative Learning.* London: WardLock Educational, 1970.

Myers, Greg. "Reality, Consensus, and Reform in the Rhetoric of Composition Teaching." *College English* 48 (1986): 154–74.

Olson, Gary. *Writing Centers: Theory and Administration.* Urbana, IL: NCTE, 1984.

Ong, Walter J. "The Writer's Audience Is Always a Fiction." *PMLA* 90 (1975): 9–21.

Reither, James A. "Writing and Knowing: Toward Redefining the Writing Process." *College English* 47 (1985): 620–28.

Woodmansee, Martha. "The Genius and the Copyright: Economic and Legal Conditions of the Emergence of the 'Author.'" *Eighteenth-Century Studies* 17 (1984): 425–48.

22 Collaboration, Control, and the Idea of a Writing Center*

The triple focus of my title reflects some problems I've been concentrating on as I thought about and prepared for the opportunity to speak at the Midwest Writing Centers Association meeting in St. Cloud, and here at the Pacific Coast/Inland Northwest Writing Centers meeting in Le Grande. I'll try as I go along to illuminate — or at least to complicate — each of these foci, and I'll conclude by sketching in what I see as a particularly compelling idea of a writing center, one informed by collaboration and, I hope, attuned to diversity.

As some of you may know, I've recently written a book on collaboration, *in* collaboration with my dearest friend and co-author, Lisa Ede. *Singular Texts/ Plural Authors: Perspectives on Collaborative Writing* was six years in the research and writing, so I would naturally gravitate to principles of collaboration in this or any other address.

Yet it's interesting to me to note that when Lisa and I began our research (see "Why Write . . . Together?" p. 27 in this collection), we didn't even use the term "collaboration"; we identified our subjects as "co- and group-writing." And when we presented our first paper on the subject at the 1985 CCCC meeting, ours was the only such paper at the conference, ours the only presentation with "collaboration" in the title. Now, as you know, the word is everywhere, in every journal, every conference program, on the tip of every scholarly tongue. So — collaboration, yes. But why control? Because as the latest pedagogical bandwagon, collaboration often masquerades as democracy when it in fact practices the same old authoritarian control. It thus stands open to abuse and can, in fact, lead to poor teaching and poor learning. And it can lead — as many of you know — to disastrous results in the writing center. So amidst the rush to embrace collaboration, I see a need for careful interrogation and some caution.

We might begin by asking where the collaboration bandwagon got rolling. Why has it gathered such steam? Because, I believe, collaboration both in

From Andrea Lunsford, in *The Writing Center Journal* 12.1 (1991): 3–10.
*Andrea A. Lunsford wrote this piece as a single author.

theory and practice reflects a broad-based epistemological shift, a shift in the way we view knowledge. The shift involves a move from viewing knowledge and reality as things exterior to or outside of us, as immediately accessible, individually knowable, measurable, and shareable — to viewing knowledge and reality as mediated by or constructed through language in social use, as socially constructed, contextualized, as, in short, the product of *collaboration.*

I'd like to suggest that collaboration as an embodiment of this theory of knowledge poses a distinct threat to one particular idea of a writing center. This idea of a writing center, what I'll call "The Center as Storehouse," holds to the earlier view of knowledge just described — knowledge as exterior to us and as directly accessible. The Center as Storehouse operates as information stations or storehouses, prescribing and handing out skills and strategies to individual learners. They often use "modules" or other kinds of individualized learning materials. They tend to view knowledge as individually derived and held, and they are not particularly amenable to collaboration, sometimes actively hostile to it. I visit lots of Storehouse Centers, and in fact I set up such a center myself, shortly after I had finished an M.A. degree and a thesis on William Faulkner.

Since Storehouse Centers do a lot of good work and since I worked very hard to set up one of them, I was loathe to complicate or critique such a center. Even after Lisa and I started studying collaboration in earnest, and in spite of the avalanche of data we gathered in support of the premise that collaboration is the norm in most professions (American Consulting Engineers Council, American Institute of Chemists, American Psychological Institute, Modern Language Association, Professional Services Management Association, International City Management Association, Society for Technical Communication), I was still a very reluctant convert.

Why? Because, I believe, collaboration posed another threat to my way of teaching, a way that informs another idea of a writing center, which I'll call "The Center as Garret." Garret Centers are informed by a deep-seated belief in individual "genius," in the Romantic sense of the term. (I need hardly point out that this belief also informs much of the humanities and, in particular, English studies.) These Centers are also informed by a deep-seated attachment to the American brand of individualism, a term coined by Alexis de Toqueville as he sought to describe the defining characteristics of this Republic.

Unlike Storehouse Centers, Garret Centers don't view knowledge as exterior, as information to be sought out or passed on mechanically. Rather they see knowledge as interior, as inside the student, and the writing center's job as helping students get in touch with this knowledge, as a way to find their unique voices, their individual and unique powers. This idea has been articulated by many, including Ken Macrorie, Peter Elbow, and Don Murray, and the idea usually gets acted out in Murray-like conferences, those in which the tutor or teacher listens, voices encouragement, and essentially serves as a validation of the students' "I-search." Obviously, collaboration problematizes Garret Centers as well, for they also view knowledge as interiorized, solitary, individually derived, individually held.

As I've indicated, I held on pretty fiercely to this idea as well as to the first one. I was still resistant to collaboration. So I took the natural path for an academic faced with this dilemma: I decided to do more research. I did *a lot* of it. And, to my chagrin, I found more and more evidence to challenge my ideas, to challenge both the idea of Centers as Storehouses or as Garrets. Not incidentally, the data I amassed mirrored what my students had been telling me for years: not the research they carried out, not their dogged writing of essays, not *me* even, but their work in groups, their *collaboration*, was the most important and helpful part of their school experience. Briefly, the data I found all support the following claims:

1. Collaboration aids in problem finding as well as problem solving.

2. Collaboration aids in learning abstractions.

3. Collaboration aids in transfer and assimilation; it fosters interdisciplinary thinking.

4. Collaboration leads not only to sharper, more critical thinking (students must explain, defend, adapt), but to deeper understanding of *others*.

5. Collaboration leads to higher achievement in general. I might mention here the Johnson and Johnson analysis of 122 studies from 1924 to 1981, which included every North American study that considered achievement or performance data in competitive, cooperative/collaborative, or individualistic classrooms. Some 60% showed that collaboration promoted higher achievement, while only 6% showed the reverse. Among studies comparing the effects of collaboration and independent work, the results are even more strongly in favor of collaboration.

   Moreover, the superiority of collaboration held for all subject areas and all age groups. See Alfie Kohn, "How to Succeed Without Even Vying," *Psychology Today*, September 1986.

6. Collaboration promotes excellence. In this regard, I am fond of quoting Hannah Arendt: "For Excellence, the presence of others is always required" (49).

7. Collaboration engages the whole student and encourages active learning; it combines reading, talking, writing, thinking; it provides practice in both synthetic and analytic skills.

Given these research findings, why am I still urging caution in using collaboration as our key term, in using collaboration as the idea of the kind of writing center I now advocate?

First, because creating a collaborative environment and truly collaborative tasks is damnably difficult. Collaborative environments and tasks must *demand* collaboration. Students, tutors, teachers must really need one another to carry out common goals. As an aside, let me note that studies of collaboration in the workplace identify three kinds of tasks that seem to call consistently for collaboration: high-order problem defining and solving; division of labor tasks, in which the job is simply too big for any one person; and division of expertise tasks. Such tasks are often difficult to come by in writing centers, particularly those based on the Storehouse or Garret models.

A collaborative environment must also be one in which goals are clearly defined and in which the jobs at hand engage everyone fairly equally, from the student clients to work-study students to peer tutors and professional staff. In other words, such an environment rejects traditional hierarchies. In addition, the kind of collaborative environment I want to encourage calls for careful and ongoing monitoring and evaluating of the collaboration or group process, again on the part of all involved. In practice, such monitoring calls on each person involved in the collaboration to build a *theory* of collaboration, a theory of group dynamics.

Building such a collaborative environment is also hard because getting groups of any kind going is hard. The students,' tutors,' and teachers' prior experiences may work against it (they probably held or still hold to Storehouse or Garret ideas); the school day and term work against it; and the drop-in nature of many centers, including my own, works against it. Against these odds, we have to figure out how to constitute groups in our centers; how to allow for evaluation and monitoring; how to teach, model, and learn about careful listening, leadership, goal setting, and negotiation — all of which are necessary to effective collaboration.

We must also recognize that collaboration is hardly a monolith. Instead, it comes in a dizzying variety of modes about which we know almost nothing. In our book, Lisa and I identify and describe two such modes, the hierarchical and the dialogic, both of which our centers need to be well versed at using. But it stands to reason that these two modes perch only at the tip of the collaborative iceberg.

As I argued earlier, I think we must be cautious in rushing to embrace collaboration because collaboration can also be used to reproduce the status quo; the rigid hierarchy of teacher-centered classrooms is replicated in the tutor-centered writing center in which the tutor is still the seat of all authority but is simply pretending it isn't so. Such a pretense of democracy sends badly mixed messages. It can also lead to the kind of homogeneity that squelches diversity, that waters down ideas to the lowest common denominator, that erases rather than values difference. This tendency is particularly troubling given our growing awareness of the roles gender and ethnicity play in all learning. So regression toward the mean is not a goal I seek in an idea of a writing center based on collaboration.

The issue of control surfaces most powerfully in this concern over a collaborative center. In the writing center ideas I put forward earlier, where is that focus of control? In Storehouse Centers, it seems to me control resides in the tutor or center staff, the possessors of information, the currency of the academy. Garret Centers, on the other hand, seem to invest power and control in the individual student knower, though I would argue that such control is often appropriated by the tutor/teacher, as I have often seen happen during Murray or Elbow style conferences. Any center based on collaboration will need to address the issue of control explicitly, and doing so will not be easy.

It won't be easy because what I think of as successful collaboration (which I'll call Burkean Parlor Centers), collaboration that is attuned to diversity, goes deeply against the grain of education in America. To illustrate, I need offer only a few representative examples:

1. Mina Shaughnessy, welcoming a supervisor to her classroom in which students were busily collaborating, was told, "Oh . . . I'll come back when you're teaching."

2. A prominent and very distinguished feminist scholar has been refused an endowed chair because most of her work had been written collaboratively.

3. A prestigious college poetry prize was withdrawn after the winning poem turned out to be written by three student collaborators.

4. A faculty member working in a writing center was threatened with dismissal for "encouraging" group-produced documents.

I have a number of such examples, all of which suggest that — used unreflectively or *un*cautiously — collaboration may harm professionally those who seek to use it and may as a result further reify a model of education as the top-down transfer of information (back to The Storehouse) or a private search for Truth (back to The Garret). As I also hope I've suggested, collaboration can easily degenerate into busy work, or what Jim Corder calls "fading into the tribe."

So I am very, very serious about the cautions I've been raising, about our need to examine carefully what we mean by collaboration and to explore how those definitions locate control. And yet I still advocate — with growing and deepening conviction — the move to collaboration in both classrooms and centers. In short, I am advocating a third, alternative idea of a writing center, one I know many of you have already brought into being. In spite of the very real risks involved, we need to embrace the idea of writing centers as Burkean Parlors, as centers for collaboration. Only in doing so can we, I believe, enable a student body and citizenry to meet the demands of the twenty-first century. A recent Labor Department report tells us, for instance, that by the mid-1990s workers will need to read at the 11th grade level for even low-paying jobs; that workers will need to be able not so much to solve prepackaged problems but to identify problems amidst a welter of information or data; that they will need to reason from complex symbol systems rather than from simple observation; most of all that they will need to be able to work with others who are different from them and to learn to negotiate power and control (Heath).

The idea of a center I want to advocate speaks directly to these needs, for its theory of knowledge is based not on positivistic principles (that's The Storehouse again), not on Platonic or absolutist ideas (that's The Garret), but on the notion of knowledge as always contextually bound, as always socially constructed. Such a center might well have as its motto Arendt's statement: "For Excellence, the presence of others is always required." Such a center would place control, power, and authority not in the tutor or staff, not in the individual student, but in the negotiating group. It would engage students not only in solving problems set by teachers but in identifying problems for themselves; not only in working as a group but in monitoring, evaluating, and building a theory of how groups work; not only in understanding and valuing collaboration but in confronting squarely the issues of control that successful collaboration inevitably raises; not only in reaching consensus but in valuing dissensus and diversity.

The idea of a center informed by a theory of knowledge as socially constructed, of power and control as constantly negotiated and shared, and of collaboration as its first principle presents quite a challenge. It challenges our ways of organizing our centers, of training our staff and tutors, of working with teachers. It even challenges our sense of where we "fit" in this idea. More importantly, however, such a center presents a challenge to the institution of higher education, an institution that insists on rigidly controlled individual performance, on evaluation as punishment, on isolation, on the kinds of values that took that poetry prize away from three young people or that accused Mina Shaughnessy of "not teaching."

This alternative, this third idea of a writing center, poses a threat as well as a challenge to the status quo in higher education. This threat is one powerful and largely invisible reason, I would argue, for the way in which many writing centers have been consistently marginalized, consistently silenced. But organizations like this one are gaining a voice, are finding ways to imagine into being centers as Burkean Parlors for collaboration, writing centers, I believe, which can lead the way in changing the face of higher education.

So, as if you didn't already know it, you're a subversive group, and I'm delighted to have been invited to participate in this collaboration. But I've been talking far too long by myself now, so I'd like to close by giving the floor to two of my student collaborators. The first — like I was — was a reluctant convert to the kind of collaboration I've been describing tonight. But here's what she wrote to me some time ago:

> Dr. Lunsford: I don't know exactly what to say here, but I want to say something. So here goes. When this Writing Center class first began, I didn't know what in the hell you meant by collaboration. I thought — hey! yo! — you're the teacher and you know a lot of stuff. And you better tell it to me. Then I can tell it to the other guys. Now I know that you know even more than I thought. I even found out I know a lot. But that's not important. What is important is knowing that knowing doesn't just happen all by itself, like the cartoons show with a little light bulb going off in a bubble over a character's head. Knowing happens with other people, figuring things out, trying to explain, talking through things. What I know is that we are all making and remaking our knowing and ourselves with each other every day — you just as much as me and the other guys, Dr. Lunsford. We're all — all of us together — collaborative recreations in process. So — well — just wish me luck.

And here's a note I received just as I got on the plane, from another student/ collaborator:

> I had believed that Ohio State had nothing more to offer me in the way of improving my writing. Happily, I was mistaken. I have great expectations

for our Writing Center Seminar class. I look forward to every one of our classes and to every session with my 110W students [two groups of three undergraduates he is tutoring]. I sometimes feel that they have more to offer me than I to them. They say the same thing, though, so I guess we're about even, all learning together. (P.S. This class and the Center have made me certain I want to attend graduate school.)

These students embody the kind of center I'm advocating, and I'm honored to join them in conversation about it, conversation we can continue together now.

WORKS CITED

Arendt, Hannah. *The Human Condition.* Chicago: U of Chicago P. 1998.

Corder, Jim W. "Hunting for Ethos Where They Say It Can't Be Found." *Rhetoric Review* 7 (Spring 1989): 299–316.

Ede, Lisa S., and Andrea A. Lunsford. *Singular Texts/Plural Authors: Perspectives on Collaborative Writing.* Carbondale, IL: Southern Illinois UP, 1990.

———. "Why Write . . . Together?" *Rhetoric Review* 1 (Jan. 1983): 150–58.

Heath, Shirley Brice. "The Fourth Vision: Literate Language at Work." *The Right to Literacy.* Ed. Andrea A. Lunsford, Helen Moglen, and James Slevin. New York: Modern Language Association, 1990. 288–306.

Johnson, D. W., and R. T. Johnson. *Cooperation and Competition: Theory and Research.* Edina, MN: Interactive Book Company. 1999.

Kohn, Alfie. "How to Succeed without Even Vying." *Psychology Today* (Sept. 1986): 22–28.

23

Some Millennial Thoughts about the Future of Writing Centers

When most writing centers in the United States were being founded and developed, colleges and universities had very few entities they labeled "centers." Today, however, centers are cropping up with increasing regularity. At our own institutions, we have (between us) Centers for Humanities, Centers for Advanced Materials Research, Centers for Cognitive Studies, Centers for the Study of First Americans — even a Center for Epigraphy. It seems worth pausing to consider this phenomenon: Where are all these centers coming from, and why are they proliferating so rapidly?

One strong possibility: Centers create spaces for the kind of work that needs to be done in higher education, work that is difficult or impossible to do within traditional disciplinary frameworks. In almost every case, for example, the previously mentioned centers allow for inter- or cross-disciplinary research and scholarship, and at their best they encourage highly productive forms of collaboration. Furthermore, they often initiate projects designed to bring college and community closer together. In short, these new centers seem to us one of the major signs of stress on old ways of taxonomizing and creating knowledge. Their growing popularity signals, we think, one institutional response to changing educational demands, populations, budgets, and technologies.

We are well aware that these are difficult times at most community colleges, colleges, and universities, and that faculty and staff in many writing centers must spend an inordinate amount of time struggling to provide basic services. Nevertheless we wish to emphasize those opportunities that we believe are available to writing centers, even those that are in various ways marginalized on their campuses. The opportunities that we will discuss involve four potentials that we see for institutional refiguration: the refiguration of institutional space, of concepts of knowledge production and intellectual property, of research paradigms and rewards, and of budget allocations.

Institutional space on traditional campuses is defined by the classroom, which in turn is carefully circumscribed and regulated. Distance education

---

From Lisa Ede and Andrea Lunsford, in *The Writing Center Journal* 20.2 (2000): 32–37.

has presented strong challenges to the sacrosanct space of the campus class-room, of course, but most often the institutional "space" available online is equally, if differently, circumscribed. In fact, students are already complaining about the lack of access to teachers in distance education courses, about the rote nature of some online work, and about their sense of isolation. Writing centers offer a clear and compelling alternative use of space, one that in many instances combines the best of face-to-face and virtual education.[1] In our centers as in many others, for example, the physical space allows for one-on-one consultations, for small group work, for individual work in quiet reading or writing comers, as well as for online access either within the physical center or from a distance. This new mix of space and use seems to us a very important but often taken-for-granted contribution writing centers make to refiguring higher education.

Perhaps even more important, writing centers make the borders of the university more permeable than they have traditionally been. That is, writing center work often moves not only across but well beyond our campuses — to outreach efforts with schools, community organizations, business, industry, and government. We believe that this feature of writing centers will be especially important as universities seek to re-imagine themselves in ways that better serve the public good. In this regard, writing centers are more like what Shirley Brice Heath calls "organizations for learning" than disciplinary-based departments. For they can, as Heath observes, respond quickly when the demands of a swiftly changing society outstrip the university's ability to respond creatively and efficiently.[2]

In traditional institutions of higher education, knowledge and intellectual property are the products of individual research and scholarship, dispensed through classroom teaching and stored in archives. In recent years, electronic forms of communication — with their ability to disseminate and duplicate material instantly — have put an enormous strain on these concepts of knowledge production and ownership. Even as we write these brief reflections, the struggle over how to regulate the production and dissemination of knowledge grows ever more intense. While writing centers can hardly resolve these struggles, they do hold out an alternative view of how knowledge can be produced and possessed. The relationship among writing tutors, academic staff, and students, for instance, is intensely collaborative. In addition, the knowledge created within writing centers is most often communal knowledge, and materials developed there are generally intended for public use.[3] In many ways, the writing center's value is figured in the way it generates and organizes knowledge (collaboratively) and circulates it (widely and freely), rather than in the creators of the knowledge or its textual representation. It is not surprising to us that writing centers have been particularly eager to take advantage of the opportunities for sharing resources via the World Wide Web.

Given the points we've just made, it seems clear that writing centers offer new and provocative ways of thinking about research paradigms and rewards. Rather than a model based on highly competitive individual research, writing centers foster team-based and collaborative research. Moreover, such research aims less toward individual advancement and more toward pro-grammatic and institutional improvement and, as a result, collapses the bi-nary between theory and practice in particularly interesting ways. In such research, theory and practice exist in a reciprocal and dialogic relationship. Finally, in writing center work, the extrinsic reward structures of the univer-sity — represented by grades and class standing for students and promotion criteria tied almost completely to individual "original" research for faculty — are replaced by intrinsic rewards measured in improved performance and sat-isfaction for students and faculty alike.

This is the moment, no doubt, to acknowledge the fact that there are downsides, as well as benefits, to resistant forms of research paradigms and rewards. Despite the increasing presence of various kinds of centers on our campuses, those involved with such efforts still must work within an institu-tional environment that values individual, rather than collaborative, efforts. Those who direct writing centers know how easily what they experience as important scholarly and pedagogical work can be valued (or more accurately devalued) as mere academic service. Many leaders in the writing center move-ment — we think here, for instance, of Lou Kelly, Muriel Harris, and Jeanne Simpson — have had to work in an almost superhuman fashion both at their local institutions and nationally to further the project of writing centers. That they have had the stamina and dedication to think and work globally as well as locally is something for which all who work for and believe in writing cen-ters must remain grateful.

And what could better link us to our next topic — the challenges that writing centers offer to traditional budgeting systems — than the notion of the superhuman. For it goes without saying that, even at institutions with a good deal of cultural capital and financial resources, writing centers have often had to struggle to establish and maintain themselves. And yet we see a potential advantage in what is from another perspective an acute disadvan-tage. For like it or not, institutions of postsecondary education are changing. Budgeting systems have traditionally been based on a model measured in terms of what we might, for lack of a better term, call disciplinary capital. This system tends to assume that some academic units merit appropriate and stable funding, while others do not. In the brave new world of academic en-trepreneurship, such assumptions no longer hold. Increasingly, all academic units are required to justify their worth and funding, and to do so not just once but continuously. Writing centers are (for better or worse) well posi-tioned for such budgeting practices and priorities. For writing centers have most often not relied upon traditional means of budgeting and have instead adopted a mixed — and decidedly entrepreneurial — approach. We know of centers that are funded through general funds allocations, private endow-ments, student fees (much like those added on for computer technology), pay-as-you-go fee structures for tutorials, "taxes" on traditional disciplines, and some form of course credit. In short, the kind of imaginative scrambling writing centers have done to build and maintain budgets may turn out, in this changing scene of higher education, to provide examples that other parts of the university can learn from.

Those whose experience of writing center work and life has been one of constant struggle for the most basic resources might well at this point exclaim, "I hope not!" So we hasten to add that we realize the potential we have sketched out here for writing centers to serve as models for institutional change and improvement is in many ways generalized and idealized. Given the limitations of space, we've necessarily been short on concrete details and examples. But we hope we've provided enough information to suggest some of the ways in which writing centers could serve as catalysts for educational reform, while also strengthening their own institutional positions.

What will it take for such a goal to be realized? The following suggestions are hardly as inclusive or specific as we might like, but they do, we hope, point in a useful direction:

- Take all the advantage that you can of your Center's multi-bordered, multi-positioned status at your institution. Be a bricoleur, trickster, inventor. Work with disciplinary and institutional capital when you can. (Lisa's Center, for instance, has recently instituted a student-fee-supported Craft of Writing lecture series that sponsors the presentations of local, regional, and national writers; novelist James Welch — co-sponsored with the English department — was the first lecturer in this series.) But work against these forces as well. Alliances with community projects or with public schools — alliances that do not necessarily command broad disciplinary or institutional attention — can nevertheless have important intrinsic and extrinsic consequences. So look for new opportunities to position and define your Center.

- Take advantage as well of broad disciplinary and institutional changes. Each time an individual writing lab or clinic redefined itself as a writing center the local impact was undoubtedly limited. (Some faculty and students perhaps never even noticed the change.) But the global impact — the long-term impact and the ability of writing center directors to argue for enabling visions of their centers — was substantial.

- When thinking about your Writing Center, think both locally and globally. The politics of location is essential in writing center work. You have to understand not only the nature and mission of your university but also the exigencies that constrain you and the opportunities that (if you can only see them) also exist. But if your vision is too local, you risk not recognizing alternative ways of re-conceiving or repositioning your Center.

- Be prepared to take significant risks. Sometimes it's necessary to say "fund us or close us."

- Finally, look to other centers, both literal and metaphorical. Does your campus have a center for excellence in teaching? A distance education program? Like your Writing Center, these units are outriders in the conventional academic hierarchies. How can you work with them to effect institutional change and to better the situation of your programs?

Working on this essay, thinking and talking about our own experiences with writing centers, we have been reminded again and again of how quickly centers and margins can shape-shift. We have each had our moments of deep despair, when we have felt that institutional arrangements would always leave our writing centers at the margins. But we have also had moments of exhilaration — moments when we felt that we had the privilege of being at the very center of a new way of thinking about writing, teaching, and learning. Center? Margin? Perhaps the new millennium will make it harder to tell the difference.

NOTES

1. In addition to the classroom, departmental and college-level offices also play an important role in defining — and claiming — institutional space. Though a mix of undergraduate students taking general education courses in a certain department may at times visit its office, in general, the circulation of students in departments is much more restricted. In this regard, writing centers again provide a more open, equitable, and flexible use of instructional space. Indeed, in many institutions, writing centers are both explicitly and implicitly defined as spaces where commitments to students and to student learning are made visible.

2. Heath argues that recent increases in the number of youth groups, groups that are completely separated from formal education but serve important educational functions, represent a similar response. Her film, *Art Show*, examines some of these organizations and provides a powerful argument for institutional change.

3. Of course, many writing center staff worry about whether they are doing too much for and with student writers — doing their work for them. But to what extent does this stance result from a desire to avoid the criticisms of those most committed to hyper-individualism and hence suspicious of any kind of collaborative work? What if (for instance) we took seriously educational research by Vygotsky and others that argues that novices learn particularly well by working with those who are within (but slightly advanced in) their "zone of proximal development"? When we think back to the process of writing our dissertations, for instance, we realize that if our Ph.D. advisors had taken the same "hands off" stance that many tutors take, we might never have graduated.

24   *Collaboration, Community, and Compromise: Writing Centers in Theory and Practice*

When we consider our writing center work in the broader context of our scholarly and pedagogical projects, we see that our commitment to writing centers in many ways fits hand in glove with our abiding scholarly interests in collaboration, in audience, and in the relationship between feminism and rhetoric. After all, as we note below, such centers serve as sites of collaboration that challenge hierarchies and traditional ways of producing knowledge, bringing student writers and peer tutors into conversations that can and often do change both them and their writing. They are also sites that allow writers and audiences to shift and merge roles and for the audience for a piece of writing to be a peer collaborator rather than an expert standing in judgment. Because they challenge institutional hierarchies and traditional ways of knowing and of producing knowledge, and because they work to enhance student agency, writing centers are also powerful sites in which to embody and explore both feminist and rhetorical theory and practice. We have come to think, then, of the writing center as an embodied space in which the differing strands of our work are woven into one. The subtitle of this essay thus echoes the subtitle of the volume as a whole. Here in the concluding essay, we draw these threads together once more in what we hope is a useful example of the interanimation of theory and practice.

While we remain committed to the ideals articulated in this opening paragraph, however, we are acutely aware that each sentence in it would profit from adding the word "potentially" to it. As embodied spaces, writing centers are deeply situated, and in multiple ways. In her 1999 *Good Intentions: Writing Center Work for Postmodern Times*, for instance, Nancy Grimm emphasizes that those committed to writing center work must "be more fully engaged with the paradox of literacy — the way that literacy both dominates and liberates, both demands submission and offers the promise of agency" (xiii). Grimm's analysis, which is echoed and elaborated on in Anne Geller, Michele Eodice, Frankie Condon, Meg Carroll, and Elizabeth Boquet's 2007 *The Everyday Writing Center: A Community of Practice*, calls attention to the need for writing center faculty and staff to challenge the comfortable view of writing centers as safe houses and instead to recognize the extent to which

This essay, written by Andrea A. Lunsford and Lisa Ede, is new to this edition.

they cannot escape larger cultural, ideological, and institutional constraints and contradictions.

Thus while writing centers hold the potential to challenge hierarchies and traditional ways of producing knowledge, they do not necessarily and inevitably do so, a point that is powerfully depicted in the "Writing Center Learning Audit" that appears in *The Everyday Writing Center*. Here the authors contrast a "pro-learning" writing center culture with an "anti-learning culture," and do so by examining a number of specific and concrete writing center practices, such as deciding whether or not to build time for reflection and inquiry into tutors' schedules (52). Reviewing this audit, we are reminded that there are many writing centers that — often for reasons beyond their control involving budgets, staffing, and other factors — finally serve institutional mandates that support traditional notions of literacy and schooling rather than expand on them. We are also reminded that if collaboration and community represent powerful writing center ideals — and often realities — they are also accompanied by conflict and compromise that are grounded in ideological, cultural, economic, and disciplinary/professional assumptions and practices. Thus it is particularly important to engage in self-critique and to be wary of totalizing narratives that turn aside from the tensions and contradictions that inevitably come with any educational enterprise.

We came dangerously close to embracing just such a narrative in an earlier draft of this essay, where we reflected in glowing terms on our own experiences with writing centers. Here are the paragraphs that originally described these experiences:

> Our own connections with writing centers are both deep and wide. Lisa directed the Center for Writing and Learning (CWL) at Oregon State University for thirty years. While over the years the CWL included additional programs — from study skills to a conversant and, most recently, supplemental instruction program — the Writing Center was always its most developed and most important program. Andrea was the founding director of Ohio State's Center for the Study and Teaching of Writing, which included the Writing Center; for the last ten years she has directed Stanford's Program in Writing and Rhetoric (PWR), in which role she had the opportunity to develop Stanford's Hume Writing Center. Andrea often remarks that her collaboration over the years with Marvin Diogenes, John Tinker, Wendy Goldberg, and Clyde Moneyhun in Stanford's Writing Center has been the most fun and rewarding administrative opportunity of her entire career. Lisa agrees that while she had held multiple positions as a writing program administrator, writing center work has been the most fulfilling — particularly in the opportunities that it has allowed for work with undergraduate writing assistants from across the disciplines.
>
> In addition to our work in our university writing centers, we have also valued our interactions with other writing center faculty and staff. Lisa particularly treasures the three years that she was involved with the International Writing Center Association's Summer Institute, where she got to know and learn from both leaders and participants. Andrea's

travels frequently take her to writing centers not only in the United States but increasingly abroad, where she is able to learn about varying models of training, interaction with faculty, curriculum, budgets, etc. Over the years, we've talked about how generative and sustaining these wide and deep connections have been and continue to be for both of us.

These words still ring true to us as generalized summaries of our decades-long involvement with writing centers, both locally and nationally: we have deeply valued and learned from these experiences. Our writing centers have also been a powerful and sustaining source of community for us. But on reflection we can also acknowledge what is missing from this picture. Absent, for instance, are Lisa's struggles in her early years of directing the Center for Writing and Learning (CWL), when most of her energy went into negotiating a minimally adequate budget for the Center and to warding off threats of closure. As Lisa notes in "Writing as a Social Process: A Theoretical Foundation for Writing Centers?" it was only when she managed to secure "a still inadequate but permanent budget" that she and her staff "had the luxury of focusing on other issues" than the Center's immediate survival (p. 350 in this collection). In reflecting on her thirty years with the CWL, Lisa realizes that funding and the potential or actuality of budget cuts were an ongoing concern throughout that entire period, which could perhaps most accurately be described as a continuing cycle of budgetary and/or institutional crises. There was an ongoing need, as well, to address misperceptions on the part of many faculty members and administrators that the writing center's function was essentially remedial.

When Andrea began teaching at a Florida community college in the late 1960s, what served as the writing center represented what she refers to in "Collaboration, Control, and the Idea of a Writing Center" (p. 358) as an example of the "Storehouse" model, one in which knowledge is prepackaged and handed out to students. And when she arrived at Ohio State a couple of decades later, the "writing center" was little more than a closet full of mimeographed handouts. As she will explain later in this essay, Stanford's Hume Writing Center has not been exempt from current budget crises and cuts. Furthermore, as we have gotten to know writing center faculty and visited writing centers throughout the United States, we have been forced to recognize how significantly writing center practices can and do vary, sometimes in unsettling or discouraging ways. Thus while we experience the "big picture" of our involvement with writing centers as largely positive, our experiences have hardly been unmixed. We know the struggles involved, in other words, in enacting the ideals we describe at the start of this essay on a day-to-day basis.

REREADING "MILLENNIAL THOUGHTS"

In this essay we want to look back on our experiences and to reflect yet again on writing center theory and practice. As the essays gathered together in this section of *Writing Together* demonstrate, over the last two decades we have (separately and together) addressed this topic. Our most recent effort to do so took the form of "Some Millennial Thoughts about the Future of Writing Centers," published in 2000 in *The Writing Center Journal* (and see p. 365). Now at the end of the first decade of the new millennium, we turn back to these thoughts, looking at them from the perspective of the present moment and musing on what the next decade may hold. As we do so we will endeavor both to reaffirm the ideals that animate much writing center work, while also recognizing that both local conditions and ideologies that circulate in the academy and in the culture at large can pose significant challenges to this effort.

While acknowledging the budgetary and institutional constraints and difficulties that many writing centers face, in "Millennial Thoughts" we chose to focus on what we saw as important opportunities available to all writing centers. These opportunities, we pointed out, involve four potentials "for institutional refiguration: the refiguration of institutional space, of concepts of knowledge production and intellectual property, of research paradigms and rewards, and of budget allocations" (p. 365). We still believe that these opportunities represent viable present and future directions for writing centers. Yet each of these "refigurations" now looks more complicated and fraught than it did ten years ago. These complications arise in part from an all-too-familiar tension: while writing centers are at the very center of university commitments to student retention and success, and to improved communication skills, they remain also too often, ironically, on the institutional margins. In what follows, we address and expand on each of the "reconfigurations" from our millennial essay from the standpoint of 2010.

Institutional Locations, Complexities, and Compromises

Whether writing centers find themselves at the center or on the margins is a matter of location, of course, in literal as well as figurative terms. A writing center's physical location on a campus can have both material and symbolic impact. In that regard, we are encouraged to see signs of greater recognition of the importance of locating writing centers in spaces that are easily accessed by students. While we can't point to a national trend, we are both aware of centers that are now housed in or near the campus library, as is the case with the centers at the University of Colorado and at Miami University in Ohio. Other writing centers reach out to campus through multiple locations. In addition to its central location, for instance, the University of Wisconsin, Madison Writing Center has locations in several of the university's libraries, residence halls, and in the multicultural student center. And yet other centers, such as the Community Writing Center that the Salt Lake City Community College Writing Center sponsors, reach out into the community.

As we noted a decade ago, writing centers have also been adept at increasing their presence in virtual space, stepping up to embrace the digital revolution, creating vigorous and productive online writing centers *without* giving up the immediacy of face-to-face contact with students. Some well-known online writing centers, such as Purdue's Online Writing Lab (OWL), provide resources for Purdue students — and anyone else with an Internet connection — while still maintaining a bustling, "live" writing lab on their West Lafayette campus. Thus, while the online component is robust (OWL mail tutors respond to anyone who emails them a brief writing-related question), it has supplemented rather than replaced the in-person writing lab. Many other writing centers have embraced both synchronous and asynchronous online conferencing as a component of what they offer. At Oregon State University's Writing Center, for instance, responses to OWL submissions comprise roughly 20 percent of all contacts in the Center.

In an educational climate where distance education and hybrid courses play increasingly important roles on our campuses, the move to supplement face-to-face conferences with online services is a wise and necessary one, especially in serving students for whom getting to the writing center is a hardship as well as those with very tight time constraints (we think of the students we know who work full time in addition to attending college). But we hope that virtual writing centers will not replace real-life centers entirely but rather enhance them and their work: there is something about sitting face-to-face with a student, talking out ideas, raising key questions, engaging in rich dialogic interaction that is difficult to duplicate online, even in video conferencing. Thus as with most aspects of writing center work, providing online services calls for deep knowledge of the local situation and for compromise as well as collaboration with students and their needs.

We have argued, and we still believe, that "centers create [both virtual and real] spaces for the kind of work . . . that is difficult or impossible to do within traditional disciplinary frameworks" (p. 365 in this collection), but we need to ask exactly where, institutionally, that work takes place. As we look across the country, we see increased efforts to streamline colleges and universities by combining units: thus a writing center may merge with other student support units or absorb other smaller units with differing missions into its space. In such situations, the original writing center faces a potential loss of autonomy and, in some circumstances, finds itself removed from the academic core or, indeed, put in competition with that core for resources. Any such merger can put at risk the foundational philosophy and mission of the center. In short, where writing centers will be located within an institution's organization — at the center, on the margins, or somewhere in between — can and often does shift its priorities, its goals, and even its services in ways that may or may not match its values and philosophy. Thus our call in "Millennial Thoughts" for a writing center advocate to be a "bricoleur, trickster, inventor" in seeking the best institutional space for the center still seems appropriate and even necessary advice. It takes a nimble, quick-witted, wise writing program administrator (WPA) to foresee the effects of such changes, to anticipate effective responses to them, and to recognize when shifting from center to margin — or vice versa — will be most advantageous to the center's work.

Even the wisest, most alert and proactive WPA, however, may be unable to forestall mergers or may possess little agency when it comes to university-mandated reporting lines: hence the "Compromises" in the heading of this section of our essay. Nancy Grimm, for example, points out in *Good Intentions* that over the years of her involvement with Michigan Technological University's Writing Center the reporting line and budget have been "moved from the Humanities Department to Dean of the Colleges of Sciences and Arts, to the Director of Special Academic Programs, back to the Dean's office, next to the Center for Teaching, Learning, and Faculty Development, and now to the Associate Provost's office" (6). (The Michigan Technological University's Writing Center, we should add, is well established, directed by a tenured scholar with a strong national reputation, and has been recognized with a 2007 Conference on College Composition and Communication [CCCC] National Writing Program of Excellence Award — thus even the savviest bricoleur is not immune to shifting university initiatives and budgets.) In reflecting on the changing locations of her Writing Center, Grimm emphasizes the difficulty of explaining "the value of a writing center to a person whose view of education, knowledge, communication, and students has probably not been affected by writing center experience" (6). She acknowledges that statistical evidence about the impact of the writing center on student retention is important in these conversations, but goes on to argue that ultimately more valuable are "theories that enable me to . . . expand my repertoire of arguments about the function and value of the writing center" (7). In so doing, Grimm observes, she is able to develop a "perspective on cultural change . . . that allows me to think my way through conflicts in conceptual systems rather than simply react to them" (8). Conflict and compromise are inevitable in writing center work, as in all educational endeavors, but there are more — and less — effective ways of negotiating their demands.

Writing Centers, Knowledge Production, and Intellectual Property

As readers of this collection may be aware, our research on collaborative writing and learning made us acutely aware of the importance of issues of intellectual property, as well as the concepts — and practices — of knowledge production. As we note in "Millennial Thoughts,"

> In many ways, the writing center's value is figured in the way it generates and organizes knowledge (collaboratively) and circulates it (widely and freely), rather than in the creators of the knowledge or its textual representation. It is not surprising to us that writing centers have been particularly eager to take advantage of the opportunities for sharing resources via the World Wide Web. (p. 366 in this collection)

We are still committed to sharing resources and to the multiple collaborations that are so characteristic of the Internet. Being able to access information on the web during a real-time tutorial has made our work more productive. Our students now go online to work collaboratively on projects, compose documents together, or "talk back" to newspaper columns or blogs — all ways in which student writers take agency and create knowledge on their own.

With legal theorist Lawrence Lessig, whose Creative Commons provides a viable alternative to traditional copyright, we have celebrated the deeply collaborative nature of the web and argued for the benefits of openness and freedom on it.

While we knew a decade ago that the struggle around who gets to share and what is able to be shared was growing more intense (Lessig, for one, bemoans the role of "big media" in sapping the creativity of the web in *Free Culture*), we would have been hard pressed to foresee that the pressures impinging on openness and freedom on the web would grow so strong or so fast. As Jonathan Zittrain argues forcefully in *The Future of the Internet — And How to Stop It*, the tension between openness and freedom and regulation and security has tipped precipitously toward regulation. Zittrain's warnings are echoed by editor in chief Chris Anderson and several writers in the September 2010 issue of *Wired*, who raise similar concerns: with the shift to mobile computing, the control that corporations such as Apple exert over what they will (and will not) allow on their platforms challenges the openness and flexibility of the web and leads to what they describe as a "locked down" system in which users have less and less control and innovation takes the form of corporation-controlled "apps." Anderson opens *Wired*'s discussion of the future of the web and Internet by saying that "As much as we love the open, unfettered Web, we're abandoning it for simpler, sleeker services [especially mobile computing devices and services] that just work" (123). He goes on to argue that the desire for devices that "just work" will carry a high but largely hidden cost as we lose the ability to alter or tweak these devices in creative and innovative ways. Thus users trade efficiency and regularity for creativity and openness.

Writing centers need to be especially attuned to these changes for several reasons. First, we are in daily contact with students who are fluent users of web technologies but who may not have thought about how new technologies and services control and/or constrain their choices. Second, writing centers, which serve as training grounds for students who will be engaged in a much more collaborative future world, need to be at the forefront not only in demonstrating how knowledge is co-created and shared but also in crafting new conventions to guide concepts such as fair use, access to web-based materials, and their own rights as content creators. Perhaps most important, writing centers need to understand and examine the consequences of a "locked down" web, or a platform where only alterations approved and sold by a company marketing a particular device (iPhone, Blackberry, etc.) can reach consumers.

What might the consequences for writing centers be, we wondered, if our students became increasingly reliant on the apps on their mobile devices? Already students can access Cliff Notes via their mobiles (for a price, of course). Sources like Wikipedia and Dictionary.com are free and only need to be downloaded. Other programs such as Cram, an app that allows users to create flash cards and other study aids, can be downloaded for (at the time this essay went to press) $6.99. Might students come to expect a writing center app for their iPhone or Blackberry, one that would take them to a locked-down, proprietary "writing center"?

This question led to yet another question: Might such a writing center app already exist? To reassure ourselves, we Googled "writing center app" and were relieved when no relevant links appeared. Then, almost without thinking, we decided to Google "writing center apps." Adding that one little "s" took us to the "Achievers Writing Center," described as "a full-service writing center in an app." Achievers Writing Center is available, along with thousands of other apps, via the iPhone App Store. Here's what the home page has to say about the Achievers Writing Center services.

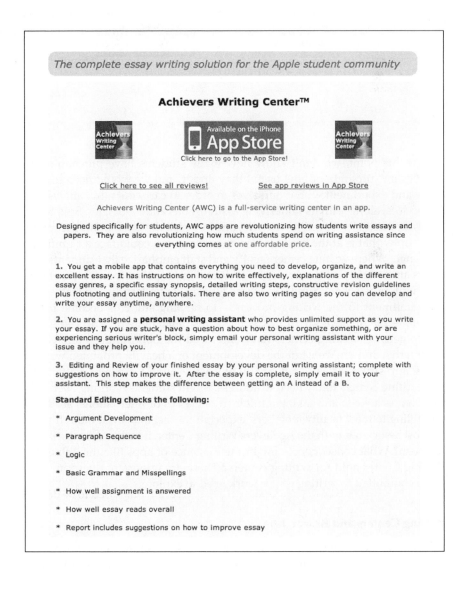

The complete essay writing solution for the Apple student community

Achievers Writing Center™

Available on the iPhone
App Store
Click here to go to the App Store!

Click here to see all reviews!   See app reviews in App Store

Achievers Writing Center (AWC) is a full-service writing center in an app.

Designed specifically for students, AWC apps are revolutionizing how students write essays and papers. They are also revolutionizing how much students spend on writing assistance since everything comes at one affordable price.

1. You get a mobile app that contains everything you need to develop, organize, and write an excellent essay. It has instructions on how to write effectively, explanations of the different essay genres, a specific essay synopsis, detailed writing steps, constructive revision guidelines plus footnoting and outlining tutorials. There are also two writing pages so you can develop and write your essay anytime, anywhere.

2. You are assigned a **personal writing assistant** who provides unlimited support as you write your essay. If you are stuck, have a question about how to best organize something, or are experiencing serious writer's block, simply email your personal writing assistant with your issue and they help you.

3. Editing and Review of your finished essay by your personal writing assistant; complete with suggestions on how to improve it. After the essay is complete, simply email it to your assistant. This step makes the difference between getting an A instead of a B.

Standard Editing checks the following:

* Argument Development

* Paragraph Sequence

* Logic

* Basic Grammar and Misspellings

* How well assignment is answered

* How well essay reads overall

* Report includes suggestions on how to improve essay

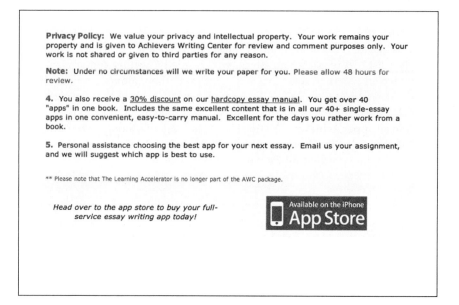

At this point, we don't know how many students have purchased the "Achievers" program or how useful they find it, and we would need to purchase and experiment with it ourselves in order to carry out a full analysis of its services, along with its underlying assumptions and ideologies. Still, to us, this is a potentially alarming scenario, one in which the collaborative learning philosophy that is at the heart of writing center work could face a significant challenge. Where writing center faculty and staff emphasize that students and tutors are co-learners, the Achievers Writing Center promotes a vision of student writers as clients. Similarly, where writing center faculty and staff share a commitment to the writing process — to helping students become better writers — the Achievers Writing Center seems much more product centered.

In general, writing centers have embraced the opportunities offered by the Internet and the web, but the development of a heavily promoted writing center app strikes us as — potentially, at least — quite a different matter, one that writing centers today need to address. Might students working twenty to forty hours a week and taking a full load of classes or international students struggling to meet faculty members' expectations feel that, even though there is a cost associated with the Achievers Writing Center, it makes the most sense for them? What consequences might the existence of apps like the Achievers Writing Center hold for writing centers? These are important questions that those committed to writing center work need to explore.

Writing Centers and Research

As we have noted, writing centers are places where students can engage in knowledge production with their peers, and as such they are sites that nurture and encourage research. Indeed, many writing centers place research and inquiry at the very heart of their endeavors, and they do so in multiple ways. As it is best understood and enacted, assessment (which is essential to most writing center work) represents a powerful and an engaged form of research. Many writing centers invite peer tutors to participate in various forms of knowledge creation — from developing new handouts and evaluating ongoing programs and practices to presenting the results of their inquiry at regional and national writing center conferences. A sign of the field's commitment to undergraduate research and to collaborative inquiry in the writing center is the decision to hold alternate International Writing Centers Association (IWCA) conferences in conjunction with the National Conference on Peer Tutoring in Writing.

As a field, writing centers have developed a rich tradition of scholarly work. Many theses and dissertations have grown out of writing center research and practice. Collaboratively edited collections have also played a key role in the field's professionalization. Here are some of the most important of these collections and their year of publication:

- 1993 *Writing Centers in Context: Twelve Case Studies*, edited by Joyce A. Kinkead and Jeanette G. Harris

- 1994 *Intersections: Theory-Practice in the Writing Center*, edited by Joan A. Mullin and Ray Wallace

- 1995 *Landmark Essays on Writing Centers*, edited by Christina Murphy and Joe Law

- 1995 *Writing Center Perspectives*, edited by Byron L. Stay, Christina Murphy, and Eric H. Hobson

- 1998 *Weaving Knowledge Together: Writing Centers and Collaboration*, edited by Carol Peterson Haviland, Maria Notarangelo, Lene Whitley-Putz, and Thia Wolf

- 2000 *Stories from the Center: Connecting Narrative and Theory in the Writing Center*, edited by Lynn Craigue Briggs and Meg Woolbright

- 2000 *Taking Flight with OWLS: Examining Electronic Writing Center Work*, edited by James Inman and Donna M. Sewell

- 2001 *The Politics of Writing Centers*, edited by Jane Nelson and Kathy Evertz

- 2002 *Writing Center Research: Extending the Conversation*, edited by Paula Gillespie, Alice Gillam, Lady Falls Brown, and Byron Stay

- 2003 *The Center Will Hold: Critical Perspectives on Writing Center Scholarship*, edited by Michael A. Pemberton and Joyce Kinkead

- 2004 *ESL Writers: A Guide for Writing Center Tutors*, edited by Shanti Bruce and Ben Rafoth

- 2005 *On Location: Theory and Practice in Classroom-Based Writing Tutoring*, edited by Candace Spigelman and Laurie Grobman

- 2006 *The Writing Center Director's Resource Book*, edited by Christina Murphy and Byron L. Stay

- 2007 *Marginal Words, Marginal Work? Tutoring the Academy in the Work of Writing Centers*, edited by William J. Macauley Jr. and Nicholas Mauriello

- 2008 *The Longman Guide to Writing Center Theory and Practice*, edited by Robert W. Barnett and Jacob S. Blumner [earlier editions published as *The Allyn and Bacon Guide to Writing Center Theory and Practice*]

- 2011 *The St. Martin's Sourcebook for Writing Tutors*, 4th edition, edited by Christina Murphy and Steve Sherwood

This is an impressive list, especially when we consider it in the context of additional research published in the *Writing Lab Newsletter, Writing Center Journal,* and such single or collaboratively authored monographs as Muriel Harris's *Teaching One-to-One: The Writing Conference*; Nancy Maloney Grimm's *Good Intentions: Writing Center Work for Postmodern Times*; Elizabeth Boquet's *Noise from the Writing Center*; and Anne Ellen Geller, Michele Eodice, Frankie Condon, Meg Carroll, and Elizabeth Boquet's *The Everyday Writing Center: A Community of Practice.*

It is easy for the kind of traditional print, peer-reviewed research that we have just described to be broadly recognized and valued. It can be more difficult for writing center faculty and staff to gain recognition for the multiple kinds of inquiry they undertake in their daily work. In this regard, for instance, see "Work in Progress: Publishing Writing Center Scholarship" by Al DeCiccio, Lisa Ede, Neal Lerner, Beth Boquet, and Muriel Harris, which argues for extending the "notion of writing and publication to include both traditional and non-traditional products" (1) such as reports, grant proposals, and so on. But putting this approach into practice can be both complicated and situated. The issues that someone directing a writing center in a tenure-line position faces can differ significantly for those doing so in professional faculty or other nontenure-line positions.

Indeed, for many directing or working in writing centers, especially if those centers are located in nonacademic units, the old maxim of "publish or perish" is simply irrelevant. Such writing center staff may be expected to engage in some form of professional development, but the time needed to carry out substantial research projects may be unavailable. On the other hand, directors who hold tenure-line positions often must serve two masters (as Lisa points out in "Writing as a Social Process," p. 349), each of whom holds radically different expectations regarding research and accompanying reward systems. Writing center directors in this position can find themselves caught in a bind — they must carry out research and publish the results of it for one master while at the same time developing curricula, training programs, and on-campus resources for the other.[1] This double bind has in some instances led to a failure to achieve tenure.

The complex institutional realities we have just described make it difficult if not impossible to generalize about an ideal scenario in terms of research and rewards for writing center staff. Nontenured positions may be accompanied by higher pay and greater flexibility than tenure-line positions. But such positions rarely come with clearly defined paths to advancement or reward, and those who hold them can be called on to fashion their own paths to job security and advancement. In short, we don't see any easy solutions or answers to the vast diversity in the research and reward systems attendant to writing centers. Many in the writing center community, painfully aware of these issues and of how they affect day-to-day lives, stand ready to undertake the kind of sustained inquiry and advocacy that could help clarify problems related to research and reward structures and lay out possible avenues of response. The good news is that we already have robust organizations, publications, conferences, and a Writing Centers Research Project to help with this endeavor. The bad news is that these professional resources are often as strapped for the kind of funding that would support ongoing and sustained inquiry as are most local writing centers. Writing center folks are accustomed to working small miracles in maddeningly difficult circumstances, however, and we have faith that ongoing efforts to keep writing centers grounded in research while creating locally effective reward systems can eventually pay off. One reason such faith seems justified is the fact that writing center faculty/staff are in general very good at collaboration and compromise: they know that two (or three) heads (and possibly also budgets) can be better than one, and they can use that to their advantage in undertaking a research project.

The film *Writing Across Borders*, written and directed by Lisa's CWL colleague Wayne Robertson (who now teaches at Whatcom Community College in Bellingham, Washington), is a good example of such a collaboration. This three-year documentary project was funded by both the CWL and by Oregon State University's Writing Intensive Curriculum Program. The film grew out of a staff meeting where international students who frequented the writing center spoke not only about their time in the writing center but also about the many cultural, rhetorical, and other adjustments they were called on to make when they moved to the United States. That experience was so inspiring and insightful that those present agreed that we should have another panel, videotape it, and use it in staff training. Vicki Tolar Burton learned of this project, recognized its value for faculty across the curriculum, and co-sponsored its production. A former writing assistant served as the videographer for the film, and all involved responded to it as it developed. Three years later, the much revised and dramatically more ambitious result was a thoughtful, well-developed, highly professional film that was recognized with a Telly award. *Writing Across Borders* has found a broad audience both nationally and internationally and has been used not only by writing center faculty and staff but in many other contexts, such as writing across the curriculum and diversity enrichment programs. It has more than surpassed its collaborators' expectations and is an excellent example of a successful collaborative project. It also provides an outstanding example of the kind of important, though nontraditional, research writing center staff often undertake, research that should in our view be recognized and rewarded as such.

The Question of Funding

Ten years ago, we noted that "these are difficult times at most community colleges, colleges, and universities," yet we were fairly optimistic about the ability of writing centers to "establish and maintain themselves," noting that writing centers are used to scrambling for budgets, patching together funding, and taking an entrepreneurial approach. What a difference a decade makes. Now that we are over two years into what some are calling the Great Recession, university budgets have been cut to the bone and the news reports of ongoing high unemployment and poor economic indicators continue.

In such a climate, writing center faculty and staff find themselves challenged more than ever simply to keep their doors open, much less to mount innovative new projects or serious research and inquiry. It is not just lore, in other words, that many writing centers in 2010 are struggling to survive and must constantly provide evidence of the need for and value of their services. Nor is it lore that writing center directors often feel that what really matters to those to whom they report is numbers on a bottom line rather than educational experiences. In fact, two years of almost continuous budget cuts, with the infighting that always accompanies them, reveal the potential vulnerability of more than a few writing centers and the staying power of disciplinary capital. In short, the credit-driven nature of most university budgets provides a relative degree of protection for academic departments offering general education courses, majors, and, often, graduate programs that does not extend to writing centers, wherever they may be located. While the economic downturn that began in 2008 respected no one, wreaking havoc across college campuses (and the world), campus units viewed as providing "support services" proved particularly at risk.

In reflecting in late 2010 on bottom lines and budgets, the very last thing we should do is generalize, since what is at stake varies drastically from center to center. One writing center might face complete closure, while another center might feel most keenly the loss of a tenure-line position dedicated to writing center work, and yet another might receive a mandate to raise funding for the center from outside the university. While we can't generalize, however, we would be hard pressed to find a center anywhere in the country that is not suffering from severe budgetary constraints. To take two personal examples, the Center for Writing and Learning at Oregon State University was recently dissolved, Lisa lost her directorial position, and the Writing Center was merged into another unit. At Stanford, budget cuts forced the layoff of a busy and badly needed administrative assistant, as well as two vital curricular positions (the director of honors writing and the director of writing in the major, both of which were housed and played central roles in the Writing Center). And while the center is still intact, it has lost some of its autonomy and moved under the umbrella of Stanford Introductory Studies, a newly created unit of the office of the Vice Provost for Undergraduate Education. While many students and faculty will not notice the change in institutional location, this move represents a diminution of both the aspirations and obligations of the writing center, which are by no means limited to introductory studies.

These times of budgetary crisis may be particularly perilous because they can serve as a smokescreen that enables central administrators to restructure departments and units, and to do so in ways that centralize power and further corporatize the university. This restructuring in response to budget crises may run counter to the best interests of writing centers and their students. We are thinking, in this regard, of a center that is downsized via administrative restructuring to the point where it cannot possibly serve its students: we know of one center that has been reduced to one table with one (occasional) tutor. Such a center cannot possibly achieve its goals, yet when Andrea visited she met tutors who wanted to volunteer their time for free — and students who were eager to take a seat at even that one table. At their best, as the example of the Michigan Tech Writing Center suggests, writing centers can survive and even thrive in shifting and tumultuous circumstances. But just because budgets are tight and organizational structures are constantly shifting doesn't mean that writing center faculty and staff should value survival over their — and the field's — guiding principles or their own steady vision of where their writing center needs to go at their particular institution.

ON THE FUTURE OF WRITING CENTERS

As we think about the current situation in higher education, the suggestions we offered at the end of our "Millennial Thoughts" essay (p. 365) still strike us as relevant. Writing centers still need to take advantage of their "multibordered, multipositioned status" and of broad disciplinary and institutional initiatives whenever possible. While it is difficult, centers benefit if those engaged in this work can think both locally and globally, attuned to the politics of location in all its multiple meanings. We also continue to believe that those committed to writing centers need to be prepared to take significant risks and to take the initiative in looking for alternative sources of funding. And we still value the potential gains offered by strategic alignments and coalition building with related units on campus.[2]

We can't predict the future of writing centers, of course, even though we would like to set out the rosiest future imaginable. But we can reiterate what look to be some constants. The tension between the principles and practices that most writing center faculty and staff embrace and the continued association of writing centers with remediation seems likely to continue. The need for writing center services will only continue to grow; students will need support for writing (and increasingly for speaking, presenting, and performing), especially in an age of new literacies. The struggle for funding will go on and on. But successful writing centers will continue to find ways within their institutional contexts to articulate and enact their deepest principles and commitments. Most important, writing centers will continue to provide a powerful and visible space in the academy where students can grow as writers, speakers, and thinkers and do so in collaboration with other students, thus honing those abilities that will carry them into their lives beyond school.

Some serendipitously situated writing centers will be able to leverage private or public funding for writing center work and to push the envelope of what writing centers can be. Such serendipity struck at Stanford as well as at Michigan, Miami of Ohio, and other universities that received endowments to support the work of the writing center. As we write this essay, we note the official opening of the Noel Studio for Academic Creativity at Eastern Kentucky University.[3] At this mid-size regional campus, a confluence of forces came together to articulate an expansive vision: the Noel Studio, located in prime property in the library, houses a "center for invention" (which might previously have been called the writing center), along with a "presentation center" with media-enhanced rehearsal and presentation spaces, a "research center" with research librarians at hand, and a discovery seminar room. This is a center (or studio) with big ambitions, and it has been fortunate to gain funding from a donor interested in supporting writing.

At Ohio State University, what started out as a writing center housed in a small closet in the 1980s has grown slowly over the years into a vibrant Center for the Study and Teaching of Writing, a unit that offers an undergraduate minor in writing and offers writing center tutorials, workshops, faculty development, and outreach across campus as well as to the larger Ohio community. While the Eastern Kentucky center attracted a major donor, the Ohio State center has been built up a bit at a time, through funding secured within the university and through some very creative grantsmanship. And while some of the newer and better-funded centers may boast beautiful spaces, high-tech equipment, and luxurious furniture, such amenities are not absolutely necessary to the centers' functioning. Indeed, many exciting elements cost little if anything. At Miami University's Center for Excellence in Writing, for instance, multilingual students are invited every week to join a "conversation corner" where they talk with undergraduate writing center consultants for extra practice with English; at other universities, including Stanford, dissertation "boot camps" draw flocks of eager graduate students to sessions run on a shoestring. Writing centers may be short on money, but they are long on imagination and vision.

As we look to the future, then, we see ongoing development and evolution for writing centers. The growing importance of visual and oral rhetorics, not to mention of the digital revolution, has challenged writing centers to extend their borders and expand their missions. Eastern Kentucky's Noel Studio embraces all elements of communication; Texas Christian now has a New Media Writing Studio to complement its writing center; Iowa State's Writing and Media Help Center works with their Written, Oral, Visual, and Electronic Communication Program (WOVE); Michigan State's Writing Center advertises services, including one-to-one consulting, creative writing consulting, digital media consulting, workshops, writing groups, and multimedia productions; Agnes Scott's center focuses on speaking as well as writing; and Clemson University not only has a writing center housed in the English department but the very successful Pearce Center for Professional Communication and its associated Class of 1941 Studio for Student Communication. These centers — and their new ways of naming themselves and identifying the work they do — mark a key moment in writing center history, as writing becomes multimodal, multimedia, multilingual, multivocal, and as writing centers move to adapt to students' shifting communicative needs.

When we reflect on these new centers, we are excited by the ways they expand and enrich traditional writing center work. (We also want to point to the growth in writing centers internationally, another very important development and one that can only enrich all writing centers.) We are mindful, to be sure, that to be effective these expansions will need to remain grounded in the best writing center principles: commitment to collaboration and dialogic interaction, to understanding of and respect for diversity, to embodied learning, to open and ongoing exploration of ideas, and to ethical communicative practices. These principles, so deeply embedded in writing center work, are what make our centers worth all the effort not just to keep them going but to expand and enrich them.

During a convocation for new students at Stanford, the Vice Provost for Undergraduate Education asked a panel of three senior students to speak to "what you most want new students to know about our campus." One student stood immediately and exclaimed, "The writing center! It's where I have practically lived for the last four years and I can't say enough about all I learned there." When we need a little encouragement, we remember this student — and legions just like her — who remind us that what we do matters.

NOTES

1. Other issues and tensions can come into play. During the years that Lisa directed the Center for Writing and Learning, she had two offices. Her CWL office, where she spent the majority of her time, was in one building; her English department office was in another. Before she was tenured, Lisa periodically took work she needed to do for the CWL to her English department office, even though she could have more conveniently and efficiently completed it at the CWL. It was important, she felt, to have a strong and visible presence in her home department.

2. There are potential risks as well as benefits in such efforts. In retrospect, Lisa can see that the development earlier in the decade of a collaborative Supplemental Instruction Program with OSU's Academic Success Center (ASC) might have helped pave the way for the dissolution of the CWL and the merger of its programs into the ASC.

3. We are interested to see centers adopting new names or labels for the work they do and are especially intrigued with the idea of the "studio." In "Collaboration, Control, and the Idea of a Writing Center" (p. 358), Andrea wrote of replacing what she saw as "Storehouse" or "Garret" metaphors for centers with a "Burkean Parlor." The new "studios" seem to fit that bill particularly well.

WORKS CITED

Anderson, Chris, and Michael Wolff. "The Web Is Dead: Long Live the Internet." *Wired* Sept. 2010: 118–27, 166. Print.

Barnett, Robert W., and Jacob S. Blumner, eds. *The Allyn and Bacon Guide to Writing Center Theory and Practice*. Needham Heights: Allyn and Bacon, 2001. Print.

Boquet, Elizabeth. *Noise From the Writing Center*. Logan: Utah State UP, 2002. Print.

Briggs, Lynn Craigue, and Meg Woolbright, eds. *Stories from the Center: Connecting Narrative and Theory in the Writing Center*. Urbana: NCTE, 2000. Print.

Bruce, Shanti, and Ben Rafoth, eds. *ESL Writers: A Guide for Writing Center Tutors.* 2nd ed. Portsmouth, NH: Boynton/Cook, 2009. Print.

DeCiccio, Al, Lisa Ede, Neal Lerner, Beth Boquet, and Muriel Harris. "Work in Progress: Publishing Writing Center Scholarship." *The Writing Lab Newsletter.* 31 Mar. 2007: 1–6. Print.

Geller, Anne Ellen, Michele Eodice, Frankie Condon, Meg Carroll, and Elizabeth H. Boquet. *The Everyday Writing Center: A Community of Practice.* Logan: Utah State UP, 2007. Print.

Gillespie, Paula, Alice Gillam, Lady Falls Brown, and Byron Stay, eds. *Writing Center Research: Extending the Conversation.* Mahwah, NJ: Erlbaum, 2002. Print.

Grimm, Nancy Maloney. *Good Intentions: Writing Center Work for Postmodern Times.* Portsmouth, NH: Boynton/Cook, 1999. Print.

Harris, Muriel. *Teaching One-to-One: The Writing Conference.* Urbana: NCTE, 1986. Print.

Haviland, Carol Peterson, Maria Notarangelo, Lene Whitley-Putz, and Thia Wolf, eds. *Weaving Knowledge Together: Writing Centers and Collaboration.* Emmitsburg, MD: NWCA P, 1998. Print.

Inman, James, and Donna M. Sewell, eds. *Taking Flight with OWLS: Examining Electronic Writing Center Work.* Mahwah, NJ: Erlbaum, 2000. Print.

Kinkead, Joyce A., and Jeanette G. Harris, eds. *Writing Centers in Context: Twelve Case Studies.* Urbana: NCTE, 1993. Print.

Lessig, Lawrence. *Free Culture: The Nature and Future of Creativity.* New York: Penguin, 2004. Print.

Macauley, William Jr., and Nicholas Mauriello, eds. *Marginal Words, Marginal Work? Tutoring the Academy in the Work of Writing Centers.* Cresskill, NJ: Hampton P, 2007. Print.

Mullin, Joan A., and Ray Wallace, eds. *Intersections: Theory-Practice in the Writing Center.* Urbana: NCTE, 1994. Print.

Murphy, Christina, and Byron L. Stay, eds. *The Writing Center Director's Resource Book.* Mahwah, NJ: Lawrence Erlbaum, 2006. Print.

Murphy, Christina, and Joe Law, eds. *Landmark Essays on Writing Centers.* Davis, CA: Hermagorus, 1995. Print.

Murphy, Christina, and Steve Sherwood, ed. *The St. Martin's Sourcebook for Writing Tutors.* 4th ed. Boston: Bedford/St. Martin's P, 2011. Print.

Nelson, Jane, and Kathy Evertz. *The Politics of Writing Centers.* Portsmouth, NH: Boynton/Cook, 2001. Print.

Niles Technology Group. *Achievers Writing Center.* Apple Inc., 2010. Web. 4 Oct. 2010.

Pemberton, Michael A., and Joyce Kinkead, eds. *The Center Will Hold: Critical Perspectives on Writing Center Scholarship.* Logan: Utah State UP, 2003. Print.

Spigelman, Candace, and Laurie Grobman. *On Location: Theory and Practice in Classroom-Based Writing Tutoring.* Logan: Utah State UP, 2005. Print.

Stay, Byron L., Christina Murphy, and Eric H. Hobson, eds. *Writing Center Perspectives.* Emmitsburg, MD: NWCA P, 1995. Print.

Zittrain, Jonathan. *The Future of the Internet — And How to Stop It.* New Haven: Yale UP, 2008. Print.

ABOUT THE AUTHORS

Lisa Ede is professor of English at Oregon State University and **Andrea A. Lunsford** is professor of English at Stanford University. In thirty years of writing together, Ede and Lunsford have coauthored twenty-three articles and book chapters. "Audience Addressed/Audience Invoked: The Role of Audience in Composition Theory and Pedagogy" won the Conference on College Composition and Communication's Richard Braddock Award in 1985 and has since been reprinted in ten anthologies on rhetoric and writing. With Robert J. Connors, Ede and Lunsford coedited *Essays on Classical Rhetoric and Modern Discourse* (1984), which received the Modern Language Association's Mina P. Shaughnessy Award in 1985. Their coauthored book, *Singular Texts/Plural Authors: Perspectives on Collaborative Writing*, appeared in 1990. In 2003 they coedited the *Selected Essays of Robert J. Connors*.

ACKNOWLEDGMENTS

Text

Calderonello, Alice Heim, Donna Beth Nelson, and Sue Carter Simmons, "An Interview with Andrea Lunsford and Lisa Ede: Collaboration as a Subversive Activity," in *Writing on the Edge*, 2.2, pp. 6–18. Copyright © 1991 Writing on the Edge. All rights reserved.

Ede, Lisa, "Writing as a Social Process: The Theoretical Foundation for Writing Centers?", in *Writing Center Journal*, vol.9, no. 2, pp. 3–14. Copyright © 1989 by Writing Center Journal. All rights reserved. Reproduced by permission.

Ede, Lisa and Andrea A. Lunsford, "Collaboration and Concepts of Authorship," in *PMLA* 116.2, 2001, pp. 354–69. Reprinted by permission of the Modern Language Association.

Ede, Lisa and Andrea Lunsford, "Audience Addressed/Audience Invoked: The Role of Audience in Composition Theory and Pedagogy," in *College Composition and Communication* 35.2, pp. 155–71. Copyright © 1984. All rights reserved. Reproduced by permission.

Ede, Lisa and Andrea Lunsford, "Collaborative Writers at Work," in *Singular Texts/Plural Authors*, ed. Lisa Ede and Andrea Lunsford, pp. 20–67. Copyright © 1990. Reprinted by permission of the Board of Trustees Southern Illinois University Press.

Ede, Lisa and Andrea Lunsford, *"Some Millennial Thoughts about the Future of Writing Centers,"* in *Writing Center Journal*, vol.20, no. 2, pp. 32–37. Copyright © 2000 by *Writing Center Journal*. All rights reserved. Reproduced by permission.

Ede, Lisa and Andrea Lunsford, "Why Write. . . Together?', in *Rhetoric Review* 1, 1983, pp. 150–57. Reprinted by permission of Taylor & Francis Ltd, http://www.informaworld.com.

Ede, Lisa, Cheryl Glenn, and Andrea Lunsford, "Border Crossings: Intersections of Rhetoric and Feminism," in *Rhetorica* 8.4, pp. 401–41. Copyright © 1995. All rights reserved. Reproduced by permission.

Lunsford, Andrea, "Collaboration, Control, and the Idea of a Writing Center" in *Writing Center Journal*, vol.12, no. 1, pp. 3–10. Copyright © 1991 by *Writing Center Journal*. All rights reserved. Reproduced by permission.

Lunsford, Andrea A. and Lisa Ede, "Collaborative Authorship and the Teaching of Writing," in *Cardozo Arts & Entertainment Law Journal* 10.2, pp. 681–702. Copyright © 1992. All rights reserved. Reproduced by permission.

Lunsford, Andrea A. and Lisa Ede, "Collaboration and Compromise: The Fine Art of Writing with a Friend," in *Writers on Writing*, >vol. 2, ed. Tom Waldrep. New York: Random House, 1988, pp. 121–27. All rights reserved. Reproduced by permission.

Lunsford, Andrea A. and Lisa Ede, "On Distinctions between Classical and Modern Rhetoric," in *Essays on Classical Rhetoric and Modern Discourse*, ed. Robert J. Connors, Lisa S. Ede, and Andrea A. Lunsford, pp. 37–49. Copyright © 1984. Reprinted by permission of the Board of Trustees, Southern Illinois University Press.

Lunsford, Andrea A. and Lisa Ede, "Representing Audience: 'Successful' Discourse and Disciplinary Critique," in *College Composition and Communication* 47.2, pp. 167–79. Copyright © 1996. All rights reserved. Reproduced by permission.

Lunsford, Andrea A. and Lisa Ede, "Rhetoric in a New Key: Women and Collaboration," in *Rhetoric Review* 1, 1983, pp. 150–57; 8.2, 1990, pp. 234–41. Reprinted by permission of the Taylor & Francis Ltd, http://www.informaworld.com.

Lunsford, Andrea and Lisa Ede, "Crimes of Writing and Reading," in *Teaching Rhetorica: Theory, Pedagogy, Practice*, ed. Kate Ronald and Joyce Ritchie. Portsmouth, NH: Boynton/Cook, pp.13–30. Copyright © 2006. All rights reserved. Reproduced by permission.

Lunsford, Andrea and Lisa Ede, "New Beginnings," in *Singular Texts/Plural Authors*, ed. Lisa Ede and Andrea Lunsford, pp. 130–43. Copyright ©1990. Reprinted by permission of the Board of Trustees, Southern Illinois University Press.

Lunsford, Andrea and Lisa Ede, "Old Beginnings," in *Singular Texts/Plural Authors*, ed. Lisa Ede and Andrea Lunsford, pp. 5–16. Copyright ©1990. Reprinted by permission of the Board of Trustees, Southern Illinois University Press.

Lunsford, Andrea and Lisa Ede, "Why Write . . . Together?: A Research Update," in *Rhetoric Review*, vol.5, no.1, pp. 71–81. Copyright © 1986. Reprinted by permission of Taylor & Francis Ltd, http://www.informaworld.com.

Lunsford, Andrea and Ede, Lisa, "Writer's Block" from *Writing on the Edge* 3.1, p. 48. Copyright © 1991. All rights reserved. Reproduced by permission.

Art

page 24: Timothy Flower; **339:** Malea Powell & 2009 FemRhet Coordinating Committee; **341:** Kirsti K. Cole is the Chair of the 2011 Feminisms & Rhetorics Conference; **378:** 2010 Niles Technology Group & Apple Inc.z

INDEX